The UCAS Guide to getting into

ART AND DESIGN

For entry to university and college in 2013

Published by: UCAS Rosehill New Barn Lane Cheltenham GL52 3LZ

Produced in conjunction with GTI Media Ltd.

UCAS, a company limited by guarantee, is registered in England and Wales number: 2839815
Registered charity number: 1024741 (England and Wales) and SC038598 (Scotland)

UCAS reference number: PU031013
Publication reference: 12_042
ISBN: 978-1-908077-12-7
Price £15.99

We have made all reasonable efforts to ensure that the information in this publication was correct at time of publication. We will not, however, accept any liability for errors, omissions or changes to information since publication. Wherever possible any changes will be updated on the UCAS website (www.ucas.com).

UCAS and its trading subsidiary, UCAS Media Limited, accept advertising for publications that promote products and services relating to higher education and career progression. Revenue generated by advertising is invested by UCAS in order to enhance our applications services and to keep the cost to applicants as low as possible. Neither UCAS nor UCAS Media Limited endorse the products and services of other organisations that appear in this publication.

Further copies available from UCAS (p&p charges apply):

Contact Publication Services PO Box 130 Cheltenham GL52 3ZF

email: publicationservices@ucas.ac.uk or fax: 01242 544 806

For further information about the UCAS application process go to www.ucas.com.

If you need to contact us, details can be found at www.ucas.com/about_us/contact_us

UCAS QUALITY AWARDS

Foreword

THINKING ABOUT ART AND DESIGN?

Finding the higher education course that's right for you at the right university or college can take time and it's important that you use all the resources and guides available to you in making this key decision. We at UCAS have teamed up with GTI Media Ltd. to provide you with *The UCAS Guide to getting into Art and Design* to show you how you can progress from being a student to careers in art and design. You will find key information on what the subject includes, entry routes and real-life case studies on how it worked out for others.

Once you know which subject area you might be interested in, you can use the listings of all the full-time higher education courses in art and design to see where you can study your subject. The course entry requirements are listed so you can check if getting in would be achievable for you. There's also advice on applying through UCAS, telling you what you need to know at each stage of the application process in just six easy steps to starting university or college.

We hope you find this publication helps you to choose and make your application to a course and university or college that is right for you.

On behalf of UCAS and GTI Media Ltd., I wish you every success in your research.

Mary Curnock Cook, Chief Executive, UCAS

At TARGETjobs we champion paid work experience for UK university students. Find internships and placements across all sectors, plus take part in the TARGETjobs Undergraduate of the Year awards.

TARGETjobs.co.uk
the best possible start to your career

Introducing
art and design

It could be you...

… creating the new look and feel of the latest women's glossy mag — graphic designer

… flying to Italy to research next season's trends in 'haute couture' — fashion designer

… seeing the look on kids' faces at the latest cartoon character you helped create — animator

… overhearing people on the tube repeat the slogan for that new ad you designed — art director

… reading rave reviews for the new exhibition you helped organise — gallery curator

… celebrating your first big sale at your latest private showing — fine artist

… and lots more besides. Could a career in art and design be for you? The aim of this guide is to help you decide.

A CAREER IN ART AND DESIGN?

- Your portfolio counts more than your grades – see **Your portfolio** page 79
- Admissions tutors look for your eye for detail and manual dexterity as well as your artistic flair – see **The career for you?** page 29
- A foundation course after A level is the most common first step on a career in art and design – see **Entry routes** page 51
- Graphic design may be the most popular at present, but ad agency work is still seen as the most 'glam'! – see **Which area?** page 17

ART AND DESIGN IN CONTEXT

Say the words 'art and design' to people outside the sector, and they'll invariably start talking about paintings. But those on the inside know it's a much more diverse field than this, with a myriad of roles, sectors and sub-sectors. In reality, very few graduates go into **fine art**, of which 'painting' is only one branch.

Most either go into art- and design-related roles, or into the **applied arts** – for example, product design, art direction, graphic design and fashion design.

If you're interested in a possible career in art and design, then this guide can help you. Read on to discover:

- the main roles on offer
- the skills that admissions tutors look for
- how to get in and the route to qualification
- advice from art and design graduates in five different sectors.

Why art and design?

Choose a career that is...

CREATIVE

Few careers can claim to be as creative as art and design. You will be paid to think creatively at all times. There is also an unrivalled sense of satisfaction and achievement in seeing your ideas come to life in the finished product.

VARIED

Your art and design background will enable you to work in a huge variety of career sectors, from manufacturing to museums, and in roles ranging from restoring great works of art to designing vacuum cleaners. Read the areas of work beginning on page 17 to find out more about the full range of art and design careers.

FUN

Read the case studies of the art and design graduates in this book and you'll find that they all really love their work. Being 'creative' and 'artistic' is something they have developed a special interest in during their studies, pursued as a hobby, or have always enjoyed doing as they grew up. Now they're getting paid to do it! As well as being an enjoyable career, art and design also makes other things fun – for example, electronic goods, which were previously dull and beige, now come in a rainbow of colours.

A STRONG INFLUENCE ON OUR DAY-TO-DAY LIVES

Art and design has a crucial influence on what we wear, read, sit on, look at, enjoy and on almost everything we buy. We wear the latest fashions on a night out, which we read about in magazines like *Cosmopolitan* or *FHM*. As a new student in higher education, you'll probably buy prints or posters for your room. The look and feel of many of the everyday objects we use is often as important to us as functionality, and well conceived and designed advertisements convince us we needed to buy those objects in the first place.

ADDING 'VALUE'

This may seem a little obscure at first, but art and design adds commercial value, preserves value and is also 'valued' by people. For example, by creating a stunning design that consumers want to buy, product and interior designers can add value to an everyday object such as a bottle opener. People will often pay more for these products and demand will rise. Restorers and conservators preserve value by restoring and maintaining treasured objects – from jewellery to great buildings. And of course, we all have an innate appreciation of art and design: a photograph, animated film or painting can give pleasure and a favourite designer shirt can make you feel better.

WHAT IS SO GOOD ABOUT A CAREER IN ART AND DESIGN?

'Along with my business partner I have founded Duke Studios, where designers can share professional workshop space and collaborate on design projects. ... Understanding how to move from making one or two items to mass production commercially is an ongoing learning curve.'
Laura Wellington, studio director and self-employed product designer, page 40

'It's nice to have a job which is both academic and where you need to be skilled with your hands to carry it out well.'
Bryony Finn, metals conservator, page 42

'I am fascinated by applied art, the application of aesthetic design and decoration to everyday, functional objects.'
Eifion Lloyd James, design assistant, page 44

'Photography is endlessly rewarding. Whether it's a solo exhibition, a publication in a high profile magazine or a cash prize for a picture, the industry is full of incentives to keep you going.'
Alex Moore, freelance photographer, page 46

'I love being involved in all stages of the design, from concept to design production, and working with a wide range of people. I particularly enjoy researching, thinking up ideas to solve problems and creating final designs.'
Fleur Isbell, design intern, page 48

Focus your career with the TARGETjobs Careers Report. Using biographical data, information about your interests and insightful psychometric testing, the Careers Report gives you a clear picture of jobs that match your skills and personality.

TARGETjobs.co.uk

the best possible start to your career

A career in art and design

A career in art and design

On graduating, of those who go into a job related to their art and design degree, the largest proportion go on to work as graphic designers and commercial artists, while only the most talented few manage to make a living as fine artists or general artists. It is also worth noting that although art and design is one of the most popular subject areas to study, many graduates start off working outside this sector after graduating. More positively though most graduates go into art and design in the long term.

WHERE THEY WORK

Freelance/self-employed

Seen in many ways as one of the hardest paths to follow early on in your career, as it relies on the reputation you build for yourself – although it is also a great way to get your foot in the door. Freelance is a common route among illustrators, graphic and interior designers, as well as more traditional fine artists, sculptors etc, all of whom rely on the strength of their portfolio.

Art galleries/museums

As curators deciding on the exhibits and collections; as exhibitions organisers, helping to set up and run temporary exhibitions; as education officers, working with local primary and secondary school pupils to bring to life the galleries' and museums' contents; as managers, ensuring the successful running of the gallery as a business; or as conservators (for example, in National Trust properties), restoring and protecting artefacts, ancient manuscripts, fabrics, furniture etc.

Industry

Either in design-based industries, eg fashion, visual communications or animation, where the core of the business is design related; or in more traditional industries that still require a design element to support what they do, eg industrial and product designers for manufacturing industry, packaging and product styling designers for consumer goods producers, and graphic designers who work on customer literature, websites and campaigns as part of the marketing team of every large organisation.

Agencies

For example, design or advertising agencies – the specialists who are called in by organisations to work on a campaign, project or account basis. Agencies will typically employ an eclectic mix of art and design graduates, including copywriters, art associates and directors to come up with the ideas, and graphic and web designers and multimedia specialists to implement them.

Trends

Different parts of the art and design sector are subject to different trends and pressures.

Economic

The state of the economy is particularly important for the advertising industry. When a company is feeling the pinch in an economic downturn, their advertising and wider marketing budget is often the first thing to be cut, which means there will be less work going for ad agencies and the creatives they employ. Similar pressures apply to product designers – if companies are on a cost-cutting programme, they may be tempted to push investment in products that are already designed and are in the market rather than new product development. However, the good news for these sectors is that UK companies are increasingly aware of the importance of keeping their customers aware of their products and of new product development to keep ahead of the competition, even in tough times.

Those wishing to work in public museums and art galleries will be facing more competition, as many of these institutions have been affected by significant funding cuts aimed at reducing Britain's deficit.

Technology

Technology affects how art is created, delivered and used. In film and photography, the big revolution of the twenty-first century so far is digital imagery, while in animation and computer games the technology is constantly evolving. It's important for you to check that the course in which you're interested offers the very latest techniques and technologies. This book was produced using a variety of different technologies such as Microsoft Word, Quark XPress and Adobe Photoshop.

Taste

Of all the things that affect art and design, trends in popular and critical taste are of vital importance. Think about fashion and product and interior design, where from one year to the next consumers' tastes can change – brown becomes the new black, or your dad's old clothing becomes 'retro'. If your experience and reputation are too closely aligned to a particular look or era, rather than a skill set, you could find yourself left behind.

Pay

Salaries vary greatly in this diverse employment sector. At the bottom end, it is common for those starting out to work voluntarily, ie for free or just for expenses, on internships or work placements in order to get a foot in the door or to build their portfolio. Starting salaries for those working for an employer in areas such as graphic design, animation or fashion design can be in the region of £14,000 to £22,000, rising to £45,000 with ten or more years of experience, and considerably more if you reach director level.

A large proportion of people in this sector also work on a self-employed or freelance basis, charging hourly, daily or per project or design. Rates depend on the sector, location and level of the person. A website designer may charge up to £600 a day, or, especially if working as part of a design agency, far more per website designed. A freelance photographer could charge between £200 and £300 per job; again, substantially more if their work is well known and sought after. Self-employed fine artists (for example Tracey Emin and co) charge per completed piece, although very few can expect to be paid £150K for their bed!

Working conditions

Your work will vary greatly according to the sector and nature of the work. Self-employed and freelance artists and designers can, in principle, set their own hours but will be under a lot of pressure to secure new work and cultivate new clients. Employed artists and designers, especially in advertising agencies, design agencies, fashion houses, and industrial and product designers employed by engineering companies, are more likely to work a 'regular' working week. However, long nights are a common feature of agency work, as creatives have to come up with ideas to meet clients' deadlines.

Which area?

There is such a range of career paths to choose from in this sector that in many ways art and design students are spoilt for choice.

Many of the skills required for some of the key roles are also highly transferable. For example, a graphic designer in print can, with relative ease and some training, move into graphic design of websites. This said, the skills required for each particular profession are in many ways becoming more precise, which means that in many art and design sectors, the further down one route you go, the harder it is to transfer across to other fields. For example, it is rare for graphic designers in an ad agency setting to move into art direction. Students would therefore be wise to take time at this stage to find out the key differences in each of the main art and design sectors before embarking on their course. This section outlines some of the main fields in which you can specialise.

ADVERTISING AGENCY ART DIRECTION

The work

Often seen as the glamorous side of art and design, this role involves the creation and development of commercial ads for organisations. They usually work in 'creative teams' of two – an art director and a copywriter. Art directors come up with the 'visual' to go with the copywriter's words or vice versa. Images can start out as basic as stick men, and the concept is then presented by the creatives to senior agency creatives, including the creative director, who reject, shape or add to it. The creative team will then rework their concept until it is ready to be presented to the client. The art director has a wider role than a graphic designer (also employed by advertising agencies). While the graphic designer takes the art director's brief and comes up with visuals to implement it, the art director oversees the whole advertisement from concept (creating the initial images and ideas) to client pitch (presenting their ideas to the client) and production (advising film crews on set).

The conditions

There's a fair bit of grind to go with the glam. The advertising sector is notorious for its long, long hours. Creative teams have to burn the midnight oil to generate the creative ideas to client deadlines. Also, getting into this sector is very tough – the unwritten, but accepted, practice is for would-be creatives to take on unpaid work on campaigns to help build their portfolio. On the plus side, this sector is known for helping its own – with successful agency creatives frequently taking time out to advise aspiring art directors on their portfolios, and even championing candidates if they think their work is good. As such, networking is an important part of the profession.

The upside

The creativity – spending all day daydreaming and being paid for it!

The downside

It can be hard to go back to the drawing board just after the fantastic idea you've nurtured for weeks is shot down by a client.

For more info

D&AD – **www.dandad.org**

The Advertising Association – **www.adassoc.org.uk**

ANIMATION

The work

As the title suggests, this is the profession that produces the 'animated' or moving content on TV, films, websites and computer or video games. The field itself is broadly divided into four main sectors – 2D drawn (where every movement and facial expression is painstakingly drawn, then transferred onto film); 2D computer generated and 3D computer generated (both of which require expertise in sophisticated software); and stop frame (using models rather than drawings as the base). Individual companies typically specialise in just one of these fields, although a few do all four.

The conditions

Most work in this sector is contract or freelance, the difference being that contract work is usually longer-lasting and less ad hoc. Some permanent positions do exist – in fact, in some of the more specialist fields, some companies are beginning to invest in their own training programmes for staff, to make up for what they see as a lack of appropriate skill-building on some courses. Contract or permanent, you will certainly face time pressures in this field and intense periods of working as films near completion.

The upside

Unlike other sectors in the audiovisual industries, animation has a number of successful centres of excellence outside London, including Manchester and Bristol.

The downside

Keeping up with the ever-advancing technology and skill sets that are required in this field.

For more info

Skillset – **www.skillset.org/animation**
BBC Design – **www.bbc.co.uk/design**

CONSERVATION/RESTORATION

The work

Art conservationists have the cultural heritage of entire nations in their hands. Where their curator colleagues have the care of the exhibition 'experience' at the core of their work (see page 23), conservators have the care of each individual artefact at the core of theirs. Individual conservators may focus on the care of individual objects, such as a rare manuscript, on particular types of objects, such as stained glass windows, murals and floors, or on the entire contents of a historic building, such as a cathedral or National Trust property. This is a highly specialised and competitive field, requiring not only an artistic sense but also scientific knowledge, manual dexterity (given the intricacy of the work), attention to detail and huge patience!

The conditions

Most people joining this field from art school go into heritage organisations (for example the National Trust, galleries and museums) on an employed basis. Their working life will be on a more regular, 9am to 5pm basis. Unlike other fields of art and design, in which freelancing is often a way to get into a profession, freelancing in this field is more of an option as a specialist adviser or consultant later in your career, once you've built your skills and a reputation in a particular field.

The upside

Unlike their commercial counterparts, restoration artists have the relative luxury of time to concentrate on this painstaking work.

The downside

Your work, though often seen by the public, is rarely noted. Restorers and conservators are the unsung heroes of the art world.

For more info

Icon – The Institute of Conservation – **www.icon.org.uk**

FASHION DESIGN

The work

Designing clothes and/or accessories is another popular field that requires not only technical hands-on design skills, but also the commercial understanding to be able to factor in production time and cost. Most people think 'couture house' when they think fashion design, but in reality the majority of fashion designers go to work for mass market design 'houses', producing recognisable high-street brands, such as Topshop, Miss Selfridge, BHS, Marks & Spencer or 'George' at Asda. The work involves drawing sketches (by hand or on a computer), selecting fabrics, and creating patterns and samples, all to an internal (for example, head of fashion) or external (for example, fashion buyer) client's brief. Some fashion designers are given very little information (for example, just the colour and fabric) and develop the product from this.

The conditions

Fashion designers may be employed or freelance. Employed designers will typically work regular office hours, although long hours to meet client deadlines should be expected. Freelance designers may charge per design or per collection. And what of the luxury lifestyle, and living it up at the fashion parties? Trips abroad to fashion shows (for research, of course!) or fabric houses are one of the perks, and you'll be first to hear of the sales at the high-end fashion houses – but you may have to wait a while to rub shoulders with Betty Jackson or Giorgio Armani.

The upside

Seeing one of your creations walking down the street towards you!

The downside

For the majority of fashion designers, having to design within tight commercial (read 'cost') constraints.

For more info

Skillset – **www.skillset.org/fashion_and_textiles**
Chartered Society of Designers – **www.csd.org.uk**

FINE ART

The work

These are the few art graduates who decide to go it alone as painters, sculptors or, to reflect the more 'modern' media, as video artists. The core of the work involves working alone to create pieces completely from scratch, which you'll try to sell. Exhibitions are the lifeblood for fine artists – to build their reputation their work must be seen, so courting galleries and gallery curators who put on the exhibitions is of crucial importance. 'Open' exhibitions, which display the work of new artists whose work is selected from an open application process (artists must apply, sometimes pay an entry fee, and submit their work for scrutiny), advertise in the key art magazines, for example *The Artist*. In between exhibitions, artists often turn their hand to commercial work (such as producing illustrations for magazines) to earn a living.

The conditions

Being self-employed may, in theory, mean that you can set your own hours and avoid the daily commute, but in reality it means that you won't have the security of a regular monthly salary, and will only be paid for what you sell.

The upside

This is probably the height of creative freedom that would suit the independent minded.

The downside

Talent rules – for every Damien Hirst, there are dozens of didn't-quite-make-its.

For more info

The Royal Society of Portrait Painters – **www.therp.co.uk**
Royal British Society of Sculptors – **www.rbs.org.uk**
a-n – The Artists Information Company – **www.a-n.co.uk**
Artquest – **www.artquest.org.uk**

GALLERY/MUSEUM CURATION

The work

Curators are responsible for organising and managing exhibitions of permanent and/or one-off collections in galleries and museums – which includes every detail of each exhibition, including buying or borrowing art and artefacts, assembling and supervising the exhibition, cataloguing collections, and even writing exhibition catalogues. The lead curator will also be involved in the commercial side of the exhibition, eg the budgeting and negotiations with exhibitors.

The conditions

On paper, this is more of a managerial role in large institutions that are at the more 'sedate' end of the art and design profession. In reality, it also involves quite anti-social hours. As these are public-facing institutions, weekend and evening work is to be expected, as is considerable pressure to cope with last-minute glitches, such as delayed arrival of artefacts, in the run-up to exhibitions.

The upside

Inspiring thousands of people who come to your gallery.

The downside

The pay – you may start on as little as £16,000 per year for a curatorial assistant in a public sector gallery or museum. However, if you're prepared to take rather more pressure, the auction houses, eg Christie's and Sotheby's, certainly pay more.

For more info

Museums Association –
www.museumsassociation.org

GRAPHIC DESIGN

The work

Also known as communication design, this field focuses on the creation of the look and feel of (traditionally) print-based materials, such as magazines, book covers, poster ads and packaging materials, although many graphic designers now specialise in design for 'new' media, principally the internet. Graphic designers are the wizards of what things should look like – from the typeface, font size and colours that should be used, to the layout and methods of reproduction. More junior graphic designers may have less of a say in the final design decisions, and will be charged with creating the look to a senior designer's specification. More senior designers will not only get to decide on the design, but will supervise the entire design from concept to publication, working with illustrators, publishers and printers along the way.

The conditions

Graphic designers may either freelance or work in-house as an employee. The freelance route is particularly common in this field, as much of the work is project based rather than ongoing – for example, designing the overall look of a new magazine or website, and creating a set of templates that more junior in-house production staff can use. In addition to the design work, much of this role (especially if freelancing) involves client meetings, and often working to very tight briefs and deadlines.

The upside

The chance to work on multiple design briefs at the same time.

The downside

This is probably the most popular destination for current art and design graduates today, which means it is becoming increasingly crowded and competitive.

For more info

Design Council – **www.designcouncil.org.uk**
Chartered Society of Designers – **www.csd.org.uk**
D&AD – **www.dandad.org**

INDUSTRIAL/PRODUCT DESIGN

The work

Purists in the art world sometimes don't count this field as part of art and design. Yet in many ways it is one of the most intricate and complex, as it requires not only artistic and creative talent and vision, but also specialist technical skills and commercial judgement. Industrial and product designers are the creators of products as diverse as cars, lamps or TV sets. They must consider many more aspects of the product than purely its look and feel. For example, critical factors include the product's safety, ergonomics, ease of use, materials (anything from aluminium to rubber), maintenance, convenience and production costs.

The conditions

This is a difficult field in which to go it alone as it often involves long timescales to bring your design to fruition. Many product designers can be found in the product development or engineering departments of large companies, where their work is usually during office hours.

The upside

Design on a large scale.

The downside

The long lead time on design products. It can take a long time to bring a new industrial product to market, so you can find yourself working on the same design or product for years.

For more info

The Institution of Engineering Designers –
www.ied.org.uk

INTERIOR DESIGN

The work

Thanks to the endless stream of home makeover TV programmes, this field of design – once the preserve of the affluent country-dweller – has left its Laura Ashley roots behind to become a high-growth field. However, the myth remains that interior design is only about decorating people's homes. In reality, the sector is much more varied, encompassing the interiors of office buildings, hotels, shops, ships and even aeroplanes. Designers typically work with their client and other professionals, such as architects, to develop a design that suits the client's taste, timescale and budget. The process involves preparing initial sketches, sourcing sample fabrics, and showing their ideas to clients as they go. This role definitely requires very honed 'interpersonal' skills for those dealing with picky clients, as well as technical design ability and creative flair.

The conditions

Interior designers working in people's homes should expect long, unsociable hours – your client's free time is your work time. Many interior designers are self-employed, which means they can't just concentrate on the design side alone but must also do the legwork, or rather 'footwork' – walking round design showrooms to spot the right furniture or flooring etc.

The upside

Having the full design remit and vision – usually interior designers work alone.

The downside

Having to bend to clients' sometimes 'quirky' – or even downright bad – taste.

For more info

The British Institute of Interior Design – **www.biid.org.uk**

PHOTOGRAPHY

The work

Photography is now part of the wider discipline of 'photo imaging' – so called to reflect the current trend towards digital imaging. However, traditional photography and image reproduction are still vibrant sectors. Photographers create permanent visual images with cameras – typically specialising in a particular type of image, for example family photography, portraits, fashion, food or even medical photography. Typically a photographer will work to a client's brief, not only selecting and taking the photos but also selecting and preparing locations and appropriate equipment, setting up the lighting, and then (if the subject is an inanimate object such as the exterior of a company building) photographing it in a way that captures the 'right' image. Photographers who work with people must have the right skills to put someone at ease to draw from them the correct look or pose.

The conditions

Freelancing is extremely common in this sector. Photographers usually pitch their portfolios and then work to briefs set by clients. Working hours – and briefs – can be long and unpredictable. You could find yourself spending perhaps more time on generating work and managing the periphery of the business (for example, equipment and supply checks, taking briefs, processing film) than on taking the photos themselves. It is now common for images to be supplied in digital format, usually on CD, DVD, or through online libraries, which may involve extensive work in digital editing suites (usually Photoshop) after the photo shoot.

The upside

The lure of the picture that really is worth a thousand words!

The downside

More than three-quarters of your time can be spent away from actual photo shoots.

For more info

British Institute of Professional Photography – **www.bipp.com**
The Royal Photographic Society – **www.rps.org**
Skillset – **www.skillset.org/photo/careers**

www.ucas.com

at the heart of connecting people to higher education

The career
for you?

Is art and design for you?

Building a successful career in art and design requires more than the ability to draw (and there are those who today dispute even the need for this skill, given the growing reliance on computer design technology). It also requires certain skills and personal qualities or 'attributes'. To help you decide if a career in art and design is for you, we suggest you think about the following three areas:

- What **you** want from your future work.
- What an art and design course typically involves.
- Which skills and qualities admissions tutors in this field typically seek in new recruits.

ANSWERING THESE QUESTIONS MAY HELP YOU TO CHOOSE YOUR CAREER

- When you think of your future, in what kind of environment do you see yourself working? For example, in an office, outdoors, 9am to 5pm, relaxed or high-pressured?
- What are your favourite hobbies outside school?
- What is it about them you enjoy? For example, working with people or finding out how things work?

- What are your favourite subjects in school and what is it about them that you enjoy most? For example, being able to create something new, or working with people?
- What do you dislike about the other subjects you're studying? (Writing 'the teacher' doesn't count!)
- Which aspects of your work experience have you most enjoyed?

WHAT DO YOU WANT IN YOUR FUTURE WORK?

You may not have an instant answer for this, but your current studies, work experience and even your hobbies can help give you clues about the kind of work you enjoy and the skills you have already started to develop. Start with a blank sheet of paper and note down the answers to the above questions to help get you thinking. Be as brutally honest with yourself as you can – don't write what you think will impress your teachers or parents. Write what really matters to you, and you'll start to see a pattern emerge…

WHAT DO ART AND DESIGN COURSES INVOLVE?

Unsurprisingly, the skills you'll require as a successful artist or designer will also be required at various stages of your studies so it is important to know what typical art and design courses entail before you apply, to be sure it's the kind of work you will enjoy. For example, one common misconception about art and design courses is that they are purely practical based. Would-be designers who've struggled through the written side of their A level course can't wait to leave their written coursework behind! While it's true that most courses assess students mostly on their practical project work, all courses include an element of written work – for example, most courses require students to produce a 500-word 'statement of intent' outlining the project they intend to produce for their final year exam. You'll also have to study the theoretical and historical side of art and design – precisely how much will depend on the individual course syllabus. As a general rule, however, all degree students will have to write a long essay or dissertation.

WHAT SKILLS DO YOU NEED?

Despite the many differences in art and design sectors, the underpinning skill set they all require is broadly the same — artistic talent, which they'll mostly discern from your portfolio. Beyond this, the following are the other key skills required of any potential art and design student:

- **creativity** – ie not just the artistic skill, but the capacity to use it to produce new perspectives or new products, or new, imaginative uses of colour, materials or media etc

- **capacity for sustained effort** – working as an artist or designer involves not just creating, but also the patience and perseverance to rework and change your work, not once, but often many times until you or your client is happy with the finished product

- **an eye for detail** – in this field, it is often the tiniest of details that alter the look or 'feel' of the finished work

- **manual dexterity** – you've got to be able to manipulate different materials and surfaces with ease

- **'interpersonal' skills** – since most roles in art and design (with the exception of fine artists who typically work alone) involve working closely together in creative teams, you need to be comfortable working with and relating to other people

- **a thick skin and a self-critical attitude** – in this field, there are few who can **create** artistic works of quality, but there are many who are prepared to **critique** it. As a student, your work will be on display, not just to your peers and tutors but (through your year-end exhibitions) also to the wider public and eventually the wider artistic community. So it is important from the outset that you learn to turn even the sharpest of criticisms into constructive feedback that you can use to improve your work.

In addition to these general skills shared and sought by all fields in art and design, admissions tutors will also look for an understanding of, and some experience of, sector-specific skills related to their field.

For example:

- would-be **animators** will need to come with a broad base of skills, including set and lighting design and even model-making — technophobes need not apply

- if you're planning on making a career as an **advertising art director**, you must come to the interview with a real sense of the style and approach of current advertisements and advertising trends

- **fashion students** must be able to talk about fashion collections that have inspired them

- **potential product or industrial designers** will also require ability with numbers and/or commercial sense, as they typically have to research how much it will cost to turn their concept into the finished product.

Alternative careers

If you're looking for something a little less mainstream, an art and design qualification can open the door to some alternative career paths.

ART THERAPIST

Art therapists are allied health professionals who typically work as part of a therapeutic team headed by a psychiatrist. They are usually employed in health authorities, hospitals, schools, prisons and mental health centres, and help in the treatment of patients by assisting their self-expression through art using a variety of media. To qualify, you typically need to take a further postgraduate diploma in art therapy. However, in addition to the formal qualifications, you'll also need great emotional sensitivity for this work, which is conducted on a one-to-one or small group basis over long periods of time.

For more info:
British Association of Art Therapists – **www.baat.org**

PICTURE RESEARCHER

As a picture researcher, you will typically be employed by a picture library, for example the Kobal Collection or Getty Images, or a design agency to source and obtain or license images to illustrate a brief. Most of the work now involves sourcing images online, although there are still smaller, specialist libraries that supply transparencies or CDs. Initially, picture researchers take a brief from internal contacts (for example, a magazine designer or editor) or external contacts (for example, the publisher or marketing manager from a client company). Before starting their search, the picture researcher must consider such factors as colours, size and target audience for the image. In terms of qualifications required, most companies seek a degree, though interestingly, it does not have to be specifically in art, and the highest qualification required is an MA in archive administration, so this is a role that could suit someone who has taken a non-art degree and is now keen to get a foot in the door.

For more info
Skillset – **www.skillset.org**
Picture Research Association (PRA) –
www.picture-research.org.uk

MEDICAL ILLUSTRATOR

Medical illustrators are often employed (freelance or in-house) by specialist publishing agencies – for example, medical publishers or health authorities – to produce images for their education, research or patient information materials. The term 'illustrator' is used loosely here, as they may be a photographer, artist or graphic designer. Medical photographers and video producers are responsible for the clinical recording of patients, using still and moving pictures working in an operating theatre, ward or clinic. Medical artists and graphic designers specialise in the design and production of artwork, scientific posters, brochures etc. Entry requirements for this field are slightly more vague – you will certainly need the relevant art and design qualification, and the Institute of Medical Illustrators recommends a postgraduate certificate in medical illustration. Whatever their medium, medical illustrators must combine technical artistic skill with an understanding of anatomy.

For more info
The Institute of Medical Illustrators – **www.imi.org.uk**

Professional bodies

Professional bodies are responsible for overseeing a particular profession or career area, ensuring that people who work in the area are fully trained and meet ethical guidelines. Professional bodies may be known as institutions, societies or associations. They generally have regulatory roles: they make sure that members of the profession are able to work successfully in their jobs without endangering lives or abusing their position.

Professional bodies are often involved in training and career development, so courses and workplace training may have to follow the body's guidelines. In order to be fully qualified and licensed to work in your profession of choice, you will have to follow the professional training route. In many areas of work, completion of the professional training results in gaining chartered status – and the addition of some extra letters after your name. Other institutions may award other types of certification once certain criteria have been met. Chartered or certified members will usually need to take further courses and training to ensure their skills are kept up to date.

What professional bodies are there?

Not all career areas have professional bodies. Those jobs that require extensive learning and training are likely to have bodies with a regulatory focus. This includes careers such as engineering, law, construction, health and finance. If you want to work in one of these areas, it's important to make sure your degree course is accredited by the professional body – otherwise you may have to undertake further study or training later on.

Other bodies may play more of a supportive role, looking after the interests of people who work in the sector. This includes journalism, management and arts-based careers. Professional bodies may also be learned bodies, providing opportunities for further learning and promoting the development of knowledge in the field.

Can I join as a student?

Many professional bodies offer student membership – sometimes free or for reduced fees. Membership can be extremely valuable as a source of advice, information and resources. You'll have the opportunity to meet other students in the field, as well as experienced professionals. It will also look good on your CV, when you come to apply for jobs.

See below for a list of professional bodies operating within the fields of art and design. You will find other support organisations listed in 'Which area' (pages 17–27).

ADVERTISING

The Advertising Association
www.adassoc.org.uk

FINE ART

Society of Graphic Fine Art
www.sgfa.org.uk

The Royal Society of Portrait Painters
www.therp.co.uk

Royal British Society of Sculptors
www.rbs.org.uk

Association of Illustrators
www.theaoi.com

The Institute of Medical Illustrators
www.imi.org.uk

The British Association of Art Therapists
www.baat.org

CONSERVATION, RESTORATION, GALLERY AND MUSEUM CURATION

The Institute of Conservation (Icon)
www.icon.org.uk

Museums Association
www.museumsassociation.org

DESIGN

Chartered Society of Designers
www.csd.org.uk

International Interior Design Association
www.iida.org

The British Institute of Interior Design
www.biid.org.uk

The Institution of Engineering Designers
www.ied.org.uk

FASHION DESIGN

The Textile Institute
www.texi.org

Chartered Society of Designers
www.csd.org.uk

UK Fashion and Textile Association
www.ukft.org

INTERACTIVE MEDIA

British Interactive Media Association
www.bima.co.uk

PHOTOGRAPHY

Association of Photographers
http://home.the-aop.org

British Institute of Professional Photography
www.bipp.com

The Royal Photographic Society
www.rps.org

Graduate destinations

Art and Design
HESA Destination of Leavers of Higher Education Survey

Each year, comprehensive statistics are collected on what graduates are doing six months after they complete their course. The survey is co-ordinated by the Higher Education Statistics Agency (HESA) and provides information about how many graduates move into employment (and what type of career) or further study and how many are believed to be unemployed.

The full results across all subject areas are published by the Higher Education Careers Service Unit (HECSU) and the Association of Graduate Careers Advisory Services (AGCAS) in *What Do Graduates Do?*, which is available from **www.ucasbooks.com**.

	Art and Fine Art	Design
In UK employment	56.3%	68.4%
In overseas employment	0.9%	1.9%
Working and studying	7.1%	4.6%
Studying in the UK for a higher degree	4.5%	2.3%
Studying in the UK for a teaching qualification	2.2%	0.9%
Undertaking other further study or training in the UK	3.1%	1.7%
Undertaking other further study or training overseas	0.2%	0.1%
Not available for employment, study or training	5.0%	3.1%
Believed to be unemployed	12.6%	10.9%
Other	8.1%	6.1%

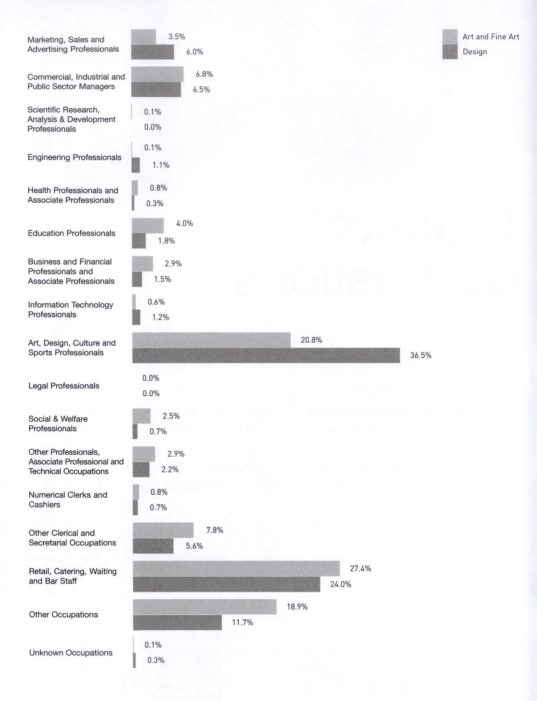

	Art and Fine Art	Design
Marketing, Sales and Advertising Professionals	3.5%	6.0%
Commercial, Industrial and Public Sector Managers	6.8%	6.5%
Scientific Research, Analysis & Development Professionals	0.1%	0.0%
Engineering Professionals	0.1%	1.1%
Health Professionals and Associate Professionals	0.8%	0.3%
Education Professionals	4.0%	1.8%
Business and Financial Professionals and Associate Professionals	2.9%	1.5%
Information Technology Professionals	0.6%	1.2%
Art, Design, Culture and Sports Professionals	20.8%	36.5%
Legal Professionals	0.0%	0.0%
Social & Welfare Professionals	2.5%	0.7%
Other Professionals, Associate Professional and Technical Occupations	2.9%	2.2%
Numerical Clerks and Cashiers	0.8%	0.7%
Other Clerical and Secretarial Occupations	7.8%	5.6%
Retail, Catering, Waiting and Bar Staff	27.4%	24.0%
Other Occupations	18.9%	11.7%
Unknown Occupations	0.1%	0.3%

Reproduced with the kind permission of HECSU/AGCAS, *What Do Graduates Do? 2011.*
Data from the HESA Destinations of Leavers from Higher Education Survey 09/10

Case studies

HEAR IT FROM THE EXPERTS

Just what can you do with an art and design degree?

The following graduate profiles show the wealth of exciting careers awaiting you! There is such a range of career paths to choose from in this sector that in many ways art and design students are spoilt for choice.

Studio director and self-employed product designer

LAURA WELLINGTON

Route into product design:

Level 3 Diploma in foundation studies – art and design, Swansea Institute of Higher Education (2003); BA design, Leeds Metropolitan University (2008)

WHY PRODUCT DESIGN?

I started my art foundation course with a career in graphic design in mind until a tutor pointed out that I approached every graphics project by working in 3D. I am fascinated by the look and feel of different materials, and tangible objects lead to ideas for me rather than the other way round. From this point onwards I moved towards 3D design.

HOW DID YOU GET TO WHERE YOU ARE TODAY?

I chose a degree where I could combine broad-based skills such as computer-aided design (CAD), with the option to specialise in furniture or product design. A major turning point for me was a three-month exchange trip (as part of my degree) through the Erasmus scheme, to study at a design academy in Finland. I was inspired by Scandinavian furniture design and then convinced that furniture and lighting design were for me.

In my third year I wrote my dissertation on setting up a business to re-use old furniture and waste products to create sustainable designs. I also had an idea for a creative space in Leeds, where designers could work collaboratively.

My best design idea was created quite by chance. On a visit to a plastics manufacturer to source perspex for a project, ever-resourceful I retrieved some colourful plastic off-cuts from their waste bin. It was while talking to a friend and absentmindedly coiling a piece of the perspex in my hand that I had the idea to create the perspex pendant light which I later christened Hula. I have been able to showcase this at a number of exhibitions including New Designers. My big breakthrough was appearing on the TV programme Britain's Next Big Thing where Habitat agreed to sell my Hula lamp in their stores.

WHAT DOES YOUR JOB INVOLVE?

Currently Hula is manufactured and sold in Habitat stores in Europe and I get royalties from this, although disappointingly Habitat no longer has many stores in the UK. I also make and sell one-off Hulas through my own business, Laura Wellington Designs. Due to the publicity from Britain's Next Big Thing, which was televised in several countries, I get orders from the UK and abroad.

However, my current focus is on setting up a creative hub in Leeds, an idea I had at university and have always wanted to pursue. Along with my business partner I have founded Duke Studios, where designers can share professional workshop space and collaborate on design projects.

WHAT HAS BEEN YOUR BIGGEST CHALLENGE?

Understanding how to move from making one or two items to mass production commercially is an ongoing learning curve. Knowing how to go about finding the best manufacturer for both quality and price is difficult.

AND THE BEST BITS?

Highlights have been doing design shows and being invited to Habitat's headquarters. I get a buzz when customers show me photos of Hula in situ and tell me how they are designing their spaces around it. At Duke Studios I get a lot of satisfaction helping other designers, encouraging co-working and contributing to the creative economy in Leeds.

LAURA'S TOP TIPS

Be proactive, treat every person you meet as a possible opportunity for the future, seize every opportunity and be a bit cheeky – if you don't ask you don't get.

Metals conservator

The British Museum

BRYONY FINN

Route into conservation and restoration:
A levels – art, chemistry, maths with statistics, German (2004); BA conservation and restoration, University of Lincoln (2007)

WHY CONSERVATION AND RESTORATION?

I chose to study a degree in conservation and restoration because it had many aspects which matched my interests. When studying art at A level I had spent a lot of time in art galleries and had a growing interest in arts, crafts and technologies. I had always had an interest in history and enjoyed visiting historic houses and museums. When I applied for the course I didn't realise how useful my A level in chemistry would be.

HOW DID YOU GET WHERE YOU ARE TODAY?

The course covered both theoretical and practical conservation and gave us opportunities from early on to work on real museum objects. I was lucky to be awarded a scholarship from the Zibby Garnett Travelling Fellowship and undertook a three-month placement as a contemporary art and sculpture intern at the Statens Museum for Kunst in Copenhagen. Working in one of Denmark's national galleries was a great experience. I then spent a lot more time volunteering in museums and as an intern in order to build experience.

After I graduated I took a variety of short-term projects including conserving wall paintings and architectural tiles, and condition-checking objects prior to moving them between collections. The British Museum employed me to conserve ceramics and glass for loan, display, research, publication and storage. I have also worked as a self-employed conservator on projects involving archaeological items, museum collections, the restoration of buildings and historic houses. I love the variety!

I have enjoyed working on a wide range of different materials ranging from contemporary to archaeological and this has informed the way I have approached my career. Although many graduates choose a specialist area of conservation, I have chosen to keep my options broad.

WHAT DOES YOUR JOB INVOLVE?

I currently work for the British Museum as a metals conservator. I am one of a small team conserving a hoard of 52,503 Roman coins that was discovered by a metal detectorist in 2010, so that the coins can be identified for cataloguing.

On a daily basis I remove corrosion from the coins using chemical and mechanical techniques to make the coins legible (identifiable by emperor, mint and coin type). At the end of the project the findings will be published along with an account of the conservation of the hoard. The job also involves presenting the work to visitors to the museum workshop.

WHAT HAS BEEN YOUR BIGGEST CHALLENGE?

It's not always easy to get jobs, especially when you are starting out, so it is important to take every opportunity to learn and gain experience. Sometimes this means spending time volunteering and on unpaid internships.

AND THE BEST BITS?

Working with an amazing collection of such special objects is a real privilege. I also enjoy the problem-solving aspects of my job and that it combines both scientific and artistic elements. It's nice to have a job which is both academic and where you need to be skilled with your hands to carry it out well.

BRYONY'S TOP TIPS

A good grounding in chemistry is useful but lots of conservation courses include conservation science to bring you up to speed. Good manual dexterity is really important as is ability to pay attention to detail. Keep a portfolio of your work showing your relevant skills (for example artistic, colour-matching or problem-solving skills) and/or objects you have worked on.

Design student

EIFION LLOYD JAMES

Route into surface pattern design:

A levels – textiles, graphic design, photography (2007); foundation diploma in art and design, Swansea Metropolitan University (2008); BA surface pattern design: contemporary applied arts practice, Swansea Metropolitan University (graduating 2012)

WHY SURFACE PATTERN DESIGN?

I started a degree in Photographic art but left after the first year realising the course wasn't right for me. I then chose Surface pattern design: Contemporary applied arts practice, as I had enjoyed the freedom of using a variety of materials and techniques on my art foundation course and had an interest in textiles. I am fascinated by applied art, the application of aesthetic design and decoration to everyday, functional objects.

TELL US ABOUT YOUR DEGREE

My degree is very broad, with three pathways: contemporary applied arts practice, textiles for fashion and textiles for interiors. We were encouraged to try all the pathways in the first year, and then decide which to opt for in the second. I chose applied arts as this involves using a range of materials including, metal, glass, textiles, plastics, wood and wire and supports innovative ideas.

The course is based in a large, creative, energetic studio that is home to students from all three years and pathways. This creates a buzz and a real mix of ideas and outcomes. The course centres on surface design in the broadest sense (including soft fabric to hard materials such as wood and metal) and there is an equal emphasis on traditional and digital techniques. Equipment includes digital textile printers and embroidery machines, laser cutters and laser engravers alongside traditional textile printing tables and facilities for dyeing and steaming. With sewing and knitting machines, printmaking, ceramics and metal workshops and a dark room I have been able to learn and combine many skills and processes.

WHAT DID YOUR WORK PLACEMENT INVOLVE?

My work placement was at Freshwest Design, a contemporary furniture and interior design company based in Pembrokeshire. I got the placement by emailing the company after becoming aware of them at a digital seminar at university.

I worked at Freshwest for about ten days in total over the summer. My responsibilities included basic tasks such as answering the phone, placing orders and making tea/coffee, but I also had the opportunity to do some design and practical work, including working on a prototype for a textile-based product.

Freshwest is a small company combining a studio and workshop where development, prototyping and fabrication happen under one roof. This meant I got an insight into both design and production.

WHAT WAS THE TOUGHEST CHALLENGE?

The biggest challenge for me was confidence. I was worried about making mistakes (and losing money for the company). Freshwest helped me overcome this by throwing me in at the deep end on the first day, tasking me to ring people and place orders!

AND THE BEST BITS?

I helped with the construction of a chandelier that was on show at Tent London, a contemporary interior design trade show taking place during the London Design Festival. Even though I had no part in the design, it was good to think that something I had worked on was in the public domain. Another high point was working on the prototype of a high end product and the fact that Freshwest listened to my ideas and valued my opinion.

EIFION'S TOP TIPS

When looking for work placements, research companies well and then send out lots of speculative emails to increase your chance of getting a reply. Having your own website (or web presence) helps at interview to enable you to show your work easily.

Freelance photographer

ALEX MOORE

Route into photography:

A levels – art and design, graphic design, English language, ICT (2007); foundation diploma in art and design, A level fine art (2008); BA photography, Staffordshire University (2011)

WHY PHOTOGRAPHY?

Initially I was interested in graphic design; I loved the subject and excelled at it but struggled to picture myself working as a designer. During my art foundation diploma I had the opportunity to practise photography, fell in love with the medium and quickly realised that it was the imagery behind the design that I had been interested in all along.

HOW DID YOU GET WHERE YOU ARE TODAY?

My photography degree was full of highs and lows but I came out of it a new person. When I reached my final year I knew I had to pull off something impressive; I wanted to stand out from the crowd. My final project was a major hit. I ended the year with a fantastic exhibition, great grades and substantial pride in what I had achieved. It was then that I realised I had the potential to work as a photographer.

I won several awards for my final project both before and long after graduation. I entered it into almost every competition going and it paid off enormously. Since then I haven't put my camera down.

WHAT DOES YOUR JOB INVOLVE?

I am working towards becoming a professional freelance photographer. My work is mainly portraiture and food photography. I use my portraits to enter competitions and as promotional material; food photography brings a much smaller but steadier income. As a photographer it is important to piece your income together from different sources as it is unlikely that any one kind of photography will earn you enough alone.

Every day I promote myself and network online. It is crucial to have an online presence. I update my website, write a blog and tweet at photographers, galleries and institutes. It is all about making your name recognisable. I also do some unpaid work for a fashion/lifestyle blog and spend a lot of time editing photographs.

I base myself at home where I have my own office; most of my photography work happens on location. If I need a studio I rent by the day.

WHAT HAS BEEN YOUR BIGGEST CHALLENGE?

Photography can never be a 9 to 5 job. It is something that you embed into your life and timetable your free time around. You never know when work is going to show up and you have to be prepared to be flexible. When I am working to a deadline it is impossible to predict how long it will take to edit 100 pictures. Expect to work unsociable hours!

AND THE BEST BITS?

Photography is endlessly rewarding. Whether it's a solo exhibition, a publication in a high profile magazine or a cash prize for a picture, the industry is full of incentives to keep you going. But aside from all that, the real reward is knowing that you are doing something that you love.

In a few years time I see myself as freelance commercial photographer living and working in London. I will divide my time between commercial/advertising photography and my personal work.

ALEX'S TOP TIPS

Don't expect to 'learn' photography from your tutors alone. If you want to be a successful photographer you have to live it. Read magazines, visit exhibitions, teach yourself techniques and always take pictures. Photography, like any business, requires an investment. Expect to spend lots of money on equipment but be realistic about what you really need.

Design intern

SAS advertising, design and marketing

FLEUR ISBELL

Route into graphic design:

A levels – product design (2006), art and design, English, physical education (2007); BA graphic communication, Bath Spa University (2011)

WHY GRAPHIC DESIGN?

I am interested in the visual language of objects around me: I like looking at patterns, shapes, texture and colours in signs, maps, buildings and typography. I also enjoy being creative, being able to experiment and make designs. Studying graphic design has allowed me to do what I love: research, solve problems, play and to be creative!

HOW DID YOU GET WHERE YOU ARE TODAY?

At university I loved the freedom to do the projects I wanted with a wide range of facilities at my disposal. I spent a lot of time in various workshops, letterpress, silkscreen, etching, textiles, book binding and in the dark room. Experimenting and combining printing and photographic methods, analogue with digital, was endlessly absorbing.

In the first year there were practical modules on film, animation, photography, illustration, design and typography. Tutors and guest lecturers helped us understand the processes involved in each of the different areas and helped me decide that I wanted to be a designer. As well as the fundamentals of design and typography I learnt a great deal about coming up with ideas and concepts and how to use design software. During my final year I started to network by going to talks and design events and found out about internships.

After graduation I had a placement at Mytton Williams design agency and took part in exhibitions, such as D&AD New Blood and Emerge Art Fair. I set up a website and blog and was featured in Creative Review magazine. Success in getting a place on the D&AD graduate academy, a five day creative bootcamp, culminated in a paid three-month internship at SAS advertising, design and marketing agency.

WHAT DOES YOUR JOB INVOLVE?

As I have always favoured an experimental way of thinking I was keen to work in an environment that was very idealistic in its approach. SAS is an advertising, design and marketing company, creating design strategies for graduate recruitment, talent schemes, employer branding and employee communications.

As a design intern I help produce work and also help with pitches. My role has involved working for clients such as BP, M&S and GlaxoSmithKline. I am involved in the design stages of brainstorming and idea generation, working with a copywriter on scamping (drawing out ideas), research and mood-boarding, and finally generating visual concepts and pieces of design work.

In January I will start a three-month internship as a junior designer with international brand consultants Wolff Olins.

WHAT HAS BEEN YOUR BIGGEST CHALLENGE?

My first placement after university was tough because as a student I was used to a certain way of working, but after a few weeks I adapted and my confidence grew.

AND THE BEST BITS?

I love being involved in all stages of the design, from concept to design production, and working with a wide range of people. I particularly enjoy researching, thinking up ideas to solve problems and creating final designs. In the future I would like to work abroad and in the distant future set up a design company.

FLEUR'S TOP TIPS

Don't be afraid, limit yourself or be scared of failure, just create! Keep inspiring yourself: go to exhibitions, design talks and workshops, read design magazines and blogs, and travel. Set up your own blog, and input your ideas, work or inspirations, such as a building you like or a sign. It's a great way to visually record your work and get other people's views.

Want to see UCAS in action?
Visit www.ucas.tv to watch

case studies

how-to guides

Entry routes

Routes to qualification

There are more art and design courses in the UK than in any other country in Europe. This helps to reduce the competition for places, but can also make it very hard to choose the right course. There is also an emerging debate about the quality and standard of some of the courses offered, especially in some key sectors such as animation, where employers have voiced concerns about whether the teaching of technology and techniques is always up to date.

Unlike many other professions, there is no one route that all students must follow to qualify. For example, some bypass the foundation course altogether; others take a foundation course only. In addition, students can stop after any stage of their studies to try to join the workforce. This said, very few people now go straight from school into art and design careers. Most employers look for individuals who have gained nationally-recognised qualifications in their particular field. There is, however, a commonly accepted or 'typical' path to qualification post-A level, involving a foundation course and/or a degree, plus a possible postgraduate course in the relevant art or design specialism.

1 foundation course +/- 2 Degree and/or Higher National Diploma (HND) +/- 3 Postgraduate course

1 FOUNDATION COURSE

This is a one-year, college-based course leading to a (level 3) diploma in foundation studies (art and design) or 'foundation course' for short. It is classified as level 3 for funding purposes (ie further education, therefore not covered by a student loan). The majority of students choose a course in their local area and, in many cases, study while living in the family home. Hundreds of courses are located in further education colleges, sixth-form colleges, art colleges and (in smaller numbers) universities.

Most courses aim to give students hands-on experience of all the major areas of art and design. Some operate on the basis of offering just a couple of focused study pathways, such as graphic design and media production. All foundation courses end with a final exhibition of students' work that is usually open to the public.

Don't confuse foundation courses with foundation degrees. Foundation degrees are 'pre-degree' vocational courses that are designed with employers to meet skills shortages at higher technician and associate professional levels. Available since 2001, they are typically two years long, and on successful completion 'graduates' may choose to go on to study for a full honours degree. Foundation degrees are available in numerous subjects, mostly linked to key skills-shortage sectors, eg the hospitality, engineering and automotive industries, although there are a growing number of courses in design and media-related fields.

FROM A STUDENT VIEWPOINT, A FOUNDATION COURSE IS DIVIDED INTO THREE MAIN STAGES

1 'EXPLORATORY' STAGE

The **autumn** term. You will be introduced to the main areas of art and design through project work. For example, as well as a general introduction to the theory and practice of art and design, you'll have the chance to experiment with different materials, such as plaster and wood.

2 'PATHWAY' STAGE

The **spring** term. You start to focus on building your portfolio in your strongest field, and you'll get to explore and research a particular area of art and design.

3 'CONFIRMATORY' STAGE

The **summer** term. Now you're ready to put together your own personal study in the form of a major piece of project work that has to show you can, for example:

- research and negotiate a project brief
- manage your project well and within the time available
- prepare and display your work in a professional manner
- evaluate your work, identifying opportunities for additional improvement.

Please note, some courses may be split into two semesters rather than three terms but will still follow the same template.

The alternative in Scotland – 'Year Zero'

Foundation courses don't exist as such in Scotland (there is currently one exception, at the Leith School of Art in Edinburgh), although some FE colleges offer courses that are similar in some respects to the foundation diplomas. Most degree courses in art and design typically take four years, ie one year longer than in England, Northern Ireland or Wales, with the first year often providing students with a broad foundation in core drawing skills, supplemented by the opportunity to try out a range of different specialisms. Students then select one area in which to specialise for the next three years. Glasgow School of Art, however, requires students to choose a specialism in the first year. It may be possible for students who have taken a foundation course elsewhere to go straight into the second year of a degree course in art and design.

Some universities elsewhere in the UK are now also starting to adopt the Scottish approach to art and design courses, by offering 'Year Zero' courses. These are basically university equivalents to foundation courses, the only difference being that they are offered as part of a longer degree. Why this trend? Universities claim it is to address the needs of students who like the idea of continuity – you won't have to up sticks at the end of your foundation course year to move to a new location and start getting to know tutors and fellow classmates all over again. However, there is another – financial – reason. Anecdotal evidence suggests that, due to financial pressures, students are increasingly likely to stay closer to home, so universities realise the importance of being able to address the needs of their local community.

There is, however, a big financial implication. 'Year Zero' students count as higher-education students, which makes them liable for tuition fees. Foundation course students, in contrast, are classed as further education students, and as such are exempt from tuition fees (so long as they are under 19 when they start the course). However, as further education students, foundation course students are also not entitled to student loans… So it just depends which is more important to you financially – that student loan or those student fees!

2 DEGREE COURSE

Don't let the vast range of courses on offer confuse you. Most courses on the same subject will follow a similar syllabus. For example, the first year of a **fine art** course typically covers core art and design skills, such as drawing, plus 'contextual' studies such as history of art, to give students greater awareness of the development of art over time. In years 2 and 3, students start to specialise and concentrate on a particular perspective. On **history of art** courses, the first year will typically serve as an introduction to the general principles of art interpretation and critique, as well as particular periods in art. In the second and third years, students will be able to focus on particular periods or forms, culminating with a dissertation in their final year, although they will probably also be able to take specialist modules, for example gallery management, and/or work placements in, for example, an auction house. However, institutions may vary in how they allocate time to each particular topic. On some courses, for example, students study subjects one after another – perhaps one week on painting, the next on art history, the next on art materials, and so on. Others prefer to teach numerous aspects of the course simultaneously through projects that last several weeks.

Please note: **sandwich courses** (which literally 'sandwich' periods of work experience in industry between periods in the studio or lecture theatre) are rare in art and design, but are a more common feature of **product** and **industrial design** degree courses.

3 POSTGRADUATE COURSE

Most students will leave their studies after their
foundation course or undergraduate degree (or HND)
to get their foot on the first rung of the art and design
profession ladder. However, most of those who stay on
at university to complete postgraduate studies do so
for one of three main reasons.

- **To specialise in a particular field** – for example,
  a graphic designer wishing to specialise in
  3D graphics.
- **To stand out from the crowd** – a postgraduate
  qualification is one way to give yourself an edge over
  other applicants in especially competitive fields, for
  example fashion or interactive media.
- **To gain a teaching qualification** – for example, a
  Postgraduate Certificate in Education (PGCE) in
  secondary art and design.

However, the possible advantage that a postgraduate
qualification may give you should be weighed against
not only the additional cost but also the additional time
you will spend away from the job market.

To research and apply for postgraduate courses at a
range of higher education institutions, go to
www.ukpass.ac.uk.

What others say...

What others say...

These are extracts from case studies in previous editions of this book. They give some insights into the experiences and thoughts of people who were once in the same position as you.

CHRIS SHIPTON – TRAINEE TEACHER, GRAPHIC ART

At art college I specialised in drawing, but also took other options such as painting and illustration. When I left college I temped for a few months until I got a proper job as a production assistant for a magazine.

When I wasn't working I continued to draw and put on exhibitions of my work. I realised that what I really wanted was to get back in touch with my artistic side and work with art in a much more direct way. I decided that teaching art would give me that opportunity, so I applied for a teacher training course in the lifelong learning sector.

One of the reasons I was drawn to teaching was that I knew it would develop my communication skills, which I didn't feel I had been using in my previous jobs. I get enormous job satisfaction from helping students on their learning journey and the sense of teamwork involved getting them from A to B.

If you want to work in art or design, it's incredibly important to develop your awareness about business alongside your creativity and studying. You need to know how to make money from your creative skills when you finish your course.

EMMA WILLIAMSON – PRODUCER

I spent the third year of my degree working in industry, as an interactive designer for a post-production company in London. I helped them build their website while I sat with their design team and gained new skills I hadn't learned on my course. Although I wasn't keen to take a year out at the time, I realise now it was an incredibly useful experience for my final year and definitely helped me get a job.

I now work as a producer at a digital advertising creative agency, project-managing pieces of work for clients. I love the fact that nearly every idea we take on has never been done before, or is a new slant on something that already exists. First reactions are nearly always 'How on earth can we do this?', but we always manage it! I love helping to create new things and seeing an idea come to life.

In this industry you need a positive 'Yes, can do' kind of attitude. It's important to build strong relationships, be good at working in a team and to be able to step back and see your role in the bigger picture.

NATALIE BOATFIELD – PHOTOGRAPHER'S PA, ART DIRECTOR AND STUDIO MANAGER

One thing I have noticed in my current role is the number of interns that come through our creative space. Most of them think they are above the small jobs, which is a definite turn off to most people – especially me, as I have to do all the horrible jobs, such as cleaning the loo or hoovering when I need to! These little tasks may not seem important, but they prove to people you can and will do anything to help out in order to progress, and that you don't expect too much too soon. Everyone started at the bottom; you have to build strong relationships and earn trust to go places.

You have to choose between leading a creative, thought-provoking life and earning lots of money. If your choice is the second, this area won't be right for you. Someone once said to me: 'When you're an assistant, you are not a photographer – there is only room for one ego. There is only one photographer and that is not you. You must wait for your turn, it will come.

JESSICA ADAMSON – FINAL YEAR FASHION DESIGN STUDENT

Once on placement, I was able to put theory into practice and see how the fashion industry operates. Everything I had learned in the first two years clicked into place.

Now in my final year, the focus is on producing my own designs and I spend most of my time working independently in the studio, completing my final project. I feel that the movement from a mix of theory and practical, to industry experience, to producing my own work has been an ideal way to prepare me for the demands of the fashion industry.

My advice would be to pick a fashion design degree with a placement and get some industry experience under your belt. If you find the theory a bit heavy, stick with it and keep your notes; I regularly refer to mine and can now appreciate why theory is important.

KIMBERLEY SELWOOD – FREELANCE JEWELLERY DESIGNER

My job is really hard work as essentially I do the work of three people: designer, maker and manager! As well as designing and creating jewellery ranges, day to day I have to do the accounts, market the business and continually look for new ways to sell my work.

My biggest challenge is money. With no regular wage I have to promote myself continually and find outlets to sell what I create. But I enjoy the freedom to schedule my own time. I love designing and the creative side of business – where it can go and how to get there. Most of all, I enjoy the successes, finding a new shop that wishes to sell my work, seeing my designs featured in the press and letters from satisfied customers.

LEWIS DARBY – PRODUCER/DIRECTOR AND FREELANCE ANIMATOR

I have always been keen on art and music. I saw an animation degree as an opportunity to combine my interest in art and sound.

There were two defining moments at university that got me to the position I'm in now. The first was in my second year, when I chose a module on 2D digital animation using After Effects (software for creating motion graphics and visual effects) and I became hooked! The second moment was in my third year. A group of us were given the opportunity to visit some animation studios in London. Being able to see people working in the industry and the kind of work I might be able to do boosted my desire to succeed.

My top tips are to make the most of any opportunities that come your way, especially as a student. Trips to studios, internships, networking and taking extra courses to boost your skills all help. I developed a good relationship with my university tytors and in return they have passed on endless opportunities to me, even 18 months after graduating.

LYNNE SEMPLE – INTERIOR DESIGNER

I am responsible for coming up with designs, interpreting designs into technical drawings for construction, building relationships with clients and project administration.

For each individual project I begin by meeting the client and discussing their needs in detail. I then produce hand-drawn sketches or use Photoshop, Powerpoint or 'sketch up' computer programmes to produce a design, a space plan and to show material finishes. When these are signed off by the clients I produce technical drawings using CAD. During construction it is important that I attend site meetings and have regular contact with the building contractor and other consultants.

You have to be prepared, initially, to work hard without a great salary, but the rewards lie in job satisfaction. Try to get industry experience in design offices while you are a student to increase your chances of finding a job after graduation.

**SIMON COOK – FREELANCE GRAPHIC
DESIGNER/ILLUSTRATOR**

As a child I loved drawing and doodling, so my desire
to be creative started at an early age. I chose graphic
design because I didn't want to be pigeonholed into one
set job title and I felt a degree in this area would give
me the necessary skills to cross over into other areas
of design.

Work as hard as you can at university and grab every
opportunity available. Make time at least once a week
to email a designer whose work you love, or graphic
design studios that you admire, to say hello and show
them your work. If illustration is what you want to do,
make sure you stand out – your style is the most
important thing!

Save with UCAS Card

If you're in Year 12, S5 or equivalent and thinking about higher education, sign up for the **FREE** UCAS Card to receive all these benefits:

- information about courses and unis
- expert advice from UCAS
- exclusive discounts for card holders

UCAS

Register today at
www.ucas.com/ucascard

find us on
Facebook

* correct at time of printing.

Applicant journey

Six easy steps to university and college

STEP 1

Choosing courses

Use Course Finder at **www.ucas.com** to find out which courses might suit you and the universities and colleges that offer them.

STEP 2

Applying

You can apply for up to five courses using the online application system at **www.ucas.com**.

STEP 3

Offers

You can check the progress of your application using Track at **www.ucas.com**, which will be updated as we receive decisions from universities and colleges. If you don't receive any offers, or decline all the offers you do receive, you may be able to use Extra, which allows eligible applicants to apply for a new choice.

STEP 4

Results

UCAS receives many exam results direct from the awarding bodies – you can check the list at **www.ucas.com**. If your qualification is listed, you don't need to send your results to UCAS or the universities and colleges. Check Track at **www.ucas.com** to see if you've got a place on your chosen course.

STEP 5

Next steps

Depending on your circumstances, you might use this step. If you have received different grades than expected, or have changed your mind, there may be other options available. You need to look at Track and course vacancies at **www.ucas.com**.

STEP 6

Starting university or college

Make sure you have everything ready, such as accommodation, finances, travel arrangements, books and equipment required for the course.

1

Choosing courses

Step 1 – Planning your application for art and design

Although this section covers routes into art and design from qualifications such as A levels and Scottish Highers, it is also possible to follow a 'vocational' route through a work-based training path, and to springboard into the profession or into higher education from there.

ENTRY REQUIREMENTS

Which subjects?

The good news for would-be artists is that the range and number of subjects you need to take at sixth form level is quite flexible. In fact, to get onto some foundation courses, you won't even need a 'full house' of qualifications, such as, for example three A levels, since a minimum of one – and more typically two – are accepted by some institutions. Admissions tutors usually place more weight on the work you've produced – as demonstrated by your portfolio – than the subjects you've studied.

Now comes the 'but' … this is not the case for all art and design courses. It is strongly recommended that you add some design or IT elements to your studies if you plan to study computer graphics, so that you're at least familiar with the technology when you start your course.

In addition, if you don't take an art or art-related subject, you will be under greater pressure when it comes to building your portfolio. Applicants who have taken Highers, A level or even AS level art are at a distinct advantage in that they are automatically able to include elements of their coursework in their portfolio. If you don't take any art or design courses at this level, you'll have to build your portfolio outside school or college from scratch which, combined with your coursework for other subjects, will be a lot more work.

Which grades?

Admissions tutors are rather ambivalent about the importance of grades. The general consensus seems to be that your grades are not as important as your artistic ability, which is good news for anyone whose more theory-based subjects may have pulled down their grade average. However, certain sectors within art and design, such as animation and computer graphics, are very competitive so the rule of thumb is that the more competitive the sector, the more important your grades. That said, a look at the average UCAS Tariff points for students accepted onto creative arts courses shows that the grade average of students starting a degree in this field is typically lower than for some other areas, for example, law and medicine.

HOW DO I FIND THE BEST COURSE FOR ME?

For courses on offer, see Course Finder at **www.ucas.com**.

Try to use various resources of information to make your choices for higher education, including the Course Finder facility at **www.ucas.com**. League tables might be a component of this research but you should bear in mind that these tables attempt to rank institutions in an overall order, which reflects the interests, preoccupations and decisions of those who have produced and edited them. The ways in which they are compiled vary greatly and you will need to look closely at the criteria that have been used. See page 74

UCAS CARD

At its simplest, the UCAS Card scheme is the start of your UCAS journey. It can save you a packet on the high street with exclusive offers to UCAS Card holders, as well as providing you with hints and tips about finding the best course at the right university or college. If that's not enough you'll also receive these benefits:

- frequent expert help from UCAS, with all the essential information you need on the application process
- free monthly newsletters providing advice, hints, tips and exclusive discounts
- tailored information on the universities and courses you're interested in
- and much more.

If you're in Year 12, S5 or equivalent and thinking about higher education for autumn 2013, sign up for your FREE UCAS Card today to receive all these benefits at **www.ucas.com/ucascard**.

Connect with us...

 www.facebook.com/ucasonline

 www.twitter.com/ucas_online

 www.youtube.com/ucasonline

> Choosing courses

1

Choosing courses

USE COURSE FINDER AT WWW.UCAS.COM TO FIND OUT WHICH COURSES MIGHT SUIT YOU, AND THE UNIVERSITIES AND COLLEGES THAT OFFER THEM.

Use the UCAS website – www.ucas.com has lots of advice on how to find a course. Go to the students' section of the website for the best advice or go straight to Course Finder to see all the courses available through UCAS. Our map of the UK at www.ucas.com/students/choosingcourses/choosinguni/map/ shows you where all the universities and colleges are located.

Watch UCAStv – at www.ucas.tv there are videos on *How to choose your course* and *Attending events*, as well as case studies from students talking about their experiences of finding a course at university or college.

Attend UCAS conventions – UCAS conventions are held throughout the UK. Universities and colleges have exhibition stands where their staff offer information about courses and institutions. Details of when the conventions are happening are shown at www.ucas.com/conventions.

Look at websites and prospectuses – universities and colleges have prospectuses and course-specific leaflets on their undergraduate courses. Your school or college library may have copies or go to the university's website to download a copy or ask them to send one to you.

Go to university and college open days – most institutions offer open days to anyone who wants to attend. See the list of universities and colleges on **www.ucas.com** and the *UCAS Open Days* publication (see the Essential Reading chapter) for information on when they are taking place. Aim to visit all of the universities and colleges you are interested in before you apply. It will help with your expectations of university life and make sure the course is the right one for you.

League tables – these can be helpful but bear in mind that they attempt to rank institutions in an overall order reflecting the views of those that produce them. They may not reflect your views and needs. Examples can be found at **www.thecompleteuniversityguide.co.uk**, **www.guardian.co.uk/education/universityguide**, **www.thetimes.co.uk** (subscription service) and **www.thesundaytimes.co.uk** (subscription service). See page xx for more information about league tables.

Do your research – speak and refer to as many trusted sources as you can find. Talk to someone already doing the job you have in mind. The section 'Which area?' on pages 17-27 will help you identify the different areas of art and design you might want to enter.

DECIDING ON YOUR COURSE CHOICES

Through UCAS you can initially apply for up to five courses. How do you find out more information to make an informed decision?

Remember you don't have to make five course choices. Only apply for a course if you're completely happy with both the course and the university or college and you would definitely be prepared to accept a place.

How do you narrow down your course choices? First of all, look up course details in this book or on Course Finder at **www.ucas.com**. This will give you an idea of the full range of courses and topics on offer. You'll quickly be able to eliminate institutions that don't offer the right course, or you can choose a 'hit list' of institutions first, and then see what they have to offer.

Once you've made a short(er) list, read the university and college websites, and generally find out as much as you can about the course, department and institution. Don't be afraid to contact them to ask for more information, request their prospectus or arrange an open day visit.

YOUR CHANCE TO CHECK OUT THE COURSES

If you don't fancy reading through endless university prospectus booklets, why not visit the 'Design Your Future' higher education exhibitions offered each year in London and Manchester (usually in November or December). For more information, visit **www.ucasevents.com/design**.

Exclusively for those interested in studying art and design or related subjects, this is an unrivalled opportunity for you to meet representatives from all the institutions around the UK who offer art and design or related courses, view artwork, attend workshops, talk to course leaders and current students, as well as collect lots of information. Not surprisingly, both events are very popular, with, in 2011, over 10,500 students taking the opportunity to check out their art and design study options. The London exhibition takes place at Olympia; the Manchester one at the Manchester Central Convention Complex.

For further details, please contact UCAS Events (tel: 01242 544 979 or e-mail: events@ucas.ac.uk). Also, art and design summer degree shows are usually held in June. With free admission, this is an ideal opportunity to find out more about particular courses you are interested in.

design
your future

Find out about art, design, media and other creative courses

The UCAS Design your future event is an excellent opportunity for students from Years 10,11,12 and foundation level to talk to representatives from a wide range of art colleges and universities, pick up prospectuses, and attend art and design study related workshops.

Some subjects covered include: Art; Design; Media; Architecture; Web Design; Fashion; Ceramics and many more…

Events are taking place in both London and Manchester and will include around one hundred exhibitors, from Universities and Colleges, to organisations of particular interest to prospective students.

TO FIND OUT MORE OR TO BOOK, PLEASE VISIT THE WEBSITE WWW.UCASEVENTS.COM/DESIGN OR CALL 01242 544645

UCAS

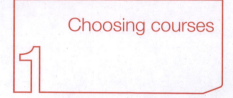

Choosing courses

1

Choosing your institution

Different people look for different things from their university or college course, but the checklist on the next page sets out the kinds of factors all prospective students should consider when choosing their university. Keep this list in mind on open days, when talking to friends about their experiences at various universities and colleges, or while reading prospectuses and websites.

TOP TIP

Don't be afraid to pick up the phone – university and college admissions officers welcome enquiries directly from students, rather than careers officers phoning on your behalf. It shows you're genuinely interested and committed to your own career early on.

WHAT TO CONSIDER WHEN CHOOSING YOUR ART AND DESIGN COURSE

Location	Do you want to stay close to home? Would you prefer to study at a city or campus university or college?
Grades required	Most studio-based art and design courses will place greater emphasis on creative potential (as evidenced in a portfolio) than on grades or points. Before applying, check university or college websites or contact the relevant art and design admissions office for clarification. Also refer to the Tariff information in this book.
Employer links	Ask the course tutor and university or college careers office about links with employers such as art galleries, advertising agencies etc. Find out if the course includes lectures from art and design professionals and where the lecturers typically come from.
Graduate prospects	Ask the careers office for their list of graduate destinations.
Cost	Ask the admissions office about tuition fees and financial assistance. Also find out what fees are charged for studio time and/or equipment.
Degree type	Think about if you want to study art on its own (single honours degree) or 50/50 with another subject, for example, 'art and history of art' (joint degree) or as one of a few subjects (combined degree).
Teaching style	How is the course taught? Ask about the number of lectures and tutorials per week, the amount of one-to-one work, and how you will build a portfolio or be involved in project work. Also ask about the balance between practical and contextual work.
Course assessment	What proportion of the assessment is based on your project work or portfolio, and how much is based on written assignments? Do you have an exhibition instead of a final exam?
Facilities for art and design students	Check out their workshop or studio facilities, and find out if you will get your own studio and storage area; unlike most subjects, where most time is spent in lecture theatres, seminars etc, art and design involves a lot of hands-on activity in workshops. In addition, find out if there is a university or college careers adviser dedicated to art and design. Also, will you be sharing facilities with part-time students?
'Fit'	Even if all the above criteria stack up, this one relies on gut feel – go and visit the art department if you can, and see if it's 'you'. For example, check out the end-of-year exhibition of final-year students' work to give you a good idea of the type and level of work the course produces. Also ask about lecturers' own particular interests; many will have personal web pages somewhere on the departmental website.

League tables

The information that follows has been provided by Dr Bernard Kingston of *The Complete University Guide*.

League tables are worth consulting early in your research and perhaps for confirmation later on. But never rely on them in isolation – always use them alongside other information sources available to you. Universities typically report that over a third of prospective students view league tables as important or very important in making their university choices. They give an insight into quality and are mainly based on data from the universities themselves. Somewhat confusingly, tables published in, say, 2012 are referred to as the 2013 tables because they are aimed at applicants going to university in that following year. The well known ones - *The Complete University Guide*, *The Guardian*, *The Times*, and *The Sunday Times* - rank the institutions and the subjects they teach using input measures (eg entry standards), throughput measures (eg student : staff ratios) and output measures (eg graduate prospects). Some tables are free to access whilst others are behind pay walls. All are interactive and enable users to create their own tables based on the measures important to them.

The universities are provided with their raw data for checking and are regularly consulted on methodology. But ultimately it is the compilers who decide what measures to use and what weights to put on them. They are competitors and rarely consult amongst themselves. So, for example, *The Times* tables differ significantly from *The Sunday Times* ones even though both newspapers belong to the same media proprietor.

Whilst the main university rankings tend to get the headlines, we would stress that the individual subject tables are as least as important, if not more so, when deciding where to study. All universities, regardless of their overall ranking, have some academic departments that rank highly in their subjects. Beware also giving much weight to an institution being a few places higher or lower in the tables – this is likely to be of little significance. This is particularly true in the lower half of the main table where overall scores show considerable bunching.

Most of the measures used to define quality come from hard factual data provided by the Higher Education Statistics Agency (HESA) but some, like student satisfaction and peer assessment, are derived from surveys of subjective impressions where you might wish to query sample size. We give a brief overview of the common measures here but please go to the individual websites for full details.

- **Student satisfaction** is derived from the annual National Student Survey (NSS) and is heavily used by *The Guardian* and *The Sunday Times*.
- **Research assessment** comes from a 2008 exercise (RAE) aimed at defining the quality of a university's research (excluded by *The Guardian*).
- **Entry standards** are based on the full UCAS Tariff scores obtained by new students.
- **Student : staff ratio** gives the number of students per member of academic staff.
- **Expenditure figures** show the costs of academic and student services.
- **Good honours** lists the proportion of graduates gaining a first or upper second honours degree.
- **Completion** indicates the proportion of students who successfully complete their studies.

- **Graduate prospects** usually reports the proportion of graduates who obtain a graduate job – not any job – or continue studying within six months of leaving.
- **Peer assessment** is used only by *The Sunday Times* which asks academics to rate other universities in their subjects.
- **Value added** is used only by *The Guardian* and compares entry standards with good honours.

All four main publishers of UK league tables (see Table 1) also publish university subject tables. *The Complete University Guide* and *The Times* are based on four measures: student satisfaction, research quality, entry standards and graduate destinations. *The Sunday Times* uses student satisfaction, entry standards, graduate destinations, graduate unemployment, good degrees and drop-out rate, while *The Guardian* uses student satisfaction (as three separate measures), entry standards, graduate destinations, student-staff ratio, spend per student and value added. This use of different measures is one reason why the different tables can yield different results (sometimes very different, especially in the case of *The Guardian* which has least in common with the other tables).

League tables compiled by *The Complete University Guide* (**www.thecompleteuniversityguide.co.uk**) and *The Guardian* (**www.guardian.co.uk**) are available in spring, those by *The Times* (**www.thetimes.co.uk**) and *The Sunday Times* (**www.thesundaytimes.co.uk**) in the summer.

Table 1 – measures used by the main publishers of UK league tables

	Universities	Measures	Subjects	Measures
The Complete University Guide	116	9	62	4
The Guardian	119	8	46	8
The Sunday Times	122	8	39	6
The Times	116	8	62	4

SOMETHING TO WATCH OUT FOR WHEN READING SUBJECT LEAGUE TABLES

- The entry standards in the tables represent the actual scores of new students in the different universities but they may not be a very important component of the entry criteria in some.

WHO PUBLISHES ART AND DESIGN LEAGUE TABLES?

The Complete University Guide	Art and design
The Guardian	Art and design
The Sunday Times	Art and design
The Times	Art and design

wondering how much higher education costs?

need information about student finance?

Visit www.ucas.com/students/studentfinance and find sources for all the information on student money matters you need.

With access to up-to-date information on bursaries, scholarships and variable fees, plus our online budget calculator. Visit us today and get the full picture.

www.ucas.com/students/studentfinance

Choosing courses

1

How will they choose you?

THE INTERVIEW

Almost all institutions interview art and design applicants, as they consider it important to be able to discuss applicants' portfolio work in person. The interview still mostly takes the form of a small interview panel interviewing students individually. However, due to increasing numbers of applicants, some art colleges and departments now run selection 'clinics' involving group interviews. The interview is mostly, though not exclusively, about your portfolio (which you may have sent them earlier as part of the application process). However, it's also about your general awareness of artistic trends and your unique perspective.

SAMPLE INTERVIEW QUESTIONS

- Which artists have had the greatest influence on you and why?
- How did you produce this piece, and why did you take this particular approach (on a piece in your portfolio)?
- When was the last time you visited an art gallery?
- Can you give us an example of a visual experience you have had that you have found particularly striking?

You also need to be aware of questions that may have an ethical dimension, for example:

- As a graphic designer, would you work on a campaign for a firearms company?
- As a fashion designer, what would your view be on the use of real fur?

1 Choosing courses

Your portfolio

Without doubt, this is the element on which admissions tutors – and eventually potential employers – place most importance when selecting candidates for their courses.

Central Saint Martins College of Art and Design, University of the Arts London, gives a number of useful tips in its guidance for applicants:

'Preparation: be prepared to adapt the portfolio according to the course you are applying to (just like you would a CV or personal statement).

Sequence: the portfolio should be well organised - so that whoever looks through it understands how you move from one idea to the next.

Scope: show the range of what you can do, concentrating on recent work. Include visual and other background research, sketches, models and prototypes - not just the finished work.

Culture-wise: it should show whatever interests you and influences your work - fashion, music, sport, environment: whatever.

Selection: be choosy. Pick work that shows ideas, skills and media, which you want to explore further in the course that you would like to do. Don't include too much and avoid repetition of one kind of work just because you think you are good at it. Generally 15-20 items for a portfolio should be enough.

Identifying yourself: if you include work that was generated as a group project, highlight what your role was in the collaboration. If you are applying from a college or school, include a signed confirmation that the work included is your own.

Explanation: the portfolio should make sense on its own. Label each piece of work with your name, a brief description and the context, for example, say what medium it is executed in and how long you spent doing it. Is it a project, self-generated, part of a group activity etc? Provide a table of contents attached to the inside front cover of the portfolio.'

On the importance of notebooks and sketchbooks, an experienced tutor at an art institute in the north-west of England says:

'Notebooks and visual diaries are a vital indicator of your ability, interest, approach, creativeness and personality. Use them constantly, of course, but never just 'page fill' to complete a book, because this will be obvious to the trained eye. Make notes at exhibitions and record your feelings and thoughts on all aspects of art and design. Frequently use a series of pages to develop a piece of work so that its evolution can be observed. Above all, do not be afraid to work experimentally rather than just making finished 'art objects'. Keep your books busy, dynamic and interesting.'

Choosing courses

1

Work experience

How much does it count for? While your portfolio is undoubtedly the most important indicator to admissions tutor of your abilities and suitability to undertake a course in art and design, work experience is also a huge plus. Work experience will increase your general skill set (eg, learning quickly, communication skills and teamwork) – which will help you perform better on your degree and produce better work for your portfolio, including actual physical pieces to add to it.

As part of the application process you'll need to write a personal statement setting out which subject you'd like to study, why you'd like to study it, and what skills and experience you bring that would make you a great student for the course. This is where your work experience will help you stand out by allowing you to describe where you've worked, what it taught you and the skills it helped you develop.

WHAT WORK EXPERIENCE?

There are no real systematic, formalised work experience schemes offered by employers in the art and design field, although some offer work placements or 'ad hoc' shadowing schemes, where you shadow, for example, a designer for a few days. There may also be the possibility of 'taster' days offered by careers organisations in conjunction with employers, and the chance of work experience placements through your school.

You'll need to be proactive: contact local companies and organisations that work in your field, explain what you want to study and ask if there is any way you could come in and help, or observe, in any capacity for a few days. Use your contacts: do you or does anyone in your family or your friends' families know someone who works in art and design and could help you out?

There is a huge range of possibilities out there: interior design companies, art galleries, museums, art shops, advertising agencies, and many more. Don't forget that getting involved in relevant activities at school (eg helping organise art exhibitions, helping design the school magazine or newsletter, helping out in art club for younger children) and voluntary work, for example for charities working in this area, counts too.

HOW TO MAKE THE MOST OF IT

Wherever you find yourself, here are a few tips to help you make the most of your work (or voluntary) experience:

- Work hard and do what's asked of you willingly.
- Ask for feedback on your work – it shows your enthusiasm and helps you develop your skills
- Write down everything you have done and what you learned. This will help you write your personal statement and at your interview if you have one.
- Make yourself useful – offer to help out.
- Build your portfolio – get copies of any work you put together (check that your employer is happy about this first).

If you only have non-art or design work experience, it will still be useful to include in your personal statement. The trick is to pull out the personal and professional skills you developed that are relevant to the work or skills required in art and design, for example interpersonal skills, working in teams, or practical hands-on work putting products together.

1

Choosing courses

The cost of higher education

The information in this section was up-to-date when this book was published. You should visit the websites mentioned in this section for the very latest information.

THE COST OF STUDYING IN THE UK

As a student, you will usually have to pay for two things: tuition fees for your course, which for most students do not need to be paid for up front, and living costs such as rent, food, books, transport and entertainment. Fees charged vary between courses, between universities and colleges and also according to your normal country of residence, so it's important to check these before you apply. Course fee information is supplied to UCAS by the universities and is displayed in Course Finder at www.ucas.com.

STUDENT LOANS

The purpose of student loans from the Government is to help cover the costs of your tuition fees and basic living costs (rent, bills, food and so on). Two types are available: a tuition fee loan to cover the tuition charges and a maintenance loan to help with accommodation and other living costs. Both types of student loan are available to all students who meet the basic eligibility requirements. Interest will be charged at inflation plus a fixed percentage while you are studying. In addition, many other commercial loans are available to students studying at university or college but the interest rate can vary considerably. Loans to help with living costs will be available for all eligible students, irrespective of family income.

Find out more information from the relevant sites below:

England: Student Finance England –
www.direct.gov.uk/studentfinance
Northern Ireland: Student Finance Northern Ireland –
www.studentfinanceni.co.uk
Scotland: Student Awards Agency for Scotland –
www.saas.gov.uk
Wales: Student Finance Wales –
www.studentfinancewales.co.uk or
www.cyllidmyfyrwyrcymru.co.uk

BURSARIES AND SCHOLARSHIPS

- The National Scholarships Programme gives financial help to students studying in England. The scheme is designed to help students whose families have lower incomes.
- Students from families with lower incomes will be entitled to a non-repayable maintenance grant to help with living costs.
- Many universities and colleges also offer non-repayable scholarships and bursaries to help students cover tuition and living costs whilst studying.
- All eligible part-time undergraduates who study for at least 25% of their time will be able to apply for a loan to cover the costs of their tuition, which means they no longer have to pay up front.

There will be extra support for disabled students and students with child or adult dependants. For more information, visit the country-specific websites listed above.

Choosing courses

1

International students

APPLYING TO STUDY IN THE UK

Deciding to go to university or college in the UK is very exciting. You need to think about what course to do, where to study, and how much it will cost. The decisions you make can have a huge effect on your future but UCAS is here to help.

HOW TO APPLY

Whatever your age or qualifications, if you want to apply for any of the 35,000 courses listed at 300 universities and colleges on the UCAS website, you must apply through UCAS at www.ucas.com. If you are unsure, your school, college, adviser, or local British Council office will be able to help. Further advice and a video guide for international students can be found on the non-UK students' section of the UCAS website at www.ucas.com/international

Students may apply on their own or through their school, college, adviser, or local British Council if they are registered with UCAS to use Apply. If you choose to use an education agent's services, check with the British Council to see if they hold a list of certificated or registered agents in your country. Check also on any charges you may need to pay. UCAS charges only the application fee (see page 86) but agents may charge for additional services.

HOW MUCH WILL MY APPLICATION COST?

If you choose to apply to more than one course, university or college you need to pay UCAS £23 GBP when you apply. If you only apply to one course at one university or college, you pay UCAS £12 GBP.

WHAT LEVEL OF ENGLISH?

UCAS provides a list of English language qualifications and grades that are acceptable to most UK universities and colleges, however you are advised to contact the institutions directly as each have their own entry requirement in English. For more information go to **www.ucas.com/students/wheretostart/ nonukstudents/englangprof**.

INTERNATIONAL STUDENT FEES

If you study in the UK, your fee status (whether you pay full-cost fees or a subsidised fee rate) will be decided by the UK university or college you plan to attend. Before you decide which university or college to attend, you need to be absolutely certain that you can pay the full cost of:

- your tuition fees (the amount is set by universities and colleges, so contact them for more information – visit their websites where many list their fees). Fee details will also be included on Course Finder at **www.ucas.com**
- the everyday living expenses for you and your family for the whole time that you are in the UK, including accommodation, food, gas and electricity bills, clothes, travel and leisure activities
- books and equipment for your course
- travel to and from your country.

You must include everything when you work out how much it will cost. You can get information to help you do this accurately from the international offices at universities and colleges, UKCISA (UK Council for International Student Affairs) and the British Council. There is a useful website tool to help you manage your money at university – **www.studentcalculator.org.uk**.

Scholarships and bursaries are offered at some universities and colleges and you should contact them for more information. In addition, you should check with your local British Council for additional scholarships available to students from your country who want to study in the UK.

LEGAL DOCUMENTS YOU WILL NEED

As you prepare to study in the UK, it is very important to think about the legal documents you will need to enter the country.

Everyone who comes to study in the UK needs a valid passport, details of which will be collected either in you UCAS application or later through Track. If you do not yet have a passport, you should apply for one as soon as possible. People from certain countries also need visas before they come into the UK. They are known as 'visa nationals'. You can check if you require a visa to travel to the UK by visiting the UK Border Agency website and selecting 'Studying in the UK', so please check the UK Border Agency website at **www.ukba.homeoffice.gov.uk** for the most up-to-date guidance and information about the United Kingdom's visa requirements.

When you apply for your visa you need to make sure you have the following documents:

- a confirmation of acceptance for studies (CAS) number from the university of college where you are going to study. The institution must be on the UKBA Register of Sponsors in order to accept international students

- a valid passport
- evidence that you have enough money to pay for your course and living costs
- certificates for all qualifications you have that are relevant to the course you have been accepted for and for any English language qualifications.

You will also have to give your biometric data.

Do check for further information from your local British Embassy or High Commission. Guidance information for international students is also available from UKCISA and from UKBA.

ADDITIONAL RESOURCES

There are a number of organisations that can provide further guidance and information to you as you prepare to study in the UK:

- British Council
  www.britishcouncil.org
- Education UK (British Council website dealing with educational matters)
  www.educationuk.org
- English UK (British Council accredited website listing English language courses in the UK)
  www.englishuk.com
- UK Border Agency (provides information on visa requirements and applications)
  www.ukba.homeoffice.gov.uk
- UKCISA (UK Council for International Student Affairs)
  www.ukcisa.org.uk
- Directgov (the official UK Government website)
  www.direct.gov.uk
- Prepare for Success
  www.prepareforsuccess.org.uk

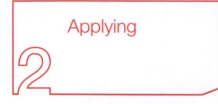

Applying

2

Step 2 – Applying

You apply through UCAS using the online application system, called Apply, at **www.ucas.com**. You can apply for a maximum of five choices, but you don't have to use them all if you don't want to. If you apply for fewer than five choices, you can add more at a later date if you want to. But be aware of the course application deadlines (you can find these in Course Finder at **www.ucas.com**).

IMPORTANT DATES FOR 2012 ENTRY

Early June 2012	UCAS Apply opens for 2013 entry registration.
Mid-September 2012	Applications can be sent to UCAS.
15 October 2012	Application deadline for the receipt at UCAS of applications for all medicine, dentistry, veterinary medicine and veterinary science courses and for all courses at the universities of Oxford and Cambridge.
15 January 2013	Application deadline for the receipt at UCAS of applications for all courses except those listed above with a 15 October deadline, and some art and design courses with a 24 March deadline.
25 February 2013	Extra starts (see page 100 for more information about Extra).
24 March 2013	Application deadline for the receipt at UCAS of applications for art and design courses except those listed on Course Finder at **www.ucas.com** with a 15 January deadline.
31 March 2013	If you apply by 15 January, the universities and colleges should aim to have sent their decisions by this date (but they can take longer).
9 May 2013	If you apply by 15 January, universities and colleges need to send their decisions by this date. If they don't, UCAS will make any outstanding choices unsuccessful on their behalf.
30 June 2013	If you send your application to us by this date, we will send it to your chosen universities and colleges. Applications received after this date are entered into Clearing (see page 114 for more information about Clearing).
3 July 2013	Last date to apply through Extra.
August 2013 (date to be confirmed)	Scottish Qualifications Authority (SQA) results are published.
15 August 2013	GCE and Advanced Diploma results are published (often known as 'A level results day'). Adjustment opens for registration (see page 115 for more information about Adjustment).

DON'T FORGET...

Universities and colleges guarantee to consider your application only if we receive it by the appropriate deadline. Check application deadlines for your courses on Course Finder at **www.ucas.com**.

If you send it to UCAS after the deadline but before 30 June 2013, universities and colleges will consider your application only if they still have places available.

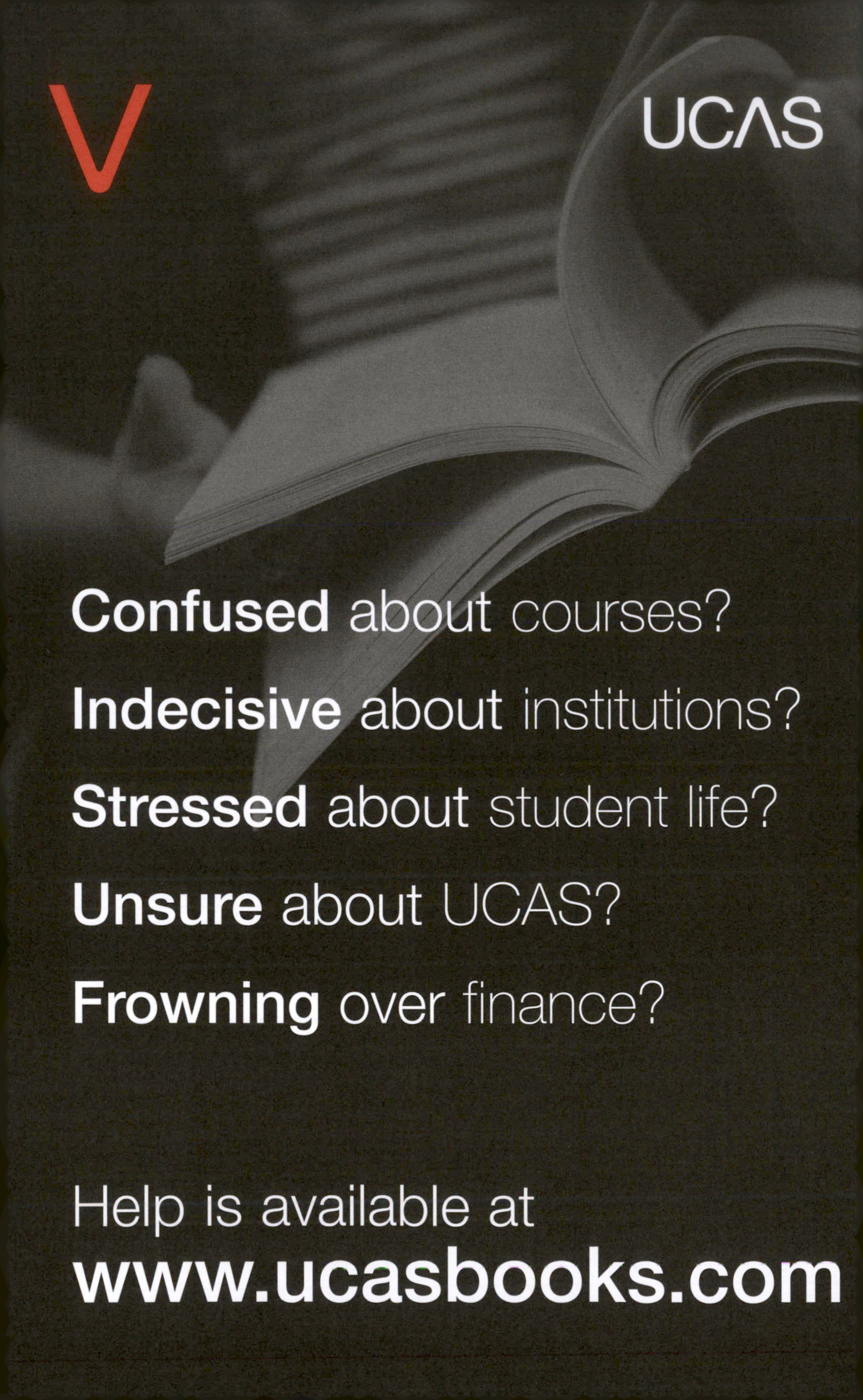
V
UCAS
Confused about courses?
Indecisive about institutions?
Stressed about student life?
Unsure about UCAS?
Frowning over finance?
Help is available at
www.ucasbooks.com

Applying

2

How to apply

There are different processes for applying to foundation courses and university degrees.

APPLYING FOR FOUNDATION COURSES

Unlike applying for a degree course, there is no single, centralised or standardised application form or process when applying for a foundation course. Instead, you should apply direct to the college concerned and not through UCAS. The exceptions are the London-based constituents of the University of the Arts London colleges, which do share a standardised, centralised application form and process. To obtain the relevant form, just contact any one of the colleges.

The London-based colleges that share a centralised application form and process are:

- Camberwell College of Arts
- Central Saint Martins College of Art and Design
- Chelsea College of Art and Design
- London College of Communication
- London College of Fashion
- Wimbledon College of Art.

All UK/EU applicants may only apply to one of the University of the Arts' colleges. If you are an international applicant, you can nominate a first and second choice college. If your first choice is unsuccessful, your application is automatically passed to your second choice.

Other than the University of the Arts London colleges, if you're applying to individual colleges, you can apply to a number (as many as you want, really) at the same time.

ART AND DESIGN COURSES – HOW TO APPLY

APPLYING FOR...	APPLY THROUGH...	APPLY BY...
Foundation course	The individual college directly, **unless** you're applying for courses at some London colleges (see list on previous page) in which case you should obtain the standard application form and then send it to your first-choice college	Usually February
Undergraduate degree or HND	UCAS Online application See **www.ucas.com** and click on 'Apply'	15 October for Ruskin College of Fine Art at Oxford University 15 January or 24 March for all other art and design courses. Visit Course Finder at **www.ucas.com** to find out which deadline is applicable for individual courses.

You apply online at **www.ucas.com** through Apply – a secure, web-based application service that is designed for all our applicants, whether they are applying through a UCAS-registered centre or as an individual, anywhere in the world. Apply is:

- easy to access – all you need is an internet connection
- easy to use – you don't have to complete your application all in one go: you can save the sections as you complete them and come back to it later
- easy to monitor – once you've applied, you can use Track to check the progress of your application, including any decisions from universities or colleges. You can also reply to your offers using Track.

Watch the UCAStv guide to applying through UCAS at **www.ucas.tv**.

If you are applying through UCAS as a foundation course student, you won't be expected to ask your old school for a reference. Your application will be handled by your foundation course tutors.

APPLICATION FEE

For 2013 entry, the fee for applying through UCAS is £23 for two or more choices and £12 for one choice.

DEFERRED ENTRY

If you want to apply for deferred entry in 2014, perhaps because you want to take a year out between school or college and higher education, you should check that the university or college will accept a deferred entry application. Occasionally, tutors are not happy to accept students who take a gap year, because it interrupts the flow of their learning. If you apply for deferred entry, you must meet the conditions of any offers by 31 August 2013, unless otherwise agreed with the university or college. If you accept a place for 2014 entry and then change your mind, you cannot reapply through us in the 2014 entry cycle unless you withdraw your original application.

INVISIBILITY OF CHOICES

Universities and colleges cannot see details of the other choices on your application until you reply to any offers or you are unsuccessful at all your choices.

You can submit only one UCAS application in each year's application cycle.

APPLYING THROUGH YOUR SCHOOL OR COLLEGE

1 GET SCHOOL OR COLLEGE 'BUZZWORD'

Ask your UCAS application coordinator (may be your sixth form tutor) for your school or college UCAS 'buzzword'. This is a password for the school or college.

2 REGISTER

Go to **www.ucas.com/students/apply** and click on **Register/Log in to use Apply** and then **register**. After you have entered your registration details, the online system will automatically generate a username for you, but you'll have to come up with a password and answers to security questions.

3 COMPLETE SEVEN SECTIONS

Complete all the sections of the application. To access any section, click on the section name at the left of the screen and follow the instructions. The sections are:

Personal details – contact details, residential status, disability status

Additional information – only UK applicants need to complete this section

Student finance – UK students can share some of their application details with their student finance company. Financial information is provided for EU and international applicants.

Choices – which courses you'd like to apply for

Education – your education and qualifications

Employment – eg work experience, holiday jobs

Statement – see page 96 for personal statement advice. Before you can send your application you need to go to the **View all details** screen and tick the **section completed** box.

4 PASS TO REFEREE

Once you've completed all the sections, send your application electronically to your referee (normally your form tutor). They'll check it, approve it and add their reference to it, and will then send it to UCAS on your behalf.

USEFUL INFORMATION ABOUT APPLY

- Important details like date of birth and course codes will be checked by Apply. It will alert you if they are not valid. We strongly recommend that the personal statement and reference are written in a word processing package and pasted in Apply.
- If you want to, you can enter European characters into certain areas of Apply.
- You can change your application at any time before it is completed and sent to UCAS.
- You can print and preview your application at any time. Before you send it you need to go to the **View all details** screen and tick the **section completed** box.
- Your school, college or centre can choose different payment methods. For example, they may want us to bill them, or you may be able to pay online by debit or credit card.

NOT APPLYING THROUGH A SCHOOL OR COLLEGE

If you're not currently studying, you'll probably be applying as an independent applicant rather than through a school, college or other UCAS-registered centre. In this case you won't be able to provide a 'buzzword', but we'll ask you a few extra questions to check you are eligible to apply.

If you're not applying through a UCAS-registered centre, the procedure you use for obtaining a reference will depend on whether or not you want your reference to be provided through a registered centre. For information on the procedures for providing references, visit **www.ucas.com/students/applying/howtoapply/reference**.

APPLICATION CHECKLIST

We want this to run smoothly for you and we also want to process your application as quickly as possible. You can help us to do this by remembering to do the following:

✓ check the closing dates for applications – see page 89
✓ check the student finance information at **www.ucas.com/students/studentfinance/** and course fees information in Course Finder at **www.ucas.com**
✓ start early and allow plenty of time for completing your application – including enough time for your referee to complete the reference section
✓ read the online instructions carefully before you start
✓ consider what each question is actually asking for – use the 'help'
✓ pay special attention to your personal statement (see page 94) and start drafting it early
✓ ask a teacher, parent, friend or careers adviser to review your draft application – particularly the personal statement
✓ if you get stuck, watch our videos on YouTube, where we answer your frequently asked questions on completing a UCAS application at **www.youtube.com/ucasonline**.
✓ if you have extra information that will not fit on your application, send it direct to your chosen universities or colleges after we have sent you your Welcome letter with your Personal ID – don't send it to us
✓ print a copy of the final version of your application, in case you are asked questions on it at an interview.

Applying

The personal statement

Next to choosing your courses, this section of your application will be the most time-consuming. It is of immense importance as many colleges and universities make their selection solely on the information in the UCAS application, rather than interviews and admissions tests. The personal statement can be the deciding factor in whether or not they offer you a place. If it is an institution that interviews, it could be the deciding factor in whether you get called for interview.

Keep a copy of your personal statement – if you are called for interview, you will almost certainly be asked questions based on it.

Tutors will look carefully at your exam results, actual and predicted, your reference and your own personal statement. Remember, they are looking for reasons to offer you a place – try to give them every opportunity to do so!

A SALES DOCUMENT

The personal statement is your opportunity to sell yourself, so do so. The university or college admissions tutor wants to get a rounded picture of you to decide whether you will make an interesting member of the university or college, both academically and socially. They want to know more about you than the subjects you are studying at school.

HOW TO START

At www.ucas.com you'll find several tools to help you write a good personal statement.

- Personal statement timeline, to help you do all your research and plan your statement over several drafts and checks.
- Personal statement mind map, which gives you reminders and hints on preparation, content and

presentation, with extra hints for mature and international applicants.

- Personal statement worksheet, which gets you to start writing by asking relevant questions so that you include everything you need. You can also check your work against a list of dos and don'ts .

Include things like hobbies, and try to link the skills you have gained to the type of course you are applying for. Describe your career plans and goals. Have you belonged to sports teams or orchestras or held positions of responsibility in the community? Try to give evidence of your ability to undertake higher level study successfully by showing your commitment and maturity. If you left full-time education a while ago, talk about the work you have done and the skills you have gathered or how you have juggled bringing up a family with other activities – that is solid evidence of time management skills. Whoever you are, make sure you explain what appeals to you about the course you are applying for.

You should say which artists and designers have inspired you and how they have influenced your work. Write enthusiastically about your portfolio to convince admissions tutors that it will be worth viewing.

Visit **www.ucas.tv** to view the video to help guide you through the process and address the most common fears and concerns about writing a personal statement.

WHAT ADMISSIONS TUTORS LOOK FOR	WHAT TO TELL THEM
<ul><li>Your reasons for wanting to take this subject in general and this particular course.</li><li>Your communication skills – not only what you say but how you say it. Your grammar and spelling must be perfect.</li><li>Relevant experience – practical things you've done that are related to your choice of course.</li><li>Evidence of your teamworking ability, leadership capability, independence.</li><li>Evidence of your skills, for example: IT skills, empathy and people skills, debating and public speaking, research and analysis.</li><li>Other activities that show your dedication and ability to apply yourself and maintain your motivation.</li></ul>	<ul><li>Why you want to do this subject – how you know it is the subject for you.</li><li>What experience you already have in this field – for example work experience, school projects, hobbies, voluntary work.</li><li>The skills and qualities you have as a person that would make you a good student, for example anything that shows your dedication, communication ability, academic achievement, initiative.</li><li>Examples that show you can knuckle down and apply yourself, for example running a marathon or your Extended Project.</li><li>If you're taking a gap year, why you've chosen this and (if possible) what you're going to do during it.</li><li>About your other interests and activities away from studying – to show you're a rounded person. (But remember that it is mainly your suitability for the particular course that they're looking to judge.)</li></ul>

Offers

3

Step 3 – Offers

Once we have sent your application to your chosen universities and colleges, they will all consider it independently and tell us if they can offer you a place. Some universities and colleges will take longer to make decisions than others. You may be asked to attend an interview, sit an additional test or provide a piece of work, such as an essay, before a decision can be made.

INTERVIEWS

Many universities (particularly the more popular ones, running competitive courses) use interviews as part of their selection process. Universities will want to find out why you want to study your chosen course at their institution, and they want to judge whether the course is suitable for you and your future career plans. Interviews also give you an opportunity to visit the university and ask any questions you may have about the course or their institution.

If you are called for interview, the key areas they are likely to cover will be:

- evidence of your academic ability
- your capacity to study hard
- your commitment to a career in art or design, best shown by work experience
- your logic and reasoning ability.

A lot of the interview will be based on information on your application, especially your personal statement. See pages 96 and 97 for tips about the personal statement.

Whenever a university or college makes a decision about your application, we record it and let you know. You can check the progress of your application using Track at **www.ucas.com**. This is our secure online service which gives you access to your application, using the same username and password you used when you applied. You can use it to find out if you have been invited for an interview or need to provide an additional piece of work, and you can check to see if you have received any offers. Whenever there is any change in your application status, we email you to advise you to check Track.

TYPES OF OFFER

Universities can make two types of offer: conditional or unconditional.

Conditional offer

A conditional offer means the university or college will offer you a place if you meet certain conditions – usually based on exam results. The conditions may be based on Tariff points (for example, 300 points from three A levels), or specify certain grades in named subjects (for example, A in art, B in history, C in English).

Unconditional offer

If you've met all the academic requirements for the course and the university or college wants to accept you, they will make you an unconditional offer. If you accept this you'll have a definite place.

However, for both types of offer, there might be other requirements, like medical or financial conditions, that you need to meet before you can start your course.

REPLYING TO OFFERS

When you have received decisions for all your choices, you must decide what you want to accept. You will be given a deadline in Track by which you have to make your replies. Before replying, get advice from family, friends or advisers, but remember that you're the one taking the course so it's your decision.

Firm acceptance

- Your firm acceptance is your first choice - this is your preferred choice out of all the offers you have received. You can have only one firm acceptance.
- If you accept an unconditional offer, you are entering a contract that you will attend the course, so you must decline any other offers.
- If you accept a conditional offer, you are agreeing that you will attend the course at that university or college if you meet the conditions of the offer. You can accept another offer as an insurance choice.

Insurance acceptance

- If your firm acceptance is a conditional offer, you can accept another offer as an insurance choice. Your insurance choice can be conditional or unconditional and acts as a back-up, so if you don't meet the conditions for your firm choice but meet the conditions for your insurance, you will be committed to the insurance choice. You can only have one insurance choice.
- The conditions for your insurance choice would usually be lower than your firm choice.
- You don't have to accept an insurance choice if you don't want one but if you do you need to be certain that it is an offer that you would accept.

For more information watch our video guides *How to use Track*, *Making sense of your offers*, and *How to reply to your offers* at **www.ucas.tv**.

WHAT IF YOU HAVE NO OFFERS?

If you have used all five choices on your application and either received no offers, or decided to turn down any offers you have received, you may be eligible to apply for another choice through Extra. Find out more about Extra on page 100.

If you are not eligible for Extra, in the summer you can contact universities and colleges with vacancies in Clearing. See page 114 for more information.

Offers

3

Extra

Extra allows you to make additional choices, one at a time, without having to wait for Clearing in July. It is completely optional and free, and is designed to encourage you to continue researching and choosing courses if you are holding no offers. You can search for courses available through Extra on Course Finder at **www.ucas.com**. The Extra service is available to eligible applicants from 25 February to early July 2012 through Track at **www.ucas.com**.

WHO IS ELIGIBLE?

You will be eligible for Extra if you have already made five choices and:

- you have had unsuccessful or withdrawal decisions from all five of your choices, or
- you have cancelled your outstanding choices and hold no offers, or

- you have received decisions from all five choices and have declined all offers made to you.

HOW DOES IT WORK?

We contact you and explain what to do if you are eligible for Extra. If you are eligible a special Extra button will be available on your Track screen. If you want to use Extra you should:

- tick the **Available in Extra** box in the Study Options section when looking for courses on Course Finder
- choose one that you would like to apply for and enter the details on your Track screen.

When you have chosen a course the university or college will be able to view your application and consider you for a place.

WHAT HAPPENS NEXT?

We give the universities and colleges a maximum of 21 days to consider your Extra application. During this time, you cannot be considered by another university or college. If you have not heard after 21 days you can apply to a different university or college if you wish, but it is a good idea to ring the one currently considering you before doing so. If you are made an offer, you can choose whether or not to accept it.

If you accept any offer, conditional or unconditional, you will not be able to take any further part in Extra.

If you are currently studying for examinations, any offer that you receive is likely to be an offer conditional on exam grades. If you already have your examination results, it is possible that a university or college may make an unconditional offer. If you accept an unconditional offer, you will be placed. If you decide to decline the offer or the university or college decides they cannot make you an offer, you will be given another opportunity to use Extra, time permitting. Your Extra button on Track will be reactivated.

Once you have accepted an offer in Extra, you are committed to it in the same way as you would be with an offer through the main UCAS system. Conditional offers made through Extra will be treated in the same way as other conditional offers, when your examination results become available.

If your results do not meet the conditions and the university or college decides that they cannot confirm your Extra offer, you will automatically become eligible for Clearing if it is too late for you to be considered by another university or college in Extra.

If you are unsuccessful, decline an offer, or do not receive an offer, or 21 days have elapsed since choosing a course through Extra, you can use Extra to apply for another course, time permitting.

ADVICE

Do the same careful research and seek guidance on your Extra choice of university or college and course as you did for your initial choices. If you applied to high-demand courses and institutions in your original application and were unsuccessful, you could consider related or alternative subjects or perhaps apply for the subject you want in combination with another. Your teachers or careers advisers or the universities and colleges themselves can provide useful guidance. Course Finder at **www.ucas.com** is another important source of information. Be flexible, that is the key to success.

But you are the only one who knows how flexible you are prepared to be. Remember that even if you decide to take a degree course other than art or design, you may be able to take an alternative route into these professions.

Visit **www.ucas.tv** to watch the video guide on how to use Extra.

Offers

3

The Tariff

Finding out what qualifications are needed for different higher education courses can be very confusing.

The UCAS Tariff is the system for allocating points to qualifications used for entry to higher education. Universities and colleges can use the UCAS Tariff to make comparisons between applicants with different qualifications. Tariff points are often used in entry requirements, although other factors are often taken into account. Information on Course Finder at **www.ucas.com** provides a fuller picture of what admissions tutors are seeking.

The tables on the following pages show the qualifications covered by the UCAS Tariff. There may have been changes to these tables since this book was printed. You should visit **www.ucas.com** to view the most up-to-date tables.

FURTHER INFORMATION?

Although Tariff points can be accumulated in a variety of ways, not all of these will necessarily be acceptable for entry to a particular higher education course. The achievement of a points score therefore does not give an automatic entitlement to entry, and many other factors are taken into account in the admissions process.

Course Finder facility at **www.ucas.com** is the best source of reference to find out what qualifications are acceptable for entry to specific courses. Updates to the Tariff, including details on how new qualifications are added, can be found at **www.ucas.com/students/ucas_tariff/**.

HOW DOES THE TARIFF WORK?

- Students can collect Tariff points from a range of different qualifications, eg GCE A level with BTEC Nationals.
- There is no ceiling to the number of points that can be accumulated.
- There is no double counting. Certain qualifications within the Tariff build on qualifications in the same subject. In these cases only the qualification with the higher Tariff score will be counted. This principle applies to:
  - GCE Advanced Subsidiary level and GCE Advanced level
  - Scottish Highers and Advanced Highers
  - Speech, drama and music awards at grades 6, 7 and 8.
- Tariff points for the Advanced Diploma come from the Progression Diploma score plus the relevant Additional and Specialist Learning (ASL) Tariff points. Please see the appropriate qualification in the Tariff tables to calculate the ASL score.
- The Extended Project Tariff points are included within the Tariff points for Progression and Advanced Diplomas. Extended Project points represented in the Tariff only count when the qualification is taken outside of these Diplomas.
- Where the Tariff tables refer to specific awarding organisations, only qualifications from these awarding organisations attract Tariff points. Qualifications with a similar title, but from a different qualification awarding organisation do not attract Tariff points.

HOW DO UNIVERSITIES AND COLLEGES USE THE TARIFF?

The Tariff provides a facility to help universities and colleges when expressing entrance requirements and when making conditional offers. Entry requirements and conditional offers expressed as Tariff points will often require a minimum level of achievement in a specified subject (for example, '300 points to include grade A at A level chemistry', or '260 points including SQA Higher grade B in mathematics').

Use of the Tariff may also vary from department to department at any one institution, and may in some cases be dependent on the programme being offered.

In July 2010, UCAS announced plans to review the qualifications information provided to universities and colleges. You can read more about the review at www.ucas.com/qireview.

WHAT QUALIFICATIONS ARE INCLUDED IN THE TARIFF?

The following qualifications are included in the UCAS Tariff. See the number on the qualification title to find the relevant section of the Tariff table.

1   AAT NVQ Level 3 in Accounting
2   AAT Level 3 Diploma in Accounting (QCF)
3   Advanced Diploma
4   Advanced Extension Awards
5   Advanced Placement Programme (US and Canada)
6   Arts Award (Gold)
7   ASDAN Community Volunteering qualification
8   Asset Languages Advanced Stage
9   British Horse Society (Stage 3 Horse Knowledge & Care, Stage 3 Riding and Preliminary Teacher's Certificate)
10 BTEC Awards (NQF)
11 BTEC Certificates and Extended Certificates (NQF)
12 BTEC Diplomas (NQF)
13 BTEC National in Early Years (NQF)
14 BTEC Nationals (NQF)
15 BTEC QCF Qualifications (Suite known as Nationals)
16 BTEC Specialist Qualifications (QCF)
17 CACHE Award, Certificate and Diploma in Child Care and Education
18 CACHE Level 3 Extended Diploma for the Children and Young People's Workforce (QCF)
19 Cambridge ESOL Examinations
20 Cambridge Pre-U
21 Certificate of Personal Effectiveness (COPE)
22 CISI Introduction to Securities and Investment
23 City & Guilds Land Based Services Level 3 Qualifications
24 Graded Dance and Vocational Graded Dance
25 Diploma in Fashion Retail
26 Diploma in Foundation Studies (Art & Design; Art, Design & Media)
27 EDI Level 3 Certificate in Accounting, Certificate in Accounting (IAS)
28 Essential Skills (Northern Ireland)
29 Essential Skills Wales
30 Extended Project (stand alone)
31 Free-standing Mathematics
32 Functional skills
33 GCE (AS, AS Double Award, A level, A level Double Award and A level (with additional AS))
34 Hong Kong Diploma of Secondary Education (from 2012 entry onwards)
35 ifs School of Finance (Certificate and Diploma in Financial Studies)
36 iMedia (OCR level Certificate/Diploma for iMedia Professionals)
37 International Baccalaureate (IB) Diploma
38 International Baccalaureate (IB) Certificate
39 Irish Leaving Certificate (Higher and Ordinary levels)
40 IT Professionals (iPRO) (Certificate and Diploma)
41 Key Skills (Levels 2, 3 and 4)
42 Music examinations (grades 6, 7 and 8)
43 OCR Level 3 Certificate in Mathematics for Engineering
44 OCR Level 3 Certificate for Young Enterprise
45 OCR Nationals (National Certificate, National Diploma and National Extended Diploma)
46 Principal Learning Wales
47 Progression Diploma
48 Rockschool Music Practitioners Qualifications
49 Scottish Qualifications
50 Speech and Drama examinations (grades 6, 7 and 8 and Performance Studies)
51 Sports Leaders UK
52 Welsh Baccalaureate Advanced Diploma (Core)

Updates on the Tariff, including details on the incorporation of any new qualifications, are posted on www.ucas.com.

UCAS TARIFF TABLES

1

AAT NVQ LEVEL 3 IN ACCOUNTING	
GRADE	TARIFF POINTS
PASS	160

2

AAT LEVEL 3 DIPLOMA IN ACCOUNTING	
GRADE	TARIFF POINTS
PASS	160

3

ADVANCED DIPLOMA

Advanced Diploma = Progression Diploma plus Additional & Specialist Learning (ASL). Please see the appropriate qualification to calculate the ASL score. Please see the Progression Diploma (Table 47) for Tariff scores

4

ADVANCED EXTENSION AWARDS	
GRADE	TARIFF POINTS
DISTINCTION	40
MERIT	20

Points for Advanced Extension Awards are over and above those gained from the A level grade

5

ADVANCED PLACEMENT PROGRAMME (US & CANADA)	
GRADE	TARIFF POINTS
Group A	
5	120
4	90
3	60
Group B	
5	50
4	35
3	20

Details of the subjects covered by each group can be found at
www.ucas.com/students/ucas_tariff/tarifftables

6

ARTS AWARD (GOLD)	
GRADE	TARIFF POINTS
PASS	35

7

ASDAN COMMUNITY VOLUNTEERING QUALIFICATION	
GRADE	TARIFF POINTS
CERTIFICATE	50
AWARD	30

8

ASSET LANGUAGES ADVANCED STAGE			
GRADE	TARIFF POINTS	GRADE	TARIFF POINTS
Speaking		Listening	
GRADE 12	28	GRADE 12	25
GRADE 11	20	GRADE 11	18
GRADE 10	12	GRADE 10	11
Reading		Writing	
GRADE 12	25	GRADE 12	25
GRADE 11	18	GRADE 11	18
GRADE 10	11	GRADE 10	11

9

BRITISH HORSE SOCIETY	
GRADE	TARIFF POINTS
Stage 3 Horse Knowledge & Care	
PASS	35
Stage 3 Riding	
PASS	35
Preliminary Teacher's Certificate	
PASS	35

Awarded by Equestrian Qualifications (GB) Ltd (EQL)

10

BTEC AWARDS (NQF) (EXCLUDING BTEC NATIONAL QUALIFICATIONS)			
GRADE	TARIFF POINTS		
	Group A	Group B	Group C
DISTINCTION	20	30	40
MERIT	13	20	26
PASS	7	10	13

Details of the subjects covered by each group can be found at
www.ucas.com/students/ucas_tariff/tarifftables

11

BTEC CERTIFICATES AND EXTENDED CERTIFICATES (NQF) (EXCLUDING BTEC NATIONAL QUALIFICATIONS)					
GRADE	TARIFF POINTS				
	Group A	Group B	Group C	Group D	Extended Certificates
DISTINCTION	40	60	80	100	60
MERIT	26	40	52	65	40
PASS	13	20	26	35	20

Details of the subjects covered by each group can be found at www.ucas.com/students/ucas_tariff/tarifftables

12

BTEC DIPLOMAS (NQF) (EXCLUDING BTEC NATIONAL QUALIFICATIONS)			
GRADE	TARIFF POINTS		
	Group A	Group B	Group C
DISTINCTION	80	100	120
MERIT	52	65	80
PASS	26	35	40

Details of the subjects covered by each group can be found at www.ucas.com/students/ucas_tariff/tarifftables

UCAS TARIFF TABLES

13

BTEC NATIONAL IN EARLY YEARS (NQF)

GRADE	TARIFF POINTS	GRADE	TARIFF POINTS	GRADE	TARIFF POINTS
Theory				Practical	
Diploma		Certificate		D	120
DDD	320	DD	200	M	80
DDM	280	DM	160	P	40
DMM	240	MM	120		
MMM	220	MP	80		
MMP	160	PP	40		
MPP	120				
PPP	80				

Points apply to the following qualifications only: BTEC National Diploma in Early Years (100/1279/5); BTEC National Certificate in Early Years (100/1280/1)

14

BTEC NATIONALS (NQF)

GRADE	TARIFF POINTS	GRADE	TARIFF POINTS	GRADE	TARIFF POINTS
Diploma		Certificate		Award	
DDD	360	DD	240	D	120
DDM	320	DM	200	M	80
DMM	280	MM	160	P	40
MMM	240	MP	120		
MMP	200	PP	80		
MPP	160				
PPP	120				

15

BTEC QUALIFICATIONS (QCF)
(SUITE OF QUALIFICATIONS KNOWN AS NATIONALS)

EXTENDED DIPLOMA	DIPLOMA	90 CREDIT DIPLOMA	SUBSIDIARY DIPLOMA	CERTIFICATE	TARIFF POINTS
D*D*D*					420
D*D*D					400
D*DD					380
DDD					360
DDM					320
DMM	D*D*				280
	D*D				260
MMM	DD				240
		D*D*			210
MMP	DM	D*D			200
		DD			180
MPP	MM	DM			160
			D*		140
PPP	MP	MM	D		120
		MP			100
	PP		M		80
				D*	70
		PP		D	60
			P	M	40
				P	20

16

BTEC SPECIALIST (QCF)

GRADE	TARIFF POINTS		
	Diploma	Certificate	Award
DISTINCTION	120	60	20
MERIT	80	40	13
PASS	40	20	7

UCAS TARIFF TABLES

17

CACHE LEVEL 3 AWARD, CERTIFICATE AND DIPLOMA IN CHILD CARE & EDUCATION

AWARD		CERTIFICATE		DIPLOMA	
GRADE	TARIFF POINTS	GRADE	TARIFF POINTS	GRADE	TARIFF POINTS
A	30	A	110	A	360
B	25	B	90	B	300
C	20	C	70	C	240
D	15	D	55	D	180
E	10	E	35	E	120

18

CACHE LEVEL 3 EXTENDED DIPLOMA FOR THE CHILDREN AND YOUNG PEOPLE'S WORKFORCE (QCF)

GRADE	TARIFF POINTS
A*	420
A	340
B	290
C	240
D	140
E	80

19

CAMBRIDGE ESOL EXAMINATIONS

GRADE	TARIFF POINTS
Certificate of Proficiency in English	
A	140
B	110
C	70
Certificate in Advanced English	
A	70

20

CAMBRIDGE PRE-U

GRADE	TARIFF POINTS	GRADE	TARIFF POINTS	GRADE	TARIFF POINTS
Principal Subject		Global Perspectives and Research		Short Course	
D1	TBC	D1	TBC	D1	TBC
D2	145	D2	140	D2	TBC
D3	130	D3	126	D3	60
M1	115	M1	112	M1	53
M2	101	M2	98	M2	46
M3	87	M3	84	M3	39
P1	73	P1	70	P1	32
P2	59	P2	56	P2	26
P3	46	P3	42	P3	20

21

CERTIFICATE OF PERSONAL EFFECTIVENESS (COPE)

GRADE	TARIFF POINTS
PASS	70

Points are awarded for the Certificate of Personal Effectiveness (CoPE) awarded by ASDAN and CCEA

22

CISI INTRODUCTION TO SECURITIES AND INVESTMENT

GRADE	TARIFF POINTS
PASS WITH DISTINCTION	60
PASS WITH MERIT	40
PASS	20

23

CITY AND GUILDS LAND BASED SERVICES LEVEL 3 QUALIFICATIONS

GRADE	TARIFF POINTS			
	EXTENDED DIPLOMA	DIPLOMA	SUBSIDIARY DIPLOMA	CERTIFICATE
DISTINCTION*	420	280	140	70
DISTINCTION	360	240	120	60
MERIT	240	160	80	40
PASS	120	80	40	20

24

GRADED DANCE AND VOCATIONAL GRADED DANCE

GRADE	TARIFF POINTS	GRADE	TARIFF POINTS	GRADE	TARIFF POINTS
Graded Dance					
Grade 8		Grade 7		Grade 6	
DISTINCTION	65	DISTINCTION	55	DISTINCTION	40
MERIT	55	MERIT	45	MERIT	35
PASS	45	PASS	35	PASS	30
Vocational Graded Dance					
Advanced Foundation		Intermediate			
DISTINCTION	70	DISTINCTION	65		
MERIT	55	MERIT	50		
PASS	45	PASS	40		

25

DIPLOMA IN FASHION RETAIL

GRADE	TARIFF POINTS
DISTINCTION	160
MERIT	120
PASS	80

Applies to the NQF and QCF versions of the qualifications awarded by ABC Awards

UCAS TARIFF TABLES

26

DIPLOMA IN FOUNDATION STUDIES (ART & DESIGN AND ART, DESIGN & MEDIA)	
GRADE	TARIFF POINTS
DISTINCTION	285
MERIT	225
PASS	165

Awarded by ABC, Edexcel, UAL and WJEC

27

EDI LEVEL 3 CERTIFICATE IN ACCOUNTING, CERTIFICATE IN ACCOUNTING (IAS)	
GRADE	TARIFF POINTS
DISTINCTION	120
MERIT	90
PASS	70

28

ESSENTIAL SKILLS (NORTHERN IRELAND)	
GRADE	TARIFF POINTS
LEVEL 2	10

Only allocated at level 2 if studied as part of a wider composite qualification such as 14-19 Diploma or Welsh Baccalaureate

29

ESSENTIAL SKILLS WALES	
GRADE	TARIFF POINTS
LEVEL 4	30
LEVEL 3	20
LEVEL 2	10

Only allocated at level 2 if studied as part of a wider composite qualification such as 14-19 Diploma or Welsh Baccalaureate

30

EXTENDED PROJECT (STAND ALONE)	
GRADE	TARIFF POINTS
A*	70
A	60
B	50
C	40
D	30
E	20

Points for the Extended Project cannot be counted if taken as part of Progression/Advanced Diploma

31

FREE-STANDING MATHEMATICS	
GRADE	TARIFF POINTS
A	20
B	17
C	13
D	10
E	7

Covers free-standing Mathematics - Additional Maths, Using and Applying Statistics, Working with Algebraic and Graphical Techniques, Modelling with Calculus

32

FUNCTIONAL SKILLS	
GRADE	TARIFF POINTS
LEVEL 2	10

Only allocated if studied as part of a wider composite qualification such as 14-19 Diploma or Welsh Baccalaureate

33

GCE AND VCE									
GRADE	TARIFF POINTS	GRADE	TARIFF POINTS	GRADE	TARIFF POINTS	GRADE	TARIFF POINTS	GRADE	TARIFF POINTS
GCE & AVCE Double Award		GCE A level with additional AS (9 units)		GCE A level & AVCE		GCE AS Double Award		GCE AS & AS VCE	
A*A*	280	A*A	200	A*	140	AA	120	A	60
A*A	260	AA	180	A	120	AB	110	B	50
AA	240	AB	170	B	100	BB	100	C	40
AB	220	BB	150	C	80	BC	90	D	30
BB	200	BC	140	D	60	CC	80	E	20
BC	180	CC	120	E	40	CD	70		
CC	160	CD	110			DD	60		
CD	140	DD	90			DE	50		
DD	120	DE	80			EE	40		
DE	100	EE	60						
EE	80								

34

HONG KONG DIPLOMA OF SECONDARY EDUCATION					
GRADE	TARIFF POINTS	GRADE	TARIFF POINTS	GRADE	TARIFF POINTS
All subjects except mathematics		Mathematics compulsory component		Mathematics optional components	
5**	No value	5**	No value	5**	No value
5*	130	5*	60	5*	70
5	120	5	45	5	60
4	80	4	35	4	50
3	40	3	25	3	40

No value for 5** pending receipt of candidate evidence (post 2012)

35

IFS SCHOOL OF FINANCE (NQF & QCF)

GRADE	TARIFF POINTS	GRADE	TARIFF POINTS
Certificate in Financial Studies (CeFS)		Diploma in Financial Studies (DipFS)	
A	60	A	120
B	50	B	100
C	40	C	80
D	30	D	60
E	20	E	40

Applicants with the ifs Diploma cannot also count points allocated to the ifs Certificate. Completion of both qualifications will result in a maximum of 120 UCAS Tariff points

36

LEVEL 3 CERTIFICATE / DIPLOMA FOR iMEDIA USERS (iMEDIA)

GRADE	TARIFF POINTS
DIPLOMA	66
CERTIFICATE	40

Awarded by OCR

37

INTERNATIONAL BACCALAUREATE (IB) DIPLOMA

GRADE	TARIFF POINTS	GRADE	TARIFF POINTS
45	720	34	479
44	698	33	457
43	676	32	435
42	654	31	413
41	632	30	392
40	611	29	370
39	589	28	348
38	567	27	326
37	545	26	304
36	523	25	282
35	501	24	260

38

INTERNATIONAL BACCALAUREATE (IB) CERTIFICATE

GRADE	TARIFF POINTS	GRADE	TARIFF POINTS	GRADE	TARIFF POINTS
Higher Level		Standard Level		Core	
7	130	7	70	3	120
6	110	6	59	2	80
5	80	5	43	1	40
4	50	4	27	0	10
3	20	3	11		

39

IRISH LEAVING CERTIFICATE

GRADE	TARIFF POINTS	GRADE	TARIFF POINTS
Higher		Ordinary	
A1	90	A1	39
A2	77	A2	26
B1	71	B1	20
B2	64	B2	14
B3	58	B3	7
C1	52		
C2	45		
C3	39		
D1	33		
D2	26		
D3	20		

40

IT PROFESSIONALS (iPRO)

GRADE	TARIFF POINTS
DIPLOMA	100
CERTIFICATE	80

Awarded by OCR

41

KEY SKILLS

GRADE	TARIFF POINTS
LEVEL 4	30
LEVEL 3	20
LEVEL 2	10

Only allocated at level 2 if studied as part of a wider composite qualification such as 14-19 Diploma or Welsh Baccalaureate

UCAS TARIFF TABLES

42

MUSIC EXAMINATIONS					
GRADE	TARIFF POINTS	GRADE	TARIFF POINTS	GRADE	TARIFF POINTS
Practical					
Grade 8		Grade 7		Grade 6	
DISTINCTION	75	DISTINCTION	60	DISTINCTION	45
MERIT	70	MERIT	55	MERIT	40
PASS	55	PASS	40	PASS	25
Theory					
Grade 8		Grade 7		Grade 6	
DISTINCTION	30	DISTINCTION	20	DISTINCTION	15
MERIT	25	MERIT	15	MERIT	10
PASS	20	PASS	10	PASS	5

Points shown are for the ABRSM, LCMM/University of West London, Rockschool and Trinity Guildhall/Trinity College London Advanced Level music examinations

43

OCR LEVEL 3 CERTIFICATE IN MATHEMATICS FOR ENGINEERING	
GRADE	TARIFF POINTS
A*	TBC
A	90
B	75
C	60
D	45
E	30

44

OCR LEVEL 3 CERTIFICATE FOR YOUNG ENTERPRISE	
GRADE	TARIFF POINTS
DISTINCTION	40
MERIT	30
PASS	20

45

OCR NATIONALS					
GRADE	TARIFF POINTS	GRADE	TARIFF POINTS	GRADE	TARIFF POINTS
National Extended Diploma		National Diploma		National Certificate	
D1	360	D	240	D	120
D2/M1	320	M1	200	M	80
M2	280	M2/P1	160	P	40
M3	240	P2	120		
P1	200	P3	80		
P2	160				
P3	120				

46

PRINCIPAL LEARNING WALES	
GRADE	TARIFF POINTS
A*	210
A	180
B	150
C	120
D	90
E	60

47

PROGRESSION DIPLOMA	
GRADE	TARIFF POINTS
A*	350
A	300
B	250
C	200
D	150
E	100

Advanced Diploma = Progression Diploma plus Additional & Specialist Learning (ASL). Please see the appropriate qualification to calculate the ASL score

48

GRADE	ROCKSCHOOL MUSIC PRACTITIONERS QUALIFICATIONS				
	TARIFF POINTS				
	Extended Diploma	Diploma	Subsidiary Diploma	Extended Certificate	Certificate
DISTINCTION	240	180	120	60	30
MERIT	160	120	80	40	20
PASS	80	60	40	20	10

49

SCOTTISH QUALIFICATIONS

GRADE	TARIFF POINTS	GRADE	TARIFF POINTS	GRADE	TARIFF POINTS	GROUP	TARIFF POINTS
Advanced Higher		Higher		Scottish Interdisciplinary Project		Scottish National Certificates	
A	130	A	80	A	65	C	125
B	110	B	65	B	55	B	100
C	90	C	50	C	45	A	75
D	72	D	36				
Ungraded Higher		NPA PC Passport					
PASS	45	PASS	45				
		Core Skills					
		HIGHER	20				

Details of the subjects covered by each Scottish National Certificate can be found at **www.ucas.com/students/ucas_tariff/tarifftables**

50

SPEECH AND DRAMA EXAMINATIONS

GRADE	TARIFF POINTS	GRADE	TARIFF POINTS	GRADE	TARIFF POINTS	GRADE	TARIFF POINTS
PCertLAM		Grade 8		Grade 7		Grade 6	
DISTINCTION	90	DISTINCTION	65	DISTINCTION	55	DISTINCTION	40
MERIT	80	MERIT	60	MERIT	50	MERIT	35
PASS	60	PASS	45	PASS	35	PASS	20

Details of the Speech and Drama Qualifications covered by the Tariff can be found at **www.ucas.com/students/ucas_tariff/tarifftables**

51

SPORTS LEADERS UK

GRADE	TARIFF POINTS
PASS	30

These points are awarded to Higher Sports Leader Award and Level 3 Certificate in Higher Sports Leadership (QCF)

52

WELSH BACCALAUREATE ADVANCED DIPLOMA (CORE)

GRADE	TARIFF POINTS
PASS	120

These points are awarded only when a candidate achieves the Welsh Baccalaureate Advanced Diploma

Results

4

Step 4 – Results

You should arrange your holidays so that you are at home when your exam results are published because, if there are any issues to discuss, admissions tutors will want to speak to you in person.

We receive many exam results direct from the exam boards – check the list at **www.ucas.com**.

If your qualification is listed, we send your results to the universities and colleges that you have accepted as your firm and insurance choices. If your qualification is not listed, you must send your exam results to the universities and colleges where you are holding offers.

After you have received your exam results check Track to find out if you have a place on your chosen course.

If you have met all the conditions for your firm choice, the university or college will confirm that you have a place. Occasionally, they may still confirm you have a place even if you have not quite met all the offer conditions; or they may offer you a place on a similar course.

If you have not met the conditions of your firm choice and the university or college has not confirmed your place, but you have met all the conditions of your insurance or second offer, your insurance university or college will confirm that you have a place.

When a university or college tells us that you have a place, we send you confirmation by letter.

RE-MARKED EXAMS

If you ask for any of your exams to be re-marked, you must tell the universities and colleges where you're holding offers. If a university or college cannot confirm your place based on the initial results, you should ask them if they would be able to reconsider their decision after the re-mark. They are under no obligation to reconsider their position even if your re-mark results in higher grades. Don't forget that re-marks may also result in lower grades.

The exam boards tell us about any re-marks that result in grade changes. We then send the revised grades to the universities and colleges where you're holding offers. As soon as you know about any grade changes, you should also tell these universities and colleges.

'CASHING IN' A LEVEL RESULTS

If you have taken A levels, your school or college must certificate or 'cash in' all your unit scores before the exam board can award final grades. If when you collect your A level results you have to add up your unit scores to find out your final grades, this means your school or college has not 'cashed in' your results.

We receive only cashed in results from the exam boards, so if your school or college has not cashed in your results, you must ask them to send a 'cash in' request to the exam board. You also need to tell the universities and colleges where you're holding offers that there'll be a delay in receiving your results and call our Customer Service Unit to find out when your results have been received.

When we receive your 'cashed in' results from the exam board we send them straight away to the universities and colleges where you're holding offers.

WHAT IF YOU DON'T HAVE A PLACE?

If you have not met the conditions of either your firm or insurance choice, and your chosen universities or colleges have not confirmed your place, you are eligible for Clearing. In Clearing you can apply for any courses that still have vacancies (but remember that admissions tutors wil still be reading your original personal statement). Clearing operates from mid-July to late September 2013 (page 114).

BETTER RESULTS THAN EXPECTED?

If you obtain exam results that meet and exceed the conditions of the offer for your firm choice, you can for a short period use a process called Adjustment to look for an alternative place, whilst still keeping your original firm choice. See page 115 for information about Adjustment.

Next steps

5

Step 5 – Next steps

You might find yourself with different exam results than you were expecting, or you may change your mind about what you want to do. If so, there may be other options open to you.

CLEARING

Clearing is a service that helps people without a place find suitable course vacancies. It runs from mid-July until the end of September, but most people use it after the exam results are published in August.

You could consider related or alternative subjects or perhaps combining your original choice of subject with another. Your teachers or careers adviser, or the universities and colleges themselves, can provide useful guidance.

Course vacancies are listed at **www.ucas.com** and in the national media following the publication of exam results in August. **Once you have your exam results**, if you're in Clearing you need to look at the vacancy listings and then contact any university or college you are interested in.

Talk to the institutions; don't be afraid to call them. Make sure you have your Personal ID and Clearing Number ready and prepare notes on what you will say to them about:

- why you want to study the course
- why you want to study at their university or college
- any relevant employment or activities you have done that relate to the course
- your grades.

Accepting an offer – you can contact as many universities and colleges as you like through Clearing, and you may informally be offered more than one place. If this happens, you will need to decide which offer you want to accept. If you're offered a place you want to be formally considered for, you enter the course details in Track, and the university or college will then let you know if they're accepting you.

ADJUSTMENT

If you receive better results than expected, and meet and exceed the conditions of your conditional firm choice, you have the opportunity to reconsider what and where you want to study. This process is called Adjustment.

Adjustment runs from A level results day on 15 August 2013 until the end of August. Your individual Adjustment period starts on A level results day or when your conditional firm choice changes to unconditional firm, whichever is the later. You then have a maximum of five calendar days to register and secure an alternative course, if you decide you want to do this. If you want to try to find an alternative course you must register in Track to use Adjustment, so universities and colleges can view your application.

There are no vacancy listings for Adjustment, so you'll need to talk to the institutions. When you contact a university or college make it clear that you are applying through Adjustment, not Clearing. If they want to consider you they will ask for your Personal ID, so they can view your application.

If you don't find an alternative place then you remain accepted at your original firm choice.

Adjustment is entirely optional; remember that nothing really beats the careful research you carried out to find the right courses before you made your UCAS application. Talk to a careers adviser at your school, college or local careers office, as they can help you decide if registering to use Adjustment is right for you.

More information about Adjustment and Clearing is available at www.ucas.com. You can also view UCAStv video guides on how to use Adjustment and Clearing at www.ucas.tv.

IF YOU ARE STILL WITHOUT A PLACE TO STUDY

If you haven't found a suitable place, or changed your mind about what you want to do, there are lots of other options. Ask for advice from your school, college or careers office. Here are some suggestions you might want to consider:

- studying a part-time course (there's a part-time course search at www.ucas.com from July until September)
- studying a foundation degree
- re-sit your exams
- getting some work experience
- studying in another country
- reapplying next year to university or college through UCAS
- taking a gap year
- doing an apprenticeship (you'll find a vacancy search on the National Apprenticeship Service (NAS) website at www.apprenticeships.org.uk)
- finding a job
- starting a business.

More advice and links to other organisations can be found on the UCAS website at www.ucas.com/students/nextsteps/advice.

Starting university or college

6

Step 6 – Starting university or college

Congratulations! Now that you have confirmed your place at university or college you will need to finalise your plans on how to get there, where to live and how to finance it. Make lists of things to do with deadlines and start contacting people whose help you can call on. Will you travel independently or ask your parents or relatives to help with transport? If you are keeping a car at uni, have you checked out parking facilities and told your insurance company?

Make sure you have everything organised, including travel arrangements, essential documents and paperwork, books and equipment required for the course. The university will send you joining information – contact the Admissions Office or the Students' Union if you have questions about anything to do with starting your course.

Freshers week will help you to settle in and make friends, but don't forget you are there to study. You may find the teaching methods rather alien at first, but remember there are plenty of sources of help, including your tutors, other students or student mentors, and the Students Union.

Where to live - unless you are planning to live at home, your university or college will usually be able to provide you with guidance on finding somewhere to live. The earlier you contact them the better your chance of finding a suitable range of options, from hall to private landlords. Find out what facilities are available at the different types of accommodation and check whether it fits within your budget. Check what you need to bring with you and what is supplied. Don't leave it all to the last minute – especially things like arranging a bank account, checking what proof of identity you might need, gathering together a few essentials like a mug and supplies of coffee, insurance cover, TV licence etc.

Student finance - you will need to budget for living costs, accommodation, travel, and books (and tuition fees if you are paying them up front). Learn about budgeting by visiting **www.ucas.com** where you will find further links to useful resources to help you manage your money. Remember that if you do get into financial difficulties the welfare office at the university will help you change tack and manage better in future, but it is always better to live within your means from the outset.

Useful contacts

CONNECTING WITH UCAS

You can follow UCAS on Twitter at **www.twitter.com/ucas_online**, and ask a question or see what others are asking on Facebook at **www.facebook.com/ucasonline**. You can also watch videos of UCAS advisers answering frequently asked questions on YouTube at **www.youtube.com/ucasonline**.

There are many UCAStv video guides to help with your journey into higher education, such as *How to choose your courses*, *Attending events*, *Open days* and *How to apply*. These can all be viewed at **www.ucas.tv** or in the relevant section of **www.ucas.com**.

If you need to speak to UCAS, please contact us on 0871 468 0 468 or 0044 871 468 0 468 from outside the UK. Calls from BT landlines within the UK will cost no more than 9p per minute. The cost of calls from mobiles and other networks may vary.

If you have hearing difficulties, you can call the Text Relay service on 18001 0871 468 0 468 (outside the UK 0044 151 494 1260). Calls are charged at normal rates.

CAREERS ADVICE

The Directgov Careers Helpline for Young People is for you if you live in England, are aged 13 to 19 and want advice on getting to where you want to be in life.

Careers advisers can give you information, advice and practical help with all sorts of things, like choosing subjects at school or mapping out your future career options. They can help you with anything that might be affecting you at school, college, work or in your personal or family life.

Contact a careers adviser at **www.direct.gov.uk/en/youngpeople/index.htm**.

Skills Development Scotland provides a starting point for anyone looking for careers information, advice or guidance.
www.myworldofwork.co.uk.

Careers Wales – Wales' national all-age careers guidance service.
www.careerswales.com
or **www.gyrfacymru.com**.

Northern Ireland Careers Service website for the new, all-age careers guidance service in Northern Ireland.
www.nidirect.gov.uk/careers.

If you're not sure what job you want or you need help to decide which course to do, give learndirect a call on 0800 101 901 or visit
www.learndirect.co.uk.

GENERAL HIGHER EDUCATION ADVICE

National Union of Students (NUS) is the national voice of students, helping them to campaign, get cheap student discounts and provide advice on living student life to the full - **www.nus.org.uk**.

STUDENTS WITH DISABILITIES

If you have a disability or specific learning difficulty, you are strongly encouraged to make early direct contact with individual institutions before submitting your application. Most universities and colleges have disability coordinators or advisers. You can find their contact details and further advice on the Disability Rights UK website - **www.disabilityalliance.org**.

There is financial help for students with disabilities, known as Disabled Students' Allowances (DSAs). More information is available on the Directgov website at **www.direct.gov.uk/disabledstudents**.

YEAR OUT

For useful information on taking a year out, see **www.gap-year.com**.

The Year Out Group website is packed with information and guidance for young people and their parents and advisers. **www.yearoutgroup.org**.

Essential reading

UCAS has brought together the best books and resources you need to make the important decisions regarding entry to higher education. With guidance on choosing courses, finding the right institution, information about student finance, admissions tests, gap years and lots more, you can find the most trusted guides at **www.ucasbooks.com**.

The publications listed on the following pages and many others are available through **www.ucasbooks.com** or from UCAS Publication Services unless otherwise stated.

UCAS PUBLICATION SERVICES

UCAS Publication Services
PO Box 130, Cheltenham, Gloucestershire GL52 3ZF

f: 01242 544 806
e: publicationservices@ucas.ac.uk
// www.ucasbooks.com

ENTIRE RESEARCH AND APPLICATION PROCESS EXPLAINED

The UCAS Guide to getting into University and College

This guide contains advice and up-to-date information about the entire research and application process, and brings together the expertise of UCAS staff, along with insights and tips from well known universities including Oxford and Cambridge, and students who are involved with or have experienced the process first-hand.

The book clearly sets out the information you need in an easy-to-read format, with myth busters, tips from students, checklists and much more; this book will be a companion for applicants throughout their entire journey into higher education.
Published by UCAS
Price £11.99
Publication date January 2011

NEED HELP COMPLETING YOUR APPLICATION?

How to Complete your UCAS Application 2013

A must for anyone applying through UCAS. Contains advice on the preparation needed, a step-by-step guide to filling out the UCAS application, information on the UCAS process and useful tips for completing the personal statement.
Published by Trotman
Price £12.99
Publication date May 2012

Insider's Guide to Applying to University

Full of honest insights, this is a thorough guide to the application process. It reveals advice from careers advisers and current students, guidance on making sense of university information and choosing courses. Also includes tips for the personal statement, interviews, admissions tests, UCAS Extra and Clearing.
Published by Trotman
Price £12.99
Publication date June 2011

How to Write a Winning UCAS Personal Statement

The personal statement is your chance to stand out from the crowd. Based on information from admissions tutors, this book will help you sell yourself. It includes specific guidance for over 30 popular subjects, common mistakes to avoid, information on what admissions tutors look for, and much more.
Published by Trotman
Price £12.99
Publication date March 2010

CHOOSING COURSES

Progression Series 2013 entry

The 'UCAS guide to getting into...' titles are designed to help you access good quality, useful information on some of the most competitive subject areas. The books cover advice on applying through UCAS, routes to qualifications, course details, job prospects, case studies and career advice.

New for 2013: information on the pros and cons of league tables and how to read them.

The UCAS Guide to getting into...
Art and Design
Economics, Finance and Accountancy
Engineering and Mathematics
Journalism, Broadcasting, Media Production and
  Performing Arts
Law
Medicine, Dentistry and Optometry
Nursing, Healthcare and Social Work
Psychology
Sports Science and Physiotherapy
Teaching and Education
Published by UCAS
Price £15.99 each
Publication date June 2012

UCAS Parent Guide

Free of charge.
Order online at www.ucas.com/parents.
Publication date February 2012

Open Days 2012

Attending open days, taster courses and higher education conventions is an important part of the application process. This publication makes planning attendance at these events quick and easy.
Published annually by UCAS.
Price £3.50
Publication date January 2012

Heap 2013: University Degree Course Offers

An independent, reliable guide to selecting university degree courses in the UK.

The guide lists degree courses available at universities and colleges throughout the UK and the grades, UCAS points or equivalent that you need to achieve to get on to each course listed.
Published by Trotman
Price £32.99
Publication date May 2012

ESSENTIAL READING

Choosing Your Degree Course & University

With so many universities and courses to choose from, it is not an easy decision for students embarking on their journey to higher education. This guide will offer expert guidance on the questions students need to ask when considering the opportunities available.
Published by Trotman
Price £24.99
Publication date April 2012

Degree Course Descriptions

Providing details of the nature of degree courses, the descriptions in this book are written by heads of departments and senior lecturers at major universities. Each description contains an overview of the course area, details of course structures, career opportunities and more.
Published by COA
Price £12.99
Publication date September 2011

CHOOSING WHERE TO STUDY

The Virgin Guide to British Universities

An insider's guide to choosing a university or college. Written by students and using independent statistics, this guide evaluates what you get from a higher education institution.
Published by Virgin
Price £15.99
Publication date May 2011

Times Good University Guide 2013

How do you find the best university for the subject you wish to study? You need a guide that evaluates the quality of what is available, giving facts, figures and comparative assessments of universities. The rankings provide hard data, analysed, interpreted and presented by a team of experts.
Published by Harper Collins
Price £16.99
Publication date June 2012

A Parent's Guide to Graduate Jobs

A must-have guide for any parent who is worried about their child's job prospects when they graduate.
In this guide, the graduate careers guru, Paul Redmond, advises parents how to help their son or daughter:

- increase their employability
- boost their earning potential
- acquire essential work skills
- use their own contacts to get them ahead
- gain the right work experience.

Published by Trotman
Price £12.99
Publication date January 2012

Which Uni?

One person's perfect uni might be hell for someone else. Picking the right one will give you the best chance of future happiness, academic success and brighter job prospects. This guide is packed with tables from a variety of sources, rating universities on everything from the quality of teaching to the make-up of the student population and much more.
Published by Trotman
Price £14.99
Publication date September 2011

Getting into the UK's Best Universities and Courses

This book is for those who set their goals high and dream of studying on a highly regarded course at a good university. It provides information on selecting the best courses for a subject, the application and personal statement, interviews, results day, timescales for applications and much more.
Published by Trotman
Price £12.99
Publication date June 2011

FINANCIAL INFORMATION

Student Finance - e-book

All students need to know about tuition fees, loans, grants, bursaries and much more. Covering all forms of income and expenditure, this comprehensive guide is produced in association with UCAS and offers great value for money.
Published by Constable Robinson
Price £4.99
Publication date May 2012

CAREERS PLANNING

A-Z of Careers and Jobs

It is vital to be well informed about career decisions and this guide will help you make the right choice. It provides full details of the wide range of opportunities on the market, the personal qualities and skills needed for each job, entry qualifications and training, realistic salary expectations and useful contact details.
Published by Kogan Page
Price £16.99
Publication date March 2012

The Careers Directory

An indispensable resource for anyone seeking careers information, covering over 350 careers. It presents up-to-date information in an innovative double-page format. Ideal for students in years 10 to 13 who are considering their futures and for other careers professionals.
Published by COA
Price £14.99
Publication date September 2011

Careers with a Science Degree

Over 100 jobs and areas of work for graduates of biological, chemical and physical sciences are described in this guide.

Whether you have yet to choose your degree subject and want to know where the various choices could lead, or are struggling for ideas about what to do with your science degree, this book will guide and inspire you. The title includes: nature of the work and potential employers, qualifications required for entry, including personal qualities and skills; training routes and opportunities for career development and postgraduate study options.
Published by Lifetime Publishing
Price £12.99
Publication date September 2010

Careers with an Arts and Humanities Degree

Covers careers and graduate opportunities related to these degrees.

The book describes over 100 jobs and areas of work suitable for graduates from a range of disciplines including: English and modern languages, history and geography, music and the fine arts. The guide highlights: graduate opportunities, training routes, postgraduate study options and entry requirements.
Published by Lifetime Publishing
Price £12.99
Publication date September 2010

'Getting into…' guides

Clear and concise guides to help applicants secure places. They include qualifications required, advice on applying, tests, interviews and case studies. The guides give an honest view and discuss current issues and careers.

Getting into Oxford and Cambridge
Publication date April 2011
Getting into Veterinary School
Publication date February 2011
Published by Trotman
Price £12.99 each

DEFERRING ENTRY

Gap Years: The Essential Guide

The essential book for all young people planning a gap year before continuing with their education. This up-to-date guide provides essential information on specialist gap year programmes, as well as the vast range of jobs and voluntary opportunities available to young people around the world.
Published by Crimson Publishing
Price £9.99
Publication date April 2012

Gap Year Guidebook 2012

This thorough and easy-to-use guide contains everything you need to know before taking a gap year. It includes real-life traveller tips, hundreds of contact details, realistic advice on everything from preparing, learning and working abroad, coping with coming home and much more.
Published by John Catt Education
Price £14.99
Publication date November 2011

Summer Jobs Worldwide 2012

This unique and specialist guide contains over 40,000 jobs for all ages. No other book includes such a variety and wealth of summer work opportunities in Britain and aboard. Anything from horse trainer in Iceland, to a guide for nature walks in Peru, to a yoga centre helper in Greece, to an animal keeper for London Zoo, can be found.
Published by Crimson Publishing
Price £14.99
Publication date November 2011

Please note all publications incur a postage and packing charge. All information was correct at the time of printing.

For a full list of publications, please visit
www.ucasbooks.com.

UCAS HIGHER EDUCATION CONVENTIONS

Meet face-to-face with over 100 UK university representatives, attend seminars on How to Apply through UCAS and Financing yourself through university.

For further details visit
www.ucas.com/conventions

Courses

Courses

Keen to get started on your art and design career? This section contains details of the various degree courses available at UK institutions.

EXPLAINING THE LIST OF COURSES

The list of courses has been divided into subject categories (see over for a list of subjects). We list the universities and colleges by their UCAS institution codes. If there is a section for non-UCAS entries, colleges are listed alphabetically. Within each institution, courses are listed first by award type (such as BA, BSc, FdA, HND, MA and many others), then alphabetically by course title.

You might find some courses showing an award type '(Mod)', which indicates a combined degree that might be modular in design. A small number of courses have award type '(FYr)'. This indicates a 12-month foundation course, after which students can choose to apply for a degree course. In either case, you should contact the university or college for further details.

Generally speaking, when a course comprises two or more subjects, the word used to connect the subjects indicates the make-up of the award: 'Subject A and Subject B' is a joint award, where both subjects carry equal weight; 'Subject A with Subject B' is a major/minor award, where Subject A accounts for at least 60% of your study. If the title shows 'Subject A/Subject B', it may indicate that students can decide on the weighting of the subjects at the end of the first year. You should check with the university or college for full details.

Each entry shows the UCAS course code and the duration of the course. Where known, the entry contains details of the minimum qualification requirements for the course, as supplied to UCAS by the universities and colleges. Bear in mind that possessing the minimum qualifications does not guarantee acceptance to the course; there may be far more applicants than places. Therefore be prepared to attend an interview and present a portfolio.

Courses with entry requirements that require applicants to disclose information about spent and unspent convictions and may require a Criminal Records Bureau (CRB) check, are marked '**CRB Check:** Required'.

Before applying for any course, you are advised to contact the university or college to check any changes in entry requirements and to see if any new courses have come on stream since the data were approved for publication. To make this easy, each institution's entry starts with their address, email, phone and fax details, as well as their website address. You will also find it useful to check Course Finder at **www.ucas.com**.

LIST OF SUBJECT CATEGORIES

The list of courses in this section has been divided into the following subject categories

3 DIMENSIONAL DESIGN

A66 THE ARTS UNIVERSITY COLLEGE AT BOURNEMOUTH (FORMERLY ARTS INSTITUTE AT BOURNEMOUTH)
WALLISDOWN
POOLE
DORSET BH12 5HH
t: 01202 363228 f: 01202 537729
e: admissions@aucb.ac.uk
// www.aucb.ac.uk

W291 BA Modelmaking
Duration: 3FT Hon
Entry Requirements: *Foundation:* Pass. *GCE:* BCC. *IB:* 24. *OCR ND:* M1 *OCR NED:* M1 Interview required. Portfolio required.

B11 BARKING AND DAGENHAM COLLEGE
DAGENHAM ROAD
ROMFORD
ESSEX RM7 0XU
t: 020 8090 3020 f: 020 8090 3021
e: engagement.services@barkingdagenhamcollege.ac.uk
// www.barkingdagenhamcollege.ac.uk

W290 FdA 3D Design
Duration: 2FT Fdg
Entry Requirements: *GCE:* 120. Portfolio required.

B20 BATH SPA UNIVERSITY
NEWTON PARK
NEWTON ST LOE
BATH BA2 9BN
t: 01225 875875 f: 01225 875444
e: enquiries@bathspa.ac.uk
// www.bathspa.ac.uk/clearing

WW2R BA Three Dimensional Design: Idea Material Object
Duration: 3FT Hon
Entry Requirements: *GCE:* 220-280. *IB:* 24. Interview required.

B23 BEDFORD COLLEGE
CAULDWELL STREET
BEDFORD MK42 9AH
t: 01234 291000 f: 01234 342674
e: info@bedford.ac.uk
// www.bedford.ac.uk

192W HNC 3D Design Crafts
Duration: 1FT HNC
Entry Requirements: *Foundation:* Pass. *GCE:* 80-120. Interview required. Portfolio required.

092W HND 3D Design Crafts
Duration: 2FT HND
Entry Requirements: *Foundation:* Pass. *GCE:* 80-120. Interview required. Portfolio required.

B25 BIRMINGHAM CITY UNIVERSITY
PERRY BARR
BIRMINGHAM B42 2SU
t: 0121 331 5595 f: 0121 331 7994
// www.bcu.ac.uk

162W HND 3D Design
Duration: 2FT HND
Entry Requirements: *GCE:* 120. *SQAH:* CCC. Interview required. Portfolio required.

B44 UNIVERSITY OF BOLTON
DEANE ROAD
BOLTON BL3 5AB
t: 01204 903903 f: 01204 399074
e: enquiries@bolton.ac.uk
// www.bolton.ac.uk

W615 BA 3-Dimensional Character Animation
Duration: 1FT Hon
Entry Requirements: Interview required. Portfolio required.

B94 BUCKINGHAMSHIRE NEW UNIVERSITY
QUEEN ALEXANDRA ROAD
HIGH WYCOMBE
BUCKINGHAMSHIRE HP11 2JZ
t: 0800 0565 660 f: 01494 605 023
e: admissions@bucks.ac.uk
// bucks.ac.uk

W700 BA Three Dimensional Contemporary Crafts and Products
Duration: 3FT Hon
Entry Requirements: *GCE:* 200-240. *IB:* 24. *OCR ND:* M1 *OCR NED:* M3 Interview required.

C22 COLEG SIR GAR / CARMARTHENSHIRE COLLEGE
SANDY ROAD
LLANELLI
CARMARTHENSHIRE SA15 4DN
t: 01554 748000 f: 01554 748170
e: admissions@colegsirgar.ac.uk
// www.colegsirgar.ac.uk

WW27 BA Three Dimensional Designer Maker (Craft Product)
Duration: 3FT Hon
Entry Requirements: Contact the institution for details.

C75 COLCHESTER INSTITUTE
SHEEPEN ROAD
COLCHESTER
ESSEX CO3 3LL
t: 01206 712777 f: 01206 712800
e: info@colchester.ac.uk
// www.colchester.ac.uk

W700 BA Art & Design - Three Dimensional Design and Craft (including Yr 0)
Duration: 4FT Hon
Entry Requirements: *Foundation:* Pass. *GCE:* 80. Interview required. Portfolio required.

W701 BA Art and Design - Three Dimensional Design & Craft
Duration: 3FT Hon
Entry Requirements: *Foundation:* Pass. *GCE:* 160. Interview required. Portfolio required.

C93 UNIVERSITY FOR THE CREATIVE ARTS
FALKNER ROAD
FARNHAM
SURREY GU9 7DS
t: 01252 892960
e: admissions@ucreative.ac.uk
// www.ucreative.ac.uk

W270 BA Three Dimensional Design (Ceramics)
Duration: 3FT Hon
Entry Requirements: *GCE:* 220. *IB:* 24. *BTEC ExtDip:* PPP. Interview required. Portfolio required.

W770 BA Three Dimensional Design (Glass)
Duration: 3FT Hon
Entry Requirements: *GCE:* 220. *IB:* 24. *BTEC ExtDip:* PPP. Interview required. Portfolio required.

W720 BA Three Dimensional Design (Metalwork & Jewellery)
Duration: 3FT Hon
Entry Requirements: *GCE:* 220. *IB:* 24. *BTEC ExtDip:* PPP. Interview required. Portfolio required.

F33 UNIVERSITY COLLEGE FALMOUTH
WOODLANE
FALMOUTH
CORNWALL TR11 4RH
t: 01326213730
e: admissions@falmouth.ac.uk
// www.falmouth.ac.uk

W250 BA(Hons) 3D Design
Duration: 3FT Hon
Entry Requirements: *GCE:* 220. *IB:* 24. Interview required. Portfolio required.

G70 UNIVERSITY OF GREENWICH
GREENWICH CAMPUS
OLD ROYAL NAVAL COLLEGE
PARK ROW
LONDON SE10 9LS
t: 020 8331 9000 f: 020 8331 8145
e: courseinfo@gre.ac.uk
// www.gre.ac.uk

GW42 BA 3D Digital Design and Animation
Duration: 3FT Hon
Entry Requirements: *Foundation:* Pass. *GCE:* 280. *IB:* 24. Interview required. Portfolio required.

WW26 FdEng CAD and 3D Animation
Duration: 2FT Fdg
Entry Requirements: *IB:* 24.

H14 HAVERING COLLEGE OF FURTHER AND HIGHER EDUCATION
ARDLEIGH GREEN ROAD
HORNCHURCH
ESSEX RM11 2LL
t: 01708 462793 f: 01708 462736
e: HE@havering-college.ac.uk
// www.havering-college.ac.uk

W290 BA 3D Design Craft
Duration: 3FT Hon
Entry Requirements: *Foundation:* Pass. Interview required. Portfolio required.

H36 UNIVERSITY OF HERTFORDSHIRE
UNIVERSITY ADMISSIONS SERVICE
COLLEGE LANE
HATFIELD
HERTS AL10 9AB
t: 01707 284800
// www.herts.ac.uk

W617 BA 3D Digital Animation
Duration: 3FT Hon
Entry Requirements: *GCE:* 240. Interview required. Portfolio required.

W280 BA 3D Games Art
Duration: 3FT Hon
Entry Requirements: *GCE:* 240. Interview required. Portfolio required.

W201 FdA Three-dimensional Design
Duration: 2FT Fdg
Entry Requirements: *GCE:* 80. Interview required. Portfolio required.

H73 HULL COLLEGE
QUEEN'S GARDENS
HULL HU1 3DG
t: 01482 329943 f: 01482 598733
e: info@hull-college.ac.uk
// www.hull-college.ac.uk/higher-education

WW72 BA 3D Design/Crafts (Ceramics/Glass and Jewellery/Metalworking) Top-Up
Duration: 1FT Hon
Entry Requirements: Contact the institution for details.

WW7F FdA 3D Design Crafts (Jewellery and Ceramics)
Duration: 2FT Fdg
Entry Requirements: Contact the institution for details.

L79 LOUGHBOROUGH UNIVERSITY
LOUGHBOROUGH
LEICESTERSHIRE LE11 3TU
t: 01509 223522 f: 01509 223905
e: admissions@lboro.ac.uk
// www.lboro.ac.uk

W790 BA Three Dimensional Design: New Practice
Duration: 3FT Hon
Entry Requirements: *GCE:* 320. *IB:* 32. *BTEC ExtDip:* DDM. Interview required. Portfolio required.

M10 THE MANCHESTER COLLEGE
OPENSHAW CAMPUS
ASHTON OLD ROAD
OPENSHAW
MANCHESTER M11 2WH
t: 0800 068 8585 f: 0161 920 4103
e: enquiries@themanchestercollege.ac.uk
// www.themanchestercollege.ac.uk

WW26 FdA 3D Modelling and Animation
Duration: 2FT Fdg
Entry Requirements: *GCE:* 160. *BTEC ExtDip:* MPP. Portfolio required.

W213 FdA 3D Visualisation
Duration: 2FT Fdg
Entry Requirements: *GCE:* 160. *BTEC ExtDip:* MPP. Portfolio required.

M40 THE MANCHESTER METROPOLITAN UNIVERSITY
ADMISSIONS OFFICE
ALL SAINTS (GMS)
ALL SAINTS
MANCHESTER M15 6BH
t: 0161 247 2000
// www.mmu.ac.uk

W240 BA Three Dimensional Design
Duration: 3FT Hon
Entry Requirements: *GCE:* 280. *IB:* 27. Interview required. Portfolio required.

M80 MIDDLESEX UNIVERSITY
MIDDLESEX UNIVERSITY
THE BURROUGHS
LONDON NW4 4BT
t: 020 8411 5555 f: 020 8411 5649
e: enquiries@mdx.ac.uk
// www.mdx.ac.uk

WP15 BA 3D Animation and Games
Duration: 3FT Hon
Entry Requirements: Interview required. Portfolio required.

N58 NORTH EAST WORCESTERSHIRE COLLEGE

PEAKMAN STREET
REDDITCH
WORCESTERSHIRE B98 8DW
t: 01527 570020 f: 01527 572901
e: admissions@ne-worcs.ac.uk
// www.ne-worcs.ac.uk

WWF9 FdA Art & Design in the Creative Industries (3D Design)

Duration: 2FT Fdg
Entry Requirements: *GCE:* 120. Interview required. Portfolio required.

N77 NORTHUMBRIA UNIVERSITY

TRINITY BUILDING
NORTHUMBERLAND ROAD
NEWCASTLE UPON TYNE NE1 8ST
t: 0191 243 7420 f: 0191 227 4561
e: er.admissions@northumbria.ac.uk
// www.northumbria.ac.uk

W260 BA 3D Design

Duration: 3FT Hon
Entry Requirements: *Foundation:* Distinction. *GCE:* 280. *SQAH:* BBCCC. *SQAAH:* BCC. *IB:* 25. *OCR NED:* M2 Interview required. Portfolio required.

N79 NORTH WARWICKSHIRE AND HINCKLEY COLLEGE

HINCKLEY ROAD
NUNEATON
WARWICKSHIRE CV11 6BH
t: 024 7624 3395
e: angela.jones@nwhc.ac.uk
// www.nwhc.ac.uk

002W HNC Three Dimensional Design Practice

Duration: 1FT HNC
Entry Requirements: Contact the institution for details.

32JW HND Three Dimensional Design Practice

Duration: 2FT HND
Entry Requirements: *GCE:* 140. Portfolio required.

P60 PLYMOUTH UNIVERSITY

DRAKE CIRCUS
PLYMOUTH PL4 8AA
t: 01752 585858 f: 01752 588055
e: admissions@plymouth.ac.uk
// www.plymouth.ac.uk

W250 BA 3D Design

Duration: 3FT Hon
Entry Requirements: *Foundation:* Merit. *GCE:* 280. *IB:* 26. *BTEC ExtDip:* DDM. Interview required. Portfolio required.

R36 ROBERT GORDON UNIVERSITY

ROBERT GORDON UNIVERSITY
SCHOOLHILL
ABERDEEN
SCOTLAND AB10 1FR
t: 01224 26 27 28 f: 01224 26 21 47
e: UGOffice@rgu.ac.uk
// www.rgu.ac.uk

W290 BA Three Dimensional Design

Duration: 4FT Hon
Entry Requirements: *GCE:* BC. *SQAH:* BBC. Interview required. Portfolio required.

S03 THE UNIVERSITY OF SALFORD

SALFORD M5 4WT
t: 0161 295 4545 f: 0161 295 4646
e: ug-admissions@salford.ac.uk
// www.salford.ac.uk

W201 BA 3D Design

Duration: 3FT Hon
Entry Requirements: Contact the institution for details.

S05 SAE INSTITUTE

297 KINGSLAND ROAD
LONDON E8 4DD
t: 020 7923 9159
e: degree.registry@sae.edu
// www.sae.edu

W615 DipHE 3D Animation

Duration: 1.5FT Dip
Entry Requirements: Contact the institution for details.

S32 SOUTH DEVON COLLEGE
LONG ROAD
PAIGNTON
DEVON TQ4 7EJ
t: 08000 213181 f: 01803 540541
e: university@southdevon.ac.uk
// www.southdevon.ac.uk/
welcome-to-university-level

W251 FdA Three Dimensional Design
Duration: 2FT Fdg
Entry Requirements: Contact the institution for details.

S72 STAFFORDSHIRE UNIVERSITY
COLLEGE ROAD
STOKE ON TRENT ST4 2DE
t: 01782 292753 f: 01782 292740
e: admissions@staffs.ac.uk
// www.staffs.ac.uk

W790 BA 3D Design: Contemporary Jewellery and Fashion Accessories
Duration: 3FT/4FT Hon
Entry Requirements: *Foundation:* Merit. *GCE:* 200-240. *IB:* 24. *BTEC Dip:* DD. *BTEC ExtDip:* MMM. Interview required. Portfolio required.

W700 BA 3D Design: Crafts
Duration: 3FT/4FT Hon
Entry Requirements: *Foundation:* Merit. *GCE:* 200-240. *IB:* 24. *BTEC Dip:* DD. *BTEC ExtDip:* MMM. Interview required. Portfolio required.

W273 BA 3D: Design: Ceramics
Duration: 3FT/4FT Hon
Entry Requirements: *Foundation:* Merit. *GCE:* 200-240. *IB:* 24. *BTEC Dip:* DD. *BTEC ExtDip:* MMM. Interview required. Portfolio required.

W282 BA Entrepreneurship in 3D Design
Duration: 1FT Hon
Entry Requirements: Interview required. Portfolio required.

S96 SWANSEA METROPOLITAN UNIVERSITY
MOUNT PLEASANT CAMPUS
SWANSEA SA1 6ED
t: 01792 481000 f: 01792 481061
e: gemma.green@smu.ac.uk
// www.smu.ac.uk

WGP4 BA 3D Computer Animation
Duration: 3FT Hon
Entry Requirements: *GCE:* 200-360. *IB:* 24. Interview required.

W130 BA Fine Art (3D and Sculptural Practice)
Duration: 3FT Hon
Entry Requirements: *Foundation:* Pass. *GCE:* 200-360. *IB:* 24. Interview required. Portfolio required.

WG64 BSc 3D Computer Animation
Duration: 3FT Hon
Entry Requirements: *GCE:* 200-360. *IB:* 24. Interview required.

U65 UNIVERSITY OF THE ARTS LONDON
272 HIGH HOLBORN
LONDON WC1V 7EY
t: 020 7514 6000x6197 f: 020 7514 6198
e: c.anderson@arts.ac.uk
// www.arts.ac.uk

W242 BA Three-Dimensional Design
Duration: 3FT Hon
Entry Requirements: *Foundation:* Pass. *GCE:* 80. *IB:* 28. Interview required. Portfolio required.

W25 WARWICKSHIRE COLLEGE
WARWICK NEW ROAD
LEAMINGTON SPA
WARWICKSHIRE CV32 5JE
t: 01926 884223 f: 01926 318 111
e: kgooch@warkscol.ac.uk
// www.warwickshire.ac.uk

007W HND 3D Design Craft
Duration: 2FT HND
Entry Requirements: *Foundation:* Pass. *GCE:* 80. Portfolio required.

Y70 YORK COLLEGE
SIM BALK LANE
YORK YO23 2BB
t: 01904 770448 f: 01904 770499
e: admissions.team@yorkcollege.ac.uk
// www.yorkcollege.ac.uk

W700 BA Three-Dimensional Contemporary Crafts
Duration: 3FT Hon
Entry Requirements: *Foundation:* Pass. *GCE:* CC. Foundation Course required. Interview required. Portfolio required.

ANIMATION AND MOVING IMAGE

A60 ANGLIA RUSKIN UNIVERSITY
BISHOP HALL LANE
CHELMSFORD
ESSEX CM1 1SQ
t: 0845 271 3333 f: 01245 251789
e: answers@anglia.ac.uk
// www.anglia.ac.uk

WW26 BA Illustration and Animation
Duration: 3FT Hon
Entry Requirements: *GCE:* 200-240. *SQAH:* CCCC. *SQAAH:* BC.
IB: 24. Interview required. Portfolio required.

A66 THE ARTS UNIVERSITY COLLEGE AT BOURNEMOUTH (FORMERLY ARTS INSTITUTE AT BOURNEMOUTH)
WALLISDOWN
POOLE
DORSET BH12 5HH
t: 01202 363228 f: 01202 537729
e: admissions@aucb.ac.uk
// www.aucb.ac.uk

W615 BA Animation Production
Duration: 3FT Hon
Entry Requirements: *Foundation:* Pass. *GCE:* BCC. *IB:* 24. *OCR ND:* M1 *OCR NED:* M1 Foundation Course required. Interview required. Portfolio required.

B11 BARKING AND DAGENHAM COLLEGE
DAGENHAM ROAD
ROMFORD
ESSEX RM7 0XU
t: 020 8090 3020 f: 020 8090 3021
e: engagement.services@barkingdagenhamcollege.ac.uk
// www.barkingdagenhamcollege.ac.uk

W690 FdA Animation and Creative Video Production
Duration: 2FT Fdg
Entry Requirements: *GCE:* 120. Portfolio required.

B22 UNIVERSITY OF BEDFORDSHIRE
PARK SQUARE
LUTON
BEDS LU1 3JU
t: 0844 8482234 f: 01582 489323
e: admissions@beds.ac.uk
// www.beds.ac.uk

W615 BA Animation
Duration: 3FT Hon
Entry Requirements: *GCE:* 200. Interview required. Portfolio required.

PW36 BA Media Production (Moving Image)
Duration: 3FT Hon
Entry Requirements: *Foundation:* Pass. *GCE:* 200. *SQAH:* BCC. *SQAAH:* BCC. *IB:* 24. *OCR ND:* M1 *OCR NED:* P1

G455 BSc Computer Animation Technology
Duration: 3FT Hon
Entry Requirements: *Foundation:* Pass. *GCE:* 200. *SQAH:* BCC. *SQAAH:* BCC. *IB:* 24. *OCR ND:* M1 *OCR NED:* P1

WG64 FdA Animation for Industry
Duration: 2FT Fdg
Entry Requirements: *GCE:* 80-120. Interview required. Portfolio required.

B25 BIRMINGHAM CITY UNIVERSITY
PERRY BARR
BIRMINGHAM B42 2SU
t: 0121 331 5595 f: 0121 331 7994
// www.bcu.ac.uk

W610 BA Visual Communication (Animation and Moving Image)
Duration: 3FT Hon
Entry Requirements: Contact the institution for details.

B40 BLACKBURN COLLEGE
FEILDEN STREET
BLACKBURN BB2 1LH
t: 01254 292594 f: 01254 679647
e: he-admissions@blackburn.ac.uk
// www.blackburn.ac.uk

WW26 BA Design (Illustration & Animation)
Duration: 3FT Hon
Entry Requirements: *GCE:* 200.

W610 BA Design (Moving Image)
Duration: 3FT Hon
Entry Requirements: *GCE:* 200.

B44 UNIVERSITY OF BOLTON
DEANE ROAD
BOLTON BL3 5AB
t: 01204 903903 f: 01204 399074
e: enquiries@bolton.ac.uk
// www.bolton.ac.uk

WW26 BA Animation & Illustration
Duration: 3FT Hon
Entry Requirements: *GCE:* 240. Interview required. Portfolio required.

WWF6 BA Animation & Illustration and Graphic Design
Duration: 3FT Hon
Entry Requirements: *GCE:* 240. Interview required. Portfolio required.

B50 BOURNEMOUTH UNIVERSITY
TALBOT CAMPUS
FERN BARROW
POOLE
DORSET BH12 5BB
t: 01202 524111
// www.bournemouth.ac.uk

GW4F BA Computer Animation Arts
Duration: 3FT Hon
Entry Requirements: *GCE:* 340. *IB:* 33. *BTEC SubDip:* D. *BTEC Dip:* DD. *BTEC ExtDip:* DDM. Interview required. Admissions Test required. Portfolio required.

W280 BA Computer Visualisation and Animation
Duration: 3FT Hon
Entry Requirements: *GCE:* 340. *IB:* 33. *BTEC SubDip:* D. *BTEC Dip:* DD. *BTEC ExtDip:* DDD. Interview required. Admissions Test required. Portfolio required.

B60 BRADFORD COLLEGE: AN ASSOCIATE COLLEGE OF LEEDS METROPOLITAN UNIVERSITY
GREAT HORTON ROAD
BRADFORD
WEST YORKSHIRE BD7 1AY
t: 01274 433008 f: 01274 431652
e: heregistry@bradfordcollege.ac.uk
// www.bradfordcollege.ac.uk/university-centre

W2G4 BA Graphic Design, Illustration, Digital Media option - Moving Image
Duration: 3FT Hon
Entry Requirements: *GCE:* 120. Interview required. Portfolio required.

W616 HND Art & Design (Animation)
Duration: 2FT HND
Entry Requirements: Contact the institution for details.

W612 HND Creative Media Production (Moving Image)
Duration: 2FT HND
Entry Requirements: Contact the institution for details.

B72 UNIVERSITY OF BRIGHTON
MITHRAS HOUSE 211
LEWES ROAD
BRIGHTON BN2 4AT
t: 01273 644644 f: 01273 642607
e: admissions@brighton.ac.uk
// www.brighton.ac.uk

W610 BA Moving Image
Duration: 3FT Hon
Entry Requirements: *GCE:* BBC. Foundation Course required. Interview required. Portfolio required.

W616 MFA Moving Image
Duration: 4FT Hon
Entry Requirements: *GCE:* BBC. Foundation Course required. Interview required. Portfolio required.

B80 UNIVERSITY OF THE WEST OF ENGLAND, BRISTOL
FRENCHAY CAMPUS
COLDHARBOUR LANE
BRISTOL BS16 1QY
t: +44 (0)117 32 83333 f: +44 (0)117 32 82810
e: admissions@uwe.ac.uk
// www.uwe.ac.uk

W615 BA Animation
Duration: 3FT Hon
Entry Requirements: *GCE:* 280. Interview required. Portfolio required.

B92 BROOKSBY MELTON COLLEGE
MELTON CAMPUS
ASFORDBY ROAD
MELTON MOWBRAY
LEICESTERSHIRE LE13 0HJ
t: 01664 850850 f: 01664 855355
e: heenquiries@brooksbymelton.ac.uk
// www.brooksbymelton.ac.uk

016W HND Media (Moving Image)
Duration: 2FT HND
Entry Requirements: *GCE:* 160. Interview required. Portfolio required.

B94 BUCKINGHAMSHIRE NEW UNIVERSITY
QUEEN ALEXANDRA ROAD
HIGH WYCOMBE
BUCKINGHAMSHIRE HP11 2JZ
t: 0800 0565 660 f: 01494 605 023
e: admissions@bucks.ac.uk
// bucks.ac.uk

W6I6 BA Animation, Games and Interactive Media
Duration: 3FT Hon
Entry Requirements: Contact the institution for details.

W694 FdA Animation & Visual Effects
Duration: 2FT Fdg
Entry Requirements: *GCE:* 100-140. *IB:* 24. *OCR ND:* P2 *OCR NED:* P3 Interview required.

C10 CANTERBURY CHRIST CHURCH UNIVERSITY
NORTH HOLMES ROAD
CANTERBURY
KENT CT1 1QU
t: 01227 782900 f: 01227 782888
e: admissions@canterbury.ac.uk
// www.canterbury.ac.uk

W615 BA Film, Radio & Television Studies (Animation)
Duration: 3FT Hon   CRB Check: Required
Entry Requirements: *GCE:* 260. *IB:* 24. Interview required.

C30 UNIVERSITY OF CENTRAL LANCASHIRE
PRESTON
LANCS PR1 2HE
t: 01772 201201 f: 01772 894954
e: uadmissions@uclan.ac.uk
// www.uclan.ac.uk

WW27 BA Animation
Duration: 3FT Hon
Entry Requirements: *GCE:* 240-300. *IB:* 26. *OCR ND:* D *OCR NED:* M3 Interview required. Portfolio required.

C71 CLEVELAND COLLEGE OF ART AND DESIGN
CHURCH SQUARE
HARTLEPOOL
CHURCH SQUARE TS24 7EX
t: 01642 288888 f: 01642 288828
e: studentrecruitment@ccad.ac.uk
// www.ccad.ac.uk

W691 FdA Creative Film and Moving Image Production
Duration: 2FT Fdg
Entry Requirements: Contact the institution for details.

C85 COVENTRY UNIVERSITY
THE STUDENT CENTRE
COVENTRY UNIVERSITY
1 GULSON RD
COVENTRY CV1 2JH
t: 024 7615 2222 f: 024 7615 2223
e: studentenquiries@coventry.ac.uk
// www.coventry.ac.uk

WW26 BA Illustration and Animation
Duration: 3FT/4SW Hon
Entry Requirements: *Foundation:* Merit. *GCE:* CCC. *SQAH:* CCCCC. *IB:* 27. *BTEC ExtDip:* MMM. *OCR NED:* M3 Interview required. Portfolio required.

C93 UNIVERSITY FOR THE CREATIVE ARTS
FALKNER ROAD
FARNHAM
SURREY GU9 7DS
t: 01252 892960
e: admissions@ucreative.ac.uk
// www.ucreative.ac.uk

W615 BA Animation
Duration: 3FT Hon
Entry Requirements: *GCE:* 220. *IB:* 24. *BTEC ExtDip:* PPP. Interview required. Portfolio required.

W281 BA CG Arts & Animation
Duration: 3FT Hon
Entry Requirements: *GCE:* 220. *IB:* 24. *BTEC ExtDip:* PPP. Interview required. Portfolio required.

D26 DE MONTFORT UNIVERSITY
THE GATEWAY
LEICESTER LE1 9BH
t: 0116 255 1551 f: 0116 250 6204
e: enquiries@dmu.ac.uk
// www.dmu.ac.uk

W615 BA Animation Design
Duration: 3FT Hon
Entry Requirements: *Foundation:* Pass. *GCE:* 260. *IB:* 28. *BTEC Dip:* D*D. *BTEC ExtDip:* MMM. Interview required. Portfolio required.

D39 UNIVERSITY OF DERBY
KEDLESTON ROAD
DERBY DE22 1GB
t: 01332 591167 f: 01332 597724
e: askadmissions@derby.ac.uk
// www.derby.ac.uk

W615 BA Animation
Duration: 3FT Hon
Entry Requirements: *Foundation:* Distinction. *GCE:* 260. *IB:* 28. *BTEC Dip:* D*D*. *BTEC ExtDip:* DMM. *OCR NED:* M2 Interview required. Portfolio required.

WW26 BA Animation
Duration: 1FT FYr
Entry Requirements: *Foundation:* Pass. *GCE:* 160. *IB:* 24. *BTEC Dip:* D*D*. *BTEC ExtDip:* DMM. *OCR ND:* M2 *OCR NED:* P2 Interview required. Portfolio required.

W618 MDes Animation
Duration: 4FT Hon
Entry Requirements: *Foundation:* Distinction. *GCE:* 260. *IB:* 28. *BTEC Dip:* D*D*. *BTEC ExtDip:* DMM. *OCR NED:* M2 Interview required. Portfolio required.

D52 DONCASTER COLLEGE
THE HUB
CHAPPELL DRIVE
SOUTH YORKSHIRE DN1 2RF
t: 01302 553610
e: he@don.ac.uk
// www.don.ac.uk

WW26 BA Illustration & Animation (top-up)
Duration: 1FT Hon
Entry Requirements: Contact the institution for details.

W610 BA Moving Image Production
Duration: 3FT Hon
Entry Requirements: Contact the institution for details.

W6G4 FdA Animation and Games Art
Duration: 2FT Fdg
Entry Requirements: *GCE:* 160.

D65 UNIVERSITY OF DUNDEE
NETHERGATE
DUNDEE DD1 4HN
t: 01382 383838 f: 01382 388150
e: contactus@dundee.ac.uk
// www.dundee.ac.uk/admissions/undergraduate/

W280 BDes Animation
Duration: 3FT Hon
Entry Requirements: Foundation Course required. Interview required. Portfolio required.

E28 UNIVERSITY OF EAST LONDON
DOCKLANDS CAMPUS
UNIVERSITY WAY
LONDON E16 2RD
t: 020 8223 3333 f: 020 8223 2978
e: study@uel.ac.uk
// www.uel.ac.uk

Q3W6 BA English Literature with Animation
Duration: 3FT Hon
Entry Requirements: *GCE:* 240. *IB:* 24.

W2WA BA Graphic Design with Animation
Duration: 3FT Hon
Entry Requirements: *GCE:* 200. *IB:* 24. Foundation Course required. Interview required. Portfolio required.

P5W6 BA Journalism Studies with Animation
Duration: 3FT Hon
Entry Requirements: *GCE:* 240. *IB:* 24.

P3W6 BA Media Studies with Animation
Duration: 3FT Hon
Entry Requirements: *GCE:* 240. *IB:* 24.

WWQ2 BA Moving Image (Extended)
Duration: 4FT Hon
Entry Requirements: *GCE:* 80. Interview required. Portfolio required.

W2WQ BA Multimedia Design Technology with Animation
Duration: 3FT Hon
Entry Requirements: *GCE:* 240.

W694 BA Photography with Animation
Duration: 3FT Hon
Entry Requirements: *GCE:* 200. *IB:* 24. Portfolio required.

W2WP BSc Computer Games Design with Animation
Duration: 3FT Hon
Entry Requirements: *GCE:* 280. *IB:* 24. Portfolio required.

E32 EAST SURREY COLLEGE (INCORPORATING REIGATE SCHOOL OF ART, DESIGN AND MEDIA)
GATTON POINT
LONDON ROAD
REDHILL RH1 2JX
t: 01737 772611 f: 01737 768641
e: fmelmoe@esc.ac.uk
// www.esc.ac.uk

62WW HND Graphic Design (Animation)
Duration: 2FT HND
Entry Requirements: Contact the institution for details.

E42 EDGE HILL UNIVERSITY
ORMSKIRK
LANCASHIRE L39 4QP
t: 01695 657000 f: 01695 584355
e: study@edgehill.ac.uk
// www.edgehill.ac.uk

W615 BA Animation
Duration: 3FT Hon
Entry Requirements: *GCE:* 280. *IB:* 26. *OCR ND:* D *OCR NED:* M2
Interview required. Portfolio required.

W617 BA Stop-Motion Animation
Duration: 3FT Hon
Entry Requirements: *GCE:* 280. *IB:* 26. *OCR ND:* D *OCR NED:* M2
Interview required. Portfolio required.

E56 THE UNIVERSITY OF EDINBURGH
STUDENT RECRUITMENT & ADMISSIONS
57 GEORGE SQUARE
EDINBURGH EH8 9JU
t: 0131 650 4360 f: 0131 651 1236
e: sra.enquiries@ed.ac.uk
// www.ed.ac.uk/studying/undergraduate/

W615 BA Animation
Duration: 4FT Hon
Entry Requirements: *Foundation:* Merit. *GCE:* BBB. *SQAH:* BBBB.
IB: 34. Portfolio required.

F33 UNIVERSITY COLLEGE FALMOUTH
WOODLANE
FALMOUTH
CORNWALL TR11 4RH
t: 01326213730
e: admissions@falmouth.ac.uk
// www.falmouth.ac.uk

WG64 BA(Hons) Digital Animation
Duration: 3FT Hon
Entry Requirements: *GCE:* 220. *IB:* 24. Interview required.
Portfolio required.

F66 FARNBOROUGH COLLEGE OF TECHNOLOGY
BOUNDARY ROAD
FARNBOROUGH
HAMPSHIRE GU14 6SB
t: 01252 407028 f: 01252 407041
e: admissions@farn-ct.ac.uk
// www.farn-ct.ac.uk

WW26 FdSc Graphic Design, Animation and Interactive Media
Duration: 2FT Fdg
Entry Requirements: *GCE:* 160.

G14 UNIVERSITY OF GLAMORGAN, CARDIFF AND PONTYPRIDD
ENQUIRIES AND ADMISSIONS UNIT
PONTYPRIDD CF37 1DL
t: 08456 434030 f: 01443 654050
e: enquiries@glam.ac.uk
// www.glam.ac.uk

W615 BA Animation
Duration: 3FT Hon
Entry Requirements: *Foundation:* Pass. *GCE:* ACC. *IB:* 24. *BTEC SubDip:* M. *BTEC Dip:* D*D*. *BTEC ExtDip:* DDM. *OCR ND:* M1
OCR NED: M2 Interview required. Portfolio required.

WW26 BA Computer Animation
Duration: 3FT Hon
Entry Requirements: *Foundation:* Pass. *GCE:* ABC. *IB:* 24. *BTEC SubDip:* M. *BTEC Dip:* DD. *BTEC ExtDip:* DDM. *OCR ND:* M1
OCR NED: P1 Interview required. Portfolio required.

W281 BA Game Art & Animation
Duration: 3FT Hon
Entry Requirements: *Foundation:* Pass. *GCE:* ACC. *IB:* 25. *BTEC SubDip:* M. *BTEC Dip:* D*D*. *BTEC ExtDip:* DMM. *OCR ND:* M1
OCR NED: M2 Interview required. Portfolio required.

G42 GLASGOW CALEDONIAN UNIVERSITY

STUDENT RECRUITMENT & ADMISSIONS SERVICE
CITY CAMPUS
COWCADDENS ROAD
GLASGOW G4 0BA
t: 0141 331 3000 f: 0141 331 8676
e: undergraduate@gcu.ac.uk
// www.gcu.ac.uk

GW4G BA Computer Games (Art and Animation)

Duration: 4FT Hon
Entry Requirements: *GCE:* CC. *SQAH:* BBB. Portfolio required.

G53 GLYNDWR UNIVERSITY

PLAS COCH
MOLD ROAD
WREXHAM LL11 2AW
t: 01978 293439 f: 01978 290008
e: sid@glyndwr.ac.uk
// www.glyndwr.ac.uk

W21F BA Design: Animation and Game Art

Duration: 3FT Hon
Entry Requirements: *GCE:* 240. Interview required. Portfolio required.

G70 UNIVERSITY OF GREENWICH

GREENWICH CAMPUS
OLD ROYAL NAVAL COLLEGE
PARK ROW
LONDON SE10 9LS
t: 020 8331 9000 f: 020 8331 8145
e: courseinfo@gre.ac.uk
// www.gre.ac.uk

W610 BA Television Production and Moving Image Culture (top up)

Duration: 1FT Hon
Entry Requirements: Contact the institution for details.

H36 UNIVERSITY OF HERTFORDSHIRE

UNIVERSITY ADMISSIONS SERVICE
COLLEGE LANE
HATFIELD
HERTS AL10 9AB
t: 01707 284800
// www.herts.ac.uk

W616 BA 2D Digital Animation

Duration: 3FT Hon
Entry Requirements: *GCE:* 240. Interview required. Portfolio required.

H60 THE UNIVERSITY OF HUDDERSFIELD

QUEENSGATE
HUDDERSFIELD HD1 3DH
t: 01484 473969 f: 01484 472765
e: admissionsandrecords@hud.ac.uk
// www.hud.ac.uk

WW63 BA Film, Animation, Music and Enterprise

Duration: 3FT/4SW Hon
Entry Requirements: *GCE:* 260.

W610 BA(Hons) Animation and Motion Graphics

Duration: 3FT/4SW Hon
Entry Requirements: *GCE:* 300. *SQAH:* BBBBB-BBBC. *IB:* 28. Interview required. Portfolio required.

H73 HULL COLLEGE

QUEEN'S GARDENS
HULL HU1 3DG
t: 01482 329943 f: 01482 598733
e: info@hull-college.ac.uk
// www.hull-college.ac.uk/higher-education

W615 BA Animation

Duration: 3FT Hon
Entry Requirements: *GCE:* 200. Foundation Course required. Interview required. Portfolio required.

K84 KINGSTON UNIVERSITY

STUDENT INFORMATION & ADVICE CENTRE
COOPER HOUSE
40-46 SURBITON ROAD
KINGSTON UPON THAMES KT1 2HX
t: 0844 8552177 f: 020 8547 7080
e: aps@kingston.ac.uk
// www.kingston.ac.uk

W220 BA Illustration & Animation

Duration: 3FT Hon
Entry Requirements: Foundation Course required. Interview required. Portfolio required.

L27 LEEDS METROPOLITAN UNIVERSITY

COURSE ENQUIRIES OFFICE
CITY CAMPUS
LEEDS LS1 3HE
t: 0113 81 23113 f: 0113 81 23129
// www.leedsmet.ac.uk

W615 BA Animation

Duration: 3FT/4SW Hon
Entry Requirements: *GCE:* 200. *IB:* 24. Interview required.

GW46 BSc Computer Animation & Special Effects
Duration: 3FT Hon
Entry Requirements: *GCE:* 200. *IB:* 24. Interview required.

L28 LEEDS COLLEGE OF ART
BLENHEIM WALK
LEEDS LS2 9AQ
t: 0113 202 8000 f: 0113 202 8001
e: info@leeds-art.ac.uk
// www.leeds-art.ac.uk

W612 BA Digital Film, Games & Animation
Duration: 3FT Hon
Entry Requirements: *Foundation:* Merit. *GCE:* 240. *IB:* 24. *BTEC Dip:* DD. *BTEC ExtDip:* MMM. Interview required. Portfolio required.

L39 UNIVERSITY OF LINCOLN
ADMISSIONS
BRAYFORD POOL
LINCOLN LN6 7TS
t: 01522 886097 f: 01522 886146
e: admissions@lincoln.ac.uk
// www.lincoln.ac.uk

W270 BA Animation
Duration: 3FT Hon
Entry Requirements: *GCE:* 280. Interview required. Portfolio required.

L51 LIVERPOOL JOHN MOORES UNIVERSITY
KINGSWAY HOUSE
HATTON GARDEN
LIVERPOOL L3 2AJ
t: 0151 231 5090 f: 0151 904 6368
e: courses@ljmu.ac.uk
// www.ljmu.ac.uk

GW42 BSc Computer Animation and Visualisation
Duration: 4SW Hon
Entry Requirements: *GCE:* 260. *IB:* 24.

L68 LONDON METROPOLITAN UNIVERSITY
166-220 HOLLOWAY ROAD
LONDON N7 8DB
t: 020 7133 4200
e: admissions@londonmet.ac.uk
// www.londonmet.ac.uk

W615 BA Media Practice (Animation)
Duration: 3FT Hon
Entry Requirements: Contact the institution for details.

M10 THE MANCHESTER COLLEGE
OPENSHAW CAMPUS
ASHTON OLD ROAD
OPENSHAW
MANCHESTER M11 2WH
t: 0800 068 8585 f: 0161 920 4103
e: enquiries@themanchestercollege.ac.uk
// www.themanchestercollege.ac.uk

W615 FdA Animation
Duration: 2FT Fdg
Entry Requirements: *Foundation:* Pass. *GCE:* 160. Portfolio required.

M40 THE MANCHESTER METROPOLITAN UNIVERSITY
ADMISSIONS OFFICE
ALL SAINTS (GMS)
ALL SAINTS
MANCHESTER M15 6BH
t: 0161 247 2000
// www.mmu.ac.uk

W217 BA Illustration with Animation
Duration: 3FT Hon
Entry Requirements: *GCE:* 280. *IB:* 27. Interview required. Portfolio required.

M80 MIDDLESEX UNIVERSITY
MIDDLESEX UNIVERSITY
THE BURROUGHS
LONDON NW4 4BT
t: 020 8411 5555 f: 020 8411 5649
e: enquiries@mdx.ac.uk
// www.mdx.ac.uk

W615 BA Animation
Duration: 3FT Hon
Entry Requirements: *GCE:* 200-300. *IB:* 28. Interview required. Portfolio required.

N23 NEWCASTLE COLLEGE
STUDENT SERVICES
RYE HILL CAMPUS
SCOTSWOOD ROAD
NEWCASTLE UPON TYNE NE4 7SA
t: 0191 200 4110 f: 0191 200 4349
e: enquiries@ncl-coll.ac.uk
// www.newcastlecollege.co.uk

WW26 FdA Animation
Duration: 2FT Fdg
Entry Requirements: *GCE:* 120-165. *OCR ND:* P2 *OCR NED:* P3 Foundation Course required. Interview required. Portfolio required.

N30 NEW COLLEGE NOTTINGHAM

ADAMS BUILDING
STONEY STREET
THE LACE MARKET
NOTTINGHAM NG1 1NG
t: 0115 910 0100 f: 0115 953 4349
e: he.team@ncn.ac.uk
// www.ncn.ac.uk

W610 FdA Multimedia (Animation and Motion)
Duration: 2FT Fdg
Entry Requirements: *GCE:* 100-240. Interview required. Portfolio required.

W600 FdA Multimedia (Photography/Moving Image)
Duration: 2FT Fdg
Entry Requirements: *GCE:* 100-240. Interview required. Portfolio required.

N37 UNIVERSITY OF WALES, NEWPORT

ADMISSIONS
LODGE ROAD
CAERLEON
NEWPORT NP18 3QT
t: 01633 432030 f: 01633 432850
e: admissions@newport.ac.uk
// www.newport.ac.uk

W615 BA Animation
Duration: 3FT Hon
Entry Requirements: *Foundation:* Merit. *GCE:* 240-260. *IB:* 24. Interview required. Portfolio required.

N39 NORWICH UNIVERSITY COLLEGE OF THE ARTS

FRANCIS HOUSE
3-7 REDWELL STREET
NORWICH NR2 4SN
t: 01603 610561 f: 01603 615728
e: admissions@nuca.ac.uk
// www.nuca.ac.uk

W615 BA Animation
Duration: 3FT Hon
Entry Requirements: *Foundation:* Merit. *OCR ND:* M1 *OCR NED:* P1 Interview required. Portfolio required.

W613 BA Film and Moving Image Production
Duration: 3FT Hon
Entry Requirements: *Foundation:* Merit. *GCE:* BBc. *OCR ND:* M1 *OCR NED:* P1 Interview required. Portfolio required.

N58 NORTH EAST WORCESTERSHIRE COLLEGE

PEAKMAN STREET
REDDITCH
WORCESTERSHIRE B98 8DW
t: 01527 570020 f: 01527 572901
e: admissions@ne-worcs.ac.uk
// www.ne-worcs.ac.uk

W610 FdA Media Production (Moving Image)
Duration: 2FT Fdg
Entry Requirements: *GCE:* 120. Interview required. Portfolio required.

N77 NORTHUMBRIA UNIVERSITY

TRINITY BUILDING
NORTHUMBERLAND ROAD
NEWCASTLE UPON TYNE NE1 8ST
t: 0191 243 7420 f: 0191 227 4561
e: er.admissions@northumbria.ac.uk
// www.northumbria.ac.uk

WW2P BA Motion Graphics & Animation Design
Duration: 3FT Hon
Entry Requirements: *Foundation:* Distinction. *GCE:* 280. *SQAH:* BBCCC. *SQAAH:* BCC. *IB:* 25. *OCR NED:* M2 Interview required. Portfolio required.

N79 NORTH WARWICKSHIRE AND HINCKLEY COLLEGE

HINCKLEY ROAD
NUNEATON
WARWICKSHIRE CV11 6BH
t: 024 7624 3395
e: angela.jones@nwhc.ac.uk
// www.nwhc.ac.uk

016W HND Media (Moving Image)
Duration: 2FT HND
Entry Requirements: *GCE:* 180-200. *IB:* 24. Interview required. Portfolio required.

P60 PLYMOUTH UNIVERSITY

DRAKE CIRCUS
PLYMOUTH PL4 8AA
t: 01752 585858 f: 01752 588055
e: admissions@plymouth.ac.uk
// www.plymouth.ac.uk

W281 BA Digital Media and Animation
Duration: 1FT Hon
Entry Requirements: Contact the institution for details.

P65 PLYMOUTH COLLEGE OF ART (FORMERLY PLYMOUTH COLLEGE OF ART AND DESIGN)
TAVISTOCK PLACE
PLYMOUTH PL4 8AT
t: 01752 203434 f: 01752 203444
e: infoservices@plymouthart.ac.uk
// www.plymouthart.ac.uk

W61M BA Animation
Duration: 3FT Hon
Entry Requirements: Contact the institution for details.

W616 BA Animation (Top-Up)
Duration: 1FT Hon
Entry Requirements: Interview required. Portfolio required. HND required.

P80 UNIVERSITY OF PORTSMOUTH
ACADEMIC REGISTRY
UNIVERSITY HOUSE
WINSTON CHURCHILL AVENUE
PORTSMOUTH PO1 2UP
t: 023 9284 8484 f: 023 9284 3082
e: admissions@port.ac.uk
// www.port.ac.uk

W615 BA Animation
Duration: 3FT/4SW Hon
Entry Requirements: *GCE:* 240-300. *IB:* 28. *BTEC SubDip:* P. *BTEC Dip:* DD. *BTEC ExtDip:* DMM. Interview required. Portfolio required.

R06 RAVENSBOURNE
6 PENROSE WAY
GREENWICH PENINSULA
LONDON SE10 0EW
t: 020 3040 3998
e: info@rave.ac.uk
// www.rave.ac.uk

WQ15 BA Animation
Duration: 3FT Hon
Entry Requirements: Contact the institution for details.

WPC5 BA Animation (with Foundation Year)
Duration: 4FT Hon
Entry Requirements: Contact the institution for details.

W616 BA Animation Production (Top-Up)
Duration: 1FT Hon
Entry Requirements: Interview required. Portfolio required.

S03 THE UNIVERSITY OF SALFORD
SALFORD M5 4WT
t: 0161 295 4545 f: 0161 295 4646
e: ug-admissions@salford.ac.uk
// www.salford.ac.uk

W615 BA Animation
Duration: 3FT Hon
Entry Requirements: *Foundation:* Distinction. *GCE:* 260. *IB:* 28. *OCR ND:* D *OCR NED:* M3

S21 SHEFFIELD HALLAM UNIVERSITY
CITY CAMPUS
HOWARD STREET
SHEFFIELD S1 1WB
t: 0114 225 5555 f: 0114 225 2167
e: admissions@shu.ac.uk
// www.shu.ac.uk

W615 BA Animation
Duration: 3FT Hon
Entry Requirements: *GCE:* 240.

W614 BA Animation and Visual Effects
Duration: 3FT Hon
Entry Requirements: *GCE:* 240.

G4W6 BSc Interactive Media with Animation
Duration: 4SW Hon
Entry Requirements: *GCE:* 240.

W616 MArt Animation
Duration: 4FT Hon
Entry Requirements: *GCE:* 260.

W617 MArt Animation and Visual Effects
Duration: 4FT Hon
Entry Requirements: *GCE:* 260.

S30 SOUTHAMPTON SOLENT UNIVERSITY
EAST PARK TERRACE
SOUTHAMPTON
HAMPSHIRE SO14 0RT
t: +44 (0) 23 8031 9039 f: + 44 (0)23 8022 2259
e: admissions@solent.ac.uk
// www.solent.ac.uk/

W615 BA Animation
Duration: 3FT Hon
Entry Requirements: *Foundation:* Merit. *GCE:* 200. *SQAAH:* AC-DDD. *IB:* 24. *BTEC ExtDip:* MMP. *OCR ND:* M1 *OCR NED:* P1 Interview required. Portfolio required.

S43 SOUTH ESSEX COLLEGE OF FURTHER & HIGHER EDUCATION

LUKER ROAD
SOUTHEND-ON-SEA
ESSEX SS1 1ND
t: 0845 52 12345 f: 01702 432320
e: Admissions@southessex.ac.uk
// www.southessex.ac.uk

W615 BA Digital Animation

Duration: 3FT Hon
Entry Requirements: *GCE:* 160. *IB:* 24. Interview required.

S72 STAFFORDSHIRE UNIVERSITY

COLLEGE ROAD
STOKE ON TRENT ST4 2DE
t: 01782 292753 f: 01782 292740
e: admissions@staffs.ac.uk
// www.staffs.ac.uk

W616 BA Animation

Duration: 3FT/4FT Hon
Entry Requirements: *GCE:* 180-220. *IB:* 24. Interview required.
Portfolio required.

W222 BA Cartoon and Comic Arts

Duration: 3FT Hon
Entry Requirements: *Foundation:* Merit. *GCE:* 200-240. *IB:* 24.
BTEC Dip: DD. *DTEC ExtDip:* MMM. Interview required. Portfolio required.

W691 BA Entrepreneurship in Moving Image

Duration: 1FT Hon
Entry Requirements: Interview required. Portfolio required.

WW67 BA Stop-motion Animation and Puppet-Making

Duration: 3FT/4FT Hon
Entry Requirements: *Foundation:* Merit. *GCE:* 200-240. *IB:* 24.
BTEC Dip: DD. *BTEC ExtDip:* MMM. Interview required. Portfolio required.

S84 UNIVERSITY OF SUNDERLAND

STUDENT HELPLINE
THE STUDENT GATEWAY
CHESTER ROAD
SUNDERLAND SR1 3SD
t: 0191 515 3000 f: 0191 515 3805
e: student.helpline@sunderland.ac.uk
// www.sunderland.ac.uk

W221 BA Animation and Design

Duration: 3FT Hon
Entry Requirements: *Foundation:* Merit. *GCE:* 220. *SQAH:* BBBC.
IB: 22. Interview required. Portfolio required.

T20 TEESSIDE UNIVERSITY

MIDDLESBROUGH TS1 3BA
t: 01642 218121 f: 01642 384201
e: registry@tees.ac.uk
// www.tees.ac.uk

GW42 BA Computer Animation

Duration: 3FT/4SW Hon
Entry Requirements: *Foundation:* Distinction. *IB:* 32. *OCR ND:* D
OCR NED: M1 Interview required. Portfolio required.

GW4G BA Computer Animation (incorporating Foundation Year)

Duration: 4FT/5SW Hon
Entry Requirements: *IB:* 28. *OCR ND:* M1 *OCR NED:* P1 Interview required.

T85 TRURO AND PENWITH COLLEGE

TRURO COLLEGE
COLLEGE ROAD
TRURO
CORNWALL TR1 3XX
t: 01872 267122 f: 01872 267526
e: heinfo@trurocollege.ac.uk
// www.truro-penwith.ac.uk

016W HND Media Moving Image

Duration: 2FT HND
Entry Requirements: *GCE:* 60. *IB:* 24. *BTEC Dip:* MP. *BTEC ExtDip:* PPP. Interview required.

U20 UNIVERSITY OF ULSTER

COLERAINE
CO. LONDONDERRY
NORTHERN IRELAND BT52 1SA
t: 028 7012 4221 f: 028 7012 4908
e: online@ulster.ac.uk
// www.ulster.ac.uk

WW26 BDes Hons Design for Interaction and Animation

Duration: 3FT/4SW Hon
Entry Requirements: *GCE:* 240. *IB:* 24. Interview required.
Portfolio required.

U40 UNIVERSITY OF THE WEST OF SCOTLAND
PAISLEY
RENFREWSHIRE
SCOTLAND PA1 2BE
t: 0141 848 3727 f: 0141 848 3623
e: admissions@uws.ac.uk
// www.uws.ac.uk

G4W2 BA Computer Animation with Digital Art
Duration: 3FT/4FT Ord/Hon
Entry Requirements: *GCE:* CC. *SQAH:* BBC.

WG66 BA/BSc Computer Animation with Games Development
Duration: 3FT/4FT Ord/Hon
Entry Requirements: *GCE:* CC. *SQAH:* BBC.

GW46 BSc Computer Animation
Duration: 3FT/4FT Ord/Hon
Entry Requirements: *GCE:* CC. *SQAH:* BBC.

G4WF BSc Computer Animation with Multimedia
Duration: 3FT/4FT Ord/Hon
Entry Requirements: *GCE:* CC. *SQAH:* BBC.

GW4P Cert HE Computer Animation & Multimedia
Duration: 1FT Cer
Entry Requirements: *GCE:* D. *SQAH:* C.

U65 UNIVERSITY OF THE ARTS LONDON
272 HIGH HOLBORN
LONDON WC1V 7EY
t: 020 7514 6000x6197 f: 020 7514 6198
e: c.anderson@arts.ac.uk
// www.arts.ac.uk

W616 BA Animation (Top-Up)
Duration: 1FT Hon
Entry Requirements: Interview required.

W281 BA Interaction and Moving Image
Duration: 3FT Hon
Entry Requirements: Contact the institution for details.

W05 THE UNIVERSITY OF WEST LONDON
ST MARY'S ROAD
EALING
LONDON W5 5RF
t: 0800 036 8888 f: 020 8566 1353
e: learning.advice@uwl.ac.uk
// www.uwl.ac.uk

W615 BA Digital Animation Specialist
Duration: 3FT Hon
Entry Requirements: *GCE:* 240. Interview required. Portfolio required.

W50 UNIVERSITY OF WESTMINSTER
2ND FLOOR, CAVENDISH HOUSE
101 NEW CAVENDISH STREET,
LONDON W1W 6XH
t: 020 7915 5511
e: course-enquiries@westminster.ac.uk
// www.westminster.ac.uk

W615 BA Animation
Duration: 3FT Hon
Entry Requirements: *GCE:* CC. *SQAH:* CCCC. *IB:* 26. *OCR ND:* M1 Interview required. Portfolio required.

GW4P BSc Multimedia Computing and Animation
Duration: 3FT/4SW Hon
Entry Requirements: *GCE:* AA-CCC. *SQAH:* BCCC-CCCCC. *IB:* 28. Interview required.

GW46 BSc Multimedia Computing and Animation with Foundation
Duration: 4FT Hon
Entry Requirements: *GCE:* CC-DDE. *IB:* 24.

W73 WIRRAL METROPOLITAN COLLEGE
CONWAY PARK CAMPUS
EUROPA BOULEVARD
BIRKENHEAD, WIRRAL
MERSEYSIDE CH41 4NT
t: 0151 551 7777 f: 0151 551 7001
// www.wmc.ac.uk

W2W6 BA Illustration with Animation
Duration: 3FT Hon
Entry Requirements: *Foundation:* Pass. Interview required. Portfolio required.

W75 UNIVERSITY OF WOLVERHAMPTON
ADMISSIONS UNIT
MX207, CAMP STREET
WOLVERHAMPTON
WEST MIDLANDS WV1 1AD
t: 01902 321000 f: 01902 321896
e: admissions@wlv.ac.uk
// www.wlv.ac.uk

W271 BA Animation
Duration: 3FT/4SW Hon
Entry Requirements: *GCE:* 200. *IB:* 24. *BTEC Dip:* DM. *BTEC ExtDip:* MMP. *OCR ND:* M1 *OCR NED:* P1 Interview required. Portfolio required.

W80 UNIVERSITY OF WORCESTER
HENWICK GROVE
WORCESTER WR2 6AJ
t: 01905 855111 f: 01905 855377
e: admissions@worc.ac.uk
// www.worcester.ac.uk

W616 BA Animation
Duration: 3FT Hon
Entry Requirements: *GCE:* 220-260. *IB:* 24. *OCR ND:* D Interview required. Portfolio required.

WW6G BA Animation and Creative Digital Media
Duration: 3FT Hon
Entry Requirements: *GCE:* 220-260. *IB:* 24. *OCR ND:* D Interview required. Portfolio required.

W690 BA Animation and Digital Film Production
Duration: 3FT Hon
Entry Requirements: *GCE:* 220-300. *IB:* 24. *OCR ND:* D Interview required. Portfolio required.

WW61 BA Animation and Fine Art Practice
Duration: 3FT Hon
Entry Requirements: *GCE:* 220-300. *IB:* 24. *OCR ND:* D Interview required. Portfolio required.

WWP2 BA Animation and Graphic Design & Multimedia
Duration: 3FT Hon
Entry Requirements: *GCE:* 220-300. *IB:* 24. *OCR ND:* D Interview required. Portfolio required.

WW6F BA Animation and Illustration
Duration: 3FT Hon
Entry Requirements: *GCE:* 220-300. *IB:* 24. *OCR ND:* D Interview required. Portfolio required.

WW68 BA Animation and Screen Writing
Duration: 3FT Hon
Entry Requirements: *GCE:* 220-300. *IB:* 24. *OCR ND:* D Interview required. Portfolio required.

WI61 BA/BSc Animation and Computing
Duration: 3FT Hon
Entry Requirements: Contact the institution for details.

ART, ART & DESIGN AND APPLIED ART

B20 BATH SPA UNIVERSITY
NEWTON PARK
NEWTON ST LOE
BATH BA2 9BN
t: 01225 875875 f: 01225 875444
e: enquiries@bathspa.ac.uk
// www.bathspa.ac.uk/clearing

WW1F BA Applied Art and Design (Top-Up)
Duration: 1FT Hon
Entry Requirements: Interview required.

WWDF BA Applied Art and Design (Work-Based)
Duration: 1FT Hon
Entry Requirements: Interview required.

WW19 BA Art/Creative Writing
Duration: 3FT Hon
Entry Requirements: *Foundation:* Pass. *GCE:* 220-280. *IB:* 24. Interview required.

WW15 BA Art/Dance
Duration: 3FT Hon
Entry Requirements: *Foundation:* Pass. *GCE:* 220-280. *IB:* 24. Interview required.

WW1L BA Art/Drama Studies
Duration: 3FT Hon
Entry Requirements: *GCE:* 220-280. *IB:* 24. Interview required.

WW13 BA Art/Music
Duration: 3FT Hon
Entry Requirements: *Foundation:* Pass. *GCE:* 220-280. *IB:* 24. Interview required.

WW12 BA Art/Textile Design Studies
Duration: 3FT Hon
Entry Requirements: *Foundation:* Pass. *GCE:* 220-280. *IB:* 24. Interview required.

WW91 DipHE Art/Creative Writing
Duration: 2FT Dip
Entry Requirements: *GCE:* 220-280. *IB:* 24.

WW1K DipHE Art/Drama Studies
Duration: 2FT Dip
Entry Requirements: *GCE:* 220-280. *IB:* 24.

WWC2 FdA Applied Art and Design
Duration: 2FT Fdg
Entry Requirements: *GCE:* 220-280. *IB:* 24. Interview required.

B22 UNIVERSITY OF BEDFORDSHIRE
PARK SQUARE
LUTON
BEDS LU1 3JU
t: 0844 8482234 f: 01582 489323
e: admissions@beds.ac.uk
// www.beds.ac.uk

W201 BA Art and Design
Duration: 3FT Hon
Entry Requirements: *GCE:* 160. Interview required. Portfolio required.

B25 BIRMINGHAM CITY UNIVERSITY
PERRY BARR
BIRMINGHAM B42 2SU
t: 0121 331 5595 f: 0121 331 7994
// www.bcu.ac.uk

W190 BA Art and Design
Duration: 3FT Hon
Entry Requirements: *GCE:* 280. *IB:* 28. Interview required. Portfolio required.

B37 BISHOP BURTON COLLEGE
BISHOP BURTON
BEVERLEY
EAST YORKSHIRE HU17 8QG
t: 01964 553000 f: 01964 553101
e: enquiries@bishopburton.ac.uk
// www.bishopburton.ac.uk

WD24 BA Floristry Design (top-up)
Duration: 1FT Hon
Entry Requirements: Contact the institution for details.

W290 FdA Floristry Design
Duration: 2FT Fdg
Entry Requirements: *GCE:* 80.

W790 FdA Floristry Design (including Year 0)
Duration: 3FT Fdg
Entry Requirements: Contact the institution for details.

B44 UNIVERSITY OF BOLTON
DEANE ROAD
BOLTON BL3 5AB
t: 01204 903903 f: 01204 399074
e: enquiries@bolton.ac.uk
// www.bolton.ac.uk

WW12 BA Art & Design
Duration: 3FT Hon
Entry Requirements: *GCE:* 240. Interview required. Portfolio required.

B60 BRADFORD COLLEGE: AN ASSOCIATE COLLEGE OF LEEDS METROPOLITAN UNIVERSITY
GREAT HORTON ROAD
BRADFORD
WEST YORKSHIRE BD7 1AY
t: 01274 433008 f: 01274 431652
e: heregistry@bradfordcollege.ac.uk
// www.bradfordcollege.ac.uk/
university-centre

WW12 BA Art and Design
Duration: 3FT Hon
Entry Requirements: *GCE:* 120. Interview required. Portfolio required.

B72 UNIVERSITY OF BRIGHTON
MITHRAS HOUSE 211
LEWES ROAD
BRIGHTON BN2 4AT
t: 01273 644644 f: 01273 642607
e: admissions@brighton.ac.uk
// www.brighton.ac.uk

WW12 BA Art and Design (Top-Up)
Duration: 1FT Hon
Entry Requirements: Interview required. Portfolio required. HND required.

W140 BA Fine Art Printmaking
Duration: 3FT Hon
Entry Requirements: *GCE:* BBC. Foundation Course required. Interview required. Portfolio required.

B80 UNIVERSITY OF THE WEST OF ENGLAND, BRISTOL
FRENCHAY CAMPUS
COLDHARBOUR LANE
BRISTOL BS16 1QY
t: +44 (0)117 32 83333 f: +44 (0)117 32 82810
e: admissions@uwe.ac.uk
// www.uwe.ac.uk

W110 BA Drawing and Applied Arts
Duration: 3FT Hon
Entry Requirements: *GCE:* 280. Interview required. Portfolio required.

B94 BUCKINGHAMSHIRE NEW UNIVERSITY
QUEEN ALEXANDRA ROAD
HIGH WYCOMBE
BUCKINGHAMSHIRE HP11 2JZ
t: 0800 0565 660 f: 01494 605 023
e: admissions@bucks.ac.uk
// bucks.ac.uk

W260 FdA Furniture Conservation & Restoration
Duration: 2FT Fdg   CRB Check: Required
Entry Requirements: Contact the institution for details.

C10 CANTERBURY CHRIST CHURCH UNIVERSITY
NORTH HOLMES ROAD
CANTERBURY
KENT CT1 1QU
t: 01227 782900 f: 01227 782888
e: admissions@canterbury.ac.uk
// www.canterbury.ac.uk

W193 BA Art: Fine and Applied Arts
Duration: 3FT Hon
Entry Requirements: *GCE:* 240. *IB:* 24. Interview required.

W192 BA Art: Fine and Applied Arts 'International Only'
Duration: 4FT Hon
Entry Requirements: Interview required.

W901 BA Art: Visual Arts and Design 'International Only'
Duration: 4FT Hon
Entry Requirements: Interview required.

GW51 BA Business Computing and Fine & Applied Arts
Duration: 3FT Hon
Entry Requirements: *GCE:* 240. *IB:* 24.

G5WC BA Business Computing with Fine & Applied Arts
Duration: 3FT Hon
Entry Requirements: *GCE:* 240. *IB:* 24.

QW31 BA English Language & Communication and Fine & Applied Arts
Duration: 3FT Hon
Entry Requirements: *GCE:* 240. *IB:* 24.

Q3WC BA English Language & Communication with Fine & Applied Arts
Duration: 3FT Hon
Entry Requirements: *GCE:* 240. *IB:* 24.

Q3W1 BA English Literature with Fine & Applied Arts
Duration: 3FT Hon
Entry Requirements: *GCE:* 240. *IB:* 24.

W1GM BA Fine & Applied Arts with Business Computing
Duration: 3FT Hon
Entry Requirements: *GCE:* 240. *IB:* 24.

W1QH BA Fine & Applied Arts with English Language & Communication
Duration: 3FT Hon
Entry Requirements: *GCE:* 240. *IB:* 24.

W1B9 BA Fine & Applied Arts with Health Studies
Duration: 3FT Hon
Entry Requirements: *GCE:* 240. *IB:* 24.

W1LG BA Fine & Applied Arts with International Relations
Duration: 3FT Hon
Entry Requirements: *GCE:* 240. *IB:* 24.

W1G4 BA Fine & Applied Arts with Internet Computing
Duration: 3FT Hon
Entry Requirements: *GCE:* 240. *IB:* 24.

BW91 BA Health Studies and Fine & Applied Arts
Duration: 3FT Hon
Entry Requirements: *GCE:* 240. *IB:* 24.

LW2C BA International Relations and Fine & Applied Arts
Duration: 3FT Hon
Entry Requirements: *GCE:* 240. *IB:* 24.

L2WD BA International Relations with Fine & Applied Arts
Duration: 3FT Hon
Entry Requirements: *GCE:* 240. *IB:* 24.

GW41 BA Internet Computing and Fine & Applied Arts
Duration: 3FT Hon
Entry Requirements: *GCE:* 240. *IB:* 24.

G4W1 BA Internet Computing with Fine & Applied Arts
Duration: 3FT Hon
Entry Requirements: *GCE:* 240. *IB:* 24.

W3W1 BA Music with Fine & Applied Arts
Duration: 3FT Hon
Entry Requirements: *GCE:* 240. *IB:* 24.

X3W1 BA/BSc Early Childhood Studies with Fine & Applied Arts
Duration: 3FT Hon   CRB Check: Required
Entry Requirements: *GCE:* 240. *IB:* 24.

XW3C BA/BSc Education Studies and Fine & Applied Arts
Duration: 3FT Hon   CRB Check: Required
Entry Requirements: *GCE:* 240. *IB:* 24.

X3WC BA/BSc Education Studies with Fine & Applied Arts
Duration: 3FT Hon   CRB Check: Required
Entry Requirements: *GCE:* 240. *IB:* 24.

W6W1 BA/BSc Film, Radio & Television Studies with Fine & Applied Arts
Duration: 3FT Hon
Entry Requirements: *GCE:* 240. *IB:* 24.

WN11 BA/BSc Fine & Applied Arts and Business Studies
Duration: 3FT Hon
Entry Requirements: *GCE:* 240. *IB:* 24.

WG15 BA/BSc Fine & Applied Arts and Computing
Duration: 3FT Hon
Entry Requirements: *GCE:* 240. *IB:* 24.

XW31 BA/BSc Fine & Applied Arts and Early Childhood Studies
Duration: 3FT Hon   CRB Check: Required
Entry Requirements: *GCE:* 240. *IB:* 24.

WQ13 BA/BSc Fine & Applied Arts and English Literature
Duration: 3FT Hon
Entry Requirements: *GCE:* 240. *IB:* 24.

WW61 BA/BSc Fine & Applied Arts and Film, Radio & Television Studies
Duration: 3FT Hon
Entry Requirements: *GCE:* 240. *IB:* 24.

RW11 BA/BSc Fine & Applied Arts and French
Duration: 3FT Hon
Entry Requirements: *GCE:* 240. *IB:* 24.

VW11 BA/BSc Fine & Applied Arts and History
Duration: 3FT Hon
Entry Requirements: *GCE:* 240. *IB:* 24.

NW51 BA/BSc Fine & Applied Arts and Marketing
Duration: 3FT Hon
Entry Requirements: *GCE:* 240. *IB:* 24.

WW13 BA/BSc Fine & Applied Arts and Music
Duration: 3FT Hon
Entry Requirements: *GCE:* 240. *IB:* 24.

CW81 BA/BSc Fine & Applied Arts and Psychology
Duration: 3FT Hon
Entry Requirements: *GCE:* 260. *IB:* 24.

WC16 BA/BSc Fine & Applied Arts and Sport & Exercise Science
Duration: 3FT Hon
Entry Requirements: *GCE:* 240. *IB:* 24.

NW81 BA/BSc Fine & Applied Arts and Tourism & Leisure Studies
Duration: 3FT Hon
Entry Requirements: *GCE:* 240. *IB:* 24.

W1N1 BA/BSc Fine & Applied Arts with Business Studies
Duration: 3FT Hon
Entry Requirements: *GCE:* 240. *IB:* 24.

W1G5 BA/BSc Fine & Applied Arts with Computing
Duration: 3FT Hon
Entry Requirements: *GCE:* 240. *IB:* 24.

W1GK BA/BSc Fine & Applied Arts with Digital Media
Duration: 3FT Hon
Entry Requirements: *GCE:* 240. *IB:* 24.

W1X3 BA/BSc Fine & Applied Arts with Early Childhood Studies
Duration: 3FT Hon   CRB Check: Required
Entry Requirements: *GCE:* 240. *IB:* 24.

W1XH BA/BSc Fine & Applied Arts with Education Studies
Duration: 3FT Hon   CRB Check: Required
Entry Requirements: *GCE:* 240. *IB:* 24.

W1Q3 BA/BSc Fine & Applied Arts with English Literature
Duration: 3FT Hon
Entry Requirements: *GCE:* 240. *IB:* 24.

W1W6 BA/BSc Fine & Applied Arts with Film, Radio & Television Studies
Duration: 3FT Hon
Entry Requirements: *GCE:* 240. *IB:* 24.

W1R1 BA/BSc Fine & Applied Arts with French
Duration: 3FT Hon
Entry Requirements: *GCE:* 240. *IB:* 24.

W1V1 BA/BSc Fine & Applied Arts with History
Duration: 3FT Hon
Entry Requirements: *GCE:* 240. *IB:* 24.

W1N5 BA/BSc Fine & Applied Arts with Marketing
Duration: 3FT Hon
Entry Requirements: *GCE:* 240. *IB:* 24.

W1W3 BA/BSc Fine & Applied Arts with Music
Duration: 3FT Hon
Entry Requirements: *GCE:* 240. *IB:* 24. Interview required.

W1C8 BA/BSc Fine & Applied Arts with Psychology
Duration: 3FT Hon
Entry Requirements: *GCE:* 260. *IB:* 24.

W1C6 BA/BSc Fine & Applied Arts with Sport & Exercise Science
Duration: 3FT Hon
Entry Requirements: *GCE:* 240. *IB:* 24.

W1N8 BA/BSc Fine & Applied Arts with Tourism & Leisure Studies
Duration: 3FT Hon
Entry Requirements: *GCE:* 240. *IB:* 24.

R1W1 BA/BSc French with Fine & Applied Arts
Duration: 3FT Hon
Entry Requirements: Contact the institution for details.

B9W1 BA/BSc Health Studies with Fine & Applied Arts
Duration: 3FT Hon
Entry Requirements: *GCE:* 240. *IB:* 24.

C8W1 BA/BSc Psychology with Fine & Applied Arts
Duration: 3FT Hon
Entry Requirements: *GCE:* 260. *IB:* 24.

N8W1 BA/BSc Tourism & Leisure Studies with Fine & Applied Arts
Duration: 3FT Hon
Entry Requirements: *GCE:* 240. *IB:* 24.

N1W1 BSc Business Studies with Fine & Applied Arts
Duration: 3FT Hon
Entry Requirements: *GCE:* 240. *IB:* 24.

N5W1 BSc Marketing with Fine & Applied Arts
Duration: 3FT Hon
Entry Requirements: *GCE:* 240. *IB:* 24.

G5W1 BSc/BA Computing with Fine & Applied Arts
Duration: 3FT Hon
Entry Requirements: *GCE:* 240. *IB:* 24.

GWK1 BSc/BA Digital Media and Fine & Applied Arts
Duration: 3FT Hon
Entry Requirements: *GCE:* 240. *IB:* 24.

G4WC BSc/BA Digital Media with Fine & Applied Arts
Duration: 3FT Hon
Entry Requirements: *GCE:* 240. *IB:* 24.

V1W1 BSc/BA History with Fine & Applied Arts
Duration: 3FT Hon
Entry Requirements: *GCE:* 240. *IB:* 24.

C6W1 BSc/BA Sport & Exercise Science with Fine & Applied Arts
Duration: 3FT Hon
Entry Requirements: *GCE:* 240. *IB:* 24.

C22 COLEG SIR GAR / CARMARTHENSHIRE COLLEGE

SANDY ROAD
LLANELLI
CARMARTHENSHIRE SA15 4DN
t: 01554 748000 f: 01554 748170
e: admissions@colegsirgar.ac.uk
// www.colegsirgar.ac.uk

W000 BA Art and Design (Multi-Disciplinary)
Duration: 3FT Hon
Entry Requirements: *GCE:* 120. Portfolio required.

W101 BA(Hons) Fine Art (Painting, Drawing and Printmaking)
Duration: 3FT Hon
Entry Requirements: Portfolio required.

C30 UNIVERSITY OF CENTRAL LANCASHIRE

PRESTON
LANCS PR1 2HE
t: 01772 201201 f: 01772 894954
e: uadmissions@uclan.ac.uk
// www.uclan.ac.uk

WW12 BA Art & Design (Foundation entry)
Duration: 4FT Hon
Entry Requirements: Interview required. Portfolio required.

C71 CLEVELAND COLLEGE OF ART AND DESIGN

CHURCH SQUARE
HARTLEPOOL
CHURCH SQUARE TS24 7EX
t: 01642 288888 f: 01642 288828
e: studentrecruitment@ccad.ac.uk
// www.ccad.ac.uk

W900 BA Applied Arts for Enterprise (Top-Up)
Duration: 1FT Hon
Entry Requirements: Interview required. Portfolio required.

W700 FdA Applied Arts
Duration: 2FT Fdg
Entry Requirements: *Foundation:* Pass. *GCE:* 120. Interview required. Portfolio required.

C75 COLCHESTER INSTITUTE

SHEEPEN ROAD
COLCHESTER
ESSEX CO3 3LL
t: 01206 712777 f: 01206 712800
e: info@colchester.ac.uk
// www.colchester.ac.uk

W231 BA Art and Design - Fashion & Textiles
Duration: 3FT Hon
Entry Requirements: *Foundation:* Pass. *GCE:* 160. Interview required. Portfolio required.

W230 BA Art and Design - Fashion and Textiles (including Year 0)
Duration: 4FT Hon
Entry Requirements: *Foundation:* Pass. *GCE:* 80. Interview required. Portfolio required.

W191 BA Art and Design - Fine Art
Duration: 3FT Hon
Entry Requirements: *Foundation:* Pass. *GCE:* 160. Interview required. Portfolio required.

W190 BA Art and Design - Fine Art (including Yr 0)
Duration: 4FT Hon
Entry Requirements: *Foundation:* Pass. *GCE:* 80. Interview required. Portfolio required.

W214 BA Art and Design - Graphic Design
Duration: 3FT Hon
Entry Requirements: *Foundation:* Pass. *GCE:* 160. Interview required. Portfolio required.

W210 BA Art and Design - Graphic Design (including Year 0)
Duration: 4FT Hon
Entry Requirements: *Foundation:* Pass. *GCE:* 80. Interview required. Portfolio required.

D65 UNIVERSITY OF DUNDEE

NETHERGATE
DUNDEE DD1 4HN
t: 01382 383838 f: 01382 388150
e: contactus@dundee.ac.uk
// www.dundee.ac.uk/admissions/undergraduate/

W100 BA Fine Art (Digital Media, Drawing and Painting, Printmaking, Sculpture)
Duration: 3FT Hon
Entry Requirements: Foundation Course required. Interview required. Portfolio required.

WW12 BA/BDes Art and Design (General Foundation)
Duration: 4FT Hon
Entry Requirements: *GCE:* CCC. *SQAH:* BBBC. *IB:* 29. Interview required. Portfolio required.

E28 UNIVERSITY OF EAST LONDON
DOCKLANDS CAMPUS
UNIVERSITY WAY
LONDON E16 2RD
t: 020 8223 3333 f: 020 8223 2978
e: study@uel.ac.uk
// www.uel.ac.uk

WW2D BA Illustration/Printmaking
Duration: 3FT Hon
Entry Requirements: *GCE:* 240.

E29 EAST RIDING COLLEGE
LONGCROFT HALL
GALLOWS LANE
BEVERLEY
EAST YORKSHIRE HU17 7DT
t: 0845 120 0037
e: info@eastridingcollege.ac.uk
// www.eastridingcollege.ac.uk/

21WW HND Art and Design
Duration: 2FT HND
Entry Requirements: Contact the institution for details.

G43 THE GLASGOW SCHOOL OF ART
167 RENFREW STREET
GLASGOW G3 6RQ
t: 0141 353 4434/4514 f: 0141 353 4408
e: admissions@gsa.ac.uk
// www.gsa.ac.uk

W120 BA Fine Art - Painting/Printmaking
Duration: 4FT Hon
Entry Requirements: *GCE:* ABB. *SQAH:* AABB-ABBB. *IB:* 30. Interview required. Portfolio required.

WW12 CertHE International Foundation (Art and Design)
Duration: 1FT FYr
Entry Requirements: Contact the institution for details.

G53 GLYNDWR UNIVERSITY
PLAS COCH
MOLD ROAD
WREXHAM LL11 2AW
t: 01978 293439 f: 01978 290008
e: sid@glyndwr.ac.uk
// www.glyndwr.ac.uk

W201 BA Design: Applied Arts
Duration: 3FT Hon
Entry Requirements: *GCE:* 240. Interview required. Portfolio required.

H18 HEREFORD COLLEGE OF ARTS
FOLLY LANE
HEREFORD HR1 1LT
t: 01432 273359 f: 01432 341099
e: headmin@hca.ac.uk
// www.hca.ac.uk

W900 BA Contemporary Applied Arts
Duration: 3FT Hon   **CRB Check:** Required
Entry Requirements: *GCE:* 200. Interview required. Portfolio required.

W790 BA Contemporary Applied Arts (top up)
Duration: 1FT Hon   **CRB Check:** Required
Entry Requirements: Interview required. Portfolio required. HND required.

H36 UNIVERSITY OF HERTFORDSHIRE
UNIVERSITY ADMISSIONS SERVICE
COLLEGE LANE
HATFIELD
HERTS AL10 9AB
t: 01707 284800
// www.herts.ac.uk

W700 BA Contemporary Applied Arts
Duration: 3FT Hon
Entry Requirements: *GCE:* 240. Interview required. Portfolio required.

H54 HOPWOOD HALL COLLEGE
ROCHDALE ROAD
MIDDLETON
MANCHESTER M24 6XH
t: 0161 643 7560 f: 0161 643 2114
e: admissions@hopwood.ac.uk
// www.hopwood.ac.uk

21WW HND Art & Design
Duration: 2FT HND
Entry Requirements: Interview required. Portfolio required.

H60 THE UNIVERSITY OF HUDDERSFIELD
QUEENSGATE
HUDDERSFIELD HD1 3DH
t: 01484 473969 f: 01484 472765
e: admissionsandrecords@hud.ac.uk
// www.hud.ac.uk

W000 BA Interdisciplinary Art & Design
Duration: 3FT Hon
Entry Requirements: *GCE:* 240. Interview required. Portfolio
required.

H73 HULL COLLEGE
QUEEN'S GARDENS
HULL HU1 3DG
t: 01482 329943 f: 01482 598733
e: info@hull-college.ac.uk
// www.hull-college.ac.uk/higher-education

W900 FdA Art and Design in the Public Realm
Duration: 2FT Hon
Entry Requirements: *GCE:* 200. Foundation Course required.
Interview required. Portfolio required.

K84 KINGSTON UNIVERSITY
STUDENT INFORMATION & ADVICE CENTRE
COOPER HOUSE
40-46 SURBITON ROAD
KINGSTON UPON THAMES KT1 2HX
t: 0844 8552177 f: 020 8547 7080
e: aps@kingston.ac.uk
// www.kingston.ac.uk

WW1F FdA Art and Design
Duration: 2FT Fdg
Entry Requirements: *GCE:* 100. Portfolio required.

K90 KIRKLEES COLLEGE
HALIFAX ROAD
DEWSBURY
WEST YORKSHIRE WF13 2AS
t: 01924 436221 f: 01924 457047
e: admissionsdc@kirkleescollege.ac.uk
// www.kirkleescollege.ac.uk

W900 BA Applied Arts
Duration: 1FT Hon
Entry Requirements: Contact the institution for details.

L23 UNIVERSITY OF LEEDS
THE UNIVERSITY OF LEEDS
WOODHOUSE LANE
LEEDS LS2 9JT
t: 0113 343 3999
e: admissions@leeds.ac.uk
// www.leeds.ac.uk

WW12 BA Art and Design
Duration: 3FT Hon
Entry Requirements: *GCE:* ABB. *SQAAH:* ABB. *IB:* 34.

L27 LEEDS METROPOLITAN UNIVERSITY
COURSE ENQUIRIES OFFICE
CITY CAMPUS
LEEDS LS1 3HE
t: 0113 81 23113 f: 0113 81 23129
// www.leedsmet.ac.uk

W210 BA Graphic Arts and Design
Duration: 3FT Hon
Entry Requirements: *Foundation:* Pass. *GCE:* 240. Interview
required. Portfolio required.

L28 LEEDS COLLEGE OF ART
BLENHEIM WALK
LEEDS LS2 9AQ
t: 0113 202 8000 f: 0113 202 8001
e: info@leeds-art.ac.uk
// www.leeds-art.ac.uk

WW12 BA Art and Design (Interdisciplinary)
Duration: 3FT Hon
Entry Requirements: *Foundation:* Merit. *GCE:* 240. *IB:* 24. *BTEC
Dip:* DD. *BTEC ExtDip:* MMM. Interview required. Portfolio
required.

L39 UNIVERSITY OF LINCOLN
ADMISSIONS
BRAYFORD POOL
LINCOLN LN6 7TS
t: 01522 886097 f: 01522 886146
e: admissions@lincoln.ac.uk
// www.lincoln.ac.uk

W160 BA Conservation & Restoration
Duration: 3FT Hon
Entry Requirements: *GCE:* 280. Interview required. Portfolio
required.

L46 LIVERPOOL HOPE UNIVERSITY
HOPE PARK
LIVERPOOL L16 9JD
t: 0151 291 3331 f: 0151 291 3434
e: administration@hope.ac.uk
// www.hope.ac.uk

VW31 BA Art & Design History and Fine Art
Duration: 3FT Hon
Entry Requirements: *GCE:* 300-320. *IB:* 25. Interview required.

L53 COLEG LLANDRILLO CYMRU
LLANDUDNO ROAD
RHOS-ON-SEA
COLWYN BAY
NORTH WALES LL28 4HZ
t: 01492 542338/339 f: 01492 543052
e: degrees@llandrillo.ac.uk
// www.llandrillo.ac.uk

WW12 FdA Art and Design
Duration: 2FT Fdg
Entry Requirements: *GCE:* 100. Interview required. Portfolio required.

L62 THE LONDON COLLEGE, UCK
VICTORIA GARDENS
NOTTING HILL GATE
LONDON W11 3PE
t: 020 7243 4000 f: 020 7243 1484
e: admissions@lcuck.ac.uk
// www.lcuck.ac.uk

202W Dip Arts and Design
Duration: 1FT Oth
Entry Requirements: Contact the institution for details.

002W HNC Art and Design
Duration: 1FT HNC
Entry Requirements: Contact the institution for details.

102W HND Art and Design
Duration: 2FT HND
Entry Requirements: Contact the institution for details.

L68 LONDON METROPOLITAN UNIVERSITY
166-220 HOLLOWAY ROAD
LONDON N7 8DB
t: 020 7133 4200
e: admissions@londonmet.ac.uk
// www.londonmet.ac.uk

W140 BA Fine Art (Printmaking)
Duration: 3FT Hon
Entry Requirements: *Foundation:* Pass. *GCE:* 280. *IB:* 28.
Foundation Course required. Interview required. Portfolio required.

M65 COLEG MENAI
FRIDDOEDD ROAD
BANGOR
GWYNEDD LL57 2TP
t: 01248 370125 f: 01248 370052
e: student.services@menai.ac.uk
// www.menai.ac.uk

WW12 FdA Art and Design
Duration: 2FT Fdg
Entry Requirements: Contact the institution for details.

M80 MIDDLESEX UNIVERSITY
MIDDLESEX UNIVERSITY
THE BURROUGHS
LONDON NW4 4BT
t: 020 8411 5555 f: 020 8411 5649
e: enquiries@mdx.ac.uk
// www.mdx.ac.uk

WW21 BA Design, Interior and Applied Arts
Duration: 3FT Hon
Entry Requirements: *GCE:* 200-300. *IB:* 28. Interview required.
Portfolio required.

WW12 FdA Art and Design (Professional Practice)
Duration: 2FT Fdg
Entry Requirements: Interview required. Portfolio required.

N23 NEWCASTLE COLLEGE
STUDENT SERVICES
RYE HILL CAMPUS
SCOTSWOOD ROAD
NEWCASTLE UPON TYNE NE4 7SA
t: 0191 200 4110 f: 0191 200 4349
e: enquiries@ncl-coll.ac.uk
// www.newcastlecollege.co.uk

W1J3 FdA Contemporary Applied Art and Design
Duration: 2FT Fdg
Entry Requirements: Contact the institution for details.

N36 NEWMAN UNIVERSITY COLLEGE, BIRMINGHAM

GENNERS LANE
BARTLEY GREEN
BIRMINGHAM B32 3NT
t: 0121 476 1181 f: 0121 476 1196
e: Admissions@newman.ac.uk
// www.newman.ac.uk

CW81 BA Applied Psychology and Art & Design
Duration: 3FT Hon
Entry Requirements: *Foundation:* Distinction. *GCE:* 260. *IB:* 24. *BTEC ExtDip:* DMM. *OCR ND:* M2 *OCR NED:* M2

WV15 BA Art & Design and Philosophy, Religion & Ethics
Duration: 3FT Hon
Entry Requirements: *Foundation:* Distinction. *GCE:* 260. *IB:* 24. *BTEC ExtDip:* DMM. *OCR ND:* M2 *OCR NED:* M2

WW41 BA Drama and Art & Design
Duration: 3FT Hon
Entry Requirements: *Foundation:* Distinction. *GCE:* 260. *IB:* 24. *BTEC ExtDip:* DMM. *OCR ND:* M2 *OCR NED:* M2

W4W1 BA Drama with Art & Design
Duration: 3FT Hon
Entry Requirements: *Foundation:* Distinction. *GCE:* 260. *IB:* 24. *BTEC ExtDip:* DMM. *OCR ND:* M2 *OCR NED:* M2

XW31 BA Education Studies and Art & Design
Duration: 3FT Hon
Entry Requirements: *Foundation:* Distinction. *GCE:* 260. *IB:* 24. *BTEC ExtDip:* DMM. *OCR ND:* M2 *OCR NED:* M2

X3W1 BA Education Studies with Art & Design
Duration: 3FT Hon
Entry Requirements: *Foundation:* Distinction. *GCE:* 260. *IB:* 24. *BTEC ExtDip:* DMM. *OCR ND:* M2 *OCR NED:* M2

VW11 BA History and Art & Design
Duration: 3FT Hon
Entry Requirements: *Foundation:* Distinction. *GCE:* 260. *IB:* 24. *BTEC ExtDip:* DMM. *OCR ND:* M2 *OCR NED:* M2

V1W1 BA History with Art & Design
Duration: 3FT Hon
Entry Requirements: *Foundation:* Distinction. *GCE:* 260. *IB:* 24. *BTEC ExtDip:* DMM. *OCR ND:* M2 *OCR NED:* M2

GW51 BA IT and Art & Design
Duration: 3FT Hon
Entry Requirements: *Foundation:* Distinction. *GCE:* 260. *IB:* 24. *BTEC ExtDip:* DMM. *OCR ND:* M2 *OCR NED:* M2

G5W0 BA IT with Art & Design
Duration: 3FT Hon
Entry Requirements: *Foundation:* Distinction. *GCE:* 260. *IB:* 24. *BTEC ExtDip:* DMM. *OCR ND:* M2 *OCR NED:* M2

PW31 BA Media & Communication and Art & Design
Duration: 3FT Hon
Entry Requirements: *Foundation:* Distinction. *GCE:* 260. *IB:* 24. *BTEC ExtDip:* DMM. *OCR ND:* M2 *OCR NED:* M2

C8W1 BA Psychology with Art & Design
Duration: 3FT Hon
Entry Requirements: *Foundation:* Distinction. *GCE:* 280. *IB:* 25. *BTEC ExtDip:* DMM. *OCR ND:* M2 *OCR NED:* M2

CW61 BA Sports Studies and Art & Design
Duration: 3FT Hon
Entry Requirements: *Foundation:* Distinction. *GCE:* 260. *IB:* 24. *BTEC ExtDip:* DMM. *OCR ND:* M2 *OCR NED:* M2

C6W1 BA Sports Studies with Art & Design
Duration: 3FT Hon
Entry Requirements: *Foundation:* Distinction. *GCE:* 280. *IB:* 25. *BTEC ExtDip:* DMM. *OCR ND:* M2 *OCR NED:* M2

VW61 BA Theology and Art & Design
Duration: 3FT Hon
Entry Requirements: *Foundation:* Distinction. *GCE:* 260. *IB:* 24. *BTEC ExtDip:* DMM. *OCR ND:* M2 *OCR NED:* M2

V6W1 BA Theology with Art & Design
Duration: 3FT Hon
Entry Requirements: *Foundation:* Merit. *GCE:* 260. *IB:* 24. *OCR ND:* M1 *OCR NED:* P1

N39 NORWICH UNIVERSITY COLLEGE OF THE ARTS

FRANCIS HOUSE
3-7 REDWELL STREET
NORWICH NR2 4SN
t: 01603 610561 f: 01603 615728
e: admissions@nuca.ac.uk
// www.nuca.ac.uk

WL21 BA Games Art and Design
Duration: 3FT Hon
Entry Requirements: *Foundation:* Merit. *GCE:* BBC. *BTEC Dip:* DM. *BTEC ExtDip:* MMM. *OCR ND:* M1 *OCR NED:* P1 Interview required. Portfolio required.

N41 NORTHBROOK COLLEGE SUSSEX
LITTLEHAMPTON ROAD
WORTHING
WEST SUSSEX BN12 6NU
t: 0845 155 6060 f: 01903 606073
e: enquiries@nbcol.ac.uk
// www.northbrook.ac.uk

W150 BA Fine Art: Printmaking
Duration: 3FT Hon
Entry Requirements: *GCE:* 160. Interview required. Portfolio required.

N58 NORTH EAST WORCESTERSHIRE COLLEGE
PEAKMAN STREET
REDDITCH
WORCESTERSHIRE B98 8DW
t: 01527 570020 f: 01527 572901
e: admissions@ne-worcs.ac.uk
// www.ne-worcs.ac.uk

WW2X FdA Art & Design in the Creative Industries (Fashion & Textiles)
Duration: 2FT Fdg
Entry Requirements: *GCE:* 120. Interview required. Portfolio required.

WW19 FdA Art & Design in the Creative Industries (Fine Art)
Duration: 2FT Fdg
Entry Requirements: *GCE:* 120. Interview required. Portfolio required.

WW29 FdA Art & Design in the Creative Industries (Graphic Design)
Duration: 2FT Fdg
Entry Requirements: *GCE:* 120. Interview required. Portfolio required.

WW69 FdA Art & Design in the Creative Industries (Photographic Practices)
Duration: 2FT Fdg
Entry Requirements: *GCE:* 120. Interview required. Portfolio required.

N79 NORTH WARWICKSHIRE AND HINCKLEY COLLEGE
HINCKLEY ROAD
NUNEATON
WARWICKSHIRE CV11 6BH
t: 024 7624 3395
e: angela.jones@nwhc.ac.uk
// www.nwhc.ac.uk

W151 DipHE Art and Design
Duration: 2FT Dip
Entry Requirements: Portfolio required.

O66 OXFORD BROOKES UNIVERSITY
ADMISSIONS OFFICE
HEADINGTON CAMPUS
GIPSY LANE
OXFORD OX3 0BP
t: 01865 483040 f: 01865 483983
e: admissions@brookes.ac.uk
// www.brookes.ac.uk

W1W3 BA/BSc Fine Art/Music
Duration: 3FT Hon
Entry Requirements: *GCE:* BCC.

WW12 FdA Creative Arts and Design Practice(Oxford & Cherwell College)
Duration: 2FT Fdg
Entry Requirements: Contact the institution for details.

P60 PLYMOUTH UNIVERSITY
DRAKE CIRCUS
PLYMOUTH PL4 8AA
t: 01752 585858 f: 01752 588055
e: admissions@plymouth.ac.uk
// www.plymouth.ac.uk

X1WX BEd Primary (Art and Design)
Duration: 3FT Hon   CRB Check: Required
Entry Requirements: *GCE:* 240. *IB:* 26. *OCR ND:* D Interview required. Portfolio required.

R48 ROEHAMPTON UNIVERSITY
ROEHAMPTON LANE
LONDON SW15 5PU
t: 020 8392 3232 f: 020 8392 3470
e: enquiries@roehampton.ac.uk
// www.roehampton.ac.uk

XWC1 BA Primary Education Foundation Stage & Key Stage 1 (Art & Design Education)
Duration: 3FT Hon   CRB Check: Required
Entry Requirements: *GCE:* 320. *IB:* 27. *BTEC ExtDip:* DDM. *OCR NED:* D2 Interview required.

XW1C BA Primary Education Key Stage 2 (Art & Design Education)
Duration: 3FT Hon **CRB Check:** Required
Entry Requirements: *GCE:* 320. *IB:* 27. *BTEC ExtDip:* DDM. *OCR NED:* D2 Interview required.

S35 SOUTHPORT COLLEGE
MORNINGTON ROAD
SOUTHPORT
MERSEYSIDE PR9 0TT
t: 08450066236 f: 01704 392610
e: guidance@southport-college.ac.uk
// www.southport-college.ac.uk

W231 HND Art & Design (Textiles)
Duration: 2FT HND
Entry Requirements: Contact the institution for details.

S76 STOCKPORT COLLEGE
WELLINGTON ROAD SOUTH
STOCKPORT SK1 3UQ
t: 0161 958 3143 f: 0161 958 3663
e: susan.kelly@stockport.ac.uk
// www.stockport.ac.uk

W210 BA Graphic Arts and Design
Duration: 3FT Hon
Entry Requirements: *GCE:* 120-240.

S82 UNIVERSITY CAMPUS SUFFOLK (UCS)
WATERFRONT BUILDING
NEPTUNE QUAY
IPSWICH
SUFFOLK IP4 1QJ
t: 01473 338833 f: 01473 339900
e: info@ucs.ac.uk
// www.ucs.ac.uk

WW12 FdA Commercial Art and Design Practice
Duration: 2FT Fdg
Entry Requirements: *GCE:* 200. *IB:* 28. *BTEC ExtDip:* DMM.
Interview required. Portfolio required.

S84 UNIVERSITY OF SUNDERLAND
STUDENT HELPLINE
THE STUDENT GATEWAY
CHESTER ROAD
SUNDERLAND SR1 3SD
t: 0191 515 3000 f: 0191 515 3805
e: student.helpline@sunderland.ac.uk
// www.sunderland.ac.uk

W102 FdA Applied Art
Duration: 2FT Fdg
Entry Requirements: *GCE:* 80-220. *SQAH:* CCCC. *IB:* 22.
Interview required. Portfolio required.

S96 SWANSEA METROPOLITAN UNIVERSITY
MOUNT PLEASANT CAMPUS
SWANSEA SA1 6ED
t: 01792 481000 f: 01792 481061
e: gemma.green@smu.ac.uk
// www.smu.ac.uk

W790 BA Surface Pattern Design (Contemporary Applied Arts Practice)
Duration: 3FT Hon
Entry Requirements: *Foundation:* Pass. *GCE:* 200-360. *IB:* 24.
Interview required. Portfolio required.

T85 TRURO AND PENWITH COLLEGE
TRURO COLLEGE
COLLEGE ROAD
TRURO
CORNWALL TR1 3XX
t: 01872 267122 f: 01872 267526
e: heinfo@trurocollege.ac.uk
// www.truro-penwith.ac.uk

W214 FdA Digital Visualisation (Art and Design)
Duration: 2FT Fdg
Entry Requirements: *GCE:* 60. *IB:* 24. *BTEC Dip:* MP. *BTEC ExtDip:* PPP. Interview required.

T90 TYNE METROPOLITAN COLLEGE
BATTLE HILL DRIVE
WALLSEND
TYNE AND WEAR NE28 9NL
t: 0191 229 5000 f: 0191 229 5301
e: enquiries@tynemet.ac.uk
// www.tynemet.ac.uk

W900 HND Art and Design (FineArt/Photograpy/Fashion)
Duration: 2FT HND
Entry Requirements: Contact the institution for details.

U20 UNIVERSITY OF ULSTER
COLERAINE
CO. LONDONDERRY
NORTHERN IRELAND BT52 1SA
t: 028 7012 4221 f: 028 7012 4908
e: online@ulster.ac.uk
// www.ulster.ac.uk

W901 BA Hons Contemporary Applied Arts
Duration: 3FT/4SW Hon
Entry Requirements: *GCE:* 240. *IB:* 24. Interview required.
Portfolio required.

WW1F BDes Art and Design (Foundation Year for Specialist Degrees)
Duration: 4FT Hon
Entry Requirements: *GCE:* 160. *IB:* 24. Interview required.
Portfolio required.

U65 UNIVERSITY OF THE ARTS LONDON
272 HIGH HOLBORN
LONDON WC1V 7EY
t: 020 7514 6000x6197 f: 020 7514 6198
e: c.anderson@arts.ac.uk
// www.arts.ac.uk

W294 BA Criticism, Communication and Curation: Arts and Design
Duration: 3FT Hon
Entry Requirements: Interview required. Portfolio required.

W75 UNIVERSITY OF WOLVERHAMPTON
ADMISSIONS UNIT
MX207, CAMP STREET
WOLVERHAMPTON
WEST MIDLANDS WV1 1AD
t: 01902 321000 f: 01902 321896
e: admissions@wlv.ac.uk
// www.wlv.ac.uk

W190 BA Applied Arts
Duration: 3FT/4SW Hon
Entry Requirements: *GCE:* 200. *IB:* 24. *BTEC Dip:* DM. *BTEC ExtDip:* MMP. *OCR ND:* M1 *OCR NED:* P1 Interview required.
Portfolio required.

WW21 BA Art and Design (with Foundation Year)
Duration: 4FT Hon
Entry Requirements: Contact the institution for details.

WW12 FdA Art and Design
Duration: 2FT Fdg
Entry Requirements: *GCE:* 120. *BTEC Dip:* MP. *BTEC ExtDip:* PPP. *OCR ND:* P2 *OCR NED:* P3 Interview required.

W76 UNIVERSITY OF WINCHESTER
WINCHESTER
HANTS SO22 4NR
t: 01962 827234 f: 01962 827288
e: course.enquiries@winchester.ac.uk
// www.winchester.ac.uk

TW7X BA American Studies and Modern Liberal Arts
Duration: 3FT Hon
Entry Requirements: *Foundation:* Distinction. *GCE:* 260-300. *IB:* 25. *OCR ND:* D *OCR NED:* M2

NW19 BA Business Management and Modern & Liberal Arts
Duration: 3FT Hon
Entry Requirements: *Foundation:* Distinction. *GCE:* 260-300. *IB:* 25. *OCR ND:* D *OCR NED:* M2

WW59 BA Choreography & Dance and Modern Liberal Arts
Duration: 3FT Hon
Entry Requirements: *Foundation:* Distinction. *GCE:* 260-300. *IB:* 25. *OCR ND:* D *OCR NED:* M2

WW8X BA Creative Writing and Modern Liberal Arts
Duration: 3FT Hon
Entry Requirements: *Foundation:* Distinction. *GCE:* 260-300. *IB:* 25. *OCR ND:* D *OCR NED:* M2

XW3Y BA Education Studies (Early Childhood) and Modern Liberal Arts
Duration: 3FT Hon
Entry Requirements: *Foundation:* Distinction. *GCE:* 260-300. *IB:* 25. *OCR ND:* D *OCR NED:* M2

XW39 BA Education Studies and Modern Liberal Arts
Duration: 3FT Hon
Entry Requirements: *Foundation:* Distinction. *GCE:* 260-300. *IB:* 25. *OCR ND:* D *OCR NED:* M2

QW39 BA English and Modern Liberal Arts
Duration: 3FT Hon
Entry Requirements: *Foundation:* Distinction. *GCE:* 260-300. *IB:* 25. *OCR ND:* D *OCR NED:* M2

NW89 BA Event Management and Modern Liberal Arts
Duration: 3FT Hon
Entry Requirements: *Foundation:* Distinction. *GCE:* 260-300. *IB:* 25. *OCR ND:* D *OCR NED:* M2

WW6X BA Film & Cinema Technology and Modern Liberal Arts
Duration: 3FT Hon
Entry Requirements: *Foundation:* Distinction. *GCE:* 260-300. *IB:* 25. *OCR ND:* D *OCR NED:* M2

VW1X BA History and Modern Liberal Arts
Duration: 3FT Hon
Entry Requirements: *Foundation:* Distinction. *GCE:* 260-300. *IB:* 25. *OCR ND:* D *OCR NED:* M2

PW5X BA Journalism Studies and Modern Liberal Arts
Duration: 3FT Hon
Entry Requirements: *Foundation:* Distinction. *GCE:* 260-300. *IB:* 25. *OCR ND:* D *OCR NED:* M2

MW1X BA Law and Modern Liberal Arts
Duration: 3FT Hon
Entry Requirements: *Foundation:* Distinction. *GCE:* 260-300. *IB:* 25. *OCR ND:* D *OCR NED:* M2

PW3Y BA Media Production and Modern Liberal Arts
Duration: 3FT Hon
Entry Requirements: *Foundation:* Distinction. *GCE:* 260-300. *IB:* 25. *OCR ND:* D *OCR NED:* M2

PW39 BA Media Studies and Modern Liberal Arts
Duration: 3FT Hon
Entry Requirements: *Foundation:* Distinction. *GCE:* 260-300. *IB:* 25. *OCR ND:* D *OCR NED:* M2

WW94 BA Modern Liberal Arts and Performing Arts (Contemporary Performance)
Duration: 3FT Hon
Entry Requirements: *Foundation:* Distinction. *GCE:* 260-300. *IB:* 25. *OCR ND:* D *OCR NED:* M2

WL9F BA Modern Liberal Arts and Politics & Global Studies
Duration: 3FT Hon
Entry Requirements: *Foundation:* Distinction. *GCE:* 260-300. *IB:* 25. *OCR ND:* D *OCR NED:* M2

WC98 BA Modern Liberal Arts and Psychology
Duration: 3FT Hon
Entry Requirements: *Foundation:* Distinction. *GCE:* 260-300. *IB:* 25. *OCR ND:* D *OCR NED:* M2

WL93 BA Modern Liberal Arts and Sociology
Duration: 3FT Hon
Entry Requirements: *Foundation:* Distinction. *GCE:* 260-300. *IB:* 25. *OCR ND:* D *OCR NED:* M2

WV9P BA Modern Liberal Arts and Theology & Religious Studies
Duration: 3FT Hon
Entry Requirements: *Foundation:* Distinction. *GCE:* 260-300. *IB:* 25. *OCR ND:* D *OCR NED:* M2

WW93 BA Modern Liberal Arts and Vocal & Choral Studies
Duration: 3FT Hon
Entry Requirements: *Foundation:* Distinction. *GCE:* 260-300. *IB:* 25. *OCR ND:* D *OCR NED:* M2

W80 UNIVERSITY OF WORCESTER
HENWICK GROVE
WORCESTER WR2 6AJ
t: 01905 855111 **f:** 01905 855377
e: admissions@worc.ac.uk
// www.worcester.ac.uk

WN19 BA Archaeology & Heritage Studies and Art & Design
Duration: 3FT Hon
Entry Requirements: *GCE:* 220-260. *IB:* 24. *OCR ND:* D Interview required. Portfolio required.

WW12 BA Art & Design
Duration: 3FT Hon
Entry Requirements: *GCE:* 220-300. *IB:* 24. *OCR ND:* D Interview required. Portfolio required.

WW18 BA Art & Design and Creative & Professional Writing
Duration: 3FT Hon
Entry Requirements: Contact the institution for details.

WW94 BA Art & Design and Drama & Performance
Duration: 3FT Hon
Entry Requirements: *GCE:* 240-260. *IB:* 24. *OCR ND:* D Interview required. Portfolio required.

WX93 BA Art & Design and Education Studies
Duration: 3FT Hon
Entry Requirements: *GCE:* 220-260. *IB:* 24. *OCR ND:* D Interview required. Portfolio required.

WQ93 BA Art & Design and English Literary Studies
Duration: 3FT Hon
Entry Requirements: *GCE:* 240-260. *IB:* 24. *OCR ND:* D Interview required. Portfolio required.

WF90 BA Art & Design and Illustration
Duration: 3FT Hon
Entry Requirements: Contact the institution for details.

WP13 BA Art & Design and Media & Cultural Studies
Duration: 3FT Hon
Entry Requirements: *GCE:* 240-260. *IB:* 24. *OCR ND:* D Interview required. Portfolio required.

WC98 BA/BSc Art & Design and Psychology
Duration: 3FT Hon
Entry Requirements: *GCE:* 280-300. *IB:* 25. *OCR ND:* D *OCR NED:* M3

W83 WORKING MEN'S COLLEGE
44 CROWNDALE ROAD
LONDON NW1 1TR
t: 020 7255 4719
e: ArtsSchool@wmcollege.ac.uk
// www.wmcollege.ac.uk

WW12 FdA Art and Design (Professional Practice)
Duration: 2FT Fdg
Entry Requirements: Contact the institution for details.

W85 WRITTLE COLLEGE
ADMISSIONS
WRITTLE COLLEGE
CHELMSFORD
ESSEX CM1 3RR
t: 01245 424200 f: 01245 420456
e: admissions@writtle.ac.uk
// www.writtle.ac.uk

WW12 BA Art and Design Practice (Top Up)
Duration: 1FT Hon
Entry Requirements: Contact the institution for details.

WW1F BA (Hons) Contemporary Art and Design
Duration: 3FT Hon
Entry Requirements: *Foundation:* Distinction. *GCE:* 260. *IB:* 24. *BTEC Dip:* D*D*. *BTEC ExtDip:* DMM. *OCR NED:* M2

WD24 CertHE Professional Floristry
Duration: 1FT Cer
Entry Requirements: *GCE:* 180. *IB:* 24. *OCR NED:* P2 Interview required.

W280 FdA Digital Art and Design
Duration: 2FT Fdg
Entry Requirements: *GCE:* 180. *IB:* 24. *BTEC Dip:* DM. *BTEC ExtDip:* MMP. *OCR NED:* P1 Foundation Course required. Interview required. Portfolio required.

DW47 FdSc Professional Floristry
Duration: 2FT Fdg
Entry Requirements: *GCE:* 180. *IB:* 24. *BTEC Dip:* DM. *BTEC ExtDip:* MMP. *OCR NED:* P1 Interview required.

CERAMICS AND GLASS

B20 BATH SPA UNIVERSITY
NEWTON PARK
NEWTON ST LOE
BATH BA2 9BN
t: 01225 875875 f: 01225 875444
e: enquiries@bathspa.ac.uk
// www.bathspa.ac.uk/clearing

WW1G BA Art/Ceramics
Duration: 3FT Hon
Entry Requirements: *Foundation:* Pass. *GCE:* 220-280. *IB:* 24. Interview required.

WW28 BA Ceramics/Creative Writing
Duration: 3FT Hon
Entry Requirements: *Foundation:* Pass. *GCE:* 220-280. *IB:* 24. Interview required.

WW2M BA Ceramics/Dance
Duration: 3FT Hon
Entry Requirements: *Foundation:* Pass. *GCE:* 220-280. *IB:* 24. Interview required.

WW2L BA Ceramics/Drama Studies
Duration: 3FT Hon
Entry Requirements: *GCE:* 220-280. *IB:* 24. Interview required.

WW2H BA Ceramics/Music
Duration: 3FT Hon
Entry Requirements: *Foundation:* Pass. *GCE:* 220-280. *IB:* 24. Interview required.

W290 BA Ceramics/Textile Design Studies
Duration: 3FT Hon
Entry Requirements: *Foundation:* Pass. *GCE:* 220-280. *IB:* 24. Interview required.

W294 BA Ceramics/Visual Design
Duration: 3FT Hon
Entry Requirements: *Foundation:* Pass. *GCE:* 220-280. *IB:* 24. Interview required.

C20 CARDIFF METROPOLITAN UNIVERSITY (UWIC)
ADMISSIONS UNIT
LLANDAFF CAMPUS
WESTERN AVENUE
CARDIFF CF5 2YB
t: 029 2041 6070 f: 029 2041 6286
e: admissions@cardiffmet.ac.uk
// www.cardiffmet.ac.uk

W232 BA Ceramics
Duration: 3FT Hon
Entry Requirements: *GCE:* 300. *IB:* 26. *BTEC ExtDip:* DDM. *OCR NED:* M1 Foundation Course required. Interview required. Portfolio required.

W270 FdA Ceramics
Duration: 2FT Fdg
Entry Requirements: Contact the institution for details.

C78 CORNWALL COLLEGE
POOL
REDRUTH
CORNWALL TR15 3RD
t: 01209 616161 f: 01209 611612
e: he.admissions@cornwall.ac.uk
// www.cornwall.ac.uk

W290 FdA Contemporary Creative Practice
Duration: 2FT Fdg
Entry Requirements: *GCE:* 120. *IB:* 24. Interview required. Portfolio required.

E56 THE UNIVERSITY OF EDINBURGH
STUDENT RECRUITMENT & ADMISSIONS
57 GEORGE SQUARE
EDINBURGH EH8 9JU
t: 0131 650 4360 f: 0131 651 1236
e: sra.enquiries@ed.ac.uk
// www.ed.ac.uk/studying/undergraduate/

W770 BA Glass
Duration: 4FT Hon
Entry Requirements: *Foundation:* Merit. *GCE:* BBB. *SQAH:* BBBB. *IB:* 34. Portfolio required.

F33 UNIVERSITY COLLEGE FALMOUTH
WOODLANE
FALMOUTH
CORNWALL TR11 4RH
t: 01326213730
e: admissions@falmouth.ac.uk
// www.falmouth.ac.uk

W271 BA(Hons) Contemporary Crafts
Duration: 3FT Hon
Entry Requirements: *GCE:* 220. *IB:* 24. Interview required. Portfolio required.

P51 PETROC
OLD STICKLEPATH HILL
BARNSTAPLE
NORTH DEVON EX31 2BQ
t: 01271 852365 f: 01271 338121
e: he@petroc.ac.uk
// www.petroc.ac.uk

W270 FdA Ceramics
Duration: 2FT Fdg
Entry Requirements: *GCE:* 80.

P65 PLYMOUTH COLLEGE OF ART (FORMERLY PLYMOUTH COLLEGE OF ART AND DESIGN)
TAVISTOCK PLACE
PLYMOUTH PL4 8AT
t: 01752 203434 f: 01752 203444
e: infoservices@plymouthart.ac.uk
// www.plymouthart.ac.uk

W771 BA (Hons) Glass
Duration: 3FT Hon
Entry Requirements: Contact the institution for details.

W770 BA (Hons) Glass (Top-Up)
Duration: 1FT Hon
Entry Requirements: Contact the institution for details.

S72 STAFFORDSHIRE UNIVERSITY
COLLEGE ROAD
STOKE ON TRENT ST4 2DE
t: 01782 292753 f: 01782 292740
e: admissions@staffs.ac.uk
// www.staffs.ac.uk

W270 BA Entrepreneurship in Ceramics
Duration: 1FT Hon
Entry Requirements: Interview required. Portfolio required.

S84 UNIVERSITY OF SUNDERLAND
STUDENT HELPLINE
THE STUDENT GATEWAY
CHESTER ROAD
SUNDERLAND SR1 3SD
t: 0191 515 3000 f: 0191 515 3805
e: student.helpline@sunderland.ac.uk
// www.sunderland.ac.uk

W266 BA Glass and Ceramics
Duration: 3FT Hon
Entry Requirements: *GCE:* 220-360. *IB:* 22. Interview required.
Portfolio required.

S96 SWANSEA METROPOLITAN UNIVERSITY
MOUNT PLEASANT CAMPUS
SWANSEA SA1 6ED
t: 01792 481000 f: 01792 481061
e: gemma.green@smu.ac.uk
// www.smu.ac.uk

W773 BA Glass
Duration: 3FT Hon
Entry Requirements: *GCE:* 200-360. *IB:* 24. Interview required.
Portfolio required.

U65 UNIVERSITY OF THE ARTS LONDON
272 HIGH HOLBORN
LONDON WC1V 7EY
t: 020 7514 6000x6197 f: 020 7514 6198
e: c.anderson@arts.ac.uk
// www.arts.ac.uk

W270 BA Ceramic Design
Duration: 3FT Hon
Entry Requirements: Interview required. Portfolio required.

COMMUNITY AND PUBLIC ARTS

C10 CANTERBURY CHRIST CHURCH UNIVERSITY
NORTH HOLMES ROAD
CANTERBURY
KENT CT1 1QU
t: 01227 782900 f: 01227 782888
e: admissions@canterbury.ac.uk
// www.canterbury.ac.uk

WN28 BA Visual Arts: Performance and Events
Duration: 3FT Hon
Entry Requirements: *GCE:* 240. *IB:* 24. Interview required.

C55 UNIVERSITY OF CHESTER
PARKGATE ROAD
CHESTER CH1 4BJ
t: 01244 511000 f: 01244 511300
e: enquiries@chester.ac.uk
// www.chester.ac.uk

WN68 BA Digital Photography and Events Management
Duration: 3FT Hon
Entry Requirements: *GCE:* 240-280. *SQAH:* BBBB. *IB:* 26.

C99 UNIVERSITY OF CUMBRIA
FUSEHILL STREET
CARLISLE
CUMBRIA CA1 2HH
t: 01228 616234 f: 01228 616235
// www.cumbria.ac.uk

WN98 FdA Performances, Festivals and Events
Duration: 2FT Fdg
Entry Requirements: *GCE:* B-cccc. *SQAH:* CC. *SQAAH:* C. Interview required. Portfolio required.

D26 DE MONTFORT UNIVERSITY
THE GATEWAY
LEICESTER LE1 9BH
t: 0116 255 1551 f: 0116 250 6204
e: enquiries@dmu.ac.uk
// www.dmu.ac.uk

WW59 BA Arts & Festivals Management and Dance
Duration: 3FT Hon
Entry Requirements: *GCE:* 260. *IB:* 28. *BTEC Dip:* D*D*. *BTEC ExtDip:* DMM.

WW94 BA Arts & Festivals Management and Drama Studies
Duration: 3FT Hon
Entry Requirements: *GCE:* 260. *IB:* 28. *BTEC Dip:* D*D*. *BTEC ExtDip:* DMM.

H73 HULL COLLEGE
QUEEN'S GARDENS
HULL HU1 3DG
t: 01482 329943 f: 01482 598733
e: info@hull-college.ac.uk
// www.hull-college.ac.uk/higher-education

W903 BA Community Performance (Top-Up)
Duration: 1FT Hon
Entry Requirements: Interview required. Admissions Test required. HND required.

K24 THE UNIVERSITY OF KENT
RECRUITMENT & ADMISSIONS OFFICE
REGISTRY
UNIVERSITY OF KENT
CANTERBURY, KENT CT2 7NZ
t: 01227 827272 f: 01227 827077
e: information@kent.ac.uk
// www.kent.ac.uk

W900 BA Event and Experience Design
Duration: 3FT Hon
Entry Requirements: *GCE:* ABB-BBB. *SQAH:* AAABB-ABBBB. *IB:* 33. *OCR ND:* D *OCR NED:* D2

N38 UNIVERSITY OF NORTHAMPTON
PARK CAMPUS
BOUGHTON GREEN ROAD
NORTHAMPTON NN2 7AL
t: 0800 358 2232 f: 01604 722083
e: admissions@northampton.ac.uk
// www.northampton.ac.uk

N8WC BA Events Management/Fine Art Painting & Drawing
Duration: 3FT Hon
Entry Requirements: *GCE:* 260-280. *SQAH:* AAA-BBBB. *IB:* 24. *BTEC Dip:* DD. *BTEC ExtDip:* DMM. *OCR ND:* D *OCR NED:* M2

W1NV BA Fine Art Painting & Drawing/Events Management
Duration: 3FT Hon
Entry Requirements: *GCE:* 260-280. *SQAH:* AAA-BBBB. *IB:* 24. *BTEC Dip:* DD. *BTEC ExtDip:* DMM. *OCR ND:* D *OCR NED:* M2

S21 SHEFFIELD HALLAM UNIVERSITY
CITY CAMPUS
HOWARD STREET
SHEFFIELD S1 1WB
t: 0114 225 5555 f: 0114 225 2167
e: admissions@shu.ac.uk
// www.shu.ac.uk

N8W9 BSc Events Management with Arts & Entertainment
Duration: 3FT/4SW Hon
Entry Requirements: *GCE:* 300.

W76 UNIVERSITY OF WINCHESTER
WINCHESTER
HANTS SO22 4NR
t: 01962 827234 f: 01962 827288
e: course.enquiries@winchester.ac.uk
// www.winchester.ac.uk

NW86 BA Event Management and Film & Cinema Technologies
Duration: 3FT Hon
Entry Requirements: *Foundation:* Distinction. *GCE:* 260-300. *IB:* 24. *OCR ND:* D *OCR NED:* M2

W900 BA Street Arts
Duration: 3FT Hon
Entry Requirements: *Foundation:* Distinction. *GCE:* 260-300. *IB:* 25. *OCR ND:* D *OCR NED:* M2

CRAFTS/DESIGN CRAFTS

B20 BATH SPA UNIVERSITY
NEWTON PARK
NEWTON ST LOE
BATH BA2 9BN
t: 01225 875875 f: 01225 875444
e: enquiries@bathspa.ac.uk
// www.bathspa.ac.uk/clearing

WW27 BA Textile Design for Fashion & Interiors
Duration: 3FT Hon
Entry Requirements: *GCE:* 220-280. *IB:* 24. Interview required.

B22 UNIVERSITY OF BEDFORDSHIRE
PARK SQUARE
LUTON
BEDS LU1 3JU
t: 0844 8482234 f: 01582 489323
e: admissions@beds.ac.uk
// www.beds.ac.uk

WW27 FdA Fashion and Surface Pattern Design
Duration: 2FT Fdg
Entry Requirements: *GCE:* 120. Interview required. Portfolio required.

B25 BIRMINGHAM CITY UNIVERSITY
PERRY BARR
BIRMINGHAM B42 2SU
t: 0121 331 5595 f: 0121 331 7994
// www.bcu.ac.uk

W790 BA Jewellery and Silversmithing Design for Industry
Duration: 1FT Hon
Entry Requirements: Interview required. Portfolio required. HND required.

067W HND Gemmology
Duration: 2FT HND
Entry Requirements: *Foundation:* Pass. *GCE:* 120. *SQAH:* BBBB. *SQAAH:* CCC. *IB:* 24. Interview required. Portfolio required.

72WW HND Jewellery and Silversmithing
Duration: 2FT HND
Entry Requirements: *Foundation:* Pass. *GCE:* 120. *SQAH:* BBBB. *SQAAH:* CCC. *IB:* 24. Interview required. Portfolio required.

B72 UNIVERSITY OF BRIGHTON
MITHRAS HOUSE 211
LEWES ROAD
BRIGHTON BN2 4AT
t: 01273 644644 f: 01273 642607
e: admissions@brighton.ac.uk
// www.brighton.ac.uk

W700 FdA Contemporary Crafts Practice
Duration: 2FT Fdg
Entry Requirements: *GCE:* 120. Interview required. Portfolio required.

B94 BUCKINGHAMSHIRE NEW UNIVERSITY
QUEEN ALEXANDRA ROAD
HIGH WYCOMBE
BUCKINGHAMSHIRE HP11 2JZ
t: 0800 0565 660 f: 01494 605 023
e: admissions@bucks.ac.uk
// bucks.ac.uk

WW72 BA Textiles & Surface Design
Duration: 3FT Hon
Entry Requirements: *GCE:* 200-240. *IB:* 24. *OCR ND:* M1 *OCR NED:* M3 Interview required.

C20 CARDIFF METROPOLITAN UNIVERSITY (UWIC)
ADMISSIONS UNIT
LLANDAFF CAMPUS
WESTERN AVENUE
CARDIFF CF5 2YB
t: 029 2041 6070 f: 029 2041 6286
e: admissions@cardiffmet.ac.uk
// www.cardiffmet.ac.uk

W790 FdA Contemporary Textile Practice
Duration: 2FT Fdg
Entry Requirements: Contact the institution for details.

C30 UNIVERSITY OF CENTRAL LANCASHIRE
PRESTON
LANCS PR1 2HE
t: 01772 201201 f: 01772 894954
e: uadmissions@uclan.ac.uk
// www.uclan.ac.uk

W700 BA Contemporary Crafts
Duration: 3FT Hon
Entry Requirements: *GCE:* 240-300. *IB:* 26. *OCR ND:* D *OCR NED:* M3 Interview required. Portfolio required.

WWF7 BA Textiles
Duration: 3FT Hon
Entry Requirements: *GCE:* 240-300. *IB:* 26. *OCR ND:* D *OCR NED:* M3 Interview required. Portfolio required.

C71 CLEVELAND COLLEGE OF ART AND DESIGN
CHURCH SQUARE
HARTLEPOOL
CHURCH SQUARE TS24 7EX
t: 01642 288888 f: 01642 288828
e: studentrecruitment@ccad.ac.uk
// www.ccad.ac.uk

W790 FdA Contemporary Textile Practice
Duration: 2FT Fdg
Entry Requirements: *Foundation:* Pass. *GCE:* 100. Interview required. Portfolio required.

C85 COVENTRY UNIVERSITY
THE STUDENT CENTRE
COVENTRY UNIVERSITY
1 GULSON RD
COVENTRY CV1 2JH
t: 024 7615 2222 f: 024 7615 2223
e: studentenquiries@coventry.ac.uk
// www.coventry.ac.uk

W700 BA Fashion Accessories
Duration: 3FT/4SW Hon
Entry Requirements: *Foundation:* Merit. *GCE:* CCC. *SQAH:* CCCCC. *IB:* 27. *BTEC ExtDip:* MMM. *OCR NED:* M3 Interview required. Portfolio required.

C93 UNIVERSITY FOR THE CREATIVE ARTS
FALKNER ROAD
FARNHAM
SURREY GU9 7DS
t: 01252 892960
e: admissions@ucreative.ac.uk
// www.ucreative.ac.uk

W700 BA Contemporary Jewellery
Duration: 3FT Hon
Entry Requirements: *GCE:* 220. *IB:* 24. *BTEC ExtDip:* PPP. Interview required. Portfolio required.

D26 DE MONTFORT UNIVERSITY
THE GATEWAY
LEICESTER LE1 9BH
t: 0116 255 1551 f: 0116 250 6204
e: enquiries@dmu.ac.uk
// www.dmu.ac.uk

W200 BA Design Crafts
Duration: 3FT Hon
Entry Requirements: *Foundation:* Pass. *GCE:* 260. *IB:* 28. *BTEC Dip:* D*D. *BTEC ExtDip:* MMM. Interview required. Portfolio required.

WW2R BA Fashion Fabrics and Accessories
Duration: 3FT Hon
Entry Requirements: *Foundation:* Pass. *GCE:* 260. *IB:* 28. *BTEC Dip:* D*D. *BTEC ExtDip:* MMM. Interview required. Portfolio required.

D52 DONCASTER COLLEGE
THE HUB
CHAPPELL DRIVE
SOUTH YORKSHIRE DN1 2RF
t: 01302 553610
e: he@don.ac.uk
// www.don.ac.uk

WW17 BA Fine Art & Crafts
Duration: 3FT Hon
Entry Requirements: *GCE:* 100.

E56 THE UNIVERSITY OF EDINBURGH
STUDENT RECRUITMENT & ADMISSIONS
57 GEORGE SQUARE
EDINBURGH EH8 9JU
t: 0131 650 4360 f: 0131 651 1236
e: sra.enquiries@ed.ac.uk
// www.ed.ac.uk/studying/undergraduate/

W721 BA Jewellery and Silversmithing
Duration: 4FT Hon
Entry Requirements: *Foundation:* Merit. *GCE:* BBB. *SQAH:* BBBB. *IB:* 34. Portfolio required.

H18 HEREFORD COLLEGE OF ARTS
FOLLY LANE
HEREFORD HR1 1LT
t: 01432 273359 f: 01432 341099
e: headmin@hca.ac.uk
// www.hca.ac.uk

W700 BA Jewellery Design
Duration: 3FT Hon   CRB Check: Required
Entry Requirements: *GCE:* 200. Interview required. Portfolio required.

H60 THE UNIVERSITY OF HUDDERSFIELD
QUEENSGATE
HUDDERSFIELD HD1 3DH
t: 01484 473969 f: 01484 472765
e: admissionsandrecords@hud.ac.uk
// www.hud.ac.uk

W2W7 BA/BSc Textiles with Surface Design
Duration: 3FT/4SW Hon
Entry Requirements: *GCE:* 300. *SQAH:* BBBB. *IB:* 28. Interview required. Portfolio required.

M10 THE MANCHESTER COLLEGE
OPENSHAW CAMPUS
ASHTON OLD ROAD
OPENSHAW
MANCHESTER M11 2WH
t: 0800 068 8585 f: 0161 920 4103
e: enquiries@themanchestercollege.ac.uk
// www.themanchestercollege.ac.uk

WW72 FdA Jewellery and Design Crafts
Duration: 2FT Fdg

Entry Requirements: *GCE:* 160. *BTEC ExtDip:* MPP.

M80 MIDDLESEX UNIVERSITY
MIDDLESEX UNIVERSITY
THE BURROUGHS
LONDON NW4 4BT
t: 020 8411 5555 f: 020 8411 5649
e: enquiries@mdx.ac.uk
// www.mdx.ac.uk

W790 BA Jewellery and Accessories
Duration: 3FT Hon

Entry Requirements: Interview required. Portfolio required.

N23 NEWCASTLE COLLEGE
STUDENT SERVICES
RYE HILL CAMPUS
SCOTSWOOD ROAD
NEWCASTLE UPON TYNE NE4 7SA
t: 0191 200 4110 f: 0191 200 4349
e: enquiries@ncl-coll.ac.uk
// www.newcastlecollege.co.uk

W751 FdA Contemporary Ceramic Practice
Duration: 2FT Fdg

Entry Requirements: *Foundation:* Pass. *GCE:* 120-165. *OCR ND:* P2 *OCR NED:* P3 Foundation Course required. Interview required. Portfolio required.

N38 UNIVERSITY OF NORTHAMPTON
PARK CAMPUS
BOUGHTON GREEN ROAD
NORTHAMPTON NN2 7AL
t: 0800 358 2232 f: 01604 722083
e: admissions@northampton.ac.uk
// www.northampton.ac.uk

W7W2 BA Surface Design & Printed Textiles
Duration: 3FT Hon

Entry Requirements: *GCE:* 260-280. *SQAH:* AAA-BBBB. *IB:* 24. *BTEC Dip:* DD. *BTEC ExtDip:* DMM. *OCR ND:* D *OCR NED:* M2 Foundation Course required. Interview required.

P65 PLYMOUTH COLLEGE OF ART (FORMERLY PLYMOUTH COLLEGE OF ART AND DESIGN)
TAVISTOCK PLACE
PLYMOUTH PL4 8AT
t: 01752 203434 f: 01752 203444
e: infoservices@plymouthart.ac.uk
// www.plymouthart.ac.uk

W702 BA (Hons) Contemporary Crafts
Duration: 3FT Hon

Entry Requirements: Contact the institution for details.

W703 BA (Hons) Contemporary Crafts (Top-Up)
Duration: 1FT Hon

Entry Requirements: Contact the institution for details.

W701 FdA Contemporary Crafts
Duration: 2FT Fdg

Entry Requirements: Contact the institution for details.

W704 FdA Contemporary Crafts (including Level 0)
Duration: 3FT Fdg

Entry Requirements: Contact the institution for details.

R51 ROSE BRUFORD COLLEGE
LAMORBEY PARK
BURNT OAK LANE
SIDCUP
KENT DA15 9DF
t: 0208 308 2600 f: 020 8308 0542
e: enquiries@bruford.ac.uk
// www.bruford.ac.uk

W4W7 BA Scenic Arts
Duration: 3FT Hon

Entry Requirements: *GCE:* 160-280.

S72 STAFFORDSHIRE UNIVERSITY
COLLEGE ROAD
STOKE ON TRENT ST4 2DE
t: 01782 292753 f: 01782 292740
e: admissions@staffs.ac.uk
// www.staffs.ac.uk

W741 BA Entrepreneurship in Surface Pattern
Duration: 1FT Hon

Entry Requirements: Interview required. Portfolio required.

W740 BA Surface Pattern Design
Duration: 3FT/4FT Hon

Entry Requirements: *Foundation:* Merit. *GCE:* 200-240. *IB:* 24. *BTEC Dip:* DD. *BTEC ExtDip:* MMM. Interview required. Portfolio required.

S82 UNIVERSITY CAMPUS SUFFOLK (UCS)
WATERFRONT BUILDING
NEPTUNE QUAY
IPSWICH
SUFFOLK IP4 1QJ
t: 01473 338833 f: 01473 339900
e: info@ucs.ac.uk
// www.ucs.ac.uk

WW27 BA Design
Duration: 3FT Hon
Entry Requirements: *GCE:* 280. *IB:* 28. *BTEC ExtDip:* DMM.
Interview required. Portfolio required.

U65 UNIVERSITY OF THE ARTS LONDON
272 HIGH HOLBORN
LONDON WC1V 7EY
t: 020 7514 6000x6197 f: 020 7514 6198
e: c.anderson@arts.ac.uk
// www.arts.ac.uk

W700 BA Fashion Jewellery
Duration: 3FT Hon
Entry Requirements: Foundation Course required. Interview
required. Portfolio required.

W740 FdA Fashion Design Technology: Surface Textiles
Duration: 2FT Fdg
Entry Requirements: Foundation Course required. Interview
required. Portfolio required.

W05 THE UNIVERSITY OF WEST LONDON
ST MARY'S ROAD
EALING
LONDON W5 5RF
t: 0800 036 8888 f: 020 8566 1353
e: learning.advice@uwl.ac.uk
// www.uwl.ac.uk

NW27 BSc Culinary Arts Management
Duration: 3FT Hon
Entry Requirements: *GCE:* 200. *IB:* 28. Interview required.

DESIGN/DESIGN & TECHNOLOGY

A30 UNIVERSITY OF ABERTAY DUNDEE
BELL STREET
DUNDEE DD1 1HG
t: 01382 308080 f: 01382 308081
e: sro@abertay.ac.uk
// www.abertay.ac.uk

GW42 BA Computer Arts
Duration: 4FT Hon
Entry Requirements: *GCE:* BBC. *SQAH:* AABB. *IB:* 26. *OCR ND:*
M1 *OCR NED:* M1 Interview required. Portfolio required.

A66 THE ARTS UNIVERSITY COLLEGE AT BOURNEMOUTH (FORMERLY ARTS INSTITUTE AT BOURNEMOUTH)
WALLISDOWN
POOLE
DORSET BH12 5HH
t: 01202 363228 f: 01202 537729
e: admissions@aucb.ac.uk
// www.aucb.ac.uk

W235 BA Fashion Design and Technology
Duration: 3FT Hon
Entry Requirements: *Foundation:* Pass. *GCE:* BCC. *IB:* 24. *OCR
ND:* M1 *OCR NED:* M1 Interview required.

B06 BANGOR UNIVERSITY
BANGOR UNIVERSITY
BANGOR
GWYNEDD LL57 2DG
t: 01248 388484 f: 01248 370451
e: admissions@bangor.ac.uk
// www.bangor.ac.uk

X1WF BSc Design & Technology
Duration: 3FT Hon
Entry Requirements: *GCE:* 200-240. *IB:* 28.

W241 BSc Dylunio Cynnyrch
Duration: 3FT Hon
Entry Requirements: *GCE:* 200-220. *IB:* 28.

B25 BIRMINGHAM CITY UNIVERSITY
PERRY BARR
BIRMINGHAM B42 2SU
t: 0121 331 5595 f: 0121 331 7994
// www.bcu.ac.uk

W2JK BA Fashion Design with Garment Technology
Duration: 3FT Hon
Entry Requirements: *GCE:* 280. *IB:* 28. Interview required.
Portfolio required.

W2N5 BA Textile Design (Retail Management)
Duration: 3FT Hon
Entry Requirements: *GCE:* 280. *IB:* 28. Interview required.
Portfolio required.

PW92 BA Visual Communication
Duration: 3FT Hon
Entry Requirements: *GCE:* 280. *IB:* 28. Interview required.
Portfolio required.

WP63 BSc Film, Production and Technology
Duration: 3FT/4SW Hon
Entry Requirements: *GCE:* 300. *IB:* 30.

HW66 BSc Television Technology and Production
Duration: 3FT/4SW Hon
Entry Requirements: *GCE:* 280. *IB:* 30.

B37 BISHOP BURTON COLLEGE
BISHOP BURTON
BEVERLEY
EAST YORKSHIRE HU17 8QG
t: 01964 553000 f: 01964 553101
e: enquiries@bishopburton.ac.uk
// www.bishopburton.ac.uk

W200 BA Design (Top Up)
Duration: 1FT Hon
Entry Requirements: Contact the institution for details.

W201 FdA Design
Duration: 2FT Fdg
Entry Requirements: *GCE:* 80. Interview required.

W202 FdA Design (including Year 0)
Duration: 3FT Fdg
Entry Requirements: Contact the institution for details.

B41 BLACKPOOL AND THE FYLDE COLLEGE AN ASSOCIATE COLLEGE OF LANCASTER UNIVERSITY
ASHFIELD ROAD
BISPHAM
BLACKPOOL
LANCS FY2 0HB
t: 01253 504346 f: 01253 504198
e: admissions@blackpool.ac.uk
// www.blackpool.ac.uk

WW6F BA Photography and Digital Design (Top-Up)
Duration: 1FT Hon
Entry Requirements: Interview required. Portfolio required. HND required.

WW62 FdA Photography and Digital Design
Duration: 2FT Fdg
Entry Requirements: *GCE:* 180. *IB:* 24. *OCR ND:* M1 Interview required. Portfolio required.

B44 UNIVERSITY OF BOLTON
DEANE ROAD
BOLTON BL3 5AB
t: 01204 903903 f: 01204 399074
e: enquiries@bolton.ac.uk
// www.bolton.ac.uk

W619 BDes Special Effects Development
Duration: 3FT Hon
Entry Requirements: *GCE:* 260. Interview required. Portfolio required.

W614 BSc Special Effects Development
Duration: 3FT Hon
Entry Requirements: *GCE:* 260. Interview required. Portfolio required.

24WG HND Games Design
Duration: 2FT HND
Entry Requirements: *GCE:* 160. Interview required.

64WG HND Special Effects Development
Duration: 2FT HND
Entry Requirements: *GCE:* 160. Interview required. Portfolio required.

B50 BOURNEMOUTH UNIVERSITY
TALBOT CAMPUS
FERN BARROW
POOLE
DORSET BH12 5BB
t: 01202 524111
// www.bournemouth.ac.uk

WN22 BA Design Business Management
Duration: 3FT/4SW Hon
Entry Requirements: *GCE:* 300. *IB:* 31. *BTEC SubDip:* D. *BTEC Dip:* DD. *BTEC ExtDip:* DDM.

B56 THE UNIVERSITY OF BRADFORD
RICHMOND ROAD
BRADFORD
WEST YORKSHIRE BD7 1DP
t: 0800 073 1225 f: 01274 235585
e: course-enquiries@bradford.ac.uk
// www.bradford.ac.uk

GW42 BA Graphics for Games
Duration: 3FT Hon
Entry Requirements: *GCE:* 240. *IB:* 24.

JW92 BSc Technology and Design with International Foundation Year
Duration: 4FT Hon
Entry Requirements: *GCE:* 120.

GW4F BSc Web Design and Technology
Duration: 3FT Hon
Entry Requirements: *GCE:* 260. *IB:* 24. Interview required.

B60 BRADFORD COLLEGE: AN ASSOCIATE COLLEGE OF LEEDS METROPOLITAN UNIVERSITY
GREAT HORTON ROAD
BRADFORD
WEST YORKSHIRE BD7 1AY
t: 01274 433008 f: 01274 431652
e: heregistry@bradfordcollege.ac.uk
// www.bradfordcollege.ac.uk/
university-centre

W2G4 BA Graphic Design, Illustration, Digital Media option - Graphic Design
Duration: 3FT Hon
Entry Requirements: *GCE:* 120. Interview required. Portfolio required.

W2G4 BA Graphic Design, Illustration, Digital Media option - Illustration
Duration: 3FT Hon
Entry Requirements: *GCE:* 120. Interview required. Portfolio required.

W2G4 BA Graphic Design, Illustration, Digital Media option - Interactive Multimedia
Duration: 3FT Hon
Entry Requirements: *GCE:* 120. Interview required. Portfolio required.

B72 UNIVERSITY OF BRIGHTON
MITHRAS HOUSE 211
LEWES ROAD
BRIGHTON BN2 4AT
t: 01273 644644 f: 01273 642607
e: admissions@brighton.ac.uk
// www.brighton.ac.uk

X1W2 BA Design and Technology Education with QTS (Secondary) (2 years)
Duration: 2FT Hon
Entry Requirements: Interview required.

W241 BSc Product Design Technology with Professional Experience
Duration: 4SW Hon
Entry Requirements: *GCE:* BBB. *IB:* 34. Interview required. Portfolio required.

W290 MDes Design and Craft
Duration: 4FT Hon
Entry Requirements: *GCE:* BBB. Interview required. Portfolio required.

B77 BRISTOL, CITY OF BRISTOL COLLEGE
SOUTH BRISTOL SKILLS ACADEMY
CITY OF BRISTOL COLLEGE
PO BOX 2887 BS2 2BB
t: 0117 312 5000
e: HEAdmissions@cityofbristol.ac.uk
// www.cityofbristol.ac.uk

W290 FdA Graphic Design with Interactive Multimedia
Duration: 2FT Fdg
Entry Requirements: *GCE:* 140. Interview required. Portfolio required.

W291 FdA Interactive Multimedia with Graphic Design
Duration: 2FT Fdg
Entry Requirements: *GCE:* 140. Interview required. Portfolio required.

B80 UNIVERSITY OF THE WEST OF ENGLAND, BRISTOL
FRENCHAY CAMPUS
COLDHARBOUR LANE
BRISTOL BS16 1QY
t: +44 (0)117 32 83333 f: +44 (0)117 32 82810
e: admissions@uwe.ac.uk
// www.uwe.ac.uk

W293 BA Filmmaking and Creative Media
Duration: 3FT Hon
Entry Requirements: *GCE:* 280. Interview required. Portfolio required.

W240 BSc Product Design Technology
Duration: 3FT/4SW Hon
Entry Requirements: *GCE:* 300. Interview required.

WW12 FdA Creative Practices
Duration: 2FT Fdg
Entry Requirements: *GCE:* 240.

B84 BRUNEL UNIVERSITY
UXBRIDGE
MIDDLESEX UB8 3PH
t: 01895 265265 f: 01895 269790
e: admissions@brunel.ac.uk
// www.brunel.ac.uk

WW28 BA Games Design and Creative Writing
Duration: 3FT Hon
Entry Requirements: *GCE:* ABB. *SQAAH:* ABB. *IB:* 33. *BTEC ExtDip:* D*DD.

WQ23 BA Games Design and English
Duration: 3FT Hon
Entry Requirements: *GCE:* AAB. *SQAAH:* AAB. *IB:* 35. *BTEC ExtDip:* D*D*D.

WW26 BA Games Design and Film & Television Studies
Duration: 3FT Hon
Entry Requirements: *GCE:* BBB. *SQAAH:* BBB. *IB:* 32. *BTEC ExtDip:* DDM.

WW2H BA Games Design and Sonic Arts
Duration: 3FT Hon
Entry Requirements: *GCE:* BBB. *SQAAH:* BBB. *IB:* 32. *BTEC ExtDip:* DDM. Admissions Test required.

HW72 BA Industrial Design and Technology
Duration: 3FT Hon
Entry Requirements: *GCE:* ABB. *SQAAH:* ABB. *IB:* 33. *BTEC ExtDip:* D*DD. Interview required.

HWR2 BA Industrial Design and Technology (4 year Thick SW)
Duration: 4SW Hon
Entry Requirements: *GCE:* ABB. *SQAAH:* ABB. *IB:* 33. *BTEC ExtDip:* D*DD. Interview required.

WW42 BA Theatre and Games Design
Duration: 3FT Hon
Entry Requirements: *GCE:* BBB. *SQAAH:* BBB. *IB:* 32. *BTEC ExtDip:* DDM.

HW62 BSc Broadcast Media (Design & Technology)
Duration: 3FT Hon
Entry Requirements: *GCE:* BBB. *SQAAH:* BBB. *IB:* 32. *BTEC SubDip:* D. *BTEC Dip:* DD. *BTEC ExtDip:* DDD. Interview required.

HW6F BSc Broadcast Media (Design & Technology) (4 year Thick SW)
Duration: 4SW Hon
Entry Requirements: *GCE:* BBB. *SQAAH:* BBB. *IB:* 32. *BTEC SubDip:* D. *BTEC Dip:* DD. *BTEC ExtDip:* DDD. Interview required.

H6W2 BSc Multimedia Technology and Design
Duration: 3FT Hon
Entry Requirements: *GCE:* BBB. *SQAAH:* BBB. *IB:* 32. *BTEC SubDip:* D. *BTEC Dip:* DD. *BTEC ExtDip:* DDD. Interview required.

H6WG BSc Multimedia Technology and Design (4 year Thick SW)
Duration: 4SW Hon
Entry Requirements: *GCE:* BBB. *SQAAH:* BBB. *IB:* 32. *BTEC SubDip:* D. *BTEC Dip:* DD. *BTEC ExtDip:* DDD. Interview required.

B92 BROOKSBY MELTON COLLEGE
MELTON CAMPUS
ASFORDBY ROAD
MELTON MOWBRAY
LEICESTERSHIRE LE13 0HJ
t: 01664 850850 f: 01664 855355
e: heenquiries@brooksbymelton.ac.uk
// www.brooksbymelton.ac.uk

W614 BSc Film Making Technology & Visual Effects (Top-Up)
Duration: 1FT Oth
Entry Requirements: Contact the institution for details.

B94 BUCKINGHAMSHIRE NEW UNIVERSITY
QUEEN ALEXANDRA ROAD
HIGH WYCOMBE
BUCKINGHAMSHIRE HP11 2JZ
t: 0800 0565 660 f: 01494 605 023
e: admissions@bucks.ac.uk
// bucks.ac.uk

GW4F BSc Web Development
Duration: 3FT Hon
Entry Requirements: *GCE:* 200-240. *IB:* 24. *OCR ND:* M1 *OCR NED:* M3

C10 CANTERBURY CHRIST CHURCH UNIVERSITY
NORTH HOLMES ROAD
CANTERBURY
KENT CT1 1QU
t: 01227 782900 f: 01227 782888
e: admissions@canterbury.ac.uk
// www.canterbury.ac.uk

WP29 BA Visual Arts: Image & Design
Duration: 3FT Hon
Entry Requirements: *GCE:* 240. *IB:* 24.

WG2L BA Web Design
Duration: 3FT Hon
Entry Requirements: *GCE:* 240. *IB:* 24.

C20 CARDIFF METROPOLITAN UNIVERSITY (UWIC)
ADMISSIONS UNIT
LLANDAFF CAMPUS
WESTERN AVENUE
CARDIFF CF5 2YB
t: 029 2041 6070 f: 029 2041 6286
e: admissions@cardiffmet.ac.uk
// www.cardiffmet.ac.uk

W291 BA Artist Designer: Maker
Duration: 3FT Hon
Entry Requirements: *GCE:* 300. *IB:* 26. *BTEC ExtDip:* DDM. *OCR NED:* M1 Foundation Course required. Interview required. Portfolio required.

W290 BSc Architectural Design & Technology
Duration: 3FT Hon
Entry Requirements: *GCE:* 300. *IB:* 26. *BTEC ExtDip:* DDM. *OCR NED:* D2 Interview required.

12KW HND Architectural Design and Technology
Duration: 2FT HND
Entry Requirements: *Foundation:* Distinction. *GCE:* 260. *IB:* 24. *BTEC ExtDip:* DMM. *OCR NED:* M2 Interview required.

42GW HND Design for Interactive Media
Duration: 2FT HND
Entry Requirements: Interview required.

C30 UNIVERSITY OF CENTRAL LANCASHIRE
PRESTON
LANCS PR1 2HE
t: 01772 201201 f: 01772 894954
e: uadmissions@uclan.ac.uk
// www.uclan.ac.uk

WN2N BA Fashion Brand Management
Duration: 3FT Hon
Entry Requirements: *GCE:* 240. *IB:* 24. *OCR ND:* D *OCR NED:* M3 Interview required. Portfolio required.

WJ2K BA Fashion Promotion (4-year sandwich)
Duration: 4SW Hon
Entry Requirements: *GCE:* 240-280. *IB:* 26. *OCR ND:* D *OCR NED:* M2 Interview required. Portfolio required.

PWH6 BA Film Production and Media Production & Technology
Duration: 3FT Hon
Entry Requirements: *GCE:* 260-300. *IB:* 28. *BTEC Dip:* D*D*. *BTEC ExtDip:* DMM. *OCR ND:* D *OCR NED:* M2

WG24 BA Games Design
Duration: 3FT Hon
Entry Requirements: *GCE:* 240-300. *IB:* 26. *OCR ND:* D *OCR NED:* M3 Interview required. Portfolio required.

NW52 FdA Visual Merchandising and Promotional Design
Duration: 2FT Fdg
Entry Requirements: *GCE:* 120. *SQAH:* CCC.

24WJ HND Furniture Design
Duration: 2FT HND
Entry Requirements: *GCE:* 80. *IB:* 24.

C55 UNIVERSITY OF CHESTER
PARKGATE ROAD
CHESTER CH1 4BJ
t: 01244 511000 f: 01244 511300
e: enquiries@chester.ac.uk
// www.chester.ac.uk

WC66 BA Digital Photography and Sport Development
Duration: 3FT Hon
Entry Requirements: *GCE:* 240-280. *SQAH:* BBBB. *IB:* 26.

C85 COVENTRY UNIVERSITY

THE STUDENT CENTRE
COVENTRY UNIVERSITY
1 GULSON RD
COVENTRY CV1 2JH
t: 024 7615 2222 f: 024 7615 2223
e: studentenquiries@coventry.ac.uk
// www.coventry.ac.uk

WWC2 BA Fine Art and Illustration

Duration: 3FT Hon

Entry Requirements: *Foundation:* Merit. *GCE:* CCC. *SQAH:*
CCCCC. *IB:* 27. *BTEC ExtDip:* MMM. *OCR NED:* M3 Interview
required. Portfolio required.

C92 CROYDON COLLEGE

COLLEGE ROAD
CROYDON CR9 1DX
t: 020 8760 5934 f: 020 8760 5880
e: admissions@croydon.ac.uk
// www.croydon.ac.uk

W280 FdA Digital Film Production

Duration: 2FT Fdg

Entry Requirements: *GCE:* 60-80. Interview required. Portfolio
required.

C93 UNIVERSITY FOR THE CREATIVE ARTS

FALKNER ROAD
FARNHAM
SURREY GU9 7DS
t: 01252 892960
e: admissions@ucreative.ac.uk
// www.ucreative.ac.uk

W280 BA Computer Games Arts

Duration: 3FT Hon

Entry Requirements: *GCE:* 220. *IB:* 24. *BTEC ExtDip:* PPP.
Interview required. Portfolio required.

WP25 BA Fashion Journalism

Duration: 3FT Hon

Entry Requirements: *GCE:* 220. *IB:* 24. *BTEC ExtDip:* PPP.
Interview required. Portfolio required.

W292 BA Graphic Media (Top-up)

Duration: 1FT Hon

Entry Requirements: Interview required. Portfolio required. HND
required.

C99 UNIVERSITY OF CUMBRIA

FUSEHILL STREET
CARLISLE
CUMBRIA CA1 2HH
t: 01228 616234 f: 01228 616235
// www.cumbria.ac.uk

W281 BA Digital Arts (with named pathway)

Duration: 1FT Hon

Entry Requirements: Contact the institution for details.

W280 FdA Art of Games Design

Duration: 2FT Fdg

Entry Requirements: *Foundation:* Pass. *GCE:* C-cccc. *SQAH:* CC.
SQAAH: C. *IB:* 25. Interview required. Portfolio required.

D26 DE MONTFORT UNIVERSITY

THE GATEWAY
LEICESTER LE1 9BH
t: 0116 255 1551 f: 0116 250 6204
e: enquiries@dmu.ac.uk
// www.dmu.ac.uk

WWF7 BA Footwear Design

Duration: 3FT Hon

Entry Requirements: *Foundation:* Pass. *GCE:* 260. *IB:* 28. *BTEC
Dip:* D*D. *BTEC ExtDip:* MMM. Interview required. Portfolio
required.

W291 BA Game Art Design

Duration: 3FT Hon

Entry Requirements: *Foundation:* Pass. *GCE:* 260. *IB:* 28. *BTEC
Dip:* D*D. *BTEC ExtDip:* MMM. Interview required. Portfolio
required.

HW66 BSc Radio Production and Technology

Duration: 3FT/4SW Hon

Entry Requirements: *GCE:* 300. *IB:* 28. *BTEC ExtDip:* DDM.
Interview required.

D65 UNIVERSITY OF DUNDEE

NETHERGATE
DUNDEE DD1 4HN
t: 01382 383838 f: 01382 388150
e: contactus@dundee.ac.uk
// www.dundee.ac.uk/admissions/
undergraduate/

WG24 BSc Digital Interaction Design

Duration: 4FT Hon

Entry Requirements: *GCE:* BCC. *SQAH:* BBBB. *IB:* 30. Interview
required. Portfolio required.

E28 UNIVERSITY OF EAST LONDON

DOCKLANDS CAMPUS
UNIVERSITY WAY
LONDON E16 2RD
t: 020 8223 3333 f: 020 8223 2978
e: study@uel.ac.uk
// www.uel.ac.uk

GWLF BA Computer Games Design (Story Development)
Duration: 3FT Hon
Entry Requirements: *GCE*: 280. *IB*: 24.

W2G5 BA Computer Games Design with Business Information Systems
Duration: 3FT Hon
Entry Requirements: *GCE*: 240. *IB*: 24.

W2P3 BA Computer Games Design with Film Studies
Duration: 3FT Hon
Entry Requirements: *GCE*: 280. *IB*: 24.

G482 BA Computer Games Design with Multimedia Design Technology
Duration: 3FT Hon
Entry Requirements: *GCE*: 280. *IB*: 24.

W235 BA Digital Fashion
Duration: 3FT Hon
Entry Requirements: *GCE*: 200. Interview required. Portfolio required.

W282 BA Interactive Media Design
Duration: 3FT Hon
Entry Requirements: *GCE*: 240. *IB*: 24.

W283 BA Interactive Media Design - Extended
Duration: 4FT Hon
Entry Requirements: *GCE*: 80. *IB*: 24.

P3WF BA Media Studies with Multimedia Design Technology
Duration: 3FT Hon
Entry Requirements: *GCE*: 240. *IB*: 24.

W2PH BA Multimedia Design Technology with Media Studies
Duration: 3FT Hon
Entry Requirements: *GCE*: 240.

W299 BSc Computer Games Design with Illustration
Duration: 3FT Hon
Entry Requirements: *GCE*: 280. *IB*: 24. Portfolio required.

I1W2 BSc Computing with Multimedia Design Technology
Duration: 3FT Hon
Entry Requirements: *GCE*: 240. *IB*: 24.

WG2K BSc Multimedia Design Technology
Duration: 3FT Hon
Entry Requirements: *GCE*: 240. *IB*: 24.

WG2L BSc Multimedia Design Technology - Extended
Duration: 4FT Hon
Entry Requirements: *GCE*: 80. *IB*: 24.

W292 BSc Multimedia Design Technology with Graphic Design
Duration: 3FT Hon
Entry Requirements: *GCE*: 240.

WQ23 BSc/BA Multimedia Design Technology / English Literature
Duration: 3FT Hon
Entry Requirements: *GCE*: 240.

WL26 BSc/BA Multimedia Design Technology/Anthropology
Duration: 3FT Hon
Entry Requirements: *GCE*: 240.

WN22 BSc/BA Multimedia Design Technology/Business Management
Duration: 3FT Hon
Entry Requirements: *GCE*: 240.

WP23 BSc/BA Multimedia Design Technology/Film Studies
Duration: 3FT Hon
Entry Requirements: *GCE*: 240.

WV21 BSc/BA Multimedia Design Technology/History
Duration: 3FT Hon
Entry Requirements: *GCE*: 240.

WL23 BSc/BA Multimedia Design Technology/Sociology
Duration: 3FT Hon
Entry Requirements: *GCE*: 240.

WL29 BSc/BA Multimedia Design Technology/Third World Development
Duration: 3FT Hon
Entry Requirements: *GCE*: 240.

E42 EDGE HILL UNIVERSITY
ORMSKIRK
LANCASHIRE L39 4QP
t: 01695 657000 f: 01695 584355
e: study@edgehill.ac.uk
// www.edgehill.ac.uk

X1W2 BSc Secondary Design and Technology Education with QTS
Duration: 2FT Hon   CRB Check: Required
Entry Requirements: Interview required. HND required.

X1WF BSc Secondary Design and Technology Education with QTS
Duration: 3FT Hon   CRB Check: Required
Entry Requirements: *Foundation:* Distinction. *GCE:* 280. *IB:* 26. *OCR ND:* M2 *OCR NED:* P1 Interview required.

E59 EDINBURGH NAPIER UNIVERSITY
CRAIGLOCKHART CAMPUS
EDINBURGH EH14 1DJ
t: +44 (0)8452 60 60 40 f: 0131 455 6464
e: info@napier.ac.uk
// www.napier.ac.uk

W290 BDes Design and Digital Arts
Duration: 1FT/2FT Ord/Hon
Entry Requirements: Interview required. Portfolio required.

W281 BSc Interactive Media Design
Duration: 3FT/4FT Ord/Hon
Entry Requirements: *GCE:* 245.

E81 EXETER COLLEGE
HELE ROAD
EXETER
DEVON EX4 4JS
t: 0845 111 6000
e: info@exe-coll.ac.uk
// www.exe-coll.ac.uk/he

WW62 FdA Photography and Digital Arts
Duration: 2FT Fdg
Entry Requirements: *GCE:* 160.

G14 UNIVERSITY OF GLAMORGAN, CARDIFF AND PONTYPRIDD
ENQUIRIES AND ADMISSIONS UNIT
PONTYPRIDD CF37 1DL
t: 08456 434030 f: 01443 654050
e: enquiries@glam.ac.uk
// www.glam.ac.uk

WNF5 BA Fashion Promotion
Duration: 4SW Hon
Entry Requirements: *GCE:* BBC. *IB:* 25. *BTEC SubDip:* M. *BTEC Dip:* D*D*. *BTEC ExtDip:* DMM. *OCR NED:* M2 Interview required. Portfolio required.

W280 BA Visual Effects and Motion Graphics
Duration: 3FT Hon
Entry Requirements: *GCE:* BBC. *BTEC SubDip:* M. *BTEC Dip:* D*D*. *BTEC ExtDip:* DMM. *OCR NED:* M2 Interview required. Portfolio required.

G28 UNIVERSITY OF GLASGOW
71 SOUTHPARK AVENUE
UNIVERSITY OF GLASGOW
GLASGOW G12 8QQ
t: 0141 330 6062 f: 0141 330 2961
e: student.recruitment@glasgow.ac.uk
// www.glasgow.ac.uk

H3W2 BEng Product Design Engineering
Duration: 4FT Hon
Entry Requirements: *GCE:* ABB. *SQAH:* AAAB-BBB. *IB:* 32.

H3WG MEng Product Design Engineering
Duration: 5FT Hon
Entry Requirements: *GCE:* AAB. *SQAH:* AAAA-AAABB. *IB:* 34.

G42 GLASGOW CALEDONIAN UNIVERSITY
STUDENT RECRUITMENT & ADMISSIONS SERVICE
CITY CAMPUS
COWCADDENS ROAD
GLASGOW G4 0BA
t: 0141 331 3000 f: 0141 331 8676
e: undergraduate@gcu.ac.uk
// www.gcu.ac.uk

W290 BA Graphic Design for Digital Media
Duration: 4FT Hon
Entry Requirements: Portfolio required.

GWK2 BSc Computer Games (Design)
Duration: 4FT Hon
Entry Requirements: Contact the institution for details.

W280 BSc Computer Games (Software Development)
Duration: 4FT/5SW Hon
Entry Requirements: *GCE:* BC. *SQAH:* ABB.

GOWER COLLEGE SWANSEA
LEARNING RESOURCE CENTRE
GORSEINON
SWANSEA SA4 6RD

G43 THE GLASGOW SCHOOL OF ART
167 RENFREW STREET
GLASGOW G3 6RQ
t: 0141 353 4434/4514 f: 0141 353 4408
e: admissions@gsa.ac.uk
// www.gsa.ac.uk

W280 BDes Digital Culture
Duration: 4FT Hon
Entry Requirements: Contact the institution for details.

HW72 BDes Product Design
Duration: 4FT Hon
Entry Requirements: *GCE:* ABB. *SQAH:* AABB-ABBB. *IB:* 30.
Interview required. Portfolio required.

G53 GLYNDWR UNIVERSITY
PLAS COCH
MOLD ROAD
WREXHAM LL11 2AW
t: 01978 293439 f: 01978 290008
e: sid@glyndwr.ac.uk
// www.glyndwr.ac.uk

HW66 BA Television Production and Technology
Duration: 3FT Hon
Entry Requirements: *GCE:* 240.

G56 GOLDSMITHS, UNIVERSITY OF LONDON
GOLDSMITHS, UNIVERSITY OF LONDON
NEW CROSS
LONDON SE14 6NW
t: 020 7048 5300 f: 020 7919 7509
e: admissions@gold.ac.uk
// www.gold.ac.uk

W200 BA Design
Duration: 3FT Hon
Entry Requirements: *GCE:* BBC. *SQAH:* BBBCC. *SQAAH:* BBC.
Interview required. Portfolio required.

W201 BA Design, Creativity and Learning
Duration: 3FT Hon
Entry Requirements: *GCE:* BBC. *SQAH:* BBCCC. *SQAAH:* BCC.
Interview required. Portfolio required.

X1W2 BA Design, Creativity and Learning (with Qualified Teacher Status)
Duration: 3FT Hon   CRB Check: Required
Entry Requirements: Interview required.

G80 GRIMSBY INSTITUTE OF FURTHER AND HIGHER EDUCATION
NUNS CORNER
GRIMSBY
NE LINCOLNSHIRE DN34 5BQ
t: 0800 328 3631
e: headmissions@grimsby.ac.uk
// www.grimsby.ac.uk

W200 BA Design
Duration: 3FT Hon
Entry Requirements: *GCE:* 160-240. Interview required.

H12 HARPER ADAMS UNIVERSITY COLLEGE
NEWPORT
SHROPSHIRE TF10 8NB
t: 01952 820280 f: 01952 813210
e: admissions@harper-adams.ac.uk
// www.harper-adams.ac.uk

23WH BSc Off-Road Vehicle Design (top-up)
Duration: 1.5FT/1FT Hon/Ord
Entry Requirements: Interview required. HND required.

H24 HERIOT-WATT UNIVERSITY, EDINBURGH
EDINBURGH CAMPUS
EDINBURGH EH14 4AS
t: 0131 449 5111 f: 0131 451 3630
e: ugadmissions@hw.ac.uk
// www.hw.ac.uk

JW42 BSc Fashion Technology
Duration: 4FT Hon
Entry Requirements: *GCE:* BBB. *SQAH:* ABBB. *IB:* 30.

H36 UNIVERSITY OF HERTFORDSHIRE
UNIVERSITY ADMISSIONS SERVICE
COLLEGE LANE
HATFIELD
HERTS AL10 9AB
t: 01707 284800
// www.herts.ac.uk

W285 BA Interactive Media Design
Duration: 3FT/4SW Hon
Entry Requirements: *GCE:* 240.

W292 BA Model Design and Model Effects
Duration: 3FT Hon
Entry Requirements: *GCE:* 240. Interview required. Portfolio required.

WH66 BSc Digital Film and Television Technology
Duration: 3FT/4SW Hon
Entry Requirements: *GCE:* 240.

WF64 BSc Digital Forensic Technology
Duration: 3FT/4SW Hon
Entry Requirements: *GCE:* 240.

WH6P BSc Digital Rights Technology
Duration: 3FT/4SW Hon
Entry Requirements: *GCE:* 240.

W286 BSc Interactive Media Software
Duration: 3FT/4SW Hon
Entry Requirements: Contact the institution for details.

W283 FdA Media Production
Duration: 2FT Fdg
Entry Requirements: *GCE:* 80. Interview required. Portfolio required.

H54 HOPWOOD HALL COLLEGE
ROCHDALE ROAD
MIDDLETON
MANCHESTER M24 6XH
t: 0161 643 7560 f: 0161 643 2114
e: admissions@hopwood.ac.uk
// www.hopwood.ac.uk

W280 FdA New Media Design
Duration: 2FT Fdg
Entry Requirements: *Foundation:* Pass. *GCE:* 60. Interview required. Portfolio required.

H60 THE UNIVERSITY OF HUDDERSFIELD
QUEENSGATE
HUDDERSFIELD HD1 3DH
t: 01484 473969 f: 01484 472765
e: admissionsandrecords@hud.ac.uk
// www.hud.ac.uk

G4W6 BA Computer Games Design
Duration: 3FT/4SW Hon
Entry Requirements: *GCE:* 320.

W4W2 BA Costume with Textiles
Duration: 4SW Hon
Entry Requirements: *GCE:* 300. *SQAH:* BBBB. *IB:* 28. Interview required. Portfolio required.

WP22 BA Fashion, Communication and Promotion
Duration: 3FT/4SW Hon
Entry Requirements: *GCE:* 300. *SQAH:* BBBB. *IB:* 28. Interview required. Portfolio required.

W228 BA(Hons) Digital Arts Practice
Duration: 3FT/4SW Hon
Entry Requirements: *GCE:* 240. Interview required. Portfolio required.

H72 THE UNIVERSITY OF HULL
THE UNIVERSITY OF HULL
COTTINGHAM ROAD
HULL HU6 7RX
t: 01482 466100 f: 01482 442290
e: admissions@hull.ac.uk
// www.hull.ac.uk

W280 BA Digital Arts
Duration: 3FT Hon
Entry Requirements: *GCE:* 260-300. *IB:* 24. *BTEC ExtDip:* DMM.

H73 HULL COLLEGE
QUEEN'S GARDENS
HULL HU1 3DG
t: 01482 329943 f: 01482 598733
e: info@hull-college.ac.uk
// www.hull-college.ac.uk/higher-education

W200 BA Applied Creative Design
Duration: 1FT Hon
Entry Requirements: Interview required. Portfolio required.

W280 BA Games Design
Duration: 3FT Hon
Entry Requirements: *GCE:* 200. Foundation Course required. Interview required. Portfolio required.

W285 BA Interactive Media
Duration: 3FT Hon
Entry Requirements: *GCE:* 200. Foundation Course required. Interview required. Portfolio required.

WW62 BA Television and Film Design
Duration: 3FT Hon
Entry Requirements: *GCE:* 200. Foundation Course required. Interview required. Portfolio required.

W281 BA Web Design
Duration: 3FT Hon
Entry Requirements: *GCE:* 200. Foundation Course required. Interview required. Portfolio required.

K24 THE UNIVERSITY OF KENT
RECRUITMENT & ADMISSIONS OFFICE
REGISTRY
UNIVERSITY OF KENT
CANTERBURY, KENT CT2 7NZ
t: 01227 827272 f: 01227 827077
e: information@kent.ac.uk
// www.kent.ac.uk

W281 BA Digital Arts
Duration: 3FT Hon
Entry Requirements: *GCE:* 320. *IB:* 33. *OCR ND:* D *OCR NED:* D2

W282 BA Digital Arts with a Year in Industry
Duration: 4FT Hon
Entry Requirements: *GCE:* 320. *IB:* 33. *OCR ND:* D *OCR NED:* D2

G4W2 BSc Multimedia Technology and Design
Duration: 3FT Hon
Entry Requirements: *GCE:* 320. *IB:* 33. *OCR ND:* D *OCR NED:* D2

G4WF BSc Multimedia Technology and Design with a year in Industry (4 years)
Duration: 4SW Hon
Entry Requirements: *GCE:* 320. *IB:* 33. *OCR ND:* D *OCR NED:* D2

K84 KINGSTON UNIVERSITY
STUDENT INFORMATION & ADVICE CENTRE
COOPER HOUSE
40-46 SURBITON ROAD
KINGSTON UPON THAMES KT1 2HX
t: 0844 8552177 f: 020 8547 7080
e: aps@kingston.ac.uk
// www.kingston.ac.uk

WN21 BA Design and Business
Duration: 3FT Hon
Entry Requirements: *GCE:* 240-320. Foundation Course required. Portfolio required.

WW26 BA Design and Film Studies
Duration: 3FT Hon
Entry Requirements: *GCE:* 240. Foundation Course required. Interview required. Portfolio required.

QW3F BA English Language & Communication and Design
Duration: 3FT Hon
Entry Requirements: *GCE:* 240-360. Interview required. Portfolio required.

W200 BA Landscape Architecture
Duration: 3FT Hon
Entry Requirements: *GCE:* 280. Interview required. Portfolio required.

WK23 BA Landscape Planning
Duration: 3FT Hon
Entry Requirements: *GCE:* 280. *IB:* 28. Interview required. Portfolio required.

W290 BA Visual & Material Culture
Duration: 3FT Hon
Entry Requirements: *GCE:* 240.

WN22 BA Visual & Material Culture and Business
Duration: 3FT Hon
Entry Requirements: *GCE:* 240-320.

W2R1 BA Visual & Material Culture with French
Duration: 3FT Hon
Entry Requirements: *GCE:* 240.

W900 BSc Creative Technology (including Foundation Year)
Duration: 4FT Hon
Entry Requirements: Contact the institution for details.

HW66 BSc Television & Video Technology
Duration: 3FT Hon
Entry Requirements: *GCE:* 240-280.

HW6P BSc Television & Video Technology
Duration: 4SW Hon
Entry Requirements: *GCE:* 240-280.

L14 LANCASTER UNIVERSITY
THE UNIVERSITY
LANCASTER
LANCASHIRE LA1 4YW
t: 01524 592029 f: 01524 846243
e: ugadmissions@lancaster.ac.uk
// www.lancs.ac.uk

NW52 BSc Marketing and Design
Duration: 3FT Hon
Entry Requirements: *GCE:* AAB. *SQAH:* ABBBB. *SQAAH:* AAB. *IB:* 35.

L23 UNIVERSITY OF LEEDS
THE UNIVERSITY OF LEEDS
WOODHOUSE LANE
LEEDS LS2 9JT
t: 0113 343 3999
e: admissions@leeds.ac.uk
// www.leeds.ac.uk

WJ29 BA/BSc Design & Technology Management
Duration: 3FT Hon
Entry Requirements: *GCE:* BBB. *SQAAH:* BBB. *IB:* 32.

L27 LEEDS METROPOLITAN UNIVERSITY
COURSE ENQUIRIES OFFICE
CITY CAMPUS
LEEDS LS1 3HE
t: 0113 81 23113 f: 0113 81 23129
// www.leedsmet.ac.uk

WW12 BA Contemporary Art Practices
Duration: 3FT Hon
Entry Requirements: *Foundation:* Pass. *GCE:* 240. Interview required. Portfolio required.

W290 BA Design
Duration: 3FT Hon
Entry Requirements: *Foundation:* Pass. *GCE:* 160. Interview required. Portfolio required.

W291 BA Design Applied Textiles
Duration: 3FT Hon
Entry Requirements: *Foundation:* Pass. *GCE:* 160. Interview required. Portfolio required.

W280 BA Design Digital
Duration: 3FT Hon
Entry Requirements: *Foundation:* Pass. *GCE:* 160. Interview required. Portfolio required.

W292 BA Design Play
Duration: 3FT Hon
Entry Requirements: *Foundation:* Pass. *GCE:* 160. Interview required. Portfolio required.

W212 BSc Creative Media Technology
Duration: 3FT Hon
Entry Requirements: *GCE:* 200. *IB:* 24. Interview required.

GW4G BSc Multimedia & Entertainment Technology (Top-up)
Duration: 1FT Hon
Entry Requirements: Contact the institution for details.

L39 UNIVERSITY OF LINCOLN
ADMISSIONS
BRAYFORD POOL
LINCOLN LN6 7TS
t: 01522 886097 f: 01522 886146
e: admissions@lincoln.ac.uk
// www.lincoln.ac.uk

WP21 BA Design for Exhibition and Museums
Duration: 3FT Hon
Entry Requirements: *GCE:* 280. Interview required. Portfolio required.

W290 BA Graphic Design
Duration: 3FT Hon
Entry Requirements: *GCE:* 280. Interview required. Portfolio required.

W219 BA Interactive Design
Duration: 3FT Hon
Entry Requirements: *GCE:* 280. Interview required. Portfolio required.

W200 BA Product Design
Duration: 3FT/4SW Hon
Entry Requirements: *GCE:* 280. Interview required. Portfolio required.

L41 THE UNIVERSITY OF LIVERPOOL
THE FOUNDATION BUILDING
BROWNLOW HILL
LIVERPOOL L69 7ZX
t: 0151 794 2000 f: 0151 708 6502
e: ugrecruitment@liv.ac.uk
// www.liv.ac.uk

WN23 BA Communication, Media and Popular Music
Duration: 3FT Hon
Entry Requirements: *GCE:* ABB. *SQAAH:* ABB. *IB:* 33.

L43 LIVERPOOL COMMUNITY COLLEGE
LIVERPOOL COMMUNITY COLLEGE
CLARENCE STREET
LIVERPOOL L3 5TP
t: 0151 252 3352 f: 0151 252 3351
e: enquiry@liv-coll.ac.uk
// www.liv-coll.ac.uk

WJ24 FdA Fashion & Clothing Technology
Duration: 2FT Fdg
Entry Requirements: Contact the institution for details.

L46 LIVERPOOL HOPE UNIVERSITY
HOPE PARK
LIVERPOOL L16 9JD
t: 0151 291 3331 f: 0151 291 3434
e: administration@hope.ac.uk
// www.hope.ac.uk

W200 BDes Design
Duration: 3FT Hon
Entry Requirements: *GCE:* 300-320. *IB:* 25. Interview required.

L51 LIVERPOOL JOHN MOORES UNIVERSITY
KINGSWAY HOUSE
HATTON GARDEN
LIVERPOOL L3 2AJ
t: 0151 231 5090 f: 0151 904 6368
e: courses@ljmu.ac.uk
// www.ljmu.ac.uk

W240 BSc Product Innovation and Development
Duration: 3FT/4SW Hon
Entry Requirements: *GCE:* 280. *OCR ND:* M2 *OCR NED:* M2
Interview required.

L62 THE LONDON COLLEGE, UCK
VICTORIA GARDENS
NOTTING HILL GATE
LONDON W11 3PE
t: 020 7243 4000 f: 020 7243 1484
e: admissions@lcuck.ac.uk
// www.lcuck.ac.uk

082W HNC Interactive Media
Duration: 1FT HNC
Entry Requirements: Contact the institution for details.

182W HND Interactive Media
Duration: 2FT HND
Entry Requirements: Contact the institution for details.

L68 LONDON METROPOLITAN UNIVERSITY
166-220 HOLLOWAY ROAD
LONDON N7 8DB
t: 020 7133 4200
e: admissions@londonmet.ac.uk
// www.londonmet.ac.uk

W000 BA Art, Media, Design Extended Degree
Duration: 4FT Hon
Entry Requirements: *GCE:* 80. *IB:* 28. Interview required. Portfolio required.

W280 BA Fine Art (Mixed Media)
Duration: 3FT Hon
Entry Requirements: *Foundation:* Pass. *GCE:* 280. *IB:* 28.
Foundation Course required. Interview required. Portfolio required.

W283 FdA Digital Media Design
Duration: 2FT Fdg
Entry Requirements: *GCE:* 160. Interview required. Portfolio required.

L75 LONDON SOUTH BANK UNIVERSITY
ADMISSIONS AND RECRUITMENT CENTRE
90 LONDON ROAD
LONDON SE1 6LN
t: 0800 923 8888 f: 020 7815 8273
e: course.enquiry@lsbu.ac.uk
// www.lsbu.ac.uk

GW52 BSc Computer Aided Design
Duration: 3FT/4SW Hon
Entry Requirements: *GCE:* 200. *IB:* 24.

L79 LOUGHBOROUGH UNIVERSITY
LOUGHBOROUGH
LEICESTERSHIRE LE11 3TU
t: 01509 223522 f: 01509 223905
e: admissions@lboro.ac.uk
// www.lboro.ac.uk

WJ24 BA Textiles: Innovation and Design
Duration: 3FT Hon
Entry Requirements: *GCE:* 320. *IB:* 32. *BTEC ExtDip:* DDM.
Interview required. Portfolio required.

M10 THE MANCHESTER COLLEGE
OPENSHAW CAMPUS
ASHTON OLD ROAD
OPENSHAW
MANCHESTER M11 2WH
t: 0800 068 8585 f: 0161 920 4103
e: enquiries@themanchestercollege.ac.uk
// www.themanchestercollege.ac.uk

W281 BA Creative Media and Visual Communication
Duration: 1FT Hon
Entry Requirements: Portfolio required. HND required.

W230 FdA Fashion and Clothing Technology
Duration: 2FT Fdg
Entry Requirements: *GCE:* 160. *BTEC ExtDip:* MPP.

W280 FdA New Media Design
Duration: 2FT Fdg
Entry Requirements: *Foundation:* Pass. *GCE:* 160. *BTEC ExtDip:* MPP. Portfolio required.

M20 THE UNIVERSITY OF MANCHESTER
RUTHERFORD BUILDING
OXFORD ROAD
MANCHESTER M13 9PL
t: 0161 275 2077 f: 0161 275 2106
e: ug-admissions@manchester.ac.uk
// www.manchester.ac.uk

W290 BSc Design Management for Fashion Retailing
Duration: 3FT Hon
Entry Requirements: *GCE:* AAB. *SQAAH:* AAB. *IB:* 35.

J4W2 BSc Textile Design and Design Management
Duration: 3FT Hon
Entry Requirements: *GCE:* AAB. *SQAAH:* AAB. *IB:* 35.

M40 THE MANCHESTER METROPOLITAN UNIVERSITY
ADMISSIONS OFFICE
ALL SAINTS (GMS)
ALL SAINTS
MANCHESTER M15 6BH
t: 0161 247 2000
// www.mmu.ac.uk

WJF4 BA Clothing Design and Technology
Duration: 3FT Hon
Entry Requirements: *GCE:* 200. *IB:* 25. Portfolio required.

WJG4 BA Fashion Design and Technology
Duration: 3FT/4SW Hon
Entry Requirements: *GCE:* 240-280. *IB:* 29.

WJ29 BSc Product Design and Technology
Duration: 3FT/4SW Hon
Entry Requirements: *GCE:* 280. *IB:* 27. *OCR NED:* M2

WJF9 BSc Product Design and Technology (Foundation)
Duration: 4FT/5SW Hon
Entry Requirements: *GCE:* 160. *IB:* 24. *BTEC Dip:* MM. *BTEC ExtDip:* MPP.

WG6L FdSc Post Production Technology for Film, TV and CGI
Duration: 2FT Fdg
Entry Requirements: *GCE:* 280. *IB:* 28.

M99 MYERSCOUGH COLLEGE
MYERSCOUGH HALL
BILSBORROW
PRESTON PR3 0RY
t: 01995 642222 f: 01995 642333
e: enquiries@myerscough.ac.uk
// www.myerscough.ac.uk

DW4F BA Commercial Floral Design (Top up)
Duration: 1FT Hon
Entry Requirements: Interview required.

WD24 FdA Commercial Floral Design
Duration: 2FT Fdg
Entry Requirements: *GCE:* A-C. *SQAH:* AA-CC. *SQAAH:* A-C. *IB:* 24. Interview required.

N23 NEWCASTLE COLLEGE
STUDENT SERVICES
RYE HILL CAMPUS
SCOTSWOOD ROAD
NEWCASTLE UPON TYNE NE4 7SA
t: 0191 200 4110 f: 0191 200 4349
e: enquiries@ncl-coll.ac.uk
// www.newcastlecollege.co.uk

WN25 FdA Creative Advertising
Duration: 2FT Fdg
Entry Requirements: *GCE:* 120-165. *OCR ND:* P2 *OCR NED:* P3 Foundation Course required. Interview required. Portfolio required.

W280 FdA Web Design
Duration: 2FT Fdg
Entry Requirements: *GCE:* 120-165. *OCR ND:* P2 *OCR NED:* P3 Foundation Course required. Interview required. Portfolio required.

WG24 FdSc Computing for Games and Interactive Media
Duration: 2FT Fdg
Entry Requirements: *GCE:* 160. *OCR ND:* P1 *OCR NED:* P2 Interview required.

WG2K FdSc Games Development
Duration: 2FT Fdg
Entry Requirements: *GCE:* 160. *OCR ND:* P1 *OCR NED:* P2 Interview required.

N30 NEW COLLEGE NOTTINGHAM
ADAMS BUILDING
STONEY STREET
THE LACE MARKET
NOTTINGHAM NG1 1NG
t: 0115 910 0100 f: 0115 953 4349
e: he.team@ncn.ac.uk
// www.ncn.ac.uk

W200 BA Design (Top-up)
Duration: 1FT Hon
Entry Requirements: Interview required. Portfolio required. HND required.

W201 FdA Design
Duration: 2FT Fdg
Entry Requirements: *GCE:* 120-240. Interview required. Portfolio required.

WN25 FdA Fashion Interpretation and Creative Cutting
Duration: 2FT Fdg
Entry Requirements: *GCE:* 80-240. Interview required. Portfolio required.

W280 FdA Multimedia (Web Design)
Duration: 2FT Fdg
Entry Requirements: *GCE:* 100-240. Interview required. Portfolio required.

N37 UNIVERSITY OF WALES, NEWPORT
ADMISSIONS
LODGE ROAD
CAERLEON
NEWPORT NP18 3QT
t: 01633 432030 f: 01633 432850
e: admissions@newport.ac.uk
// www.newport.ac.uk

WGF4 BA Computer Games Design
Duration: 3FT Hon
Entry Requirements: *Foundation:* Merit. *GCE:* 240-260. *IB:* 24. Interview required. Portfolio required.

X1WG BSc Secondary Design and Technology with QTS
Duration: 3FT Hon   CRB Check: Required
Entry Requirements: *GCE:* 200. *IB:* 24. Interview required.

X1W2 BSc Secondary Design and Technology with QTS (2 years)
Duration: 2FT Ord   CRB Check: Required
Entry Requirements: Interview required.

N38 UNIVERSITY OF NORTHAMPTON
PARK CAMPUS
BOUGHTON GREEN ROAD
NORTHAMPTON NN2 7AL
t: 0800 358 2232 f: 01604 722083
e: admissions@northampton.ac.uk
// www.northampton.ac.uk

NWM2 BA Fashion Marketing
Duration: 3FT Hon
Entry Requirements: *GCE:* 260-300. *SQAH:* ABBB. *IB:* 25. *BTEC Dip:* DD. *BTEC ExtDip:* DMM. *OCR ND:* D *OCR NED:* M2

W6L9 BA Film & Television Studies/International Development
Duration: 3FT Hon
Entry Requirements: *GCE:* 260-280. *SQAH:* AAA-BBBB. *IB:* 24. *BTEC Dip:* DD. *BTEC ExtDip:* DMM. *OCR ND:* D *OCR NED:* M2

W1LX BA Fine Art Painting & Drawing/International Development
Duration: 3FT Hon
Entry Requirements: *GCE:* 260-280. *SQAH:* AAA-BBBB. *IB:* 24. *BTEC Dip:* DD. *BTEC ExtDip:* DMM. *OCR ND:* D *OCR NED:* M2

L9W6 BA International Development./Film & Television Studies
Duration: 3FT Hon
Entry Requirements: *GCE:* 260-280. *SQAH:* AAA-BBBB. *IB:* 24. *BTEC Dip:* DD. *BTEC ExtDip:* DMM. *OCR ND:* D *OCR NED:* M2

L9WC BA International Development/Fine Art Painting and Drawing
Duration: 3FT Hon
Entry Requirements: *GCE:* 260-280. *SQAH:* AAA-BBBB. *IB:* 24. *BTEC Dip:* DD. *BTEC ExtDip:* DMM. *OCR ND:* D *OCR NED:* M2

42GW HND Interactive Digital Media
Duration: 2FT HND
Entry Requirements: *GCE:* 140-160. *SQAH:* BC-CCC. *IB:* 24. *BTEC Dip:* MP. *BTEC ExtDip:* MPP. *OCR ND:* P1 *OCR NED:* P2 Interview required.

N58 NORTH EAST WORCESTERSHIRE COLLEGE
PEAKMAN STREET
REDDITCH
WORCESTERSHIRE B98 8DW
t: 01527 570020 f: 01527 572901
e: admissions@ne-worcs.ac.uk
// www.ne-worcs.ac.uk

WG24 FdA Interactive Media and Games Development
Duration: 2FT Fdg
Entry Requirements: *GCE:* 120. Interview required.

N61 NORTH GLASGOW COLLEGE

123 FLEMINGTON ST
SPRINGBURN
GLASGOW G21 4TD
t: 0141 630 5150
e: g.mcdonald@north-gla.ac.uk
// northglasgowcollege.ac.uk

W290 BA Hons Jewellery Design and Technology
Duration: 1FT Hon
Entry Requirements: Contact the institution for details.

N77 NORTHUMBRIA UNIVERSITY

TRINITY BUILDING
NORTHUMBERLAND ROAD
NEWCASTLE UPON TYNE NE1 8ST
t: 0191 243 7420 f: 0191 227 4561
e: er.admissions@northumbria.ac.uk
// www.northumbria.ac.uk

W280 BA Interactive Media Design
Duration: 3FT Hon
Entry Requirements: *Foundation:* Distinction. *GCE:* 280. *SQAH:* BBCCC. *SQAAH:* BCC. *IB:* 25. *OCR NED:* M2 Interview required. Portfolio required.

WJ29 BA Transportation Design
Duration: 4SW Hon
Entry Requirements: *Foundation:* Distinction. *GCE:* 300. *SQAH:* BBBBC. *SQAAH:* BBC. *IB:* 26. *BTEC Dip:* DM. *BTEC ExtDip:* DDM. *OCR NED:* M2 Interview required. Portfolio required.

GW42 BSc Computer Games Design and Production
Duration: 4SW Hon
Entry Requirements: *GCE:* 280. *SQAH:* BBCCC. *SQAAH:* BCC. *IB:* 25. *BTEC Dip:* D*D*. *BTEC ExtDip:* DMM. *OCR NED:* M2

WJ2X BSc Product Design Technology
Duration: 3FT/4SW Hon
Entry Requirements: *GCE:* 280. *SQAH:* BBCCC. *SQAAH:* BCC. *IB:* 25. *BTEC ExtDip:* DMM. *OCR NED:* M3 Interview required. Portfolio required.

WJ2Y BSc Product Design Technology
Duration: 4FT/5SW Hon
Entry Requirements: *GCE:* 200. *SQAH:* CCCC. *IB:* 24. *BTEC Dip:* DM. *OCR ND:* M1 *OCR NED:* P1

N79 NORTH WARWICKSHIRE AND HINCKLEY COLLEGE

HINCKLEY ROAD
NUNEATON
WARWICKSHIRE CV11 6BH
t: 024 7624 3395
e: angela.jones@nwhc.ac.uk
// www.nwhc.ac.uk

312W HND Visual Communication
Duration: 2FT HND
Entry Requirements: *GCE:* 140. Portfolio required.

N91 NOTTINGHAM TRENT UNIVERSITY

DRYDEN BUILDING
BURTON STREET
NOTTINGHAM NG1 4BU
t: +44 (0) 115 848 4200 f: +44 (0) 115 848 8869
e: applications@ntu.ac.uk
// www.ntu.ac.uk

W280 BA Design for Film and Television
Duration: 3FT Hon
Entry Requirements: *GCE:* 280. Interview required. Portfolio required.

NWP0 BA Marketing, Design and Communication
Duration: 3FT Hon
Entry Requirements: *GCE:* 300. *OCR NED:* D2

XWC2 BSc Secondary Design and Technology Education
Duration: 3FT Hon **CRB Check:** Required
Entry Requirements: *GCE:* 240. *BTEC ExtDip:* MMM. *OCR NED:* M3 Interview required. Admissions Test required.

P35 PEMBROKESHIRE COLLEGE (ACCREDITED COLLEGE OF UNIVERSITY OF GLAMORGAN)

HAVERFORDWEST
PEMBROKESHIRE SA61 1SZ
t: 01437 753000 f: 01437 753001
e: admissions@pembrokeshire.ac.uk
// www.pembrokeshire.ac.uk

W200 BA Design Studies
Duration: 3FT Hon
Entry Requirements: *GCE:* 140.

P60 PLYMOUTH UNIVERSITY
DRAKE CIRCUS
PLYMOUTH PL4 8AA
t: 01752 585858 f: 01752 588055
e: admissions@plymouth.ac.uk
// www.plymouth.ac.uk

GW4X BA Digital Art and Technology
Duration: 3FT Hon
Entry Requirements: *Foundation:* Distinction. *GCE:* 280. *IB:* 26.
BTEC ExtDip: DMM.

W200 BA Media Arts
Duration: 3FT Hon
Entry Requirements: *GCE:* 280. *IB:* 27. *BTEC ExtDip:* DMM.

GW49 BSc Digital Art and Technology
Duration: 3FT Hon
Entry Requirements: *GCE:* 280. *IB:* 25. *BTEC ExtDip:* DMM.

P65 PLYMOUTH COLLEGE OF ART (FORMERLY PLYMOUTH COLLEGE OF ART AND DESIGN)
TAVISTOCK PLACE
PLYMOUTH PL4 8AT
t: 01752 203434 f: 01752 203444
e: infoservices@plymouthart.ac.uk
// www.plymouthart.ac.uk

WWDF BA Contemporary Art and Media Practice
Duration: 3FT Hon
Entry Requirements: Contact the institution for details.

W200 BA Interdisciplinary Design
Duration: 3FT Hon
Entry Requirements: Contact the institution for details.

WWCG FdA Contemporary Art and Media Practice
Duration: 2FT Fdg
Entry Requirements: Contact the institution for details.

WW1G FdA Contemporary Art and Media Practice (with Year 0)
Duration: 3FT Fdg
Entry Requirements: Contact the institution for details.

P80 UNIVERSITY OF PORTSMOUTH
ACADEMIC REGISTRY
UNIVERSITY HOUSE
WINSTON CHURCHILL AVENUE
PORTSMOUTH PO1 2UP
t: 023 9284 8484 f: 023 9284 3082
e: admissions@port.ac.uk
// www.port.ac.uk

PW36 BA Media Studies and Entertainment Technology
Duration: 3FT Hon
Entry Requirements: *GCE:* 240-300. *IB:* 25. *BTEC SubDip:* P.
BTEC Dip: DD. *BTEC ExtDip:* DMM.

GW42 BSc Computing and the Digital Image
Duration: 3FT/4SW Hon
Entry Requirements: *GCE:* 260-300. *IB:* 26. *BTEC SubDip:* P.
BTEC Dip: PP. *BTEC ExtDip:* DMM.

Q50 QUEEN MARY, UNIVERSITY OF LONDON
QUEEN MARY, UNIVERSITY OF LONDON
MILE END ROAD
LONDON E1 4NS
t: 020 7882 5555 f: 020 7882 5500
e: admissions@qmul.ac.uk
// www.qmul.ac.uk

WH21 BEng Design & Innovation
Duration: 3FT Hon
Entry Requirements: *GCE:* 300. *IB:* 32. Interview required.
Portfolio required.

W242 BEng Design and Innovation with Industrial Experience
Duration: 4FT Hon
Entry Requirements: *GCE:* 300. *IB:* 32. Interview required.
Portfolio required.

W240 MEng Design and Innovation
Duration: 4FT Hon
Entry Requirements: *GCE:* 360. *IB:* 36. Interview required.
Portfolio required.

W241 MEng Design and Innovation with Industrial Experience
Duration: 5FT Hon
Entry Requirements: *GCE:* 360. *IB:* 36. Interview required.
Portfolio required.

R06 RAVENSBOURNE

6 PENROSE WAY
GREENWICH PENINSULA
LONDON SE10 0EW
t: 020 3040 3998
e: info@rave.ac.uk
// www.rave.ac.uk

W281 BA Design Interactions

Duration: 3FT Hon
Entry Requirements: *Foundation:* Pass. *GCE:* AA-CC. *IB:* 28.
Interview required. Portfolio required.

W283 BA Design Interactions (Fast-Track)

Duration: 2FT Hon
Entry Requirements: Contact the institution for details.

W282 BA Design Interactions (with Foundation Year)

Duration: 4FT Hon
Entry Requirements: *Foundation:* Pass. *GCE:* A-E. *IB:* 28.
Interview required. Portfolio required.

NWM2 BA Digital Advertising and Design (Fast-Track)

Duration: 2FT Hon
Entry Requirements: Contact the institution for details.

NW5F BA Digital Advertising and Design (with Foundation Year)

Duration: 4FT Hon
Entry Requirements: Contact the institution for details.

NWN2 BA Fashion Promotion (Fast-Track)

Duration: 2FT Hon
Entry Requirements: Contact the institution for details.

W280 BA Motion Graphics

Duration: 3FT Hon
Entry Requirements: *Foundation:* Pass. *GCE:* AA-CC. *IB:* 28.
Interview required. Portfolio required.

W284 BA Motion Graphics (Fast-Track)

Duration: 2FT Hon
Entry Requirements: Contact the institution for details.

R20 RICHMOND, THE AMERICAN INTERNATIONAL UNIVERSITY IN LONDON

QUEENS ROAD
RICHMOND
SURREY TW10 6JP
t: 020 8332 9000 f: 020 8332 1596
e: enroll@richmond.ac.uk
// www.richmond.ac.uk

WW12 BA Creative Arts and Communications: Art, Design and Media

Duration: 3FT/4FT Hon
Entry Requirements: *GCE:* 260. *IB:* 33.

R51 ROSE BRUFORD COLLEGE

LAMORBEY PARK
BURNT OAK LANE
SIDCUP
KENT DA15 9DF
t: 0208 308 2600 f: 020 8308 0542
e: enquiries@bruford.ac.uk
// www.bruford.ac.uk

W4W2 BA Lighting Design

Duration: 3FT Hon
Entry Requirements: *GCE:* 160-280.

S05 SAE INSTITUTE

297 KINGSLAND ROAD
LONDON E8 4DD
t: 020 7923 9159
e: degree.registry@sae.edu
// www.sae.edu

W281 BA/BSc Web Development

Duration: 2FT Hon
Entry Requirements: Contact the institution for details.

W282 DipHE Web Development

Duration: 1.5FT Dip
Entry Requirements: Contact the institution for details.

S21 SHEFFIELD HALLAM UNIVERSITY

CITY CAMPUS
HOWARD STREET
SHEFFIELD S1 1WB
t: 0114 225 5555 f: 0114 225 2167
e: admissions@shu.ac.uk
// www.shu.ac.uk

W280 BA Games Design

Duration: 3FT Hon
Entry Requirements: *GCE:* 260.

HW12 BSc Computer-Aided Design Technology
Duration: 3FT/4SW Hon
Entry Requirements: *GCE:* 240.

WH21 BSc Design Technology
Duration: 3FT/4SW Hon
Entry Requirements: *GCE:* 240.

XW12 BSc Design and Technology with Education and Qualified Teacher Status
Duration: 3FT Hon
Entry Requirements: *GCE:* 200.

GWP2 BSc Games & Interactive Media Technologies (Top-Up)
Duration: 1FT Hon
Entry Requirements: HND required.

XWC2 BSc Secondary Education in Design and Technology for QTS (2 years)
Duration: 2FT Hon
Entry Requirements: Contact the institution for details.

W281 MArt Games Design
Duration: 4FT Hon
Entry Requirements: *GCE:* 280.

S28 SOMERSET COLLEGE OF ARTS AND TECHNOLOGY
WELLINGTON ROAD
TAUNTON
SOMERSET TA1 5AX
t: 01823 366331 f: 01823 366418
e: enquiries@somerset.ac.uk
// www.somerset.ac.uk/student-area/considering-a-degree.html

JW52 BA Design: Packaging (Top-Up)
Duration: 1FT Hon
Entry Requirements: HND required.

S30 SOUTHAMPTON SOLENT UNIVERSITY
EAST PARK TERRACE
SOUTHAMPTON
HAMPSHIRE SO14 0RT
t: +44 (0) 23 8031 9039 f: + 44 (0)23 8022 2259
e: admissions@solent.ac.uk
// www.solent.ac.uk/

W2NB BA Fashion Management with Marketing
Duration: 3FT Hon
Entry Requirements: *Foundation:* Distinction. *GCE:* 240. *SQAAH:* AA-CCD. *IB:* 24. *BTEC ExtDip:* MMM. *OCR ND:* D *OCR NED:* M3

W290 BA Fashion Styling
Duration: 3FT Hon
Entry Requirements: *Foundation:* Merit. *GCE:* 200. *SQAAH:* AC-DDD. *IB:* 24. *BTEC ExtDip:* MMP. *OCR ND:* M1 *OCR NED:* P1 Interview required. Portfolio required.

W29D BA Fashion Writing (Top-Up)
Duration: 1FT Hon
Entry Requirements: Interview required. HND required.

WJ26 BEng Yacht & Powercraft Design wth International Foundation Year (Intl only, Jan)
Duration: 4FT Hon
Entry Requirements: Contact the institution for details.

W243 BSc Watersports Technology
Duration: 3FT Hon
Entry Requirements: *GCE:* 180.

W244 BSc Watersports Technology (with Foundation Year)
Duration: 4FT Hon
Entry Requirements: Contact the institution for details.

S35 SOUTHPORT COLLEGE
MORNINGTON ROAD
SOUTHPORT
MERSEYSIDE PR9 0TT
t: 08450066236 f: 01704 392610
e: guidance@southport-college.ac.uk
// www.southport-college.ac.uk

WG24 FdSc New Media Design & Technology
Duration: 2FT Fdg
Entry Requirements: *GCE:* 160.

S41 SOUTH CHESHIRE COLLEGE
DANE BANK AVENUE
CREWE CW2 8AB
t: 01270 654654 f: 01270 651515
e: admissions@s-cheshire.ac.uk
// www.s-cheshire.ac.uk

W280 FdA Graphics and Digital Media
Duration: 2FT Fdg
Entry Requirements: Interview required. Portfolio required.

S43 SOUTH ESSEX COLLEGE OF FURTHER & HIGHER EDUCATION
LUKER ROAD
SOUTHEND-ON-SEA
ESSEX SS1 1ND
t: 0845 52 12345 f: 01702 432320
e: Admissions@southessex.ac.uk
// www.southessex.ac.uk

WG24 BSc Computer Games Design
Duration: 3FT Hon
Entry Requirements: *GCE:* 160. *IB:* 24. Interview required.

S46 SOUTH NOTTINGHAM COLLEGE
WEST BRIDGFORD CENTRE
GREYTHORN DRIVE
WEST BRIDGFORD
NOTTINGHAM NG2 7GA
t: 0115 914 6400 f: 0115 914 6444
e: enquiries@snc.ac.uk
// www.snc.ac.uk

W212 FdA Computer Games and Interactive Media (Arts Route)
Duration: 2FT Fdg
Entry Requirements: *GCE:* 160. Interview required.

W280 FdSc Computer Games and Interactive Media (Science Route)
Duration: 2FT Fdg
Entry Requirements: *GCE:* 160. Interview required.

S51 ST HELENS COLLEGE
WATER STREET
ST HELENS
MERSEYSIDE WA10 1PP
t: 01744 733766 f: 01744 623400
e: enquiries@sthelens.ac.uk
// www.sthelens.ac.uk

W282 BA Game Art
Duration: 3FT Hon
Entry Requirements: Contact the institution for details.

S72 STAFFORDSHIRE UNIVERSITY
COLLEGE ROAD
STOKE ON TRENT ST4 2DE
t: 01782 292753 f: 01782 292740
e: admissions@staffs.ac.uk
// www.staffs.ac.uk

W201 BA Design with Foundation Year
Duration: 4FT Hon
Entry Requirements: *Foundation:* Merit. *GCE:* 200-240. *IB:* 24.
BTEC Dip: DD. *BTEC ExtDip:* MMM. Interview required. Portfolio required.

W294 BA Entrepreneurship in Graphics and Digital Media
Duration: 1FT Hon
Entry Requirements: Interview required. Portfolio required.

W283 BA Entrepreneurship in New Media
Duration: 1FT Hon
Entry Requirements: Interview required. Portfolio required.

W293 BA Transport Design
Duration: 3FT/4FT Hon
Entry Requirements: *Foundation:* Merit. *GCE:* 200-240. *IB:* 24.
BTEC Dip: DD. *BTEC ExtDip:* MMM. Interview required. Portfolio required.

W200 BA VFX: Visual Effects and Concept Design
Duration: 3FT/4FT Hon
Entry Requirements: *Foundation:* Merit. *GCE:* 200-240. *IB:* 24.
BTEC Dip: DD. *BTEC ExtDip:* MMM. Interview required. Portfolio required.

W618 BSc Digital Film and Post Production Technology
Duration: 3FT/4SW Hon
Entry Requirements: *GCE:* 240-280. *IB:* 24.

W610 BSc Film Production Technology
Duration: 3FT Hon
Entry Requirements: *GCE:* 240-280. *IB:* 24.

W690 BSc Film Production Technology (Top-Up)
Duration: 2FT Hon
Entry Requirements: Contact the institution for details.

P3W6 FdSc Film and Television Production Technology with Sound
Duration: 2FT Fdg
Entry Requirements: *GCE:* 120. Interview required.

S76 STOCKPORT COLLEGE
WELLINGTON ROAD SOUTH
STOCKPORT SK1 3UQ
t: 0161 958 3143 f: 0161 958 3663
e: susan.kelly@stockport.ac.uk
// www.stockport.ac.uk

WN25 FdA Design and Advertising
Duration: 2FT Fdg
Entry Requirements: Contact the institution for details.

S78 THE UNIVERSITY OF STRATHCLYDE
GLASGOW G1 1XQ
t: 0141 552 4400 f: 0141 552 0775
// www.strath.ac.uk

W240 BSc Product Design and Innovation
Duration: 4FT Hon
Entry Requirements: *GCE:* A*AA-ABB. *SQAH:* AAAA-AAABBB. *IB:*
34. Interview required.

S79 STRANMILLIS UNIVERSITY COLLEGE: A COLLEGE OF QUEEN'S UNIVERSITY BELFAST
STRANMILLIS ROAD
BELFAST BT9 5DY
t: 028 9038 1271 f: 028 9038 4444
e: Registry@stran.ac.uk
// www.stran.ac.uk

XW12 BEd Technology & Design with Education
Duration: 4FT Hon   CRB Check: Required
Entry Requirements: *GCE:* BCC. *OCR ND:* M2 *OCR NED:* M2
Interview required.

S82 UNIVERSITY CAMPUS SUFFOLK (UCS)
WATERFRONT BUILDING
NEPTUNE QUAY
IPSWICH
SUFFOLK IP4 1QJ
t: 01473 338833 f: 01473 339900
e: info@ucs.ac.uk
// www.ucs.ac.uk

GW42 BA Computer Games Design
Duration: 3FT Hon
Entry Requirements: *GCE:* 240-280. *IB:* 28. *BTEC ExtDip:* DMM.
Interview required. Portfolio required.

S84 UNIVERSITY OF SUNDERLAND
STUDENT HELPLINE
THE STUDENT GATEWAY
CHESTER ROAD
SUNDERLAND SR1 3SD
t: 0191 515 3000 f: 0191 515 3805
e: student.helpline@sunderland.ac.uk
// www.sunderland.ac.uk

W280 BA Design: Multimedia and Graphics
Duration: 3FT Hon
Entry Requirements: *Foundation:* Merit. *GCE:* 220. *SQAH:* BBBC.
IB: 22. Interview required. Portfolio required.

H3WF BEng Automotive Engineering
Duration: 3FT/4SW Hon
Entry Requirements: *GCE:* 260. *IB:* 24. *OCR ND:* D *OCR NED:* M3

H3W2 BEng Mechanical Engineering
Duration: 3FT/4SW Hon
Entry Requirements: *GCE:* 260. *IB:* 24. *OCR ND:* D *OCR NED:* M3

S96 SWANSEA METROPOLITAN UNIVERSITY
MOUNT PLEASANT CAMPUS
SWANSEA SA1 6ED
t: 01792 481000 f: 01792 481061
e: gemma.green@smu.ac.uk
// www.smu.ac.uk

W283 BA Creative Computer Games Design
Duration: 3FT Hon
Entry Requirements: *GCE:* 200-360. *IB:* 24. Interview required.

WG24 BA Interactive Digital Media
Duration: 3FT Hon
Entry Requirements: *GCE:* 200-360. *IB:* 24. Interview required.

W284 BSc Product Design
Duration: 3FT Hon
Entry Requirements: *GCE:* 240-360. *IB:* 24. Interview required.
Portfolio required.

T20 TEESSIDE UNIVERSITY
MIDDLESBROUGH TS1 3BA
t: 01642 218121 f: 01642 384201
e: registry@tees.ac.uk
// www.tees.ac.uk

W212 BA Computer Games Art
Duration: 3FT/4SW Hon
Entry Requirements: *Foundation:* Distinction. *IB:* 30. *OCR ND:* D
OCR NED: M2 Interview required. Portfolio required.

W283 BA Computer Games Art (incorporating Foundation Year)
Duration: 4FT/5SW Hon
Entry Requirements: *IB:* 28. *OCR ND:* M1 *OCR NED:* P1 Interview required.

GWL2 BA Computer Games Design (incorporating Foundation Year)
Duration: 4FT/5SW Hon
Entry Requirements: *IB:* 28. *OCR ND:* M1 *OCR NED:* P1 Interview required.

T80 UNIVERSITY OF WALES TRINITY SAINT DAVID
COLLEGE ROAD
CARMARTHEN SA31 3EP
t: 01267 676767 f: 01267 676766
e: registry@trinitysaintdavid.ac.uk
// www.tsd.ac.uk

WW12 BA Celf a Dylunio
Duration: 3FT Hon
Entry Requirements: Contact the institution for details.

U20 UNIVERSITY OF ULSTER
COLERAINE
CO. LONDONDERRY
NORTHERN IRELAND BT52 1SA
t: 028 7012 4221 f: 028 7012 4908
e: online@ulster.ac.uk
// www.ulster.ac.uk

W900 BA Creative Technologies
Duration: 3FT Hon
Entry Requirements: *GCE:* 240. *IB:* 24. Interview required. Portfolio required.

H1W2 BSc Technology with Design
Duration: 4SW Hon
Entry Requirements: *GCE:* 280. *IB:* 24. Interview required. Admissions Test required.

U40 UNIVERSITY OF THE WEST OF SCOTLAND
PAISLEY
RENFREWSHIRE
SCOTLAND PA1 2BE
t: 0141 848 3727 f: 0141 848 3623
e: admissions@uws.ac.uk
// www.uws.ac.uk

W901 BA Contemporary Art Practice
Duration: 1FT/2FT Ord/Hon
Entry Requirements: Contact the institution for details.

W290 BA Digital Art
Duration: 3FT/4FT Ord/Hon
Entry Requirements: *GCE:* CC. *SQAH:* BCC. Portfolio required.

U65 UNIVERSITY OF THE ARTS LONDON
272 HIGH HOLBORN
LONDON WC1V 7EY
t: 020 7514 6000x6197 f: 020 7514 6198
e: c.anderson@arts.ac.uk
// www.arts.ac.uk

W245 BA Cordwainers Fashion Accessories: Product Design and Development
Duration: 3FT Hon
Entry Requirements: Foundation Course required. Interview required. Portfolio required.

W243 BA Cordwainers Footwear: Product Design and Development
Duration: 3FT Hon
Entry Requirements: Foundation Course required. Interview required. Portfolio required.

W290 BA Creative Direction for Fashion
Duration: 3FT Hon
Entry Requirements: Interview required. Portfolio required.

W292 BA Design for Graphic Communication (Top-Up)
Duration: 1FT Hon
Entry Requirements: Contact the institution for details.

W2V3 BA Fashion (Fashion History & Theory)
Duration: 3FT/4SW Hon
Entry Requirements: Interview required. Portfolio required.

W293 BA Fashion Design Technology: Menswear
Duration: 3FT Hon
Entry Requirements: Foundation Course required. Interview required. Portfolio required.

W291 BA Fashion Design Technology: Womenswear
Duration: 3FT Hon
Entry Requirements: Foundation Course required. Interview required. Portfolio required.

W241 BA Fashion Design and Development
Duration: 3FT Hon
Entry Requirements: Foundation Course required. Interview required. Portfolio required.

WPF3 BA Illustration and Visual Media
Duration: 3FT Hon
Entry Requirements: Contact the institution for details.

W284 BA Interactive Games Design (Top-Up)
Duration: 1FT Hon
Entry Requirements: Contact the institution for details.

W206 BA Jewellery Design
Duration: 3FT Hon
Entry Requirements: Interview required.

WJF4 FdA Cordwainers Footwear Design
Duration: 2FT Fdg
Entry Requirements: Foundation Course required. Interview required. Portfolio required.

WJ24 FdA Fashion Design Technology: Designer Pattern Cutter
Duration: 2FT Fdg
Entry Requirements: Foundation Course required. Interview required. Portfolio required.

W2JL FdA Fashion Design Technology: Knitwear
Duration: 2FT Fdg
Entry Requirements: Foundation Course required. Interview required. Portfolio required.

W201 FdA Graphic Design
Duration: 2FT Fdg
Entry Requirements: Interview required. Portfolio required.

W295 FdA Hair and Make up for Fashion
Duration: 2FT Fdg
Entry Requirements: *IB:* 28. Foundation Course required. Interview required. Portfolio required.

W296 FdA Hair and Make up for Film and TV
Duration: 2FT Fdg
Entry Requirements: *IB:* 28. Foundation Course required. Interview required. Portfolio required.

W297 MSc Cosmetic Science
Duration: 3FT/4FT/5SW Hon
Entry Requirements: Contact the institution for details.

W05 THE UNIVERSITY OF WEST LONDON
ST MARY'S ROAD
EALING
LONDON W5 5RF
t: 0800 036 8888 f: 020 8566 1353
e: learning.advice@uwl.ac.uk
// www.uwl.ac.uk

WW42 BA Acting for Stage and Media
Duration: 3FT Hon
Entry Requirements: *GCE:* 160. *IB:* 24. Interview required.

W280 BA Digital Arts
Duration: 3FT Hon
Entry Requirements: *GCE:* 200. *IB:* 28. Interview required. Portfolio required.

W28C BA Graphic Design (Visual Communication & Illustration)
Duration: 3FT Hon
Entry Requirements: *GCE:* 240. Interview required. Portfolio required.

JW96 BA Music Technology and Video Production
Duration: 3FT Hon
Entry Requirements: *GCE:* 200. *IB:* 28. Interview required. Portfolio required.

W08 WAKEFIELD COLLEGE
MARGARET STREET
WAKEFIELD
WEST YORKSHIRE WF1 2DH
t: 01924 789111 f: 01924 789281
e: courseinfo@wakefield.ac.uk
// www.wakefield.ac.uk

W280 FdA Web Design
Duration: 2FT Fdg
Entry Requirements: *GCE:* 120-240. Interview required.

W50 UNIVERSITY OF WESTMINSTER
2ND FLOOR, CAVENDISH HOUSE
101 NEW CAVENDISH STREET,
LONDON W1W 6XH
t: 020 7915 5511
e: course-enquiries@westminster.ac.uk
// www.westminster.ac.uk

WP23 BA Mixed Media Fine Art
Duration: 3FT Hon
Entry Requirements: *GCE:* CC. *IB:* 28. Interview required. Portfolio required.

WJ65 BSc Photography and Digital Imaging Technologies
Duration: 3FT Hon
Entry Requirements: *GCE:* CC. *SQAH:* CCCC. *IB:* 26. Interview required.

W67 WIGAN AND LEIGH COLLEGE

PO BOX 53
PARSON'S WALK
WIGAN
GREATER MANCHESTER WN1 1RS
t: 01942 761605 f: 01942 761164
e: applications@wigan-leigh.ac.uk
// www.wigan-leigh.ac.uk

W230 FdA Fashion & Clothing Technology
Duration: 2FT Fdg
Entry Requirements: Interview required. Portfolio required.

W75 UNIVERSITY OF WOLVERHAMPTON

ADMISSIONS UNIT
MX207, CAMP STREET
WOLVERHAMPTON
WEST MIDLANDS WV1 1AD
t: 01902 321000 f: 01902 321896
e: admissions@wlv.ac.uk
// www.wlv.ac.uk

W284 BA Computer Games Design
Duration: 3FT/4SW Hon
Entry Requirements: *GCE:* 200. *IB:* 24. *BTEC Dip:* DM. *BTEC ExtDip:* MMP. *OCR ND:* M1 *OCR NED:* P1 Interview required. Portfolio required.

W76 UNIVERSITY OF WINCHESTER

WINCHESTER
HANTS SO22 4NR
t: 01962 827234 f: 01962 827288
e: course.enquiries@winchester.ac.uk
// www.winchester.ac.uk

TW76 BA American Studies and Film & Cinema Technologies
Duration: 3FT Hon
Entry Requirements: *Foundation:* Distinction. *GCE:* 260-300. *IB:* 24. *OCR ND:* D *OCR NED:* M2

VWK6 BA Archaeology and Film & Cinema Technology
Duration: 3FT Hon
Entry Requirements: *Foundation:* Distinction. *GCE:* 260-300. *IB:* 24. *OCR ND:* D *OCR NED:* M2

WW56 BA Choreography & Dance and Film & Cinema Technologies
Duration: 3FT Hon
Entry Requirements: *Foundation:* Distinction. *GCE:* 260-300. *IB:* 25. *OCR ND:* D *OCR NED:* M2

WW86 BA Creative Writing and Film & Cinema Technologies
Duration: 3FT Hon
Entry Requirements: *Foundation:* Distinction. *GCE:* 260-300. *IB:* 25. *OCR ND:* D *OCR NED:* M2

LW36 BA Criminology and Film & Cinema Technology
Duration: 3FT Hon
Entry Requirements: *Foundation:* Distinction. *GCE:* 260-300. *IB:* 24. *OCR ND:* D *OCR NED:* M2

W280 BA Digital Media Design
Duration: 3FT Hon
Entry Requirements: *Foundation:* Distinction. *GCE:* 260-300. *IB:* 25. *OCR ND:* D *OCR NED:* M2

WW46 BA Drama and Film & Cinema Technologies
Duration: 3FT Hon
Entry Requirements: *Foundation:* Distinction. *GCE:* 260-300. *IB:* 25. *OCR ND:* D *OCR NED:* M2

XW36 BA Education Studies (Early Childhood) and Film & Cinema Technologies
Duration: 3FT Hon
Entry Requirements: *Foundation:* Distinction. *GCE:* 260-300. *IB:* 24. *OCR ND:* D *OCR NED:* M2

XW3P BA Education Studies and Film & Cinema Technologies
Duration: 3FT Hon
Entry Requirements: *Foundation:* Distinction. *GCE:* 260-300. *IB:* 24. *OCR ND:* D *OCR NED:* M2

QW36 BA English Language Studies and Film & Cinema Technologies
Duration: 3FT Hon
Entry Requirements: *Foundation:* Distinction. *GCE:* 260-300. *IB:* 25. *OCR ND:* D *OCR NED:* M2

WQ63 BA Film & Cinema Technologies and English
Duration: 3FT Hon
Entry Requirements: *Foundation:* Distinction. *GCE:* 260-300. *IB:* 25. *OCR ND:* D *OCR NED:* M2

WP65 BA Film & Cinema Technologies and Journalism Studies
Duration: 3FT Hon
Entry Requirements: Contact the institution for details.

WM61 BA Film & Cinema Technologies and Law
Duration: 3FT Hon
Entry Requirements: *Foundation:* Distinction. *GCE:* 260-300. *IB:* 25. *OCR ND:* D *OCR NED:* M2

WP6H BA Film & Cinema Technologies and Media Production
Duration: 3FT Hon
Entry Requirements: *Foundation:* Distinction. *GCE:* 260-300. *IB:* 24. *OCR ND:* D *OCR NED:* M2

WP63 BA Film & Cinema Technologies and Media Studies
Duration: 3FT Hon
Entry Requirements: *Foundation:* Distinction. *GCE:* 260-300. *IB:* 25. *OCR ND:* D *OCR NED:* M2

WW64 BA Film & Cinema Technologies and Performing Arts (Contemporary Performance)
Duration: 3FT Hon
Entry Requirements: *Foundation:* Distinction. *GCE:* 260-300. *IB:* 24. *OCR ND:* D *OCR NED:* M2

WC68 BA Film & Cinema Technologies and Psychology
Duration: 3FT Hon
Entry Requirements: *Foundation:* Distinction. *GCE:* 260-300. *IB:* 25. *OCR ND:* D *OCR NED:* M2

WN6V BA Film & Cinema Technologies and Sports Management
Duration: 3FT Hon
Entry Requirements: *Foundation:* Pass. *GCE:* 260-300. *IB:* 24. *OCR ND:* D

WV66 BA Film & Cinema Technologies and Theology & Religious Studies
Duration: 3FT Hon
Entry Requirements: *Foundation:* Distinction. *GCE:* 260-300. *IB:* 25. *OCR ND:* D

WW6H BA Film & Cinema Technology and Vocal & Choral Studies
Duration: 3FT Hon
Entry Requirements: *Foundation:* Distinction. *GCE:* 260-300. *IB:* 24. *OCR ND:* D *OCR NED:* M2

PW36 BA Film Studies and Film & Cinema Technologies
Duration: 3FT Hon
Entry Requirements: *Foundation:* Distinction. *GCE:* 260-300. *IB:* 24. *OCR ND:* D *OCR NED:* M2

WPQ3 BA Film and Cinema Technologies
Duration: 3FT Hon
Entry Requirements: *Foundation:* Distinction. *GCE:* 260-300. *IB:* 24. *OCR ND:* D *OCR NED:* M2

LW26 BA Politics & Global Studies and Film & Cinema Technologies
Duration: 3FT Hon
Entry Requirements: *Foundation:* Distinction. *GCE:* 260-300. *IB:* 24. *OCR ND:* D

GW42 BSc Digital Media Development
Duration: 3FT Hon
Entry Requirements: *Foundation:* Distinction. *GCE:* 260-300. *IB:* 24. *OCR ND:* D *OCR NED:* M2

W85 WRITTLE COLLEGE
ADMISSIONS
WRITTLE COLLEGE
CHELMSFORD
ESSEX CM1 3RR
t: 01245 424200 f: 01245 420456
e: admissions@writtle.ac.uk
// www.writtle.ac.uk

WK23 BSc Landscape Architecture
Duration: 3FT Hon
Entry Requirements: *Foundation:* Distinction. *GCE:* 260. *IB:* 24. *BTEC Dip:* D*D*. *BTEC ExtDip:* DMM. *OCR NED:* M2

Y75 YORK ST JOHN UNIVERSITY
LORD MAYOR'S WALK
YORK YO31 7EX
t: 01904 876598 f: 01904 876940/876921
e: admissions@yorksj.ac.uk
// w3.yorksj.ac.uk

WWC2 BA Fine Arts
Duration: 3FT Hon
Entry Requirements: *Foundation:* Pass. *GCE:* 200-240. *IB:* 24. Interview required. Portfolio required.

DIGITAL AND MEDIA ART & DESIGN

A40 ABERYSTWYTH UNIVERSITY
ABERYSTWYTH UNIVERSITY, WELCOME CENTRE
PENGLAIS CAMPUS
ABERYSTWYTH
CEREDIGION SY23 3FB
t: 01970 622021 f: 01970 627410
e: ug-admissions@aber.ac.uk
// www.aber.ac.uk

W620 BA Film & Television Studies
Duration: 3FT Hon
Entry Requirements: *GCE:* 300-320.

WW64 BA Film & Television Studies/Drama & Theatre Studies
Duration: 3FT Hon
Entry Requirements: *GCE:* 300-320. *IB:* 32.

WX63 BA Film & Television Studies/Education
Duration: 3FT Hon
Entry Requirements: *GCE:* 300-320. *IB:* 32.

QW36 BA Film & Television Studies/English Literature
Duration: 3FT Hon
Entry Requirements: *GCE:* 300-320. *IB:* 32.

WW16 BA Film & Television Studies/Fine Art
Duration: 3FT Hon
Entry Requirements: *GCE:* 300-320. *IB:* 32. Portfolio required.

RW16 BA French/Film & Television Studies (4 years)
Duration: 4FT Hon
Entry Requirements: *GCE:* 300-320. *IB:* 32.

VW16 BA History/Film & Television Studies
Duration: 3FT Hon
Entry Requirements: *GCE:* 300-320. *IB:* 29.

LW26 BA International Politics/Film & Television Studies
Duration: 3FT Hon
Entry Requirements: *GCE:* 300-320. *IB:* 29.

GW16 BA Mathematics/Film & Television Studies
Duration: 3FT Hon
Entry Requirements: *GCE:* 320. *IB:* 27.

LWF6 BA Politics/Film & Television Studies
Duration: 3FT Hon
Entry Requirements: *GCE:* 300-320. *IB:* 29.

WP43 BA Scenography & Theatre Design/Film & Television Studies
Duration: 3FT Hon
Entry Requirements: *GCE:* 300-320. *IB:* 32.

RW46 BA Spanish/Film & Television Studies (4 years)
Duration: 4FT Hon
Entry Requirements: *GCE:* 300-320. *IB:* 32.

VWF6 BA Welsh History/Film & Television Studies
Duration: 3FT Hon
Entry Requirements: *GCE:* 300-320. *IB:* 29.

A44 ACCRINGTON & ROSSENDALE COLLEGE
BROAD OAK ROAD,
ACCRINGTON,
LANCASHIRE, BB5 2AW.
t: 01254 389933 f: 01254 354001
e: info@accross.ac.uk
// www.accrosshighereducation.co.uk/

WP63 BA (Hons) Film and Digital Media
Duration: 3FT Hon
Entry Requirements: *GCE:* 160. Interview required.

A60 ANGLIA RUSKIN UNIVERSITY
BISHOP HALL LANE
CHELMSFORD
ESSEX CM1 1SQ
t: 0845 271 3333 f: 01245 251789
e: answers@anglia.ac.uk
// www.anglia.ac.uk

W612 BA Film and Television Production
Duration: 3FT Hon
Entry Requirements: *GCE:* 200-240. *SQAH:* BCCC. *SQAAH:* CC. *IB:* 24. Interview required. Portfolio required.

B20 BATH SPA UNIVERSITY
NEWTON PARK
NEWTON ST LOE
BATH BA2 9BN
t: 01225 875875 f: 01225 875444
e: enquiries@bathspa.ac.uk
// www.bathspa.ac.uk/clearing

W103 BA Fine Art (Media)
Duration: 3FT Hon
Entry Requirements: *GCE:* 220-280. *IB:* 24. Interview required. Portfolio required.

WPQ3 BA Photography and Digital Media
Duration: 3FT Hon
Entry Requirements: *GCE:* 220-280. *IB:* 24. Interview required. Portfolio required.

W640 FdA Digital Design: Photography & Motion Graphics
Duration: 2FT Fdg
Entry Requirements: *GCE:* 220-280. *IB:* 24. Interview required.

B22 UNIVERSITY OF BEDFORDSHIRE
PARK SQUARE
LUTON
BEDS LU1 3JU
t: 0844 8482234 f: 01582 489323
e: admissions@beds.ac.uk
// www.beds.ac.uk

W213 BA Advertising Design
Duration: 3FT Hon
Entry Requirements: *GCE:* 160. Interview required. Portfolio required.

PW3G BA Media Production (New Media)
Duration: 3FT Hon
Entry Requirements: *Foundation:* Pass. *GCE:* 200. *SQAH:* BCC. *SQAAH:* BCC. *IB:* 24. *OCR ND:* M1 *OCR NED:* P1

W610 BA Television Production
Duration: 3FT Hon
Entry Requirements: *Foundation:* Pass. *GCE:* 200. *SQAH:* BCC. *SQAAH:* BCC. *IB:* 24. *OCR ND:* M1 *OCR NED:* P1

WNF5 FdA Graphic Design and Advertising
Duration: 2FT Fdg
Entry Requirements: *GCE:* 80-120.

B25 BIRMINGHAM CITY UNIVERSITY
PERRY BARR
BIRMINGHAM B42 2SU
t: 0121 331 5595 f: 0121 331 7994
// www.bcu.ac.uk

W290 BA Fashion Design with Fashion Communication
Duration: 3FT Hon
Entry Requirements: *GCE:* 280. *SQAH:* BBBB. *SQAAH:* CCC. *IB:* 28. Interview required. Portfolio required.

P9WP BA Media and Communication (Television)
Duration: 3FT Hon
Entry Requirements: *Foundation:* Pass. *GCE:* BBC. *SQAH:* ABBB. *SQAAH:* BBC. *IB:* 30.

B30 BIRMINGHAM METROPOLITAN COLLEGE (FORMERLY MATTHEW BOULTON COLLEGE)
JENNENS ROAD
BIRMINGHAM B4 7PS
t: 0121 446 4545 f: 0121 503 8590
e: HEEnquiries@bmetc.ac.uk
// www.bmetc.ac.uk/

I620 HND Interactive and Visual Design
Duration: 2FT HND
Entry Requirements: Contact the institution for details.

B40 BLACKBURN COLLEGE
FEILDEN STREET
BLACKBURN BB2 1LH
t: 01254 292594 f: 01254 679647
e: he-admissions@blackburn.ac.uk
// www.blackburn.ac.uk

W216 BA Design (New Media)
Duration: 3FT Hon
Entry Requirements: *GCE:* 200.

B44 UNIVERSITY OF BOLTON
DEANE ROAD
BOLTON BL3 5AB
t: 01204 903903 f: 01204 399074
e: enquiries@bolton.ac.uk
// www.bolton.ac.uk

W219 BA Digital Graphic Design
Duration: 1FT Hon
Entry Requirements: Interview required. Portfolio required.

W601 BSc Film Production for the Advertising & Music Industries
Duration: 3FT Hon
Entry Requirements: *GCE:* 260. Interview required.

W602 FdSc Film Production for the Advertising & Music Industries
Duration: 2FT Fdg
Entry Requirements: *GCE:* 160. Interview required.

B50 BOURNEMOUTH UNIVERSITY
TALBOT CAMPUS
FERN BARROW
POOLE
DORSET BH12 5BB
t: 01202 524111
// www.bournemouth.ac.uk

W620 BA Scriptwriting for Film and Television
Duration: 3FT Hon
Entry Requirements: *GCE:* 320. *IB:* 32. *BTEC SubDip:* M. *BTEC Dip:* DM. *BTEC ExtDip:* DDM. Admissions Test required. Portfolio required.

W621 BA Television Production
Duration: 3FT Hon
Entry Requirements: *GCE:* 340. *IB:* 33. *BTEC SubDip:* D. *BTEC Dip:* DD. *BTEC ExtDip:* DDD. Interview required. Portfolio required.

W212 FdA Creative Multimedia Design
Duration: 2FT Fdg
Entry Requirements: *GCE:* 120. *IB:* 24. Interview required.

B56 THE UNIVERSITY OF BRADFORD
RICHMOND ROAD
BRADFORD
WEST YORKSHIRE BD7 1DP
t: 0800 073 1225 f: 01274 235585
e: course-enquiries@bradford.ac.uk
// www.bradford.ac.uk

WW26 BA Digital and Creative Enterprise
Duration: 1FT Hon
Entry Requirements: Interview required. HND required.

P3W6 BA Media Studies with Cinematics
Duration: 3FT Hon
Entry Requirements: *GCE:* 240. *IB:* 24.

WP63 BA Photography for Digital Media
Duration: 3FT Hon
Entry Requirements: *GCE:* 240. *IB:* 24. Interview required.

GW46 BSc Digital Media
Duration: 3FT Hon
Entry Requirements: *GCE:* 260. *IB:* 28. Interview required.

B60 BRADFORD COLLEGE: AN ASSOCIATE COLLEGE OF LEEDS METROPOLITAN UNIVERSITY
GREAT HORTON ROAD
BRADFORD
WEST YORKSHIRE BD7 1AY
t: 01274 433008 f: 01274 431652
e: heregistry@bradfordcollege.ac.uk
// www.bradfordcollege.ac.uk/ university-centre

W2G4 BA Graphic Design, Illustration, Digital Media
Duration: 3FT Hon
Entry Requirements: *GCE:* 220. Interview required. Portfolio required.

W212 FdSc Multimedia & Design
Duration: 2FT Fdg
Entry Requirements: *GCE:* 60-120.

B72 UNIVERSITY OF BRIGHTON
MITHRAS HOUSE 211
LEWES ROAD
BRIGHTON BN2 4AT
t: 01273 644644 f: 01273 642607
e: admissions@brighton.ac.uk
// www.brighton.ac.uk

W214 BA Digital Media Design (Top-Up)
Duration: 1FT Hon
Entry Requirements: Interview required. Portfolio required. HND required.

W612 FdA Digital Post Production
Duration: 2FT Fdg
Entry Requirements: *GCE:* 160. *IB:* 24.

B84 BRUNEL UNIVERSITY
UXBRIDGE
MIDDLESEX UB8 3PH
t: 01895 265265 f: 01895 269790
e: admissions@brunel.ac.uk
// www.brunel.ac.uk

Q3W6 BA English and Film & Television Studies
Duration: 3FT Hon
Entry Requirements: *GCE:* AAB. *SQAAH:* AAB. *IB:* 35. *BTEC ExtDip:* D*D*D.

W620 BA Film & Television Studies
Duration: 3FT Hon
Entry Requirements: *GCE:* BBB. *SQAAH:* BBB. *IB:* 32. *BTEC ExtDip:* DDM.

B94 BUCKINGHAMSHIRE NEW UNIVERSITY
QUEEN ALEXANDRA ROAD
HIGH WYCOMBE
BUCKINGHAMSHIRE HP11 2JZ
t: 0800 0565 660 f: 01494 605 023
e: admissions@bucks.ac.uk
// bucks.ac.uk

WN25 BA Advertising: Creative
Duration: 3FT Hon
Entry Requirements: *GCE:* 200-240. *IB:* 24. *OCR ND:* M1 *OCR NED:* M3 Interview required.

W693 FdA Photography & Digital Imaging
Duration: 2FT Fdg
Entry Requirements: *GCE:* 100-140. *IB:* 24. *OCR ND:* P2 *OCR NED:* P3 Interview required.

C10 CANTERBURY CHRIST CHURCH UNIVERSITY
NORTH HOLMES ROAD
CANTERBURY
KENT CT1 1QU
t: 01227 782900 f: 01227 782888
e: admissions@canterbury.ac.uk
// www.canterbury.ac.uk

QW3P BA English Language & Communication and Film, Radio & Television
Duration: 3FT Hon
Entry Requirements: *GCE:* 240. *IB:* 24.

Q3WP BA English Language & Communication with Film, Radio & Television Studies
Duration: 3FT Hon
Entry Requirements: *GCE:* 240. *IB:* 24.

W620 BA Film, Radio & Television Studies
Duration: 3FT Hon   CRB Check: Required
Entry Requirements: *GCE:* 260. *IB:* 24. Interview required.

W6QH BA Film, Radio & Television Studies with English Language & Communication
Duration: 3FT Hon
Entry Requirements: *GCE:* 240. *IB:* 24.

TW76 BA/BSc American Studies and Film, Radio & Television Studies
Duration: 3FT Hon
Entry Requirements: *GCE:* 240. *IB:* 24.

T7W6 BA/BSc American Studies with Film, Radio & Television Studies
Duration: 3FT Hon
Entry Requirements: *GCE:* 240. *IB:* 24.

NW16 BA/BSc Business Studies and Film, Radio & Television Studies
Duration: 3FT Hon
Entry Requirements: *GCE:* 240. *IB:* 24.

XW36 BA/BSc Early Childhood Studies and Film, Radio & Television Studies
Duration: 3FT Hon   CRB Check: Required
Entry Requirements: *GCE:* 240. *IB:* 24.

QW36 BA/BSc English Literature and Film, Radio & Television Studies
Duration: 3FT Hon
Entry Requirements: *GCE:* 240. *IB:* 24.

Q3W6 BA/BSc English Literature with Film, Radio & Television Studies
Duration: 3FT Hon
Entry Requirements: *GCE:* 240. *IB:* 24.

WR61 BA/BSc Film, Radio & Television Studies and French
Duration: 3FT Hon
Entry Requirements: *GCE:* 240. *IB:* 24.

W6P3 BA/BSc Film, Radio & Television Studies and Media and Communications
Duration: 3FT Hon
Entry Requirements: *GCE:* 240. *IB:* 24.

WV66 BA/BSc Film, Radio & Television Studies and Religious Studies
Duration: 3FT Hon
Entry Requirements: *GCE:* 240. *IB:* 24.

NW86 BA/BSc Film, Radio & Television Studies and Tourism & Leisure Studies
Duration: 3FT Hon
Entry Requirements: *GCE:* 240. *IB:* 24.

W6T7 BA/BSc Film, Radio & Television Studies with American Studies
Duration: 3FT Hon
Entry Requirements: *GCE:* 240. *IB:* 24.

W6N1 BA/BSc Film, Radio & Television Studies with Business Studies
Duration: 3FT Hon
Entry Requirements: *GCE:* 240. *IB:* 24.

W6G4 BA/BSc Film, Radio & Television Studies with Digital Media
Duration: 3FT Hon
Entry Requirements: *GCE:* 240. *IB:* 24.

W6X3 BA/BSc Film, Radio & Television Studies with Early Childhood Studies
Duration: 3FT Hon   CRB Check: Required
Entry Requirements: *GCE:* 240. *IB:* 24.

W6Q3 BA/BSc Film, Radio & Television Studies with English Literature
Duration: 3FT Hon
Entry Requirements: *GCE:* 240. *IB:* 24.

W6R1 BA/BSc Film, Radio & Television Studies with French
Duration: 3FT Hon
Entry Requirements: *GCE:* 240. *IB:* 24.

W6L7 BA/BSc Film, Radio & Television Studies with Geography
Duration: 3FT Hon
Entry Requirements: *GCE:* 240. *IB:* 24.

W6V1 BA/BSc Film, Radio & Television Studies with History
Duration: 3FT Hon
Entry Requirements: *GCE:* 240. *IB:* 24.

W6N5 BA/BSc Film, Radio & Television Studies with Marketing
Duration: 3FT Hon
Entry Requirements: *GCE:* 240. *IB:* 24.

W6W3 BA/BSc Film, Radio & Television Studies with Music
Duration: 3FT Hon
Entry Requirements: *GCE:* 240. *IB:* 24. Interview required.

W6C8 BA/BSc Film, Radio & Television Studies with Psychology
Duration: 3FT Hon
Entry Requirements: *GCE:* 260. *IB:* 24.

W6V6 BA/BSc Film, Radio & Television Studies with Religious Studies
Duration: 3FT Hon
Entry Requirements: *GCE:* 240. *IB:* 24.

W6N8 BA/BSc Film, Radio & Television Studies with Tourism & Leisure Studies
Duration: 3FT Hon
Entry Requirements: *GCE:* 240. *IB:* 24.

WL67 BA/BSc Geography and Film, Radio & Television Studies
Duration: 3FT Hon
Entry Requirements: *GCE:* 240. *IB:* 24.

VW16 BA/BSc History and Film, Radio & Television Studies
Duration: 3FT Hon
Entry Requirements: *GCE:* 240. *IB:* 24.

WN65 BA/BSc Marketing and Film, Radio & Television Studies
Duration: 3FT Hon
Entry Requirements: *GCE:* 240. *IB:* 24.

PW36 BA/BSc Media and Communications and Film, Radio and Television Studies
Duration: 3FT Hon
Entry Requirements: *GCE:* 240. *IB:* 24.

P3W6 BA/BSc Media and Communications with Film, Radio and Television Studies
Duration: 3FT Hon
Entry Requirements: *GCE:* 240. *IB:* 24.

G4WQ BA/BSc Multimedia Design with Photography
Duration: 3FT Hon
Entry Requirements: *GCE:* 240. *IB:* 24.

WW63 BA/BSc Music and Film, Radio & Television Studies
Duration: 3FT Hon
Entry Requirements: *GCE:* 240. *IB:* 24.

W3W6 BA/BSc Music with Film, Radio & Television Studies
Duration: 3FT Hon
Entry Requirements: *GCE:* 240. *IB:* 24.

CW86 BA/BSc Psychology and Film, Radio & Television Studies
Duration: 3FT Hon
Entry Requirements: *GCE:* 260. *IB:* 24.

C8W6 BA/BSc Psychology with Film, Radio & Television Studies
Duration: 3FT Hon
Entry Requirements: *GCE:* 260. *IB:* 24.

V6W6 BA/BSc Religious Studies with Film, Radio & Television Studies
Duration: 3FT Hon
Entry Requirements: *GCE:* 240. *IB:* 24.

N8W6 BA/BSc Tourism & Leisure Studies with Film, Radio & Television Studies
Duration: 3FT Hon
Entry Requirements: *GCE:* 240. *IB:* 24.

N1W6 BSc Business Studies with Film, Radio & Television Studies
Duration: 3FT Hon
Entry Requirements: *GCE:* 240. *IB:* 24.

N5W6 BSc Marketing with Film, Radio & Television Studies
Duration: 3FT Hon
Entry Requirements: *GCE:* 240. *IB:* 24.

GW46 BSc/BA Digital Media and Film, Radio & Television Studies
Duration: 3FT Hon
Entry Requirements: *GCE:* 240. *IB:* 24.

G4W6 BSc/BA Digital Media with Film, Radio & Television Studies
Duration: 3FT Hon
Entry Requirements: *GCE:* 240. *IB:* 24.

X3W6 BSc/BA Early Childhood Studies with Film, Radio & Television Studies
Duration: 3FT Hon   **CRB Check:** Required
Entry Requirements: *GCE:* 240. *IB:* 24.

L7W6 BSc/BA Geography with Film, Radio & Television Studies
Duration: 3FT Hon
Entry Requirements: *GCE:* 240. *IB:* 24.

V1W6 BSc/BA History with Film, Radio & Television Studies
Duration: 3FT Hon
Entry Requirements: *GCE:* 240. *IB:* 24.

C22 COLEG SIR GAR / CARMARTHENSHIRE COLLEGE
SANDY ROAD
LLANELLI
CARMARTHENSHIRE SA15 4DN
t: 01554 748000 **f:** 01554 748170
e: admissions@colegsirgar.ac.uk
// www.colegsirgar.ac.uk

W221 BA (Hons) Digital Illustration
Duration: 3FT Hon
Entry Requirements: Portfolio required.

C30 UNIVERSITY OF CENTRAL LANCASHIRE
PRESTON
LANCS PR1 2HE
t: 01772 201201 **f:** 01772 894954
e: uadmissions@uclan.ac.uk
// www.uclan.ac.uk

W211 BA Advertising
Duration: 3FT Hon
Entry Requirements: *GCE:* 240-300. *IB:* 26. *OCR ND:* D *OCR NED:* M3 Interview required. Portfolio required.

W212 BA Digital Design for Fashion
Duration: 3FT Hon
Entry Requirements: *GCE:* 240. *IB:* 24. *OCR ND:* D *OCR NED:* M3 Interview required. Portfolio required.

WG2L BA Digital Graphics
Duration: 3FT Hon
Entry Requirements: *GCE:* 240-300. *IB:* 26. *OCR ND:* D *OCR NED:* M3 Interview required. Portfolio required.

PW36 BA Film and Media Studies
Duration: 3FT Hon
Entry Requirements: *GCE:* 240-260. *IB:* 28. *OCR ND:* D *OCR NED:* M3

WN2M BA Visual Merchandising & Promotional Design (Top-Up)
Duration: 1FT Hon
Entry Requirements: HND required.

WP23 BSc Film and Television Graphics Production
Duration: 3FT Hon
Entry Requirements: *GCE:* 300. *SQAH:* AAAB. *IB:* 30. *OCR ND:* D *OCR NED:* D2

GW42 BSc Infographics
Duration: 3FT Hon
Entry Requirements: *GCE:* 300. *IB:* 28. *OCR ND:* D *OCR NED:* D2

WGF4 BSc Interactive Digital Media
Duration: 3FT Hon
Entry Requirements: *GCE:* 300. *SQAH:* AAAB. *IB:* 30. *OCR ND:* D *OCR NED:* D2

C55 UNIVERSITY OF CHESTER
PARKGATE ROAD
CHESTER CH1 4BJ
t: 01244 511000 f: 01244 511300
e: enquiries@chester.ac.uk
// www.chester.ac.uk

WN65 BA Digital Photography and Advertising
Duration: 3FT Hon
Entry Requirements: *GCE:* 240-280. *SQAH:* BBBB. *IB:* 24.

WN62 BA Digital Photography and Business Management
Duration: 3FT Hon
Entry Requirements: *GCE:* 240-280. *SQAH:* BBBB. *IB:* 26.

WJ69 BA Digital Photography and Commercial Music Production
Duration: 3FT Hon
Entry Requirements: *Foundation:* Pass. *GCE:* 260-300. *SQAH:* BBBB. *IB:* 28.

WP63 BA Digital Photography and Film Studies
Duration: 3FT Hon
Entry Requirements: *GCE:* 240-280. *SQAH:* BBBB. *IB:* 26.

WP6M BA Digital Photography and Journalism
Duration: 3FT Hon
Entry Requirements: *GCE:* 240-280. *SQAH:* BBBB. *IB:* 26.

WP6H BA Digital Photography and Media Studies
Duration: 3FT Hon
Entry Requirements: *GCE:* 240-280. *SQAH:* BBBB. *IB:* 26.

WP6J BA Digital Photography and Radio Production
Duration: 3FT Hon
Entry Requirements: *Foundation:* Pass. *GCE:* 260-300. *SQAH:* BBBB. *IB:* 28.

WPP3 BA Digital Photography and TV Production
Duration: 3FT Hon
Entry Requirements: *Foundation:* Pass. *GCE:* 260-300. *SQAH:* BBBB. *IB:* 28.

PW26 BA Marketing & Public Relations and Digital Photography
Duration: 3FT Hon
Entry Requirements: *GCE:* 240-280. *SQAH:* BBBB. *IB:* 26.

C78 CORNWALL COLLEGE
POOL
REDRUTH
CORNWALL TR15 3RD
t: 01209 616161 f: 01209 611612
e: he.admissions@cornwall.ac.uk
// www.cornwall.ac.uk

36WP HNC Creative Media Production
Duration: 1FT HNC   CRB Check: Required
Entry Requirements: Contact the institution for details.

63PW HND Creative Media Production
Duration: 2FT HND   CRB Check: Required
Entry Requirements: Contact the institution for details.

C93 UNIVERSITY FOR THE CREATIVE ARTS
FALKNER ROAD
FARNHAM
SURREY GU9 7DS
t: 01252 892960
e: admissions@ucreative.ac.uk
// www.ucreative.ac.uk

W218 BA Advertising and Brand Communication
Duration: 3FT Hon
Entry Requirements: *GCE:* 220. *IB:* 24. *BTEC ExtDip:* PPP.
Interview required. Portfolio required.

W690 BA Digital Film and Screen Arts
Duration: 3FT Hon
Entry Requirements: *GCE:* 220. *IB:* 24. *BTEC ExtDip:* PPP.
Interview required. Portfolio required.

W213 BA Graphic Design: New Media
Duration: 3FT Hon
Entry Requirements: *GCE:* 220. *IB:* 24. *BTEC ExtDip:* PPP.
Interview required. Portfolio required.

D26 DE MONTFORT UNIVERSITY
THE GATEWAY
LEICESTER LE1 9BH
t: 0116 255 1551 f: 0116 250 6204
e: enquiries@dmu.ac.uk
// www.dmu.ac.uk

WP63 FdSc Digital Video and Broadcast Production
Duration: 2FT Fdg
Entry Requirements: *GCE:* 120. *IB:* 24. *OCR NED:* P2

D39 UNIVERSITY OF DERBY
KEDLESTON ROAD
DERBY DE22 1GB
t: 01332 591167 f: 01332 597724
e: askadmissions@derby.ac.uk
// www.derby.ac.uk

W622 BA Film and Television Studies
Duration: 3FT Hon
Entry Requirements: *Foundation:* Distinction. *GCE:* 240. *IB:* 26.
BTEC Dip: D*D*. *BTEC ExtDip:* DMM. *OCR ND:* D *OCR NED:* M3

D65 UNIVERSITY OF DUNDEE
NETHERGATE
DUNDEE DD1 4HN
t: 01382 383838 f: 01382 388150
e: contactus@dundee.ac.uk
// www.dundee.ac.uk/admissions/
undergraduate/

W690 BA Time Based Art and Digital Film
Duration: 3FT Hon
Entry Requirements: Foundation Course required. Interview
required. Portfolio required.

E14 UNIVERSITY OF EAST ANGLIA
NORWICH NR4 7TJ
t: 01603 591515 f: 01603 591523
e: admissions@uea.ac.uk
// www.uea.ac.uk

W610 BA Film and Television Studies
Duration: 3FT Hon   CRB Check: Required
Entry Requirements: *GCE:* AAB. *SQAAH:* AAB. *IB:* 33. *BTEC*
ExtDip: DDD. Interview required.

E28 UNIVERSITY OF EAST LONDON
DOCKLANDS CAMPUS
UNIVERSITY WAY
LONDON E16 2RD
t: 020 8223 3333 f: 020 8223 2978
e: study@uel.ac.uk
// www.uel.ac.uk

WGN2 BA Digital Fashion with Business Management
Duration: 3FT Hon
Entry Requirements: *GCE:* 240. *IB:* 24. Portfolio required.

WFX3 BA Digital Fashion with Education Studies
Duration: 3FT Hon
Entry Requirements: *GCE:* 240. *IB:* 24. Portfolio required.

WG90 BA Digital Fashion with Graphic Design
Duration: 3FT Hon
Entry Requirements: *GCE:* 240. *IB:* 24. Portfolio required.

WFW6 BA Digital Fashion with Photography
Duration: 3FT Hon
Entry Requirements: *GCE:* 240. *IB:* 24. Portfolio required.

WFC8 BA Digital Fashion with Psychology
Duration: 3FT Hon
Entry Requirements: *GCE:* 240. *IB:* 24. Portfolio required.

WN2M BA Graphic Design / Advertising
Duration: 3FT Hon
Entry Requirements: *GCE:* 200. *IB:* 24.

W2PJ BA Graphic Design with Media Studies
Duration: 3FT Hon
Entry Requirements: *GCE:* 240. *IB:* 24.

W6P3 BA Photography with Media Studies
Duration: 3FT Hon
Entry Requirements: *GCE:* 240. *IB:* 24. Portfolio required.

E32 EAST SURREY COLLEGE (INCORPORATING REIGATE SCHOOL OF ART, DESIGN AND MEDIA)
GATTON POINT
LONDON ROAD
REDHILL RH1 2JX
t: 01737 772611 f: 01737 768641
e: fmelmoe@esc.ac.uk
// www.esc.ac.uk

046W HND Digital Photography
Duration: 2FT HND
Entry Requirements: *GCE:* 80. Interview required. Portfolio
required.

E42 EDGE HILL UNIVERSITY
ORMSKIRK
LANCASHIRE L39 4QP
t: 01695 657000 f: 01695 584355
e: study@edgehill.ac.uk
// www.edgehill.ac.uk

W600 BA Film & Television Production
Duration: 3FT Hon
Entry Requirements: *GCE:* 280. *IB:* 26. *OCR ND:* D *OCR NED:* M2
Interview required. Portfolio required.

E56 THE UNIVERSITY OF EDINBURGH
STUDENT RECRUITMENT & ADMISSIONS
57 GEORGE SQUARE
EDINBURGH EH8 9JU
t: 0131 650 4360 f: 0131 651 1236
e: sra.enquiries@ed.ac.uk
// www.ed.ac.uk/studying/undergraduate/

W900 BA Intermedia Art
Duration: 4FT Hon
Entry Requirements: **Foundation:** Merit. **GCE:** BBB. **SQAH:** BBBB.
IB: 34. Portfolio required.

F66 FARNBOROUGH COLLEGE OF TECHNOLOGY
BOUNDARY ROAD
FARNBOROUGH
HAMPSHIRE GU14 6SB
t: 01252 407028 f: 01252 407041
e: admissions@farn-ct.ac.uk
// www.farn-ct.ac.uk

PW36 BA Media Production (Photography)
Duration: 3FT Hon
Entry Requirements: **GCE:** 180-200. **OCR ND:** M2 **OCR NED:** M3
Admissions Test required.

W641 BA Media Production (Photography) (Top Up)
Duration: 1FT Hon
Entry Requirements: Contact the institution for details.

G14 UNIVERSITY OF GLAMORGAN, CARDIFF AND PONTYPRIDD
ENQUIRIES AND ADMISSIONS UNIT
PONTYPRIDD CF37 1DL
t: 08456 434030 f: 01443 654050
e: enquiries@glam.ac.uk
// www.glam.ac.uk

W212 BA Graphic Communication
Duration: 3FT Hon
Entry Requirements: **Foundation:** Pass. **GCE:** BBC. **IB:** 25. **BTEC SubDip:** M. **BTEC Dip:** D*D*. **BTEC ExtDip:** DMM. **OCR ND:** M1 **OCR NED:** M2 Interview required. Portfolio required.

G28 UNIVERSITY OF GLASGOW
71 SOUTHPARK AVENUE
UNIVERSITY OF GLASGOW
GLASGOW G12 8QQ
t: 0141 330 6062 f: 0141 330 2961
e: student.recruitment@glasgow.ac.uk
// www.glasgow.ac.uk

VW46 MA Archaeology/Film & Television Studies
Duration: 4FT Hon
Entry Requirements: **GCE:** ABB. **SQAH:** AAAB-ABBB. **IB:** 34.

GL57 MA Digital Media & Information Studies/Geography
Duration: 4FT Hon
Entry Requirements: **GCE:** ABB. **SQAH:** AAAB-ABBB. **IB:** 34.

GL52 MA Digital Media & Information Studies/Politics
Duration: 4FT Hon
Entry Requirements: **GCE:** ABB. **SQAH:** AAAB-ABBB. **IB:** 34.

GL56 MA Digital Media & Information Studies/Sociology
Duration: 4FT Hon
Entry Requirements: **GCE:** ABB. **SQAH:** AAAB-ABBB. **IB:** 34.

QW3P MA English Literature/Film & Television Studies
Duration: 4FT Hon
Entry Requirements: **GCE:** ABB. **SQAH:** AAAB-ABBB. **IB:** 36.

RW16 MA Film & Television Studies/French
Duration: 5FT Hon
Entry Requirements: **GCE:** ABB. **SQAH:** AAAB-ABBB. **IB:** 36.

RW26 MA Film & Television Studies/German
Duration: 5FT Hon
Entry Requirements: **GCE:** ABB. **SQAH:** AAAB-ABBB. **IB:** 36.

VW16 MA Film & Television Studies/History
Duration: 4FT Hon
Entry Requirements: **GCE:** ABB. **SQAH:** AAAB-ABBB. **IB:** 36.

VW36 MA Film & Television Studies/History of Art
Duration: 4FT Hon
Entry Requirements: **GCE:** ABB. **SQAH:** AAAB-ABBB. **IB:** 36.

QW66 MA Film & Television Studies/Latin
Duration: 4FT Hon
Entry Requirements: **GCE:** ABB. **SQAH:** AAAB-ABBB. **IB:** 36.

WW36 MA Film & Television Studies/Music
Duration: 4FT Hon
Entry Requirements: **GCE:** ABB. **SQAH:** AAAB-ABBB. **IB:** 36.

VW56 MA Film & Television Studies/Philosophy
Duration: 4FT Hon
Entry Requirements: *GCE:* ABB. *SQAH:* AAAB-ABBB. *IB:* 36.

FW36 MA Film & Television Studies/Physics
Duration: 4FT Hon
Entry Requirements: *GCE:* ABB. *SQAH:* AAAB-ABBB. *IB:* 36.

LW26 MA Film & Television Studies/Politics
Duration: 4FT Hon
Entry Requirements: *GCE:* ABB. *SQAH:* AAAB-ABBB. *IB:* 36.

LW46 MA Film & Television Studies/Public Policy
Duration: 4FT Hon
Entry Requirements: *GCE:* ABB. *SQAH:* AAAB-ABBB. *IB:* 36.

RW76 MA Film & Television Studies/Russian
Duration: 5FT Hon
Entry Requirements: *GCE:* ABB. *SQAH:* AAAB-ABBB. *IB:* 36.

VWF6 MA Film & Television Studies/Scottish History
Duration: 4FT Hon
Entry Requirements: *GCE:* ABB. *SQAH:* AAAB-ABBB. *IB:* 36.

QW26 MA Film & Television Studies/Scottish Literature
Duration: 4FT Hon
Entry Requirements: *GCE:* ABB. *SQAH:* AAAB-ABBB. *IB:* 36.

LW36 MA Film & Television Studies/Sociology
Duration: 4FT Hon
Entry Requirements: *GCE:* ABB. *SQAH:* AAAB-ABBB. *IB:* 36.

WW46 MA Film & Television Studies/Theatre Studies
Duration: 4FT Hon
Entry Requirements: *GCE:* ABB. *SQAH:* AAAB-ABBB. *IB:* 36.

G45 GLOUCESTERSHIRE COLLEGE
PRINCESS ELIZABETH WAY
CHELTENHAM GL51 7SJ
t: 01242 532008 f: 01242 532023
e: admissions@gloscol.ac.uk
// www.gloscol.ac.uk

012W HND Graphic Design/Multimedia
Duration: 2FT HND
Entry Requirements: *GCE:* 160. Interview required. Portfolio required.

G50 THE UNIVERSITY OF GLOUCESTERSHIRE
PARK CAMPUS
THE PARK
CHELTENHAM GL50 2RH
t: 01242 714501 f: 01242 714869
e: admissions@glos.ac.uk
// www.glos.ac.uk

W640 BA Photography - Editorial and Advertising
Duration: 3FT Hon
Entry Requirements: *GCE:* 280-300. Interview required. Portfolio required.

G452 BSc Multimedia Web Design
Duration: 2FT Hon
Entry Requirements: Contact the institution for details.

G53 GLYNDWR UNIVERSITY
PLAS COCH
MOLD ROAD
WREXHAM LL11 2AW
t: 01978 293439 f: 01978 290008
e: sid@glyndwr.ac.uk
// www.glyndwr.ac.uk

W991 BA Design: Graphic Design and Multimedia
Duration: 3FT Hon
Entry Requirements: *GCE:* 240. Interview required. Portfolio required.

G70 UNIVERSITY OF GREENWICH
GREENWICH CAMPUS
OLD ROYAL NAVAL COLLEGE
PARK ROW
LONDON SE10 9LS
t: 020 8331 9000 f: 020 8331 8145
e: courseinfo@gre.ac.uk
// www.gre.ac.uk

W210 BA Graphic and Digital Design
Duration: 3FT Hon
Entry Requirements: *Foundation:* Pass. *GCE:* 280. *IB:* 24. Interview required. Portfolio required.

W612 BSc Digital Film Production
Duration: 3FT Hon
Entry Requirements: *GCE:* 280. *IB:* 24.

52NW HND Graphic Design and Advertising
Duration: 2FT HND
Entry Requirements: *GCE:* 100. *IB:* 24.

012W HND Graphic and Digital Design
Duration: 2FT HND
Entry Requirements: *Foundation:* Pass. *GCE:* 180. Interview required. Portfolio required.

H36 UNIVERSITY OF HERTFORDSHIRE
UNIVERSITY ADMISSIONS SERVICE
COLLEGE LANE
HATFIELD
HERTS AL10 9AB
t: 01707 284800
// www.herts.ac.uk

W600 BA Film and Television Documentary
Duration: 3FT Hon
Entry Requirements: *GCE:* 300. Interview required. Portfolio required.

WP63 BA Film and Television Entertainment
Duration: 3FT Hon
Entry Requirements: *GCE:* 300. Interview required. Portfolio required.

WW68 BA Film and Television Fiction
Duration: 3FT Hon
Entry Requirements: *GCE:* 300. Interview required. Portfolio required.

H49 UNIVERSITY OF THE HIGHLANDS AND ISLANDS
UHI EXECUTIVE OFFICE
NESS WALK
INVERNESS
SCOTLAND IV3 5SQ
t: 01463 279000 f: 01463 279001
e: info@uhi.ac.uk
// www.uhi.ac.uk

316W HNC Sound Production
Duration: 1FT HNC
Entry Requirements: *GCE:* D. *SQAH:* C. Interview required.

309W HND Contemporary Art Practice
Duration: 2FT HND
Entry Requirements: Interview required. Portfolio required.

H72 THE UNIVERSITY OF HULL
THE UNIVERSITY OF HULL
COTTINGHAM ROAD
HULL HU6 7RX
t: 01482 466100 f: 01482 442290
e: admissions@hull.ac.uk
// www.hull.ac.uk

GW42 BA Applied Digital Media (1 year top-up)
Duration: 1FT Hon
Entry Requirements: Contact the institution for details.

W212 BA Design for Digital Media
Duration: 3FT Hon
Entry Requirements: *GCE:* 260-300. *IB:* 24. *BTEC ExtDip:* DMM.

W214 BA Digital Media Studies
Duration: 3FT Hon
Entry Requirements: *GCE:* 260-300. *IB:* 24. *BTEC ExtDip:* DMM.

K90 KIRKLEES COLLEGE
HALIFAX ROAD
DEWSBURY
WEST YORKSHIRE WF13 2AS
t: 01924 436221 f: 01924 457047
e: admissionsdc@kirkleescollege.ac.uk
// www.kirkleescollege.ac.uk

W641 FdA Digital Photography
Duration: 2FT Fdg
Entry Requirements: *GCE:* 180.

L27 LEEDS METROPOLITAN UNIVERSITY
COURSE ENQUIRIES OFFICE
CITY CAMPUS
LEEDS LS1 3HE
t: 0113 81 23113 f: 0113 81 23129
// www.leedsmet.ac.uk

GW42 BSc Games Design
Duration: 3FT/4SW Hon
Entry Requirements: *GCE:* 200. *IB:* 24. Interview required.

L28 LEEDS COLLEGE OF ART

BLENHEIM WALK
LEEDS LS2 9AQ
t: 0113 202 8000 f: 0113 202 8001
e: info@leeds-art.ac.uk
// www.leeds-art.ac.uk

W900 BA Creative Advertising
Duration: 3FT Hon
Entry Requirements: *Foundation:* Merit. *GCE:* 240. *IB:* 24. *BTEC Dip:* DD. *BTEC ExtDip:* MMM. Interview required. Portfolio required.

L39 UNIVERSITY OF LINCOLN

ADMISSIONS
BRAYFORD POOL
LINCOLN LN6 7TS
t: 01522 886097 f: 01522 886146
e: admissions@lincoln.ac.uk
// www.lincoln.ac.uk

W213 BA Creative Advertising
Duration: 3FT Hon
Entry Requirements: *GCE:* 280. Interview required. Portfolio required.

PW36 BA Film & Television
Duration: 3FT Hon
Entry Requirements: *GCE:* 280.

L53 COLEG LLANDRILLO CYMRU

LLANDUDNO ROAD
RHOS-ON-SEA
COLWYN BAY
NORTH WALES LL28 4HZ
t: 01492 542338/339 f: 01492 543052
e: degrees@llandrillo.ac.uk
// www.llandrillo.ac.uk

WP63 FdA Digital Media and Television Production
Duration: 2FT Fdg
Entry Requirements: *GCE:* 180. Interview required.

L68 LONDON METROPOLITAN UNIVERSITY

166-220 HOLLOWAY ROAD
LONDON N7 8DB
t: 020 7133 4200
e: admissions@londonmet.ac.uk
// www.londonmet.ac.uk

W212 FdA Multimedia Games Design
Duration: 2FT Fdg
Entry Requirements: Contact the institution for details.

L75 LONDON SOUTH BANK UNIVERSITY

ADMISSIONS AND RECRUITMENT CENTRE
90 LONDON ROAD
LONDON SE1 6LN
t: 0800 923 8888 f: 020 7815 8273
e: course.enquiry@lsbu.ac.uk
// www.lsbu.ac.uk

W690 BA Digital Film and Video
Duration: 3FT Hon
Entry Requirements: *GCE:* 240. *IB:* 24.

W640 BA Digital Photography
Duration: 3FT Hon
Entry Requirements: *GCE:* 240. *IB:* 24.

M10 THE MANCHESTER COLLEGE

OPENSHAW CAMPUS
ASHTON OLD ROAD
OPENSHAW
MANCHESTER M11 2WH
t: 0800 068 8585 f: 0161 920 4103
e: enquiries@themanchestercollege.ac.uk
// www.themanchestercollege.ac.uk

W210 FdA Digital Graphic Design
Duration: 2FT Fdg
Entry Requirements: *GCE:* 160. *BTEC ExtDip:* MPP. Portfolio required.

WN2M FdA Graphic Design and Advertising
Duration: 2FT Fdg
Entry Requirements: *GCE:* 160. *BTEC ExtDip:* MPP. Portfolio required.

W640 FdA Photography and Digital Imaging
Duration: 2FT Fdg
Entry Requirements: *Foundation:* Pass. *GCE:* 160. *BTEC ExtDip:* MPP. Portfolio required.

M40 THE MANCHESTER METROPOLITAN UNIVERSITY

ADMISSIONS OFFICE
ALL SAINTS (GMS)
ALL SAINTS
MANCHESTER M15 6BH
t: 0161 247 2000
// www.mmu.ac.uk

NW16 BA Business/Film & Television Studies
Duration: 3FT Hon
Entry Requirements: *GCE:* 280. *IB:* 28. *BTEC Dip:* D*D*. *BTEC ExtDip:* DMM.

WX63 BA Childhood & Youth Studies/Film & Television Studies
Duration: 3FT Hon
Entry Requirements: *GCE:* 280. *IB:* 28. *BTEC Dip:* D*D*. *BTEC ExtDip:* DMM.

W212 BA Creative Multimedia
Duration: 3FT Hon
Entry Requirements: *GCE:* 280. *IB:* 27. Interview required. Portfolio required.

WW3Q BA Creative Music Production/Film & Television Studies
Duration: 3FT Hon
Entry Requirements: *GCE:* 280. *IB:* 28. *BTEC Dip:* D*D*. *BTEC ExtDip:* DMM. Interview required.

WW86 BA Creative Writing/Film & Television Studies
Duration: 3FT Hon
Entry Requirements: *GCE:* 280. *IB:* 28. *BTEC Dip:* D*D*. *BTEC ExtDip:* DMM. Portfolio required.

LW3P BA Crime Studies/Film & Television Studies
Duration: 3FT Hon
Entry Requirements: *GCE:* 280. *IB:* 28. *BTEC Dip:* D*D*. *BTEC ExtDip:* DMM.

WW46 BA Drama/Film & Television Studies
Duration: 3FT Hon
Entry Requirements: *GCE:* 280. *IB:* 28. *BTEC Dip:* D*D*. *BTEC ExtDip:* DMM. Interview required.

QW36 BA English/Film & Television Studies
Duration: 3FT Hon
Entry Requirements: *GCE:* 280. *IB:* 28. *BTEC Dip:* D*D*. *BTEC ExtDip:* DMM.

NW56 BA Film & Television Studies/Marketing
Duration: 3FT Hon
Entry Requirements: *GCE:* 280. *IB:* 28. *BTEC Dip:* D*D*. *BTEC ExtDip:* DMM.

WW36 BA Film & Television Studies/Music
Duration: 3FT Hon
Entry Requirements: *GCE:* 280. *IB:* 28. *BTEC Dip:* D*D*. *BTEC ExtDip:* DMM. Interview required.

VW56 BA Film & Television Studies/Philosophy
Duration: 3FT Hon
Entry Requirements: *GCE:* 280. *IB:* 28. *BTEC Dip:* D*D*. *BTEC ExtDip:* DMM.

LWJ6 BA Film & Television Studies/Sociology
Duration: 3FT Hon
Entry Requirements: *GCE:* 280. *IB:* 28. *BTEC Dip:* D*D*. *BTEC ExtDip:* DMM.

VW36 BA Film and Media Studies option - Film and Media Studies
Duration: 3FT Hon
Entry Requirements: Contact the institution for details.

VW36 BA Film and Media Studies
Duration: 3FT Hon
Entry Requirements: *GCE:* 280. *IB:* 27. Interview required.

W920 BA Interactive Arts
Duration: 3FT Hon
Entry Requirements: *GCE:* 280. *IB:* 27. Interview required. Portfolio required.

CW66 BA/BSc Film & Television Studies/Sport
Duration: 3FT Hon
Entry Requirements: *GCE:* 280. *IB:* 28. *BTEC Dip:* D*D*. *BTEC ExtDip:* DMM.

N23 NEWCASTLE COLLEGE
STUDENT SERVICES
RYE HILL CAMPUS
SCOTSWOOD ROAD
NEWCASTLE UPON TYNE NE4 7SA
t: 0191 200 4110 f: 0191 200 4349
e: enquiries@ncl-coll.ac.uk
// www.newcastlecollege.co.uk

WP63 BA Television & Media Practice (Top-up)
Duration: 1FT Hon
Entry Requirements: Interview required. Portfolio required. HND required.

W6P3 FdA Television and Media Practice
Duration: 2FT Fdg CRB Check: Required
Entry Requirements: *GCE:* 120-160. *OCR ND:* P2 *OCR NED:* P3 Interview required.

N30 NEW COLLEGE NOTTINGHAM
ADAMS BUILDING
STONEY STREET
THE LACE MARKET
NOTTINGHAM NG1 1NG
t: 0115 910 0100 f: 0115 953 4349
e: he.team@ncn.ac.uk
// www.ncn.ac.uk

W214 BA Digital Media Design (Top-up)
Duration: 1FT Hon
Entry Requirements: Interview required. Portfolio required.

W215 FdA Multimedia (Multimedia Design)
Duration: 2FT Fdg
Entry Requirements: *GCE:* 100-240. Interview required. Portfolio required.

N37 UNIVERSITY OF WALES, NEWPORT
ADMISSIONS
LODGE ROAD
CAERLEON
NEWPORT NP18 3QT
t: 01633 432030 f: 01633 432850
e: admissions@newport.ac.uk
// www.newport.ac.uk

WN25 BA Advertising Design
Duration: 3FT Hon
Entry Requirements: *Foundation:* Merit. *GCE:* 240. *IB:* 24. Interview required. Portfolio required.

W614 BA Documentary Film and Television
Duration: 3FT Hon
Entry Requirements: *Foundation:* Merit. *GCE:* 240-260. *IB:* 24. Interview required. Portfolio required.

W642 BA Photography for Fashion and Advertising
Duration: 3FT Hon
Entry Requirements: *Foundation:* Merit. *GCE:* 240-260. *IB:* 24. Interview required. Portfolio required.

N38 UNIVERSITY OF NORTHAMPTON
PARK CAMPUS
BOUGHTON GREEN ROAD
NORTHAMPTON NN2 7AL
t: 0800 358 2232 f: 01604 722083
e: admissions@northampton.ac.uk
// www.northampton.ac.uk

N4W6 BA Accounting/Film & Television Studies
Duration: 3FT Hon
Entry Requirements: *GCE:* 260-280. *SQAH:* AAA-BBBB. *IB:* 24. *BTEC Dip:* DD. *BTEC ExtDip:* DMM. *OCR ND:* D *OCR NED:* M2

N5WP BA Advertising/Film & Television Studies
Duration: 3FT Hon
Entry Requirements: *GCE:* 260-280. *SQAH:* AAA-BBBB. *IB:* 24. *BTEC Dip:* DD. *BTEC ExtDip:* DMM. *OCR ND:* D *OCR NED:* M2

N5WC BA Advertising/Fine Art Painting & Drawing
Duration: 3FT Hon
Entry Requirements: *GCE:* 260-280. *SQAH:* AAA-BBBB. *IB:* 24. *BTEC Dip:* DD. *BTEC ExtDip:* DMM. *OCR ND:* D *OCR NED:* M2

N1WP BA Business Entrepreneurship/Film & Television Studies
Duration: 3FT Hon
Entry Requirements: *GCE:* 260-280. *SQAH:* AAA-BBBB. *IB:* 24. *BTEC Dip:* DD. *BTEC ExtDip:* DMM. *OCR ND:* D *OCR NED:* M2

W8W6 BA Creative Writing/Film & Television Studies
Duration: 3FT Hon
Entry Requirements: *GCE:* 260-280. *SQAH:* AAA-BBBB. *IB:* 24. *BTEC Dip:* DD. *BTEC ExtDip:* DMM. *OCR ND:* D *OCR NED:* M2

M9W6 BA Criminology/Film & Television Studies
Duration: 3FT Hon
Entry Requirements: *GCE:* 260-280. *SQAH:* AAA-BBBB. *IB:* 24. *BTEC Dip:* DD. *BTEC ExtDip:* DMM. *OCR ND:* D *OCR NED:* M2

W5W6 BA Dance/Film & Television Studies
Duration: 3FT Hon
Entry Requirements: *GCE:* 260-280. *SQAH:* AAA-BBBB. *IB:* 24. *BTEC Dip:* DD. *BTEC ExtDip:* DMM. *OCR ND:* D *OCR NED:* M2 Interview required.

L1W6 BA Economics/Film & Television Studies
Duration: 3FT Hon
Entry Requirements: *GCE:* 260-280. *SQAH:* AAA-BBBB. *IB:* 24. *BTEC Dip:* DD. *BTEC ExtDip:* DMM. *OCR ND:* D *OCR NED:* M2

Q3W6 BA English/Film & Television Studies
Duration: 3FT Hon
Entry Requirements: *GCE:* 260-280. *SQAH:* AAA-BBBB. *IB:* 24. *BTEC Dip:* DD. *BTEC ExtDip:* DMM. *OCR ND:* D *OCR NED:* M2

W620 BA Film & Television Studies
Duration: 3FT Hon
Entry Requirements: *GCE:* 260-280. *SQAH:* AAA-BBBB. *IB:* 24. *BTEC Dip:* DD. *BTEC ExtDip:* DMM. *OCR ND:* D *OCR NED:* M2

W6N2 BA Film & Television Studies with Applied Management
Duration: 3FT Hon
Entry Requirements: *GCE:* 260-280. *SQAH:* AAA-BBBB. *IB:* 24.
BTEC Dip: DD. *BTEC ExtDip:* DMM. *OCR ND:* D *OCR NED:* M2

W6N4 BA Film & Television Studies/Accounting
Duration: 3FT Hon
Entry Requirements: *GCE:* 260-280. *SQAH:* AAA-BBBB. *IB:* 24.
BTEC Dip: DD. *BTEC ExtDip:* DMM. *OCR ND:* D *OCR NED:* M2

W6NM BA Film & Television Studies/Advertising
Duration: 3FT Hon
Entry Requirements: *GCE:* 260-280. *SQAH:* AAA-BBBB. *IB:* 24.
BTEC Dip: DD. *BTEC ExtDip:* DMM. *OCR ND:* D *OCR NED:* M2

W6G5 BA Film & Television Studies/Business Computing Systems
Duration: 3FT Hon
Entry Requirements: *GCE:* 260-280. *SQAH:* AAA-BBBB. *IB:* 24.
BTEC Dip: DD. *BTEC ExtDip:* DMM. *OCR ND:* D *OCR NED:* M2

W6N1 BA Film & Television Studies/Business Entrepreneurship
Duration: 3FT Hon
Entry Requirements: *GCE:* 260-280. *SQAH:* AAA-BBBB. *IB:* 24.
BTEC Dip: DD. *BTEC ExtDip:* DMM. *OCR ND:* D *OCR NED:* M2

W6G4 BA Film & Television Studies/Computing
Duration: 3FT Hon
Entry Requirements: *GCE:* 260-280. *SQAH:* AAA-BBBB. *IB:* 24.
BTEC Dip: DD. *BTEC ExtDip:* DMM. *OCR ND:* D *OCR NED:* M2

W6W8 BA Film & Television Studies/Creative Writing
Duration: 3FT Hon
Entry Requirements: *GCE:* 260-280. *SQAH:* AAA-BBBB. *IB:* 24.
BTEC Dip: DD. *BTEC ExtDip:* DMM. *OCR ND:* D *OCR NED:* M2

W6M9 BA Film & Television Studies/Criminology
Duration: 3FT Hon
Entry Requirements: *GCE:* 260-280. *SQAH:* AAA-BBBB. *IB:* 24.
BTEC Dip: DD. *BTEC ExtDip:* DMM. *OCR ND:* D *OCR NED:* M2

W6W5 BA Film & Television Studies/Dance
Duration: 3FT Hon
Entry Requirements: *GCE:* 260-280. *SQAH:* AAA-BBBB. *IB:* 24.
BTEC Dip: DD. *BTEC ExtDip:* DMM. *OCR ND:* D *OCR NED:* M2
Interview required.

W6L1 BA Film & Television Studies/Economics
Duration: 3FT Hon
Entry Requirements: *GCE:* 260-280. *SQAH:* AAA-BBBB. *IB:* 24.
BTEC Dip: DD. *BTEC ExtDip:* DMM. *OCR ND:* D *OCR NED:* M2

W6Q3 BA Film & Television Studies/English
Duration: 3FT Hon
Entry Requirements: *GCE:* 260-280. *SQAH:* AAA-BBBB. *IB:* 24.
BTEC Dip: DD. *BTEC ExtDip:* DMM. *OCR ND:* D *OCR NED:* M2

W6W1 BA Film & Television Studies/Fine Art Painting & Drawing
Duration: 3FT Hon
Entry Requirements: *GCE:* 260-280. *SQAH:* AAA-BBBB. *IB:* 24.
BTEC Dip: DD. *BTEC ExtDip:* DMM. *OCR ND:* D *OCR NED:* M2

W6R1 BA Film & Television Studies/French
Duration: 3FT Hon
Entry Requirements: *GCE:* 260-280. *SQAH:* AAA-BBBB. *IB:* 24.
BTEC Dip: DD. *BTEC ExtDip:* DMM. *OCR ND:* D *OCR NED:* M2

W6V1 BA Film & Television Studies/History
Duration: 3FT Hon
Entry Requirements: *GCE:* 260-280. *SQAH:* AAA-BBBB. *IB:* 24.
BTEC Dip: DD. *BTEC ExtDip:* DMM. *OCR ND:* D *OCR NED:* M2

W6B1 BA Film & Television Studies/Human Bioscience
Duration: 3FT Hon
Entry Requirements: *GCE:* 260-280. *SQAH:* AAA-BBBB. *IB:* 24.
BTEC Dip: DD. *BTEC ExtDip:* DMM. *OCR ND:* D *OCR NED:* M2

W6L7 BA Film & Television Studies/Human Geography
Duration: 3FT Hon
Entry Requirements: *GCE:* 260-280. *SQAH:* AAA-BBBB. *IB:* 24.
BTEC Dip: DD. *BTEC ExtDip:* DMM. *OCR ND:* D *OCR NED:* M2

W6N6 BA Film & Television Studies/Human Resource Management
Duration: 3FT Hon
Entry Requirements: *GCE:* 260-280. *SQAH:* AAA-BBBB. *IB:* 24.
BTEC Dip: DD. *BTEC ExtDip:* DMM. *OCR ND:* D *OCR NED:* M2

W6P5 BA Film & Television Studies/Journalism
Duration: 3FT Hon
Entry Requirements: *GCE:* 260-280. *SQAH:* AAA-BBBB. *IB:* 24.
BTEC Dip: DD. *BTEC ExtDip:* DMM. *OCR ND:* D *OCR NED:* M2

W6M1 BA Film & Television Studies/Law
Duration: 3FT Hon
Entry Requirements: *GCE:* 260-280. *SQAH:* AAA-BBBB. *IB:* 24.
BTEC Dip: DD. *BTEC ExtDip:* DMM. *OCR ND:* D *OCR NED:* M2

W6N5 BA Film & Television Studies/Marketing
Duration: 3FT Hon

Entry Requirements: *GCE:* 260-280. *SQAH:* AAA-BBBB. *IB:* 24. *BTEC Dip:* DD. *BTEC ExtDip:* DMM. *OCR ND:* D *OCR NED:* M2

W6PH BA Film & Television Studies/Media Production
Duration: 3FT Hon

Entry Requirements: *GCE:* 260-280. *SQAH:* AAA-BBBB. *IB:* 24. *BTEC Dip:* DD. *BTEC ExtDip:* DMM. *OCR ND:* D *OCR NED:* M2

W6F8 BA Film & Television Studies/Physical Geography
Duration: 3FT Hon

Entry Requirements: *GCE:* 260-280. *SQAH:* AAA-BBBB. *IB:* 24. *BTEC Dip:* DD. *BTEC ExtDip:* DMM. *OCR ND:* D *OCR NED:* M2

W6L2 BA Film & Television Studies/Politics
Duration: 3FT Hon

Entry Requirements: *GCE:* 260-280. *SQAH:* AAA-BBBB. *IB:* 24. *BTEC Dip:* DD. *BTEC ExtDip:* DMM. *OCR ND:* D *OCR NED:* M2

W6W3 BA Film & Television Studies/Popular Music
Duration: 3FT Hon

Entry Requirements: *GCE:* 260-280. *SQAH:* AAA-BBBB. *IB:* 24. *BTEC Dip:* DD. *BTEC ExtDip:* DMM. *OCR ND:* D *OCR NED:* M2
Interview required.

W6C8 BA Film & Television Studies/Psychology
Duration: 3FT Hon

Entry Requirements: *GCE:* 260-280. *SQAH:* AAA-BBBB. *IB:* 24. *BTEC Dip:* DD. *BTEC ExtDip:* DMM. *OCR ND:* D *OCR NED:* M2

W6L5 BA Film & Television Studies/Social Care
Duration: 3FT Hon

Entry Requirements: *GCE:* 260-280. *SQAH:* AAA-BBBB. *IB:* 24. *BTEC Dip:* DD. *BTEC ExtDip:* DMM. *OCR ND:* D *OCR NED:* M2

W6C6 BA Film & Television Studies/Sport Studies
Duration: 3FT Hon

Entry Requirements: *GCE:* 260-280. *SQAH:* AAA-BBBB. *IB:* 24. *BTEC Dip:* DD. *BTEC ExtDip:* DMM. *OCR ND:* D *OCR NED:* M2

W6N8 BA Film & Television Studies/Tourism
Duration: 3FT Hon

Entry Requirements: *GCE:* 260-280. *SQAH:* AAA-BBBB. *IB:* 24. *BTEC Dip:* DD. *BTEC ExtDip:* DMM. *OCR ND:* D *OCR NED:* M2

W6GK BA Film & Television Studies/Web Design
Duration: 3FT Hon

Entry Requirements: *GCE:* 260-280. *SQAH:* AAA-BBBB. *IB:* 24. *BTEC Dip:* DD. *BTEC ExtDip:* DMM. *OCR ND:* D *OCR NED:* M2

W1NM BA Fine Art Painting & Drawing/Advertising
Duration: 3FT Hon

Entry Requirements: *GCE:* 260-280. *SQAH:* AAA-BBBB. *IB:* 24. *BTEC Dip:* DD. *BTEC ExtDip:* DMM. *OCR ND:* D *OCR NED:* M2

W1W6 BA Fine Art Painting & Drawing/Film & Television Studies
Duration: 3FT Hon

Entry Requirements: *GCE:* 260-280. *SQAH:* AAA-BBBB. *IB:* 24. *BTEC Dip:* DD. *BTEC ExtDip:* DMM. *OCR ND:* D *OCR NED:* M2

W1PH BA Fine Art Painting & Drawing/Media Production
Duration: 3FT Hon

Entry Requirements: *GCE:* 260-280. *SQAH:* AAA-BBBB. *IB:* 24. *BTEC Dip:* DD. *BTEC ExtDip:* DMM. *OCR ND:* D *OCR NED:* M2

W1GK BA Fine Art Painting & Drawing/Web Design
Duration: 3FT Hon

Entry Requirements: *GCE:* 260-280. *SQAH:* AAA-BBBB. *IB:* 24. *BTEC Dip:* DD. *BTEC ExtDip:* DMM. *OCR ND:* D *OCR NED:* M2

R1W6 BA French/Film & Television Studies
Duration: 3FT Hon

Entry Requirements: *GCE:* 260-280. *SQAH:* AAA-BBBB. *IB:* 24. *BTEC Dip:* DD. *BTEC ExtDip:* DMM. *OCR ND:* D *OCR NED:* M2

V1W6 BA History/Film & Television Studies
Duration: 3FT Hon

Entry Requirements: *GCE:* 260-280. *SQAH:* AAA-BBBB. *IB:* 24. *BTEC Dip:* DD. *BTEC ExtDip:* DMM. *OCR ND:* D *OCR NED:* M2

L7W6 BA Human Geography/Film & Television Studies
Duration: 3FT Hon

Entry Requirements: *GCE:* 260-280. *SQAH:* AAA-BBBB. *IB:* 24. *BTEC Dip:* DD. *BTEC ExtDip:* DMM. *OCR ND:* D *OCR NED:* M2

N6W6 BA Human Resource Management/Film & Television Studies
Duration: 3FT Hon

Entry Requirements: *GCE:* 260-280. *SQAH:* AAA-BBBB. *IB:* 24. *BTEC Dip:* DD. *BTEC ExtDip:* DMM. *OCR ND:* D *OCR NED:* M2

P5W6 BA Journalism/Film & Television Studies
Duration: 3FT Hon
Entry Requirements: **GCE:** 260-280. **SQAH:** AAA-BBBB. **IB:** 24. **BTEC Dip:** DD. **BTEC ExtDip:** DMM. **OCR ND:** D **OCR NED:** M2

M1W6 BA Law/Film & Television Studies
Duration: 3FT Hon
Entry Requirements: **GCE:** 260-280. **SQAH:** AAA-BBBB. **IB:** 24. **BTEC Dip:** DD. **BTEC ExtDip:** DMM. **OCR ND:** D **OCR NED:** M2

N5W6 BA Marketing/Film & Television Studies
Duration: 3FT Hon
Entry Requirements: **GCE:** 260-280. **SQAH:** AAA-BBBB. **IB:** 24. **BTEC Dip:** DD. **BTEC ExtDip:** DMM. **OCR ND:** D **OCR NED:** M2

P3WP BA Media Production/Film & Television Studies
Duration: 3FT Hon
Entry Requirements: **GCE:** 260-280. **SQAH:** AAA-BBBB. **IB:** 24. **BTEC Dip:** DD. **BTEC ExtDip:** DMM. **OCR ND:** D **OCR NED:** M2

P3WC BA Media Production/Fine Art Painting & Drawing
Duration: 3FT Hon
Entry Requirements: **GCE:** 260-280. **SQAH:** AAA-BBBB. **IB:** 24. **BTEC Dip:** DD. **BTEC ExtDip:** DMM. **OCR ND:** D **OCR NED:** M2

L2W6 BA Politics/Film & Television Studies
Duration: 3FT Hon
Entry Requirements: **GCE:** 260-280. **SQAH:** AAA-BBBB. **IB:** 24. **BTEC Dip:** DD. **BTEC ExtDip:** DMM. **OCR ND:** D **OCR NED:** M2

W3W6 BA Popular Music/Film & Television Studies
Duration: 3FT Hon
Entry Requirements: **GCE:** 260-280. **SQAH:** AAA-BBBB. **IB:** 24. **BTEC Dip:** DD. **BTEC ExtDip:** DMM. **OCR ND:** D **OCR NED:** M2
Interview required.

C8W6 BA Psychology/Film & Television Studies
Duration: 3FT Hon
Entry Requirements: **GCE:** 260-280. **SQAH:** AAA-BBBB. **IB:** 24. **BTEC Dip:** DD. **BTEC ExtDip:** DMM. **OCR ND:** D **OCR NED:** M2

L5W6 BA Social Care/Film & Television Studies
Duration: 3FT Hon
Entry Requirements: **GCE:** 260-280. **SQAH:** AAA-BBBB. **IB:** 24. **BTEC Dip:** DD. **BTEC ExtDip:** DMM. **OCR ND:** D **OCR NED:** M2

C6W6 BA Sport Studies/Film & Television Studies
Duration: 3FT Hon
Entry Requirements: **GCE:** 260-280. **SQAH:** AAA-BBBB. **IB:** 24. **BTEC Dip:** DD. **BTEC ExtDip:** DMM. **OCR ND:** D **OCR NED:** M2

N8W6 BA Tourism/Film & Television Studies
Duration: 3FT Hon
Entry Requirements: **GCE:** 260-280. **SQAH:** AAA-BBBB. **IB:** 24. **BTEC Dip:** DD. **BTEC ExtDip:** DMM. **OCR ND:** D **OCR NED:** M2

G5W6 BSc Business Computing Systems/Film & Television Studies
Duration: 3FT Hon
Entry Requirements: **GCE:** 260-280. **SQAH:** AAA-BBBB. **IB:** 24. **BTEC Dip:** DD. **BTEC ExtDip:** DMM. **OCR ND:** D **OCR NED:** M2

G4W6 BSc Computing/Film & Television Studies
Duration: 3FT Hon
Entry Requirements: **GCE:** 260-280. **SQAH:** AAA-BBBB. **IB:** 24. **BTEC Dip:** DD. **BTEC ExtDip:** DMM. **OCR ND:** D **OCR NED:** M2

B1W6 BSc Human Bioscience/Film & Television Studies
Duration: 3FT Hon
Entry Requirements: **GCE:** 260-280. **SQAH:** AAA-BBBB. **IB:** 24. **BTEC Dip:** DD. **BTEC ExtDip:** DMM. **OCR ND:** D **OCR NED:** M2

F8W6 BSc Physical Geography/Film & Television Studies
Duration: 3FT Hon
Entry Requirements: **GCE:** 260-280. **SQAH:** AAA-BBBB. **IB:** 24. **BTEC Dip:** DD. **BTEC ExtDip:** DMM. **OCR ND:** D **OCR NED:** M2

G4WP BSc Web Design/Film & Television Studies
Duration: 3FT Hon
Entry Requirements: **GCE:** 260-280. **SQAH:** AAA-BBBB. **IB:** 24. **BTEC Dip:** DD. **BTEC ExtDip:** DMM. **OCR ND:** D **OCR NED:** M2

G4WC BSc Web Design/Fine Art Painting & Drawing
Duration: 3FT Hon
Entry Requirements: **GCE:** 260-280. **SQAH:** AAA-BBBB. **IB:** 24. **BTEC Dip:** DD. **BTEC ExtDip:** DMM. **OCR ND:** D **OCR NED:** M2

216W HND Digital Film-Making
Duration: 2FT HND
Entry Requirements: **GCE:** 140-160. **SQAH:** BC-CCC. **IB:** 24. **BTEC Dip:** MP. **BTEC ExtDip:** MPP. **OCR ND:** P1 **OCR NED:** P2

N41 NORTHBROOK COLLEGE SUSSEX
LITTLEHAMPTON ROAD
WORTHING
WEST SUSSEX BN12 6NU
t: 0845 155 6060 f: 01903 606073
e: enquiries@nbcol.ac.uk
// www.northbrook.ac.uk

W642 FdA Photography (Fashion, Advertising and Editorial)
Duration: 2FT Fdg
Entry Requirements: *GCE:* 160. Interview required. Portfolio required.

N84 THE UNIVERSITY OF NOTTINGHAM
THE ADMISSIONS OFFICE
THE UNIVERSITY OF NOTTINGHAM
UNIVERSITY PARK
NOTTINGHAM NG7 2RD
t: 0115 951 5151 f: 0115 951 4668
// www.nottingham.ac.uk

W630 BA Film and Television Studies
Duration: 3FT Hon
Entry Requirements: *GCE:* ABB. *SQAAH:* ABB. *IB:* 32.

P60 PLYMOUTH UNIVERSITY
DRAKE CIRCUS
PLYMOUTH PL4 8AA
t: 01752 585858 f: 01752 588055
e: admissions@plymouth.ac.uk
// www.plymouth.ac.uk

WW46 BA Digital Performance Arts
Duration: 1FT Hon
Entry Requirements: HND required.

P65 PLYMOUTH COLLEGE OF ART (FORMERLY PLYMOUTH COLLEGE OF ART AND DESIGN)
TAVISTOCK PLACE
PLYMOUTH PL4 8AT
t: 01752 203434 f: 01752 203444
e: infoservices@plymouthart.ac.uk
// www.plymouthart.ac.uk

W690 FdA Film & Media Production
Duration: 2FT Fdg
Entry Requirements: *Foundation:* Pass. *IB:* 24. *OCR ND:* M1 *OCR NED:* P1 Interview required. Portfolio required.

W691 FdA Film and Media Production (including Level 0)
Duration: 3FT Fdg
Entry Requirements: *IB:* 24. *OCR ND:* P3 *OCR NED:* P3 Interview required. Portfolio required.

P80 UNIVERSITY OF PORTSMOUTH
ACADEMIC REGISTRY
UNIVERSITY HOUSE
WINSTON CHURCHILL AVENUE
PORTSMOUTH PO1 2UP
t: 023 9284 8484 f: 023 9284 3082
e: admissions@port.ac.uk
// www.port.ac.uk

W612 BA Television and Film Production
Duration: 3FT/4SW Hon
Entry Requirements: *GCE:* 240-300. *IB:* 28. *BTEC SubDip:* P. *BTEC Dip:* DD. *BTEC ExtDip:* DMM.

R06 RAVENSBOURNE
6 PENROSE WAY
GREENWICH PENINSULA
LONDON SE10 0EW
t: 020 3040 3998
e: info@rave.ac.uk
// www.rave.ac.uk

NW52 BA Digital Advertising and Design
Duration: 3FT Hon
Entry Requirements: Contact the institution for details.

W611 BA Digital Film Production (with Foundation Year)
Duration: 4FT Hon
Entry Requirements: *Foundation:* Pass. *GCE:* A-E. *IB:* 28. Interview required. Admissions Test required.

W640 BA Digital Photography
Duration: 3FT Hon
Entry Requirements: *Foundation:* Pass. *GCE:* AA-CC. *IB:* 28. Interview required. Portfolio required.

WP40 BA Digital Photography (Fast-Track)
Duration: 2FT Hon
Entry Requirements: Contact the institution for details.

W641 BA Digital Photography (with Foundation Year)
Duration: 4FT Hon
Entry Requirements: Contact the institution for details.

W617 BA Sound Design
Duration: 3FT Hon
Entry Requirements: *Foundation:* Pass. *GCE:* AA-CC. *IB:* 28. Interview required. Portfolio required.

W614 BA Sound Design (Fast-Track)
Duration: 2FT Hon
Entry Requirements: Contact the institution for details.

W613 BA Sound Design (with Foundation Year)
Duration: 4FT Hon
Entry Requirements: *Foundation:* Pass. *GCE:* A-E. *IB:* 28.
Interview required. Portfolio required.

R18 REGENT'S COLLEGE, LONDON (INCORPORATING REGENT'S BUSINESS SCHOOL, LONDON)
INNER CIRCLE, REGENT'S COLLEGE
REGENT'S PARK
LONDON NW1 4NS
t: +44(0)20 7487 7505 f: +44(0)20 7487 7425
e: exrel@regents.ac.uk
// www.regents.ac.uk/

W6P3 BA Film, Television and Digital Media Production
Duration: 3FT Hon
Entry Requirements: *SQAH:* BBCC. *SQAAH:* CC.

R72 ROYAL HOLLOWAY, UNIVERSITY OF LONDON
ROYAL HOLLOWAY, UNIVERSITY OF LONDON
EGHAM
SURREY TW20 0EX
t: 01784 414944 f: 01784 473662
e: Admissions@rhul.ac.uk
// www.rhul.ac.uk

W625 BA Media Arts
Duration: 3FT Hon
Entry Requirements: *GCE:* ABB-ABbb. *SQAH:* AABBB. *SQAAH:* ABB. *IB:* 34.

S05 SAE INSTITUTE
297 KINGSLAND ROAD
LONDON E8 4DD
t: 020 7923 9159
e: degree.registry@sae.edu
// www.sae.edu

W612 BA/BSc Digital Film Making
Duration: 2FT Hon
Entry Requirements: Contact the institution for details.

W601 DipHE Digital Film Making
Duration: 1.5FT Dip
Entry Requirements: Contact the institution for details.

S21 SHEFFIELD HALLAM UNIVERSITY
CITY CAMPUS
HOWARD STREET
SHEFFIELD S1 1WB
t: 0114 225 5555 f: 0114 225 2167
e: admissions@shu.ac.uk
// www.shu.ac.uk

W212 BA Digital Media Production
Duration: 3FT Hon
Entry Requirements: *GCE:* 240.

W215 MArt Digital Media Production
Duration: 4FT Hon
Entry Requirements: *GCE:* 260.

S26 SOLIHULL COLLEGE
BLOSSOMFIELD ROAD
SOLIHULL
WEST MIDLANDS B91 1SB
t: 0121 678 7006 f: 0121 678 7200
e: enquiries@solihull.ac.uk
// www.solihull.ac.uk

066W HND Photography & Digital Imaging
Duration: 2FT HND
Entry Requirements: *Foundation:* Merit. *GCE:* A-E. *IB:* 24. *BTEC Dip:* MM. *BTEC ExtDip:* MMM. *OCR ND:* M2 *OCR NED:* M3
Interview required. Portfolio required.

S30 SOUTHAMPTON SOLENT UNIVERSITY
EAST PARK TERRACE
SOUTHAMPTON
HAMPSHIRE SO14 0RT
t: +44 (0) 23 8031 9039 f: + 44 (0)23 8022 2259
e: admissions@solent.ac.uk
// www.solent.ac.uk/

W990 BA Promotional Media (Top-Up)
Duration: 1FT Hon
Entry Requirements: Interview required. HND required.

S64 ST MARY'S UNIVERSITY COLLEGE, TWICKENHAM
WALDEGRAVE ROAD
STRAWBERRY HILL
MIDDLESEX TW1 4SX
t: 020 8240 4029 f: 020 8240 2361
e: admit@smuc.ac.uk
// www.smuc.ac.uk

PW3P BA Film & Popular Culture and Media Arts
Duration: 3FT Hon
Entry Requirements: *GCE:* 240. *SQAH:* BBBC. *IB:* 28. *OCR ND:* D *OCR NED:* M3 Interview required.

S72 STAFFORDSHIRE UNIVERSITY
COLLEGE ROAD
STOKE ON TRENT ST4 2DE
t: 01782 292753 f: 01782 292740
e: admissions@staffs.ac.uk
// www.staffs.ac.uk

WNF5 BA Advertising and Brand Management
Duration: 3FT/4FT Hon
Entry Requirements: *Foundation:* Merit. *GCE:* 200-240. *IB:* 24. *BTEC Dip:* DD. *BTEC ExtDip:* MMM. Interview required. Portfolio required.

WN65 BA Advertising and Commercial Film Production
Duration: 3FT/4FT Hon
Entry Requirements: *Foundation:* Merit. *GCE:* 200-240. *IB:* 24. *BTEC Dip:* DD. *BTEC ExtDip:* MMM. Interview required. Portfolio required.

W620 BA Film, Television and Radio Studies
Duration: 3FT Hon
Entry Requirements: *GCE:* 200-240. *IB:* 24. *BTEC Dip:* DD. *BTEC ExtDip:* MMM.

WP90 BSc CGI and Digital Effects
Duration: 3FT/4SW Hon
Entry Requirements: Contact the institution for details.

S82 UNIVERSITY CAMPUS SUFFOLK (UCS)
WATERFRONT BUILDING
NEPTUNE QUAY
IPSWICH
SUFFOLK IP4 1QJ
t: 01473 338833 f: 01473 339900
e: info@ucs.ac.uk
// www.ucs.ac.uk

W212 BA Graphic Design
Duration: 3FT Hon
Entry Requirements: *GCE:* 240-280. *IB:* 28. *BTEC ExtDip:* DMM. Interview required. Portfolio required.

W640 BA Photographic & Digital Media
Duration: 3FT Hon
Entry Requirements: *GCE:* 280. *IB:* 28. *BTEC ExtDip:* DMM. Interview required. Portfolio required.

S84 UNIVERSITY OF SUNDERLAND
STUDENT HELPLINE
THE STUDENT GATEWAY
CHESTER ROAD
SUNDERLAND SR1 3SD
t: 0191 515 3000 f: 0191 515 3805
e: student.helpline@sunderland.ac.uk
// www.sunderland.ac.uk

W220 BA Advertising & Design
Duration: 3FT Hon
Entry Requirements: *Foundation:* Merit. *GCE:* 220. *SQAH:* BBBC. *IB:* 22. Interview required. Portfolio required.

W612 BA Digital Film Production
Duration: 3FT Hon
Entry Requirements: *GCE:* 260-360. *IB:* 30. Interview required. Portfolio required.

WP63 BA Media Studies and Photography
Duration: 3FT Hon
Entry Requirements: *GCE:* 260-360. *IB:* 32. *OCR ND:* D *OCR NED:* M3

P3W6 BA Media Studies with Photography
Duration: 3FT Hon
Entry Requirements: *GCE:* 260-360. *IB:* 32. *OCR ND:* D *OCR NED:* M3

W651 BA Photography, Video and Digital Imaging
Duration: 3FT Hon
Entry Requirements: *GCE:* 220-360. *SQAH:* BBCCC. *IB:* 22. Interview required. Portfolio required.

S96 SWANSEA METROPOLITAN UNIVERSITY
MOUNT PLEASANT CAMPUS
SWANSEA SA1 6ED
t: 01792 481000 f: 01792 481061
e: gemma.green@smu.ac.uk
// www.smu.ac.uk

W221 BA Advertising and Brand Design
Duration: 3FT Hon
Entry Requirements: *Foundation:* Pass. *GCE:* 200-360. *IB:* 24. Interview required. Portfolio required.

W610 BA Digital Film and Television Production
Duration: 3FT Hon
Entry Requirements: *Foundation:* Pass. *GCE:* 200-360. *IB:* 24. Interview required. Portfolio required.

W601 BA Digital Film and Television Production (4 year programme)
Duration: 4FT Hon
Entry Requirements: *Foundation:* Pass. *GCE:* 200-360. *IB:* 24. Interview required. Portfolio required.

W214 BSc Multimedia
Duration: 3FT Hon
Entry Requirements: *GCE:* 200-360. *IB:* 24. Interview required.

S98 SWINDON COLLEGE
NORTH STAR AVENUE
SWINDON
WILTSHIRE SN2 1DY
t: 0800 731 2250 f: 01793 430503
e: headmissions@swindon-college.ac.uk
// www.swindon-college.ac.uk

W21F HND Interactive Media
Duration: 2FT HND
Entry Requirements: Contact the institution for details.

T20 TEESSIDE UNIVERSITY
MIDDLESBROUGH TS1 3BA
t: 01642 218121 f: 01642 384201
e: registry@tees.ac.uk
// www.tees.ac.uk

WGC4 BA Creative Digital Media
Duration: 3FT/4SW Hon
Entry Requirements: *IB:* 30. *OCR ND:* D *OCR NED:* M2 Interview required.

GW49 BA Web and Multimedia Design
Duration: 3FT/4SW Hon
Entry Requirements: *IB:* 30. *OCR ND:* D *OCR NED:* M2 Interview required.

T85 TRURO AND PENWITH COLLEGE
TRURO COLLEGE
COLLEGE ROAD
TRURO
CORNWALL TR1 3XX
t: 01872 267122 f: 01872 267526
e: heinfo@trurocollege.ac.uk
// www.truro-penwith.ac.uk

W640 FdA Photography and Digital Imaging
Duration: 2FT Fdg
Entry Requirements: *GCE:* 60. *IB:* 24. *BTEC Dip:* MP. *BTEC ExtDip:* PPP. Interview required.

U20 UNIVERSITY OF ULSTER
COLERAINE
CO. LONDONDERRY
NORTHERN IRELAND BT52 1SA
t: 028 7012 4221 f: 028 7012 4908
e: online@ulster.ac.uk
// www.ulster.ac.uk

P3WP BA Media Studies with Photo-Imaging
Duration: 3FT Hon
Entry Requirements: *GCE:* 280. *IB:* 24.

U65 UNIVERSITY OF THE ARTS LONDON
272 HIGH HOLBORN
LONDON WC1V 7EY
t: 020 7514 6000x6197 f: 020 7514 6198
e: c.anderson@arts.ac.uk
// www.arts.ac.uk

W601 BA Film and Television
Duration: 3FT Hon
Entry Requirements: *IB:* 28. Foundation Course required. Interview required. Portfolio required.

W212 BA Graphic and Media Design
Duration: 3FT/4SW Hon
Entry Requirements: Interview required.

W25 WARWICKSHIRE COLLEGE
WARWICK NEW ROAD
LEAMINGTON SPA
WARWICKSHIRE CV32 5JE
t: 01926 884223 f: 01926 318 111
e: kgooch@warkscol.ac.uk
// www.warwickshire.ac.uk

016W HND Digital Film & Video
Duration: 2FT HND
Entry Requirements: Contact the institution for details.

W50 UNIVERSITY OF WESTMINSTER
2ND FLOOR, CAVENDISH HOUSE
101 NEW CAVENDISH STREET,
LONDON W1W 6XH
t: 020 7915 5511
e: course-enquiries@westminster.ac.uk
// www.westminster.ac.uk

W620 BA Film and Television Production
Duration: 3FT Hon
Entry Requirements: *GCE:* ABB. *SQAH:* AAAAA-AAABB. *SQAAH:* AAA-ABB. *IB:* 30. *OCR ND:* D Interview required. Portfolio required.

W67 WIGAN AND LEIGH COLLEGE
PO BOX 53
PARSON'S WALK
WIGAN
GREATER MANCHESTER WN1 1RS
t: 01942 761605 f: 01942 761164
e: applications@wigan-leigh.ac.uk
// www.wigan-leigh.ac.uk

W612 FdA Media Production and Technician
Duration: 2FT Fdg
Entry Requirements: Interview required.

W76 UNIVERSITY OF WINCHESTER
WINCHESTER
HANTS SO22 4NR
t: 01962 827234 f: 01962 827288
e: course.enquiries@winchester.ac.uk
// www.winchester.ac.uk

P3W6 BA Media Studies
Duration: 3FT Hon
Entry Requirements: *Foundation:* Distinction. *GCE:* 260-300. *IB:* 25. *OCR ND:* D *OCR NED:* M2

W80 UNIVERSITY OF WORCESTER
HENWICK GROVE
WORCESTER WR2 6AJ
t: 01905 855111 f: 01905 855377
e: admissions@worc.ac.uk
// www.worcester.ac.uk

W212 BA Creative Digital Media
Duration: 3FT Hon
Entry Requirements: *GCE:* 220-300. *IB:* 24. *OCR ND:* D Interview required. Portfolio required.

PW3G BA Creative Digital Media and Graphic Design & Multimedia
Duration: 3FT Hon
Entry Requirements: Contact the institution for details.

W612 BA Digital Film Production
Duration: 3FT Hon
Entry Requirements: *GCE:* 220-300. *IB:* 24. *OCR ND:* D Interview required. Portfolio required.

PW36 BA Digital Film Production and Film Studies
Duration: 3FT Hon
Entry Requirements: *GCE:* 240-260. *IB:* 24. *OCR ND:* D Interview required. Portfolio required.

WW6V BA Digital Film Production and Screen Writing
Duration: 3FT Hon
Entry Requirements: *GCE:* 220-300. *IB:* 24. *OCR ND:* D Interview required. Portfolio required.

W210 BA Graphic Design & Multimedia
Duration: 3FT Hon
Entry Requirements: *GCE:* 220-300. *IB:* 24. *OCR ND:* D Interview required. Portfolio required.

W292 BA Graphic Design & Multimedia and Illustration
Duration: 3FT Hon
Entry Requirements: *GCE:* 220-300. *IB:* 24. *OCR ND:* D Interview required. Portfolio required.

WPFH BA Graphic Design & Multimedia and Media & Cultural Studies
Duration: 3FT Hon
Entry Requirements: Contact the institution for details.

GWKF BA/BSc Computing and Graphic Design & Multimedia
Duration: 3FT Hon
Entry Requirements: *GCE:* 240-260. *IB:* 24. *OCR ND:* D Interview required. Portfolio required.

Y50 THE UNIVERSITY OF YORK
STUDENT RECRUITMENT AND ADMISSIONS
UNIVERSITY OF YORK
HESLINGTON
YORK YO10 5DD
t: 01904 324000 f: 01904 323538
e: ug-admissions@york.ac.uk
// www.york.ac.uk

W600 BSc Film and Television Production
Duration: 3FT Hon
Entry Requirements: *GCE:* AAB. *SQAH:* AAAAB. *SQAAH:* AB. *IB:* 35. *BTEC ExtDip:* DDD.

Y75 YORK ST JOHN UNIVERSITY
LORD MAYOR'S WALK
YORK YO31 7EX
t: 01904 876598 f: 01904 876940/876921
e: admissions@yorksj.ac.uk
// w3.yorksj.ac.uk

W600 BA Film & Television Production
Duration: 3FT Hon
Entry Requirements: *GCE:* 240-260. *IB:* 24.

WW64 BA Film & Television Production (for international applicants only)
Duration: 4FT Hon
Entry Requirements: *GCE:* 240-260. *IB:* 24.

FASHION

A50 AMERICAN INTERCONTINENTAL UNIVERSITY - LONDON
110 MARYLEBONE HIGH STREET
LONDON W1U 4RY
t: 020 7467 5640 f: 020 7467 5641
e: admissions@aiulondon.ac.uk
// www.aiulondon.ac.uk

W230 BA Fashion Design
Duration: 4FT Hon
Entry Requirements: Contact the institution for details.

WNF5 BA Fashion Marketing
Duration: 4FT Hon
Entry Requirements: Contact the institution for details.

WF30 BFA Fashion Marketing and Design
Duration: 4FT Deg
Entry Requirements: Contact the institution for details.

WC30 BFA Fashion Marketing specialisation Fashion Retailing
Duration: 4FT Deg
Entry Requirements: Contact the institution for details.

A60 ANGLIA RUSKIN UNIVERSITY
BISHOP HALL LANE
CHELMSFORD
ESSEX CM1 1SQ
t: 0845 271 3333 f: 01245 251789
e: answers@anglia.ac.uk
// www.anglia.ac.uk

W230 BA Fashion Design
Duration: 3FT Hon
Entry Requirements: *GCE:* 200-240. *SQAH:* CCCC. *SQAAH:* BC.
IB: 24. Interview required. Portfolio required.

A66 THE ARTS UNIVERSITY COLLEGE AT BOURNEMOUTH (FORMERLY ARTS INSTITUTE AT BOURNEMOUTH)
WALLISDOWN
POOLE
DORSET BH12 5HH
t: 01202 363228 f: 01202 537729
e: admissions@aucb.ac.uk
// www.aucb.ac.uk

W230 BA Fashion Studies
Duration: 3FT Hon
Entry Requirements: *Foundation:* Pass. *GCE:* BCC. *IB:* 24. *OCR ND:* M1 *OCR NED:* M1 Interview required. Portfolio required.

B15 BASINGSTOKE COLLEGE OF TECHNOLOGY
WORTING ROAD
BASINGSTOKE RG21 8TN
t: (Main) 01256 354141 f: 01256 306444
e: admissions@bcot.ac.uk
// www.bcot.ac.uk

W230 BA Textiles for Fashion
Duration: 3FT Hon
Entry Requirements: *GCE:* 240. Portfolio required.

B20 BATH SPA UNIVERSITY
NEWTON PARK
NEWTON ST LOE
BATH BA2 9BN
t: 01225 875875 f: 01225 875444
e: enquiries@bathspa.ac.uk
// www.bathspa.ac.uk/clearing

W233 BA Fashion Design
Duration: 3FT Hon
Entry Requirements: *GCE:* 220-280. *IB:* 24. Interview required.

W232 FdA Fashion & Textile Design Skills
Duration: 2FT Fdg
Entry Requirements: *GCE:* 220-280. *IB:* 24. Interview required.

B22 UNIVERSITY OF BEDFORDSHIRE
PARK SQUARE
LUTON
BEDS LU1 3JU
t: 0844 8482234 f: 01582 489323
e: admissions@beds.ac.uk
// www.beds.ac.uk

W231 BA Fashion Design
Duration: 3FT Hon
Entry Requirements: *GCE:* 200. Interview required.

W291 BA Fashion Design (Level 3 only)
Duration: 1FT Hon
Entry Requirements: Interview required.

W230 FdA Fashion & Textile Design
Duration: 2FT Fdg
Entry Requirements: *GCE:* 120. Interview required. Portfolio required.

B23 BEDFORD COLLEGE
CAULDWELL STREET
BEDFORD MK42 9AH
t: 01234 291000 f: 01234 342674
e: info@bedford.ac.uk
// www.bedford.ac.uk

232W HNC Fashion and Textiles
Duration: 1FT HNC
Entry Requirements: *Foundation:* Pass. *GCE:* 80-120. Interview required. Portfolio required.

132W HND Fashion and Textiles
Duration: 2FT HND
Entry Requirements: *Foundation:* Pass. *GCE:* 80-120. Interview required. Portfolio required.

B25 BIRMINGHAM CITY UNIVERSITY
PERRY BARR
BIRMINGHAM B42 2SU
t: 0121 331 5595 f: 0121 331 7994
// www.bcu.ac.uk

W230 BA Fashion Design
Duration: 3FT Hon
Entry Requirements: *GCE:* 280. *SQAH:* BBBB. *SQAAH:* CCC. *IB:* 28. Interview required. Portfolio required.

W2W4 BA Fashion Design with Design for Performance
Duration: 3FT Hon
Entry Requirements: *GCE:* 280. *IB:* 28. Interview required. Portfolio required.

W233 BA Fashion Design with Fashion Accessories
Duration: 3FT Hon
Entry Requirements: Contact the institution for details.

W3N2 BA Fashion Design with Fashion Management and Buying
Duration: 3FT Hon
Entry Requirements: Contact the institution for details.

W2N2 BA Fashion Retail Management
Duration: 3FT Hon
Entry Requirements: *GCE:* 280. *IB:* 28. Interview required. Portfolio required.

W239 BA Jewellery Design and Related Products
Duration: 3FT Hon
Entry Requirements: Contact the institution for details.

B37 BISHOP BURTON COLLEGE
BISHOP BURTON
BEVERLEY
EAST YORKSHIRE HU17 8QG
t: 01964 553000 f: 01964 553101
e: enquiries@bishopburton.ac.uk
// www.bishopburton.ac.uk

W230 BA Fashion and Clothing
Duration: 3FT Hon
Entry Requirements: *IB:* 24.

W232 FdA Fashion and Clothing
Duration: 2FT Fdg
Entry Requirements: Interview required.

W233 FdA Fashion and Clothing (including Foundation Year)
Duration: 3FT Fdg
Entry Requirements: Contact the institution for details.

B40 BLACKBURN COLLEGE
FEILDEN STREET
BLACKBURN BB2 1LH
t: 01254 292594 f: 01254 679647
e: he-admissions@blackburn.ac.uk
// www.blackburn.ac.uk

W23Y BA Contemporary Fashion (Top-Up)
Duration: 1FT Hon
Entry Requirements: Contact the institution for details.

W230 FdA Fashion
Duration: 2FT Fdg
Entry Requirements: Contact the institution for details.

B60 BRADFORD COLLEGE: AN ASSOCIATE COLLEGE OF LEEDS METROPOLITAN UNIVERSITY

GREAT HORTON ROAD
BRADFORD
WEST YORKSHIRE BD7 1AY
t: 01274 433008 f: 01274 431652
e: heregistry@bradfordcollege.ac.uk
// www.bradfordcollege.ac.uk/
university-centre

W232 BA Fashion Design
Duration: 3FT Hon
Entry Requirements: *GCE:* 220. Interview required. Portfolio required.

B72 UNIVERSITY OF BRIGHTON

MITHRAS HOUSE 211
LEWES ROAD
BRIGHTON BN2 4AT
t: 01273 644644 f: 01273 642607
e: admissions@brighton.ac.uk
// www.brighton.ac.uk

W2N2 BA Fashion with Business Studies
Duration: 3FT/4SW Hon
Entry Requirements: *GCE:* BBB. Foundation Course required. Interview required. Portfolio required.

W2N1 MDes Fashion with Business Studies
Duration: 4FT/5SW Hon
Entry Requirements: *GCE:* BBB. Foundation Course required. Interview required. Portfolio required.

B80 UNIVERSITY OF THE WEST OF ENGLAND, BRISTOL

FRENCHAY CAMPUS
COLDHARBOUR LANE
BRISTOL BS16 1QY
t: +44 (0)117 32 83333 f: +44 (0)117 32 82810
e: admissions@uwe.ac.uk
// www.uwe.ac.uk

W230 BA Fashion
Duration: 3FT Hon
Entry Requirements: *GCE:* 280. Interview required. Portfolio required.

C22 COLEG SIR GAR / CARMARTHENSHIRE COLLEGE

SANDY ROAD
LLANELLI
CARMARTHENSHIRE SA15 4DN
t: 01554 748000 f: 01554 748170
e: admissions@colegsirgar.ac.uk
// www.colegsirgar.ac.uk

W2H0 BA (Hons) Fashion (Apparel Design and Construction)
Duration: 3FT Hon
Entry Requirements: Portfolio required.

W232 BA (Hons) Textiles (Art, Design and Craft)
Duration: 3FT Hon
Entry Requirements: Portfolio required.

C30 UNIVERSITY OF CENTRAL LANCASHIRE

PRESTON
LANCS PR1 2HE
t: 01772 201201 f: 01772 894954
e: uadmissions@uclan.ac.uk
// www.uclan.ac.uk

W232 BA Eastern Fashion Design
Duration: 3FT Hon
Entry Requirements: *GCE:* 220. *IB:* 24. *OCR ND:* D *OCR NED:* M3 Interview required. Portfolio required.

N5W6 BA Fashion & Brand Promotion and Photography
Duration: 3FT Hon
Entry Requirements: *Foundation:* Distinction. *GCE:* 260-300. *IB:* 25. *BTEC Dip:* D*D*. *BTEC ExtDip:* DMM. *OCR NED:* M2 Interview required. Portfolio required.

W231 BA Fashion (4-year sandwich)
Duration: 4SW Hon
Entry Requirements: *GCE:* 240-280. *IB:* 26. Interview required. Portfolio required.

WN21 BA Fashion Entrepreneurship
Duration: 3FT Hon
Entry Requirements: *GCE:* 240. *IB:* 24. *OCR ND:* D *OCR NED:* M3 Interview required. Portfolio required.

W2N5 BA Fashion Promotion with Styling
Duration: 3FT Hon
Entry Requirements: *GCE:* 240-280. *IB:* 26. *OCR ND:* D *OCR NED:* M2 Interview required. Portfolio required.

N5W2 BA Marketing Management with Fashion (sandwich)
Duration: 4SW Hon
Entry Requirements: Contact the institution for details.

N553 BA Retail Management (Fashion)
Duration: 3FT Hon
Entry Requirements: *GCE:* 260-300. *SQAH:* AABB-BBBC. *IB:* 28. *OCR ND:* D

C71 CLEVELAND COLLEGE OF ART AND DESIGN
CHURCH SQUARE
HARTLEPOOL
CHURCH SQUARE TS24 7EX
t: 01642 288888 f: 01642 288828
e: studentrecruitment@ccad.ac.uk
// www.ccad.ac.uk

W232 BA(Hons) Fashion Enterprise
Duration: 3FT Hon
Entry Requirements: *Foundation:* Pass. *GCE:* 120. Interview required. Portfolio required.

W230 BA(Hons) Textiles and Surface Design
Duration: 3FT Hon
Entry Requirements: *Foundation:* Pass. *GCE:* 120. Interview required. Portfolio required.

WJ24 FdA Creative Fashion Practices
Duration: 2FT Fdg
Entry Requirements: *Foundation:* Pass. *GCE:* 120. Interview required. Portfolio required.

C85 COVENTRY UNIVERSITY
THE STUDENT CENTRE
COVENTRY UNIVERSITY
1 GULSON RD
COVENTRY CV1 2JH
t: 024 7615 2222 f: 024 7615 2223
e: studentenquiries@coventry.ac.uk
// www.coventry.ac.uk

WN25 BA Fashion
Duration: 3FT/4SW Hon
Entry Requirements: *Foundation:* Merit. *GCE:* CCC. *SQAH:* CCCCC. *IB:* 27. *BTEC ExtDip:* MMM. *OCR NED:* M3 Interview required. Portfolio required.

C92 CROYDON COLLEGE
COLLEGE ROAD
CROYDON CR9 1DX
t: 020 8760 5934 f: 020 8760 5880
e: admissions@croydon.ac.uk
// www.croydon.ac.uk

W2N1 BA Fashion Design with Business
Duration: 3FT Hon
Entry Requirements: *GCE:* 80-100. Interview required. Portfolio required.

WJ24 FdA Fashion Design, Pattern Cutting and Construction
Duration: 2FT Fdg
Entry Requirements: Contact the institution for details.

C93 UNIVERSITY FOR THE CREATIVE ARTS
FALKNER ROAD
FARNHAM
SURREY GU9 7DS
t: 01252 892960
e: admissions@ucreative.ac.uk
// www.ucreative.ac.uk

W230 BA Fashion
Duration: 3FT Hon
Entry Requirements: *GCE:* 220. *IB:* 24. *BTEC ExtDip:* PPP. Interview required. Portfolio required.

W237 BA Fashion Atelier
Duration: 3FT Hon
Entry Requirements: *GCE:* 220. *IB:* 24. *BTEC ExtDip:* PPP. Interview required. Portfolio required.

W233 BA Fashion Design
Duration: 3FT Hon
Entry Requirements: *GCE:* 220. *IB:* 24. *BTEC ExtDip:* PPP. Interview required. Portfolio required.

WN2N BA Fashion Management & Marketing
Duration: 3FT Hon
Entry Requirements: *GCE:* 220. *IB:* 24. *BTEC ExtDip:* PPP. Interview required. Portfolio required.

W226 BA Fashion Promotion
Duration: 3FT Hon
Entry Requirements: *GCE:* 220. *IB:* 24. *BTEC ExtDip:* PPP. Interview required. Portfolio required.

WN65 BA Fashion Promotion & Imaging
Duration: 3FT Hon
Entry Requirements: *GCE:* 220. *IB:* 24. *BTEC ExtDip:* PPP. Interview required. Portfolio required.

W231 BA Fashion Textiles
Duration: 3FT Hon
Entry Requirements: *GCE:* 220. *IB:* 24. *BTEC ExtDip:* PPP.
Interview required. Portfolio required.

W234 BA Textiles for Fashion & Interiors
Duration: 3FT Hon
Entry Requirements: *GCE:* 220. *IB:* 24. *BTEC ExtDip:* PPP.
Interview required. Portfolio required.

D26 DE MONTFORT UNIVERSITY
THE GATEWAY
LEICESTER LE1 9BH
t: 0116 255 1551 f: 0116 250 6204
e: enquiries@dmu.ac.uk
// www.dmu.ac.uk

W235 BA Contour Fashion
Duration: 3FT Hon
Entry Requirements: *Foundation:* Pass. *GCE:* 260. *IB:* 28. *BTEC Dip:* D*D. *BTEC ExtDip:* MMM. Interview required. Portfolio required.

W224 BA Fashion Buying (with Design)
Duration: 3FT Hon
Entry Requirements: *Foundation:* Pass. *GCE:* 260. *IB:* 28. *BTEC Dip:* D*D. *BTEC ExtDip:* MMM. Interview required. Portfolio required.

WN25 BA Fashion Buying (with Marketing)
Duration: 3FT/4SW Hon
Entry Requirements: *Foundation:* Pass. *GCE:* 260. *IB:* 28. *BTEC Dip:* D*D. *BTEC ExtDip:* MMM. Interview required.

W230 BA Fashion Design
Duration: 3FT Hon
Entry Requirements: *Foundation:* Pass. *GCE:* 260. *IB:* 28. *BTEC Dip:* D*D. *BTEC ExtDip:* MMM. Interview required. Portfolio required.

WJ74 FdA Footwear
Duration: 2FT Fdg
Entry Requirements: *GCE:* 80. Interview required. Portfolio required.

D39 UNIVERSITY OF DERBY
KEDLESTON ROAD
DERBY DE22 1GB
t: 01332 591167 f: 01332 597724
e: askadmissions@derby.ac.uk
// www.derby.ac.uk

W221 BA Fashion Studies
Duration: 3FT Hon
Entry Requirements: *Foundation:* Distinction. *GCE:* 260. *IB:* 28. *BTEC Dip:* D*D*. *BTEC ExtDip:* DMM. *OCR NED:* M2 Interview required. Portfolio required.

W230 BA Textile Design
Duration: 3FT Hon
Entry Requirements: *Foundation:* Distinction. *GCE:* 260. *IB:* 28. *BTEC Dip:* D*D*. *BTEC ExtDip:* DMM. *OCR NED:* M2 Interview required. Portfolio required.

W233 FYr Fashion Studies (Year 0)
Duration: 1FT FYr
Entry Requirements: *Foundation:* Pass. *GCE:* 160. *IB:* 24. *BTEC Dip:* D*D*. *BTEC ExtDip:* DMM. *OCR ND:* M2 *OCR NED:* P2 Interview required. Portfolio required.

D52 DONCASTER COLLEGE
THE HUB
CHAPPELL DRIVE
SOUTH YORKSHIRE DN1 2RF
t: 01302 553610
e: he@don.ac.uk
// www.don.ac.uk

W292 BA Fashion and Textiles Design
Duration: 3FT Hon
Entry Requirements: *GCE:* 100.

D58 DUDLEY COLLEGE OF TECHNOLOGY
THE BROADWAY
DUDLEY DY1 4AS
t: 01384 363277/6 f: 01384 363311
e: admissions@dudleycol.ac.uk
// www.dudleycol.ac.uk

022W HND Design (Fashion and Textiles)
Duration: 2FT HND
Entry Requirements: *GCE:* 40-80.

E28 UNIVERSITY OF EAST LONDON
DOCKLANDS CAMPUS
UNIVERSITY WAY
LONDON E16 2RD
t: 020 8223 3333 f: 020 8223 2978
e: study@uel.ac.uk
// www.uel.ac.uk

W230 BA Fashion Design
Duration: 3FT Hon
Entry Requirements: *GCE:* 200. Interview required. Portfolio required.

W233 BA Fashion Design (Extended)
Duration: 4FT/5SW Hon
Entry Requirements: *GCE:* 80. Interview required. Portfolio required.

W231 BA Fashion Design (with Placement Year)
Duration: 4SW Hon
Entry Requirements: *GCE:* 200. Interview required. Portfolio required.

E56 THE UNIVERSITY OF EDINBURGH
STUDENT RECRUITMENT & ADMISSIONS
57 GEORGE SQUARE
EDINBURGH EH8 9JU
t: 0131 650 4360 f: 0131 651 1236
e: sra.enquiries@ed.ac.uk
// www.ed.ac.uk/studying/undergraduate/

W230 BA Fashion
Duration: 4FT Hon
Entry Requirements: *Foundation:* Merit. *GCE:* BBB. *SQAH:* BBBB. *IB:* 34. Portfolio required.

F33 UNIVERSITY COLLEGE FALMOUTH
WOODLANE
FALMOUTH
CORNWALL TR11 4RH
t: 01326213730
e: admissions@falmouth.ac.uk
// www.falmouth.ac.uk

W232 BA(Hons) Fashion Design
Duration: 3FT Hon
Entry Requirements: *GCE:* 220. *IB:* 24. Interview required. Portfolio required.

W641 BA(Hons) Fashion Photography
Duration: 3FT Hon
Entry Requirements: *GCE:* 220. *IB:* 24. Interview required. Portfolio required.

W233 BA(Hons) Performance Sportswear Design
Duration: 3FT Hon
Entry Requirements: *GCE:* 220. *IB:* 24. Interview required. Portfolio required.

W230 BA(Hons) Textile Design
Duration: 3FT Hon
Entry Requirements: *GCE:* 220. *IB:* 24. Interview required. Portfolio required.

G14 UNIVERSITY OF GLAMORGAN, CARDIFF AND PONTYPRIDD
ENQUIRIES AND ADMISSIONS UNIT
PONTYPRIDD CF37 1DL
t: 08456 434030 f: 01443 654050
e: enquiries@glam.ac.uk
// www.glam.ac.uk

W230 BA Fashion Design
Duration: 3FT Hon
Entry Requirements: *Foundation:* Pass. *GCE:* BBC. *IB:* 24. *BTEC SubDip:* M. *BTEC Dip:* D*D*. *BTEC ExtDip:* DMM. *OCR ND:* M1 *OCR NED:* M2 Interview required. Portfolio required.

W231 BA Fashion Design
Duration: 4SW Hon
Entry Requirements: *GCE:* BBC. *IB:* 25. *BTEC SubDip:* M. *BTEC Dip:* D*D*. *BTEC ExtDip:* DMM. *OCR NED:* M2 Interview required. Portfolio required.

WN25 BA Fashion Promotion
Duration: 3FT Hon
Entry Requirements: *Foundation:* Pass. *GCE:* BBC. *IB:* 25. *BTEC SubDip:* M. *BTEC Dip:* D*D*. *BTEC ExtDip:* DMM. *OCR ND:* M1 *OCR NED:* M2 Interview required. Portfolio required.

G42 GLASGOW CALEDONIAN UNIVERSITY
STUDENT RECRUITMENT & ADMISSIONS SERVICE
CITY CAMPUS
COWCADDENS ROAD
GLASGOW G4 0BA
t: 0141 331 3000 f: 0141 331 8676
e: undergraduate@gcu.ac.uk
// www.gcu.ac.uk

W2N5 BA International Fashion Branding
Duration: 4FT Hon
Entry Requirements: *GCE:* CCC. *SQAH:* BBBC. *IB:* 24.

G43 THE GLASGOW SCHOOL OF ART
167 RENFREW STREET
GLASGOW G3 6RQ
t: 0141 353 4434/4514 f: 0141 353 4408
e: admissions@gsa.ac.uk
// www.gsa.ac.uk

W230 BDes Fashion Design
Duration: 4FT Hon
Entry Requirements: *GCE:* ABB. *SQAH:* AABB-ABBB. *IB:* 30.
Interview required. Portfolio required.

H14 HAVERING COLLEGE OF FURTHER AND HIGHER EDUCATION
ARDLEIGH GREEN ROAD
HORNCHURCH
ESSEX RM11 2LL
t: 01708 462793 f: 01708 462736
e: HE@havering-college.ac.uk
// www.havering-college.ac.uk

032W HNC Fashion
Duration: 1FT HNC
Entry Requirements: Contact the institution for details.

H24 HERIOT-WATT UNIVERSITY, EDINBURGH
EDINBURGH CAMPUS
EDINBURGH EH14 4AS
t: 0131 449 5111 f: 0131 451 3630
e: ugadmissions@hw.ac.uk
// www.hw.ac.uk

W232 BA Design for Textiles (Fashion, Interior, Art)
Duration: 4FT Hon
Entry Requirements: *GCE:* BBB. *SQAH:* ABBB. *IB:* 30. Portfolio required.

W230 BA Fashion
Duration: 4FT Hon
Entry Requirements: *GCE:* BBB. *SQAH:* ABBB. *IB:* 30. Portfolio required.

W640 BA Fashion Communication
Duration: 4FT Hon
Entry Requirements: *GCE:* BBB. *SQAH:* ABBB. *IB:* 30. Portfolio required.

WN25 BA Fashion Marketing & Retailing
Duration: 4FT Hon
Entry Requirements: *GCE:* BBB. *SQAH:* ABBB. *IB:* 30.

W234 BA Fashion Menswear
Duration: 4FT Hon
Entry Requirements: *GCE:* BBB. *SQAH:* ABBB. *IB:* 30. Portfolio required.

W233 BA Fashion Womenswear
Duration: 4FT Hon
Entry Requirements: *GCE:* BBB. *SQAH:* ABBB. *IB:* 30. Portfolio required.

H36 UNIVERSITY OF HERTFORDSHIRE
UNIVERSITY ADMISSIONS SERVICE
COLLEGE LANE
HATFIELD
HERTS AL10 9AB
t: 01707 284800
// www.herts.ac.uk

W230 BA Fashion
Duration: 3FT Hon
Entry Requirements: *GCE:* 240. Interview required. Portfolio required.

N5W2 BA Marketing with Fashion
Duration: 3FT/4SW Hon
Entry Requirements: *GCE:* 280. *IB:* 28.

W232 FdA Fashion & Textiles
Duration: 2FT Fdg
Entry Requirements: *GCE:* 80. Interview required. Portfolio required.

H60 THE UNIVERSITY OF HUDDERSFIELD
QUEENSGATE
HUDDERSFIELD HD1 3DH
t: 01484 473969 f: 01484 472765
e: admissionsandrecords@hud.ac.uk
// www.hud.ac.uk

W2N5 BA Fashion Design with Marketing & Production
Duration: 3FT/4SW Hon
Entry Requirements: *GCE:* 300. *SQAH:* BBBB. *IB:* 28. Interview required. Portfolio required.

W239 BA Fashion Design with Textiles
Duration: 3FT/4SW Hon
Entry Requirements: *GCE:* 300. *SQAH:* BBBB. *IB:* 28. Interview required. Portfolio required.

W231 BA(Hons) Fashion and Textile Buying Management
Duration: 3FT/4SW Hon
Entry Requirements: *GCE:* 300. *SQAH:* BBBB. *IB:* 28. Interview required. Portfolio required.

H73 HULL COLLEGE

QUEEN'S GARDENS
HULL HU1 3DG
t: 01482 329943 f: 01482 598733
e: info@hull-college.ac.uk
// www.hull-college.ac.uk/higher-education

W230 FdA Fashion Design and Interpretation
Duration: 2FT Fdg
Entry Requirements: *GCE:* 200. Foundation Course required.
Interview required. Portfolio required.

WJ24 FdA Fashion Design and Production
Duration: 2FT Fdg
Entry Requirements: *GCE:* 80. Interview required. Portfolio
required.

WN25 FdA Fashion Marketing and Retail
Duration: 2FT Fdg
Entry Requirements: *GCE:* 80. Interview required. Portfolio
required.

K24 THE UNIVERSITY OF KENT

RECRUITMENT & ADMISSIONS OFFICE
REGISTRY
UNIVERSITY OF KENT
CANTERBURY, KENT CT2 7NZ
t: 01227 827272 f: 01227 827077
e: information@kent.ac.uk
// www.kent.ac.uk

W234 BA Fashion and Textiles
Duration: 1FT Hon
Entry Requirements: Contact the institution for details.

W232 BA Fashion and Textiles (top-up)
Duration: 1FT Hon
Entry Requirements: Interview required. Portfolio required.

W230 FdA Fashion and Textiles
Duration: 2FT Fdg
Entry Requirements: *GCE:* 40. Interview required. Portfolio
required.

W233 FdA Textiles and Fashion
Duration: 2FT Deg
Entry Requirements: *OCR NED:* M2 Interview required. Portfolio
required.

K84 KINGSTON UNIVERSITY

STUDENT INFORMATION & ADVICE CENTRE
COOPER HOUSE
40-46 SURBITON ROAD
KINGSTON UPON THAMES KT1 2HX
t: 0844 8552177 f: 020 8547 7080
e: aps@kingston.ac.uk
// www.kingston.ac.uk

W230 BA Fashion
Duration: 3FT Hon
Entry Requirements: *IB:* 28. Foundation Course required. Interview
required. Portfolio required.

K90 KIRKLEES COLLEGE

HALIFAX ROAD
DEWSBURY
WEST YORKSHIRE WF13 2AS
t: 01924 436221 f: 01924 457047
e: admissionsdc@kirkleescollege.ac.uk
// www.kirkleescollege.ac.uk

W230 BA Fashion (Top-Up)
Duration: 1FT Hon
Entry Requirements: HND required.

WJ24 FdA Fashion Design & Manufacture
Duration: 2FT Fdg
Entry Requirements: *GCE:* 180.

WN25 FdA Fashion Styling & Promotion
Duration: 2FT Fdg
Entry Requirements: *GCE:* 180.

L23 UNIVERSITY OF LEEDS

THE UNIVERSITY OF LEEDS
WOODHOUSE LANE
LEEDS LS2 9JT
t: 0113 343 3999
e: admissions@leeds.ac.uk
// www.leeds.ac.uk

W230 BA Fashion Design
Duration: 3FT Hon
Entry Requirements: *GCE:* ABB. *SQAAH:* ABB. *IB:* 34.

W231 BA Fashion Marketing
Duration: 3FT Hon
Entry Requirements: *GCE:* BBB. *SQAAH:* BBB. *IB:* 32.

L28 LEEDS COLLEGE OF ART
BLENHEIM WALK
LEEDS LS2 9AQ
t: 0113 202 8000 f: 0113 202 8001
e: info@leeds-art.ac.uk
// www.leeds-art.ac.uk

W221 BA Fashion
Duration: 3FT Hon
Entry Requirements: *Foundation:* Merit. *GCE:* 240. *IB:* 24. *BTEC Dip:* DD. *BTEC ExtDip:* MMM. Interview required. Portfolio required.

L36 LEICESTER COLLEGE
FREEMEN'S PARK CAMPUS
AYLESTONE ROAD
LEICESTER LE2 7LW
t: 0116 224 2240 f: 0116 224 2041
e: info@leicestercollege.ac.uk
// www.leicestercollege.ac.uk

WJ24 FdA Fashion and Costume
Duration: 2FT Fdg
Entry Requirements: *GCE:* 80. Foundation Course required. Interview required. Portfolio required.

L39 UNIVERSITY OF LINCOLN
ADMISSIONS
BRAYFORD POOL
LINCOLN LN6 7TS
t: 01522 886097 f: 01522 886146
e: admissions@lincoln.ac.uk
// www.lincoln.ac.uk

W230 BA Fashion Studies
Duration: 3FT Hon
Entry Requirements: *GCE:* 280. Interview required. Portfolio required.

L51 LIVERPOOL JOHN MOORES UNIVERSITY
KINGSWAY HOUSE
HATTON GARDEN
LIVERPOOL L3 2AJ
t: 0151 231 5090 f: 0151 904 6368
e: courses@ljmu.ac.uk
// www.ljmu.ac.uk

W2H0 BA Fashion
Duration: 3FT Hon
Entry Requirements: *GCE:* 280-320. Foundation Course required. Interview required. Portfolio required.

L68 LONDON METROPOLITAN UNIVERSITY
166-220 HOLLOWAY ROAD
LONDON N7 8DB
t: 020 7133 4200
e: admissions@londonmet.ac.uk
// www.londonmet.ac.uk

W230 FdA Fashion with Textiles
Duration: 2FT Fdg
Entry Requirements: *GCE:* 160. Interview required. Portfolio required.

M10 THE MANCHESTER COLLEGE
OPENSHAW CAMPUS
ASHTON OLD ROAD
OPENSHAW
MANCHESTER M11 2WH
t: 0800 068 8585 f: 0161 920 4103
e: enquiries@themanchestercollege.ac.uk
// www.themanchestercollege.ac.uk

W231 FdA Fashion Design and Realisation
Duration: 2FT Fdg
Entry Requirements: Contact the institution for details.

WN25 FdSc International Fashion Marketing
Duration: 2FT Fdg
Entry Requirements: *GCE:* 160. *BTEC ExtDip:* MPP.

M40 THE MANCHESTER METROPOLITAN UNIVERSITY
ADMISSIONS OFFICE
ALL SAINTS (GMS)
ALL SAINTS
MANCHESTER M15 6BH
t: 0161 247 2000
// www.mmu.ac.uk

W230 BA Fashion
Duration: 3FT Hon
Entry Requirements: *GCE:* 280. *IB:* 27. Interview required. Portfolio required.

W233 BA International Fashion Practice
Duration: 1FT Hon
Entry Requirements: Contact the institution for details.

M77 MID CHESHIRE COLLEGE
HARTFORD CAMPUS
NORTHWICH
CHESHIRE CW8 1LJ
t: 01606 74444 f: 01606 720700
e: eandrews@midchesh.ac.uk
// www.midchesh.ac.uk

W232 FdA Fashion Design
Duration: 2FT Fdg
Entry Requirements: *GCE:* 120. Interview required.

M80 MIDDLESEX UNIVERSITY
MIDDLESEX UNIVERSITY
THE BURROUGHS
LONDON NW4 4BT
t: 020 8411 5555 f: 020 8411 5649
e: enquiries@mdx.ac.uk
// www.mdx.ac.uk

W230 BA Fashion
Duration: 3FT Hon
Entry Requirements: Interview required. Portfolio required.

W239 BA Fashion Design, Styling and Promotion
Duration: 3FT Hon
Entry Requirements: *GCE:* 200-300. *IB:* 28. Interview required. Portfolio required.

W232 BA Fashion Textiles
Duration: 3FT Hon
Entry Requirements: *GCE:* 200-300. *IB:* 28. Interview required. Portfolio required.

N23 NEWCASTLE COLLEGE
STUDENT SERVICES
RYE HILL CAMPUS
SCOTSWOOD ROAD
NEWCASTLE UPON TYNE NE4 7SA
t: 0191 200 4110 f: 0191 200 4349
e: enquiries@ncl-coll.ac.uk
// www.newcastlecollege.co.uk

W230 FdA Fashion
Duration: 2FT Fdg
Entry Requirements: *Foundation:* Pass. *GCE:* 120-165. *OCR ND:* P2 *OCR NED:* P3 Foundation Course required. Interview required. Portfolio required.

W234 FdA Fashion Retail and Enterprise
Duration: 2FT Fdg
Entry Requirements: Contact the institution for details.

N30 NEW COLLEGE NOTTINGHAM
ADAMS BUILDING
STONEY STREET
THE LACE MARKET
NOTTINGHAM NG1 1NG
t: 0115 910 0100 f: 0115 953 4349
e: he.team@ncn.ac.uk
// www.ncn.ac.uk

W230 FdA Fashion Design
Duration: 2FT Fdg
Entry Requirements: *GCE:* 80-240. Interview required. Portfolio required.

N37 UNIVERSITY OF WALES, NEWPORT
ADMISSIONS
LODGE ROAD
CAERLEON
NEWPORT NP18 3QT
t: 01633 432030 f: 01633 432850
e: admissions@newport.ac.uk
// www.newport.ac.uk

W230 BA Fashion Design
Duration: 3FT Hon
Entry Requirements: *Foundation:* Merit. *GCE:* 240-260. *IB:* 24. Interview required. Portfolio required.

N38 UNIVERSITY OF NORTHAMPTON
PARK CAMPUS
BOUGHTON GREEN ROAD
NORTHAMPTON NN2 7AL
t: 0800 358 2232 f: 01604 722083
e: admissions@northampton.ac.uk
// www.northampton.ac.uk

W230 BA Fashion
Duration: 3FT Hon
Entry Requirements: *GCE:* 260-280. *SQAH:* AAA-BBBB. *IB:* 24. *BTEC Dip:* DD. *BTEC ExtDip:* DMM. *OCR ND:* D *OCR NED:* M2 Foundation Course required. Interview required.

W232 BA Fashion (Footwear and Accessories)
Duration: 3FT Hon
Entry Requirements: *GCE:* 260-280. *SQAH:* AAA-BBBB. *IB:* 24. *BTEC Dip:* DD. *BTEC ExtDip:* DMM. *OCR ND:* D *OCR NED:* M2 Foundation Course required. Interview required.

W231 BA Fashion (Printed Textiles for Fashion)
Duration: 3FT Hon
Entry Requirements: *GCE:* 260-280. *SQAH:* AAA-BBBB. *IB:* 24. *BTEC Dip:* DD. *BTEC ExtDip:* DMM. *OCR ND:* D *OCR NED:* M2 Foundation Course required. Interview required.

N39 NORWICH UNIVERSITY COLLEGE OF THE ARTS
FRANCIS HOUSE
3-7 REDWELL STREET
NORWICH NR2 4SN
t: 01603 610561 f: 01603 615728
e: admissions@nuca.ac.uk
// www.nuca.ac.uk

W233 BA Fashion
Duration: 3FT Hon
Entry Requirements: *Foundation:* Merit. *GCE:* BBc. *OCR ND:* M1 *OCR NED:* P1 Interview required. Portfolio required.

N41 NORTHBROOK COLLEGE SUSSEX
LITTLEHAMPTON ROAD
WORTHING
WEST SUSSEX BN12 6NU
t: 0845 155 6060 f: 01903 606073
e: enquiries@nbcol.ac.uk
// www.northbrook.ac.uk

W232 BA Fashion Design
Duration: 3FT Hon
Entry Requirements: *GCE:* 160. Interview required. Portfolio required.

N77 NORTHUMBRIA UNIVERSITY
TRINITY BUILDING
NORTHUMBERLAND ROAD
NEWCASTLE UPON TYNE NE1 8ST
t: 0191 243 7420 f: 0191 227 4561
e: er.admissions@northumbria.ac.uk
// www.northumbria.ac.uk

W230 BA Fashion
Duration: 4SW Hon
Entry Requirements: *Foundation:* Distinction. *GCE:* 320. *SQAH:* BBBBB. *SQAAH:* BBB. *IB:* 27. *BTEC Dip:* DM. *BTEC ExtDip:* DDM. *OCR ND:* M1 *OCR NED:* M1 Interview required. Portfolio required.

WP29 BA Fashion Communication
Duration: 3FT Hon
Entry Requirements: *Foundation:* Distinction. *GCE:* 320. *SQAH:* BBBBB. *SQAAH:* BBB. *IB:* 27. *BTEC Dip:* DM. *BTEC ExtDip:* DDM. *OCR ND:* M1 *OCR NED:* M1 Interview required. Portfolio required.

W231 BA Fashion Marketing
Duration: 4SW Hon
Entry Requirements: *Foundation:* Distinction. *GCE:* 320. *SQAH:* BBBBB. *SQAAH:* BBB. *IB:* 27. *BTEC Dip:* DM. *BTEC ExtDip:* DDM. *OCR ND:* M1 *OCR NED:* M1 Interview required. Portfolio required.

N79 NORTH WARWICKSHIRE AND HINCKLEY COLLEGE
HINCKLEY ROAD
NUNEATON
WARWICKSHIRE CV11 6BH
t: 024 7624 3395
e: angela.jones@nwhc.ac.uk
// www.nwhc.ac.uk

232W HNC Design for Fashion and Textiles
Duration: 1FT HNC
Entry Requirements: Contact the institution for details.

032W HND Design for Fashion and Textiles
Duration: 2FT HND
Entry Requirements: *GCE:* 120. *IB:* 24. Interview required. Portfolio required.

N91 NOTTINGHAM TRENT UNIVERSITY
DRYDEN BUILDING
BURTON STREET
NOTTINGHAM NG1 4BU
t: +44 (0) 115 848 4200 f: +44 (0) 115 848 8869
e: applications@ntu.ac.uk
// www.ntu.ac.uk

WN2M BA Fashion Communication & Promotion
Duration: 3FT Hon
Entry Requirements: *GCE:* 340. *BTEC ExtDip:* DDM.

W230 BA Fashion Design
Duration: 3FT Hon
Entry Requirements: *GCE:* 280. *BTEC Dip:* D*D*. *BTEC ExtDip:* DMM. *OCR NED:* M2 Interview required. Portfolio required.

W222 BA Fashion Knitwear Design and Knitted Textiles
Duration: 4SW Hon
Entry Requirements: *Foundation:* Distinction. *GCE:* 240. *BTEC Dip:* DD. *BTEC ExtDip:* MMM. *OCR ND:* D *OCR NED:* M3 Interview required. Portfolio required.

JW42 BA Fashion Management
Duration: 4SW Hon
Entry Requirements: *GCE:* 340. *BTEC ExtDip:* DDM.

WN25 BA Fashion Marketing and Branding
Duration: 3FT Hon
Entry Requirements: *GCE:* 340. *BTEC ExtDip:* DDM.

W232 BA (Hons) International Fashion Business
Duration: 1FT Hon
Entry Requirements: Interview required.

W231 BA Hons Fashion Accessory Design
Duration: 3FT Hon
Entry Requirements: *GCE:* 240. *OCR ND:* D Interview required. Portfolio required.

P65 PLYMOUTH COLLEGE OF ART (FORMERLY PLYMOUTH COLLEGE OF ART AND DESIGN)
TAVISTOCK PLACE
PLYMOUTH PL4 8AT
t: 01752 203434 f: 01752 203444
e: infoservices@plymouthart.ac.uk
// www.plymouthart.ac.uk

W230 BA Fashion (Top-Up)
Duration: 1FT Hon
Entry Requirements: Interview required. Portfolio required. HND required.

W290 BA (Hons) Fashion
Duration: 3FT Hon
Entry Requirements: Contact the institution for details.

WN22 FdA Fashion
Duration: 2FT Fdg
Entry Requirements: *Foundation:* Pass. *IB:* 24. *OCR ND:* M1 *OCR NED:* P1 Interview required. Portfolio required.

W232 FdA Fashion (including Level 0)
Duration: 3FT Fdg
Entry Requirements: *IB:* 24. *OCR ND:* P3 *OCR NED:* P3 Interview required. Portfolio required.

P80 UNIVERSITY OF PORTSMOUTH
ACADEMIC REGISTRY
UNIVERSITY HOUSE
WINSTON CHURCHILL AVENUE
PORTSMOUTH PO1 2UP
t: 023 9284 8484 f: 023 9284 3082
e: admissions@port.ac.uk
// www.port.ac.uk

W230 BA Fashion and Textile Design with Enterprise
Duration: 3FT Hon
Entry Requirements: *GCE:* 240-300. *IB:* 26. *BTEC SubDip:* P. *BTEC Dip:* DD. *BTEC ExtDip:* DMM. Interview required. Portfolio required.

R06 RAVENSBOURNE
6 PENROSE WAY
GREENWICH PENINSULA
LONDON SE10 0EW
t: 020 3040 3998
e: info@rave.ac.uk
// www.rave.ac.uk

W230 BA Fashion
Duration: 3FT Hon
Entry Requirements: *Foundation:* Pass. *GCE:* AA-CC. *IB:* 28. Interview required. Portfolio required.

WF30 BA Fashion (Fast-Track)
Duration: 2FT Hon
Entry Requirements: Contact the institution for details.

W234 BA Fashion (with Foundation Year)
Duration: 4FT Hon
Entry Requirements: *Foundation:* Pass. *GCE:* A-E. *IB:* 28. Interview required. Portfolio required.

W231 BA Fashion Lifestyle Products
Duration: 3FT Hon
Entry Requirements: Contact the institution for details.

WF31 BA Fashion Lifestyle Products (Fast-Track)
Duration: 2FT Hon
Entry Requirements: Contact the institution for details.

WG30 BA Fashion Lifestyle Products (with Foundation Year)
Duration: 4FT Hon
Entry Requirements: Contact the institution for details.

WN25 BA Fashion Promotion (with Foundation Year)
Duration: 4FT Hon
Entry Requirements: Contact the institution for details.

R36 ROBERT GORDON UNIVERSITY
ROBERT GORDON UNIVERSITY
SCHOOLHILL
ABERDEEN
SCOTLAND AB10 1FR
t: 01224 26 27 28 f: 01224 26 21 47
e: UGOffice@rgu.ac.uk
// www.rgu.ac.uk

WN22 BA Fashion Management
Duration: 4FT Hon
Entry Requirements: *GCE:* BCC. *SQAH:* BBBC. *IB:* 27.

W291 BA (Hons) Fashion and Textiles Design
Duration: 4FT Hon
Entry Requirements: *GCE:* BC. *SQAH:* BBC. Interview required. Portfolio required.

S03 THE UNIVERSITY OF SALFORD
SALFORD M5 4WT
t: 0161 295 4545 f: 0161 295 4646
e: ug-admissions@salford.ac.uk
// www.salford.ac.uk

W225 BA Fashion
Duration: 3FT Hon
Entry Requirements: *Foundation:* Pass. *GCE:* 260. *IB:* 26. *OCR ND:* D *OCR NED:* M3 Interview required. Portfolio required.

S21 SHEFFIELD HALLAM UNIVERSITY
CITY CAMPUS
HOWARD STREET
SHEFFIELD S1 1WB
t: 0114 225 5555 f: 0114 225 2167
e: admissions@shu.ac.uk
// www.shu.ac.uk

W232 BA Fashion Design
Duration: 3FT Hon
Entry Requirements: *GCE:* 280.

W230 MDes Fashion Design
Duration: 4FT Hon
Entry Requirements: *GCE:* 300.

S22 SHEFFIELD COLLEGE
THE SHEFFIELD COLLEGE
HE UNIT
HILLSBOROUGH COLLEGE AT THE BARRACKS
SHEFFIELD S6 2LR
t: 0114 260 2597
e: heunit@sheffcol.ac.uk
// www.sheffcol.ac.uk

WJ24 FdA Fashion Design and Manufacture
Duration: 2FT Fdg
Entry Requirements: Interview required. Portfolio required.

S27 UNIVERSITY OF SOUTHAMPTON
HIGHFIELD
SOUTHAMPTON SO17 1BJ
t: 023 8059 4732 f: 023 8059 3037
e: admissions@soton.ac.uk
// www.southampton.ac.uk

WN25 BA Fashion Marketing
Duration: 3FT Hon
Entry Requirements: Contact the institution for details.

WJ24 BA Fashion and Textile Design
Duration: 3FT Hon
Entry Requirements: *Foundation:* Pass. *GCE:* ABB. *IB:* 32. Interview required. Portfolio required.

S28 SOMERSET COLLEGE OF ARTS AND TECHNOLOGY
WELLINGTON ROAD
TAUNTON
SOMERSET TA1 5AX
t: 01823 366331 f: 01823 366418
e: enquiries@somerset.ac.uk
// www.somerset.ac.uk/student-area/considering-a-degree.html

W230 BA Design (Fashion)
Duration: 3FT Hon
Entry Requirements: *Foundation:* Pass. *GCE:* 180. *IB:* 24. Interview required. Portfolio required.

W221 BA Design (Fashion/Textiles)
Duration: 3FT Hon
Entry Requirements: *Foundation:* Pass. *GCE:* 180. *IB:* 24. Interview required. Portfolio required.

S30 SOUTHAMPTON SOLENT UNIVERSITY
EAST PARK TERRACE
SOUTHAMPTON
HAMPSHIRE SO14 0RT
t: +44 (0) 23 8031 9039 f: + 44 (0)23 8022 2259
e: admissions@solent.ac.uk
// www.solent.ac.uk/

W235 BA Fashion
Duration: 3FT Hon
Entry Requirements: *Foundation:* Merit. *GCE:* 200. *SQAAH:* AC-DDD. *IB:* 24. *BTEC ExtDip:* MMP. *OCR ND:* M1 *OCR NED:* P1 Portfolio required.

W234 BA Fashion (Top-Up)
Duration: 1FT Hon
Entry Requirements: Contact the institution for details.

W293 BA Fashion Graphics
Duration: 3FT Hon
Entry Requirements: *Foundation:* Merit. *GCE:* 200. *SQAAH:* AC-DDD. *IB:* 24. *BTEC ExtDip:* MMP. *OCR ND:* M1 *OCR NED:* P1 Portfolio required.

W2NN BA Fashion Management with Marketing
Duration: 4SW Hon
Entry Requirements: *Foundation:* Distinction. *GCE:* 240. *SQAAH:* AA-CCD. *IB:* 24. *BTEC ExtDip:* MMM. *OCR ND:* D *OCR NED:* M3

W645 BA Fashion Photography (Top-up)
Duration: 1FT Hon
Entry Requirements: Portfolio required.

W231 BA Fashion Styling & Make-Up for Media (Top-Up)
Duration: 1FT Hon
Entry Requirements: Contact the institution for details.

W640 BA Fashion with Photography
Duration: 3FT Hon
Entry Requirements: *Foundation:* Merit. *GCE:* 200. *SQAAH:* AC-DDD. *IB:* 24. *BTEC ExtDip:* MMP. *OCR ND:* M1 *OCR NED:* P1 Interview required. Portfolio required.

W2P2 BA Fashion with Public Relations
Duration: 3FT Hon
Entry Requirements: *Foundation:* Distinction. *GCE:* 240. *SQAAH:* AA-CCD. *IB:* 24. *BTEC ExtDip:* MMM. *OCR ND:* D *OCR NED:* M3 Portfolio required.

S43 SOUTH ESSEX COLLEGE OF FURTHER & HIGHER EDUCATION
LUKER ROAD
SOUTHEND-ON-SEA
ESSEX SS1 1ND
t: 0845 52 12345 f: 01702 432320
e: Admissions@southessex.ac.uk
// www.southessex.ac.uk

WN2M BA Fashion Communication & Marketing
Duration: 1FT Hon
Entry Requirements: Contact the institution for details.

W220 BA Fashion Design
Duration: 3FT Hon
Entry Requirements: *GCE:* 160. *IB:* 24. Interview required.

W232 CertHE Fashion Design
Duration: 1FT Cer
Entry Requirements: *GCE:* 40. *IB:* 24. Interview required.

W233 DipHE Fashion Design
Duration: 2FT Dip
Entry Requirements: *GCE:* 40. *IB:* 24. Interview required.

WJ24 FdA Fashion & Textiles
Duration: 2FT Fdg
Entry Requirements: Interview required.

WN25 FdA Fashion Communication & Marketing
Duration: 2FT Fdg
Entry Requirements: *GCE:* 40. *IB:* 24. Interview required.

S72 STAFFORDSHIRE UNIVERSITY
COLLEGE ROAD
STOKE ON TRENT ST4 2DE
t: 01782 292753 f: 01782 292740
e: admissions@staffs.ac.uk
// www.staffs.ac.uk

W2N1 BA Entrepreneurship in Fashion (Top-Up)
Duration: 1FT Hon
Entry Requirements: Interview required. Portfolio required.

W230 FdA Creative and Cultural Industries (Fashion Studies)
Duration: 2FT Hon
Entry Requirements: Contact the institution for details.

W2H0 HND Fashion
Duration: 2FT HND
Entry Requirements: Interview required.

S82 UNIVERSITY CAMPUS SUFFOLK (UCS)
WATERFRONT BUILDING
NEPTUNE QUAY
IPSWICH
SUFFOLK IP4 1QJ
t: 01473 338833 f: 01473 339900
e: info@ucs.ac.uk
// www.ucs.ac.uk

W230 FdA Fashion & Textiles
Duration: 2FT Fdg
Entry Requirements: *GCE:* 200. *IB:* 28. *BTEC ExtDip:* DMM. Interview required. Portfolio required.

S84 UNIVERSITY OF SUNDERLAND
STUDENT HELPLINE
THE STUDENT GATEWAY
CHESTER ROAD
SUNDERLAND SR1 3SD
t: 0191 515 3000 f: 0191 515 3805
e: student.helpline@sunderland.ac.uk
// www.sunderland.ac.uk

WN25 BA Fashion Product and Promotion
Duration: 3FT Hon
Entry Requirements: *Foundation:* Merit. *GCE:* 220. *SQAH:* BBBC. *IB:* 22. Interview required. Portfolio required.

S96 SWANSEA METROPOLITAN UNIVERSITY

MOUNT PLEASANT CAMPUS
SWANSEA SA1 6ED
t: 01792 481000 f: 01792 481061
e: gemma.green@smu.ac.uk
// www.smu.ac.uk

W230 BA Fashion Styling, Design and Embellishment

Duration: 3FT Hon

Entry Requirements: *Foundation:* Pass. *GCE:* 200-360. *IB:* 24. Interview required. Portfolio required.

W234 BA Surface Pattern Design (Textiles for Fashion)

Duration: 3FT Hon

Entry Requirements: *Foundation:* Pass. *GCE:* 200-360. *IB:* 24. Interview required. Portfolio required.

S98 SWINDON COLLEGE

NORTH STAR AVENUE
SWINDON
WILTSHIRE SN2 1DY
t: 0800 731 2250 f: 01793 430503
e: headmissions@swindon-college.ac.uk
// www.swindon-college.ac.uk

W290 HND Fashion and Textiles

Duration: 2FT HND

Entry Requirements: Contact the institution for details.

U20 UNIVERSITY OF ULSTER

COLERAINE
CO. LONDONDERRY
NORTHERN IRELAND BT52 1SA
t: 028 7012 4221 f: 028 7012 4908
e: online@ulster.ac.uk
// www.ulster.ac.uk

W232 BDes Hons Textile Art, Design and Fashion

Duration: 3FT/4SW Hon

Entry Requirements: Contact the institution for details.

U65 UNIVERSITY OF THE ARTS LONDON

272 HIGH HOLBORN
LONDON WC1V 7EY
t: 020 7514 6000x6197 f: 020 7514 6198
e: c.anderson@arts.ac.uk
// www.arts.ac.uk

W230 BA Bespoke Tailoring

Duration: 3FT Hon

Entry Requirements: Foundation Course required. Interview required. Portfolio required.

W236 BA Fashion (Fashion Communication with Promotion)

Duration: 3FT/4SW Hon

Entry Requirements: Foundation Course required. Interview required.

W238 BA Fashion (Fashion Design Menswear)

Duration: 3FT/4SW Hon

Entry Requirements: *IB:* 28. Foundation Course required. Interview required.

W234 BA Fashion (Fashion Design Womenswear)

Duration: 3FT/4SW Hon

Entry Requirements: *IB:* 28. Foundation Course required. Interview required.

W228 BA Fashion (Fashion Design with Knitwear)

Duration: 3FT/4SW Hon

Entry Requirements: Foundation Course required. Interview required.

W237 BA Fashion (Fashion Design with Marketing)

Duration: 3FT/4SW Hon

Entry Requirements: Foundation Course required. Interview required.

W239 BA Fashion (Fashion Print)

Duration: 3FT/4SW Hon

Entry Requirements: Foundation Course required. Interview required.

W233 BA Fashion Contour

Duration: 4SW Hon

Entry Requirements: Foundation Course required. Interview required. Portfolio required.

W221 BA Fashion Illustration

Duration: 3FT Hon

Entry Requirements: Interview required. Portfolio required.

WN22 BA Fashion Management

Duration: 3FT/4SW Hon

Entry Requirements: *IB:* 28. Interview required.

W641 BA Fashion Photography

Duration: 3FT Hon

Entry Requirements: *IB:* 28. Foundation Course required. Interview required. Portfolio required.

WP22 BA Fashion Public Relations

Duration: 3FT Hon

Entry Requirements: *IB:* 28. Interview required.

W232 BA Fashion Sportswear
Duration: 3FT Hon
Entry Requirements: Foundation Course required. Interview required. Portfolio required.

W220 BA Fashion Textiles
Duration: 3FT Hon
Entry Requirements: Foundation Course required. Interview required. Portfolio required.

WF13 Cert HE Fashion Retail Merchandising
Duration: 1FT Cer
Entry Requirements: Interview required.

WN25 FdA Fashion Design and Marketing
Duration: 2FT Fdg
Entry Requirements: Foundation Course required. Interview required. Portfolio required.

W213 FdA Fashion Retail Branding and Visual Merchandising
Duration: 2FT Fdg
Entry Requirements: *IB:* 28. Interview required.

WN2F FdA Fashion Retail Management
Duration: 2FT Fdg
Entry Requirements: Interview required.

W642 FdA Fashion Styling and Photography
Duration: 2FT Fdg
Entry Requirements: *IB:* 28. Foundation Course required. Interview required. Portfolio required.

WJ2L FdA Tailoring
Duration: 2FT Fdg
Entry Requirements: Interview required. Portfolio required.

WNG2 MDes International Fashion Production Management
Duration: 4FT Hon
Entry Requirements: Interview required. Portfolio required.

WNF2 MSc International Fashion Management
Duration: 4FT Hon
Entry Requirements: Contact the institution for details.

W05 THE UNIVERSITY OF WEST LONDON
ST MARY'S ROAD
EALING
LONDON W5 5RF
t: 0800 036 8888 f: 020 8566 1353
e: learning.advice@uwl.ac.uk
// www.uwl.ac.uk

W232 BA Fashion and Textiles
Duration: 3FT Hon
Entry Requirements: *GCE:* 240. Interview required. Portfolio required.

W230 FdA Fashion and Textiles
Duration: 2FT Fdg
Entry Requirements: *GCE:* 160. *IB:* 24. Interview required. Portfolio required.

W12 WALSALL COLLEGE
WALSALL COLLEGE
LITTLETON STREET WEST
WALSALL
WEST MIDLANDS WS2 8ES
t: 01922 657000 f: 01922 657083
e: ckemp@walsallcollege.ac.uk
// www.walsallcollege.ac.uk

122W HNC Fashion & Textiles
Duration: 1FT HNC
Entry Requirements: *Foundation:* Pass. *GCE:* 80-240. Interview required. Portfolio required.

522W HND Fashion & Textiles
Duration: 2FT HND
Entry Requirements: *Foundation:* Pass. *GCE:* 80-240. Interview required. Portfolio required.

W50 UNIVERSITY OF WESTMINSTER
2ND FLOOR, CAVENDISH HOUSE
101 NEW CAVENDISH STREET,
LONDON W1W 6XH
t: 020 7915 5511
e: course-enquiries@westminster.ac.uk
// www.westminster.ac.uk

W230 BA Fashion Design
Duration: 3FT Hon
Entry Requirements: *Foundation:* Merit. *SQAH:* CCCC. *IB:* 26. Portfolio required.

W232 BA Fashion Design (Sandwich)
Duration: 4SW Hon
Entry Requirements: *SQAH:* CCCC. *IB:* 26. Portfolio required.

WN25 BA Fashion Merchandise Management

Duration: 4SW Hon

Entry Requirements: *GCE:* BBC. *IB:* 28. Interview required. Admissions Test required.

W74 WILTSHIRE COLLEGE

WILTSHIRE COLLEGE LACKHAM
LACOCK
CHIPPENHAM
WILTSHIRE SN15 2NY
t: 01249 466806 f: 01249 444474
e: HEAdmissions@wiltshire.ac.uk
// www.wiltshire.ac.uk

W231 BA Fashion and Textiles

Duration: 3FT Hon

Entry Requirements: *Foundation:* Merit. *GCE:* 220. *IB:* 24. Interview required. Portfolio required.

W75 UNIVERSITY OF WOLVERHAMPTON

ADMISSIONS UNIT
MX207, CAMP STREET
WOLVERHAMPTON
WEST MIDLANDS WV1 1AD
t: 01902 321000 f: 01902 321896
e: admissions@wlv.ac.uk
// www.wlv.ac.uk

W295 BA Fashion and Textiles

Duration: 3FT/4SW Hon

Entry Requirements: *GCE:* 200. *IB:* 24. *BTEC Dip:* DM. *BTEC ExtDip:* MMP. *OCR ND:* M1 *OCR NED:* P1 Interview required. Portfolio required.

Y70 YORK COLLEGE

SIM BALK LANE
YORK YO23 2BB
t: 01904 770448 f: 01904 770499
e: admissions.team@yorkcollege.ac.uk
// www.yorkcollege.ac.uk

W232 BA Fashion Design (Top-Up)

Duration: 1FT Hon

Entry Requirements: Contact the institution for details.

W230 FdA Fashion Design

Duration: 2FT Fdg

Entry Requirements: *Foundation:* Pass. *GCE:* CC.

FINE ART

A20 THE UNIVERSITY OF ABERDEEN

UNIVERSITY OFFICE
KING'S COLLEGE
ABERDEEN AB24 3FX
t: +44 (0) 1224 273504 f: +44 (0) 1224 272034
e: sras@abdn.ac.uk
// www.abdn.ac.uk/sras

WV63 MA Film & Visual Culture and History of Art

Duration: 4FT Hon

Entry Requirements: *GCE:* BBB. *SQAH:* BBBB. *IB:* 30.

A40 ABERYSTWYTH UNIVERSITY

ABERYSTWYTH UNIVERSITY, WELCOME CENTRE
PENGLAIS CAMPUS
ABERYSTWYTH
CEREDIGION SY23 3FB
t: 01970 622021 f: 01970 627410
e: ug-admissions@aber.ac.uk
// www.aber.ac.uk

V3W1 BA Art History with Fine Art

Duration: 3FT Hon

Entry Requirements: *GCE:* 280. *IB:* 29. Portfolio required.

WW14 BA Drama & Theatre Studies/Fine Art

Duration: 3FT Hon

Entry Requirements: *GCE:* 300-320. *IB:* 32. Portfolio required.

WX13 BA Education/Fine Art

Duration: 3FT Hon

Entry Requirements: *GCE:* 280. *IB:* 29. Portfolio required.

W100 BA Fine Art

Duration: 3FT Hon

Entry Requirements: *GCE:* 280. *IB:* 30. Portfolio required.

W1V3 BA Fine Art with Art History

Duration: 3FT Hon

Entry Requirements: *GCE:* 280. *IB:* 29. Portfolio required.

WV13 BA Fine Art/Art History

Duration: 3FT Hon

Entry Requirements: *GCE:* 280. *IB:* 29. Portfolio required.

WQ1N BA Fine Art/Cymraeg

Duration: 3FT Hon

Entry Requirements: *GCE:* 280. *IB:* 29. Portfolio required.

WQ13 BA Fine Art/English Literature

Duration: 3FT Hon

Entry Requirements: *GCE:* 300. *IB:* 28. Portfolio required.

WQ1M BA Fine Art/Gwyddeleg Iaith a Llen
Duration: 4SW Hon
Entry Requirements: *GCE:* 280. *IB:* 29. Portfolio required.

WV11 BA Fine Art/History
Duration: 3FT Hon
Entry Requirements: *GCE:* 300. *IB:* 29. Portfolio required.

WQ15 BA Irish Language & Literature/Fine Art
Duration: 3FT Hon
Entry Requirements: *GCE:* 280. *IB:* 29. Portfolio required.

A60 ANGLIA RUSKIN UNIVERSITY
BISHOP HALL LANE
CHELMSFORD
ESSEX CM1 1SQ
t: 0845 271 3333 f: 01245 251789
e: answers@anglia.ac.uk
// www.anglia.ac.uk

W105 BA Fine Art
Duration: 3FT Hon
Entry Requirements: *GCE:* 200-240. *SQAH:* CCCC. *SQAAH:* BC.
IB: 24. Interview required. Portfolio required.

A66 THE ARTS UNIVERSITY COLLEGE AT BOURNEMOUTH (FORMERLY ARTS INSTITUTE AT BOURNEMOUTH)
WALLISDOWN
POOLE
DORSET BH12 5HH
t: 01202 363228 f: 01202 537729
e: admissions@aucb.ac.uk
// www.aucb.ac.uk

W100 BA Fine Art
Duration: 3FT Hon
Entry Requirements: *Foundation:* Pass. *GCE:* BBC. *IB:* 24. *OCR ND:* M1 *OCR NED:* M1 Interview required. Portfolio required.

B11 BARKING AND DAGENHAM COLLEGE
DAGENHAM ROAD
ROMFORD
ESSEX RM7 0XU
t: 020 8090 3020 f: 020 8090 3021
e: engagement.services@barkingdagenhamcollege.ac.uk
// www.barkingdagenhamcollege.ac.uk

001W HND Fine Art
Duration: 2FT HND
Entry Requirements: Interview required. Portfolio required.

B20 BATH SPA UNIVERSITY
NEWTON PARK
NEWTON ST LOE
BATH BA2 9BN
t: 01225 875875 f: 01225 875444
e: enquiries@bathspa.ac.uk
// www.bathspa.ac.uk/clearing

WWCF BA Art/Visual Design
Duration: 3FT Hon
Entry Requirements: *Foundation:* Pass. *GCE:* 220-280. *IB:* 24. Interview required.

W190 BA Contemporary Arts Practice
Duration: 3FT Hon
Entry Requirements: *GCE:* 220-280. Interview required.

XW11 BA Education/Art
Duration: 3FT Hon   CRB Check: Required
Entry Requirements: *GCE:* 220-280. *IB:* 24.

W101 BA Fine Art (Painting)
Duration: 3FT Hon
Entry Requirements: *GCE:* 220-280. *IB:* 24. Interview required. Portfolio required.

W102 BA Fine Art (Sculpture)
Duration: 3FT Hon
Entry Requirements: *GCE:* 220-280. *IB:* 24. Interview required. Portfolio required.

B22 UNIVERSITY OF BEDFORDSHIRE
PARK SQUARE
LUTON
BEDS LU1 3JU
t: 0844 8482234 f: 01582 489323
e: admissions@beds.ac.uk
// www.beds.ac.uk

W101 BA Fine Art
Duration: 3FT Hon
Entry Requirements: *GCE:* 200. Interview required. Portfolio required.

W102 FdA Contemporary Fine Art Practice
Duration: 2FT Fdg
Entry Requirements: *GCE:* 120. Interview required. Portfolio required.

B23 BEDFORD COLLEGE
CAULDWELL STREET
BEDFORD MK42 9AH
t: 01234 291000 f: 01234 342674
e: info@bedford.ac.uk
// www.bedford.ac.uk

101W HNC Fine Arts
Duration: 1FT HNC
Entry Requirements: *Foundation:* Pass. *GCE:* 80-120. Interview required. Portfolio required.

001W HND Fine Arts
Duration: 2FT HND
Entry Requirements: *Foundation:* Pass. *GCE:* 80-120. Interview required. Portfolio required.

B24 BIRKBECK, UNIVERSITY OF LONDON
MALET STREET
LONDON WC1E 7HX
t: 020 7631 6316
e: webform: www.bbk.ac.uk/ask
// www.bbk.ac.uk/ask

QW31 BA Arts and Humanities
Duration: 3FT Hon
Entry Requirements: *GCE:* BBB. *SQAH:* BBBBB-BBBCC. *IB:* 30. Interview required.

B25 BIRMINGHAM CITY UNIVERSITY
PERRY BARR
BIRMINGHAM B42 2SU
t: 0121 331 5595 f: 0121 331 7994
// www.bcu.ac.uk

W101 BA Fine Art
Duration: 3FT Hon
Entry Requirements: *GCE:* 280. *IB:* 28. Interview required. Portfolio required.

001W HND Fine Art
Duration: 2FT HND
Entry Requirements: *GCE:* 120. *IB:* 24. Interview required. Portfolio required.

B38 BISHOP GROSSETESTE UNIVERSITY COLLEGE LINCOLN
BISHOP GROSSETESTE UNIVERSITY COLLEGE
LINCOLN LN1 3DY
t: 01522 583658 f: 01522 530243
e: admissions@bishopg.ac.uk
// www.bishopg.ac.uk/courses

WW41 BA Applied Drama and Visual Arts
Duration: 3FT Hon   CRB Check: Required
Entry Requirements: Interview required. Portfolio required.

W4W1 BA Applied Drama with Visual Arts
Duration: 3FT Hon   CRB Check: Required
Entry Requirements: Contact the institution for details.

XW31 BA Early Childhood Studies and Visual Arts
Duration: 3FT Hon   CRB Check: Required
Entry Requirements: Contact the institution for details.

X3W1 BA Early Childhood Studies with Visual Arts
Duration: 3FT Hon   CRB Check: Required
Entry Requirements: Contact the institution for details.

X1W1 BA Education Studies and Visual Arts
Duration: 3FT Hon   CRB Check: Required
Entry Requirements: *Foundation:* Pass. *GCE:* 220.

X3WD BA Education Studies with Visual Arts
Duration: 3FT Hon   CRB Check: Required
Entry Requirements: *Foundation:* Pass. *GCE:* 220.

QW31 BA English and Visual Arts
Duration: 3FT Hon   CRB Check: Required
Entry Requirements: Contact the institution for details.

Q3W1 BA English with Visual Arts
Duration: 3FT Hon   CRB Check: Required
Entry Requirements: Contact the institution for details.

XW3C BA Special Educational Needs & Inclusion and Visual Arts
Duration: 3FT Hon   CRB Check: Required
Entry Requirements: Contact the institution for details.

WV11 BA Visual Arts and History
Duration: 3FT Hon   CRB Check: Required
Entry Requirements: Contact the institution for details.

B40 BLACKBURN COLLEGE
FEILDEN STREET
BLACKBURN BB2 1LH
t: 01254 292594 f: 01254 679647
e: he-admissions@blackburn.ac.uk
// www.blackburn.ac.uk

W101 BA Fine Art (Integrated Media)
Duration: 3FT Hon
Entry Requirements: *GCE:* 200.

B41 BLACKPOOL AND THE FYLDE COLLEGE AN ASSOCIATE COLLEGE OF LANCASTER UNIVERSITY
ASHFIELD ROAD
BISPHAM
BLACKPOOL
LANCS FY2 0HB
t: 01253 504346 f: 01253 504198
e: admissions@blackpool.ac.uk
// www.blackpool.ac.uk

W100 BA Fine Art and Professional Practice
Duration: 3FT Hon
Entry Requirements: *Foundation:* Merit. *GCE:* 220. *IB:* 24.
Interview required. Portfolio required.

B44 UNIVERSITY OF BOLTON
DEANE ROAD
BOLTON BL3 5AB
t: 01204 903903 f: 01204 399074
e: enquiries@bolton.ac.uk
// www.bolton.ac.uk

W101 BA Fine Arts
Duration: 3FT Hon
Entry Requirements: *GCE:* 240. Interview required. Portfolio required.

B60 BRADFORD COLLEGE: AN ASSOCIATE COLLEGE OF LEEDS METROPOLITAN UNIVERSITY
GREAT HORTON ROAD
BRADFORD
WEST YORKSHIRE BD7 1AY
t: 01274 433008 f: 01274 431652
e: heregistry@bradfordcollege.ac.uk
// www.bradfordcollege.ac.uk/
university-centre

W100 BA Fine Art
Duration: 3FT Hon
Entry Requirements: *GCE:* 220. Interview required. Portfolio required.

B72 UNIVERSITY OF BRIGHTON
MITHRAS HOUSE 211
LEWES ROAD
BRIGHTON BN2 4AT
t: 01273 644644 f: 01273 642607
e: admissions@brighton.ac.uk
// www.brighton.ac.uk

W100 BA Critical Fine Art Practice
Duration: 3FT Hon
Entry Requirements: *GCE:* BBC. Foundation Course required. Interview required. Portfolio required.

W120 BA Fine Art Painting
Duration: 3FT Hon
Entry Requirements: *GCE:* BBC. Foundation Course required. Interview required. Portfolio required.

W130 BA Fine Art Sculpture
Duration: 3FT Hon
Entry Requirements: *GCE:* BBC. Foundation Course required. Interview required. Portfolio required.

WW31 BA Music and Visual Art
Duration: 3FT Hon
Entry Requirements: *GCE:* BBC. Foundation Course required. Interview required. Portfolio required.

W5W1 BA Performance and Visual Arts (Dance)
Duration: 3FT Hon
Entry Requirements: *GCE:* BBC. Foundation Course required. Interview required. Portfolio required.

W4WD BA Performance and Visual Arts (Theatre)
Duration: 3FT Hon
Entry Requirements: *GCE:* BBC. Foundation Course required. Interview required. Portfolio required.

W101 FdA Contemporary Fine Art Practice
Duration: 2FT Fdg
Entry Requirements: *GCE:* 120. Interview required. Portfolio required.

B80 UNIVERSITY OF THE WEST OF ENGLAND, BRISTOL
FRENCHAY CAMPUS
COLDHARBOUR LANE
BRISTOL BS16 1QY
t: +44 (0)117 32 83333 f: +44 (0)117 32 82810
e: admissions@uwe.ac.uk
// www.uwe.ac.uk

W101 BA Fine Arts
Duration: 3FT Hon
Entry Requirements: *GCE:* 280. Interview required. Portfolio required.

B94 BUCKINGHAMSHIRE NEW UNIVERSITY
QUEEN ALEXANDRA ROAD
HIGH WYCOMBE
BUCKINGHAMSHIRE HP11 2JZ
t: 0800 0565 660 f: 01494 605 023
e: admissions@bucks.ac.uk
// bucks.ac.uk

W100 BA Fine Art
Duration: 3FT Hon
Entry Requirements: *GCE:* 200-240. *IB:* 24. *OCR ND:* M1 *OCR NED:* M3 Interview required.

C10 CANTERBURY CHRIST CHURCH UNIVERSITY
NORTH HOLMES ROAD
CANTERBURY
KENT CT1 1QU
t: 01227 782900 f: 01227 782888
e: admissions@canterbury.ac.uk
// www.canterbury.ac.uk

C8WC BA/BSc Sport & Exercise Psychology with Art
Duration: 3FT Hon
Entry Requirements: Contact the institution for details.

C20 CARDIFF METROPOLITAN UNIVERSITY (UWIC)
ADMISSIONS UNIT
LLANDAFF CAMPUS
WESTERN AVENUE
CARDIFF CF5 2YB
t: 029 2041 6070 f: 029 2041 6286
e: admissions@cardiffmet.ac.uk
// www.cardiffmet.ac.uk

W100 BA Fine Art
Duration: 3FT Hon
Entry Requirements: *GCE:* 300. *IB:* 26. *BTEC ExtDip:* DDM. *OCR NED:* M1 Foundation Course required. Interview required. Portfolio required.

C22 COLEG SIR GAR / CARMARTHENSHIRE COLLEGE
SANDY ROAD
LLANELLI
CARMARTHENSHIRE SA15 4DN
t: 01554 748000 f: 01554 748170
e: admissions@colegsirgar.ac.uk
// www.colegsirgar.ac.uk

W130 BA Fine Art Sculpture
Duration: 3FT Hon
Entry Requirements: *Foundation:* Pass. Portfolio required.

W100 BA (Hons) Fine Art (Contemporary Practice)
Duration: 3FT Hon
Entry Requirements: Portfolio required.

C30 UNIVERSITY OF CENTRAL LANCASHIRE
PRESTON
LANCS PR1 2HE
t: 01772 201201 f: 01772 894954
e: uadmissions@uclan.ac.uk
// www.uclan.ac.uk

WW1F BA Drawing and Image Making
Duration: 3FT Hon
Entry Requirements: *GCE:* 240. *IB:* 24. *OCR ND:* D *OCR NED:* M3 Interview required. Portfolio required.

W101 BA Fine Art
Duration: 3FT Hon
Entry Requirements: *GCE:* 240. *IB:* 24. *OCR ND:* D *OCR NED:* M3 Interview required. Portfolio required.

W102 FdA Fine Art
Duration: 2FT Fdg
Entry Requirements: *GCE:* 80. Interview required. Portfolio required.

C55 UNIVERSITY OF CHESTER
PARKGATE ROAD
CHESTER CH1 4BJ
t: 01244 511000 f: 01244 511300
e: enquiries@chester.ac.uk
// www.chester.ac.uk

XW31 BA Education Studies and Fine Art
Duration: 3FT Hon
Entry Requirements: *GCE:* 240-280. *SQAH:* BBBB. *IB:* 26.

W100 BA Fine Art
Duration: 3FT Hon
Entry Requirements: *Foundation:* Pass. *GCE:* 240-280. *SQAH:* BBBB. *IB:* 26. Interview required. Portfolio required.

WW94 BA Fine Art and Drama & Theatre Studies
Duration: 3FT Hon
Entry Requirements: *GCE:* 260-300. *SQAH:* BBBB. *IB:* 28.

WQ93 BA Fine Art and English
Duration: 3FT Hon
Entry Requirements: *GCE:* 260-300. *SQAH:* BBBB. *IB:* 28.

RW19 BA Fine Art and French
Duration: 4FT Hon
Entry Requirements: *Foundation:* Pass. *GCE:* 240-280. *SQAH:* BBBB. *IB:* 26.

WW12 BA Fine Art and Graphic Design
Duration: 3FT Hon
Entry Requirements: *GCE:* 240-280. *SQAH:* BBBB. *IB:* 26.

RW49 BA Fine Art and Spanish
Duration: 4FT Hon
Entry Requirements: *Foundation:* Pass. *GCE:* 240-280. *SQAH:* BBBB. *IB:* 26.

WW16 BA Photography and Fine Art
Duration: 3FT Hon
Entry Requirements: *Foundation:* Pass. *GCE:* 240-280. *SQAH:* BBBB. *IB:* 26. Interview required. Portfolio required.

C58 UNIVERSITY OF CHICHESTER
BISHOP OTTER CAMPUS
COLLEGE LANE
CHICHESTER
WEST SUSSEX PO19 6PE
t: 01243 816002 f: 01243 816161
e: admissions@chi.ac.uk
// www.chiuni.ac.uk

W100 BA Fine Art
Duration: 3FT Hon
Entry Requirements: *GCE:* BCC. *SQAAH:* BCC. *IB:* 28. *BTEC Dip:* DD. *BTEC ExtDip:* DMM. Interview required. Portfolio required.

W1QH BA Fine Art and International English Studies
Duration: 3FT Hon
Entry Requirements: *GCE:* BCC. *SQAAH:* BCC. *IB:* 28. *BTEC Dip:* DD. *BTEC ExtDip:* DMM. Interview required. Portfolio required.

W1QJ BA Fine Art with International English Studies
Duration: 3FT Hon
Entry Requirements: *GCE:* BCC. *SQAAH:* BCC. *IB:* 28. *BTEC Dip:* DD. *BTEC ExtDip:* DMM. Interview required. Portfolio required.

C85 COVENTRY UNIVERSITY
THE STUDENT CENTRE
COVENTRY UNIVERSITY
1 GULSON RD
COVENTRY CV1 2JH
t: 024 7615 2222 f: 024 7615 2223
e: studentenquiries@coventry.ac.uk
// www.coventry.ac.uk

W100 BA Fine Art
Duration: 3FT/4SW Hon
Entry Requirements: *Foundation:* Merit. *GCE:* CCC. *SQAH:* CCCCC. *IB:* 27. *BTEC ExtDip:* MMM. *OCR NED:* M3 Interview required. Portfolio required.

C88 CRAVEN COLLEGE
HIGH STREET
SKIPTON
NORTH YORKSHIRE BD23 1JY
t: 01756 791411 f: 01756 794872
e: enquiries@craven-college.ac.uk
// www.craven-college.ac.uk

W100 BA Fine Art
Duration: 3FT Hon
Entry Requirements: Contact the institution for details.

001W HND Fine Art
Duration: 2FT HND
Entry Requirements: *Foundation:* Pass. *GCE:* 160. Interview required. Portfolio required.

C92 CROYDON COLLEGE
COLLEGE ROAD
CROYDON CR9 1DX
t: 020 8760 5934 f: 020 8760 5880
e: admissions@croydon.ac.uk
// www.croydon.ac.uk

W100 BA Fine Art
Duration: 3FT Hon
Entry Requirements: Contact the institution for details.

C93 UNIVERSITY FOR THE CREATIVE ARTS
FALKNER ROAD
FARNHAM
SURREY GU9 7DS
t: 01252 892960
e: admissions@ucreative.ac.uk
// www.ucreative.ac.uk

WP13 BA Arts & Media
Duration: 3FT Hon
Entry Requirements: *GCE:* 220. *IB:* 24. *BTEC ExtDip:* PPP. Interview required. Portfolio required.

W100 BA Fine Art
Duration: 3FT Hon
Entry Requirements: *GCE:* 220. *IB:* 24. *BTEC ExtDip:* PPP. Interview required. Portfolio required.

W101 BA Fine Art
Duration: 3FT Hon
Entry Requirements: *GCE:* 220. *IB:* 24. *BTEC ExtDip:* PPP. Interview required. Portfolio required.

C99 UNIVERSITY OF CUMBRIA
FUSEHILL STREET
CARLISLE
CUMBRIA CA1 2HH
t: 01228 616234 f: 01228 616235
// www.cumbria.ac.uk

W100 BA Fine Art
Duration: 3FT Hon
Entry Requirements: *Foundation:* Merit. *GCE:* 240. *SQAH:* BBC. *SQAAH:* CC. *IB:* 30. *OCR ND:* D Interview required. Portfolio required.

W108 BA Fine Art (with Year 0)
Duration: 4FT Hon
Entry Requirements: *Foundation:* Pass. *GCE:* C-cccc. *SQAH:* CC. *SQAAH:* C. *IB:* 25. Interview required. Portfolio required.

W104 DipHE Fine Art
Duration: 2FT Dip
Entry Requirements: Contact the institution for details.

W110 FdA Drawing
Duration: 2FT Fdg
Entry Requirements: *Foundation:* Pass. *GCE:* C-cccc. *SQAH:* CC. *SQAAH:* C. *IB:* 25. Interview required. Portfolio required.

D26 DE MONTFORT UNIVERSITY
THE GATEWAY
LEICESTER LE1 9BH
t: 0116 255 1551 f: 0116 250 6204
e: enquiries@dmu.ac.uk
// www.dmu.ac.uk

W100 BA Fine Art
Duration: 3FT Hon
Entry Requirements: *Foundation:* Pass. *GCE:* 260. *IB:* 28. *BTEC Dip:* D*D. *BTEC ExtDip:* MMM. Interview required. Portfolio required.

D39 UNIVERSITY OF DERBY
KEDLESTON ROAD
DERBY DE22 1GB
t: 01332 591167 f: 01332 597724
e: askadmissions@derby.ac.uk
// www.derby.ac.uk

NW21 BA Business Management and Popular Music (Production)
Duration: 3FT Hon
Entry Requirements: *Foundation:* Distinction. *GCE:* 260-300. *IB:* 28. *BTEC Dip:* D*D*. *BTEC ExtDip:* DMM. *OCR NED:* M2

W191 BA Creative Expressive Therapies (Art)
Duration: 3FT Hon **CRB Check:** Required
Entry Requirements: *Foundation:* Distinction. *GCE:* 280. *IB:* 28. *BTEC Dip:* D*D*. *BTEC ExtDip:* DMM. *OCR NED:* M2 Interview required.

W100 BA Fine Art
Duration: 3FT Hon
Entry Requirements: *Foundation:* Distinction. *GCE:* 240. *IB:* 28. *BTEC Dip:* D*D*. *BTEC ExtDip:* DMM. *OCR ND:* D *OCR NED:* M3 Interview required. Portfolio required.

W101 FYr Fine Art (Year 0)
Duration: 1FT Hon
Entry Requirements: *Foundation:* Pass. *GCE:* 160. *IB:* 24. *BTEC Dip:* D*D*. *BTEC ExtDip:* DMM. *OCR ND:* M2 *OCR NED:* P2 Interview required. Portfolio required.

D65 UNIVERSITY OF DUNDEE
NETHERGATE
DUNDEE DD1 4HN
t: 01382 383838 f: 01382 388150
e: contactus@dundee.ac.uk
// www.dundee.ac.uk/admissions/undergraduate/

WV15 BA Art, Philosophy, Contemporary Practices
Duration: 3FT Hon
Entry Requirements: Foundation Course required. Interview required. Portfolio required.

E28 UNIVERSITY OF EAST LONDON
DOCKLANDS CAMPUS
UNIVERSITY WAY
LONDON E16 2RD
t: 020 8223 3333 f: 020 8223 2978
e: study@uel.ac.uk
// www.uel.ac.uk

W100 BA Fine Art
Duration: 3FT Hon
Entry Requirements: *GCE:* 200. Interview required. Portfolio required.

W108 BA Fine Art (Extended)
Duration: 4FT Hon
Entry Requirements: *GCE:* 80. Interview required. Portfolio required.

W1L6 BA Fine Art with Cultural Studies
Duration: 3FT Hon
Entry Requirements: *GCE:* 240. *IB:* 24.

W1Q3 BA Fine Art with English Literature
Duration: 3FT Hon
Entry Requirements: *GCE:* 240. *IB:* 24.

W1L2 BA Fine Art with International Politics
Duration: 3FT Hon
Entry Requirements: *GCE:* 240. *IB:* 24.

W1C8 BA Fine Art with Psychosocial Studies
Duration: 3FT Hon
Entry Requirements: *GCE:* 240. *IB:* 24.

WW12 BA Fine Art/Graphic Design
Duration: 3FT Hon
Entry Requirements: *GCE:* 200. *IB:* 24.

V1W1 BA History with Fine Art
Duration: 3FT Hon
Entry Requirements: *GCE:* 240. *IB:* 24.

W2W1 BA Illustration with Fine Art
Duration: 3FT Hon
Entry Requirements: *GCE:* 240.

E32 EAST SURREY COLLEGE (INCORPORATING REIGATE SCHOOL OF ART, DESIGN AND MEDIA)
GATTON POINT
LONDON ROAD
REDHILL RH1 2JX
t: 01737 772611 f: 01737 768641
e: fmelmoe@esc.ac.uk
// www.esc.ac.uk

001W HND Fine Art
Duration: 2FT HND
Entry Requirements: *GCE:* 80.

E56 THE UNIVERSITY OF EDINBURGH
STUDENT RECRUITMENT & ADMISSIONS
57 GEORGE SQUARE
EDINBURGH EH8 9JU
t: 0131 650 4360 f: 0131 651 1236
e: sra.enquiries@ed.ac.uk
// www.ed.ac.uk/studying/undergraduate/

W100 BA Art
Duration: 4FT Hon
Entry Requirements: *GCE:* BBB. *SQAH:* BBBB. *IB:* 34. Portfolio required.

W120 BA Painting
Duration: 4FT Hon
Entry Requirements: *Foundation:* Merit. *GCE:* BBB. *SQAH:* BBBB. *IB:* 34. Portfolio required.

W130 BA Sculpture
Duration: 4FT Hon
Entry Requirements: *Foundation:* Merit. *GCE:* BBB. *SQAH:* BBBB. *IB:* 34. Portfolio required.

W150 MA Fine Art
Duration: 5FT Hon
Entry Requirements: *GCE:* BBB. *SQAH:* ABBB-BBBB. *IB:* 34. Portfolio required.

E70 THE UNIVERSITY OF ESSEX
WIVENHOE PARK
COLCHESTER
ESSEX CO4 3SQ
t: 01206 873666 f: 01206 874477
e: admit@essex.ac.uk
// www.essex.ac.uk

VW36 BA Film Studies and History of Art
Duration: 3FT Hon
Entry Requirements: *GCE:* ABB-BBB. *SQAH:* AAAB-AABB. *BTEC ExtDip:* DDM. Interview required.

E81 EXETER COLLEGE
HELE ROAD
EXETER
DEVON EX4 4JS
t: 0845 111 6000
e: info@exe-coll.ac.uk
// www.exe-coll.ac.uk/he

W100 FdA Fine Art
Duration: 2FT Fdg
Entry Requirements: *GCE:* 160.

E84 UNIVERSITY OF EXETER
LAVER BUILDING
NORTH PARK ROAD
EXETER
DEVON EX4 4QE
t: 01392 723044 f: 01392 722479
e: admissions@exeter.ac.uk
// www.exeter.ac.uk

VW31 BA Art History and Visual Culture
Duration: 3FT Hon
Entry Requirements: *GCE:* AAA-AAB. *SQAH:* AAAAB-AAABB. *SQAAH:* AAB-ABB. *BTEC ExtDip:* DDD.

F33 UNIVERSITY COLLEGE FALMOUTH
WOODLANE
FALMOUTH
CORNWALL TR11 4RH
t: 01326213730
e: admissions@falmouth.ac.uk
// www.falmouth.ac.uk

W110 BA(Hons) Drawing
Duration: 3FT Hon
Entry Requirements: *GCE:* 220. *IB:* 24. Interview required. Portfolio required.

W100 BA(Hons) Fine Art
Duration: 3FT Hon
Entry Requirements: *GCE:* 220. *IB:* 24. Interview required. Portfolio required.

G14 UNIVERSITY OF GLAMORGAN, CARDIFF AND PONTYPRIDD
ENQUIRIES AND ADMISSIONS UNIT
PONTYPRIDD CF37 1DL
t: 08456 434030 f: 01443 654050
e: enquiries@glam.ac.uk
// www.glam.ac.uk

W111 FdA Art Practice
Duration: 2FT Fdg
Entry Requirements: Interview required.

G28 UNIVERSITY OF GLASGOW
71 SOUTHPARK AVENUE
UNIVERSITY OF GLASGOW
GLASGOW G12 8QQ
t: 0141 330 6062 f: 0141 330 2961
e: student.recruitment@glasgow.ac.uk
// www.glasgow.ac.uk

VW31 MA History of Art and Art-world Practice
Duration: 4FT Hon
Entry Requirements: Contact the institution for details.

G43 THE GLASGOW SCHOOL OF ART
167 RENFREW STREET
GLASGOW G3 6RQ
t: 0141 353 4434/4514 f: 0141 353 4408
e: admissions@gsa.ac.uk
// www.gsa.ac.uk

W130 BA Fine Art - Environmental Art/Sculpture
Duration: 4FT Hon
Entry Requirements: *GCE:* ABB. *SQAH:* AABB-ABBB. *IB:* 30. Interview required. Portfolio required.

W640 BA Fine Art - Photography
Duration: 4FT Hon
Entry Requirements: *GCE:* ABB. *SQAH:* AABB-ABBB. *IB:* 30. Interview required. Portfolio required.

G50 THE UNIVERSITY OF GLOUCESTERSHIRE
PARK CAMPUS
THE PARK
CHELTENHAM GL50 2RH
t: 01242 714501 f: 01242 714869
e: admissions@glos.ac.uk
// www.glos.ac.uk

W100 BA Fine Art
Duration: 3FT Hon
Entry Requirements: Interview required. Portfolio required.

W190 BA Fine Art (Photography)
Duration: 3FT Hon
Entry Requirements: *GCE:* 280-300. Interview required. Portfolio required.

G53 GLYNDWR UNIVERSITY
PLAS COCH
MOLD ROAD
WREXHAM LL11 2AW
t: 01978 293439 f: 01978 290008
e: sid@glyndwr.ac.uk
// www.glyndwr.ac.uk

W000 BA Fine Art
Duration: 3FT Hon
Entry Requirements: *GCE:* 240. Portfolio required.

G56 GOLDSMITHS, UNIVERSITY OF LONDON
GOLDSMITHS, UNIVERSITY OF LONDON
NEW CROSS
LONDON SE14 6NW
t: 020 7048 5300 f: 020 7919 7509
e: admissions@gold.ac.uk
// www.gold.ac.uk

W190 BA Fine Art
Duration: 3FT Hon
Entry Requirements: *GCE:* BBC. *SQAH:* BBBCC. *SQAAH:* BBC.
Foundation Course required. Interview required. Portfolio required.

W191 BA Fine Art (Extension Degree)
Duration: 4FT Hon
Entry Requirements: *SQAH:* BBBCC. *SQAAH:* BBC. Interview
required. Portfolio required.

VW31 BA Fine Art and History of Art
Duration: 3FT Hon
Entry Requirements: *Foundation:* Pass. Foundation Course
required. Interview required. Portfolio required.

G70 UNIVERSITY OF GREENWICH
GREENWICH CAMPUS
OLD ROYAL NAVAL COLLEGE
PARK ROW
LONDON SE10 9LS
t: 020 8331 9000 f: 020 8331 8145
e: courseinfo@gre.ac.uk
// www.gre.ac.uk

W100 FdA Art Practice
Duration: 2FT Fdg
Entry Requirements: Interview required. Portfolio required.

G80 GRIMSBY INSTITUTE OF FURTHER AND HIGHER EDUCATION
NUNS CORNER
GRIMSBY
NE LINCOLNSHIRE DN34 5BQ
t: 0800 328 3631
e: headmissions@grimsby.ac.uk
// www.grimsby.ac.uk

W102 BA Fine Art Practice
Duration: 3FT Hon
Entry Requirements: Contact the institution for details.

H14 HAVERING COLLEGE OF FURTHER AND HIGHER EDUCATION
ARDLEIGH GREEN ROAD
HORNCHURCH
ESSEX RM11 2LL
t: 01708 462793 f: 01708 462736
e: HE@havering-college.ac.uk
// www.havering-college.ac.uk

W100 BA Fine Art
Duration: 3FT Hon
Entry Requirements: Foundation Course required. Interview
required. Portfolio required.

H18 HEREFORD COLLEGE OF ARTS
FOLLY LANE
HEREFORD HR1 1LT
t: 01432 273359 f: 01432 341099
e: headmin@hca.ac.uk
// www.hca.ac.uk

W102 BA Fine Art
Duration: 3FT Hon   CRB Check: Required
Entry Requirements: *GCE:* 200. Interview required. Portfolio
required.

W101 BA Fine Art (top-up)
Duration: 1FT Hon   CRB Check: Required
Entry Requirements: Interview required. Portfolio required. HND
required.

H36 UNIVERSITY OF HERTFORDSHIRE
UNIVERSITY ADMISSIONS SERVICE
COLLEGE LANE
HATFIELD
HERTS AL10 9AB
t: 01707 284800
// www.herts.ac.uk

W100 BA Fine Art
Duration: 3FT Hon
Entry Requirements: *Foundation:* Pass. *GCE:* 240. Interview
required. Portfolio required.

W190 FdA Fine Art Practice

Duration: 2FT Fdg

Entry Requirements: *GCE:* 80. Interview required. Portfolio required.

H49 UNIVERSITY OF THE HIGHLANDS AND ISLANDS

UHI EXECUTIVE OFFICE
NESS WALK
INVERNESS
SCOTLAND IV3 5SQ
t: 01463 279000 f: 01463 279001
e: info@uhi.ac.uk
// www.uhi.ac.uk

W100 BA Fine Art

Duration: 4FT Hon

Entry Requirements: *GCE:* CC. *SQAH:* CCC. Portfolio required.

WW12 BA Hons Fine Art Textiles

Duration: 4FT Hon

Entry Requirements: *GCE:* CC. *SQAH:* CCC. Portfolio required.

H60 THE UNIVERSITY OF HUDDERSFIELD

QUEENSGATE
HUDDERSFIELD HD1 3DH
t: 01484 473969 f: 01484 472765
e: admissionsandrecords@hud.ac.uk
// www.hud.ac.uk

W1W0 BA(Hons) Contemporary Art and Illustration

Duration: 3FT/4SW Hon

Entry Requirements: *GCE:* 300. *SQAH:* BBBB. *IB:* 28. Interview required. Portfolio required.

H73 HULL COLLEGE

QUEEN'S GARDENS
HULL HU1 3DG
t: 01482 329943 f: 01482 598733
e: info@hull-college.ac.uk
// www.hull-college.ac.uk/higher-education

W100 BA Contemporary Fine Art Practice

Duration: 3FT Hon

Entry Requirements: *GCE:* 200. Foundation Course required. Interview required. Portfolio required.

WW14 FdA Visual Arts

Duration: 2FT Fdg

Entry Requirements: *GCE:* 80. Interview required. Portfolio required.

K24 THE UNIVERSITY OF KENT

RECRUITMENT & ADMISSIONS OFFICE
REGISTRY
UNIVERSITY OF KENT
CANTERBURY, KENT CT2 7NZ
t: 01227 827272 f: 01227 827077
e: information@kent.ac.uk
// www.kent.ac.uk

W100 BA Fine Art

Duration: 3FT Hon

Entry Requirements: *GCE:* ABB-BBB. *SQAH:* AABBB-ABBBB. *SQAAH:* ABB-BBB. *IB:* 33. *OCR ND:* D *OCR NED:* D2 Interview required. Portfolio required.

W101 BA Fine Art (Top-up)

Duration: 1FT Hon

Entry Requirements: Interview required. Portfolio required.

K84 KINGSTON UNIVERSITY

STUDENT INFORMATION & ADVICE CENTRE
COOPER HOUSE
40-46 SURBITON ROAD
KINGSTON UPON THAMES KT1 2HX
t: 0844 8552177 f: 020 8547 7080
e: aps@kingston.ac.uk
// www.kingston.ac.uk

KW11 BA Art Market

Duration: 3FT Hon

Entry Requirements: *GCE:* 300. *IB:* 28. Interview required.

KW1C BA Art Market

Duration: 4SW Hon

Entry Requirements: *GCE:* 300. *IB:* 28. Interview required.

W100 BA Fine Art

Duration: 3FT Hon

Entry Requirements: Foundation Course required. Interview required. Portfolio required.

WV1H BA Fine Art and Art History

Duration: 3FT Hon

Entry Requirements: Foundation Course required. Interview required. Portfolio required.

VW32 BA Visual & Material Culture and History of Art, Design and Film

Duration: 3FT Hon

Entry Requirements: *GCE:* 240.

K90 KIRKLEES COLLEGE
HALIFAX ROAD
DEWSBURY
WEST YORKSHIRE WF13 2AS
t: 01924 436221 f: 01924 457047
e: admissionsdc@kirkleescollege.ac.uk
// www.kirkleescollege.ac.uk

W100 BA Fine Art for Design
Duration: 3FT Hon
Entry Requirements: *GCE:* 200. *IB:* 28. Interview required.
Portfolio required.

L05 LAKES COLLEGE - WEST CUMBRIA
HALLWOOD ROAD
LILLYHALL
WORKINGTON CA14 4JN
t: 01946 839300 f: 01946 839302
e: student.services@lcwc.ac.uk
// www.lcwc.ac.uk

W100 HND Fine Art
Duration: 2FT HND
Entry Requirements: Contact the institution for details.

L14 LANCASTER UNIVERSITY
THE UNIVERSITY
LANCASTER
LANCASHIRE LA1 4YW
t: 01524 592029 f: 01524 846243
e: ugadmissions@lancaster.ac.uk
// www.lancs.ac.uk

W100 BA Fine Art
Duration: 3FT Hon
Entry Requirements: *GCE:* AAB. *SQAH:* ABBBB. *SQAAH:* AAB. *IB:*
35. Portfolio required.

L23 UNIVERSITY OF LEEDS
THE UNIVERSITY OF LEEDS
WOODHOUSE LANE
LEEDS LS2 9JT
t: 0113 343 3999
e: admissions@leeds.ac.uk
// www.leeds.ac.uk

W150 BA Fine Art
Duration: 3FT Hon
Entry Requirements: *GCE:* ABB. *SQAH:* BBBBB. *SQAAH:* ABB. *IB:*
34. Interview required. Portfolio required.

L27 LEEDS METROPOLITAN UNIVERSITY
COURSE ENQUIRIES OFFICE
CITY CAMPUS
LEEDS LS1 3HE
t: 0113 81 23113 f: 0113 81 23129
// www.leedsmet.ac.uk

W100 BA Fine Art
Duration: 3FT Hon
Entry Requirements: *Foundation:* Pass. *GCE:* 80. Interview
required. Portfolio required.

L28 LEEDS COLLEGE OF ART
BLENHEIM WALK
LEEDS LS2 9AQ
t: 0113 202 8000 f: 0113 202 8001
e: info@leeds-art.ac.uk
// www.leeds-art.ac.uk

W100 BA Fine Art
Duration: 3FT Hon
Entry Requirements: *Foundation:* Merit. *GCE:* 240. *IB:* 24. *BTEC
Dip:* DD. *BTEC ExtDip:* MMM. Interview required. Portfolio
required.

L39 UNIVERSITY OF LINCOLN
ADMISSIONS
BRAYFORD POOL
LINCOLN LN6 7TS
t: 01522 886097 f: 01522 886146
e: admissions@lincoln.ac.uk
// www.lincoln.ac.uk

W101 BA Fine Art
Duration: 3FT Hon
Entry Requirements: *GCE:* 280. Interview required. Portfolio
required.

L43 LIVERPOOL COMMUNITY COLLEGE
LIVERPOOL COMMUNITY COLLEGE
CLARENCE STREET
LIVERPOOL L3 5TP
t: 0151 252 3352 f: 0151 252 3351
e: enquiry@liv-coll.ac.uk
// www.liv-coll.ac.uk

W100 FdA Fine Art
Duration: 2FT Fdg
Entry Requirements: Contact the institution for details.

L46 LIVERPOOL HOPE UNIVERSITY
HOPE PARK
LIVERPOOL L16 9JD
t: 0151 291 3331 f: 0151 291 3434
e: administration@hope.ac.uk
// www.hope.ac.uk

WW41 BA Drama & Theatre Studies and Fine Art
Duration: 3FT Hon
Entry Requirements: *GCE:* 300-320. *IB:* 25. Interview required.

XWJ1 BA Education and Fine Art
Duration: 3FT Hon   CRB Check: Required
Entry Requirements: *GCE:* 300-320. *IB:* 25. Interview required.

QW3C BA English Language and Fine Art
Duration: 3FT Hon
Entry Requirements: *GCE:* 300-320. *IB:* 25. Interview required.

W101 BA Fine Art
Duration: 3FT Hon
Entry Requirements: *GCE:* 300-320. *IB:* 25. Interview required.
Portfolio required.

W1V5 BA Fine Art & Philosophy & Ethics
Duration: 3FT Hon
Entry Requirements: *GCE:* 300-320. *IB:* 25.

W1L2 BA Fine Art & Politics
Duration: 3FT Hon
Entry Requirements: *GCE:* 300-320. *IB:* 25.

W1C8 BA Fine Art & Psychology
Duration: 3FT Hon
Entry Requirements: *GCE:* 300-320. *IB:* 25.

WP1H BA Fine Art and Media & Communication
Duration: 3FT Hon
Entry Requirements: *GCE:* 300-320. *IB:* 25. Interview required.
Portfolio required.

WW1H BA Fine Art and Music
Duration: 3FT Hon
Entry Requirements: *GCE:* 300-320. *IB:* 25. Interview required.
Portfolio required.

X1W1 BA Primary Teaching with Fine Art
Duration: 4FT Hon   CRB Check: Required
Entry Requirements: *GCE:* 300-320. *IB:* 25. Interview required.
Admissions Test required.

L51 LIVERPOOL JOHN MOORES UNIVERSITY
KINGSWAY HOUSE
HATTON GARDEN
LIVERPOOL L3 2AJ
t: 0151 231 5090 f: 0151 904 6368
e: courses@ljmu.ac.uk
// www.ljmu.ac.uk

W100 BA Fine Art
Duration: 3FT Hon
Entry Requirements: *GCE:* 280-320. Foundation Course required.
Interview required. Portfolio required.

L68 LONDON METROPOLITAN UNIVERSITY
166-220 HOLLOWAY ROAD
LONDON N7 8DB
t: 020 7133 4200
e: admissions@londonmet.ac.uk
// www.londonmet.ac.uk

W101 BA Fine Art
Duration: 3FT Hon
Entry Requirements: *Foundation:* Pass. *GCE:* 280. *IB:* 28.
Foundation Course required. Interview required. Portfolio required.

W120 BA Fine Art (Painting)
Duration: 3FT Hon
Entry Requirements: *Foundation:* Pass. *GCE:* 280. *IB:* 28.
Foundation Course required. Interview required. Portfolio required.

W641 BA Fine Art (Photography)
Duration: 3FT Hon
Entry Requirements: *Foundation:* Pass. *GCE:* 280. *IB:* 28.
Foundation Course required. Interview required. Portfolio required.

W130 BA Fine Art (Sculpture and Installation)
Duration: 3FT Hon
Entry Requirements: *Foundation:* Pass. *GCE:* 280. *IB:* 28.
Foundation Course required. Interview required. Portfolio required.

L79 LOUGHBOROUGH UNIVERSITY
LOUGHBOROUGH
LEICESTERSHIRE LE11 3TU
t: 01509 223522 f: 01509 223905
e: admissions@lboro.ac.uk
// www.lboro.ac.uk

W100 BA Fine Art
Duration: 3FT Hon
Entry Requirements: *IB:* 32. *BTEC ExtDip:* DDM. Interview
required. Portfolio required.

M10 THE MANCHESTER COLLEGE
OPENSHAW CAMPUS
ASHTON OLD ROAD
OPENSHAW
MANCHESTER M11 2WH
t: 0800 068 8585 f: 0161 920 4103
e: enquiries@themanchestercollege.ac.uk
// www.themanchestercollege.ac.uk

W100 FdA Fine Art
Duration: 2FT Fdg
Entry Requirements: Contact the institution for details.

M40 THE MANCHESTER METROPOLITAN UNIVERSITY
ADMISSIONS OFFICE
ALL SAINTS (GMS)
ALL SAINTS
MANCHESTER M15 6BH
t: 0161 247 2000
// www.mmu.ac.uk

W100 BA Fine Art
Duration: 3FT Hon
Entry Requirements: *GCE:* 280. *IB:* 27. Interview required. Portfolio required.

M65 COLEG MENAI
FRIDDOEDD ROAD
BANGOR
GWYNEDD LL57 2TP
t: 01248 370125 f: 01248 370052
e: student.services@menai.ac.uk
// www.menai.ac.uk

W190 BA Fine Art
Duration: 3FT Hon
Entry Requirements: Contact the institution for details.

M80 MIDDLESEX UNIVERSITY
MIDDLESEX UNIVERSITY
THE BURROUGHS
LONDON NW4 4BT
t: 020 8411 5555 f: 020 8411 5649
e: enquiries@mdx.ac.uk
// www.mdx.ac.uk

W101 BA Fine Art
Duration: 3FT Hon
Entry Requirements: *GCE:* 200-300. *IB:* 28. Interview required. Portfolio required.

N21 NEWCASTLE UNIVERSITY
KING'S GATE
NEWCASTLE UPON TYNE NE1 7RU
t: 01912083333
// www.ncl.ac.uk

W150 BA Fine Art
Duration: 4FT Hon
Entry Requirements: *Foundation:* Pass. *GCE:* AAB-BBB. *SQAH:* AAABB-AABB. Interview required. Portfolio required.

N23 NEWCASTLE COLLEGE
STUDENT SERVICES
RYE HILL CAMPUS
SCOTSWOOD ROAD
NEWCASTLE UPON TYNE NE4 7SA
t: 0191 200 4110 f: 0191 200 4349
e: enquiries@ncl-coll.ac.uk
// www.newcastlecollege.co.uk

W100 FdA Fine Art Practice
Duration: 2FT Fdg   CRB Check: Required
Entry Requirements: *Foundation:* Pass. *GCE:* 120-165. *OCR ND:* P2 *OCR NED:* P3 Foundation Course required. Interview required. Portfolio required.

N36 NEWMAN UNIVERSITY COLLEGE, BIRMINGHAM
GENNERS LANE
BARTLEY GREEN
BIRMINGHAM B32 3NT
t: 0121 476 1181 f: 0121 476 1196
e: Admissions@newman.ac.uk
// www.newman.ac.uk

XW11 BA Primary Education (QTS) Art
Duration: 3FT/4FT Hon   CRB Check: Required
Entry Requirements: *Foundation:* Merit. *GCE:* 280. *IB:* 25. *OCR ND:* M2 *OCR NED:* M2 Interview required. Admissions Test required.

N38 UNIVERSITY OF NORTHAMPTON
PARK CAMPUS
BOUGHTON GREEN ROAD
NORTHAMPTON NN2 7AL
t: 0800 358 2232 f: 01604 722083
e: admissions@northampton.ac.uk
// www.northampton.ac.uk

N1W1 BA Business/Fine Art Painting & Drawing
Duration: 3FT Hon
Entry Requirements: *GCE:* 260-280. *SQAH:* AAA-BBBB. *IB:* 24. *BTEC Dip:* DD. *BTEC ExtDip:* DMM. *OCR ND:* D *OCR NED:* M2

W8W1 BA Creative Writing/Fine Art Painting & Drawing
Duration: 3FT Hon
Entry Requirements: *GCE:* 260-280. *SQAH:* AAA-BBBB. *IB:* 24. *BTEC Dip:* DD. *BTEC ExtDip:* DMM. *OCR ND:* D *OCR NED:* M2

W4W1 BA Drama/Fine Art Painting & Drawing
Duration: 3FT Hon
Entry Requirements: *GCE:* 260-280. *SQAH:* AAA-BBBB. *IB:* 24. *BTEC Dip:* DD. *BTEC ExtDip:* DMM. *OCR ND:* D *OCR NED:* M2
Interview required.

L1W1 BA Economics/Fine Art Painting & Drawing
Duration: 3FT Hon
Entry Requirements: *GCE:* 260-280. *SQAH:* AAA-BBBB. *IB:* 24. *BTEC Dip:* DD. *BTEC ExtDip:* DMM. *OCR ND:* D *OCR NED:* M2

X3W1 BA Education Studies/Fine Art Painting & Drawing
Duration: 3FT Hon
Entry Requirements: *GCE:* 260-280. *SQAH:* AAA-BBBB. *IB:* 24. *BTEC Dip:* DD. *BTEC ExtDip:* DMM. *OCR ND:* D *OCR NED:* M2

Q3W1 BA English/Fine Art Painting & Drawing
Duration: 3FT Hon
Entry Requirements: *GCE:* 260-280. *SQAH:* AAA-BBBB. *IB:* 24. *BTEC Dip:* DD. *BTEC ExtDip:* DMM. *OCR ND:* D *OCR NED:* M2

W100 BA Fine Art
Duration: 3FT Hon
Entry Requirements: *GCE:* 240-280. *SQAH:* AAB-BBBC. *IB:* 24. *BTEC Dip:* DD. *BTEC ExtDip:* DMM. *OCR ND:* D *OCR NED:* M2
Foundation Course required. Interview required.

W120 BA Fine Art Painting & Drawing
Duration: 3FT Hon
Entry Requirements: *GCE:* 240-280. *SQAH:* AAB-BBBC. *IB:* 24. *BTEC Dip:* DD. *BTEC ExtDip:* DMM. *OCR ND:* D *OCR NED:* M2
Foundation Course required. Interview required.

W1D4 BA Fine Art Painting & Drawing with Applied Equine Studies
Duration: 3FT Hon
Entry Requirements: *GCE:* 260-280. *SQAH:* AAA-BBBB. *IB:* 24. *BTEC Dip:* DD. *BTEC ExtDip:* DMM. *OCR ND:* D *OCR NED:* M2

W1NG BA Fine Art Painting & Drawing with Applied Management
Duration: 3FT Hon
Entry Requirements: *GCE:* 260-280. *SQAH:* AAA-BBBB. *IB:* 24. *BTEC Dip:* DD. *BTEC ExtDip:* DMM. *OCR ND:* D *OCR NED:* M2

W1C1 BA Fine Art Painting & Drawing/Biological Conservation
Duration: 3FT Hon
Entry Requirements: *GCE:* 260-280. *SQAH:* AAA-BBBB. *IB:* 24. *BTEC Dip:* DD. *BTEC ExtDip:* DMM. *OCR ND:* D *OCR NED:* M2

W1N1 BA Fine Art Painting & Drawing/Business
Duration: 3FT Hon
Entry Requirements: *GCE:* 260-280. *SQAH:* AAA-BBBB. *IB:* 24. *BTEC Dip:* DD. *BTEC ExtDip:* DMM. *OCR ND:* D *OCR NED:* M2

W1G5 BA Fine Art Painting & Drawing/Business Computing Systems
Duration: 3FT Hon
Entry Requirements: *GCE:* 260-280. *SQAH:* AAA-BBBB. *IB:* 24. *BTEC Dip:* DD. *BTEC ExtDip:* DMM. *OCR ND:* D *OCR NED:* M2

W1G4 BA Fine Art Painting & Drawing/Computing
Duration: 3FT Hon
Entry Requirements: *GCE:* 260-280. *SQAH:* AAA-BBBB. *IB:* 24. *BTEC Dip:* DD. *BTEC ExtDip:* DMM. *OCR ND:* D *OCR NED:* M2

W1W8 BA Fine Art Painting & Drawing/Creative Writing
Duration: 3FT Hon
Entry Requirements: *GCE:* 260-280. *SQAH:* AAA-BBBB. *IB:* 24. *BTEC Dip:* DD. *BTEC ExtDip:* DMM. *OCR ND:* D *OCR NED:* M2

W1W4 BA Fine Art Painting & Drawing/Drama
Duration: 3FT Hon
Entry Requirements: *GCE:* 260-280. *SQAH:* AAA-BBBB. *IB:* 24. *BTEC Dip:* DD. *BTEC ExtDip:* DMM. *OCR ND:* D *OCR NED:* M2
Interview required.

W1L1 BA Fine Art Painting & Drawing/Economics
Duration: 3FT Hon
Entry Requirements: *GCE:* 260-280. *SQAH:* AAA-BBBB. *IB:* 24. *BTEC Dip:* DD. *BTEC ExtDip:* DMM. *OCR ND:* D *OCR NED:* M2

W1X3 BA Fine Art Painting & Drawing/Education Studies
Duration: 3FT Hon
Entry Requirements: *GCE:* 260-280. *SQAH:* AAA-BBBB. *IB:* 24. *BTEC Dip:* DD. *BTEC ExtDip:* DMM. *OCR ND:* D *OCR NED:* M2

W1Q3 BA Fine Art Painting & Drawing/English
Duration: 3FT Hon
Entry Requirements: *GCE:* 260-280. *SQAH:* AAA-BBBB. *IB:* 24. *BTEC Dip:* DD. *BTEC ExtDip:* DMM. *OCR ND:* D *OCR NED:* M2

W1L4 BA Fine Art Painting & Drawing/Health Studies
Duration: 3FT Hon
Entry Requirements: *GCE:* 260-280. *SQAH:* AAA-BBBB. *IB:* 24.
BTEC Dip: DD. *BTEC ExtDip:* DMM. *OCR ND:* D *OCR NED:* M2

W1M1 BA Fine Art Painting & Drawing/Law
Duration: 3FT Hon
Entry Requirements: *GCE:* 260-280. *SQAH:* AAA-BBBB. *IB:* 24.
BTEC Dip: DD. *BTEC ExtDip:* DMM. *OCR ND:* D *OCR NED:* M2

W1N2 BA Fine Art Painting & Drawing/Management
Duration: 3FT Hon
Entry Requirements: *GCE:* 260-280. *SQAH:* AAA-BBBB. *IB:* 24.
BTEC Dip: DD. *BTEC ExtDip:* DMM. *OCR ND:* D *OCR NED:* M2

W1N5 BA Fine Art Painting & Drawing/Marketing
Duration: 3FT Hon
Entry Requirements: *GCE:* 260-280. *SQAH:* AAA-BBBB. *IB:* 24.
BTEC Dip: DD. *BTEC ExtDip:* DMM. *OCR ND:* D *OCR NED:* M2

W1F8 BA Fine Art Painting & Drawing/Physical Geography
Duration: 3FT Hon
Entry Requirements: *GCE:* 260-280. *SQAH:* AAA-BBBB. *IB:* 24.
BTEC Dip: DD. *BTEC ExtDip:* DMM. *OCR ND:* D *OCR NED:* M2

W1L2 BA Fine Art Painting & Drawing/Politics
Duration: 3FT Hon
Entry Requirements: *GCE:* 260-280. *SQAH:* AAA-BBBB. *IB:* 24.
BTEC Dip: DD. *BTEC ExtDip:* DMM. *OCR ND:* D *OCR NED:* M2

W1W3 BA Fine Art Painting & Drawing/Popular Music
Duration: 3FT Hon
Entry Requirements: *GCE:* 260-280. *SQAH:* AAA-BBBB. *IB:* 24.
BTEC Dip: DD. *BTEC ExtDip:* DMM. *OCR ND:* D *OCR NED:* M2
Interview required.

W1C8 BA Fine Art Painting & Drawing/Psychology
Duration: 3FT Hon
Entry Requirements: *GCE:* 260-280. *SQAH:* AAA-BBBB. *IB:* 24.
BTEC Dip: DD. *BTEC ExtDip:* DMM. *OCR ND:* D *OCR NED:* M2

W1L3 BA Fine Art Painting & Drawing/Sociology
Duration: 3FT Hon
Entry Requirements: *GCE:* 260-280. *SQAH:* AAA-BBBB. *IB:* 24.
BTEC Dip: DD. *BTEC ExtDip:* DMM. *OCR ND:* D *OCR NED:* M2

W1C6 BA Fine Art Painting & Drawing/Sport Studies
Duration: 3FT Hon
Entry Requirements: *GCE:* 260-280. *SQAH:* AAA-BBBB. *IB:* 24.
BTEC Dip: DD. *BTEC ExtDip:* DMM. *OCR ND:* D *OCR NED:* M2

W1N8 BA Fine Art Painting & Drawing/Tourism
Duration: 3FT Hon
Entry Requirements: *GCE:* 260-280. *SQAH:* AAA-BBBB. *IB:* 24.
BTEC Dip: DD. *BTEC ExtDip:* DMM. *OCR ND:* D *OCR NED:* M2

W1FV BA Fine Art Painting & Drawing/Wastes Management
Duration: 3FT Hon
Entry Requirements: *GCE:* 260-280. *SQAH:* AAA-BBBB. *IB:* 24.
BTEC Dip: DD. *BTEC ExtDip:* DMM. *OCR ND:* D *OCR NED:* M2

L4W1 BA Health Studies/Fine Art Painting & Drawing
Duration: 3FT Hon
Entry Requirements: *GCE:* 260-280. *SQAH:* AAA-BBBB. *IB:* 24.
BTEC Dip: DD. *BTEC ExtDip:* DMM. *OCR ND:* D *OCR NED:* M2

N2W1 BA Management/Fine Art Painting & Drawing
Duration: 3FT Hon
Entry Requirements: *GCE:* 260-280. *SQAH:* AAA-BBBB. *IB:* 24.
BTEC Dip: DD. *BTEC ExtDip:* DMM. *OCR ND:* D *OCR NED:* M2

N5W1 BA Marketing/Fine Art Painting & Drawing
Duration: 3FT Hon
Entry Requirements: *GCE:* 260-280. *SQAH:* AAA-BBBB. *IB:* 24.
BTEC Dip: DD. *BTEC ExtDip:* DMM. *OCR ND:* D *OCR NED:* M2

F8W1 BA Physical Geography/Fine Art Painting & Drawing
Duration: 3FT Hon
Entry Requirements: *GCE:* 260-280. *SQAH:* AAA-BBBB. *IB:* 24.
BTEC Dip: DD. *BTEC ExtDip:* DMM. *OCR ND:* D *OCR NED:* M2

L2W1 BA Politics/Fine Art Painting & Drawing
Duration: 3FT Hon
Entry Requirements: *GCE:* 260-280. *SQAH:* AAA-BBBB. *IB:* 24.
BTEC Dip: DD. *BTEC ExtDip:* DMM. *OCR ND:* D *OCR NED:* M2

W3W1 BA Popular Music/Fine Art Painting & Drawing
Duration: 3FT Hon
Entry Requirements: *GCE:* 260-280. *SQAH:* AAA-BBBB. *IB:* 24.
BTEC Dip: DD. *BTEC ExtDip:* DMM. *OCR ND:* D *OCR NED:* M2
Interview required.

C8W1 BA Psychology/Fine Art Painting & Drawing
Duration: 3FT Hon
Entry Requirements: *GCE:* 260-280. *SQAH:* AAA-BBBB. *IB:* 24. *BTEC Dip:* DD. *BTEC ExtDip:* DMM. *OCR ND:* D *OCR NED:* M2

L3W1 BA Sociology/Fine Art Painting & Drawing
Duration: 3FT Hon
Entry Requirements: *GCE:* 260-280. *SQAH:* AAA-BBBB. *IB:* 24. *BTEC Dip:* DD. *BTEC ExtDip:* DMM. *OCR ND:* D *OCR NED:* M2

XW31 BA Special Educational Needs & Inclusion/Fine Art Painting & Drawing
Duration: 3FT Hon
Entry Requirements: *GCE:* 260-280. *SQAH:* AAA-BBBB. *IB:* 24. *BTEC Dip:* DD. *BTEC ExtDip:* DMM. *OCR ND:* D *OCR NED:* M2

C6W1 BA Sport Studies/Fine Art Painting & Drawing
Duration: 3FT Hon
Entry Requirements: *GCE:* 260-280. *SQAH:* AAA-BBBB. *IB:* 24. *BTEC Dip:* DD. *BTEC ExtDip:* DMM. *OCR ND:* D *OCR NED:* M2

N8W1 BA Tourism/Fine Art Painting & Drawing
Duration: 3FT Hon
Entry Requirements: *GCE:* 260-280. *SQAH:* AAA-BBBB. *IB:* 24. *BTEC Dip:* DD. *BTEC ExtDip:* DMM. *OCR ND:* D *OCR NED:* M2

C1W1 BSc Biological Conservation/Fine Art Painting & Drawing
Duration: 3FT Hon
Entry Requirements: *GCE:* 260-280. *SQAH:* AAA-BBBB. *IB:* 24. *BTEC Dip:* DD. *BTEC ExtDip:* DMM. *OCR ND:* D *OCR NED:* M2

G5W1 BSc Business Computing Systems/Fine Art Painting & Drawing
Duration: 3FT Hon
Entry Requirements: *GCE:* 260-280. *SQAH:* AAA-BBBB. *IB:* 24. *BTEC Dip:* DD. *BTEC ExtDip:* DMM. *OCR ND:* D *OCR NED:* M2

G4W1 BSc Computing/Fine Art Painting & Drawing
Duration: 3FT Hon
Entry Requirements: *GCE:* 260-280. *SQAH:* AAA-BBBB. *IB:* 24. *BTEC Dip:* DD. *BTEC ExtDip:* DMM. *OCR ND:* D *OCR NED:* M2

F8WC BSc Wastes Management/Fine Art Painting & Drawing
Duration: 3FT Hon
Entry Requirements: *GCE:* 260-280. *SQAH:* AAA-BBBB. *IB:* 24. *BTEC Dip:* DD. *BTEC ExtDip:* DMM. *OCR ND:* D *OCR NED:* M2

W101 FdA Fine Art
Duration: 2FT Fdg
Entry Requirements: *GCE:* 140-160. *SQAH:* BC-CCC. *IB:* 24. *BTEC Dip:* MP. *BTEC ExtDip:* MPP. *OCR ND:* P1 *OCR NED:* P2
Interview required. Portfolio required.

N39 NORWICH UNIVERSITY COLLEGE OF THE ARTS
FRANCIS HOUSE
3-7 REDWELL STREET
NORWICH NR2 4SN
t: 01603 610561 f: 01603 615728
e: admissions@nuca.ac.uk
// www.nuca.ac.uk

W101 BA Fine Art
Duration: 3FT Hon
Entry Requirements: *Foundation:* Merit. *GCE:* BBc. *OCR ND:* M1 *OCR NED:* P1 Interview required. Portfolio required.

W102 BA Fine Art (including Level 0)
Duration: 4FT Hon
Entry Requirements: *Foundation:* Merit. *OCR ND:* M1 *OCR NED:* P1 Interview required. Portfolio required.

N41 NORTHBROOK COLLEGE SUSSEX
LITTLEHAMPTON ROAD
WORTHING
WEST SUSSEX BN12 6NU
t: 0845 155 6060 f: 01903 606073
e: enquiries@nbcol.ac.uk
// www.northbrook.ac.uk

W102 BA Fine Art
Duration: 3FT Hon
Entry Requirements: *GCE:* 160. Interview required. Portfolio required.

W110 BA Fine Art: Drawing
Duration: 3FT Hon
Entry Requirements: *GCE:* 160. Interview required. Portfolio required.

W190 BA Fine Art: Installation
Duration: 3FT Hon
Entry Requirements: *GCE:* 160. Interview required. Portfolio required.

W100 BA Fine Art: Painting
Duration: 3FT Hon
Entry Requirements: *GCE:* 160. Interview required. Portfolio required.

W643 BA Fine Art: Photography

Duration: 3FT Hon

Entry Requirements: *GCE:* 160. Interview required. Portfolio required.

W101 BA Fine Art: Sculpture

Duration: 3FT Hon

Entry Requirements: *GCE:* 160. Interview required. Portfolio required.

N61 NORTH GLASGOW COLLEGE

123 FLEMINGTON ST
SPRINGBURN
GLASGOW G21 4TD
t: 0141 630 5150
e: g.mcdonald@north-gla.ac.uk
// northglasgowcollege.ac.uk

W100 BA (Hons) Visual Arts

Duration: 1FT Hon

Entry Requirements: Contact the institution for details.

N77 NORTHUMBRIA UNIVERSITY

TRINITY BUILDING
NORTHUMBERLAND ROAD
NEWCASTLE UPON TYNE NE1 8ST
t: 0191 243 7420 f: 0191 227 4561
e: er.admissions@northumbria.ac.uk
// www.northumbria.ac.uk

W100 BA Fine Art

Duration: 3FT Hon

Entry Requirements: *Foundation:* Distinction. *GCE:* 300. *SQAH:* BBBBC. *SQAAH:* BBC. *IB:* 26. *OCR NED:* M1 Interview required. Portfolio required.

N91 NOTTINGHAM TRENT UNIVERSITY

DRYDEN BUILDING
BURTON STREET
NOTTINGHAM NG1 4BU
t: +44 (0) 115 848 4200 f: +44 (0) 115 848 8869
e: applications@ntu.ac.uk
// www.ntu.ac.uk

W170 BA Decorative Arts

Duration: 3FT Hon

Entry Requirements: *GCE:* 280. Interview required. Portfolio required.

W100 BA Fine Art

Duration: 3FT Hon

Entry Requirements: *GCE:* 280. *BTEC Dip:* D*D*. *BTEC ExtDip:* DMM. *OCR NED:* M2 Interview required. Portfolio required.

O33 OXFORD UNIVERSITY

UNDERGRADUATE ADMISSIONS OFFICE
UNIVERSITY OF OXFORD
WELLINGTON SQUARE
OXFORD OX1 2JD
t: 01865 288000 f: 01865 270212
e: undergraduate.admissions@admin.ox.ac.uk
// www.admissions.ox.ac.uk

W100 BA Fine Art

Duration: 3FT Hon

Entry Requirements: *GCE:* AAA. *SQAH:* AAAAA-AAAAB. *SQAAH:* AAB. Interview required. Admissions Test required. Portfolio required.

O66 OXFORD BROOKES UNIVERSITY

ADMISSIONS OFFICE
HEADINGTON CAMPUS
GIPSY LANE
OXFORD OX3 0BP
t: 01865 483040 f: 01865 483983
e: admissions@brookes.ac.uk
// www.brookes.ac.uk

W100 BA Fine Art

Duration: 3FT Hon

Entry Requirements: Portfolio required.

W110 BA Fine Art: Drawing for Fine Art Practice (Swindon College)

Duration: 3FT Hon

Entry Requirements: Interview required. Portfolio required.

W1R4 BA/BSc Fine Art with Spanish (Minor)

Duration: 4SW Hon

Entry Requirements: *GCE:* BCC. *IB:* 31.

W1P3 BA/BSc Fine Art/Film Studies

Duration: 3FT Hon

Entry Requirements: Contact the institution for details.

W1F1 BA/BSc Fine Art/French Studies

Duration: 4SW Hon

Entry Requirements: *GCE:* BCC. *IB:* 31.

W1V3 BA/BSc Fine Art/History of Art

Duration: 3FT Hon

Entry Requirements: Contact the institution for details.

W1P4 BA/BSc Fine Art/Publishing Media

Duration: 3FT Hon

Entry Requirements: *GCE:* BBC.

P51 PETROC
OLD STICKLEPATH HILL
BARNSTAPLE
NORTH DEVON EX31 2BQ
t: 01271 852365 f: 01271 338121
e: he@petroc.ac.uk
// www.petroc.ac.uk

W101 FdA Fine Art
Duration: 2FT Fdg
Entry Requirements: *GCE:* 80.

P60 PLYMOUTH UNIVERSITY
DRAKE CIRCUS
PLYMOUTH PL4 8AA
t: 01752 585858 f: 01752 588055
e: admissions@plymouth.ac.uk
// www.plymouth.ac.uk

W100 BA Fine Art
Duration: 3FT Hon
Entry Requirements: *Foundation:* Pass. *GCE:* 280. *SQAH:* CCC.
IB: 26. *BTEC ExtDip:* DMM. Interview required. Portfolio required.

VW31 BA Fine Art and Art History
Duration: 3FT Hon
Entry Requirements: *Foundation:* Pass. *GCE:* 260. *IB:* 26. *BTEC ExtDip:* DMM. Interview required. Portfolio required.

P65 PLYMOUTH COLLEGE OF ART (FORMERLY PLYMOUTH COLLEGE OF ART AND DESIGN)
TAVISTOCK PLACE
PLYMOUTH PL4 8AT
t: 01752 203434 f: 01752 203444
e: infoservices@plymouthart.ac.uk
// www.plymouthart.ac.uk

W101 BA Fine Art
Duration: 3FT Hon
Entry Requirements: *Foundation:* Pass. *IB:* 24. *OCR ND:* M1 *OCR NED:* P1 Interview required. Portfolio required.

W100 BA Fine Art (Top-Up)
Duration: 1FT Hon
Entry Requirements: Interview required. Portfolio required. HND required.

P80 UNIVERSITY OF PORTSMOUTH
ACADEMIC REGISTRY
UNIVERSITY HOUSE
WINSTON CHURCHILL AVENUE
PORTSMOUTH PO1 2UP
t: 023 9284 8484 f: 023 9284 3082
e: admissions@port.ac.uk
// www.port.ac.uk

W101 BA Contemporary Fine Art
Duration: 3FT Hon
Entry Requirements: *GCE:* 240-300. *IB:* 26. *BTEC SubDip:* P. *BTEC Dip:* DD. *BTEC ExtDip:* DMM. Interview required. Portfolio required.

R12 THE UNIVERSITY OF READING
THE UNIVERSITY OF READING
PO BOX 217
READING RG6 6AH
t: 0118 378 8619 f: 0118 378 8924
e: student.recruitment@reading.ac.uk
// www.reading.ac.uk

W150 BA Art
Duration: 4FT Hon
Entry Requirements: *Foundation:* Pass. *GCE:* 80-340. Interview required. Portfolio required.

QW31 BA Art and English Literature
Duration: 4FT Hon
Entry Requirements: *Foundation:* Pass. *GCE:* ABC-BBB. *SQAH:* ABBBC-BBBBB. *SQAAH:* ABC-BBB. Interview required. Portfolio required.

WW41 BA Art and Film & Theatre
Duration: 4FT Hon
Entry Requirements: *Foundation:* Pass. *GCE:* ABC-BBB. *SQAH:* ABBBC-BBBBB. *SQAAH:* ABC-BBB. Interview required. Portfolio required.

VW31 BA Art and History of Art
Duration: 4FT Hon
Entry Requirements: *Foundation:* Pass. *GCE:* ABC-BBB. *SQAH:* ABBBC-BBBBB. *SQAAH:* ABC-BBB. Interview required. Portfolio required.

VW51 BA Art and Philosophy
Duration: 4FT Hon
Entry Requirements: *Foundation:* Pass. *GCE:* AAC-ABB. *SQAH:* AAACC-ABBBB. *SQAAH:* AAC-ABB. Interview required. Portfolio required.

CW81 BA Art and Psychology
Duration: 4FT Hon
Entry Requirements: *GCE:* AAB. *SQAH:* AAABB. *SQAAH:* AAB. *BTEC Dip:* DD. *BTEC ExtDip:* DDD. Interview required. Portfolio required.

W101 BA Fine Art
Duration: 3FT Hon
Entry Requirements: *Foundation:* Pass. *GCE:* 205. Foundation Course required. Interview required. Portfolio required.

X1W1 BA Primary Education with Art
Duration: 3FT Hon   **CRB Check:** Required
Entry Requirements: *Foundation:* Pass. *GCE:* 180. *BTEC Dip:* DM. *BTEC ExtDip:* MMP. Interview required.

R36 ROBERT GORDON UNIVERSITY
ROBERT GORDON UNIVERSITY
SCHOOLHILL
ABERDEEN
SCOTLAND AB10 1FR
t: 01224 26 27 28 f: 01224 26 21 47
e: UGOffice@rgu.ac.uk
// www.rgu.ac.uk

W120 BA Painting
Duration: 4FT Hon
Entry Requirements: *GCE:* BC. *SQAH:* BBC. Interview required. Portfolio required.

WW61 BA (Hons) Contemporary Art Practice
Duration: 4FT Hon
Entry Requirements: *GCE:* BC. *SQAH:* BBC. Interview required. Portfolio required.

S03 THE UNIVERSITY OF SALFORD
SALFORD M5 4WT
t: 0161 295 4545 f: 0161 295 4646
e: ug-admissions@salford.ac.uk
// www.salford.ac.uk

W100 BA Visual Arts
Duration: 3FT Hon
Entry Requirements: *Foundation:* Pass. *GCE:* 260. *IB:* 26. *OCR ND:* D *OCR NED:* M3 Interview required. Portfolio required.

S21 SHEFFIELD HALLAM UNIVERSITY
CITY CAMPUS
HOWARD STREET
SHEFFIELD S1 1WB
t: 0114 225 5555 f: 0114 225 2167
e: admissions@shu.ac.uk
// www.shu.ac.uk

W192 BA Creative Art Practice
Duration: 3FT Hon
Entry Requirements: *GCE:* 260.

W102 BA (Hons) Fine Art
Duration: 3FT Hon
Entry Requirements: *GCE:* 260.

W103 MArt Fine Art
Duration: 4FT Deg
Entry Requirements: *GCE:* 280.

S26 SOLIHULL COLLEGE
BLOSSOMFIELD ROAD
SOLIHULL
WEST MIDLANDS B91 1SB
t: 0121 678 7006 f: 0121 678 7200
e: enquiries@solihull.ac.uk
// www.solihull.ac.uk

001W HND Fine Art
Duration: 2FT HND
Entry Requirements: *Foundation:* Merit. *GCE:* A-E. *IB:* 24. *BTEC Dip:* MM. *BTEC ExtDip:* MMM. *OCR ND:* M2 *OCR NED:* M3 Interview required. Portfolio required.

S27 UNIVERSITY OF SOUTHAMPTON
HIGHFIELD
SOUTHAMPTON SO17 1BJ
t: 023 8059 4732 f: 023 8059 3037
e: admissions@soton.ac.uk
// www.southampton.ac.uk

W190 BA Fine Art
Duration: 3FT Hon
Entry Requirements: *Foundation:* Pass. *GCE:* ABB. *IB:* 32. Interview required. Portfolio required.

S28 SOMERSET COLLEGE OF ARTS AND TECHNOLOGY
WELLINGTON ROAD
TAUNTON
SOMERSET TA1 5AX
t: 01823 366331 f: 01823 366418
e: enquiries@somerset.ac.uk
// www.somerset.ac.uk/student-area/considering-a-degree.html

W101 BA Fine Art (Top-Up)
Duration: 1FT Hon
Entry Requirements: Contact the institution for details.

W100 FdA Fine Art
Duration: 2FT Fdg
Entry Requirements: Foundation: Pass. GCE: 160. IB: 24. Interview required. Portfolio required.

S30 SOUTHAMPTON SOLENT UNIVERSITY
EAST PARK TERRACE
SOUTHAMPTON
HAMPSHIRE SO14 0RT
t: +44 (0) 23 8031 9039 f: + 44 (0)23 8022 2259
e: admissions@solent.ac.uk
// www.solent.ac.uk/

W100 BA Fine Art
Duration: 3FT Hon
Entry Requirements: Foundation: Merit. GCE: 200. SQAAH: AC-DDD. IB: 24. BTEC ExtDip: MMP. OCR ND: M1 OCR NED: P1 Interview required. Portfolio required.

W102 BA Visual Arts (Top-Up)
Duration: 1FT Hon
Entry Requirements: Portfolio required. HND required.

S36 UNIVERSITY OF ST ANDREWS
ST KATHARINE'S WEST
16 THE SCORES
ST ANDREWS
FIFE KY16 9AX
t: 01334 462150 f: 01334 463330
e: admissions@st-andrews.ac.uk
// www.st-andrews.ac.uk

TW61 MA Arabic and Art History (European & North American Art) with Integrated Yr Abroad
Duration: 5FT Hon
Entry Requirements: GCE: AAB. SQAH: AABB. IB: 35.

S43 SOUTH ESSEX COLLEGE OF FURTHER & HIGHER EDUCATION
LUKER ROAD
SOUTHEND-ON-SEA
ESSEX SS1 1ND
t: 0845 52 12345 f: 01702 432320
e: Admissions@southessex.ac.uk
// www.southessex.ac.uk

W100 BA Fine Art
Duration: 3FT Hon
Entry Requirements: GCE: 160. IB: 24. Interview required.

W101 CertHE Fine Art
Duration: 1FT Cer
Entry Requirements: Contact the institution for details.

S46 SOUTH NOTTINGHAM COLLEGE
WEST BRIDGFORD CENTRE
GREYTHORN DRIVE
WEST BRIDGFORD
NOTTINGHAM NG2 7GA
t: 0115 914 6400 f: 0115 914 6444
e: enquiries@snc.ac.uk
// www.snc.ac.uk

WW16 FdA Visual Arts Practice
Duration: 2FT Fdg
Entry Requirements: GCE: 160. Interview required.

S51 ST HELENS COLLEGE
WATER STREET
ST HELENS
MERSEYSIDE WA10 1PP
t: 01744 733766 f: 01744 623400
e: enquiries@sthelens.ac.uk
// www.sthelens.ac.uk

W120 BA Fine Art Painting
Duration: 3FT Hon
Entry Requirements: GCE: 120. Interview required.

S72 STAFFORDSHIRE UNIVERSITY
COLLEGE ROAD
STOKE ON TRENT ST4 2DE
t: 01782 292753 f: 01782 292740
e: admissions@staffs.ac.uk
// www.staffs.ac.uk

W102 BA Art Foundation Year
Duration: 4FT Hon
Entry Requirements: Foundation: Merit. GCE: 200-240. IB: 24. BTEC Dip: DD. BTEC ExtDip: MMM. Interview required. Portfolio required.

W101 BA Entrepreneurship in Fine Art
Duration: 1FT Hon
Entry Requirements: Interview required. Portfolio required.

W100 BA Fine Art
Duration: 3FT/4FT Hon
Entry Requirements: *Foundation:* Merit. *GCE:* 200-240. *IB:* 24. *BTEC Dip:* DD. *BTEC ExtDip:* MMM. Interview required. Portfolio required.

W641 BA Fine Art: Photography
Duration: 3FT/4FT Hon
Entry Requirements: *Foundation:* Merit. *GCE:* 200-240. *IB:* 24. *BTEC Dip:* DD. *BTEC ExtDip:* MMM. Interview required. Portfolio required.

W900 FdA Creative and Cultural Industries (Contemporary Art Practice)
Duration: 2FT Fdg
Entry Requirements: Interview required.

S77 STOURBRIDGE COLLEGE
HAGLEY ROAD
STOURBRIDGE
WEST MIDLANDS DY8 1QU
t: 01384 344344 f: 01384 344600
e: info@stourbridge.ac.uk
// www.stourbridge.ac.uk

101W HNC Fine Arts
Duration: 2FT HNC
Entry Requirements: Foundation Course required. Interview required. Portfolio required.

001W HND Fine Arts
Duration: 2FT HND
Entry Requirements: *Foundation:* Pass. Interview required.

S82 UNIVERSITY CAMPUS SUFFOLK (UCS)
WATERFRONT BUILDING
NEPTUNE QUAY
IPSWICH
SUFFOLK IP4 1QJ
t: 01473 338833 f: 01473 339900
e: info@ucs.ac.uk
// www.ucs.ac.uk

W100 BA Fine Art
Duration: 3FT Hon
Entry Requirements: *GCE:* 240-280. *IB:* 28. *BTEC ExtDip:* DMM. Interview required. Portfolio required.

S84 UNIVERSITY OF SUNDERLAND
STUDENT HELPLINE
THE STUDENT GATEWAY
CHESTER ROAD
SUNDERLAND SR1 3SD
t: 0191 515 3000 f: 0191 515 3805
e: student.helpline@sunderland.ac.uk
// www.sunderland.ac.uk

W100 BA Fine Art
Duration: 3FT Hon
Entry Requirements: *GCE:* 220-360. *SQAH:* BBCCC. *IB:* 22. Interview required. Portfolio required.

W150 FdA Calligraphy and Design
Duration: 2FT Fdg
Entry Requirements: Contact the institution for details.

S96 SWANSEA METROPOLITAN UNIVERSITY
MOUNT PLEASANT CAMPUS
SWANSEA SA1 6ED
t: 01792 481000 f: 01792 481061
e: gemma.green@smu.ac.uk
// www.smu.ac.uk

W100 BA Fine Art (Combined Media)
Duration: 3FT Hon
Entry Requirements: *Foundation:* Pass. *GCE:* 200-360. *IB:* 24. Interview required. Portfolio required.

W101 BA Fine Art (Painting and Drawing)
Duration: 3FT Hon
Entry Requirements: *Foundation:* Pass. *GCE:* 200-360. *IB:* 24. Interview required. Portfolio required.

T20 TEESSIDE UNIVERSITY
MIDDLESBROUGH TS1 3BA
t: 01642 218121 f: 01642 384201
e: registry@tees.ac.uk
// www.tees.ac.uk

W100 BA Fine Art
Duration: 3FT Hon
Entry Requirements: *Foundation:* Distinction. *GCE:* 300. *IB:* 25. Interview required. Portfolio required.

T90 TYNE METROPOLITAN COLLEGE
BATTLE HILL DRIVE
WALLSEND
TYNE AND WEAR NE28 9NL
t: 0191 229 5000 f: 0191 229 5301
e: enquiries@tynemet.ac.uk
// www.tynemet.ac.uk

001W HND Fine Art
Duration: 2FT HND
Entry Requirements: Contact the institution for details.

U20 UNIVERSITY OF ULSTER
COLERAINE
CO. LONDONDERRY
NORTHERN IRELAND BT52 1SA
t: 028 7012 4221 f: 028 7012 4908
e: online@ulster.ac.uk
// www.ulster.ac.uk

W100 BA Hons Fine Art
Duration: 3FT/4SW Hon
Entry Requirements: *GCE:* 240. *IB:* 24. Interview required. Portfolio required.

U65 UNIVERSITY OF THE ARTS LONDON
272 HIGH HOLBORN
LONDON WC1V 7EY
t: 020 7514 6000x6197 f: 020 7514 6190
e: c.anderson@arts.ac.uk
// www.arts.ac.uk

W110 BA Drawing
Duration: 3FT Hon
Entry Requirements: *Foundation:* Pass. *GCE:* 80. *IB:* 28. Interview required. Portfolio required.

W100 BA Fine Art
Duration: 3FT/4SW Hon
Entry Requirements: Interview required.

W104 BA Fine Art
Duration: 3FT Hon
Entry Requirements: *Foundation:* Pass. *GCE:* 80. *IB:* 28. Foundation Course required. Interview required. Portfolio required.

W121 BA Fine Art (Painting)
Duration: 3FT Hon
Entry Requirements: *Foundation:* Pass. *GCE:* 80. *IB:* 28. Foundation Course required. Portfolio required.

W105 BA Fine Art (Print and Time-Based Media)
Duration: 3FT Hon
Entry Requirements: *Foundation:* Pass. *GCE:* 80. *IB:* 28. Foundation Course required. Portfolio required.

W131 BA Fine Art (Sculpture)
Duration: 3FT Hon
Entry Requirements: *Foundation:* Pass. *GCE:* 80. *IB:* 28. Foundation Course required. Portfolio required.

W120 BA Painting
Duration: 3FT Hon
Entry Requirements: *Foundation:* Pass. *GCE:* 80. *IB:* 28. Interview required. Portfolio required.

W130 BA Sculpture
Duration: 3FT Hon
Entry Requirements: *Foundation:* Pass. *GCE:* 80. *IB:* 28. Interview required. Portfolio required.

U80 UNIVERSITY COLLEGE LONDON (UNIVERSITY OF LONDON)
GOWER STREET
LONDON WC1E 6BT
t: 020 7679 3000 f: 020 7679 3001
// www.ucl.ac.uk

W100 BA Fine Art (4 years)
Duration: 4FT Hon
Entry Requirements: *GCE:* ABBe. *SQAAH:* ABB. *IB:* 34. *BTEC ExtDip:* DDD. Interview required. Portfolio required.

W101 BFA Fine Art
Duration: 3FT Hon
Entry Requirements: *GCE:* ABBe. *SQAAH:* ABB. *IB:* 34. *BTEC ExtDip:* DDD. Interview required. Portfolio required.

W25 WARWICKSHIRE COLLEGE
WARWICK NEW ROAD
LEAMINGTON SPA
WARWICKSHIRE CV32 5JE
t: 01926 884223 f: 01926 318 111
e: kgooch@warkscol.ac.uk
// www.warwickshire.ac.uk

W100 DipHE Fine Art
Duration: 2FT Dip
Entry Requirements: *Foundation:* Pass. *GCE:* 200. Portfolio required.

W73 WIRRAL METROPOLITAN COLLEGE
CONWAY PARK CAMPUS
EUROPA BOULEVARD
BIRKENHEAD, WIRRAL
MERSEYSIDE CH41 4NT
t: 0151 551 7777 f: 0151 551 7001
// www.wmc.ac.uk

W100 BA Fine Art
Duration: 3FT Hon
Entry Requirements: *Foundation:* Pass. Foundation Course required. Interview required. Portfolio required.

W75 UNIVERSITY OF WOLVERHAMPTON
ADMISSIONS UNIT
MX207, CAMP STREET
WOLVERHAMPTON
WEST MIDLANDS WV1 1AD
t: 01902 321000 f: 01902 321896
e: admissions@wlv.ac.uk
// www.wlv.ac.uk

W100 BA Fine Art
Duration: 3FT/4SW Hon
Entry Requirements: *GCE:* 200. *IB:* 24. *BTEC Dip:* DM. *BTEC ExtDip:* MMP. *OCR ND:* M1 *OCR NED:* P1 Interview required. Portfolio required.

W76 UNIVERSITY OF WINCHESTER
WINCHESTER
HANTS SO22 4NR
t: 01962 827234 f: 01962 827288
e: course.enquiries@winchester.ac.uk
// www.winchester.ac.uk

XWC1 BA Art: Primary (3 years QTS)
Duration: 3FT Hon   CRB Check: Required
Entry Requirements: *Foundation:* Distinction. *GCE:* 260-300. *IB:* 24. Interview required.

W80 UNIVERSITY OF WORCESTER
HENWICK GROVE
WORCESTER WR2 6AJ
t: 01905 855111 f: 01905 855377
e: admissions@worc.ac.uk
// www.worcester.ac.uk

WW41 BA Drama & Performance and Fine Art Practice
Duration: 3FT Hon
Entry Requirements: *GCE:* 240-260. *IB:* 24. *OCR ND:* D Interview required. Portfolio required.

XW31 BA Education Studies and Fine Art Practice
Duration: 3FT Hon
Entry Requirements: *GCE:* 220-300. *IB:* 24. *OCR ND:* D Interview required. Portfolio required.

QW31 BA English Literary Studies and Fine Art Practice
Duration: 3FT Hon
Entry Requirements: *GCE:* 240-260. *IB:* 24. *OCR ND:* D Interview required. Portfolio required.

W100 BA Fine Art Practice
Duration: 3FT Hon
Entry Requirements: *GCE:* 220-300. *IB:* 24. *OCR ND:* D Interview required. Portfolio required.

WW1F BA Fine Art Practice and Illustration
Duration: 3FT Hon
Entry Requirements: *GCE:* 220-300. *IB:* 24. *OCR ND:* D Interview required. Portfolio required.

Y80 YORKSHIRE COAST COLLEGE OF FURTHER AND HIGHER EDUCATION
LADY EDITH'S DRIVE
SCARBOROUGH
NORTH YORKSHIRE YO12 5RN
t: 01723 372105 f: 01723 501918
e: admissions@ycoastco.ac.uk
// www.yorkshirecoastcollege.ac.uk

W100 BA Fine Art
Duration: 3FT Hon
Entry Requirements: *Foundation:* Pass. *GCE:* 160-240. Interview required. Portfolio required.

FURNITURE

B94 BUCKINGHAMSHIRE NEW UNIVERSITY
QUEEN ALEXANDRA ROAD
HIGH WYCOMBE
BUCKINGHAMSHIRE HP11 2JZ
t: 0800 0565 660 f: 01494 605 023
e: admissions@bucks.ac.uk
// bucks.ac.uk

W262 BA Furniture
Duration: 3FT Hon   CRB Check: Required
Entry Requirements: Contact the institution for details.

W26A BA Furniture Design and Make
Duration: 1FT Hon   CRB Check: Required
Entry Requirements: Contact the institution for details.

W261 FdA Furniture Design and Make
Duration: 2FT Fdg
Entry Requirements: *GCE:* 100-140. *IB:* 24. *OCR ND:* M1 *OCR NED:* M3

017W HND Furniture Studies
Duration: 2FT HND
Entry Requirements: *GCE:* 200-240. *IB:* 24. *OCR ND:* M1 *OCR NED:* M3 Interview required.

C20 CARDIFF METROPOLITAN UNIVERSITY (UWIC)
ADMISSIONS UNIT
LLANDAFF CAMPUS
WESTERN AVENUE
CARDIFF CF5 2YB
t: 029 2041 6070 f: 029 2041 6286
e: admissions@cardiffmet.ac.uk
// www.cardiffmet.ac.uk

W260 FdA Contemporary Furniture Design
Duration: 2FT Fdg
Entry Requirements: Interview required.

C30 UNIVERSITY OF CENTRAL LANCASHIRE
PRESTON
LANCS PR1 2HE
t: 01772 201201 f: 01772 894954
e: uadmissions@uclan.ac.uk
// www.uclan.ac.uk

W260 BA Interior Design
Duration: 3FT Hon
Entry Requirements: *GCE:* 240-300. *IB:* 26. *OCR ND:* D *OCR NED:* M3 Interview required. Portfolio required.

C78 CORNWALL COLLEGE
POOL
REDRUTH
CORNWALL TR15 3RD
t: 01209 616161 f: 01209 611612
e: he.admissions@cornwall.ac.uk
// www.cornwall.ac.uk

WJ25 FdA Furniture Design & Make
Duration: 2FT Fdg
Entry Requirements: Contact the institution for details.

D26 DE MONTFORT UNIVERSITY
THE GATEWAY
LEICESTER LE1 9BH
t: 0116 255 1551 f: 0116 250 6204
e: enquiries@dmu.ac.uk
// www.dmu.ac.uk

W261 BA Furniture Design
Duration: 3FT Hon
Entry Requirements: *Foundation:* Pass. *GCE:* 260. *IB:* 28. *BTEC Dip:* D*D. *BTEC ExtDip:* MMM. Interview required. Portfolio required.

W293 BA Product and Furniture Design
Duration: 3FT Hon
Entry Requirements: *Foundation:* Pass. *GCE:* 260. *IB:* 28. *BTEC Dip:* D*D. *BTEC ExtDip:* MMM. Interview required. Portfolio required.

K84 KINGSTON UNIVERSITY
STUDENT INFORMATION & ADVICE CENTRE
COOPER HOUSE
40-46 SURBITON ROAD
KINGSTON UPON THAMES KT1 2HX
t: 0844 8552177 f: 020 8547 7080
e: aps@kingston.ac.uk
// www.kingston.ac.uk

W260 BA Product & Furniture Design
Duration: 3FT Hon
Entry Requirements: Interview required. Portfolio required.

L27 LEEDS METROPOLITAN UNIVERSITY
COURSE ENQUIRIES OFFICE
CITY CAMPUS
LEEDS LS1 3HE
t: 0113 81 23113 f: 0113 81 23129
// www.leedsmet.ac.uk

W260 BA Design Furniture
Duration: 3FT Hon
Entry Requirements: *Foundation:* Pass. *GCE:* 160. Interview required. Portfolio required.

L68 LONDON METROPOLITAN UNIVERSITY
166-220 HOLLOWAY ROAD
LONDON N7 8DB
t: 020 7133 4200
e: admissions@londonmet.ac.uk
// www.londonmet.ac.uk

W260 BA Furniture and Product Design
Duration: 3FT Hon
Entry Requirements: *Foundation:* Pass. *GCE:* 240. *IB:* 28. Interview required. Portfolio required.

WJ2M FdA Furniture
Duration: 2.5FT Fdg
Entry Requirements: *Foundation:* Pass. *GCE:* 80. *IB:* 28.
Interview required. Portfolio required.

N23 NEWCASTLE COLLEGE
STUDENT SERVICES
RYE HILL CAMPUS
SCOTSWOOD ROAD
NEWCASTLE UPON TYNE NE4 7SA
t: 0191 200 4110 f: 0191 200 4349
e: enquiries@ncl-coll.ac.uk
// www.newcastlecollege.co.uk

W251 FdA Furniture and Fine Product
Duration: 2FT Fdg
Entry Requirements: Contact the institution for details.

N91 NOTTINGHAM TRENT UNIVERSITY
DRYDEN BUILDING
BURTON STREET
NOTTINGHAM NG1 4BU
t: +44 (0) 115 848 4200 f: +44 (0) 115 848 8869
e: applications@ntu.ac.uk
// www.ntu.ac.uk

W240 BA Furniture and Product Design
Duration: 3FT/4SW Hon
Entry Requirements: *GCE:* 280. *OCR NED:* M2 Interview required.
Portfolio required.

S21 SHEFFIELD HALLAM UNIVERSITY
CITY CAMPUS
HOWARD STREET
SHEFFIELD S1 1WB
t: 0114 225 5555 f: 0114 225 2167
e: admissions@shu.ac.uk
// www.shu.ac.uk

W260 BA Furniture and Product Design
Duration: 3FT Hon
Entry Requirements: *GCE:* 240. Portfolio required.

W261 MDes Furniture and Product Design
Duration: 4FT Hon
Entry Requirements: *GCE:* 260.

U20 UNIVERSITY OF ULSTER
COLERAINE
CO. LONDONDERRY
NORTHERN IRELAND BT52 1SA
t: 028 7012 4221 f: 028 7012 4908
e: online@ulster.ac.uk
// www.ulster.ac.uk

W260 BDes Hons Product and Furniture Design
Duration: 3FT/4SW Hon
Entry Requirements: *GCE:* 240. *IB:* 24. Interview required.
Portfolio required.

W75 UNIVERSITY OF WOLVERHAMPTON
ADMISSIONS UNIT
MX207, CAMP STREET
WOLVERHAMPTON
WEST MIDLANDS WV1 1AD
t: 01902 321000 f: 01902 321896
e: admissions@wlv.ac.uk
// www.wlv.ac.uk

W262 BA Interior Design
Duration: 3FT/4SW Hon
Entry Requirements: *GCE:* 200. *IB:* 24. *BTEC Dip:* DM. *BTEC ExtDip:* MMP. *OCR ND:* M1 *OCR NED:* P1 Interview required.
Portfolio required.

GRAPHIC DESIGN

A50 AMERICAN INTERCONTINENTAL UNIVERSITY - LONDON
110 MARYLEBONE HIGH STREET
LONDON W1U 4RY
t: 020 7467 5640 f: 020 7467 5641
e: admissions@aiulondon.ac.uk
// www.aiulondon.ac.uk

W210 BA Visual Communication - Graphic Design
Duration: 4FT Hon
Entry Requirements: Contact the institution for details.

A60 ANGLIA RUSKIN UNIVERSITY
BISHOP HALL LANE
CHELMSFORD
ESSEX CM1 1SQ
t: 0845 271 3333 f: 01245 251789
e: answers@anglia.ac.uk
// www.anglia.ac.uk

W200 BA Graphic Design
Duration: 3FT Hon
Entry Requirements: *GCE:* 200-240. *SQAH:* CCCC. *SQAAH:* BC.
IB: 24. Interview required. Portfolio required.

W210 FdA Graphic Design
Duration: 2FT Fdg
Entry Requirements: *GCE:* 120.

A66 THE ARTS UNIVERSITY COLLEGE AT BOURNEMOUTH (FORMERLY ARTS INSTITUTE AT BOURNEMOUTH)
WALLISDOWN
POOLE
DORSET BH12 5HH
t: 01202 363228 f: 01202 537729
e: admissions@aucb.ac.uk
// www.aucb.ac.uk

W210 BA Graphic Design
Duration: 3FT Hon
Entry Requirements: *Foundation:* Pass. *GCE:* BBC. *IB:* 24. *OCR ND:* M1 *OCR NED:* M1 Interview required. Portfolio required.

B11 BARKING AND DAGENHAM COLLEGE
DAGENHAM ROAD
ROMFORD
ESSEX RM7 0XU
t: 020 8090 3020 f: 020 8090 3021
e: engagement.services@barkingdagenhamcollege.ac.uk
// www.barkingdagenhamcollege.ac.uk

W210 FdA Graphic Design
Duration: 2FT Fdg
Entry Requirements: *GCE:* 120.

B20 BATH SPA UNIVERSITY
NEWTON PARK
NEWTON ST LOE
BATH BA2 9BN
t: 01225 875875 f: 01225 875444
e: enquiries@bathspa.ac.uk
// www.bathspa.ac.uk/clearing

W214 BA Creative Industries: Graphic Design (Work-based)
Duration: 1FT Hon
Entry Requirements: Interview required.

W200 BA Graphic Communication
Duration: 3FT Hon
Entry Requirements: *GCE:* 220-280. *IB:* 24. Interview required. Portfolio required.

W210 FdA Graphic Design
Duration: 2FT Fdg
Entry Requirements: *GCE:* 220-280. *IB:* 24. Interview required.

B22 UNIVERSITY OF BEDFORDSHIRE
PARK SQUARE
LUTON
BEDS LU1 3JU
t: 0844 8482234 f: 01582 489323
e: admissions@beds.ac.uk
// www.beds.ac.uk

W211 BA Graphic Design
Duration: 3FT Hon
Entry Requirements: *GCE:* 160-240. *SQAH:* CCC. *SQAAH:* CCC. *IB:* 30. Interview required. Portfolio required.

B23 BEDFORD COLLEGE
CAULDWELL STREET
BEDFORD MK42 9AH
t: 01234 291000 f: 01234 342674
e: info@bedford.ac.uk
// www.bedford.ac.uk

112W HNC Graphic Design
Duration: 1FT HNC
Entry Requirements: *Foundation:* Pass. *GCE:* 80-120. Interview required. Portfolio required.

012W HND Graphic Design
Duration: 2FT HND
Entry Requirements: *Foundation:* Pass. *GCE:* 80-120. Interview required. Portfolio required.

B25 BIRMINGHAM CITY UNIVERSITY
PERRY BARR
BIRMINGHAM B42 2SU
t: 0121 331 5595 f: 0121 331 7994
// www.bcu.ac.uk

W211 BA Visual Communication (Graphic Communication)
Duration: 3FT Hon
Entry Requirements: *GCE:* 280. *IB:* 28. Interview required.
Portfolio required.

B40 BLACKBURN COLLEGE
FEILDEN STREET
BLACKBURN BB2 1LH
t: 01254 292594 f: 01254 679647
e: he-admissions@blackburn.ac.uk
// www.blackburn.ac.uk

W210 BA Design (Graphic Communication)
Duration: 3FT Hon
Entry Requirements: *GCE:* 200.

W217 BA Design (Graphic Communication) Top up
Duration: 1FT Hon
Entry Requirements: Contact the institution for details.

W641 BA Photographic Media (Top-Up)
Duration: 1FT Hon
Entry Requirements: Contact the institution for details.

W215 FdA Graphic Design
Duration: 2FT Fdg
Entry Requirements: *GCE:* 120. Interview required. Portfolio
required.

W640 FdA Photographic Media
Duration: 2FT Fdg
Entry Requirements: *GCE:* 120.

B41 BLACKPOOL AND THE FYLDE COLLEGE AN ASSOCIATE COLLEGE OF LANCASTER UNIVERSITY
ASHFIELD ROAD
BISPHAM
BLACKPOOL
LANCS FY2 0HB
t: 01253 504346 f: 01253 504198
e: admissions@blackpool.ac.uk
// www.blackpool.ac.uk

W211 BA Graphic Design
Duration: 3FT Hon
Entry Requirements: *Foundation:* Merit. *GCE:* 220. *IB:* 24.
Interview required. Portfolio required.

B44 UNIVERSITY OF BOLTON
DEANE ROAD
BOLTON BL3 5AB
t: 01204 903903 f: 01204 399074
e: enquiries@bolton.ac.uk
// www.bolton.ac.uk

W210 BA Graphic Design
Duration: 3FT Hon
Entry Requirements: *GCE:* 240. Interview required. Portfolio
required.

WWG6 BA Graphic Design and Photography
Duration: 3FT Hon
Entry Requirements: *GCE:* 240. Interview required. Portfolio
required.

B72 UNIVERSITY OF BRIGHTON
MITHRAS HOUSE 211
LEWES ROAD
BRIGHTON BN2 4AT
t: 01273 644644 f: 01273 642607
e: admissions@brighton.ac.uk
// www.brighton.ac.uk

W210 BA Graphic Design
Duration: 3FT Hon
Entry Requirements: *GCE:* BBC. Foundation Course required.
Interview required. Portfolio required.

W215 FdA Graphic Communication
Duration: 2FT Fdg
Entry Requirements: *GCE:* 120. Interview required. Portfolio
required.

W216 MDes Graphic Design
Duration: 4FT Hon
Entry Requirements: *GCE:* BBC. Foundation Course required.
Interview required. Portfolio required.

B80 UNIVERSITY OF THE WEST OF ENGLAND, BRISTOL

FRENCHAY CAMPUS
COLDHARBOUR LANE
BRISTOL BS16 1QY
t: +44 (0)117 32 83333 f: +44 (0)117 32 82810
e: admissions@uwe.ac.uk
// www.uwe.ac.uk

W211 BA Graphic Design
Duration: 3FT Hon
Entry Requirements: *GCE:* 280. Interview required. Portfolio required.

B94 BUCKINGHAMSHIRE NEW UNIVERSITY

QUEEN ALEXANDRA ROAD
HIGH WYCOMBE
BUCKINGHAMSHIRE HP11 2JZ
t: 0800 0565 660 f: 01494 605 023
e: admissions@bucks.ac.uk
// bucks.ac.uk

W210 BA Graphic Arts
Duration: 3FT Hon
Entry Requirements: *GCE:* 200-240. *IB:* 24. *OCR ND:* M1 *OCR NED:* M3 Interview required.

W214 FdA Graphic Design
Duration: 2FT Fdg
Entry Requirements: *GCE:* 100-140. *IB:* 24. *OCR ND:* P2 *OCR NED:* P3 Interview required.

C10 CANTERBURY CHRIST CHURCH UNIVERSITY

NORTH HOLMES ROAD
CANTERBURY
KENT CT1 1QU
t: 01227 782900 f: 01227 782888
e: admissions@canterbury.ac.uk
// www.canterbury.ac.uk

W210 BA Graphic Design
Duration: 3FT Hon
Entry Requirements: *GCE:* 240. *IB:* 24. Interview required.

WW62 BA Video and Motion Graphics
Duration: 3FT Hon
Entry Requirements: *GCE:* 240. *IB:* 24.

C20 CARDIFF METROPOLITAN UNIVERSITY (UWIC)

ADMISSIONS UNIT
LLANDAFF CAMPUS
WESTERN AVENUE
CARDIFF CF5 2YB
t: 029 2041 6070 f: 029 2041 6286
e: admissions@cardiffmet.ac.uk
// www.cardiffmet.ac.uk

W210 BA Graphic Communication
Duration: 3FT Hon
Entry Requirements: *GCE:* 300. *IB:* 26. *BTEC ExtDip:* DDM. *OCR NED:* M1 Foundation Course required. Interview required. Portfolio required.

W640 BA Photographic Practice
Duration: 3FT Hon
Entry Requirements: Interview required.

W213 FdA Graphic Communication
Duration: 2FT Fdg
Entry Requirements: Contact the institution for details.

C22 COLEG SIR GAR / CARMARTHENSHIRE COLLEGE

SANDY ROAD
LLANELLI
CARMARTHENSHIRE SA15 4DN
t: 01554 748000 f: 01554 748170
e: admissions@colegsirgar.ac.uk
// www.colegsirgar.ac.uk

W290 BA (Hons) Graphic Communication
Duration: 3FT Hon
Entry Requirements: Portfolio required.

C30 UNIVERSITY OF CENTRAL LANCASHIRE

PRESTON
LANCS PR1 2HE
t: 01772 201201 f: 01772 894954
e: uadmissions@uclan.ac.uk
// www.uclan.ac.uk

W210 BA Graphic Design (3-year full-time/4-year sandwich)
Duration: 3FT/4SW Hon
Entry Requirements: *GCE:* 240-300. *IB:* 26. *OCR ND:* D *OCR NED:* M3 Interview required. Portfolio required.

W214 FdA Graphic Design
Duration: 2FT Fdg
Entry Requirements: *GCE:* 200. Interview required. Portfolio required.

C55 UNIVERSITY OF CHESTER
PARKGATE ROAD
CHESTER CH1 4BJ
t: 01244 511000 f: 01244 511300
e: enquiries@chester.ac.uk
// www.chester.ac.uk

W213 BA Graphic Design
Duration: 3FT Hon
Entry Requirements: *Foundation:* Pass. *GCE:* 240-280. *SQAH:* BBBB. *IB:* 26. Interview required. Portfolio required.

WW2P BA Photography and Graphic Design
Duration: 3FT Hon
Entry Requirements: *Foundation:* Pass. *GCE:* 240-280. *SQAH:* BBBB. *IB:* 26. Interview required. Portfolio required.

C65 CITY AND ISLINGTON COLLEGE
COURSE INFORMATION UNIT
THE MARLBOROUGH BUILDING
383 HOLLOWAY ROAD
LONDON N7 0RN
t: 020 7700 9200
e: hedegrees@candi.ac.uk
// www.candi.ac.uk/HE

012W HND Graphic Design
Duration: 2FT HND
Entry Requirements: Interview required. Portfolio required.

C71 CLEVELAND COLLEGE OF ART AND DESIGN
CHURCH SQUARE
HARTLEPOOL
CHURCH SQUARE TS24 7EX
t: 01642 288888 f: 01642 288828
e: studentrecruitment@ccad.ac.uk
// www.ccad.ac.uk

W210 FdA Graphic Design
Duration: 2FT Fdg
Entry Requirements: *Foundation:* Pass. *GCE:* 100. Interview required. Portfolio required.

C85 COVENTRY UNIVERSITY
THE STUDENT CENTRE
COVENTRY UNIVERSITY
1 GULSON RD
COVENTRY CV1 2JH
t: 024 7615 2222 f: 024 7615 2223
e: studentenquiries@coventry.ac.uk
// www.coventry.ac.uk

W211 BA Graphic Design
Duration: 3FT/4SW Hon
Entry Requirements: *Foundation:* Merit. *GCE:* CCC. *SQAH:* CCCCC. *IB:* 27. *BTEC ExtDip:* MMM. *OCR NED:* M3 Interview required. Portfolio required.

W291 BA Illustration and Graphics
Duration: 3FT/4SW Hon
Entry Requirements: *Foundation:* Merit. *GCE:* CCC. *SQAH:* CCCCC. *IB:* 27. *BTEC ExtDip:* MMM. *OCR NED:* M3 Interview required. Portfolio required.

C92 CROYDON COLLEGE
COLLEGE ROAD
CROYDON CR9 1DX
t: 020 8760 5934 f: 020 8760 5880
e: admissions@croydon.ac.uk
// www.croydon.ac.uk

W211 BA Graphic Design
Duration: 3FT Hon
Entry Requirements: *GCE:* 80-100. Interview required. Portfolio required.

C93 UNIVERSITY FOR THE CREATIVE ARTS
FALKNER ROAD
FARNHAM
SURREY GU9 7DS
t: 01252 892960
e: admissions@ucreative.ac.uk
// www.ucreative.ac.uk

W217 BA Graphic Communication
Duration: 3FT Hon
Entry Requirements: *GCE:* 220. *IB:* 24. *BTEC ExtDip:* PPP. Interview required. Portfolio required.

W210 BA Graphic Design
Duration: 3FT Hon
Entry Requirements: *GCE:* 220. *IB:* 24. *BTEC ExtDip:* PPP. Interview required. Portfolio required.

C99 UNIVERSITY OF CUMBRIA
FUSEHILL STREET
CARLISLE
CUMBRIA CA1 2HH
t: 01228 616234 f: 01228 616235
// www.cumbria.ac.uk

W210 BA Graphic Design
Duration: 3FT Hon
Entry Requirements: *Foundation:* Pass. *GCE:* 240. *SQAH:* BBC. *SQAAH:* CC. *IB:* 30. *OCR ND:* D Interview required. Portfolio required.

W215 BA Graphic Design (with Year 0)
Duration: 4FT Hon
Entry Requirements: *Foundation:* Pass. *GCE:* C-cccc. *SQAH:* CC. *SQAAH:* C. *IB:* 25. Interview required. Portfolio required.

D26 DE MONTFORT UNIVERSITY
THE GATEWAY
LEICESTER LE1 9BH
t: 0116 255 1551 f: 0116 250 6204
e: enquiries@dmu.ac.uk
// www.dmu.ac.uk

W219 BA Graphic Design
Duration: 3FT Hon
Entry Requirements: *Foundation:* Pass. *GCE:* 260. *IB:* 28. *BTEC Dip:* D*D. *BTEC ExtDip:* MMM. Interview required. Portfolio required.

W221 BA Graphic Design and Illustration
Duration: 3FT Hon
Entry Requirements: *Foundation:* Pass. *GCE:* 260. *IB:* 28. *BTEC Dip:* D*D. *BTEC ExtDip:* MMM. Interview required. Portfolio required.

D39 UNIVERSITY OF DERBY
KEDLESTON ROAD
DERBY DE22 1GB
t: 01332 591167 f: 01332 597724
e: askadmissions@derby.ac.uk
// www.derby.ac.uk

W211 BA Graphic Design
Duration: 3FT Hon
Entry Requirements: *Foundation:* Distinction. *GCE:* 260. *IB:* 28. *BTEC Dip:* D*D*. *BTEC ExtDip:* DMM. *OCR NED:* M2 Interview required. Portfolio required.

W210 FYr Graphic Design
Duration: 1FT FYr
Entry Requirements: *Foundation:* Pass. *GCE:* 160. *IB:* 24. *BTEC Dip:* D*D*. *BTEC ExtDip:* DMM. *OCR ND:* M2 *OCR NED:* P2 Interview required. Portfolio required.

W216 MDes Graphic Design
Duration: 4FT Hon
Entry Requirements: *Foundation:* Distinction. *GCE:* 260. *IB:* 28. *BTEC Dip:* D*D*. *BTEC ExtDip:* DMM. *OCR NED:* M2 Interview required. Portfolio required.

D52 DONCASTER COLLEGE
THE HUB
CHAPPELL DRIVE
SOUTH YORKSHIRE DN1 2RF
t: 01302 553610
e: he@don.ac.uk
// www.don.ac.uk

W291 BA Graphic Design
Duration: 3FT Hon
Entry Requirements: *GCE:* 100.

D65 UNIVERSITY OF DUNDEE
NETHERGATE
DUNDEE DD1 4HN
t: 01382 383838 f: 01382 388150
e: contactus@dundee.ac.uk
// www.dundee.ac.uk/admissions/undergraduate/

W210 BDes Graphic Design
Duration: 3FT Hon
Entry Requirements: Foundation Course required. Interview required. Portfolio required.

E28 UNIVERSITY OF EAST LONDON
DOCKLANDS CAMPUS
UNIVERSITY WAY
LONDON E16 2RD
t: 020 8223 3333 f: 020 8223 2978
e: study@uel.ac.uk
// www.uel.ac.uk

N2WF BA Business Management with Graphic Design
Duration: 3FT Hon
Entry Requirements: *GCE:* 240. *IB:* 24. Portfolio required.

W216 BA Graphic Design
Duration: 3FT Hon
Entry Requirements: *GCE:* 200. Interview required. Portfolio required.

W219 BA Graphic Design (Extended)
Duration: 4FT Hon
Entry Requirements: *GCE:* 80. Interview required. Portfolio required.

WF90 BA Graphic Design and Printed Textile Design
Duration: 3FT Hon
Entry Requirements: *GCE:* 200.

W2I1 BA Graphic Design with Computing
Duration: 3FT Hon
Entry Requirements: *GCE:* 200. *IB:* 24. Interview required. Portfolio required.

W2W9 BA Graphic Design with Illustration
Duration: 3FT Hon
Entry Requirements: *GCE:* 240. *IB:* 24. Foundation Course required. Interview required. Portfolio required.

WW2Q BA Graphic Design/Photography
Duration: 3FT Hon
Entry Requirements: *GCE:* 200. *IB:* 24. Foundation Course required. Interview required. Portfolio required.

W296 BA Illustration with Graphic Design
Duration: 3FT Hon
Entry Requirements: *GCE:* 200. *IB:* 24.

W291 BA Illustration/Graphic Design
Duration: 3FT Hon
Entry Requirements: *GCE:* 200. *IB:* 24.

WWPG BA Photography/Graphic Design
Duration: 3FT Hon
Entry Requirements: *GCE:* 200. *IB:* 24. Portfolio required.

IW12 BA/BSc Computing and Graphic Design
Duration: 3FT Hon
Entry Requirements: *GCE:* 240. *IB:* 24. Portfolio required.

C8W2 BSc Psychology with Graphic Design
Duration: 3FT Hon
Entry Requirements: *GCE:* 240. *IB:* 24.

E32 EAST SURREY COLLEGE (INCORPORATING REIGATE SCHOOL OF ART, DESIGN AND MEDIA)
GATTON POINT
LONDON ROAD
REDHILL RH1 2JX
t: 01737 772611 f: 01737 768641
e: fmelmoe@esc.ac.uk
// www.esc.ac.uk

012W HND Graphic Design
Duration: 2FT HND
Entry Requirements: Foundation Course required. Interview required. Portfolio required.

022W HND Graphic Design (Illustration)
Duration: 2FT HND
Entry Requirements: *GCE:* 80. Foundation Course required. Interview required. Portfolio required.

E56 THE UNIVERSITY OF EDINBURGH
STUDENT RECRUITMENT & ADMISSIONS
57 GEORGE SQUARE
EDINBURGH EH8 9JU
t: 0131 650 4360 f: 0131 651 1236
e: sra.enquiries@ed.ac.uk
// www.ed.ac.uk/studying/undergraduate/

W210 BA Graphic Design
Duration: 4FT Hon
Entry Requirements: *Foundation:* Merit. *GCE:* BBB. *SQAH:* BBBB. *IB:* 34. Portfolio required.

E59 EDINBURGH NAPIER UNIVERSITY
CRAIGLOCKHART CAMPUS
EDINBURGH EH14 1DJ
t: +44 (0)8452 60 60 40 f: 0131 455 6464
e: info@napier.ac.uk
// www.napier.ac.uk

W210 BDes Graphic Design
Duration: 4FT Hon
Entry Requirements: *GCE:* 240. Interview required. Portfolio required.

E81 EXETER COLLEGE
HELE ROAD
EXETER
DEVON EX4 4JS
t: 0845 111 6000
e: info@exe-coll.ac.uk
// www.exe-coll.ac.uk/he

WP23 FdA Graphic Communication
Duration: 2FT Fdg
Entry Requirements: *GCE:* 160.

F33 UNIVERSITY COLLEGE FALMOUTH
WOODLANE
FALMOUTH
CORNWALL TR11 4RH
t: 01326213730
e: admissions@falmouth.ac.uk
// www.falmouth.ac.uk

W214 BA(Hons) Graphic Design
Duration: 3FT Hon
Entry Requirements: *GCE:* 220. *IB:* 24. Interview required. Portfolio required.

G14 UNIVERSITY OF GLAMORGAN, CARDIFF AND PONTYPRIDD

ENQUIRIES AND ADMISSIONS UNIT
PONTYPRIDD CF37 1DL
t: 08456 434030 f: 01443 654050
e: enquiries@glam.ac.uk
// www.glam.ac.uk

WF13 BA Graphic Communication
Duration: 4SW Hon
Entry Requirements: *GCE:* BBC. *IB:* 25. *BTEC SubDip:* M. *BTEC Dip:* D*D*. *BTEC ExtDip:* DMM. *OCR NED:* M2 Interview required. Portfolio required.

G45 GLOUCESTERSHIRE COLLEGE

PRINCESS ELIZABETH WAY
CHELTENHAM GL51 7SJ
t: 01242 532008 f: 01242 532023
e: admissions@gloscol.ac.uk
// www.gloscol.ac.uk

WWW6 HND Creative Practices
Duration: 2FT HND
Entry Requirements: Contact the institution for details.

G50 THE UNIVERSITY OF GLOUCESTERSHIRE

PARK CAMPUS
THE PARK
CHELTENHAM GL50 2RH
t: 01242 714501 f: 01242 714869
e: admissions@glos.ac.uk
// www.glos.ac.uk

W210 BA Graphic Design
Duration: 3FT Hon
Entry Requirements: *GCE:* 280-300. Interview required. Portfolio required.

G53 GLYNDWR UNIVERSITY

PLAS COCH
MOLD ROAD
WREXHAM LL11 2AW
t: 01978 293439 f: 01978 290008
e: sid@glyndwr.ac.uk
// www.glyndwr.ac.uk

W222 BA Design: Illustration, Graphic Novels and Children's Publishing
Duration: 3FT Hon
Entry Requirements: *GCE:* 240. Interview required. Portfolio required.

G80 GRIMSBY INSTITUTE OF FURTHER AND HIGHER EDUCATION

NUNS CORNER
GRIMSBY
NE LINCOLNSHIRE DN34 5BQ
t: 0800 328 3631
e: headmissions@grimsby.ac.uk
// www.grimsby.ac.uk

W611 BA Motion Graphics
Duration: 3FT Hon
Entry Requirements: Interview required.

H14 HAVERING COLLEGE OF FURTHER AND HIGHER EDUCATION

ARDLEIGH GREEN ROAD
HORNCHURCH
ESSEX RM11 2LL
t: 01708 462793 f: 01708 462736
e: HE@havering-college.ac.uk
// www.havering-college.ac.uk

W210 BA Graphic Design
Duration: 3FT Hon
Entry Requirements: Interview required. Portfolio required.

H18 HEREFORD COLLEGE OF ARTS

FOLLY LANE
HEREFORD HR1 1LT
t: 01432 273359 f: 01432 341099
e: headmin@hca.ac.uk
// www.hca.ac.uk

W216 BA Graphic & Media Design
Duration: 3FT Hon   **CRB Check:** Required
Entry Requirements: *GCE:* 200. Interview required. Portfolio required.

W214 BA Graphic and Media Design (top-up)
Duration: 1FT Hon   **CRB Check:** Required
Entry Requirements: Interview required. Portfolio required. HND required.

H36 UNIVERSITY OF HERTFORDSHIRE

UNIVERSITY ADMISSIONS SERVICE
COLLEGE LANE
HATFIELD
HERTS AL10 9AB
t: 01707 284800
// www.herts.ac.uk

W211 BA Graphic Design and Illustration
Duration: 3FT Hon
Entry Requirements: *Foundation:* Pass. *GCE:* 240. Interview required. Portfolio required.

W216 FdA Graphic Design
Duration: 2FT Fdg
Entry Requirements: *GCE:* 80. Interview required. Portfolio required.

H60 THE UNIVERSITY OF HUDDERSFIELD
QUEENSGATE
HUDDERSFIELD HD1 3DH
t: 01484 473969 f: 01484 472765
e: admissionsandrecords@hud.ac.uk
// www.hud.ac.uk

W216 BA Graphic Design
Duration: 3FT/4SW Hon
Entry Requirements: *GCE:* 300. *SQAH:* BBBB. *IB:* 28. Interview required. Portfolio required.

H73 HULL COLLEGE
QUEEN'S GARDENS
HULL HU1 3DG
t: 01482 329943 f: 01482 598733
e: info@hull-college.ac.uk
// www.hull-college.ac.uk/higher-education

W215 BA Graphic Design
Duration: 3FT Hon
Entry Requirements: *GCE:* 200. Foundation Course required. Interview required. Portfolio required.

K24 THE UNIVERSITY OF KENT
RECRUITMENT & ADMISSIONS OFFICE
REGISTRY
UNIVERSITY OF KENT
CANTERBURY, KENT CT2 7NZ
t: 01227 827272 f: 01227 827077
e: information@kent.ac.uk
// www.kent.ac.uk

W210 BA Graphic Design (Top-up)
Duration: 1FT Hon
Entry Requirements: Interview required. Portfolio required.

012W HND Graphic Design
Duration: 2FT HND
Entry Requirements: Interview required. Portfolio required.

K84 KINGSTON UNIVERSITY
STUDENT INFORMATION & ADVICE CENTRE
COOPER HOUSE
40-46 SURBITON ROAD
KINGSTON UPON THAMES KT1 2HX
t: 0844 8552177 f: 020 8547 7080
e: aps@kingston.ac.uk
// www.kingston.ac.uk

W210 BA Graphic Design
Duration: 3FT Hon
Entry Requirements: Foundation Course required. Interview required. Portfolio required.

WW6F BA Graphic Design and Photography
Duration: 3FT Hon
Entry Requirements: Foundation Course required. Interview required. Portfolio required.

K90 KIRKLEES COLLEGE
HALIFAX ROAD
DEWSBURY
WEST YORKSHIRE WF13 2AS
t: 01924 436221 f: 01924 457047
e: admissionsdc@kirkleescollege.ac.uk
// www.kirkleescollege.ac.uk

W214 BA Graphic Communication (Top-up)
Duration: 1FT Hon
Entry Requirements: Contact the institution for details.

W210 FdA Graphic Communication
Duration: 2FT Fdg
Entry Requirements: *GCE:* 180.

L23 UNIVERSITY OF LEEDS
THE UNIVERSITY OF LEEDS
WOODHOUSE LANE
LEEDS LS2 9JT
t: 0113 343 3999
e: admissions@leeds.ac.uk
// www.leeds.ac.uk

W290 BA Graphic and Communication Design
Duration: 3FT Hon
Entry Requirements: *GCE:* ABB. *SQAAH:* ABB. *IB:* 34.

L27 LEEDS METROPOLITAN UNIVERSITY
COURSE ENQUIRIES OFFICE
CITY CAMPUS
LEEDS LS1 3HE
t: 0113 81 23113 f: 0113 81 23129
// www.leedsmet.ac.uk

WP65 BSc Photographic Journalism
Duration: 3FT Hon
Entry Requirements: *GCE:* 200. *IB:* 24. Interview required.

L28 LEEDS COLLEGE OF ART
BLENHEIM WALK
LEEDS LS2 9AQ
t: 0113 202 8000 f: 0113 202 8001
e: info@leeds-art.ac.uk
// www.leeds-art.ac.uk

W214 BA Graphic Design
Duration: 3FT Hon
Entry Requirements: *Foundation:* Merit. *GCE:* 240. *IB:* 24. *BTEC Dip:* DD. *BTEC ExtDip:* MMM. Interview required. Portfolio required.

L51 LIVERPOOL JOHN MOORES UNIVERSITY
KINGSWAY HOUSE
HATTON GARDEN
LIVERPOOL L3 2AJ
t: 0151 231 5090 f: 0151 904 6368
e: courses@ljmu.ac.uk
// www.ljmu.ac.uk

W210 BA Graphic Design and Illustration
Duration: 3FT Hon
Entry Requirements: *GCE:* 280-320. Foundation Course required. Interview required. Portfolio required.

L62 THE LONDON COLLEGE, UCK
VICTORIA GARDENS
NOTTING HILL GATE
LONDON W11 3PE
t: 020 7243 4000 f: 020 7243 1484
e: admissions@lcuck.ac.uk
// www.lcuck.ac.uk

412W HNC Graphic Design
Duration: 1FT HNC
Entry Requirements: Contact the institution for details.

012W HND Graphic Design
Duration: 2FT HND
Entry Requirements: Contact the institution for details.

L68 LONDON METROPOLITAN UNIVERSITY
166-220 HOLLOWAY ROAD
LONDON N7 8DB
t: 020 7133 4200
e: admissions@londonmet.ac.uk
// www.londonmet.ac.uk

W214 BA Graphic Design
Duration: 3FT Hon
Entry Requirements: *Foundation:* Pass. *GCE:* 280. *IB:* 28. Foundation Course required. Interview required. Portfolio required.

L79 LOUGHBOROUGH UNIVERSITY
LOUGHBOROUGH
LEICESTERSHIRE LE11 3TU
t: 01509 223522 f: 01509 223905
e: admissions@lboro.ac.uk
// www.lboro.ac.uk

W900 BA Graphic Communication and Illustration
Duration: 3FT/4SW Hon
Entry Requirements: *IB:* 32. *BTEC ExtDip:* DDM. Interview required. Portfolio required.

M40 THE MANCHESTER METROPOLITAN UNIVERSITY
ADMISSIONS OFFICE
ALL SAINTS (GMS)
ALL SAINTS
MANCHESTER M15 6BH
t: 0161 247 2000
// www.mmu.ac.uk

W210 BA Graphic Design
Duration: 3FT Hon
Entry Requirements: *GCE:* 280. *IB:* 27. Interview required. Portfolio required.

M77 MID CHESHIRE COLLEGE
HARTFORD CAMPUS
NORTHWICH
CHESHIRE CW8 1LJ
t: 01606 74444 f: 01606 720700
e: eandrews@midchesh.ac.uk
// www.midchesh.ac.uk

W210 FdA Graphic Design
Duration: 2FT Fdg
Entry Requirements: *GCE:* 120. Interview required.

M80 MIDDLESEX UNIVERSITY
MIDDLESEX UNIVERSITY
THE BURROUGHS
LONDON NW4 4BT
t: 020 8411 5555 f: 020 8411 5649
e: enquiries@mdx.ac.uk
// www.mdx.ac.uk

W210 BA Graphic Design
Duration: 3FT Hon
Entry Requirements: *GCE:* 200-300. *IB:* 28. Interview required.
Portfolio required.

N23 NEWCASTLE COLLEGE
STUDENT SERVICES
RYE HILL CAMPUS
SCOTSWOOD ROAD
NEWCASTLE UPON TYNE NE4 7SA
t: 0191 200 4110 f: 0191 200 4349
e: enquiries@ncl-coll.ac.uk
// www.newcastlecollege.co.uk

W640 FdA Commercial Photographic Practice
Duration: 2FT Fdg
Entry Requirements: *GCE:* 120-165. *OCR ND:* P2 *OCR NED:* P3
Foundation Course required. Interview required. Portfolio required.

W210 FdA Graphic Design
Duration: 2FT Fdg
Entry Requirements: *GCE:* 120-165. *OCR ND:* P2 *OCR NED:* P3
Foundation Course required. Interview required. Portfolio required.

N28 NEW COLLEGE DURHAM
FRAMWELLGATE MOOR CAMPUS
DURHAM DH1 5ES
t: 0191 375 4210/4211 f: 0191 375 4222
e: admissions@newdur.ac.uk
// www.newcollegedurham.ac.uk

W210 FdA Graphic Design
Duration: 2FT Fdg
Entry Requirements: *GCE:* 40. Portfolio required.

N33 NEW COLLEGE STAMFORD
DRIFT ROAD
STAMFORD
LINCOLNSHIRE PE9 1XA
t: 01780 484300 f: 01780 484301
e: enquiries@stamford.ac.uk
// www.stamford.ac.uk

W210 HND Graphic Design
Duration: 2FT HND
Entry Requirements: Interview required.

N37 UNIVERSITY OF WALES, NEWPORT
ADMISSIONS
LODGE ROAD
CAERLEON
NEWPORT NP18 3QT
t: 01633 432030 f: 01633 432850
e: admissions@newport.ac.uk
// www.newport.ac.uk

W641 BA Photographic Art
Duration: 3FT Hon
Entry Requirements: *Foundation:* Merit. *GCE:* 240-260. *IB:* 24.
Interview required. Portfolio required.

N38 UNIVERSITY OF NORTHAMPTON
PARK CAMPUS
BOUGHTON GREEN ROAD
NORTHAMPTON NN2 7AL
t: 0800 358 2232 f: 01604 722083
e: admissions@northampton.ac.uk
// www.northampton.ac.uk

W210 BA Graphic Communications
Duration: 3FT Hon
Entry Requirements: *GCE:* 240-280. *SQAH:* AAB-BBBC. *IB:* 24.
BTEC Dip: DD. *BTEC ExtDip:* DMM. *OCR ND:* D *OCR NED:* M2
Foundation Course required. Interview required.

W640 BA Photographic Practice
Duration: 3FT Hon
Entry Requirements: *GCE:* 240-280. *SQAH:* AAB-BBBC. *IB:* 24.
BTEC Dip: DD. *BTEC ExtDip:* DMM. *OCR ND:* D *OCR NED:* M2
Foundation Course required. Interview required.

W214 FdA Graphic Design
Duration: 2FT Fdg
Entry Requirements: *GCE:* 140-160. *SQAH:* BC-CCC. *IB:* 24.
BTEC Dip: MP. *BTEC ExtDip:* MPP. *OCR ND:* P1 *OCR NED:* P2
Interview required.

N39 NORWICH UNIVERSITY COLLEGE OF THE ARTS
FRANCIS HOUSE
3-7 REDWELL STREET
NORWICH NR2 4SN
t: 01603 610561 f: 01603 615728
e: admissions@nuca.ac.uk
// www.nuca.ac.uk

W213 BA Graphic Communication
Duration: 3FT Hon
Entry Requirements: *Foundation:* Merit. *GCE:* BBC. *BTEC Dip:*
DM. *BTEC ExtDip:* MMM. *OCR ND:* M1 *OCR NED:* P1 Interview
required. Portfolio required.

W210 BA Graphic Design
Duration: 3FT Hon
Entry Requirements: *Foundation:* Merit. *GCE:* BBC. *BTEC Dip:*
DM. *BTEC ExtDip:* MMM. *OCR ND:* M1 *OCR NED:* P1 Interview
required. Portfolio required.

W216 BA Graphic Design (including Level 0)
Duration: 4FT Hon
Entry Requirements: *Foundation:* Merit. *OCR ND:* M1 *OCR NED:*
P1 Interview required. Portfolio required.

N41 NORTHBROOK COLLEGE SUSSEX
LITTLEHAMPTON ROAD
WORTHING
WEST SUSSEX BN12 6NU
t: 0845 155 6060 **f:** 01903 606073
e: enquiries@nbcol.ac.uk
// www.northbrook.ac.uk

W641 BA Contemporary Photographic Arts Practice
Duration: 3FT Hon
Entry Requirements: *GCE:* 160. Interview required. Portfolio
required.

W210 FdA Graphic Design
Duration: 2FT Fdg
Entry Requirements: *GCE:* 160. Interview required. Portfolio
required.

N77 NORTHUMBRIA UNIVERSITY
TRINITY BUILDING
NORTHUMBERLAND ROAD
NEWCASTLE UPON TYNE NE1 8ST
t: 0191 243 7420 **f:** 0191 227 4561
e: er.admissions@northumbria.ac.uk
// www.northumbria.ac.uk

W640 BA Contemporary Photographic Practice
Duration: 3FT Hon
Entry Requirements: *Foundation:* Distinction. *GCE:* 300. *SQAH:*
BBBBC. *SQAAH:* BBC. *IB:* 26. *OCR NED:* M1 Interview required.
Portfolio required.

W210 BA Graphic Design
Duration: 3FT Hon
Entry Requirements: *Foundation:* Distinction. *GCE:* 320. *SQAH:*
BBBBB. *SQAAH:* BBB. *IB:* 27. *BTEC Dip:* DM. *BTEC ExtDip:* DDM.
OCR ND: M1 *OCR NED:* M1 Interview required. Portfolio required.

N91 NOTTINGHAM TRENT UNIVERSITY
DRYDEN BUILDING
BURTON STREET
NOTTINGHAM NG1 4BU
t: +44 (0) 115 848 4200 **f:** +44 (0) 115 848 8869
e: applications@ntu.ac.uk
// www.ntu.ac.uk

W211 BA Graphic Design
Duration: 3FT Hon
Entry Requirements: *GCE:* 280. Interview required. Portfolio
required.

O25 OXFORD & CHERWELL VALLEY COLLEGE
BANBURY CAMPUS
BROUGHTON ROAD
BANBURY
OXON OX16 9QA
t: 01865 551691 **f:** 01865 551777
e: uni@ocvc.ac.uk
// www.ocvc.ac.uk

W210 HND Graphic Design
Duration: 2FT HND
Entry Requirements: Contact the institution for details.

O66 OXFORD BROOKES UNIVERSITY
ADMISSIONS OFFICE
HEADINGTON CAMPUS
GIPSY LANE
OXFORD OX3 0BP
t: 01865 483040 **f:** 01865 483983
e: admissions@brookes.ac.uk
// www.brookes.ac.uk

W210 BA Graphic Design (Swindon College)
Duration: 3FT Hon
Entry Requirements: Interview required. Portfolio required.

P60 PLYMOUTH UNIVERSITY
DRAKE CIRCUS
PLYMOUTH PL4 8AA
t: 01752 585858 **f:** 01752 588055
e: admissions@plymouth.ac.uk
// www.plymouth.ac.uk

W215 BA Graphic Communication and Typography
Duration: 3FT Hon
Entry Requirements: *Foundation:* Pass. *GCE:* 280. *IB:* 26. *BTEC
ExtDip:* DMM. Interview required. Portfolio required.

P65 PLYMOUTH COLLEGE OF ART (FORMERLY PLYMOUTH COLLEGE OF ART AND DESIGN)

TAVISTOCK PLACE
PLYMOUTH PL4 8AT
t: 01752 203434 f: 01752 203444
e: infoservices@plymouthart.ac.uk
// www.plymouthart.ac.uk

W214 BA Graphic Design

Duration: 3FT Hon
Entry Requirements: *Foundation:* Pass. *IB:* 24. *OCR ND:* M1 *OCR NED:* P1 Interview required. Portfolio required.

W216 BA Graphic Design (Top-Up)

Duration: 1FT Hon
Entry Requirements: Interview required. Portfolio required. HND required.

W210 FdA Graphic Design

Duration: 2FT Fdg
Entry Requirements: *Foundation:* Pass. *IB:* 24. *OCR ND:* M1 *OCR NED:* P1 Interview required. Portfolio required.

W217 FdA Graphic Design (including Level 0)

Duration: 3FT Fdg
Entry Requirements: *IB:* 24. *OCR ND:* P3 *OCR NED:* P3 Interview required. Portfolio required.

P80 UNIVERSITY OF PORTSMOUTH

ACADEMIC REGISTRY
UNIVERSITY HOUSE
WINSTON CHURCHILL AVENUE
PORTSMOUTH PO1 2UP
t: 023 9284 8484 f: 023 9284 3082
e: admissions@port.ac.uk
// www.port.ac.uk

W210 BA Graphic Design

Duration: 3FT Hon
Entry Requirements: *GCE:* 240-300. *IB:* 26. *BTEC SubDip:* P. *BTEC Dip:* DD. *BTEC ExtDip:* DMM. Interview required. Portfolio required.

R06 RAVENSBOURNE

6 PENROSE WAY
GREENWICH PENINSULA
LONDON SE10 0EW
t: 020 3040 3998
e: info@rave.ac.uk
// www.rave.ac.uk

W210 BA Graphic Design

Duration: 3FT Hon
Entry Requirements: *Foundation:* Pass. *GCE:* AA-CC. *IB:* 28. Interview required. Portfolio required.

W211 BA Graphic Design (Fast-Track)

Duration: 2FT Hon
Entry Requirements: Contact the institution for details.

W215 BA Graphic Design (with Foundation Year)

Duration: 4FT Hon
Entry Requirements: *Foundation:* Pass. *GCE:* A-E. *IB:* 28. Interview required. Portfolio required.

W610 BA Motion Graphics (with Foundation Year)

Duration: 4FT Hon
Entry Requirements: *Foundation:* Pass. *GCE:* A-E. *IB:* 28. Interview required. Portfolio required.

R12 THE UNIVERSITY OF READING

THE UNIVERSITY OF READING
PO BOX 217
READING RG6 6AH
t: 0118 378 8619 f: 0118 378 8924
e: student.recruitment@reading.ac.uk
// www.reading.ac.uk

W213 BA Graphic Communication

Duration: 3FT Hon
Entry Requirements: *Foundation:* Pass. *GCE:* ABC-BBB. *SQAH:* ABBBC-BBBBB. *SQAAH:* ABC-BBB. Interview required. Portfolio required.

R36 ROBERT GORDON UNIVERSITY

ROBERT GORDON UNIVERSITY
SCHOOLHILL
ABERDEEN
SCOTLAND AB10 1FR
t: 01224 26 27 28 f: 01224 26 21 47
e: UGOffice@rgu.ac.uk
// www.rgu.ac.uk

WW26 BA (Hons) Communication Design

Duration: 4FT Hon
Entry Requirements: *GCE:* BC. *SQAH:* BBC. Interview required. Portfolio required.

R52 ROTHERHAM COLLEGE OF ARTS AND TECHNOLOGY

EASTWOOD LANE
ROTHERHAM
SOUTH YORKSHIRE S65 1EG
t: 08080 722777 f: 01709 373053
e: info@rotherham.ac.uk
// www.rotherham.ac.uk

W210 FdA Graphic Design

Duration: 2FT Fdg
Entry Requirements: *Foundation:* Pass. *GCE:* 120. Interview required. Portfolio required.

S03 THE UNIVERSITY OF SALFORD

SALFORD M5 4WT
t: 0161 295 4545 f: 0161 295 4646
e: ug-admissions@salford.ac.uk
// www.salford.ac.uk

W211 BA Graphic Design

Duration: 3FT Hon
Entry Requirements: *Foundation:* Pass. *GCE:* 280. *IB:* 28. *OCR ND:* D *OCR NED:* M2 Interview required. Portfolio required.

S21 SHEFFIELD HALLAM UNIVERSITY

CITY CAMPUS
HOWARD STREET
SHEFFIELD S1 1WB
t: 0114 225 5555 f: 0114 225 2167
e: admissions@shu.ac.uk
// www.shu.ac.uk

W210 BA Graphic Design

Duration: 3FT Hon
Entry Requirements: *GCE:* 280.

W214 MDes Graphic Design

Duration: 4FT Hon
Entry Requirements: *GCE:* 300.

S22 SHEFFIELD COLLEGE

THE SHEFFIELD COLLEGE
HE UNIT
HILLSBOROUGH COLLEGE AT THE BARRACKS
SHEFFIELD S6 2LR
t: 0114 260 2597
e: heunit@sheffcol.ac.uk
// www.sheffcol.ac.uk

W210 FdA Graphic Design

Duration: 2FT Fdg
Entry Requirements: *GCE:* 120.

S26 SOLIHULL COLLEGE

BLOSSOMFIELD ROAD
SOLIHULL
WEST MIDLANDS B91 1SB
t: 0121 678 7006 f: 0121 678 7200
e: enquiries@solihull.ac.uk
// www.solihull.ac.uk

012W HND Graphic Design

Duration: 2FT HND
Entry Requirements: *Foundation:* Merit. *GCE:* A-E. *IB:* 24. *BTEC Dip:* MM. *BTEC ExtDip:* MMM. *OCR ND:* M2 *OCR NED:* M3 Foundation Course required. Interview required. Portfolio required.

S27 UNIVERSITY OF SOUTHAMPTON

HIGHFIELD
SOUTHAMPTON SO17 1BJ
t: 023 8059 4732 f: 023 8059 3037
e: admissions@soton.ac.uk
// www.southampton.ac.uk

W210 BA Graphic Arts

Duration: 3FT Hon
Entry Requirements: *Foundation:* Pass. *GCE:* ABB. *IB:* 32. Interview required. Portfolio required.

S28 SOMERSET COLLEGE OF ARTS AND TECHNOLOGY

WELLINGTON ROAD
TAUNTON
SOMERSET TA1 5AX
t: 01823 366331 f: 01823 366418
e: enquiries@somerset.ac.uk
// www.somerset.ac.uk/student-area/ considering-a-degree.html

W214 BA Design: Graphics (Top-Up)

Duration: 1FT Hon
Entry Requirements: HND required.

W210 FdA Graphic Design

Duration: 2FT Fdg
Entry Requirements: *Foundation:* Pass. *GCE:* 160. *IB:* 24. Interview required. Portfolio required.

S30 SOUTHAMPTON SOLENT UNIVERSITY
EAST PARK TERRACE
SOUTHAMPTON
HAMPSHIRE SO14 0RT
t: +44 (0) 23 8031 9039 f: + 44 (0)23 8022 2259
e: admissions@solent.ac.uk
// www.solent.ac.uk/

W215 BA Graphic Design
Duration: 3FT Hon
Entry Requirements: *Foundation:* Merit. *GCE:* 200. *SQAAH:* AC-DDD. *IB:* 24. *BTEC ExtDip:* MMP. *OCR ND:* M1 *OCR NED:* P1 Portfolio required.

WF10 BA Graphic Design (Top-Up)
Duration: 1FT Hon
Entry Requirements: Interview required. Portfolio required. HND required.

S35 SOUTHPORT COLLEGE
MORNINGTON ROAD
SOUTHPORT
MERSEYSIDE PR9 0TT
t: 08450066236 f: 01704 392610
e: guidance@southport-college.ac.uk
// www.southport-college.ac.uk

W210 HND Graphic Design
Duration: 2FT HND
Entry Requirements: Contact the institution for details.

S43 SOUTH ESSEX COLLEGE OF FURTHER & HIGHER EDUCATION
LUKER ROAD
SOUTHEND-ON-SEA
ESSEX SS1 1ND
t: 0845 52 12345 f: 01702 432320
e: Admissions@southessex.ac.uk
// www.southessex.ac.uk

W210 BA Graphic Design
Duration: 3FT Hon
Entry Requirements: *GCE:* 160. *IB:* 24. Interview required. Portfolio required.

W214 CertHE Graphic Design
Duration: 1FT Cer
Entry Requirements: Contact the institution for details.

W215 DipHE Graphic Design
Duration: 2FT Dip
Entry Requirements: Contact the institution for details.

S51 ST HELENS COLLEGE
WATER STREET
ST HELENS
MERSEYSIDE WA10 1PP
t: 01744 733766 f: 01744 623400
e: enquiries@sthelens.ac.uk
// www.sthelens.ac.uk

W211 BA Graphic Design
Duration: 3FT Hon
Entry Requirements: Contact the institution for details.

W215 BA Graphic Design (Top-Up)
Duration: 1FT Hon
Entry Requirements: Interview required. Portfolio required.

W210 FdA Graphic Design
Duration: 2FT Fdg
Entry Requirements: *Foundation:* Pass. *GCE:* 40-80. *IB:* 18.

S72 STAFFORDSHIRE UNIVERSITY
COLLEGE ROAD
STOKE ON TRENT ST4 2DE
t: 01782 292753 f: 01782 292740
e: admissions@staffs.ac.uk
// www.staffs.ac.uk

W211 BA Graphic Design
Duration: 3FT/4FT Hon
Entry Requirements: *Foundation:* Merit. *GCE:* 200-240. *IB:* 24. *BTEC Dip:* DD. *BTEC ExtDip:* MMM. Interview required. Portfolio required.

S76 STOCKPORT COLLEGE
WELLINGTON ROAD SOUTH
STOCKPORT SK1 3UQ
t: 0161 958 3143 f: 0161 958 3663
e: susan.kelly@stockport.ac.uk
// www.stockport.ac.uk

W215 BA Illustration
Duration: 3FT Hon
Entry Requirements: *GCE:* 120-240. Portfolio required.

S82 UNIVERSITY CAMPUS SUFFOLK (UCS)
WATERFRONT BUILDING
NEPTUNE QUAY
IPSWICH
SUFFOLK IP4 1QJ
t: 01473 338833 f: 01473 339900
e: info@ucs.ac.uk
// www.ucs.ac.uk

W214 BA Graphic Communication (Level 3 entry only)
Duration: 1FT Hon
Entry Requirements: Interview required. Portfolio required.

W293 BA Graphic Design (Graphic Illustration)
Duration: 3FT Hon
Entry Requirements: *GCE:* 280. *IB:* 28. *BTEC ExtDip:* DMM.
Interview required. Portfolio required.

W210 FdA Graphic Design
Duration: 2FT Fdg
Entry Requirements: *GCE:* 200. *IB:* 28. *BTEC ExtDip:* DMM.
Interview required. Portfolio required..

S84 UNIVERSITY OF SUNDERLAND
STUDENT HELPLINE
THE STUDENT GATEWAY
CHESTER ROAD
SUNDERLAND SR1 3SD
t: 0191 515 3000 f: 0191 515 3805
e: student.helpline@sunderland.ac.uk
// www.sunderland.ac.uk

W210 BA Graphic Communication and Design
Duration: 3FT Hon
Entry Requirements: *Foundation:* Merit. *GCE:* 220. *SQAH:* BBBC. *IB:* 22. Interview required. Portfolio required.

W214 BA Graphic Design (Top-up)
Duration: 1FT Hon
Entry Requirements: Interview required. Portfolio required. HND required.

W215 BA Illustration and Design
Duration: 3FT Hon
Entry Requirements: *Foundation:* Merit. *GCE:* 220. *SQAH:* BBBC. *IB:* 22. Interview required. Portfolio required.

S96 SWANSEA METROPOLITAN UNIVERSITY
MOUNT PLEASANT CAMPUS
SWANSEA SA1 6ED
t: 01792 481000 f: 01792 481061
e: gemma.green@smu.ac.uk
// www.smu.ac.uk

W210 BA Graphic Design
Duration: 3FT Hon
Entry Requirements: *Foundation:* Pass. *GCE:* 200-360. *IB:* 24.
Interview required. Portfolio required.

T20 TEESSIDE UNIVERSITY
MIDDLESBROUGH TS1 3BA
t: 01642 218121 f: 01642 384201
e: registry@tees.ac.uk
// www.tees.ac.uk

W210 BA Graphic Design
Duration: 3FT Hon
Entry Requirements: *Foundation:* Distinction. *GCE:* 300. *IB:* 25.
Interview required. Portfolio required.

W2W9 FdA Design for the Creative Industries
Duration: 2FT Fdg
Entry Requirements: *GCE:* 200-240. *IB:* 24. Interview required.
Portfolio required.

T90 TYNE METROPOLITAN COLLEGE
BATTLE HILL DRIVE
WALLSEND
TYNE AND WEAR NE28 9NL
t: 0191 229 5000 f: 0191 229 5301
e: enquiries@tynemet.ac.uk
// www.tynemet.ac.uk

012W HND Graphic Design
Duration: 2FT HND
Entry Requirements: Interview required. Portfolio required.

U65 UNIVERSITY OF THE ARTS LONDON
272 HIGH HOLBORN
LONDON WC1V 7EY
t: 020 7514 6000x6197 f: 020 7514 6198
e: c.anderson@arts.ac.uk
// www.arts.ac.uk

W210 BA Graphic Design
Duration: 3FT Hon
Entry Requirements: *Foundation:* Pass. *GCE:* 80. *IB:* 28.
Portfolio required.

W211 BA Graphic Design
Duration: 3FT Hon
Entry Requirements: Interview required.

W216 BA Graphic Design Communication
Duration: 3FT Hon
Entry Requirements: *Foundation:* Pass. *GCE:* 80. *IB:* 28.
Foundation Course required. Portfolio required.

W12 WALSALL COLLEGE
WALSALL COLLEGE
LITTLETON STREET WEST
WALSALL
WEST MIDLANDS WS2 8ES
t: 01922 657000 f: 01922 657083
e: ckemp@walsallcollege.ac.uk
// www.walsallcollege.ac.uk

112W HNC Graphic Design
Duration: 1FT HNC
Entry Requirements: Interview required.

012W HND Graphic Design
Duration: 2FT HND
Entry Requirements: *GCE:* 120-240. Interview required. Portfolio required.

W50 UNIVERSITY OF WESTMINSTER
2ND FLOOR, CAVENDISH HOUSE
101 NEW CAVENDISH STREET,
LONDON W1W 6XH
t: 020 7915 5511
e: course-enquiries@westminster.ac.uk
// www.westminster.ac.uk

W211 BA Graphic Communication Design
Duration: 3FT Hon
Entry Requirements: *GCE:* BB. *SQAH:* BBBB. *IB:* 28. Interview required. Portfolio required.

W640 BA Photographic Arts
Duration: 3FT Hon
Entry Requirements: *GCE:* BB. *SQAH:* AAAAA-BBBBB. *SQAAH:* AAA-BBB. *IB:* 28. Interview required. Portfolio required.

W67 WIGAN AND LEIGH COLLEGE
PO BOX 53
PARSON'S WALK
WIGAN
GREATER MANCHESTER WN1 1RS
t: 01942 761605 f: 01942 761164
e: applications@wigan-leigh.ac.uk
// www.wigan-leigh.ac.uk

W210 FdA Graphic Design
Duration: 2FT Fdg
Entry Requirements: Interview required. Portfolio required.

W74 WILTSHIRE COLLEGE
WILTSHIRE COLLEGE LACKHAM
LACOCK
CHIPPENHAM
WILTSHIRE SN15 2NY
t: 01249 466806 f: 01249 444474
e: HEAdmissions@wiltshire.ac.uk
// www.wiltshire.ac.uk

W210 HND Graphic Design
Duration: 2FT HND
Entry Requirements: *Foundation:* Pass. *GCE:* 120. *IB:* 24. *OCR ND:* P2 *OCR NED:* P3 Interview required. Portfolio required.

W75 UNIVERSITY OF WOLVERHAMPTON
ADMISSIONS UNIT
MX207, CAMP STREET
WOLVERHAMPTON
WEST MIDLANDS WV1 1AD
t: 01902 321000 f: 01902 321896
e: admissions@wlv.ac.uk
// www.wlv.ac.uk

W211 BA Graphic Communication
Duration: 3FT/4SW Hon
Entry Requirements: *GCE:* 200. *IB:* 24. *BTEC Dip:* DM. *BTEC ExtDip:* MMP. *OCR ND:* M1 *OCR NED:* P1 Interview required. Portfolio required.

W292 BA Graphic Communication and Illustration
Duration: 3FT Hon
Entry Requirements: *GCE:* 200. *IB:* 24. *BTEC Dip:* DM. *BTEC ExtDip:* MMP. *OCR ND:* M1 *OCR NED:* P1 Interview required. Portfolio required.

W81 WORCESTER COLLEGE OF TECHNOLOGY
DEANSWAY
WORCESTER WR1 2JF
t: 01905 725555 f: 01905 28906
// www.wortech.ac.uk

412W HND Graphic Design
Duration: 2FT HND
Entry Requirements: *GCE:* 240. Interview required. Portfolio required.

Y70 YORK COLLEGE
SIM BALK LANE
YORK YO23 2BB
t: 01904 770448 f: 01904 770499
e: admissions.team@yorkcollege.ac.uk
// www.yorkcollege.ac.uk

W210 BA Graphic Design
Duration: 3FT Hon
Entry Requirements: *Foundation:* Pass. *GCE:* CC.

ILLUSTRATION AND BOOK ART

A50 AMERICAN INTERCONTINENTAL UNIVERSITY - LONDON
110 MARYLEBONE HIGH STREET
LONDON W1U 4RY
t: 020 7467 5640 f: 020 7467 5641
e: admissions@aiulondon.ac.uk
// www.aiulondon.ac.uk

W220 BA Visual Communication - Illustration
Duration: 4FT Hon
Entry Requirements: Contact the institution for details.

A60 ANGLIA RUSKIN UNIVERSITY
BISHOP HALL LANE
CHELMSFORD
ESSEX CM1 1SQ
t: 0845 271 3333 f: 01245 251789
e: answers@anglia.ac.uk
// www.anglia.ac.uk

W225 BA Illustration
Duration: 3FT Hon
Entry Requirements: *GCE:* 200-240. *SQAH:* CCCC. *SQAAH:* BC.
IB: 24. Interview required. Portfolio required.

A66 THE ARTS UNIVERSITY COLLEGE AT BOURNEMOUTH (FORMERLY ARTS INSTITUTE AT BOURNEMOUTH)
WALLISDOWN
POOLE
DORSET BH12 5HH
t: 01202 363228 f: 01202 537729
e: admissions@aucb.ac.uk
// www.aucb.ac.uk

W220 BA Illustration
Duration: 3FT Hon
Entry Requirements: *Foundation:* Pass. *GCE:* BBC. *IB:* 24. *OCR ND:* M1 *OCR NED:* M1 Interview required. Portfolio required.

B22 UNIVERSITY OF BEDFORDSHIRE
PARK SQUARE
LUTON
BEDS LU1 3JU
t: 0844 8482234 f: 01582 489323
e: admissions@beds.ac.uk
// www.beds.ac.uk

W220 BA Illustration
Duration: 3FT Hon
Entry Requirements: *GCE:* 160. Interview required. Portfolio required.

B25 BIRMINGHAM CITY UNIVERSITY
PERRY BARR
BIRMINGHAM B42 2SU
t: 0121 331 5595 f: 0121 331 7994
// www.bcu.ac.uk

W222 BA Textile Design (Constructed Textiles)
Duration: 3FT Hon
Entry Requirements: *GCE:* 280. *IB:* 28. Interview required. Portfolio required.

W223 BA Textile Design (Embroidery)
Duration: 3FT Hon
Entry Requirements: *GCE:* 280. *IB:* 28. Interview required. Portfolio required.

W220 BA Visual Communication (Illustration)
Duration: 3FT Hon
Entry Requirements: *GCE:* 280. *IB:* 28. Interview required. Portfolio required.

B41 BLACKPOOL AND THE FYLDE COLLEGE AN ASSOCIATE COLLEGE OF LANCASTER UNIVERSITY
ASHFIELD ROAD
BISPHAM
BLACKPOOL
LANCS FY2 0HB
t: 01253 504346 f: 01253 504198
e: admissions@blackpool.ac.uk
// www.blackpool.ac.uk

W220 BA Illustration
Duration: 3FT Hon
Entry Requirements: *Foundation:* Merit. *GCE:* 220. *IB:* 24. Interview required. Portfolio required.

B72 UNIVERSITY OF BRIGHTON

MITHRAS HOUSE 211
LEWES ROAD
BRIGHTON BN2 4AT
t: 01273 644644 f: 01273 642607
e: admissions@brighton.ac.uk
// www.brighton.ac.uk

W220 BA Illustration
Duration: 3FT Hon
Entry Requirements: *GCE:* BBC. Foundation Course required.
Interview required. Portfolio required.

W221 FdA Illustration
Duration: 2FT Fdg
Entry Requirements: *GCE:* 120. Interview required. Portfolio
required.

W222 MDes Illustration
Duration: 4FT Hon
Entry Requirements: *GCE:* BBC. Foundation Course required.
Interview required. Portfolio required.

B80 UNIVERSITY OF THE WEST OF ENGLAND, BRISTOL

FRENCHAY CAMPUS
COLDHARBOUR LANE
BRISTOL BS16 1QY
t: +44 (0)117 32 83333 f: +44 (0)117 32 82810
e: admissions@uwe.ac.uk
// www.uwe.ac.uk

W224 BA Illustration
Duration: 3FT Hon
Entry Requirements: *GCE:* 280. Interview required. Portfolio
required.

C20 CARDIFF METROPOLITAN UNIVERSITY (UWIC)

ADMISSIONS UNIT
LLANDAFF CAMPUS
WESTERN AVENUE
CARDIFF CF5 2YB
t: 029 2041 6070 f: 029 2041 6286
e: admissions@cardiffmet.ac.uk
// www.cardiffmet.ac.uk

W220 BA Illustration
Duration: 3FT Hon
Entry Requirements: *GCE:* 300. *IB:* 26. *BTEC ExtDip:* DDM. *OCR
NED:* M1 Foundation Course required. Interview required. Portfolio
required.

C30 UNIVERSITY OF CENTRAL LANCASHIRE

PRESTON
LANCS PR1 2HE
t: 01772 201201 f: 01772 894954
e: uadmissions@uclan.ac.uk
// www.uclan.ac.uk

W225 BA Illustration
Duration: 3FT Hon
Entry Requirements: *GCE:* 240-300. *IB:* 26. *OCR ND:* D *OCR
NED:* M3 Interview required. Portfolio required.

C93 UNIVERSITY FOR THE CREATIVE ARTS

FALKNER ROAD
FARNHAM
SURREY GU9 7DS
t: 01252 892960
e: admissions@ucreative.ac.uk
// www.ucreative.ac.uk

W220 BA Illustration
Duration: 3FT Hon
Entry Requirements: *GCE:* 220. *IB:* 24. *BTEC ExtDip:* PPP.
Interview required. Portfolio required.

C99 UNIVERSITY OF CUMBRIA

FUSEHILL STREET
CARLISLE
CUMBRIA CA1 2HH
t: 01228 616234 f: 01228 616235
// www.cumbria.ac.uk

W220 BA Illustration
Duration: 3FT Hon
Entry Requirements: *Foundation:* Pass. *GCE:* 240. *SQAH:* BBC.
SQAAH: CC. *IB:* 30. *OCR ND:* D Interview required. Portfolio
required.

W222 BA Illustration (with Year 0)
Duration: 4FT Hon
Entry Requirements: *Foundation:* Pass. *GCE:* C-cccc. *SQAH:* CC.
SQAAH: C. *IB:* 25. Interview required. Portfolio required.

D39 UNIVERSITY OF DERBY

KEDLESTON ROAD
DERBY DE22 1GB
t: 01332 591167 f: 01332 597724
e: askadmissions@derby.ac.uk
// www.derby.ac.uk

W220 BA Illustration
Duration: 3FT Hon
Entry Requirements: *Foundation:* Distinction. *GCE:* 260. *IB:* 28.
BTEC Dip: D*D*. *BTEC ExtDip:* DMM. *OCR NED:* M2 Interview
required. Portfolio required.

W290 FYr Illustration
Duration: 1FT FYr
Entry Requirements: *Foundation:* Pass. *GCE:* 160. *IB:* 24. *BTEC Dip:* D*D*. *BTEC ExtDip:* DMM. *OCR ND:* M2 *OCR NED:* P2 Interview required. Portfolio required.

W222 MDes Illustration
Duration: 4FT Hon
Entry Requirements: *Foundation:* Distinction. *GCE:* 260. *IB:* 28. *BTEC Dip:* D*D*. *BTEC ExtDip:* DMM. *OCR NED:* M2 Interview required. Portfolio required.

D65 UNIVERSITY OF DUNDEE
NETHERGATE
DUNDEE DD1 4HN
t: 01382 383838 f: 01382 388150
e: contactus@dundee.ac.uk
// www.dundee.ac.uk/admissions/ undergraduate/

W220 BDes Illustration
Duration: 3FT Hon
Entry Requirements: Foundation Course required. Interview required. Portfolio required.

E28 UNIVERSITY OF EAST LONDON
DOCKLANDS CAMPUS
UNIVERSITY WAY
LONDON E16 2RD
t: 020 8223 3333 f: 020 8223 2978
e: study@uel.ac.uk
// www.uel.ac.uk

W8W2 BA Creative & Professional Writing with Illustration
Duration: 3FT Hon
Entry Requirements: *GCE:* 240. *IB:* 24.

XW32 BA Early Childhood Studies and Illustration
Duration: 3FT Hon
Entry Requirements: *GCE:* 240. *IB:* 24.

WW6F BA Illustration/Photography
Duration: 3FT Hon
Entry Requirements: *GCE:* 200. *IB:* 24.

W6WA BA Photography with Illustration
Duration: 3FT Hon
Entry Requirements: *GCE:* 200. *IB:* 24. Portfolio required.

W228 BA Printed Textile Design (Extended)
Duration: 4FT Hon
Entry Requirements: *GCE:* 80. Interview required. Portfolio required.

WFW2 BA Printed Textile Design with Illustration
Duration: 3FT Hon
Entry Requirements: *GCE:* 200. *IB:* 24. Portfolio required.

E56 THE UNIVERSITY OF EDINBURGH
STUDENT RECRUITMENT & ADMISSIONS
57 GEORGE SQUARE
EDINBURGH EH8 9JU
t: 0131 650 4360 f: 0131 651 1236
e: sra.enquiries@ed.ac.uk
// www.ed.ac.uk/studying/undergraduate/

W220 BA Illustration
Duration: 4FT Hon
Entry Requirements: *Foundation:* Merit. *GCE:* BBB. *SQAH:* BBBB. *IB:* 34. Portfolio required.

F33 UNIVERSITY COLLEGE FALMOUTH
WOODLANE
FALMOUTH
CORNWALL TR11 4RH
t: 01326213730
e: admissions@falmouth.ac.uk
// www.falmouth.ac.uk

W221 BA(Hons) Illustration
Duration: 3FT Hon
Entry Requirements: *GCE:* 220. *IB:* 24. Interview required. Portfolio required.

G50 THE UNIVERSITY OF GLOUCESTERSHIRE
PARK CAMPUS
THE PARK
CHELTENHAM GL50 2RH
t: 01242 714501 f: 01242 714869
e: admissions@glos.ac.uk
// www.glos.ac.uk

W220 BA Illustration
Duration: 3FT Hon
Entry Requirements: *GCE:* 280-300. Interview required. Portfolio required.

H18 HEREFORD COLLEGE OF ARTS
FOLLY LANE
HEREFORD HR1 1LT
t: 01432 273359 f: 01432 341099
e: headmin@hca.ac.uk
// www.hca.ac.uk

W220 BA Illustration
Duration: 3FT Hon **CRB Check:** Required
Entry Requirements: *GCE:* 200. Interview required. Portfolio required.

W221 BA Illustration (top up)

Duration: 1FT Hon   **CRB Check:** Required
Entry Requirements: Interview required. Portfolio required. HND required.

H36 UNIVERSITY OF HERTFORDSHIRE

UNIVERSITY ADMISSIONS SERVICE
COLLEGE LANE
HATFIELD
HERTS AL10 9AB
t: 01707 284800
// www.herts.ac.uk

W220 FdA Illustration

Duration: 2FT Fdg
Entry Requirements: *GCE:* 80. Interview required. Portfolio required.

H60 THE UNIVERSITY OF HUDDERSFIELD

QUEENSGATE
HUDDERSFIELD HD1 3DH
t: 01484 473969 **f:** 01484 472765
e: admissionsandrecords@hud.ac.uk
// www.hud.ac.uk

W221 BA Illustration

Duration: 3FT/4SW Hon
Entry Requirements: *GCE:* 300. *SQAH:* BBBB. *IB:* 28. Interview required. Portfolio required.

H73 HULL COLLEGE

QUEEN'S GARDENS
HULL HU1 3DG
t: 01482 329943 **f:** 01482 598733
e: info@hull-college.ac.uk
// www.hull-college.ac.uk/higher-education

W220 BA Illustration

Duration: 3FT Hon
Entry Requirements: *GCE:* 200. Foundation Course required. Interview required. Portfolio required.

L39 UNIVERSITY OF LINCOLN

ADMISSIONS
BRAYFORD POOL
LINCOLN LN6 7TS
t: 01522 886097 **f:** 01522 886146
e: admissions@lincoln.ac.uk
// www.lincoln.ac.uk

W220 BA Illustration

Duration: 3FT Hon
Entry Requirements: *GCE:* 280. Interview required. Portfolio required.

L68 LONDON METROPOLITAN UNIVERSITY

166-220 HOLLOWAY ROAD
LONDON N7 8DB
t: 020 7133 4200
e: admissions@londonmet.ac.uk
// www.londonmet.ac.uk

W220 BA Illustration

Duration: 3FT Hon
Entry Requirements: *Foundation:* Merit. *GCE:* 240. *IB:* 28. Foundation Course required. Interview required. Portfolio required.

M80 MIDDLESEX UNIVERSITY

MIDDLESEX UNIVERSITY
THE BURROUGHS
LONDON NW4 4BT
t: 020 8411 5555 **f:** 020 8411 5649
e: enquiries@mdx.ac.uk
// www.mdx.ac.uk

W220 BA Illustration

Duration: 3FT Hon
Entry Requirements: *GCE:* 200-300. *IB:* 28. Interview required. Portfolio required.

N33 NEW COLLEGE STAMFORD

DRIFT ROAD
STAMFORD
LINCOLNSHIRE PE9 1XA
t: 01780 484300 **f:** 01780 484301
e: enquiries@stamford.ac.uk
// www.stamford.ac.uk

W220 FdA Illustration

Duration: 2FT Fdg
Entry Requirements: Interview required.

N38 UNIVERSITY OF NORTHAMPTON

PARK CAMPUS
BOUGHTON GREEN ROAD
NORTHAMPTON NN2 7AL
t: 0800 358 2232 **f:** 01604 722083
e: admissions@northampton.ac.uk
// www.northampton.ac.uk

W220 BA Illustration

Duration: 3FT Hon
Entry Requirements: *GCE:* 240-280. *SQAH:* AAB-BBBC. *IB:* 24. *BTEC Dip:* DD. *BTEC ExtDip:* DMM. *OCR ND:* D *OCR NED:* M2 Foundation Course required. Interview required.

N39 NORWICH UNIVERSITY COLLEGE OF THE ARTS

FRANCIS HOUSE
3-7 REDWELL STREET
NORWICH NR2 4SN
t: 01603 610561 f: 01603 615728
e: admissions@nuca.ac.uk
// www.nuca.ac.uk

W220 BA Illustration
Duration: 3FT Hon
Entry Requirements: *Foundation:* Merit. *GCE:* BBC. *BTEC Dip:* DM. *BTEC ExtDip:* MMM. *OCR ND:* M1 *OCR NED:* P1 Interview required. Portfolio required.

N41 NORTHBROOK COLLEGE SUSSEX

LITTLEHAMPTON ROAD
WORTHING
WEST SUSSEX BN12 6NU
t: 0845 155 6060 f: 01903 606073
e: enquiries@nbcol.ac.uk
// www.northbrook.ac.uk

W221 FdA Illustration
Duration: 2FT Fdg
Entry Requirements: *GCE:* 160. Interview required. Portfolio required.

N91 NOTTINGHAM TRENT UNIVERSITY

DRYDEN BUILDING
BURTON STREET
NOTTINGHAM NG1 4BU
t: +44 (0) 115 848 4200 f: +44 (0) 115 848 8869
e: applications@ntu.ac.uk
// www.ntu.ac.uk

W221 BA Textile Design
Duration: 3FT Hon
Entry Requirements: *GCE:* 280. *OCR NED:* M2 Interview required. Portfolio required.

O66 OXFORD BROOKES UNIVERSITY

ADMISSIONS OFFICE
HEADINGTON CAMPUS
GIPSY LANE
OXFORD OX3 0BP
t: 01865 483040 f: 01865 483983
e: admissions@brookes.ac.uk
// www.brookes.ac.uk

W220 BA Illustration-Narrative and Sequential (Swindon College)
Duration: 3FT Hon
Entry Requirements: Interview required. Portfolio required.

P51 PETROC

OLD STICKLEPATH HILL
BARNSTAPLE
NORTH DEVON EX31 2BQ
t: 01271 852365 f: 01271 338121
e: he@petroc.ac.uk
// www.petroc.ac.uk

W220 FdA Illustration
Duration: 2FT Fdg
Entry Requirements: *GCE:* 80.

P60 PLYMOUTH UNIVERSITY

DRAKE CIRCUS
PLYMOUTH PL4 8AA
t: 01752 585858 f: 01752 588055
e: admissions@plymouth.ac.uk
// www.plymouth.ac.uk

W222 BA Illustration
Duration: 3FT Hon
Entry Requirements: *Foundation:* Pass. *GCE:* 280. *IB:* 26. *BTEC ExtDip:* DMM. Interview required. Portfolio required.

P65 PLYMOUTH COLLEGE OF ART (FORMERLY PLYMOUTH COLLEGE OF ART AND DESIGN)

TAVISTOCK PLACE
PLYMOUTH PL4 8AT
t: 01752 203434 f: 01752 203444
e: infoservices@plymouthart.ac.uk
// www.plymouthart.ac.uk

W220 BA Illustration
Duration: 3FT Hon
Entry Requirements: *Foundation:* Pass. *IB:* 24. *OCR ND:* M1 *OCR NED:* P1 Interview required. Portfolio required.

WW2C BA Illustration (Top-Up)
Duration: 1FT Hon
Entry Requirements: Interview required. Portfolio required. HND required.

WW21 FdA Illustration
Duration: 2FT Fdg
Entry Requirements: *Foundation:* Pass. *IB:* 24. *OCR ND:* M1 *OCR NED:* P1 Interview required. Portfolio required.

WP24 FdA Illustration (including Level 0)
Duration: 3FT Fdg
Entry Requirements: *IB:* 24. *OCR ND:* P3 *OCR NED:* P3 Interview required. Portfolio required.

P80 UNIVERSITY OF PORTSMOUTH
ACADEMIC REGISTRY
UNIVERSITY HOUSE
WINSTON CHURCHILL AVENUE
PORTSMOUTH PO1 2UP
t: 023 9284 8484 f: 023 9284 3082
e: admissions@port.ac.uk
// www.port.ac.uk

W220 BA Illustration
Duration: 3FT Hon
Entry Requirements: *GCE:* 240-300. *IB:* 26. *BTEC SubDip:* P.
BTEC Dip: DD. *BTEC ExtDip:* DMM. Interview required. Portfolio required.

S30 SOUTHAMPTON SOLENT UNIVERSITY
EAST PARK TERRACE
SOUTHAMPTON
HAMPSHIRE SO14 0RT
t: +44 (0) 23 8031 9039 f: + 44 (0)23 8022 2259
e: admissions@solent.ac.uk
// www.solent.ac.uk/

W221 BA Illustration
Duration: 3FT Hon
Entry Requirements: *Foundation:* Merit. *GCE:* 200. *SQAAH:* AC-DDD. *IB:* 24. *BTEC ExtDip:* MMP. *OCR ND:* M1 *OCR NED:* P1
Portfolio required.

S32 SOUTH DEVON COLLEGE
LONG ROAD
PAIGNTON
DEVON TQ4 7EJ
t: 08000 213181 f: 01803 540541
e: university@southdevon.ac.uk
// www.southdevon.ac.uk/
welcome-to-university-level

W213 FdA Illustration Arts
Duration: 2FT Fdg
Entry Requirements: Contact the institution for details.

S72 STAFFORDSHIRE UNIVERSITY
COLLEGE ROAD
STOKE ON TRENT ST4 2DE
t: 01782 292753 f: 01782 292740
e: admissions@staffs.ac.uk
// www.staffs.ac.uk

W221 BA Entrepreneurship in Illustration
Duration: 1FT Hon
Entry Requirements: Interview required. Portfolio required.

W220 BA Illustration
Duration: 3FT/4FT Hon
Entry Requirements: *GCE:* 180-220. *IB:* 24. *BTEC Dip:* DD.
BTEC ExtDip: MMM. Interview required. Portfolio required.

S96 SWANSEA METROPOLITAN UNIVERSITY
MOUNT PLEASANT CAMPUS
SWANSEA SA1 6ED
t: 01792 481000 f: 01792 481061
e: gemma.green@smu.ac.uk
// www.smu.ac.uk

W220 BA General Illustration
Duration: 3FT Hon
Entry Requirements: *Foundation:* Pass. *GCE:* 200-360. *IB:* 24.
Interview required. Portfolio required.

U65 UNIVERSITY OF THE ARTS LONDON
272 HIGH HOLBORN
LONDON WC1V 7EY
t: 020 7514 6000x6197 f: 020 7514 6198
e: c.anderson@arts.ac.uk
// www.arts.ac.uk

W222 BA Illustration
Duration: 3FT Hon
Entry Requirements: *Foundation:* Pass. *GCE:* 80. *IB:* 28.
Interview required. Portfolio required.

W224 FdA Illustration
Duration: 2FT Fdg
Entry Requirements: *IB:* 28. Interview required. Portfolio required.

W50 UNIVERSITY OF WESTMINSTER
2ND FLOOR, CAVENDISH HOUSE
101 NEW CAVENDISH STREET,
LONDON W1W 6XH
t: 020 7915 5511
e: course-enquiries@westminster.ac.uk
// www.westminster.ac.uk

W220 BA Illustration and Visual Communication
Duration: 3FT Hon
Entry Requirements: *GCE:* CC. *SQAH:* CCCC. *IB:* 26. *OCR ND:* M1
Interview required. Portfolio required.

W75 UNIVERSITY OF WOLVERHAMPTON

ADMISSIONS UNIT
MX207, CAMP STREET
WOLVERHAMPTON
WEST MIDLANDS WV1 1AD
t: 01902 321000 f: 01902 321896
e: admissions@wlv.ac.uk
// www.wlv.ac.uk

W220 BA Illustration

Duration: 3FT/4SW Hon
Entry Requirements: *GCE:* 200. *IB:* 24. *BTEC Dip:* DM. *BTEC ExtDip:* MMP. *OCR ND:* M1 *OCR NED:* P1 Interview required. Portfolio required.

W80 UNIVERSITY OF WORCESTER

HENWICK GROVE
WORCESTER WR2 6AJ
t: 01905 855111 f: 01905 855377
e: admissions@worc.ac.uk
// www.worcester.ac.uk

WW82 BA Creative & Professional Writing and Illustration

Duration: 3FT Hon
Entry Requirements: Contact the institution for details.

QWF2 BA English Language Studies and Illustration

Duration: 3FT Hon
Entry Requirements: Contact the institution for details.

W220 BA Illustration

Duration: 3FT Hon
Entry Requirements: *GCE:* 220-300. *IB:* 24. *OCR ND:* D Interview required. Portfolio required.

INTERIOR, SPATIAL AND STRUCTURAL DESIGN

A50 AMERICAN INTERCONTINENTAL UNIVERSITY - LONDON

110 MARYLEBONE HIGH STREET
LONDON W1U 4RY
t: 020 7467 5640 f: 020 7467 5641
e: admissions@aiulondon.ac.uk
// www.aiulondon.ac.uk

W250 BA Interior Design

Duration: 4FT Hon
Entry Requirements: Contact the institution for details.

A60 ANGLIA RUSKIN UNIVERSITY

BISHOP HALL LANE
CHELMSFORD
ESSEX CM1 1SQ
t: 0845 271 3333 f: 01245 251789
e: answers@anglia.ac.uk
// www.anglia.ac.uk

W250 BA Interior Design

Duration: 3FT Hon
Entry Requirements: *GCE:* 200-240. *SQAH:* CCCC. *SQAAH:* BC. *IB:* 24. Interview required. Portfolio required.

A66 THE ARTS UNIVERSITY COLLEGE AT BOURNEMOUTH (FORMERLY ARTS INSTITUTE AT BOURNEMOUTH)

WALLISDOWN
POOLE
DORSET BH12 5HH
t: 01202 363228 f: 01202 537729
e: admissions@aucb.ac.uk
// www.aucb.ac.uk

KW12 BA Interior Architecture and Design

Duration: 3FT Hon
Entry Requirements: *Foundation:* Pass. *GCE:* BCC. *IB:* 24. *OCR ND:* M1 *OCR NED:* M1 Interview required. Portfolio required.

B22 UNIVERSITY OF BEDFORDSHIRE

PARK SQUARE
LUTON
BEDS LU1 3JU
t: 0844 8482234 f: 01582 489323
e: admissions@beds.ac.uk
// www.beds.ac.uk

W235 BA Interior Design

Duration: 3FT Hon
Entry Requirements: *GCE:* 160-240. *SQAH:* BCC. *SQAAH:* BCC. *IB:* 30. Interview required. Portfolio required.

B25 BIRMINGHAM CITY UNIVERSITY

PERRY BARR
BIRMINGHAM B42 2SU
t: 0121 331 5595 f: 0121 331 7994
// www.bcu.ac.uk

W250 BA Interior Design

Duration: 3FT Hon
Entry Requirements: *GCE:* 280. *IB:* 28. Interview required. Portfolio required.

W241 BA Interior Products Design

Duration: 3FT Hon
Entry Requirements: *GCE:* 280. *IB:* 28. Interview required. Portfolio required.

B40 BLACKBURN COLLEGE
FEILDEN STREET
BLACKBURN BB2 1LH
t: 01254 292594 f: 01254 679647
e: he-admissions@blackburn.ac.uk
// www.blackburn.ac.uk

W251 BA Design (Interiors, Top-Up)
Duration: 1FT Hon
Entry Requirements: HND required.

W250 FdA Interior Design
Duration: 2FT Fdg
Entry Requirements: *GCE:* 120.

B44 UNIVERSITY OF BOLTON
DEANE ROAD
BOLTON BL3 5AB
t: 01204 903903 f: 01204 399074
e: enquiries@bolton.ac.uk
// www.bolton.ac.uk

W252 BA Interior Design
Duration: 3FT Hon
Entry Requirements: *GCE:* 240. Interview required. Portfolio required.

B60 BRADFORD COLLEGE: AN ASSOCIATE COLLEGE OF LEEDS METROPOLITAN UNIVERSITY
GREAT HORTON ROAD
BRADFORD
WEST YORKSHIRE BD7 1AY
t: 01274 433008 f: 01274 431652
e: heregistry@bradfordcollege.ac.uk
// www.bradfordcollege.ac.uk/
university-centre

W250 BA Interior Design
Duration: 1FT Hon
Entry Requirements: Interview required. Portfolio required. HND required.

B72 UNIVERSITY OF BRIGHTON
MITHRAS HOUSE 211
LEWES ROAD
BRIGHTON BN2 4AT
t: 01273 644644 f: 01273 642607
e: admissions@brighton.ac.uk
// www.brighton.ac.uk

W250 BA Interior Architecture
Duration: 3FT Hon
Entry Requirements: *GCE:* BBB. *IB:* 30. Interview required. Portfolio required.

C85 COVENTRY UNIVERSITY
THE STUDENT CENTRE
COVENTRY UNIVERSITY
1 GULSON RD
COVENTRY CV1 2JH
t: 024 7615 2222 f: 024 7615 2223
e: studentenquiries@coventry.ac.uk
// www.coventry.ac.uk

W250 BA Interior Design
Duration: 3FT/4SW Hon
Entry Requirements: *Foundation:* Merit. *GCE:* CCC. *SQAH:* CCCCC. *IB:* 27. *BTEC ExtDip:* MMM. *OCR NED:* M3 Interview required. Portfolio required.

W251 MDes Interior Design
Duration: 4FT Hon
Entry Requirements: *Foundation:* Merit. *GCE:* CCC. *SQAH:* CCCCC. *IB:* 27. *BTEC ExtDip:* MMM. *OCR NED:* M3 Interview required. Portfolio required.

C93 UNIVERSITY FOR THE CREATIVE ARTS
FALKNER ROAD
FARNHAM
SURREY GU9 7DS
t: 01252 892960
e: admissions@ucreative.ac.uk
// www.ucreative.ac.uk

W251 BA Interior Architecture and Design
Duration: 3FT Hon
Entry Requirements: *GCE:* 220. *IB:* 24. *BTEC ExtDip:* PPP. Interview required. Portfolio required.

W252 BA Interior Architecture and Design
Duration: 3FT Hon
Entry Requirements: *GCE:* 220. *IB:* 24. *BTEC ExtDip:* PPP. Interview required. Portfolio required.

D26 DE MONTFORT UNIVERSITY
THE GATEWAY
LEICESTER LE1 9BH
t: 0116 255 1551 f: 0116 250 6204
e: enquiries@dmu.ac.uk
// www.dmu.ac.uk

W250 BA Interior Design
Duration: 3FT Hon
Entry Requirements: *Foundation:* Pass. *GCE:* 260. *IB:* 28. *BTEC Dip:* D*D. *BTEC ExtDip:* MMM. Interview required. Portfolio required.

W252 FdA Interior Design
Duration: 2FT Fdg
Entry Requirements: *GCE:* 80. *IB:* 26. Interview required. Portfolio required.

NW22 FdA Leadership & Enterprise (Interior Design)
Duration: 2FT Fdg
Entry Requirements: *GCE:* 80. *IB:* 26. Interview required. Portfolio required.

W253 MDes Interior Design
Duration: 4FT Hon
Entry Requirements: *Foundation:* Pass. *GCE:* 280. *IB:* 30. *BTEC Dip:* D*D*. *BTEC ExtDip:* DMM. Interview required. Portfolio required.

D65 UNIVERSITY OF DUNDEE
NETHERGATE
DUNDEE DD1 4HN
t: 01382 383838 f: 01382 388150
e: contactus@dundee.ac.uk
// www.dundee.ac.uk/admissions/undergraduate/

W250 BDes Interior Environmental Design
Duration: 3FT Hon
Entry Requirements: Foundation Course required. Interview required. Portfolio required.

E56 THE UNIVERSITY OF EDINBURGH
STUDENT RECRUITMENT & ADMISSIONS
57 GEORGE SQUARE
EDINBURGH EH8 9JU
t: 0131 650 4360 f: 0131 651 1236
e: sra.enquiries@ed.ac.uk
// www.ed.ac.uk/studying/undergraduate/

W250 BA Interior Design
Duration: 4FT Hon
Entry Requirements: *Foundation:* Merit. *GCE:* BBB. *SQAH:* BBBB. *IB:* 34. Portfolio required.

E59 EDINBURGH NAPIER UNIVERSITY
CRAIGLOCKHART CAMPUS
EDINBURGH EH14 1DJ
t: +44 (0)8452 60 60 40 f: 0131 455 6464
e: info@napier.ac.uk
// www.napier.ac.uk

W251 BDes Interior and Spatial Design
Duration: 3FT/4FT Ord/Hon
Entry Requirements: Contact the institution for details.

F33 UNIVERSITY COLLEGE FALMOUTH
WOODLANE
FALMOUTH
CORNWALL TR11 4RH
t: 01326213730
e: admissions@falmouth.ac.uk
// www.falmouth.ac.uk

W252 BA(Hons) Interior Design
Duration: 3FT Hon
Entry Requirements: *GCE:* 220. *IB:* 24. Interview required. Portfolio required.

G14 UNIVERSITY OF GLAMORGAN, CARDIFF AND PONTYPRIDD
ENQUIRIES AND ADMISSIONS UNIT
PONTYPRIDD CF37 1DL
t: 08456 434030 f: 01443 654050
e: enquiries@glam.ac.uk
// www.glam.ac.uk

W250 BA Interior Design
Duration: 3FT Hon
Entry Requirements: *Foundation:* Pass. *GCE:* BBC. *IB:* 25. *BTEC SubDip:* M. *BTEC Dip:* D*D*. *BTEC ExtDip:* DMM. *OCR ND:* M1 *OCR NED:* M2 Interview required. Portfolio required.

W252 BA Interior Design
Duration: 4SW Hon
Entry Requirements: *GCE:* BBC. *IB:* 25. *BTEC SubDip:* M. *BTEC Dip:* D*D*. *BTEC ExtDip:* DMM. *OCR NED:* M2 Interview required. Portfolio required.

G42 GLASGOW CALEDONIAN UNIVERSITY
STUDENT RECRUITMENT & ADMISSIONS SERVICE
CITY CAMPUS
COWCADDENS ROAD
GLASGOW G4 0BA
t: 0141 331 3000 f: 0141 331 8676
e: undergraduate@gcu.ac.uk
// www.gcu.ac.uk

W250 BA Interior Design (Top-Up)
Duration: 1FT/2FT Hon
Entry Requirements: Interview required. Portfolio required. HND required.

G43 THE GLASGOW SCHOOL OF ART
167 RENFREW STREET
GLASGOW G3 6RQ
t: 0141 353 4434/4514 f: 0141 353 4408
e: admissions@gsa.ac.uk
// www.gsa.ac.uk

W250 BA Interior Design
Duration: 4FT Hon
Entry Requirements: *GCE:* ABB. *SQAH:* AABB-ABBB. *IB:* 30.
Interview required. Portfolio required.

H24 HERIOT-WATT UNIVERSITY, EDINBURGH
EDINBURGH CAMPUS
EDINBURGH EH14 4AS
t: 0131 449 5111 f: 0131 451 3630
e: ugadmissions@hw.ac.uk
// www.hw.ac.uk

W250 BA Interior Design (Top-Up)
Duration: 2FT Hon
Entry Requirements: Portfolio required.

H36 UNIVERSITY OF HERTFORDSHIRE
UNIVERSITY ADMISSIONS SERVICE
COLLEGE LANE
HATFIELD
HERTS AL10 9AB
t: 01707 284800
// www.herts.ac.uk

W251 BA Interior Architecture and Design
Duration: 3FT Hon
Entry Requirements: *GCE:* 240. Interview required. Portfolio required.

H60 THE UNIVERSITY OF HUDDERSFIELD
QUEENSGATE
HUDDERSFIELD HD1 3DH
t: 01484 473969 f: 01484 472765
e: admissionsandrecords@hud.ac.uk
// www.hud.ac.uk

W250 BA Interior Design
Duration: 3FT/4SW Hon
Entry Requirements: *GCE:* 300. *SQAH:* BBBB. *IB:* 28. Interview required. Portfolio required.

H73 HULL COLLEGE
QUEEN'S GARDENS
HULL HU1 3DG
t: 01482 329943 f: 01482 598733
e: info@hull-college.ac.uk
// www.hull-college.ac.uk/higher-education

W252 FdA Interior Architectural Design
Duration: 2FT Fdg
Entry Requirements: *GCE:* 80. Interview required. Portfolio required.

K84 KINGSTON UNIVERSITY
STUDENT INFORMATION & ADVICE CENTRE
COOPER HOUSE
40-46 SURBITON ROAD
KINGSTON UPON THAMES KT1 2HX
t: 0844 8552177 f: 020 8547 7080
e: aps@kingston.ac.uk
// www.kingston.ac.uk

W250 BA Interior Design
Duration: 3FT Hon
Entry Requirements: Interview required. Portfolio required.

L27 LEEDS METROPOLITAN UNIVERSITY
COURSE ENQUIRIES OFFICE
CITY CAMPUS
LEEDS LS1 3HE
t: 0113 81 23113 f: 0113 81 23129
// www.leedsmet.ac.uk

W251 BA Interior Architecture and Design
Duration: 3FT Hon
Entry Requirements: *GCE:* 280-300. Interview required. Portfolio required.

L39 UNIVERSITY OF LINCOLN
ADMISSIONS
BRAYFORD POOL
LINCOLN LN6 7TS
t: 01522 886097 f: 01522 886146
e: admissions@lincoln.ac.uk
// www.lincoln.ac.uk

W250 BA Interior Architecture and Design
Duration: 3FT Hon
Entry Requirements: *GCE:* 280. Interview required. Portfolio required.

L51 LIVERPOOL JOHN MOORES UNIVERSITY
KINGSWAY HOUSE
HATTON GARDEN
LIVERPOOL L3 2AJ
t: 0151 231 5090 f: 0151 904 6368
e: courses@ljmu.ac.uk
// www.ljmu.ac.uk

W250 BA Spatial Design
Duration: 3FT Hon
Entry Requirements: GCE: 260. IB: 28. Interview required.
Portfolio required.

L68 LONDON METROPOLITAN UNIVERSITY
166-220 HOLLOWAY ROAD
LONDON N7 8DB
t: 020 7133 4200
e: admissions@londonmet.ac.uk
// www.londonmet.ac.uk

KW12 BA Architecture and Interior Design Extended degree
Duration: 4FT Hon
Entry Requirements: GCE: 120. IB: 28. Interview required.
Portfolio required.

WK21 BA Interior Design
Duration: 3FT Hon
Entry Requirements: Foundation: Pass. GCE: 280. IB: 28.
Foundation Course required. Interview required. Portfolio required.

W251 FdA Interior Design
Duration: 2FT Fdg
Entry Requirements: Foundation: Pass. GCE: 80. IB: 28.
Foundation Course required. Interview required. Portfolio required.

M10 THE MANCHESTER COLLEGE
OPENSHAW CAMPUS
ASHTON OLD ROAD
OPENSHAW
MANCHESTER M11 2WH
t: 0800 068 8585 f: 0161 920 4103
e: enquiries@themanchestercollege.ac.uk
// www.themanchestercollege.ac.uk

W250 FdA Interior Design
Duration: 2FT Fdg
Entry Requirements: Contact the institution for details.

M40 THE MANCHESTER METROPOLITAN UNIVERSITY
ADMISSIONS OFFICE
ALL SAINTS (GMS)
ALL SAINTS
MANCHESTER M15 6BH
t: 0161 247 2000
// www.mmu.ac.uk

W250 BA Interior Design
Duration: 3FT Hon
Entry Requirements: GCE: 280-300. IB: 29. Interview required.

M80 MIDDLESEX UNIVERSITY
MIDDLESEX UNIVERSITY
THE BURROUGHS
LONDON NW4 4BT
t: 020 8411 5555 f: 020 8411 5649
e: enquiries@mdx.ac.uk
// www.mdx.ac.uk

W250 BA Interior Architecture and Design
Duration: 3FT Hon
Entry Requirements: GCE: 200-300. IB: 28. Interview required.
Portfolio required.

N23 NEWCASTLE COLLEGE
STUDENT SERVICES
RYE HILL CAMPUS
SCOTSWOOD ROAD
NEWCASTLE UPON TYNE NE4 7SA
t: 0191 200 4110 f: 0191 200 4349
e: enquiries@ncl-coll.ac.uk
// www.newcastlecollege.co.uk

W250 FdA Interior Architecture
Duration: 2FT Fdg
Entry Requirements: Foundation: Pass. GCE: 120-165. OCR ND:
P2 OCR NED: P3 Foundation Course required. Interview required.
Portfolio required.

N38 UNIVERSITY OF NORTHAMPTON
PARK CAMPUS
BOUGHTON GREEN ROAD
NORTHAMPTON NN2 7AL
t: 0800 358 2232 f: 01604 722083
e: admissions@northampton.ac.uk
// www.northampton.ac.uk

W250 BA Interior Design
Duration: 3FT Hon
Entry Requirements: GCE: 240-280. SQAH: AAB-BBBC. IB: 24.
BTEC Dip: DD. BTEC ExtDip: DMM. OCR ND: D OCR NED: M2
Foundation Course required. Interview required.

W251 BA Interior Design (top-up)
Duration: 1FT Hon
Entry Requirements: Interview required. HND required.

052W HND Interior Design
Duration: 2FT HND
Entry Requirements: *GCE:* 80-120. *SQAH:* BC-CCC. *IB:* 24. *BTEC Dip:* MP. *BTEC ExtDip:* MPP. *OCR ND:* P1 *OCR NED:* P2 Interview required. Portfolio required.

N77 NORTHUMBRIA UNIVERSITY
TRINITY BUILDING
NORTHUMBERLAND ROAD
NEWCASTLE UPON TYNE NE1 8ST
t: 0191 243 7420 f: 0191 227 4561
e: er.admissions@northumbria.ac.uk
// www.northumbria.ac.uk

W251 BA Interior Architecture
Duration: 3FT Hon
Entry Requirements: *GCE:* 300. *SQAH:* BBBBC. *SQAAH:* BBC. *IB:* 26. *BTEC ExtDip:* DDM. *OCR ND:* D Interview required. Portfolio required.

W250 BA Honours Interior Design
Duration: 3FT Hon
Entry Requirements: *Foundation:* Distinction. *GCE:* 300. *SQAH:* BBBBC. *SQAAH:* BBC. *IB:* 26. *BTEC Dip:* DM. *BTEC ExtDip:* DDM. *OCR NED:* M2 Interview required. Portfolio required.

N91 NOTTINGHAM TRENT UNIVERSITY
DRYDEN BUILDING
BURTON STREET
NOTTINGHAM NG1 4BU
t: +44 (0) 115 848 4200 f: +44 (0) 115 848 8869
e: applications@ntu.ac.uk
// www.ntu.ac.uk

W250 BA Interior Architecture and Design
Duration: 3FT/4SW Hon
Entry Requirements: *GCE:* 340. *BTEC ExtDip:* DDD. *OCR NED:* D1

O66 OXFORD BROOKES UNIVERSITY
ADMISSIONS OFFICE
HEADINGTON CAMPUS
GIPSY LANE
OXFORD OX3 0BP
t: 01865 483040 f: 01865 483983
e: admissions@brookes.ac.uk
// www.brookes.ac.uk

W250 BA Interior Architecture
Duration: 3FT Hon
Entry Requirements: *GCE:* ABB.

P80 UNIVERSITY OF PORTSMOUTH
ACADEMIC REGISTRY
UNIVERSITY HOUSE
WINSTON CHURCHILL AVENUE
PORTSMOUTH PO1 2UP
t: 023 9284 8484 f: 023 9284 3082
e: admissions@port.ac.uk
// www.port.ac.uk

W251 BA Interior Design
Duration: 3FT Hon
Entry Requirements: *GCE:* 220-320. *IB:* 28. *BTEC SubDip:* P. *BTEC Dip:* DD. *BTEC ExtDip:* MMM.

R06 RAVENSBOURNE
6 PENROSE WAY
GREENWICH PENINSULA
LONDON SE10 0EW
t: 020 3040 3998
e: info@rave.ac.uk
// www.rave.ac.uk

WK21 BA Interior Design Environment Architecture (with Foundation Year)
Duration: 4FT Hon
Entry Requirements: *Foundation:* Pass. *GCE:* A-E. *IB:* 28. Interview required. Portfolio required.

W250 BA Interior Design Environment Architectures
Duration: 3FT Hon
Entry Requirements: *Foundation:* Pass. *GCE:* AA-CC. *IB:* 28. Interview required. Portfolio required.

W251 BA Interior Design Environment Architectures (Fast-track)
Duration: 2FT Hon
Entry Requirements: Contact the institution for details.

S21 SHEFFIELD HALLAM UNIVERSITY
CITY CAMPUS
HOWARD STREET
SHEFFIELD S1 1WB
t: 0114 225 5555 f: 0114 225 2167
e: admissions@shu.ac.uk
// www.shu.ac.uk

W250 BA Interior Design
Duration: 3FT Hon
Entry Requirements: *Foundation:* Pass. *GCE:* 260. Interview required. Portfolio required.

W251 MDes Interior Design
Duration: 4FT Hon
Entry Requirements: *Foundation:* Pass. *GCE:* 280.

S28 SOMERSET COLLEGE OF ARTS AND TECHNOLOGY
WELLINGTON ROAD
TAUNTON
SOMERSET TA1 5AX
t: 01823 366331 f: 01823 366418
e: enquiries@somerset.ac.uk
// www.somerset.ac.uk/student-area/
considering-a-degree.html

W235 BA Design (Interior Textiles & Surface Design)
Duration: 3FT Hon
Entry Requirements: *Foundation:* Pass. *GCE:* 180. *IB:* 24.
Interview required. Portfolio required.

W237 BA Design (Interior Textiles)
Duration: 3FT Hon
Entry Requirements: *Foundation:* Pass. *GCE:* 180. *IB:* 24.
Interview required. Portfolio required.

S30 SOUTHAMPTON SOLENT UNIVERSITY
EAST PARK TERRACE
SOUTHAMPTON
HAMPSHIRE SO14 0RT
t: +44 (0) 23 8031 9039 f: + 44 (0)23 8022 2259
e: admissions@solent.ac.uk
// www.solent.ac.uk/

W250 BA Interior Design
Duration: 3FT Hon
Entry Requirements: *GCE:* 120.

W252 BA Interior Design (Decoration)
Duration: 3FT Hon
Entry Requirements: *Foundation:* Merit. *GCE:* 200. *SQAAH:* AC-DDD. *IB:* 24. *BTEC ExtDip:* MMP. *OCR ND:* M1 *OCR NED:* P1
Portfolio required.

W251 BA Interior Design (with foundation)
Duration: 4FT Hon
Entry Requirements: *GCE:* 40.

S43 SOUTH ESSEX COLLEGE OF FURTHER & HIGHER EDUCATION
LUKER ROAD
SOUTHEND-ON-SEA
ESSEX SS1 1ND
t: 0845 52 12345 f: 01702 432320
e: Admissions@southessex.ac.uk
// www.southessex.ac.uk

W250 BA Interior Design
Duration: 3FT Hon
Entry Requirements: *GCE:* 160. *IB:* 24. Interview required.
Portfolio required.

W251 CertHE Interior Design
Duration: 1FT Cer
Entry Requirements: Contact the institution for details.

W252 DipHE Interior Design
Duration: 2FT Dip
Entry Requirements: Contact the institution for details.

S76 STOCKPORT COLLEGE
WELLINGTON ROAD SOUTH
STOCKPORT SK1 3UQ
t: 0161 958 3143 f: 0161 958 3663
e: susan.kelly@stockport.ac.uk
// www.stockport.ac.uk

W250 FdA Interior Design with Sustainability
Duration: 2FT Fdg
Entry Requirements: Interview required. Portfolio required.

S82 UNIVERSITY CAMPUS SUFFOLK (UCS)
WATERFRONT BUILDING
NEPTUNE QUAY
IPSWICH
SUFFOLK IP4 1QJ
t: 01473 338833 f: 01473 339900
e: info@ucs.ac.uk
// www.ucs.ac.uk

W261 BA Interior Architecture and Design
Duration: 3FT Hon
Entry Requirements: *GCE:* 240-280. *IB:* 28. *BTEC ExtDip:* DMM.
Interview required. Portfolio required.

S84 UNIVERSITY OF SUNDERLAND
STUDENT HELPLINE
THE STUDENT GATEWAY
CHESTER ROAD
SUNDERLAND SR1 3SD
t: 0191 515 3000 f: 0191 515 3805
e: student.helpline@sunderland.ac.uk
// www.sunderland.ac.uk

W250 BA Interior Design
Duration: 3FT Hon
Entry Requirements: *Foundation:* Merit. *GCE:* 220. *SQAH:* BBBC.
IB: 22. Interview required. Portfolio required.

S96 SWANSEA METROPOLITAN UNIVERSITY
MOUNT PLEASANT CAMPUS
SWANSEA SA1 6ED
t: 01792 481000 f: 01792 481061
e: gemma.green@smu.ac.uk
// www.smu.ac.uk

W235 BA Surface Pattern Design (Textiles for Interiors)
Duration: 3FT Hon
Entry Requirements: *Foundation:* Pass. *GCE:* 200-360. *IB:* 24.
Interview required. Portfolio required.

T20 TEESSIDE UNIVERSITY
MIDDLESBROUGH TS1 3BA
t: 01642 218121 f: 01642 384201
e: registry@tees.ac.uk
// www.tees.ac.uk

W255 BA Interior Architecture
Duration: 3FT Hon
Entry Requirements: *Foundation:* Distinction. *GCE:* 280. *IB:* 25.
Interview required. Portfolio required.

W250 BA Interior Design
Duration: 3FT Hon
Entry Requirements: *Foundation:* Distinction. *GCE:* 280. *IB:* 25.
Interview required. Portfolio required.

T85 TRURO AND PENWITH COLLEGE
TRURO COLLEGE
COLLEGE ROAD
TRURO
CORNWALL TR1 3XX
t: 01872 267122 f: 01872 267526
e: heinfo@trurocollege.ac.uk
// www.truro-penwith.ac.uk

W250 FdA Interior Design Practice
Duration: 2FT Fdg
Entry Requirements: *GCE:* 60. *IB:* 24. *BTEC Dip:* MP. *BTEC ExtDip:* PPP. Interview required.

U20 UNIVERSITY OF ULSTER
COLERAINE
CO. LONDONDERRY
NORTHERN IRELAND BT52 1SA
t: 028 7012 4221 f: 028 7012 4908
e: online@ulster.ac.uk
// www.ulster.ac.uk

W250 BDes Design for Creative Practice
Duration: 3FT/4SW Hon
Entry Requirements: *GCE:* CCC. *IB:* 24. Interview required.
Portfolio required.

W251 BDes Hons Interior Design
Duration: 3FT/4SW Hon
Entry Requirements: Interview required. Portfolio required.

U65 UNIVERSITY OF THE ARTS LONDON
272 HIGH HOLBORN
LONDON WC1V 7EY
t: 020 7514 6000x6197 f: 020 7514 6198
e: c.anderson@arts.ac.uk
// www.arts.ac.uk

W250 BA Interior and Spatial Design
Duration: 3FT Hon
Entry Requirements: *Foundation:* Pass. *GCE:* 80. *IB:* 28.
Foundation Course required. Portfolio required.

W12 WALSALL COLLEGE
WALSALL COLLEGE
LITTLETON STREET WEST
WALSALL
WEST MIDLANDS WS2 8ES
t: 01922 657000 f: 01922 657083
e: ckemp@walsallcollege.ac.uk
// www.walsallcollege.ac.uk

05FW HNC Interior Design
Duration: 1FT HNC
Entry Requirements: Contact the institution for details.

02MW HND Interior Design
Duration: 2FT HND
Entry Requirements: Contact the institution for details.

W50 UNIVERSITY OF WESTMINSTER
2ND FLOOR, CAVENDISH HOUSE
101 NEW CAVENDISH STREET,
LONDON W1W 6XH
t: 020 7915 5511
e: course-enquiries@westminster.ac.uk
// www.westminster.ac.uk

W250 BA Interior Architecture
Duration: 3FT Hon
Entry Requirements: *GCE:* BBB. Interview required.

W85 WRITTLE COLLEGE
ADMISSIONS
WRITTLE COLLEGE
CHELMSFORD
ESSEX CM1 3RR
t: 01245 424200 f: 01245 420456
e: admissions@writtle.ac.uk
// www.writtle.ac.uk

W251 BA Interior Architecture
Duration: 3FT Hon
Entry Requirements: *Foundation:* Distinction. *GCE:* 260. *IB:* 24.
BTEC Dip: D*D*. *BTEC ExtDip:* DMM. *OCR NED:* M2

W250 BA Interior Design
Duration: 3FT Hon
Entry Requirements: *Foundation:* Distinction. *GCE:* 260. *IB:* 24.
BTEC Dip: D*D*. *BTEC ExtDip:* DMM. *OCR NED:* M2

W290 FdA Interior Design - Commercial and Residential
Duration: 2FT Fdg
Entry Requirements: *GCE:* 180. *IB:* 24. *BTEC Dip:* DM. *BTEC ExtDip:* MMP. *OCR NED:* P1 Foundation Course required. Interview required. Portfolio required.

JEWELLERY AND DESIGNED METAL

B25 BIRMINGHAM CITY UNIVERSITY
PERRY BARR
BIRMINGHAM B42 2SU
t: 0121 331 5595 f: 0121 331 7994
// www.bcu.ac.uk

W723 BA Horology
Duration: 3FT Hon
Entry Requirements: Contact the institution for details.

C93 UNIVERSITY FOR THE CREATIVE ARTS
FALKNER ROAD
FARNHAM
SURREY GU9 7DS
t: 01252 892960
e: admissions@ucreative.ac.uk
// www.ucreative.ac.uk

W721 BA Silversmithing, Goldsmithing and Jewellery
Duration: 3FT Hon
Entry Requirements: *GCE:* 220. *IB:* 24. *BTEC ExtDip:* PPP.
Interview required. Portfolio required.

D65 UNIVERSITY OF DUNDEE
NETHERGATE
DUNDEE DD1 4HN
t: 01382 383838 f: 01382 388150
e: contactus@dundee.ac.uk
// www.dundee.ac.uk/admissions/
undergraduate/

W720 BDes Jewellery & Metal Design
Duration: 3FT Hon
Entry Requirements: Foundation Course required. Interview required. Portfolio required.

G43 THE GLASGOW SCHOOL OF ART
167 RENFREW STREET
GLASGOW G3 6RQ
t: 0141 353 4434/4514 f: 0141 353 4408
e: admissions@gsa.ac.uk
// www.gsa.ac.uk

W721 BA Silversmithing & Jewellery Design
Duration: 4FT Hon
Entry Requirements: *GCE:* ABB. *SQAH:* AABB-ABBB. *IB:* 30.
Interview required. Portfolio required.

H18 HEREFORD COLLEGE OF ARTS
FOLLY LANE
HEREFORD HR1 1LT
t: 01432 273359 f: 01432 341099
e: headmin@hca.ac.uk
// www.hca.ac.uk

W720 BA Artist Blacksmithing
Duration: 3FT Hon **CRB Check:** Required
Entry Requirements: *GCE:* 200. Interview required. Portfolio required.

W721 BA Jewellery Design (Top-Up)
Duration: 1FT Hon **CRB Check:** Required
Entry Requirements: Interview required. Portfolio required. HND required.

L39 UNIVERSITY OF LINCOLN
ADMISSIONS
BRAYFORD POOL
LINCOLN LN6 7TS
t: 01522 886097 f: 01522 886146
e: admissions@lincoln.ac.uk
// www.lincoln.ac.uk

W720 BA Jewellery and Object
Duration: 3FT Hon
Entry Requirements: *GCE:* 280. Interview required. Portfolio required.

L68 LONDON METROPOLITAN UNIVERSITY
166-220 HOLLOWAY ROAD
LONDON N7 8DB
t: 020 7133 4200
e: admissions@londonmet.ac.uk
// www.londonmet.ac.uk

W724 BA Jewellery and Silversmithing
Duration: 3FT Hon
Entry Requirements: *Foundation:* Merit. *GCE:* 240. *IB:* 28. Foundation Course required. Interview required. Portfolio required.

P65 PLYMOUTH COLLEGE OF ART (FORMERLY PLYMOUTH COLLEGE OF ART AND DESIGN)
TAVISTOCK PLACE
PLYMOUTH PL4 8AT
t: 01752 203434 f: 01752 203444
e: infoservices@plymouthart.ac.uk
// www.plymouthart.ac.uk

W722 BA (Hons) Jewellery and Silversmithing
Duration: 3FT Hon
Entry Requirements: Contact the institution for details.

W721 BA (Hons) Jewellery and Silversmithing (Top-Up)
Duration: 1FT Hon
Entry Requirements: Contact the institution for details.

S21 SHEFFIELD HALLAM UNIVERSITY
CITY CAMPUS
HOWARD STREET
SHEFFIELD S1 1WB
t: 0114 225 5555 f: 0114 225 2167
e: admissions@shu.ac.uk
// www.shu.ac.uk

W721 BA Metalwork and Jewellery
Duration: 3FT Hon
Entry Requirements: *GCE:* 240. Interview required. Portfolio required.

W724 MDes Metalwork and Jewellery
Duration: 4FT Hon
Entry Requirements: *GCE:* 260. Interview required. Portfolio required.

T85 TRURO AND PENWITH COLLEGE
TRURO COLLEGE
COLLEGE ROAD
TRURO
CORNWALL TR1 3XX
t: 01872 267122 f: 01872 267526
e: heinfo@trurocollege.ac.uk
// www.truro-penwith.ac.uk

W724 BA (Hons) Silversmithing and Jewellery
Duration: 1FT Deg
Entry Requirements: Interview required.

W721 FdA Silversmithing and Jewellery
Duration: 2FT Fdg
Entry Requirements: *GCE:* 60. *IB:* 24. *BTEC Dip:* MP. *BTEC ExtDip:* PPP. Interview required.

PHOTOGRAPHY, VIDEO & LENS MEDIA

A20 THE UNIVERSITY OF ABERDEEN
UNIVERSITY OFFICE
KING'S COLLEGE
ABERDEEN AB24 3FX
t: +44 (0) 1224 273504 f: +44 (0) 1224 272034
e: sras@abdn.ac.uk
// www.abdn.ac.uk/sras

LW66 MA Anthropology and Film & Visual Culture
Duration: 4FT Hon
Entry Requirements: *GCE:* BBB. *SQAH:* BBBB. *IB:* 30.

VW66 MA Divinity and Film & Visual Culture
Duration: 4FT Hon
Entry Requirements: *GCE:* BBB. *SQAH:* BBBB. *IB:* 30.

QW36 MA English and Film & Visual Culture
Duration: 4FT Hon
Entry Requirements: *GCE:* BBB. *SQAH:* BBBB. *IB:* 30.

WR61 MA Film & Visual Culture and French
Duration: 4FT Hon
Entry Requirements: *GCE:* BBB. *SQAH:* BBBB. *IB:* 30.

WR6C MA Film & Visual Culture and French
Duration: 5FT Hon
Entry Requirements: *GCE:* BBB. *SQAH:* BBBB. *IB:* 30.

QW56 MA Film & Visual Culture and Gaelic Studies
Duration: 4FT Hon
Entry Requirements: *GCE:* BBB. *SQAH:* BBBB. *IB:* 30.

WR62 MA Film & Visual Culture and German
Duration: 4FT Hon
Entry Requirements: *GCE:* BBB. *SQAH:* BBBB. *IB:* 30.

WR6F MA Film & Visual Culture and German
Duration: 5FT Hon
Entry Requirements: *GCE:* BBB. *SQAH:* BBBB. *IB:* 30.

WR64 MA Film & Visual Culture and Hispanic Studies
Duration: 4FT Hon
Entry Requirements: *GCE:* BBB. *SQAH:* BBBB. *IB:* 30.

WR6K MA Film & Visual Culture and Hispanic Studies
Duration: 5FT Hon
Entry Requirements: *GCE:* BBB. *SQAH:* BBBB. *IB:* 30.

WV61 MA Film & Visual Culture and History
Duration: 4FT Hon
Entry Requirements: *GCE:* BBB. *SQAH:* BBBB. *IB:* 30.

WL62 MA Film & Visual Culture and International Relations
Duration: 4FT Hon
Entry Requirements: *GCE:* BBB. *SQAH:* BBBB. *IB:* 30.

WQ62 MA Film & Visual Culture and Literature in a World Context
Duration: 4FT Hon
Entry Requirements: *GCE:* BBB. *SQAH:* BBBB. *IB:* 30.

WV65 MA Film & Visual Culture and Philosophy
Duration: 4FT Hon
Entry Requirements: *GCE:* BBB. *SQAH:* BBBB. *IB:* 30.

WL6F MA Film & Visual Culture and Politics
Duration: 4FT Hon
Entry Requirements: *GCE:* BBB. *SQAH:* BBBB. *IB:* 30.

WV66 MA Film & Visual Culture and Religious Studies
Duration: 4FT Hon
Entry Requirements: *GCE:* BBB. *SQAH:* BBBB. *IB:* 30.

LW36 MA Film & Visual Culture and Sociology
Duration: 4FT Hon
Entry Requirements: *GCE:* BBB. *SQAH:* BBBB. *IB:* 30.

W690 MA Film and Visual Culture
Duration: 4FT/3FT Hon/Ord
Entry Requirements: *GCE:* BBB. *SQAH:* BBBB. *IB:* 30.

A30 UNIVERSITY OF ABERTAY DUNDEE
BELL STREET
DUNDEE DD1 1HG
t: 01382 308080 f: 01382 308081
e: sro@abertay.ac.uk
// www.abertay.ac.uk

WW26 BA Visual Communication and Media Design
Duration: 4FT Hon
Entry Requirements: *GCE:* CCD. *SQAH:* BBBB. *IB:* 26. *OCR ND:* M1 *OCR NED:* M1 Interview required. Portfolio required.

A40 ABERYSTWYTH UNIVERSITY
ABERYSTWYTH UNIVERSITY, WELCOME CENTRE
PENGLAIS CAMPUS
ABERYSTWYTH
CEREDIGION SY23 3FB
t: 01970 622021 f: 01970 627410
e: ug-admissions@aber.ac.uk
// www.aber.ac.uk

W621 BA Astudiaethau Ffilm a Theledu
Duration: 3FT Hon
Entry Requirements: *GCE:* 300-320. *IB:* 32.

QWM6 BA Cymraeg ac Astudiathau Ffilm a Theledu
Duration: 3FT Hon
Entry Requirements: *GCE:* 300-320. *IB:* 30.

LWR6 BA Daearyddiaeth ac Astudiaethau Ffilm a Theledu
Duration: 3FT Hon
Entry Requirements: *GCE:* 300-320.

WWP4 BA Drama ac Astudiaethau Theatr/Astudiaethau Ffilm a Theledu
Duration: 3FT Hon
Entry Requirements: *GCE:* 300-320. *IB:* 32.

LWG6 BA Gwleidyddiaeth Ryngwladol ac Astudiaethau Ffilm a Theledu
Duration: 3FT Hon
Entry Requirements: *GCE:* 300-320. *IB:* 29.

QP53 BA Gwyddeleg: Iaith a Lln/Astudiaethau Ffilm a Theledu
Duration: 4FT Hon
Entry Requirements: *GCE:* 300-320. *IB:* 32.

VW26 BA Hanes Cymru ac Astudiaethau Ffilm a Theledu
Duration: 3FT Hon
Entry Requirements: *GCE:* 300-320. *IB:* 29.

A60 ANGLIA RUSKIN UNIVERSITY
BISHOP HALL LANE
CHELMSFORD
ESSEX CM1 1SQ
t: 0845 271 3333 f: 01245 251789
e: answers@anglia.ac.uk
// www.anglia.ac.uk

W640 BA Photography
Duration: 3FT Hon
Entry Requirements: *GCE:* 260. *SQAH:* CCCC. *SQAAH:* BC. *IB:* 24. Interview required. Portfolio required.

W641 FdA Professional Photography
Duration: 2FT Fdg
Entry Requirements: Contact the institution for details.

A66 THE ARTS UNIVERSITY COLLEGE AT BOURNEMOUTH (FORMERLY ARTS INSTITUTE AT BOURNEMOUTH)
WALLISDOWN
POOLE
DORSET BH12 5HH
t: 01202 363228 f: 01202 537729
e: admissions@aucb.ac.uk
// www.aucb.ac.uk

W644 BA Commercial Photography
Duration: 3FT Hon
Entry Requirements: *Foundation:* Pass. *GCE:* BCC. *IB:* 24. *OCR ND:* M1 *OCR NED:* M1 Interview required. Portfolio required.

W610 BA Film Production
Duration: 3FT Hon
Entry Requirements: *Foundation:* Pass. *GCE:* BCC. *IB:* 24. *OCR ND:* M1 *OCR NED:* M1 Interview required. Portfolio required.

W640 BA Photography
Duration: 3FT Hon
Entry Requirements: *Foundation:* Pass. *GCE:* BCC. *IB:* 24. *OCR ND:* M1 *OCR NED:* M1 Interview required. Portfolio required.

B06 BANGOR UNIVERSITY
BANGOR UNIVERSITY
BANGOR
GWYNEDD LL57 2DG
t: 01248 388484 f: 01248 370451
e: admissions@bangor.ac.uk
// www.bangor.ac.uk

Q3WP BA English Language with Film Studies
Duration: 3FT Hon
Entry Requirements: *GCE:* 240-300. *IB:* 28.

W620 BA Film Studies
Duration: 3FT Hon
Entry Requirements: *GCE:* 260-300. *IB:* 28.

V1W6 BA History with Film Studies
Duration: 3FT Hon
Entry Requirements: *GCE:* 240-280. *IB:* 28.

WW36 BA Music and Film Studies
Duration: 3FT Hon
Entry Requirements: *GCE:* 260-300. *IB:* 28.

B11 BARKING AND DAGENHAM COLLEGE
DAGENHAM ROAD
ROMFORD
ESSEX RM7 0XU
t: 020 8090 3020 f: 020 8090 3021
e: engagement.services@barkingdagenhamcollege.ac.uk
// www.barkingdagenhamcollege.ac.uk

W641 BA Hons Photography (Top-Up)
Duration: 1FT Hon
Entry Requirements: Contact the institution for details.

W640 FdA Photography
Duration: 2FT Fdg
Entry Requirements: *GCE:* 120.

B20 BATH SPA UNIVERSITY
NEWTON PARK
NEWTON ST LOE
BATH BA2 9BN
t: 01225 875875 f: 01225 875444
e: enquiries@bathspa.ac.uk
// www.bathspa.ac.uk/clearing

WW86 BA Creative Writing/Film & Screen Studies
Duration: 3FT Hon
Entry Requirements: *GCE:* 220-280. *IB:* 24.

W620 BA Film & Screen Studies
Duration: 3FT Hon
Entry Requirements: *GCE:* 220-280. *IB:* 24.

CW16 BA/BSc Biology/Film & Screen Studies
Duration: 3FT Hon
Entry Requirements: *GCE:* 220-280. *IB:* 24.

NW16 BA/BSc Business & Management/Film & Screen Studies
Duration: 3FT Hon
Entry Requirements: *GCE:* 220-280. *IB:* 24.

NW1P BA/BSc Business & Management/Film & Screen Studies
Duration: 2FT Dip
Entry Requirements: *GCE:* 220-280. *IB:* 24.

WW56 BA/BSc Dance/Film & Screen Studies
Duration: 3FT Hon
Entry Requirements: *GCE:* 220-280. *IB:* 24. Interview required.

WW46 BA/BSc Drama Studies/Film & Screen Studies
Duration: 3FT Hon
Entry Requirements: *GCE:* 220-280. *IB:* 24.

XW36 BA/BSc Education/Film & Screen Studies
Duration: 3FT Hon   CRB Check: Required
Entry Requirements: *GCE:* 220-280. *IB:* 24.

QWH6 BA/BSc English Literature/Film and Screen Studies
Duration: 3FT Hon
Entry Requirements: *GCE:* 220-280. *IB:* 24.

WD66 BA/BSc Film & Screen Studies/Food & Nutrition
Duration: 3FT Hon
Entry Requirements: *GCE:* 220-280. *IB:* 24.

WL67 BA/BSc Film & Screen Studies/Geography
Duration: 3FT Hon
Entry Requirements: *GCE:* 220-280. *IB:* 24.

WP6H BA/BSc Film & Screen Studies/Media Communications
Duration: 3FT Hon
Entry Requirements: *GCE:* 220-280. *IB:* 24.

WW63 BA/BSc Film & Screen Studies/Music
Duration: 3FT Hon
Entry Requirements: *GCE:* 220-280. *IB:* 24. Interview required.

WC68 BA/BSc Film & Screen Studies/Psychology
Duration: 3FT Hon
Entry Requirements: *GCE:* 220-280. *IB:* 24.

WL63 BA/BSc Film & Screen Studies/Sociology
Duration: 3FT Hon
Entry Requirements: *GCE:* 220-280. *IB:* 24.

WV66 BA/BSc Film & Screen Studies/Study of Religions
Duration: 3FT Hon
Entry Requirements: *GCE:* 220-280. *IB:* 24.

CW1P DipHE Biology/Film & Screen Studies
Duration: 2FT Dip
Entry Requirements: *GCE:* 220-280. *IB:* 24.

WW68 DipHE Creative Writing/Film & Screen Studies
Duration: 2FT Dip
Entry Requirements: *GCE:* 220-280. *IB:* 24.

WW4P DipHE Drama Studies/Film & Screen Studies
Duration: 2FT Dip
Entry Requirements: *GCE:* 220-280. *IB:* 24.

XW3P DipHE Education/Film & Screen Studies
Duration: 2FT Dip
Entry Requirements: *GCE:* 220-280. *IB:* 24.

QW3Q DipHE English Literature/Film and Screen Studies
Duration: 2FT Dip
Entry Requirements: *GCE:* 220-280. *IB:* 24.

W621 DipHE Film & Screen Studies
Duration: 2FT Dip
Entry Requirements: *GCE:* 220-280. *IB:* 24.

WD6P DipHE Film & Screen Studies/Food & Nutrition
Duration: 2FT Dip
Entry Requirements: *GCE:* 220-280. *IB:* 24.

WL6R DipHE Film & Screen Studies/Geography
Duration: 2FT Dip
Entry Requirements: *GCE:* 220-280. *IB:* 24.

WPP3 DipHE Film & Screen Studies/Media Communications
Duration: 2FT Dip
Entry Requirements: *GCE:* 220-280. *IB:* 24.

WC6V DipHE Film & Screen Studies/Psychology
Duration: 2FT Dip
Entry Requirements: *GCE:* 220-280. *IB:* 24.

WL6H DipHE Film & Screen Studies/Sociology
Duration: 2FT Dip
Entry Requirements: *GCE:* 220-280. *IB:* 24.

WV6P DipHE Film & Screen Studies/Study of Religions
Duration: 2FT Dip
Entry Requirements: *GCE:* 220-280. *IB:* 24.

W641 FdA Photography
Duration: 2FT Fdg
Entry Requirements: Interview required.

B22 UNIVERSITY OF BEDFORDSHIRE
PARK SQUARE
LUTON
BEDS LU1 3JU
t: 0844 8482234 f: 01582 489323
e: admissions@beds.ac.uk
// www.beds.ac.uk

W600 BA Photography and Video Art
Duration: 3FT Hon
Entry Requirements: *GCE:* 200. Interview required. Portfolio required.

W640 FdA Creative & Editorial Photography
Duration: 2FT Fdg
Entry Requirements: *GCE:* 120. Interview required. Portfolio required.

B23 BEDFORD COLLEGE
CAULDWELL STREET
BEDFORD MK42 9AH
t: 01234 291000 f: 01234 342674
e: info@bedford.ac.uk
// www.bedford.ac.uk

04PW HNC Photography
Duration: 1FT HNC
Entry Requirements: Contact the institution for details.

046W HND Photography
Duration: 2FT HND
Entry Requirements: *GCE:* 80-120. *OCR ND:* P1 *OCR NED:* P1
Interview required. Portfolio required.

B25 BIRMINGHAM CITY UNIVERSITY
PERRY BARR
BIRMINGHAM B42 2SU
t: 0121 331 5595 f: 0121 331 7994
// www.bcu.ac.uk

P9W6 BA Media and Communication (Media Photography)
Duration: 3FT Hon
Entry Requirements: *Foundation:* Pass. *GCE:* BBC. *SQAH:* ABBB. *SQAAH:* BBC. *IB:* 30.

W640 BA Visual Communication (Photography)
Duration: 3FT Hon
Entry Requirements: *GCE:* 280. *IB:* 28. Interview required. Portfolio required.

B41 BLACKPOOL AND THE FYLDE COLLEGE AN ASSOCIATE COLLEGE OF LANCASTER UNIVERSITY
ASHFIELD ROAD
BISPHAM
BLACKPOOL
LANCS FY2 0HB
t: 01253 504346 f: 01253 504198
e: admissions@blackpool.ac.uk
// www.blackpool.ac.uk

W640 BA Photography
Duration: 3FT Hon
Entry Requirements: *Foundation:* Merit. *GCE:* 220. *IB:* 24. Interview required. Portfolio required.

B44 UNIVERSITY OF BOLTON
DEANE ROAD
BOLTON BL3 5AB
t: 01204 903903 f: 01204 399074
e: enquiries@bolton.ac.uk
// www.bolton.ac.uk

W640 BA Photography
Duration: 3FT Hon
Entry Requirements: *GCE:* 240. Interview required. Portfolio required.

B50 BOURNEMOUTH UNIVERSITY
TALBOT CAMPUS
FERN BARROW
POOLE
DORSET BH12 5BB
t: 01202 524111
// www.bournemouth.ac.uk

PW36 BA Film Production and Cinematography
Duration: 3FT Hon
Entry Requirements: *GCE:* 340. *IB:* 33. *BTEC SubDip:* D. *BTEC Dip:* DD. *BTEC ExtDip:* DDD. Interview required.

W640 BA Photography
Duration: 3FT Hon
Entry Requirements: *GCE:* 340. *IB:* 33. *BTEC SubDip:* D. *BTEC Dip:* DD. *BTEC ExtDip:* DDD. Interview required.

B60 BRADFORD COLLEGE: AN ASSOCIATE COLLEGE OF LEEDS METROPOLITAN UNIVERSITY
GREAT HORTON ROAD
BRADFORD
WEST YORKSHIRE BD7 1AY
t: 01274 433008 f: 01274 431652
e: heregistry@bradfordcollege.ac.uk
// www.bradfordcollege.ac.uk/university-centre

W640 BA Photography
Duration: 1FT Hon
Entry Requirements: Interview required. Portfolio required. HND required.

W641 BA Photography
Duration: 3FT Hon
Entry Requirements: *GCE:* 220.

B72 UNIVERSITY OF BRIGHTON
MITHRAS HOUSE 211
LEWES ROAD
BRIGHTON BN2 4AT
t: 01273 644644 f: 01273 642607
e: admissions@brighton.ac.uk
// www.brighton.ac.uk

W640 BA Photography
Duration: 3FT Hon
Entry Requirements: *GCE:* BBC. Foundation Course required. Interview required. Portfolio required.

W642 MFA Photography
Duration: 4FT Hon
Entry Requirements: *GCE:* BBC. Foundation Course required. Interview required. Portfolio required.

B77 BRISTOL, CITY OF BRISTOL COLLEGE
SOUTH BRISTOL SKILLS ACADEMY
CITY OF BRISTOL COLLEGE
PO BOX 2887 BS2 2BB
t: 0117 312 5000
e: HEAdmissions@cityofbristol.ac.uk
// www.cityofbristol.ac.uk

W641 FdA Professional Photography
Duration: 2FT Fdg
Entry Requirements: *GCE:* 140. Interview required. Portfolio required.

B80 UNIVERSITY OF THE WEST OF ENGLAND, BRISTOL
FRENCHAY CAMPUS
COLDHARBOUR LANE
BRISTOL BS16 1QY
t: +44 (0)117 32 83333 f: +44 (0)117 32 82810
e: admissions@uwe.ac.uk
// www.uwe.ac.uk

W640 BA Photography
Duration: 3FT Hon
Entry Requirements: *GCE:* 280. Interview required. Portfolio required.

B84 BRUNEL UNIVERSITY
UXBRIDGE
MIDDLESEX UB8 3PH
t: 01895 265265 f: 01895 269790
e: admissions@brunel.ac.uk
// www.brunel.ac.uk

WW46 BA Theatre and Film & TV Studies
Duration: 3FT Hon
Entry Requirements: *GCE:* BBB. *SQAAH:* BBB. *IB:* 32. *BTEC ExtDip:* DDM.

B94 BUCKINGHAMSHIRE NEW UNIVERSITY
QUEEN ALEXANDRA ROAD
HIGH WYCOMBE
BUCKINGHAMSHIRE HP11 2JZ
t: 0800 0565 660 f: 01494 605 023
e: admissions@bucks.ac.uk
// bucks.ac.uk

PW36 BA Film and TV Production
Duration: 3FT Hon
Entry Requirements: *GCE:* 200-240. *IB:* 24. *OCR ND:* M1 *OCR NED:* M3

C10 CANTERBURY CHRIST CHURCH UNIVERSITY
NORTH HOLMES ROAD
CANTERBURY
KENT CT1 1QU
t: 01227 782900 f: 01227 782888
e: admissions@canterbury.ac.uk
// www.canterbury.ac.uk

NW26 BA Business Management and Photography
Duration: 3FT Hon
Entry Requirements: *GCE:* 240. *IB:* 24.

W640 BA Photography
Duration: 3FT Hon
Entry Requirements: *GCE:* 200. *IB:* 24. Interview required.
Portfolio required.

WJ69 BA Photography and Music Production
Duration: 3FT Hon
Entry Requirements: *GCE:* 240. *IB:* 24.

W6N2 BA Photography with Business Management
Duration: 3FT Hon
Entry Requirements: *GCE:* 240. *IB:* 24.

TWR6 BA/BSc American Studies and Film, Radio & TV (With a Year in USA)
Duration: 4FT Hon
Entry Requirements: Contact the institution for details.

WPT7 BA/BSc Film, Radio & TV with American Studies (With a Year in USA)
Duration: 4FT Hon
Entry Requirements: Contact the institution for details.

C22 COLEG SIR GAR / CARMARTHENSHIRE COLLEGE
SANDY ROAD
LLANELLI
CARMARTHENSHIRE SA15 4DN
t: 01554 748000 f: 01554 748170
e: admissions@colegsirgar.ac.uk
// www.colegsirgar.ac.uk

W640 BA Photography
Duration: 3FT Hon
Entry Requirements: *Foundation:* Pass. Portfolio required.

C30 UNIVERSITY OF CENTRAL LANCASHIRE
PRESTON
LANCS PR1 2HE
t: 01772 201201 f: 01772 894954
e: uadmissions@uclan.ac.uk
// www.uclan.ac.uk

PW3P BA Film & Media and Film Production
Duration: 3FT Hon
Entry Requirements: *GCE:* 260-300. *IB:* 28. *BTEC Dip:* D*D*. *BTEC ExtDip:* DMM. *OCR ND:* D *OCR NED:* M2

WP6J BA Film Production
Duration: 3FT Hon
Entry Requirements: *GCE:* 240-260. *IB:* 28. *OCR ND:* D *OCR NED:* M3 Portfolio required.

WP6H BA Photography
Duration: 3FT Hon
Entry Requirements: *GCE:* 240-260. *IB:* 28. *OCR ND:* D *OCR NED:* M3

C55 UNIVERSITY OF CHESTER
PARKGATE ROAD
CHESTER CH1 4BJ
t: 01244 511000 f: 01244 511300
e: enquiries@chester.ac.uk
// www.chester.ac.uk

PW5P BA Photography and Journalism
Duration: 3FT Hon
Entry Requirements: *Foundation:* Pass. *GCE:* 240-280. *SQAH:* BBBB. *IB:* 26. Interview required. Portfolio required.

C57 CHICHESTER COLLEGE
WESTGATE FIELDS
CHICHESTER
WEST SUSSEX PO19 1SB
t: 01243 786321 x2127 f: 01243 539481
e: sally.billingham@chichester.ac.uk
// www.chichester.ac.uk

36PW HND Film Making
Duration: 2FT/1FT HND/HNC
Entry Requirements: *Foundation:* Merit. *GCE:* AA-DD. *SQAH:* AAAAA-DDDDD. *SQAAH:* AAA-CCC. *OCR ND:* M2 *OCR NED:* M3 Interview required. Portfolio required.

C65 CITY AND ISLINGTON COLLEGE
COURSE INFORMATION UNIT
THE MARLBOROUGH BUILDING
383 HOLLOWAY ROAD
LONDON N7 0RN
t: 020 7700 9200
e: hedegrees@candi.ac.uk
// www.candi.ac.uk/HE

046W HND Photography
Duration: 2FT HND
Entry Requirements: Interview required. Portfolio required.

C71 CLEVELAND COLLEGE OF ART AND DESIGN
CHURCH SQUARE
HARTLEPOOL
CHURCH SQUARE TS24 7EX
t: 01642 288888 f: 01642 288828
e: studentrecruitment@ccad.ac.uk
// www.ccad.ac.uk

W640 BA(Hons) Photography
Duration: 3FT Hon
Entry Requirements: *Foundation:* Pass. *GCE:* 120. Interview required. Portfolio required.

W641 FdA Commercial Photography
Duration: 2FT Fdg
Entry Requirements: *Foundation:* Pass. *GCE:* 100. Interview required. Portfolio required.

C75 COLCHESTER INSTITUTE
SHEEPEN ROAD
COLCHESTER
ESSEX CO3 3LL
t: 01206 712777 f: 01206 712800
e: info@colchester.ac.uk
// www.colchester.ac.uk

W640 BA Photography
Duration: 3FT Hon
Entry Requirements: *Foundation:* Pass. *GCE:* 160. Interview required. Portfolio required.

W641 FdA Photography
Duration: 2FT Fdg
Entry Requirements: *Foundation:* Pass. *GCE:* 80. Interview required. Portfolio required.

C85 COVENTRY UNIVERSITY
THE STUDENT CENTRE
COVENTRY UNIVERSITY
1 GULSON RD
COVENTRY CV1 2JH
t: 024 7615 2222 f: 024 7615 2223
e: studentenquiries@coventry.ac.uk
// www.coventry.ac.uk

W640 BA Photography
Duration: 3FT/4SW Hon
Entry Requirements: *GCE:* BCC. *SQAH:* BCCCC. *IB:* 28. *BTEC ExtDip:* DMM. *OCR NED:* M2 Interview required. Portfolio required.

C88 CRAVEN COLLEGE
HIGH STREET
SKIPTON
NORTH YORKSHIRE BD23 1JY
t: 01756 791411 f: 01756 794872
e: enquiries@craven-college.ac.uk
// www.craven-college.ac.uk

W640 FdA Photography
Duration: 2FT Fdg
Entry Requirements: *GCE:* 100. Interview required. Portfolio required.

C93 UNIVERSITY FOR THE CREATIVE ARTS
FALKNER ROAD
FARNHAM
SURREY GU9 7DS
t: 01252 892960
e: admissions@ucreative.ac.uk
// www.ucreative.ac.uk

W600 BA Film Production
Duration: 3FT Hon
Entry Requirements: *GCE:* 220. *IB:* 24. *BTEC ExtDip:* PPP. Interview required. Portfolio required.

W640 BA Photography
Duration: 3FT Hon
Entry Requirements: *GCE:* 220. *IB:* 24. *BTEC ExtDip:* PPP. Interview required. Portfolio required.

W642 BA Photography (Contemporary Practice)
Duration: 3FT Hon
Entry Requirements: *GCE:* 220. *IB:* 24. *BTEC ExtDip:* PPP. Interview required. Portfolio required.

C99 UNIVERSITY OF CUMBRIA
FUSEHILL STREET
CARLISLE
CUMBRIA CA1 2HH
t: 01228 616234 f: 01228 616235
// www.cumbria.ac.uk

W641 BA Photography
Duration: 3FT Hon
Entry Requirements: *Foundation:* Merit. *GCE:* 240. *SQAH:* BBC.
SQAAH: CC. *IB:* 30. *OCR ND:* D Interview required. Portfolio
required.

W640 BA Photography (with Year 0)
Duration: 4FT Hon
Entry Requirements: *Foundation:* Pass. *GCE:* C-cccc. *SQAH:* CC.
SQAAH: C. *IB:* 25. Interview required. Portfolio required.

CW36 BA Wildlife and Media
Duration: 3FT Hon
Entry Requirements: *GCE:* 240. *IB:* 24. Interview required.

D26 DE MONTFORT UNIVERSITY
THE GATEWAY
LEICESTER LE1 9BH
t: 0116 255 1551 f: 0116 250 6204
e: enquiries@dmu.ac.uk
// www.dmu.ac.uk

WQ63 BA English and Film Studies
Duration: 3FT Hon
Entry Requirements: *GCE:* 260. *IB:* 28. *BTEC Dip:* D*D*. *BTEC
ExtDip:* DMM.

W640 BA Photography & Video
Duration: 3FT Hon
Entry Requirements: *Foundation:* Pass. *GCE:* 260. *IB:* 28. *BTEC
Dip:* D*D. *BTEC ExtDip:* MMM. Interview required. Portfolio
required.

D39 UNIVERSITY OF DERBY
KEDLESTON ROAD
DERBY DE22 1GB
t: 01332 591167 f: 01332 597724
e: askadmissions@derby.ac.uk
// www.derby.ac.uk

W640 BA Commercial Photography
Duration: 3FT Hon
Entry Requirements: *Foundation:* Distinction. *GCE:* 260. *IB:* 28.
BTEC Dip: D*D*. *BTEC ExtDip:* DMM. *OCR NED:* M2 Interview
required. Portfolio required.

W600 BA Film Studies
Duration: 3FT Hon
Entry Requirements: *Foundation:* Distinction. *GCE:* 240. *IB:* 26.
BTEC Dip: D*D*. *BTEC ExtDip:* DMM. *OCR ND:* D *OCR NED:* M3

W621 BA Film and Video Production
Duration: 3FT Hon
Entry Requirements: *Foundation:* Distinction. *GCE:* 260. *IB:* 28.
BTEC Dip: D*D*. *BTEC ExtDip:* DMM. *OCR NED:* M2 Interview
required. Portfolio required.

W650 BA Photography
Duration: 3FT Hon
Entry Requirements: *Foundation:* Distinction. *GCE:* 260. *IB:* 28.
BTEC Dip: D*D*. *BTEC ExtDip:* DMM. *OCR NED:* M2 Interview
required. Portfolio required.

W645 FYr Commercial Photography (Year 0)
Duration: 1FT FYr
Entry Requirements: *Foundation:* Pass. *GCE:* 160. *IB:* 24. *BTEC
Dip:* D*D*. *BTEC ExtDip:* DMM. *OCR ND:* M2 *OCR NED:* P2
Interview required.

W619 FYr Film and Video Production (Year 0)
Duration: 1FT FYr
Entry Requirements: *Foundation:* Pass. *GCE:* 160. *IB:* 24. *BTEC
Dip:* D*D*. *BTEC ExtDip:* DMM. *OCR ND:* M2 *OCR NED:* P2
Interview required. Portfolio required.

W644 FYr Photography (Year 0)
Duration: 1FT FYr
Entry Requirements: *Foundation:* Distinction. *GCE:* 240. *IB:* 26.
BTEC Dip: D*D*. *BTEC ExtDip:* DMM. *OCR ND:* D *OCR NED:* M3
Interview required. Portfolio required.

D65 UNIVERSITY OF DUNDEE
NETHERGATE
DUNDEE DD1 4HN
t: 01382 383838 f: 01382 388150
e: contactus@dundee.ac.uk
// www.dundee.ac.uk/admissions/
undergraduate/

QW36 MA English and Film Studies
Duration: 4FT Hon
Entry Requirements: *GCE:* BCC. *SQAH:* ABBB. *IB:* 30.

E14 UNIVERSITY OF EAST ANGLIA
NORWICH NR4 7TJ
t: 01603 591515 f: 01603 591523
e: admissions@uea.ac.uk
// www.uea.ac.uk

WV63 BA Film Studies and Art History
Duration: 3FT Hon CRB Check: Required
Entry Requirements: *GCE:* AAB. *SQAAH:* AAB. *IB:* 33. *BTEC
ExtDip:* DDD. Interview required.

TW76 BA Film and American Studies (4 years)
Duration: 4FT Hon   **CRB Check:** Required
Entry Requirements: *GCE:* AAB. *SQAAH:* AAB. *IB:* 33. *BTEC*
ExtDip: DDD. Interview required.

QW36 BA Film and English Studies
Duration: 3FT Hon   **CRB Check:** Required
Entry Requirements: *GCE:* AAB. *SQAAH:* AAB. *IB:* 33. *BTEC*
ExtDip: DDD. Interview required.

E28 UNIVERSITY OF EAST LONDON
DOCKLANDS CAMPUS
UNIVERSITY WAY
LONDON E16 2RD
t: 020 8223 3333 f: 020 8223 2978
e: study@uel.ac.uk
// www.uel.ac.uk

W8W6 BA Creative and Professional Writing and Photography
Duration: 3FT Hon
Entry Requirements: *GCE:* 240. *IB:* 24.

L6W6 BA Cultural Studies with Photography
Duration: 3FT Hon
Entry Requirements: *GCE:* 240. *IB:* 24.

QWH6 BA English Literature and Photography
Duration: 3FT Hon
Entry Requirements: *GCE:* 240.

P3WP BA Film Studies with Photography
Duration: 3FT Hon
Entry Requirements: *GCE:* 240. *IB:* 24.

W622 BA Film and Video - Theory and Practice Extended
Duration: 4FT Hon
Entry Requirements: *GCE:* 80. *IB:* 24.

W620 BA Film and Video: Theory & Practice
Duration: 3FT Hon
Entry Requirements: *GCE:* 240. *IB:* 24.

N2W6 BA Music Industry Management with Photography
Duration: 3FT Hon
Entry Requirements: *GCE:* 240. *IB:* 24.

W641 BA Photography
Duration: 3FT Hon
Entry Requirements: *GCE:* 200. Interview required. Portfolio required.

W642 BA Photography (Extended)
Duration: 4FT Hon
Entry Requirements: *GCE:* 80. Interview required. Portfolio required.

WWQF BA Photography and Printed Textile Design
Duration: 3FT Hon
Entry Requirements: *GCE:* 200. Interview required.

W6W8 BA Photography with Creative & Professional Writing
Duration: 3FT Hon
Entry Requirements: *GCE:* 200. *IB:* 24. Portfolio required.

W6QJ BA Photography with English Literature
Duration: 3FT Hon
Entry Requirements: *GCE:* 200. *IB:* 24. Portfolio required.

W6F4 BA Photography with Forensic Science
Duration: 3FT Hon
Entry Requirements: *GCE:* 200. *IB:* 24. Portfolio required.

WL66 BA Photography/Cultural Studies
Duration: 3FT Hon
Entry Requirements: *GCE:* 240. *IB:* 24. Portfolio required.

E42 EDGE HILL UNIVERSITY
ORMSKIRK
LANCASHIRE L39 4QP
t: 01695 657000 f: 01695 584355
e: study@edgehill.ac.uk
// www.edgehill.ac.uk

WW69 BA Creative Writing and Film Studies
Duration: 3FT Hon
Entry Requirements: *GCE:* 280. *IB:* 26. *OCR ND:* D *OCR NED:* M2

Q1W6 BA English Language with Film Studies
Duration: 3FT Hon
Entry Requirements: *GCE:* 280. *IB:* 26. *OCR ND:* D *OCR NED:* M2

WQ63 BA English and Film Studies
Duration: 3FT Hon
Entry Requirements: *GCE:* 280. *IB:* 26. *OCR ND:* D *OCR NED:* M2

Q3W6 BA English with Film Studies
Duration: 3FT Hon
Entry Requirements: *GCE:* 280. *IB:* 26. *OCR ND:* D *OCR NED:* M2

WV61 BA Film Studies and History
Duration: 3FT Hon
Entry Requirements: *GCE:* 280. *IB:* 26. *OCR ND:* D *OCR NED:* M2

WP69 BA Film Studies and Media
Duration: 3FT Hon
Entry Requirements: *GCE:* 280. *IB:* 26. *OCR ND:* D *OCR NED:* M2

P3W6 BA Film Studies with Film Production
Duration: 3FT Hon
Entry Requirements: *GCE:* 280. *IB:* 26. *OCR ND:* D *OCR NED:* M2

V1W6 BA History with Film Studies
Duration: 3FT Hon
Entry Requirements: *GCE:* 280. *IB:* 26. *OCR ND:* D *OCR NED:* M2

E56 THE UNIVERSITY OF EDINBURGH
STUDENT RECRUITMENT & ADMISSIONS
57 GEORGE SQUARE
EDINBURGH EH8 9JU
t: 0131 650 4360 f: 0131 651 1236
e: sra.enquiries@ed.ac.uk
// www.ed.ac.uk/studying/undergraduate/

W640 BA Photography
Duration: 4FT Hon
Entry Requirements: *Foundation:* Merit. *GCE:* BBB. *SQAH:* BBBB.
IB: 34. Portfolio required.

E59 EDINBURGH NAPIER UNIVERSITY
CRAIGLOCKHART CAMPUS
EDINBURGH EH14 1DJ
t: +44 (0)8452 60 60 40 f: 0131 455 6464
e: info@napier.ac.uk
// www.napier.ac.uk

W600 BA Photography & Film
Duration: 3FT/4FT Ord/Hon
Entry Requirements: *GCE:* 240. Interview required. Portfolio
required.

E70 THE UNIVERSITY OF ESSEX
WIVENHOE PARK
COLCHESTER
ESSEX CO4 3SQ
t: 01206 873666 f: 01206 874477
e: admit@essex.ac.uk
// www.essex.ac.uk

**T7W6 BA American (United States) Studies
with Film (Including Year Abroad)**
Duration: 4FT Hon
Entry Requirements: *GCE:* ABB-BBB. *SQAH:* AAAB-AABB. Interview
required.

W620 BA Film Studies
Duration: 3FT Hon
Entry Requirements: *GCE:* ABB-BBB. *SQAH:* AAAB-AABB. *BTEC
ExtDip:* DDM.

QW26 BA Film Studies and Literature
Duration: 3FT Hon
Entry Requirements: *GCE:* ABB-BBB. *SQAH:* AAAB-AABB. *BTEC
ExtDip:* DDM.

VW16 BA History and Film Studies
Duration: 3FT Hon
Entry Requirements: *GCE:* ABB-BBB. *SQAH:* AAAB-AABB. *IB:* 32.

**V1WQ BA History and Film Studies (Including
Year Abroad)**
Duration: 4FT Hon
Entry Requirements: *GCE:* ABB-BBB. *SQAH:* AAAB-AABB. *IB:* 32.

V1W6 BA History with Film Studies
Duration: 3FT Hon
Entry Requirements: *GCE:* ABB-BBB. *SQAH:* AAAB-AABB. *IB:* 32.

**V1WP BA History with Film Studies (Including
Year Abroad)**
Duration: 4FT Hon
Entry Requirements: *GCE:* ABB-BBB. *SQAH:* AAAB-AABB. *IB:* 32.

E84 UNIVERSITY OF EXETER
LAVER BUILDING
NORTH PARK ROAD
EXETER
DEVON EX4 4QE
t: 01392 723044 f: 01392 722479
e: admissions@exeter.ac.uk
// www.exeter.ac.uk

Q3W6 BA English and Film Studies
Duration: 3FT Hon
Entry Requirements: *GCE:* AAB-ABB. *SQAH:* AAABB-AABBB.
SQAAH: ABB-BBB.

WR61 BA Film Studies and French (4 years)
Duration: 4FT Hon
Entry Requirements: *GCE:* AAB-ABB. *SQAH:* AAABB-AABBB.
SQAAH: ABB-BBB. *BTEC ExtDip:* DDM.

WR62 BA Film Studies and German (4 years)
Duration: 4FT Hon
Entry Requirements: *GCE:* AAB-ABB. *SQAH:* AAABB-AABBB.
SQAAH: ABB-BBB. *BTEC ExtDip:* DDM.

**WR63 BA Film Studies and Italian (Italian for
beginners available) (4 years)**
Duration: 4FT Hon
Entry Requirements: *GCE:* AAB-ABB. *SQAH:* AAABB-AABBB.
SQAAH: ABB-BBB.

**WR67 BA Film Studies and Russian (Russian
for beginners available) (4 years)**
Duration: 4FT Hon
Entry Requirements: *GCE:* AAB-ABB. *SQAH:* AAABB-AABBB.
SQAAH: ABB-BBB.

WR64 BA Film Studies and Spanish (Spanish for beginners available) (4 years)
Duration: 4FT Hon
Entry Requirements: *GCE:* AAB-ABB. *SQAH:* AAABB-AABBB. *SQAAH:* ABB-BBB. *BTEC ExtDip:* DDM.

F33 UNIVERSITY COLLEGE FALMOUTH
WOODLANE
FALMOUTH
CORNWALL TR11 4RH
t: 01326213730
e: admissions@falmouth.ac.uk
// www.falmouth.ac.uk

W610 BA(Hons) Film
Duration: 3FT Hon
Entry Requirements: *GCE:* 220. *IB:* 24. Interview required.

WF67 BA(Hons) Marine and Natural History Photography
Duration: 3FT Hon
Entry Requirements: *GCE:* 220. *IB:* 24. Interview required.
Portfolio required.

W640 BA(Hons) Photography
Duration: 3FT Hon
Entry Requirements: *GCE:* 220. *IB:* 24. Interview required.
Portfolio required.

WP65 BA(Hons) Press & Editorial Photography
Duration: 3FT Hon
Entry Requirements: *GCE:* 220. *IB:* 24. Interview required.
Portfolio required.

F66 FARNBOROUGH COLLEGE OF TECHNOLOGY
BOUNDARY ROAD
FARNBOROUGH
HAMPSHIRE GU14 6SB
t: 01252 407028 f: 01252 407041
e: admissions@farn-ct.ac.uk
// www.farn-ct.ac.uk

W640 FdA Photography
Duration: 2FT Fdg
Entry Requirements: *GCE:* 160.

G14 UNIVERSITY OF GLAMORGAN, CARDIFF AND PONTYPRIDD
ENQUIRIES AND ADMISSIONS UNIT
PONTYPRIDD CF37 1DL
t: 08456 434030 f: 01443 654050
e: enquiries@glam.ac.uk
// www.glam.ac.uk

W600 BA Film Studies
Duration: 3FT Hon
Entry Requirements: *GCE:* BBC. *IB:* 25. *BTEC SubDip:* M. *BTEC Dip:* D*D*. *BTEC ExtDip:* DMM. *OCR NED:* M2 Interview required.

PW36 BA Photography
Duration: 3FT Hon
Entry Requirements: *GCE:* BBB. *IB:* 26. *BTEC SubDip:* M. *BTEC Dip:* DD. *BTEC ExtDip:* DMM. *OCR NED:* M2 Interview required.
Portfolio required.

W601 FdA Creative Industries (Film and Video)
Duration: 2FT Fdg
Entry Requirements: *GCE:* CCC. *BTEC SubDip:* M. *BTEC Dip:* DD. *BTEC ExtDip:* MMM. Interview required.

W640 FdA Creative Industries (Photography)
Duration: 2FT Fdg
Entry Requirements: *GCE:* CCC. *BTEC SubDip:* M. *BTEC Dip:* DD. *BTEC ExtDip:* MMM.

G50 THE UNIVERSITY OF GLOUCESTERSHIRE
PARK CAMPUS
THE PARK
CHELTENHAM GL50 2RH
t: 01242 714501 f: 01242 714869
e: admissions@glos.ac.uk
// www.glos.ac.uk

WP65 BA Photojournalism and Documentary Photography
Duration: 3FT Hon
Entry Requirements: *GCE:* 280-300. Interview required. Portfolio required.

W642 FdA Professional Photography
Duration: 2FT Fdg
Entry Requirements: *GCE:* 120. Interview required. Portfolio required.

G53 GLYNDWR UNIVERSITY
PLAS COCH
MOLD ROAD
WREXHAM LL11 2AW
t: 01978 293439 f: 01978 290008
e: sid@glyndwr.ac.uk
// www.glyndwr.ac.uk

W990 BA Design:Film and Photography
Duration: 3FT Hon
Entry Requirements: *GCE:* 240. Portfolio required.

G70 UNIVERSITY OF GREENWICH
GREENWICH CAMPUS
OLD ROYAL NAVAL COLLEGE
PARK ROW
LONDON SE10 9LS
t: 020 8331 9000 f: 020 8331 8145
e: courseinfo@gre.ac.uk
// www.gre.ac.uk

W641 BA Photography (Stage 3 Top up)
Duration: 1FT Hon
Entry Requirements: Contact the institution for details.

W640 FdA Photography
Duration: 2FT Fdg
Entry Requirements: Contact the institution for details.

G80 GRIMSBY INSTITUTE OF FURTHER AND HIGHER EDUCATION
NUNS CORNER
GRIMSBY
NE LINCOLNSHIRE DN34 5BQ
t: 0800 328 3631
e: headmissions@grimsby.ac.uk
// www.grimsby.ac.uk

WN61 BA Commercial Photography
Duration: 3FT Hon
Entry Requirements: *GCE:* 120-240. Interview required.

H14 HAVERING COLLEGE OF FURTHER AND HIGHER EDUCATION
ARDLEIGH GREEN ROAD
HORNCHURCH
ESSEX RM11 2LL
t: 01708 462793 f: 01708 462736
e: HE@havering-college.ac.uk
// www.havering-college.ac.uk

046W HNC Photography
Duration: 1FT HNC
Entry Requirements: Interview required. Portfolio required.

H18 HEREFORD COLLEGE OF ARTS
FOLLY LANE
HEREFORD HR1 1LT
t: 01432 273359 f: 01432 341099
e: headmin@hca.ac.uk
// www.hca.ac.uk

W643 BA Photography
Duration: 3FT Hon   CRB Check: Required
Entry Requirements: *GCE:* 200. Interview required. Portfolio required.

W641 BA Photography (top up)
Duration: 1FT Hon   CRB Check: Required
Entry Requirements: Interview required. Portfolio required. HND required.

W642 FdA Commercial Photography
Duration: 2FT Fdg   CRB Check: Required
Entry Requirements: *Foundation:* Pass. *GCE:* 150-200. Interview required. Portfolio required.

H36 UNIVERSITY OF HERTFORDSHIRE
UNIVERSITY ADMISSIONS SERVICE
COLLEGE LANE
HATFIELD
HERTS AL10 9AB
t: 01707 284800
// www.herts.ac.uk

W641 BA Photography
Duration: 3FT Hon
Entry Requirements: Interview required. Portfolio required.

W614 BA Visual Effects
Duration: 3FT Hon
Entry Requirements: *Foundation:* Pass. Interview required. Portfolio required.

HW66 BSc Film and TV Production
Duration: 3FT/4SW Hon
Entry Requirements: *GCE:* 240.

W640 FdA Photography
Duration: 2FT Fdg
Entry Requirements: *GCE:* 80. Interview required. Portfolio required.

H60 THE UNIVERSITY OF HUDDERSFIELD
QUEENSGATE
HUDDERSFIELD HD1 3DH
t: 01484 473969 f: 01484 472765
e: admissionsandrecords@hud.ac.uk
// www.hud.ac.uk

W640 BA Photography
Duration: 3FT Hon
Entry Requirements: *GCE:* 300. *SQAH:* BBBB. *IB:* 28. Interview required. Portfolio required.

H72 THE UNIVERSITY OF HULL
THE UNIVERSITY OF HULL
COTTINGHAM ROAD
HULL HU6 7RX
t: 01482 466100 f: 01482 442290
e: admissions@hull.ac.uk
// www.hull.ac.uk

WW86 BA Creative Writing and Film Studies
Duration: 3FT Hon
Entry Requirements: *GCE:* 280-320. *IB:* 30. *BTEC ExtDip:* DDM.

W631 BA Film Studies
Duration: 3FT Hon
Entry Requirements: *GCE:* 280-320. *IB:* 28. *BTEC ExtDip:* DMM.

H73 HULL COLLEGE
QUEEN'S GARDENS
HULL HU1 3DG
t: 01482 329943 f: 01482 598733
e: info@hull-college.ac.uk
// www.hull-college.ac.uk/higher-education

W641 BA Lens Based Photo Media
Duration: 1FT Hon
Entry Requirements: Foundation Course required. Interview required. Portfolio required. HND required.

W640 FdA Lens Based Photo Media
Duration: 2FT Fdg
Entry Requirements: *GCE:* 200. Foundation Course required. Interview required. Portfolio required.

K24 THE UNIVERSITY OF KENT
RECRUITMENT & ADMISSIONS OFFICE
REGISTRY
UNIVERSITY OF KENT
CANTERBURY, KENT CT2 7NZ
t: 01227 827272 f: 01227 827077
e: information@kent.ac.uk
// www.kent.ac.uk

WV63 BA Art and Film
Duration: 3FT Hon
Entry Requirements: *GCE:* ABB. *SQAH:* AAAAB-AAABB. *SQAAH:* AAB-ABB. *IB:* 33. *OCR ND:* D *OCR NED:* D1

VW96 BA Cultural Studies and Film Studies
Duration: 3FT Hon
Entry Requirements: *GCE:* ABB. *SQAH:* AABBB. *SQAAH:* ABB. *IB:* 33. *OCR ND:* D *OCR NED:* D2

W612 BA European Arts (Film Studies)
Duration: 4FT Hon
Entry Requirements: *GCE:* AAB-ABB. *SQAH:* AAAAB-AAABB. *SQAAH:* AAB-ABB. *IB:* 33. *OCR ND:* D *OCR NED:* D1

W610 BA Film Studies
Duration: 3FT Hon
Entry Requirements: *GCE:* AAB-ABB. *SQAH:* AAAAB-AAABB. *SQAAH:* AAB-ABB. *IB:* 33. *OCR ND:* D *OCR NED:* D1 Interview required.

QW86 BA Film Studies and Classical & Archaeological Studies
Duration: 3FT Hon
Entry Requirements: *GCE:* AAB-ABB. *SQAH:* AAAAB-AAABB. *SQAAH:* AAB-ABB. *IB:* 33. *OCR ND:* D *OCR NED:* D1

WQ62 BA Film Studies and Comparative Literature
Duration: 3FT Hon
Entry Requirements: *GCE:* ABB. *SQAH:* AAABB. *SQAAH:* ABB. *IB:* 35. *OCR ND:* D *OCR NED:* M1

WG64 BA Film Studies and Computing
Duration: 3FT Hon
Entry Requirements: *GCE:* AAB-ABB. *SQAH:* AAAAB-AAABB. *SQAAH:* AAB-ABB. *IB:* 33. *OCR ND:* D *OCR NED:* D1

WW46 BA Film Studies and Drama & Theatre Studies
Duration: 3FT Hon
Entry Requirements: *GCE:* AAB-ABB. *SQAH:* AAAAB-AAABB. *SQAAH:* AAB-ABB. *IB:* 33. *OCR ND:* D *OCR NED:* D1

QW36 BA Film Studies and English & American Literature
Duration: 3FT Hon
Entry Requirements: *GCE:* AAB. *SQAH:* AAABB. *SQAAH:* AAB. *IB:* 33. *OCR ND:* D *OCR NED:* M2

WQ63 BA Film Studies and English, American & Post-Colonial Literatures
Duration: 3FT Hon
Entry Requirements: *GCE:* AAB. *SQAH:* AAABB. *SQAAH:* AAB. *IB:* 33. *OCR ND:* D *OCR NED:* M2

RW16 BA Film Studies and French
Duration: 4FT Hon
Entry Requirements: *GCE:* ABB. *SQAH:* AAABB. *SQAAH:* ABB. *IB:* 33. *OCR ND:* D *OCR NED:* D2

RW26 BA Film Studies and German
Duration: 4FT Hon
Entry Requirements: *GCE:* ABB. *SQAH:* AAABB. *SQAAH:* ABB. *IB:* 33. *OCR ND:* M1 *OCR NED:* M3

WR64 BA Film Studies and Hispanic Studies
Duration: 4FT Hon
Entry Requirements: *GCE:* ABB. *SQAH:* AAABB. *SQAAH:* ABB. *IB:* 35. *OCR ND:* D *OCR NED:* M1

VW16 BA Film Studies and History
Duration: 3FT Hon
Entry Requirements: *GCE:* ABB. *SQAH:* AAABB. *SQAAH:* ABB. *IB:* 33. *OCR ND:* D *OCR NED:* D2

VW36 BA Film Studies and History & Philosophy of Art
Duration: 3FT Hon
Entry Requirements: *GCE:* ABB. *SQAH:* AAAAB-AAABB. *SQAAH:* AAB-ABB. *IB:* 33. *OCR ND:* D *OCR NED:* D1

RW36 BA Film Studies and Italian
Duration: 4FT Hon
Entry Requirements: *GCE:* BBB. *SQAH:* AABBB. *SQAAH:* BBB. *IB:* 35. *OCR ND:* D *OCR NED:* M1

VW56 BA Film Studies and Philosophy
Duration: 3FT Hon
Entry Requirements: *GCE:* ABB. *SQAH:* AAABB. *SQAAH:* ABB. *IB:* 33. *OCR ND:* D *OCR NED:* M1

VW66 BA Film Studies and Religious Studies
Duration: 3FT Hon
Entry Requirements: *GCE:* AAB-ABB. *SQAH:* AAAAB-AAABB. *SQAAH:* AAB-ABB. *IB:* 33. *OCR ND:* D *OCR NED:* D1

W611 BA Film Studies with a Placement Year
Duration: 4FT Hon
Entry Requirements: *GCE:* AAB-ABB. *SQAH:* AAAAB-AAABB. *SQAAH:* AAB-ABB. *IB:* 33. *OCR ND:* D *OCR NED:* D1 Interview required.

W616 BA Film Studies with a Year Abroad
Duration: 4FT Hon
Entry Requirements: *GCE:* AAB-ABB. *SQAH:* AAAAB-AAABB. *SQAAH:* AAB-ABB. *IB:* 33. *OCR ND:* D *OCR NED:* D1 Interview required.

W640 BA Photography (Top-up)
Duration: 1FT Hon
Entry Requirements: Interview required. Portfolio required. HND required.

W641 FdA Photography
Duration: 2FT Fdg
Entry Requirements: Interview required. Portfolio required.

046W HND Photography
Duration: 2FT HND
Entry Requirements: *OCR NED:* M2 Interview required. Portfolio required.

K84 KINGSTON UNIVERSITY
STUDENT INFORMATION & ADVICE CENTRE
COOPER HOUSE
40-46 SURBITON ROAD
KINGSTON UPON THAMES KT1 2HX
t: 0844 8552177 f: 020 8547 7080
e: aps@kingston.ac.uk
// www.kingston.ac.uk

NW16 BA Business and Film Studies
Duration: 3FT Hon
Entry Requirements: *GCE:* 280. *IB:* 30.

WP63 BA Film Making
Duration: 3FT Hon
Entry Requirements: *Foundation:* Pass. *GCE:* 240. Interview required. Portfolio required.

W610 BA Film Studies
Duration: 3FT Hon
Entry Requirements: *GCE:* 240. *IB:* 30.

W6R1 BA Film Studies with French
Duration: 3FT Hon
Entry Requirements: *GCE:* 240-360.

W6R4 BA Film Studies with Spanish
Duration: 3FT Hon
Entry Requirements: *GCE:* 240-360.

W640 BA Photography
Duration: 3FT Hon
Entry Requirements: Foundation Course required. Interview required. Portfolio required.

K90 KIRKLEES COLLEGE
HALIFAX ROAD
DEWSBURY
WEST YORKSHIRE WF13 2AS
t: 01924 436221 f: 01924 457047
e: admissionsdc@kirkleescollege.ac.uk
// www.kirkleescollege.ac.uk

W642 BA Photography
Duration: 1FT Hon
Entry Requirements: Contact the institution for details.

L21 LEEDS CITY COLLEGE
TECHNOLOGY CAMPUS
COOKRIDGE STREET
LEEDS LS2 8BL
t: 0113 216 2406 f: 0113 216 2401
e: helen.middleton@leedscitycollege.ac.uk
// www.leedscitycollege.ac.uk

W641 BA Photography
Duration: 1FT Ord
Entry Requirements: Contact the institution for details.

W640 FdA Photography
Duration: 2FT Fdg
Entry Requirements: Contact the institution for details.

L23 UNIVERSITY OF LEEDS
THE UNIVERSITY OF LEEDS
WOODHOUSE LANE
LEEDS LS2 9JT
t: 0113 343 3999
e: admissions@leeds.ac.uk
// www.leeds.ac.uk

QW46 BA Arabic and World Cinemas
Duration: 4FT Hon
Entry Requirements: *GCE:* ABB. *SQAAH:* ABB. *IB:* 34.

TW16 BA Chinese and World Cinemas
Duration: 4FT Hon
Entry Requirements: *GCE:* ABB. *SQAAH:* ABB. *IB:* 34.

W600 BA Cinema and Photography
Duration: 3FT Hon
Entry Requirements: *GCE:* BBB. *SQAH:* AAABB-AABBB. *SQAAH:* BBB. *IB:* 32.

RW16 BA French and World Cinemas
Duration: 4FT Hon
Entry Requirements: *GCE:* ABB. *SQAAH:* ABB. *IB:* 34.

RW26 BA German and World Cinemas
Duration: 4FT Hon
Entry Requirements: *GCE:* ABB. *SQAAH:* ABB. *IB:* 34.

RW36 BA Italian A and World Cinemas
Duration: 4FT Hon
Entry Requirements: *GCE:* ABB. *SQAAH:* ABB. *IB:* 34.

RW3P BA Italian B and World Cinemas
Duration: 4FT Hon
Entry Requirements: *GCE:* ABB. *SQAAH:* ABB. *IB:* 34.

TW26 BA Japanese and World Cinemas
Duration: 4FT Hon
Entry Requirements: *GCE:* AAB. *SQAAH:* AAB. *IB:* 36.

RW56 BA Portuguese and World Cinemas
Duration: 4FT Hon
Entry Requirements: *GCE:* ABB. *SQAAH:* ABB. *IB:* 34.

RW76 BA Russian A and World Cinemas
Duration: 4FT Hon
Entry Requirements: *GCE:* ABB. *SQAAH:* ABB. *IB:* 34.

RW7P BA Russian B and World Cinemas
Duration: 4FT Hon
Entry Requirements: *GCE:* ABB. *SQAAH:* ABB. *IB:* 34.

RW46 BA Spanish and World Cinemas
Duration: 4FT Hon
Entry Requirements: *GCE:* ABB. *SQAAH:* ABB. *IB:* 34.

L28 LEEDS COLLEGE OF ART
BLENHEIM WALK
LEEDS LS2 9AQ
t: 0113 202 8000 f: 0113 202 8001
e: info@leeds-art.ac.uk
// www.leeds-art.ac.uk

W642 BA Photography
Duration: 3FT Hon
Entry Requirements: *Foundation:* Merit. *GCE:* 240. *IB:* 24. *BTEC Dip:* DD. *BTEC ExtDip:* MMM. Interview required. Portfolio required.

L36 LEICESTER COLLEGE
FREEMEN'S PARK CAMPUS
AYLESTONE ROAD
LEICESTER LE2 7LW
t: 0116 224 2240 f: 0116 224 2041
e: info@leicestercollege.ac.uk
// www.leicestercollege.ac.uk

W640 FdA Photography (with Video)
Duration: 2FT Fdg
Entry Requirements: *GCE:* 80. Interview required. Portfolio required.

W690 FdA Video (with Photography)
Duration: 2FT Fdg
Entry Requirements: *GCE:* 80. Interview required. Portfolio required.

L39 UNIVERSITY OF LINCOLN
ADMISSIONS
BRAYFORD POOL
LINCOLN LN6 7TS
t: 01522 886097 f: 01522 886146
e: admissions@lincoln.ac.uk
// www.lincoln.ac.uk

W600 BA Contemporary Lens Media
Duration: 3FT Hon
Entry Requirements: *GCE:* 280. Interview required. Portfolio required.

L51 LIVERPOOL JOHN MOORES UNIVERSITY
KINGSWAY HOUSE
HATTON GARDEN
LIVERPOOL L3 2AJ
t: 0151 231 5090 f: 0151 904 6368
e: courses@ljmu.ac.uk
// www.ljmu.ac.uk

WW86 BA Creative Writing and Film Studies
Duration: 3FT Hon
Entry Requirements: *GCE:* 280. *IB:* 29.

L53 COLEG LLANDRILLO CYMRU
LLANDUDNO ROAD
RHOS-ON-SEA
COLWYN BAY
NORTH WALES LL28 4HZ
t: 01492 542338/339 f: 01492 543052
e: degrees@llandrillo.ac.uk
// www.llandrillo.ac.uk

046W HND Photography
Duration: 2FT HND
Entry Requirements: *GCE:* 80. Interview required. Portfolio required.

L68 LONDON METROPOLITAN UNIVERSITY
166-220 HOLLOWAY ROAD
LONDON N7 8DB
t: 020 7133 4200
e: admissions@londonmet.ac.uk
// www.londonmet.ac.uk

W640 FdA Photography
Duration: 2FT Fdg
Entry Requirements: *GCE:* 160. Interview required. Portfolio required.

L75 LONDON SOUTH BANK UNIVERSITY
ADMISSIONS AND RECRUITMENT CENTRE
90 LONDON ROAD
LONDON SE1 6LN
t: 0800 923 8888 f: 020 7815 8273
e: course.enquiry@lsbu.ac.uk
// www.lsbu.ac.uk

W600 BA Film Studies
Duration: 3FT Hon
Entry Requirements: *GCE:* 240. *IB:* 24.

M10 THE MANCHESTER COLLEGE
OPENSHAW CAMPUS
ASHTON OLD ROAD
OPENSHAW
MANCHESTER M11 2WH
t: 0800 068 8585 f: 0161 920 4103
e: enquiries@themanchestercollege.ac.uk
// www.themanchestercollege.ac.uk

W690 FdA TV and Film Production
Duration: 2FT Fdg
Entry Requirements: *Foundation:* Pass. *GCE:* 160. *BTEC ExtDip:* MPP. Portfolio required.

M20 THE UNIVERSITY OF MANCHESTER
RUTHERFORD BUILDING
OXFORD ROAD
MANCHESTER M13 9PL
t: 0161 275 2077 f: 0161 275 2106
e: ug-admissions@manchester.ac.uk
// www.manchester.ac.uk

TW16 BA Chinese and Screen Studies
Duration: 4FT Hon
Entry Requirements: *GCE:* AAB-ABB. *SQAAH:* AAB-ABB.

WW46 BA Drama and Screen Studies
Duration: 3FT Hon
Entry Requirements: *GCE:* AAB-BBB. *SQAAH:* AAB-BBB. Interview required.

QW36 BA English Language and Screen Studies
Duration: 3FT Hon
Entry Requirements: *GCE:* AAB-BBB. *SQAAH:* AAB-BBB.

RW16 BA French and Screen Studies
Duration: 4FT Hon
Entry Requirements: *GCE:* AAB-ABB. *SQAAH:* AAB-ABB.

RW26 BA German and Screen Studies
Duration: 4FT Hon
Entry Requirements: *GCE:* AAB-BBB. *SQAAH:* AAB-BBB.

RW36 BA Italian and Screen Studies
Duration: 4FT Hon
Entry Requirements: *GCE:* AAB-BBB. *SQAAH:* AAB-BBB.

TW26 BA Japanese and Screen Studies
Duration: 4FT Hon
Entry Requirements: *GCE:* AAB-ABB. *SQAAH:* AAB-ABB.

TW76 BA Latin American Studies and Screen Studies
Duration: 4FT Hon
Entry Requirements: *GCE:* AAB-BBB. *SQAAH:* AAB-BBB.

QW16 BA Linguistics and Screen Studies
Duration: 3FT Hon
Entry Requirements: *GCE:* AAB-BBB. *SQAAH:* AAB-BBB.

TW66 BA Middle Eastern Studies and Screen Studies
Duration: 4FT Hon
Entry Requirements: *GCE:* AAB-BBC. *SQAAH:* AAB-BBC.

RW56 BA Portuguese and Screen Studies
Duration: 4FT Hon
Entry Requirements: *GCE:* AAB-BBB. *SQAAH:* AAB-BBB.

RW76 BA Russian and Screen Studies
Duration: 4FT Hon
Entry Requirements: *GCE:* AAB-BBB. *SQAAH:* AAB-BBB.

RW46 BA Spanish and Screen Studies
Duration: 4FT Hon
Entry Requirements: *GCE:* AAB-ABB. *SQAAH:* AAB-ABB.

M40 THE MANCHESTER METROPOLITAN UNIVERSITY
ADMISSIONS OFFICE
ALL SAINTS (GMS)
ALL SAINTS
MANCHESTER M15 6BH
t: 0161 247 2000
// www.mmu.ac.uk

QWH6 BA English and Film
Duration: 3FT Hon
Entry Requirements: *GCE:* 280. *IB:* 28.

W640 BA Photography
Duration: 3FT Hon
Entry Requirements: *GCE:* 280. *IB:* 27. Interview required. Portfolio required.

M77 MID CHESHIRE COLLEGE
HARTFORD CAMPUS
NORTHWICH
CHESHIRE CW8 1LJ
t: 01606 74444 f: 01606 720700
e: eandrews@midchesh.ac.uk
// www.midchesh.ac.uk

W641 FdA Contemporary Photography Practice
Duration: 2FT Fdg
Entry Requirements: *GCE:* 120. Interview required. Portfolio required.

M80 MIDDLESEX UNIVERSITY
MIDDLESEX UNIVERSITY
THE BURROUGHS
LONDON NW4 4BT
t: 020 8411 5555 f: 020 8411 5649
e: enquiries@mdx.ac.uk
// www.mdx.ac.uk

W640 BA Photography
Duration: 3FT Hon
Entry Requirements: *GCE:* 200-300. *IB:* 28. Interview required. Portfolio required.

M99 MYERSCOUGH COLLEGE
MYERSCOUGH HALL
BILSBORROW
PRESTON PR3 0RY
t: 01995 642222 f: 01995 642333
e: enquiries@myerscough.ac.uk
// www.myerscough.ac.uk

W640 FdA Location Photography
Duration: 2FT Fdg
Entry Requirements: Interview required.

N33 NEW COLLEGE STAMFORD
DRIFT ROAD
STAMFORD
LINCOLNSHIRE PE9 1XA
t: 01780 484300 f: 01780 484301
e: enquiries@stamford.ac.uk
// www.stamford.ac.uk

046W HND Photography
Duration: 2FT HND
Entry Requirements: Interview required.

N37 UNIVERSITY OF WALES, NEWPORT
ADMISSIONS
LODGE ROAD
CAERLEON
NEWPORT NP18 3QT
t: 01633 432030 f: 01633 432850
e: admissions@newport.ac.uk
// www.newport.ac.uk

W617 BA Creative Music
Duration: 3FT Hon
Entry Requirements: Foundation: Merit. GCE: 240-260. IB: 24.
Interview required. Portfolio required.

W640 BA Documentary Photography
Duration: 3FT Hon
Entry Requirements: Foundation: Merit. GCE: 240-260. IB: 24.
Interview required. Portfolio required.

W620 BA Film and Video
Duration: 3FT Hon
Entry Requirements: Foundation: Merit. GCE: 240-260. IB: 24.
Interview required. Portfolio required.

N38 UNIVERSITY OF NORTHAMPTON
PARK CAMPUS
BOUGHTON GREEN ROAD
NORTHAMPTON NN2 7AL
t: 0800 358 2232 f: 01604 722083
e: admissions@northampton.ac.uk
// www.northampton.ac.uk

056W HND Photography
Duration: 2FT HND
Entry Requirements: GCE: 140-160. SQAH: BC-CCC. IB: 24.
BTEC Dip: MP. BTEC ExtDip: MPP. OCR ND: P1 OCR NED: P2
Interview required.

N39 NORWICH UNIVERSITY COLLEGE OF THE ARTS
FRANCIS HOUSE
3-7 REDWELL STREET
NORWICH NR2 4SN
t: 01603 610561 f: 01603 615728
e: admissions@nuca.ac.uk
// www.nuca.ac.uk

W640 BA Photography
Duration: 3FT Hon
Entry Requirements: Foundation: Merit. GCE: BBC. BTEC Dip:
DM. BTEC ExtDip: MMM. OCR ND: M1 OCR NED: P1 Interview
required. Portfolio required.

N49 NESCOT, SURREY
REIGATE ROAD
EWELL
EPSOM
SURREY KT17 3DS
t: 020 8394 3038 f: 020 8394 3030
e: info@nescot.ac.uk
// www.nescot.ac.uk

W620 FdSc Photo Imaging
Duration: 2FT Fdg
Entry Requirements: GCE: 200. Portfolio required.

N78 NORTHUMBERLAND COLLEGE
COLLEGE ROAD
ASHINGTON
NORTHUMBERLAND NE63 9RG
t: 01670 841200 f: 01670 841201
e: advice.centre@northland.ac.uk
// www.northland.ac.uk

W640 HND Photography
Duration: 2FT HND
Entry Requirements: Contact the institution for details.

N79 NORTH WARWICKSHIRE AND HINCKLEY COLLEGE
HINCKLEY ROAD
NUNEATON
WARWICKSHIRE CV11 6BH
t: 024 7624 3395
e: angela.jones@nwhc.ac.uk
// www.nwhc.ac.uk

046W HND Photography
Duration: 2FT HND
Entry Requirements: Contact the institution for details.

N84 THE UNIVERSITY OF NOTTINGHAM
THE ADMISSIONS OFFICE
THE UNIVERSITY OF NOTTINGHAM
UNIVERSITY PARK
NOTTINGHAM NG7 2RD
t: 0115 951 5151 f: 0115 951 4668
// www.nottingham.ac.uk

TW76 BA Film and American Studies
Duration: 3FT Hon
Entry Requirements: *GCE:* ABC-BBB. *SQAAH:* ABC-BBB. *IB:* 30.

N91 NOTTINGHAM TRENT UNIVERSITY
DRYDEN BUILDING
BURTON STREET
NOTTINGHAM NG1 4BU
t: +44 (0) 115 848 4200 f: +44 (0) 115 848 8869
e: applications@ntu.ac.uk
// www.ntu.ac.uk

W640 BA Photography/Photography in Europe
Duration: 3FT Hon
Entry Requirements: *GCE:* 280. *BTEC Dip:* D*D*. *BTEC ExtDip:* DMM. Interview required. Portfolio required.

P60 PLYMOUTH UNIVERSITY
DRAKE CIRCUS
PLYMOUTH PL4 8AA
t: 01752 585858 f: 01752 588055
e: admissions@plymouth.ac.uk
// www.plymouth.ac.uk

W640 BA Photography
Duration: 3FT Hon
Entry Requirements: *Foundation:* Pass. *GCE:* 280. *IB:* 26. *BTEC ExtDip:* DMM. Interview required. Portfolio required.

W600 BA TV Arts
Duration: 1FT Hon
Entry Requirements: Contact the institution for details.

P65 PLYMOUTH COLLEGE OF ART (FORMERLY PLYMOUTH COLLEGE OF ART AND DESIGN)
TAVISTOCK PLACE
PLYMOUTH PL4 8AT
t: 01752 203434 f: 01752 203444
e: infoservices@plymouthart.ac.uk
// www.plymouthart.ac.uk

W692 BA Film
Duration: 3FT Hon
Entry Requirements: Contact the institution for details.

W620 BA Film (Top-Up)
Duration: 1FT Hon
Entry Requirements: Interview required. Portfolio required. HND required.

W645 BA Photography
Duration: 3FT Hon
Entry Requirements: Contact the institution for details.

W640 BA Photography (Top-Up)
Duration: 1FT Hon
Entry Requirements: Interview required. Portfolio required. HND required.

W643 FdA Commercial Photography
Duration: 2FT Fdg
Entry Requirements: Contact the institution for details.

W641 FdA Commercial Photography (including Level 0)
Duration: 3FT Fdg
Entry Requirements: *IB:* 24. *OCR ND:* P3 *OCR NED:* P3 Interview required. Portfolio required.

P80 UNIVERSITY OF PORTSMOUTH
ACADEMIC REGISTRY
UNIVERSITY HOUSE
WINSTON CHURCHILL AVENUE
PORTSMOUTH PO1 2UP
t: 023 9284 8484 f: 023 9284 3082
e: admissions@port.ac.uk
// www.port.ac.uk

QW36 BA English and Film Studies
Duration: 3FT Hon
Entry Requirements: *GCE:* 240-300. *IB:* 26. *BTEC SubDip:* P. *BTEC Dip:* DD. *BTEC ExtDip:* DMM.

W670 BA Film Studies
Duration: 3FT Hon
Entry Requirements: *GCE:* 240-300. *IB:* 25. *BTEC SubDip:* P. *BTEC Dip:* DD. *BTEC ExtDip:* DMM.

W640 BA Photography
Duration: 3FT Hon
Entry Requirements: *GCE:* 240-300. *IB:* 26. *BTEC SubDip:* P.
BTEC Dip: DD. *BTEC ExtDip:* DMM. Interview required. Portfolio
required.

Q25 QUEEN MARGARET UNIVERSITY, EDINBURGH
QUEEN MARGARET UNIVERSITY DRIVE
EDINBURGH EH21 6UU
t: 0131474 0000 f: 0131 474 0001
e: admissions@qmu.ac.uk
// www.qmu.ac.uk

WW46 BA Theatre and Film Studies
Duration: 4FT Hon
Entry Requirements: *GCE:* 300. *IB:* 30.

Q50 QUEEN MARY, UNIVERSITY OF LONDON
QUEEN MARY, UNIVERSITY OF LONDON
MILE END ROAD
LONDON E1 4NS
t: 020 7882 5555 f: 020 7882 5500
e: admissions@qmul.ac.uk
// www.qmul.ac.uk

QW36 BA English and Film Studies
Duration: 3FT Hon
Entry Requirements: *GCE:* 360. *IB:* 36.

WW46 BA Film Studies and Drama
Duration: 3FT Hon
Entry Requirements: *GCE:* 360. *IB:* 36.

RW16 BA Film Studies and French (4 years)
Duration: 4FT Hon
Entry Requirements: *GCE:* 340. *IB:* 34.

RW26 BA Film Studies and German (4 years)
Duration: 4FT Hon
Entry Requirements: *GCE:* 320. *IB:* 32.

RW46 BA Film Studies and Hispanic Studies (4 years)
Duration: 4FT Hon
Entry Requirements: *GCE:* 320. *IB:* 32.

VW16 BA Film Studies and History
Duration: 3FT Hon
Entry Requirements: *GCE:* 340. *IB:* 34.

RW76 BA Film Studies and Russian (4 years)
Duration: 4FT Hon
Entry Requirements: *GCE:* 320. *IB:* 32.

Q75 QUEEN'S UNIVERSITY BELFAST
UNIVERSITY ROAD
BELFAST BT7 1NN
t: 028 9097 3838 f: 028 9097 5151
e: admissions@qub.ac.uk
// www.qub.ac.uk

WW46 BA Drama and Film Studies
Duration: 3FT Hon
Entry Requirements: *GCE:* BBB-BBCb. *SQAH:* BBBBB. *SQAAH:*
BBB. *IB:* 32.

QW36 BA English and Film Studies
Duration: 3FT Hon
Entry Requirements: *GCE:* BBB-BBCb. *SQAH:* BBBBB. *SQAAH:*
BBB. *IB:* 32.

W600 BA Film Studies
Duration: 3FT Hon
Entry Requirements: *GCE:* BBB-BBCb. *SQAH:* BBBBB. *SQAAH:*
BBB. *IB:* 32.

R06 RAVENSBOURNE
6 PENROSE WAY
GREENWICH PENINSULA
LONDON SE10 0EW
t: 020 3040 3998
e: info@rave.ac.uk
// www.rave.ac.uk

W690 BA Editing & Post Production (with Foundation Year)
Duration: 4FT Hon
Entry Requirements: *Foundation:* Pass. *GCE:* A-E. *IB:* 28.
Interview required. Admissions Test required.

R18 REGENT'S COLLEGE, LONDON (INCORPORATING REGENT'S BUSINESS SCHOOL, LONDON)
INNER CIRCLE, REGENT'S COLLEGE
REGENT'S PARK
LONDON NW1 4NS
t: +44(0)20 7487 7505 f: +44(0)20 7487 7425
e: exrel@regents.ac.uk
// www.regents.ac.uk/

WW86 BA Screen Writing and Producing
Duration: 3FT Hon
Entry Requirements: *SQAH:* BBCC. *SQAAH:* CC.

R36 ROBERT GORDON UNIVERSITY
ROBERT GORDON UNIVERSITY
SCHOOLHILL
ABERDEEN
SCOTLAND AB10 1FR
t: 01224 26 27 28 f: 01224 26 21 47
e: UGOffice@rgu.ac.uk
// www.rgu.ac.uk

W641 BA Commercial Photography
Duration: 1FT Ord
Entry Requirements: Contact the institution for details.

R48 ROEHAMPTON UNIVERSITY
ROEHAMPTON LANE
LONDON SW15 5PU
t: 020 8392 3232 f: 020 8392 3470
e: enquiries@roehampton.ac.uk
// www.roehampton.ac.uk

W600 BA Film
Duration: 3FT Hon
Entry Requirements: *GCE:* 300. *IB:* 26. *BTEC ExtDip:* DDM. *OCR NED:* D2 Interview required.

W640 BA Photography
Duration: 3FT Hon
Entry Requirements: *GCE:* 300. *IB:* 26. *BTEC ExtDip:* DDM. *OCR NED:* D2 Interview required.

WW68 BA Photography and Creative Writing
Duration: 3FT Hon
Entry Requirements: *GCE:* 300. *IB:* 26. *BTEC ExtDip:* DDM. *OCR NED:* D2 Interview required.

WP63 BA Photography and Film
Duration: 3FT Hon
Entry Requirements: *GCE:* 300. *IB:* 26. *BTEC ExtDip:* DDM. *OCR NED:* D2 Interview required.

WP65 BA Photography and Journalism
Duration: 3FT Hon
Entry Requirements: *GCE:* 300. *IB:* 26. *BTEC ExtDip:* DDM. *OCR NED:* D2 Interview required.

WR64 BA Photography and Spanish
Duration: 4FT Hon
Entry Requirements: *GCE:* 300. *IB:* 26. *BTEC ExtDip:* DDM. *OCR NED:* D2 Interview required.

PW36 BA/BSc Media & Culture and Photography
Duration: 3FT Hon
Entry Requirements: *GCE:* 300. *IB:* 26. *BTEC ExtDip:* DDM. *OCR NED:* D2 Interview required.

WM69 BA/BSc Photography and Criminology
Duration: 3FT Hon
Entry Requirements: *GCE:* 300. *IB:* 26. *BTEC ExtDip:* DDM. *OCR NED:* D2 Interview required.

WV65 BA/BSc Photography and Philosophy
Duration: 3FT Hon
Entry Requirements: *GCE:* 300. *IB:* 26. *BTEC ExtDip:* DDM. *OCR NED:* D2 Interview required.

R52 ROTHERHAM COLLEGE OF ARTS AND TECHNOLOGY
EASTWOOD LANE
ROTHERHAM
SOUTH YORKSHIRE S65 1EG
t: 08080 722777 f: 01709 373053
e: info@rotherham.ac.uk
// www.rotherham.ac.uk

W640 FdA Photography
Duration: 2FT Fdg
Entry Requirements: *Foundation:* Pass. *GCE:* 120. Interview required. Portfolio required.

R72 ROYAL HOLLOWAY, UNIVERSITY OF LONDON
ROYAL HOLLOWAY, UNIVERSITY OF LONDON
EGHAM
SURREY TW20 0EX
t: 01784 414944 f: 01784 473662
e: Admissions@rhul.ac.uk
// www.rhul.ac.uk

Q2W6 BA Comparative Literature and Culture with Visual Arts
Duration: 3FT Hon
Entry Requirements: Contact the institution for details.

W620 BA Film Studies
Duration: 3FT Hon
Entry Requirements: *GCE:* ABB-ABbb. *SQAH:* AABBB. *SQAAH:* ABB. *IB:* 34.

W6V5 BA Film Studies with Philosophy
Duration: 3FT Hon
Entry Requirements: *GCE:* ABB-ABbb. *SQAH:* AABBB. *SQAAH:* ABB. *IB:* 34.

R1W6 BA French with Visual Arts
Duration: 4FT Hon
Entry Requirements: Contact the institution for details.

Q1W6 BA Multilingual Studies with Visual Arts
Duration: 4FT Hon
Entry Requirements: Contact the institution for details.

R4W6 BA Spanish with Visual Arts
Duration: 4FT Hon
Entry Requirements: Contact the institution for details.

S03 THE UNIVERSITY OF SALFORD
SALFORD M5 4WT
t: 0161 295 4545 f: 0161 295 4646
e: ug-admissions@salford.ac.uk
// www.salford.ac.uk

W640 BA Photography
Duration: 3FT Hon
Entry Requirements: *GCE:* 260. Interview required. Portfolio required.

S05 SAE INSTITUTE
297 KINGSLAND ROAD
LONDON E8 4DD
t: 020 7923 9159
e: degree.registry@sae.edu
// www.sae.edu

W616 BA/BSc Audio Production
Duration: 2FT Hon
Entry Requirements: Contact the institution for details.

W600 DipHE Audio Engineering
Duration: 1.5FT Dip
Entry Requirements: Contact the institution for details.

S21 SHEFFIELD HALLAM UNIVERSITY
CITY CAMPUS
HOWARD STREET
SHEFFIELD S1 1WB
t: 0114 225 5555 f: 0114 225 2167
e: admissions@shu.ac.uk
// www.shu.ac.uk

W640 BA Photography
Duration: 3FT Hon
Entry Requirements: *GCE:* 300.

W641 MArt Photography
Duration: 4FT Hon
Entry Requirements: *GCE:* 320.

S22 SHEFFIELD COLLEGE
THE SHEFFIELD COLLEGE
HE UNIT
HILLSBOROUGH COLLEGE AT THE BARRACKS
SHEFFIELD S6 2LR
t: 0114 260 2597
e: heunit@sheffcol.ac.uk
// www.sheffcol.ac.uk

W640 FdA Photography
Duration: 2FT Fdg
Entry Requirements: *GCE:* 120. Interview required. Portfolio required.

S27 UNIVERSITY OF SOUTHAMPTON
HIGHFIELD
SOUTHAMPTON SO17 1BJ
t: 023 8059 4732 f: 023 8059 3037
e: admissions@soton.ac.uk
// www.southampton.ac.uk

QW36 BA Film and English
Duration: 3FT Hon
Entry Requirements: *GCE:* AAB. *IB:* 34.

RW16 BA Film and French (4 years)
Duration: 4FT Hon
Entry Requirements: *GCE:* AAB. *IB:* 34.

RW26 BA Film and German (4 years)
Duration: 4FT Hon
Entry Requirements: *GCE:* AAB. *IB:* 34.

WV61 BA Film and History
Duration: 3FT Hon
Entry Requirements: *GCE:* AAB. *IB:* 34.

WV65 BA Film and Philosophy
Duration: 3FT Hon
Entry Requirements: *GCE:* AAB. *IB:* 34.

RW46 BA Film and Spanish (4 years)
Duration: 4FT Hon
Entry Requirements: *GCE:* AAB. *IB:* 34.

S30 SOUTHAMPTON SOLENT UNIVERSITY
EAST PARK TERRACE
SOUTHAMPTON
HAMPSHIRE SO14 0RT
t: +44 (0) 23 8031 9039 f: + 44 (0)23 8022 2259
e: admissions@solent.ac.uk
// www.solent.ac.uk/

W610 BA Film
Duration: 3FT Hon
Entry Requirements: *Foundation:* Distinction. *GCE:* 260. *SQAAH:* AA-CCC. *IB:* 24. *BTEC ExtDip:* DDM. *OCR NED:* M2 Interview required.

W651 BA Photography
Duration: 3FT Hon
Entry Requirements: *Foundation:* Distinction. *GCE:* 260. *SQAAH:* AA-CCC. *IB:* 24. *BTEC ExtDip:* DDM. *OCR NED:* M2 Portfolio required.

W642 BA Photography (Top-Up)
Duration: 1FT Hon
Entry Requirements: Interview required. Portfolio required. HND required.

W644 BA Photography with International Foundation Year
Duration: 4FT Hon
Entry Requirements: Contact the institution for details.

W614 BA Special Effects
Duration: 3FT Hon
Entry Requirements: *Foundation:* Merit. *GCE:* 200. *SQAAH:* AC-DDD. *IB:* 24. *BTEC ExtDip:* MMP. *OCR ND:* M1 *OCR NED:* P1 Interview required. Portfolio required.

S35 SOUTHPORT COLLEGE
MORNINGTON ROAD
SOUTHPORT
MERSEYSIDE PR9 0TT
t: 08450066236 f: 01704 392610
e: guidance@southport-college.ac.uk
// www.southport-college.ac.uk

W640 HND Photography
Duration: 2FT HND
Entry Requirements: Contact the institution for details.

S43 SOUTH ESSEX COLLEGE OF FURTHER & HIGHER EDUCATION
LUKER ROAD
SOUTHEND-ON-SEA
ESSEX SS1 1ND
t: 0845 52 12345 f: 01702 432320
e: Admissions@southessex.ac.uk
// www.southessex.ac.uk

W642 BA Photography
Duration: 3FT Hon
Entry Requirements: *GCE:* 160. *IB:* 24. Interview required.

W643 CertHE Photography
Duration: 1FT Cer
Entry Requirements: *GCE:* 120. *IB:* 24. Interview required.

W641 DipHE Photography
Duration: 2FT Dip
Entry Requirements: *GCE:* 120. *IB:* 24. Interview required. Admissions Test required.

S46 SOUTH NOTTINGHAM COLLEGE
WEST BRIDGFORD CENTRE
GREYTHORN DRIVE
WEST BRIDGFORD
NOTTINGHAM NG2 7GA
t: 0115 914 6400 f: 0115 914 6444
e: enquiries@snc.ac.uk
// www.snc.ac.uk

W640 FdA Photography
Duration: 2FT Fdg
Entry Requirements: *GCE:* 160. Interview required.

S51 ST HELENS COLLEGE
WATER STREET
ST HELENS
MERSEYSIDE WA10 1PP
t: 01744 733766 f: 01744 623400
e: enquiries@sthelens.ac.uk
// www.sthelens.ac.uk

W640 BA Photography
Duration: 3FT Hon
Entry Requirements: *GCE:* 120.

S72 STAFFORDSHIRE UNIVERSITY
COLLEGE ROAD
STOKE ON TRENT ST4 2DE
t: 01782 292753 f: 01782 292740
e: admissions@staffs.ac.uk
// www.staffs.ac.uk

W642 BA Entrepreneurship in Photography
Duration: 1FT Hon
Entry Requirements: Interview required. Portfolio required.

W600 BA Media (Film) Production
Duration: 3FT/4FT Hon
Entry Requirements: *Foundation:* Merit. *GCE:* 200-240. *IB:* 24. *BTEC Dip:* DD. *BTEC ExtDip:* MMM. Interview required. Portfolio required.

W640 BA Photography
Duration: 3FT/4FT Hon
Entry Requirements: *Foundation:* Merit. *GCE:* 200-240. *IB:* 24. *BTEC Dip:* DD. *BTEC ExtDip:* MMM. Interview required. Portfolio required.

WP65 BA Photojournalism
Duration: 3FT/4FT Hon
Entry Requirements: *Foundation:* Merit. *GCE:* 200-240. *IB:* 24. *BTEC Dip:* DD. *BTEC ExtDip:* MMM. Interview required. Portfolio required.

S74 STRATFORD UPON AVON COLLEGE
THE WILLOWS NORTH
ALCESTER ROAD
STRATFORD-UPON-AVON
WARWICKSHIRE CV37 9QR
t: 01789 266245 f: 01789 267524
e: college@stratford.ac.uk
// www.stratford.ac.uk

W640 HND Photography
Duration: 2FT HND
Entry Requirements: Contact the institution for details.

S76 STOCKPORT COLLEGE
WELLINGTON ROAD SOUTH
STOCKPORT SK1 3UQ
t: 0161 958 3143 f: 0161 958 3663
e: susan.kelly@stockport.ac.uk
// www.stockport.ac.uk

W640 BA Photography
Duration: 3FT Hon
Entry Requirements: Contact the institution for details.

W641 FdA Commercial Photography
Duration: 2FT Fdg
Entry Requirements: Portfolio required.

S82 UNIVERSITY CAMPUS SUFFOLK (UCS)
WATERFRONT BUILDING
NEPTUNE QUAY
IPSWICH
SUFFOLK IP4 1QJ
t: 01473 338833 f: 01473 339900
e: info@ucs.ac.uk
// www.ucs.ac.uk

W601 BA Photography
Duration: 3FT Hon
Entry Requirements: *GCE:* 240-280. *IB:* 28. *BTEC ExtDip:* DMM. Interview required. Portfolio required.

S84 UNIVERSITY OF SUNDERLAND
STUDENT HELPLINE
THE STUDENT GATEWAY
CHESTER ROAD
SUNDERLAND SR1 3SD
t: 0191 515 3000 f: 0191 515 3805
e: student.helpline@sunderland.ac.uk
// www.sunderland.ac.uk

WN61 BA Business Management and Photography
Duration: 3FT Hon
Entry Requirements: *GCE:* 260-360. *IB:* 31. *OCR ND:* D *OCR NED:* M3

N2W6 BA Business Management with Photography
Duration: 3FT Hon
Entry Requirements: *GCE:* 260-360. *IB:* 31. *OCR ND:* D *OCR NED:* M3

XWH6 BA Childhood Studies and Photography
Duration: 3FT Hon
Entry Requirements: *GCE:* 260-360.

X3W6 BA Childhood Studies with Photography
Duration: 3FT Hon
Entry Requirements: *GCE:* 260-360.

WM69 BA Criminology and Photography
Duration: 3FT Hon
Entry Requirements: *GCE:* 260-360. *OCR ND:* D *OCR NED:* M3

M9W6 BA Criminology with Photography
Duration: 3FT Hon
Entry Requirements: *GCE:* 260-360. *OCR ND:* D *OCR NED:* M3

WW56 BA Dance and Photography
Duration: 3FT Hon
Entry Requirements: *GCE:* 260-360. *IB:* 31. *OCR ND:* D *OCR NED:* M3

W5W6 BA Dance with Photography
Duration: 3FT Hon
Entry Requirements: *GCE:* 220-360. *IB:* 31. *OCR ND:* D *OCR NED:* M3

W4W6 BA Drama with Photography
Duration: 3FT Hon
Entry Requirements: *GCE:* 260-360. *OCR ND:* D *OCR NED:* M3

Q1W6 BA English Language & Linguistics with Photography
Duration: 3FT Hon
Entry Requirements: *GCE:* 260-360. *OCR ND:* D *OCR NED:* M3

WQ63 BA English and Photography
Duration: 3FT Hon
Entry Requirements: *GCE:* 260-360. *IB:* 31. *OCR ND:* D *OCR NED:* M3

Q3W6 BA English with Photography
Duration: 3FT Hon
Entry Requirements: *GCE:* 260-360. *IB:* 31. *OCR ND:* D *OCR NED:* M3

PW36 BA Film and Media
Duration: 3FT Hon
Entry Requirements: *GCE:* 260-360. *IB:* 30.

LW56 BA Health & Social Care and Photography
Duration: 3FT Hon
Entry Requirements: *GCE:* 260-360.

WV61 BA History and Photography
Duration: 3FT Hon
Entry Requirements: *GCE:* 260-360. *IB:* 31. *OCR ND:* D *OCR NED:* M3

V1W6 BA History with Photography
Duration: 3FT Hon
Entry Requirements: *GCE:* 260-360. *IB:* 31. *OCR ND:* D *OCR NED:* M3

PW56 BA Journalism and Photography
Duration: 3FT Hon
Entry Requirements: *GCE:* 260-360. *IB:* 32. *OCR ND:* D *OCR NED:* M3

P5W6 BA Journalism with Photography
Duration: 3FT Hon
Entry Requirements: *GCE:* 260-360. *IB:* 32. *OCR ND:* D *OCR NED:* M3

RW16 BA Modern Foreign Languages (French) and Photography
Duration: 3FT Hon
Entry Requirements: *GCE:* 260-360. *IB:* 31. *OCR ND:* D *OCR NED:* M3

RW26 BA Modern Foreign Languages (German) and Photography
Duration: 3FT Hon
Entry Requirements: *GCE:* 260-360. *IB:* 31. *OCR ND:* D *OCR NED:* M3

RW46 BA Modern Foreign Languages (Spanish) and Photography
Duration: 3FT Hon
Entry Requirements: *GCE:* 260-360. *IB:* 31. *OCR ND:* D *OCR NED:* M3

WW46 BA Photography and Drama
Duration: 3FT Hon
Entry Requirements: *GCE:* 260-360. *OCR ND:* D *OCR NED:* M3

WX63 BA Photography and Education
Duration: 3FT Hon
Entry Requirements: *GCE:* 260-360. *OCR ND:* D *OCR NED:* M3

WQ61 BA Photography and English Language/Linguistics
Duration: 3FT Hon
Entry Requirements: *GCE:* 260-360. *OCR ND:* D *OCR NED:* M3

WL62 BA Photography and Politics
Duration: 3FT Hon
Entry Requirements: *GCE:* 260-360. *OCR ND:* D *OCR NED:* M3

WC68 BA Photography and Psychology
Duration: 3FT Hon
Entry Requirements: *GCE:* 260-360. *OCR ND:* D *OCR NED:* M3

WL63 BA Photography and Sociology
Duration: 3FT Hon
Entry Requirements: *GCE:* 260-360. *OCR ND:* D *OCR NED:* M3

WX61 BA Photography and TESOL
Duration: 3FT Hon
Entry Requirements: *GCE:* 260-360. *OCR ND:* D *OCR NED:* M3

W6W5 BA Photography with Dance
Duration: 3FT Hon
Entry Requirements: *GCE:* 260-360.

W6L5 BA Photography with Health & Social Care
Duration: 3FT Hon
Entry Requirements: *GCE:* 260-360.

PW26 BA Public Relations and Photography
Duration: 3FT Hon
Entry Requirements: *GCE:* 260-360. *OCR ND:* D *OCR NED:* M3

P2W6 BA Public Relations with Photography
Duration: 3FT Hon
Entry Requirements: *GCE:* 260-360. *OCR ND:* D *OCR NED:* M3

L3W6 BA Sociology with Photography
Duration: 3FT Hon
Entry Requirements: *GCE:* 260-360. *IB:* 31. *OCR ND:* D *OCR NED:* M3

X1W6 BA TESOL with Photography
Duration: 3FT Hon
Entry Requirements: *GCE:* 260-360. *OCR ND:* D *OCR NED:* M3

NW86 BA Tourism and Photography
Duration: 3FT Hon
Entry Requirements: *GCE:* 260-360. *IB:* 31. *OCR ND:* D *OCR NED:* M3

N8W6 BA Tourism with Photography
Duration: 3FT Hon
Entry Requirements: *GCE:* 220-360. *IB:* 31. *OCR ND:* D *OCR NED:* M3

CW66 BA/BSc Sport and Photography
Duration: 3FT Hon
Entry Requirements: *GCE:* 260-360. *OCR ND:* D *OCR NED:* M3

C8W6 BSc Psychology with Photography
Duration: 3FT Hon
Entry Requirements: *GCE:* 260-360. *IB:* 32. *OCR ND:* D *OCR NED:* M3

C6W6 BSc Sport with Photography
Duration: 3FT Hon
Entry Requirements: *GCE:* 260-360. *OCR ND:* D *OCR NED:* M3

W640 FdA Applied Photography
Duration: 2FT Fdg
Entry Requirements: *GCE:* 80-220. *SQAH:* CCCC. *IB:* 22.
Interview required.

S85 UNIVERSITY OF SURREY
STAG HILL
GUILDFORD
SURREY GU2 7XH
t: +44(0)1483 689305 f: +44(0)1483 689388
e: ugteam@surrey.ac.uk
// www.surrey.ac.uk

W620 BA Film Studies (3 or 4 years)
Duration: 3FT/4SW Hon
Entry Requirements: *GCE:* ABB. *IB:* 34.

W6W8 BA (Hons) Film Studies with Creative Writing (3 or 4 years)
Duration: 3FT/4SW Hon
Entry Requirements: *GCE:* ABB. *IB:* 34.

S96 SWANSEA METROPOLITAN UNIVERSITY
MOUNT PLEASANT CAMPUS
SWANSEA SA1 6ED
t: 01792 481000 f: 01792 481061
e: gemma.green@smu.ac.uk
// www.smu.ac.uk

W600 BA Documentary Video
Duration: 3FT Hon
Entry Requirements: *Foundation:* Pass. *GCE:* 200-360. *IB:* 24.
Interview required. Portfolio required.

W643 BA Photography in the Arts
Duration: 3FT Hon
Entry Requirements: *Foundation:* Pass. *GCE:* 200-360. *IB:* 24.
Interview required. Portfolio required.

W640 BA Photography in the Arts (4-year programme)
Duration: 4FT Hon
Entry Requirements: *Foundation:* Pass. *GCE:* 200-360. *IB:* 24.
Interview required. Portfolio required.

W6P5 BA Photojournalism
Duration: 3FT Hon
Entry Requirements: *Foundation:* Pass. *GCE:* 200-360. *IB:* 24.
Interview required. Portfolio required.

WP65 BA Photojournalism (4 Year Programme)
Duration: 4FT Hon
Entry Requirements: *Foundation:* Pass. *GCE:* 200-360. *IB:* 24.
Interview required. Portfolio required.

W611 BA Video Arts
Duration: 3FT Hon
Entry Requirements: *Foundation:* Pass. *GCE:* 200-360. *IB:* 24.
Interview required. Portfolio required.

S98 SWINDON COLLEGE
NORTH STAR AVENUE
SWINDON
WILTSHIRE SN2 1DY
t: 0800 731 2250 f: 01793 430503
e: headmissions@swindon-college.ac.uk
// www.swindon-college.ac.uk

046W HND Photography
Duration: 2FT HND
Entry Requirements: *Foundation:* Pass. *IB:* 24. Foundation
Course required. Interview required. Portfolio required.

T85 TRURO AND PENWITH COLLEGE
TRURO COLLEGE
COLLEGE ROAD
TRURO
CORNWALL TR1 3XX
t: 01872 267122 f: 01872 267526
e: heinfo@trurocollege.ac.uk
// www.truro-penwith.ac.uk

W610 FdA Action Photography
Duration: 2FT Fdg
Entry Requirements: *GCE:* 60. *IB:* 24. *BTEC Dip:* MP. *BTEC*
ExtDip: PPP. Interview required.

U20 UNIVERSITY OF ULSTER
COLERAINE
CO. LONDONDERRY
NORTHERN IRELAND BT52 1SA
t: 028 7012 4221 f: 028 7012 4908
e: online@ulster.ac.uk
// www.ulster.ac.uk

Q3W6 BA English with Photo-Imaging
Duration: 3FT Hon
Entry Requirements: *GCE:* 280. *IB:* 24.

P3W6 BA Film Studies with Photo-Imaging
Duration: 3FT Hon
Entry Requirements: *GCE:* BBC. *IB:* 24.

R1W6 BA French with Photo-Imaging
Duration: 3FT Hon
Entry Requirements: *GCE:* 260. *IB:* 24.

R2W6 BA German with Photo-Imaging
Duration: 3FT Hon
Entry Requirements: *GCE:* 260. *IB:* 24.

V1W6 BA History with Photo-Imaging
Duration: 3FT Hon
Entry Requirements: *GCE:* 280. *IB:* 24.

P5W6 BA Journalism with Photo Imaging
Duration: 3FT Hon
Entry Requirements: *GCE:* 280-300.

W641 BA Photography
Duration: 3FT Hon
Entry Requirements: *GCE:* 240. *IB:* 24. Interview required.
Portfolio required.

R4W6 BA Spanish with Photo-Imaging
Duration: 3FT Hon
Entry Requirements: *GCE:* 260. *IB:* 24.

U40 UNIVERSITY OF THE WEST OF SCOTLAND
PAISLEY
RENFREWSHIRE
SCOTLAND PA1 2BE
t: 0141 848 3727 f: 0141 848 3623
e: admissions@uws.ac.uk
// www.uws.ac.uk

WW68 BA Filmmaking and Screen Writing
Duration: 4FT Hon
Entry Requirements: *GCE:* BC-CC. *SQAH:* BBC. Interview required.
Portfolio required.

W690 BA Photography
Duration: 1FT Ord
Entry Requirements: Interview required. HND required.

U65 UNIVERSITY OF THE ARTS LONDON
272 HIGH HOLBORN
LONDON WC1V 7EY
t: 020 7514 6000x6197 f: 020 7514 6198
e: c.anderson@arts.ac.uk
// www.arts.ac.uk

W640 BA Photography
Duration: 3FT Hon
Entry Requirements: *IB:* 28. Foundation Course required. Interview
required. Portfolio required.

W643 BA Photography
Duration: 3FT Hon
Entry Requirements: *Foundation:* Pass. *GCE:* 80. *IB:* 28.
Interview required. Portfolio required.

W05 THE UNIVERSITY OF WEST LONDON
ST MARY'S ROAD
EALING
LONDON W5 5RF
t: 0800 036 8888 f: 020 8566 1353
e: learning.advice@uwl.ac.uk
// www.uwl.ac.uk

W600 BA Practical Filmmaking (Met Film School)
Duration: 2FT Hon
Entry Requirements: *GCE:* 160. *IB:* 24. Interview required.

W642 BA (Hons) Photography
Duration: 3FT Hon
Entry Requirements: *GCE:* 240. Interview required. Portfolio required.

W620 CertHE Cinematography (Met Film School)
Duration: 1FT Cer
Entry Requirements: *GCE:* 50. Interview required.

W601 CertHE Practical Filmmaking (Met Film School)
Duration: 1FT Cer
Entry Requirements: *GCE:* 50. Interview required.

316W DipHE Practical Film Making
Duration: 2FT Dip
Entry Requirements: *GCE:* 100. *IB:* 24. Interview required.

W641 FdA Photography
Duration: 2FT Fdg
Entry Requirements: *GCE:* 180. *IB:* 24. Interview required. Portfolio required.

W08 WAKEFIELD COLLEGE
MARGARET STREET
WAKEFIELD
WEST YORKSHIRE WF1 2DH
t: 01924 789111 f: 01924 789281
e: courseinfo@wakefield.ac.uk
// www.wakefield.ac.uk

W641 FdA Photography (Commercial)
Duration: 2FT Fdg
Entry Requirements: *GCE:* 120.

W12 WALSALL COLLEGE
WALSALL COLLEGE
LITTLETON STREET WEST
WALSALL
WEST MIDLANDS WS2 8ES
t: 01922 657000 f: 01922 657083
e: ckemp@walsallcollege.ac.uk
// www.walsallcollege.ac.uk

W640 HNC Photography
Duration: 1FT HNC
Entry Requirements: Contact the institution for details.

046W HND Photography
Duration: 2FT HND
Entry Requirements: Contact the institution for details.

W20 THE UNIVERSITY OF WARWICK
COVENTRY CV4 8UW
t: 024 7652 3723 f: 024 7652 4649
e: ugadmissions@warwick.ac.uk
// www.warwick.ac.uk

W620 BA Film Studies
Duration: 3FT Hon
Entry Requirements: *GCE:* AABb. *SQAAH:* AA. *IB:* 36. Interview required.

QW26 BA Film and Literature
Duration: 3FT Hon
Entry Requirements: *GCE:* AABb. *SQAAH:* AA. *IB:* 36. Interview required.

R1W6 BA French with Film Studies
Duration: 4FT Hon
Entry Requirements: *GCE:* AAB. *SQAAH:* AA. *IB:* 36.

R3W6 BA Italian with Film Studies (4 years including year abroad)
Duration: 4FT Hon
Entry Requirements: *GCE:* AAB. *SQAAH:* AA. *IB:* 36.

W50 UNIVERSITY OF WESTMINSTER
2ND FLOOR, CAVENDISH HOUSE
101 NEW CAVENDISH STREET,
LONDON W1W 6XH
t: 020 7915 5511
e: course-enquiries@westminster.ac.uk
// www.westminster.ac.uk

WB69 BSc Clinical Photography
Duration: 3FT Hon
Entry Requirements: *GCE:* CC. *SQAH:* CCCC. *IB:* 26. Interview required.

W51 CITY OF WESTMINSTER COLLEGE

CITY OF WESTMINSTER COLLEGE
PADDINGTON GREEN CAMPUS
25 PADDINGTON GREEN
LONDON W2 1NB
t: 020 7723 8826
e: customer.services@cwc.ac.uk
// www.cwc.ac.uk

W640 FdA Professional Photography
Duration: 2FT Fdg
Entry Requirements: Interview required. Portfolio required.

W75 UNIVERSITY OF WOLVERHAMPTON

ADMISSIONS UNIT
MX207, CAMP STREET
WOLVERHAMPTON
WEST MIDLANDS WV1 1AD
t: 01902 321000 f: 01902 321896
e: admissions@wlv.ac.uk
// www.wlv.ac.uk

WQ63 BA Film Studies and English
Duration: 3FT Hon
Entry Requirements: GCE: 160-220. IB: 28.

WPQ3 BA Film Studies and Media & Cultural Studies
Duration: 3FT Hon
Entry Requirements: GCE: 160-220. IB: 24.

PWH6 BA Media & Communication Studies and Film Studies
Duration: 3FT Hon
Entry Requirements: GCE: 160-220. IB: 28.

W640 BA Photography
Duration: 3FT/4SW Hon
Entry Requirements: GCE: 200. IB: 24. BTEC Dip: DM. BTEC ExtDip: MMP. OCR ND: M1 OCR NED: P1 Interview required. Portfolio required.

W613 BA Video and Film Production
Duration: 3FT/4SW Hon
Entry Requirements: GCE: 200. IB: 24. BTEC Dip: DM. BTEC ExtDip: MMP. OCR ND: M1 OCR NED: P1 Interview required. Portfolio required.

W612 FdA Commercial Video Production
Duration: 1FT Fdg
Entry Requirements: GCE: 160. IB: 24. BTEC Dip: MM. BTEC ExtDip: MPP. OCR ND: M2 OCR NED: P2 Interview required. Portfolio required.

146W HND Photography
Duration: 2FT HND
Entry Requirements: GCE: 40. Interview required. Portfolio required.

PRODUCT DESIGN

A30 UNIVERSITY OF ABERTAY DUNDEE

BELL STREET
DUNDEE DD1 1HG
t: 01382 308080 f: 01382 308081
e: sro@abertay.ac.uk
// www.abertay.ac.uk

D610 BSc Food Product Design
Duration: 4FT Hon
Entry Requirements: GCE: CDD. SQAH: BBC. IB: 26.

A80 ASTON UNIVERSITY, BIRMINGHAM

ASTON TRIANGLE
BIRMINGHAM B4 7ET
t: 0121 204 4444 f: 0121 204 3696
e: admissions@aston.ac.uk (automatic response)
// www.aston.ac.uk/prospective-students/ug

H772 BSc Industrial Product Design
Duration: 3FT/4SW Hon
Entry Requirements: GCE: 300-320. IB: 32. OCR NED: D1

H773 BSc Product Design and Management
Duration: 3FT/4SW Hon
Entry Requirements: GCE: 300-320. IB: 32. OCR NED: D1

H331 BSc Transport Product Design
Duration: 3FT/4SW Hon
Entry Requirements: IB: 32.

B06 BANGOR UNIVERSITY

BANGOR UNIVERSITY
BANGOR
GWYNEDD LL57 2DG
t: 01248 388484 f: 01248 370451
e: admissions@bangor.ac.uk
// www.bangor.ac.uk

W240 BSc Product Design
Duration: 3FT Hon
Entry Requirements: GCE: 200-220. IB: 28.

B25 BIRMINGHAM CITY UNIVERSITY
PERRY BARR
BIRMINGHAM B42 2SU
t: 0121 331 5595 f: 0121 331 7994
// www.bcu.ac.uk

W243 BA Product Design
Duration: 3FT Hon
Entry Requirements: *GCE:* 280. *IB:* 28. Interview required.
Portfolio required.

B50 BOURNEMOUTH UNIVERSITY
TALBOT CAMPUS
FERN BARROW
POOLE
DORSET BH12 5BB
t: 01202 524111
// www.bournemouth.ac.uk

W242 BA Industrial Design
Duration: 3FT/4SW Hon
Entry Requirements: *GCE:* 300. *IB:* 31. *BTEC SubDip:* D. *BTEC Dip:* DD. *BTEC ExtDip:* DDM. Interview required. Portfolio required.

W240 BA Product Design
Duration: 4SW Hon
Entry Requirements: *GCE:* 320. *IB:* 32. *BTEC SubDip:* D. *BTEC Dip:* DD. *BTEC ExtDip:* DDM. Interview required. Portfolio required.

B56 THE UNIVERSITY OF BRADFORD
RICHMOND ROAD
BRADFORD
WEST YORKSHIRE BD7 1DP
t: 0800 073 1225 f: 01274 235585
e: course-enquiries@bradford.ac.uk
// www.bradford.ac.uk

HW72 BSc Product Design
Duration: 3FT Hon
Entry Requirements: *GCE:* 240. *IB:* 24. Interview required.

HWR2 BSc Product Design (4 years)
Duration: 4SW Hon
Entry Requirements: *GCE:* 240. *IB:* 24. Interview required.

B72 UNIVERSITY OF BRIGHTON
MITHRAS HOUSE 211
LEWES ROAD
BRIGHTON BN2 4AT
t: 01273 644644 f: 01273 642607
e: admissions@brighton.ac.uk
// www.brighton.ac.uk

W240 BA Design and Craft
Duration: 3FT Hon
Entry Requirements: *GCE:* BBB. Interview required. Portfolio required.

W242 BSc Product Design with Professional Experience
Duration: 4SW Hon
Entry Requirements: *GCE:* BBB. *IB:* 36. Interview required. Portfolio required.

W243 BSc Sustainable Product Design with Professional Experience
Duration: 3FT/4SW Deg/Hon
Entry Requirements: *GCE:* BBB. *IB:* 34. Interview required. Portfolio required.

B84 BRUNEL UNIVERSITY
UXBRIDGE
MIDDLESEX UB8 3PH
t: 01895 265265 f: 01895 269790
e: admissions@brunel.ac.uk
// www.brunel.ac.uk

WH27 BSc Product Design Engineering
Duration: 3FT Hon
Entry Requirements: *GCE:* ABB. *SQAAH:* ABB. *IB:* 33. *BTEC ExtDip:* D*DD. Interview required.

WHF7 BSc Product Design Engineering (4 year Thick SW)
Duration: 4SW Hon
Entry Requirements: *GCE:* ABB. *SQAAH:* ABB. *IB:* 33. *BTEC ExtDip:* D*DD. Interview required.

B94 BUCKINGHAMSHIRE NEW UNIVERSITY
QUEEN ALEXANDRA ROAD
HIGH WYCOMBE
BUCKINGHAMSHIRE HP11 2JZ
t: 0800 0565 660 f: 01494 605 023
e: admissions@bucks.ac.uk
// bucks.ac.uk

W241 BA Product Design
Duration: 3FT Hon
Entry Requirements: *GCE:* 200-240. *IB:* 24. *OCR ND:* M1 *OCR NED:* M3 Interview required.

W240 BA Spatial Design
Duration: 3FT Hon
Entry Requirements: *GCE:* 200-240. *IB:* 24. *OCR ND:* M1 *OCR NED:* M3 Interview required.

HW72 BSc Product Design
Duration: 3FT Hon
Entry Requirements: *GCE:* 200-240. *IB:* 24. *OCR ND:* M1 *OCR NED:* M3 Interview required.

C20 CARDIFF METROPOLITAN UNIVERSITY (UWIC)
ADMISSIONS UNIT
LLANDAFF CAMPUS
WESTERN AVENUE
CARDIFF CF5 2YB
t: 029 2041 6070 f: 029 2041 6286
e: admissions@cardiffmet.ac.uk
// www.cardiffmet.ac.uk

W240 BA Product Design
Duration: 3FT Hon
Entry Requirements: *GCE:* 300. *IB:* 26. *BTEC ExtDip:* DDM. *OCR NED:* D2 Foundation Course required. Interview required. Portfolio required.

C30 UNIVERSITY OF CENTRAL LANCASHIRE
PRESTON
LANCS PR1 2HE
t: 01772 201201 f: 01772 894954
e: uadmissions@uclan.ac.uk
// www.uclan.ac.uk

W241 BA Product Design
Duration: 3FT Hon
Entry Requirements: *GCE:* 240-300. *IB:* 26. *OCR ND:* D *OCR NED:* M3 Interview required. Portfolio required.

W240 BSc Product Design
Duration: 3FT Hon
Entry Requirements: *GCE:* 240-300. *IB:* 26. *OCR ND:* D *OCR NED:* M3 Interview required. Portfolio required.

C85 COVENTRY UNIVERSITY
THE STUDENT CENTRE
COVENTRY UNIVERSITY
1 GULSON RD
COVENTRY CV1 2JH
t: 024 7615 2222 f: 024 7615 2223
e: studentenquiries@coventry.ac.uk
// www.coventry.ac.uk

WHG3 BA Automotive Design
Duration: 3FT/4SW Hon
Entry Requirements: *Foundation:* Merit. *GCE:* BCC. *SQAH:* BCCCC. *IB:* 27. *BTEC ExtDip:* MMM. *OCR NED:* M3 Interview required. Portfolio required.

W24D BA Product Design
Duration: 4SW/3FT Hon
Entry Requirements: *Foundation:* Merit. *GCE:* CCC. *SQAH:* CCCCC. *IB:* 27. *BTEC ExtDip:* MMM. *OCR NED:* M3 Interview required. Portfolio required.

WH22 BA Transport Design
Duration: 3FT/4SW Hon
Entry Requirements: *Foundation:* Merit. *GCE:* BCC. *SQAH:* BCCCC. *IB:* 27. *BTEC ExtDip:* MMM. *OCR NED:* M3 Interview required. Portfolio required.

W241 MDes Automotive Design
Duration: 4FT Hon
Entry Requirements: *Foundation:* Merit. *GCE:* BCC. *SQAH:* BCCCC. *IB:* 27. *BTEC ExtDip:* MMM. *OCR NED:* M3 Interview required. Portfolio required.

W243 MDes Product Design
Duration: 4FT Hon
Entry Requirements: *Foundation:* Merit. *GCE:* CCC. *SQAH:* CCCCC. *IB:* 27. *BTEC ExtDip:* MMM. *OCR NED:* M3 Interview required. Portfolio required.

WH27 MDes Transport Design
Duration: 4FT Hon
Entry Requirements: *Foundation:* Merit. *GCE:* BCC. *SQAH:* BCCCC. *IB:* 27. *BTEC ExtDip:* MMM. *OCR NED:* M3 Interview required. Portfolio required.

C93 UNIVERSITY FOR THE CREATIVE ARTS
FALKNER ROAD
FARNHAM
SURREY GU9 7DS
t: 01252 892960
e: admissions@ucreative.ac.uk
// www.ucreative.ac.uk

W240 BA Product Design
Duration: 3FT Hon
Entry Requirements: *GCE:* 220. *IB:* 24. *BTEC ExtDip:* PPP.
Interview required. Portfolio required.

W242 BA Product Design and Interaction
Duration: 3FT Hon
Entry Requirements: *GCE:* 220. *IB:* 24. *BTEC ExtDip:* PPP.
Interview required. Portfolio required.

D26 DE MONTFORT UNIVERSITY
THE GATEWAY
LEICESTER LE1 9BH
t: 0116 255 1551 f: 0116 250 6204
e: enquiries@dmu.ac.uk
// www.dmu.ac.uk

W240 BA Product Design
Duration: 3FT Hon
Entry Requirements: *Foundation:* Pass. *GCE:* 260. *IB:* 28. *BTEC
Dip:* D*D. *BTEC ExtDip:* MMM. Interview required. Portfolio
required.

W242 BSc Product Design
Duration: 3FT/4SW Hon
Entry Requirements: *Foundation:* Pass. *GCE:* 260. *IB:* 28. *BTEC
Dip:* D*D. *BTEC ExtDip:* MMM. Interview required. Portfolio
required.

WH21 MDes Design Products
Duration: 4FT Hon
Entry Requirements: *Foundation:* Pass. *GCE:* 280. *IB:* 30. *BTEC
Dip:* D*D*. *BTEC ExtDip:* DMM. Interview required. Portfolio
required.

D39 UNIVERSITY OF DERBY
KEDLESTON ROAD
DERBY DE22 1GB
t: 01332 591167 f: 01332 597724
e: askadmissions@derby.ac.uk
// www.derby.ac.uk

W241 BA Product Design
Duration: 3FT Hon
Entry Requirements: *Foundation:* Distinction. *GCE:* 260. *IB:* 28.
BTEC Dip: D*D*. *BTEC ExtDip:* DMM. *OCR NED:* M2 Interview
required.

W242 BSc Product Design
Duration: 3FT Hon
Entry Requirements: *Foundation:* Distinction. *GCE:* 260. *IB:* 28.
BTEC Dip: D*D*. *BTEC ExtDip:* DMM. *OCR NED:* M2 Interview
required.

W240 FYr Product Design (Year 0)
Duration: 1FT FYr
Entry Requirements: *Foundation:* Pass. *GCE:* 160. *IB:* 24. *BTEC
Dip:* D*D*. *BTEC ExtDip:* DMM. *OCR ND:* M2 *OCR NED:* P2

D65 UNIVERSITY OF DUNDEE
NETHERGATE
DUNDEE DD1 4HN
t: 01382 383838 f: 01382 388150
e: contactus@dundee.ac.uk
// www.dundee.ac.uk/admissions/
undergraduate/

W240 BSc Product Design
Duration: 4FT Hon
Entry Requirements: *GCE:* BBC. *SQAH:* ABBB. *IB:* 30. Interview
required. Portfolio required.

E56 THE UNIVERSITY OF EDINBURGH
STUDENT RECRUITMENT & ADMISSIONS
57 GEORGE SQUARE
EDINBURGH EH8 9JU
t: 0131 650 4360 f: 0131 651 1236
e: sra.enquiries@ed.ac.uk
// www.ed.ac.uk/studying/undergraduate/

W240 BA Product Design
Duration: 4FT Hon
Entry Requirements: *Foundation:* Merit. *GCE:* BBB. *SQAH:* BBBB.
IB: 34. Portfolio required.

E59 EDINBURGH NAPIER UNIVERSITY
CRAIGLOCKHART CAMPUS
EDINBURGH EH14 1DJ
t: +44 (0)8452 60 60 40 f: 0131 455 6464
e: info@napier.ac.uk
// www.napier.ac.uk

W241 BDes Product Design
Duration: 3FT/4FT Ord/Hon
Entry Requirements: *GCE:* 240. Interview required. Portfolio
required.

G42 GLASGOW CALEDONIAN UNIVERSITY
STUDENT RECRUITMENT & ADMISSIONS SERVICE
CITY CAMPUS
COWCADDENS ROAD
GLASGOW G4 0BA
t: 0141 331 3000 f: 0141 331 8676
e: undergraduate@gcu.ac.uk
// www.gcu.ac.uk

W240 BA International Product Design
Duration: 2FT Hon
Entry Requirements: Interview required. Portfolio required. HND required.

G70 UNIVERSITY OF GREENWICH
GREENWICH CAMPUS
OLD ROYAL NAVAL COLLEGE
PARK ROW
LONDON SE10 9LS
t: 020 8331 9000 f: 020 8331 8145
e: courseinfo@gre.ac.uk
// www.gre.ac.uk

W241 FdEng Product Design
Duration: 2FT Fdg
Entry Requirements: IB: 24.

H12 HARPER ADAMS UNIVERSITY COLLEGE
NEWPORT
SHROPSHIRE TF10 8NB
t: 01952 820280 f: 01952 813210
e: admissions@harper-adams.ac.uk
// www.harper-adams.ac.uk

HW32 FdSc Off-Road Vehicle Design
Duration: 3SW Fdg
Entry Requirements: GCE: 120-160. SQAH: CCC. Interview required.

H36 UNIVERSITY OF HERTFORDSHIRE
UNIVERSITY ADMISSIONS SERVICE
COLLEGE LANE
HATFIELD
HERTS AL10 9AB
t: 01707 284800
// www.herts.ac.uk

W240 BA Product Design
Duration: 3FT Hon
Entry Requirements: GCE: 240. Interview required. Portfolio required.

W241 BSc Industrial Design
Duration: 3FT Hon
Entry Requirements: GCE: 240. Interview required. Portfolio required.

H60 THE UNIVERSITY OF HUDDERSFIELD
QUEENSGATE
HUDDERSFIELD HD1 3DH
t: 01484 473969 f: 01484 472765
e: admissionsandrecords@hud.ac.uk
// www.hud.ac.uk

W242 BA/BSc Product Design
Duration: 3FT/4SW Hon
Entry Requirements: GCE: 300. SQAH: BBBB. IB: 28. Interview required. Portfolio required.

H72 THE UNIVERSITY OF HULL
THE UNIVERSITY OF HULL
COTTINGHAM ROAD
HULL HU6 7RX
t: 01482 466100 f: 01482 442290
e: admissions@hull.ac.uk
// www.hull.ac.uk

HW12 BSc Electronic Product Design
Duration: 3FT Hon
Entry Requirements: GCE: 260. IB: 26. BTEC ExtDip: MMM.

K84 KINGSTON UNIVERSITY
STUDENT INFORMATION & ADVICE CENTRE
COOPER HOUSE
40-46 SURBITON ROAD
KINGSTON UPON THAMES KT1 2HX
t: 0844 8552177 f: 020 8547 7080
e: aps@kingston.ac.uk
// www.kingston.ac.uk

WH21 BSc Product Design
Duration: 3FT Hon
Entry Requirements: GCE: 240. Interview required. Portfolio required.

L27 LEEDS METROPOLITAN UNIVERSITY
COURSE ENQUIRIES OFFICE
CITY CAMPUS
LEEDS LS1 3HE
t: 0113 81 23113 f: 0113 81 23129
// www.leedsmet.ac.uk

W240 BA Design Product
Duration: 3FT Hon
Entry Requirements: Foundation: Pass. GCE: 160. Interview required. Portfolio required.

L41 THE UNIVERSITY OF LIVERPOOL
THE FOUNDATION BUILDING
BROWNLOW HILL
LIVERPOOL L69 7ZX
t: 0151 794 2000 f: 0151 708 6502
e: ugrecruitment@liv.ac.uk
// www.liv.ac.uk

H1WF BEng Engineering with Product Design
Duration: 3FT Hon
Entry Requirements: *GCE:* ABB. *SQAAH:* ABB. *IB:* 33. Interview required.

H1WG MEng Engineering with Product Design (4 years)
Duration: 4FT Hon
Entry Requirements: *GCE:* AAB. *SQAAH:* AAB. *IB:* 35. Interview required.

M80 MIDDLESEX UNIVERSITY
MIDDLESEX UNIVERSITY
THE BURROUGHS
LONDON NW4 4BT
t: 020 8411 5555 f: 020 8411 5649
e: enquiries@mdx.ac.uk
// www.mdx.ac.uk

W240 BA Product Design
Duration: 3FT/4SW Hon
Entry Requirements: *GCE:* 200-300. *IB:* 28. Interview required. Portfolio required.

W244 BSc Product Design
Duration: 3FT/4SW Hon
Entry Requirements: *GCE:* 200-300. *IB:* 28. Interview required. Portfolio required.

N38 UNIVERSITY OF NORTHAMPTON
PARK CAMPUS
BOUGHTON GREEN ROAD
NORTHAMPTON NN2 7AL
t: 0800 358 2232 f: 01604 722083
e: admissions@northampton.ac.uk
// www.northampton.ac.uk

W240 BSc Product Design
Duration: 3FT Hon
Entry Requirements: *GCE:* 260-280. *SQAH:* AAA-BBBB. *IB:* 24. *BTEC Dip:* DD. *BTEC ExtDip:* DMM. *OCR ND:* D *OCR NED:* M2 Interview required. Portfolio required.

042W HND Product Design
Duration: 2FT HND
Entry Requirements: *GCE:* 80-120. *SQAH:* BC-CCC. *IB:* 24. *BTEC Dip:* MP. *BTEC ExtDip:* MPP. *OCR ND:* P1 *OCR NED:* P2 Interview required. Portfolio required.

N77 NORTHUMBRIA UNIVERSITY
TRINITY BUILDING
NORTHUMBERLAND ROAD
NEWCASTLE UPON TYNE NE1 8ST
t: 0191 243 7420 f: 0191 227 4561
e: er.admissions@northumbria.ac.uk
// www.northumbria.ac.uk

W240 BA Design for Industry
Duration: 4FT Hon
Entry Requirements: *Foundation:* Distinction. *GCE:* 300. *SQAH:* BBBBC. *SQAAH:* BBC. *IB:* 26. *BTEC Dip:* DM. *BTEC ExtDip:* DDM. *OCR NED:* M2 Interview required. Portfolio required.

N91 NOTTINGHAM TRENT UNIVERSITY
DRYDEN BUILDING
BURTON STREET
NOTTINGHAM NG1 4BU
t: +44 (0) 115 848 4200 f: +44 (0) 115 848 8869
e: applications@ntu.ac.uk
// www.ntu.ac.uk

W241 BA Product Design
Duration: 3FT/4SW Hon
Entry Requirements: *Foundation:* Distinction. *GCE:* 280. *BTEC Dip:* D*D*. *BTEC ExtDip:* DMM. *OCR NED:* M2 Interview required. Portfolio required.

R06 RAVENSBOURNE
6 PENROSE WAY
GREENWICH PENINSULA
LONDON SE10 0EW
t: 020 3040 3998
e: info@rave.ac.uk
// www.rave.ac.uk

W240 BA Design Products
Duration: 3FT Hon
Entry Requirements: *Foundation:* Pass. *GCE:* AA-CC. *IB:* 28. Interview required. Portfolio required.

W242 BA Design Products (Fast-Track)
Duration: 2FT Hon
Entry Requirements: Contact the institution for details.

W241 BA Design Products (with Foundation Year)
Duration: 4FT Hon
Entry Requirements: *Foundation:* Pass. *GCE:* A-E. *IB:* 28. Interview required. Portfolio required.

S21 SHEFFIELD HALLAM UNIVERSITY
CITY CAMPUS
HOWARD STREET
SHEFFIELD S1 1WB
t: 0114 225 5555 f: 0114 225 2167
e: admissions@shu.ac.uk
// www.shu.ac.uk

W240 BA Product Design
Duration: 3FT Hon
Entry Requirements: *Foundation:* Pass. *GCE:* 280. Interview required. Portfolio required.

W242 MDes Product Design
Duration: 4FT Hon
Entry Requirements: *Foundation:* Pass. *GCE:* 300. Interview required. Portfolio required.

S30 SOUTHAMPTON SOLENT UNIVERSITY
EAST PARK TERRACE
SOUTHAMPTON
HAMPSHIRE SO14 0RT
t: +44 (0) 23 8031 9039 f: + 44 (0)23 8022 2259
e: admissions@solent.ac.uk
// www.solent.ac.uk/

W241 BA Product Design
Duration: 3FT Hon
Entry Requirements: *Foundation:* Distinction. *GCE:* 240. *SQAAH:* AA-CCD. *IB:* 24. *BTEC ExtDip:* MMM *OCR ND:* D *OCR NED:* M3 Portfolio required.

S72 STAFFORDSHIRE UNIVERSITY
COLLEGE ROAD
STOKE ON TRENT ST4 2DE
t: 01782 292753 f: 01782 292740
e: admissions@staffs.ac.uk
// www.staffs.ac.uk

W240 BA Product Design
Duration: 3FT/4FT Hon
Entry Requirements: *Foundation:* Merit. *GCE:* 200-240. *IB:* 24. *BTEC Dip:* DD. *BTEC ExtDip:* MMM. Interview required. Portfolio required.

S90 UNIVERSITY OF SUSSEX
UNDERGRADUATE ADMISSIONS
SUSSEX HOUSE
UNIVERSITY OF SUSSEX
BRIGHTON BN1 9RH
t: 01273 678416 f: 01273 678545
e: ug.applicants@sussex.ac.uk
// www.sussex.ac.uk

HW12 BSc Product Design
Duration: 3FT Hon
Entry Requirements: *GCE:* ABB-BBB. *SQAH:* AABBB-ABBBB. *IB:* 32. *BTEC SubDip:* D. *BTEC Dip:* DD. *BTEC ExtDip:* DDD. *OCR ND:* D *OCR NED:* D2

HW1F BSc Product Design (with a professional placement year)
Duration: 4SW Hon
Entry Requirements: *GCE:* ABB-BBB. *SQAH:* AABBB-ABBBB. *IB:* 32. *BTEC SubDip:* D. *BTEC Dip:* DD. *BTEC ExtDip:* DDD. *OCR ND:* D *OCR NED:* D2

S96 SWANSEA METROPOLITAN UNIVERSITY
MOUNT PLEASANT CAMPUS
SWANSEA SA1 6ED
t: 01792 481000 f: 01792 481061
e: gemma.green@smu.ac.uk
// www.smu.ac.uk

W240 BA Automotive Design
Duration: 3FT Hon
Entry Requirements: *GCE:* 240-360. *IB:* 24. Interview required. Portfolio required.

W242 BA Product Design
Duration: 3FT Hon
Entry Requirements: *GCE:* 240-360. *IB:* 24. Interview required. Portfolio required.

T20 TEESSIDE UNIVERSITY
MIDDLESBROUGH TS1 3BA
t: 01642 218121 f: 01642 384201
e: registry@tees.ac.uk
// www.tees.ac.uk

W240 BA Product Design
Duration: 3FT Hon
Entry Requirements: *Foundation:* Distinction. *GCE:* 280. *IB:* 25. Interview required. Portfolio required.

W241 BSc Product Design
Duration: 3FT Hon
Entry Requirements: *Foundation:* Distinction. *GCE:* 280. *IB:* 25. Interview required. Portfolio required.

U65 UNIVERSITY OF THE ARTS LONDON
272 HIGH HOLBORN
LONDON WC1V 7EY
t: 020 7514 6000x6197 f: 020 7514 6198
e: c.anderson@arts.ac.uk
// www.arts.ac.uk

W240 BA Product Design
Duration: 3FT Hon
Entry Requirements: Interview required.

W75 UNIVERSITY OF WOLVERHAMPTON
ADMISSIONS UNIT
MX207, CAMP STREET
WOLVERHAMPTON
WEST MIDLANDS WV1 1AD
t: 01902 321000 f: 01902 321896
e: admissions@wlv.ac.uk
// www.wlv.ac.uk

W241 BDes Product Design
Duration: 3FT/4SW Hon
Entry Requirements: *GCE:* 200. *IB:* 24. *BTEC Dip:* DM. *BTEC ExtDip:* MMP. *OCR ND:* M1 *OCR NED:* P1 Interview required. Portfolio required.

Y75 YORK ST JOHN UNIVERSITY
LORD MAYOR'S WALK
YORK YO31 7EX
t: 01904 876598 f: 01904 876940/876921
e: admissions@yorksj.ac.uk
// w3.yorksj.ac.uk

W290 BA Product Design
Duration: 3FT Hon
Entry Requirements: *Foundation:* Pass. *GCE:* 200-240. *IB:* 24. Interview required. Portfolio required.

W241 BA Product Design (for International applicants only)
Duration: 4FT Hon
Entry Requirements: *Foundation:* Pass. *GCE:* 200-240. *IB:* 24. Interview required. Portfolio required.

TEXTILE, FABRIC AND PATTERN DESIGN

A66 THE ARTS UNIVERSITY COLLEGE AT BOURNEMOUTH (FORMERLY ARTS INSTITUTE AT BOURNEMOUTH)
WALLISDOWN
POOLE
DORSET BH12 5HH
t: 01202 363228 f: 01202 537729
e: admissions@aucb.ac.uk
// www.aucb.ac.uk

W236 BA Textiles
Duration: 3FT Hon
Entry Requirements: *Foundation:* Pass. *GCE:* BCC. *IB:* 24. *OCR ND:* M1 *OCR NED:* M1 Interview required. Portfolio required.

B20 BATH SPA UNIVERSITY
NEWTON PARK
NEWTON ST LOE
BATH BA2 9BN
t: 01225 875875 f: 01225 875444
e: enquiries@bathspa.ac.uk
// www.bathspa.ac.uk/clearing

WWX2 BA Creative Writing/Textile Design Studies
Duration: 3FT Hon
Entry Requirements: *Foundation:* Pass. *GCE:* 220-280. *IB:* 24. Interview required.

WW52 BA Dance/Textile Design Studies
Duration: 3FT Hon
Entry Requirements: *Foundation:* Pass. *GCE:* 220-280. *IB:* 24. Interview required.

WW2K BA Drama Studies/Textile Design Studies
Duration: 3FT Hon
Entry Requirements: *GCE:* 220-280. *IB:* 24. Interview required.

XWC2 BA Education/Textile Design Studies
Duration: 3FT Hon   CRB Check: Required
Entry Requirements: *GCE:* 220-280. *IB:* 24. Interview required.

WWH2 BA Music/Textile Design Studies
Duration: 3FT Hon
Entry Requirements: *GCE:* 220-280. *IB:* 24. Interview required. Portfolio required.

W295 BA Textile Design Studies/Visual Design
Duration: 3FT Hon
Entry Requirements: *Foundation:* Pass. *GCE:* 220-280. *IB:* 24. Interview required.

B25 BIRMINGHAM CITY UNIVERSITY
PERRY BARR
BIRMINGHAM B42 2SU
t: 0121 331 5595 f: 0121 331 7994
// www.bcu.ac.uk

W231 BA Textile Design
Duration: 3FT Hon
Entry Requirements: *GCE:* 280. *IB:* 28. Interview required.
Portfolio required.

W232 BA Textile Design (Printed Textiles and Surface Design)
Duration: 3FT Hon
Entry Requirements: Contact the institution for details.

B40 BLACKBURN COLLEGE
FEILDEN STREET
BLACKBURN BB2 1LH
t: 01254 292594 f: 01254 679647
e: he-admissions@blackburn.ac.uk
// www.blackburn.ac.uk

W232 BA Design (Contemporary Textiles, Top-Up)
Duration: 1FT Hon
Entry Requirements: Interview required. Portfolio required. HND required.

W231 FdA Textiles
Duration: 2FT Fdg
Entry Requirements: *GCE:* 120.

B44 UNIVERSITY OF BOLTON
DEANE ROAD
BOLTON BL3 5AB
t: 01204 903903 f: 01204 399074
e: enquiries@bolton.ac.uk
// www.bolton.ac.uk

W231 BA Textile/Surface Design
Duration: 3FT Hon
Entry Requirements: *GCE:* 240. Interview required. Portfolio required.

B60 BRADFORD COLLEGE: AN ASSOCIATE COLLEGE OF LEEDS METROPOLITAN UNIVERSITY
GREAT HORTON ROAD
BRADFORD
WEST YORKSHIRE BD7 1AY
t: 01274 433008 f: 01274 431652
e: heregistry@bradfordcollege.ac.uk
// www.bradfordcollege.ac.uk/university-centre

W233 BA Contemporary Surface Design and Textiles
Duration: 3FT Hon
Entry Requirements: *GCE:* 220. Interview required. Portfolio required.

B72 UNIVERSITY OF BRIGHTON
MITHRAS HOUSE 211
LEWES ROAD
BRIGHTON BN2 4AT
t: 01273 644644 f: 01273 642607
e: admissions@brighton.ac.uk
// www.brighton.ac.uk

W2NC BA Textiles with Business Studies
Duration: 3FT/4SW Hon
Entry Requirements: *GCE:* BBB. Foundation Course required. Interview required. Portfolio required.

W2ND MDes Textiles with Business Studies
Duration: 4FT/5SW Hon
Entry Requirements: *GCE:* BBB. Foundation Course required. Interview required. Portfolio required.

C20 CARDIFF METROPOLITAN UNIVERSITY (UWIC)
ADMISSIONS UNIT
LLANDAFF CAMPUS
WESTERN AVENUE
CARDIFF CF5 2YB
t: 029 2041 6070 f: 029 2041 6286
e: admissions@cardiffmet.ac.uk
// www.cardiffmet.ac.uk

W231 BA Textiles
Duration: 3FT Hon
Entry Requirements: *GCE:* 300. *IB:* 26. *BTEC ExtDip:* DDM. *OCR NED:* M1 Foundation Course required. Interview required. Portfolio required.

C93 UNIVERSITY FOR THE CREATIVE ARTS
FALKNER ROAD
FARNHAM
SURREY GU9 7DS
t: 01252 892960
e: admissions@ucreative.ac.uk
// www.ucreative.ac.uk

WR11 BA Hand Embroidery (Top-Up)
Duration: 1FT Hon
Entry Requirements: Interview required. Portfolio required. HND required.

W711 FdA Hand Embroidery
Duration: 2FT Hon
Entry Requirements: *GCE:* 80. Interview required. Portfolio required.

D26 DE MONTFORT UNIVERSITY
THE GATEWAY
LEICESTER LE1 9BH
t: 0116 255 1551 f: 0116 250 6204
e: enquiries@dmu.ac.uk
// www.dmu.ac.uk

W231 BA Textile Design (pathways in Constructed, Mixed Media, Printed)
Duration: 3FT/4SW Hon
Entry Requirements: *Foundation:* Pass. *GCE:* 260. *IB:* 28. *BTEC Dip:* D*D. *BTEC ExtDip:* MMM. Interview required. Portfolio required.

D39 UNIVERSITY OF DERBY
KEDLESTON ROAD
DERBY DE22 1GB
t: 01332 591167 f: 01332 597724
e: askadmissions@derby.ac.uk
// www.derby.ac.uk

W231 Fyr Textile Design (Year 0)
Duration: 1FT FYr
Entry Requirements: *Foundation:* Pass. *GCE:* 160. *IB:* 24. *BTEC Dip:* D*D*. *BTEC ExtDip:* DMM. *OCR ND:* M2 *OCR NED:* P2 Interview required. Portfolio required.

D65 UNIVERSITY OF DUNDEE
NETHERGATE
DUNDEE DD1 4HN
t: 01382 383838 f: 01382 388150
e: contactus@dundee.ac.uk
// www.dundee.ac.uk/admissions/undergraduate/

W231 BDes Textile Design
Duration: 3FT Hon
Entry Requirements: Foundation Course required. Interview required. Portfolio required.

E28 UNIVERSITY OF EAST LONDON
DOCKLANDS CAMPUS
UNIVERSITY WAY
LONDON E16 2RD
t: 020 8223 3333 f: 020 8223 2978
e: study@uel.ac.uk
// www.uel.ac.uk

NCW2 BA Business Management and Printed Textile Design
Duration: 3FT Hon
Entry Requirements: *GCE:* 240. *IB:* 24. *OCR ND:* M1 *OCR NED:* P1 Portfolio required.

N2WG BA Business Management with Printed Textile Design
Duration: 3FT Hon
Entry Requirements: *GCE:* 240. *IB:* 24. Portfolio required.

W232 BA Printed Textile Design
Duration: 3FT Hon
Entry Requirements: *GCE:* 200. Interview required. Portfolio required.

W2P9 BA Printed Textile Design with Communication Studies
Duration: 3FT Hon
Entry Requirements: *GCE:* 200. *IB:* 24. Portfolio required.

G43 THE GLASGOW SCHOOL OF ART
167 RENFREW STREET
GLASGOW G3 6RQ
t: 0141 353 4434/4514 f: 0141 353 4408
e: admissions@gsa.ac.uk
// www.gsa.ac.uk

W231 BDes Textile Design
Duration: 4FT Hon
Entry Requirements: *GCE:* ABB. *SQAH:* AABB-ABBB. *IB:* 30. Interview required. Portfolio required.

H18 HEREFORD COLLEGE OF ARTS
FOLLY LANE
HEREFORD HR1 1LT
t: 01432 273359 f: 01432 341099
e: headmin@hca.ac.uk
// www.hca.ac.uk

W231 BA Textile Design
Duration: 3FT Hon CRB Check: Required
Entry Requirements: *GCE:* 200. Interview required. Portfolio required.

W235 BA Textile Design (top-up)
Duration: 1FT Hon CRB Check: Required
Entry Requirements: Interview required. Portfolio required. HND required.

H49 UNIVERSITY OF THE HIGHLANDS AND ISLANDS
UHI EXECUTIVE OFFICE
NESS WALK
INVERNESS
SCOTLAND IV3 5SQ
t: 01463 279000 f: 01463 279001
e: info@uhi.ac.uk
// www.uhi.ac.uk

W231 BA Contemporary Textiles
Duration: 4FT Hon
Entry Requirements. *GCE:* CC. *SQAH:* CCC. Portfolio required.

H73 HULL COLLEGE
QUEEN'S GARDENS
HULL HU1 3DG
t: 01482 329943 f: 01482 598733
e: info@hull-college.ac.uk
// www.hull-college.ac.uk/higher-education

W231 FdA Textiles
Duration: 2FT Fdg
Entry Requirements: *GCE:* 200. Foundation Course required. Interview required. Portfolio required.

L23 UNIVERSITY OF LEEDS
THE UNIVERSITY OF LEEDS
WOODHOUSE LANE
LEEDS LS2 9JT
t: 0113 343 3999
e: admissions@leeds.ac.uk
// www.leeds.ac.uk

W232 BA Textile Design
Duration: 3FT Hon
Entry Requirements: *GCE:* BBB. *SQAAH:* BBB. *IB:* 32.

L28 LEEDS COLLEGE OF ART
BLENHEIM WALK
LEEDS LS2 9AQ
t: 0113 202 8000 f: 0113 202 8001
e: info@leeds-art.ac.uk
// www.leeds-art.ac.uk

W222 BA Printed Textiles and Surface Pattern Design
Duration: 3FT Hon
Entry Requirements: *Foundation:* Merit. *GCE:* 240. *IB:* 24. *BTEC Dip:* DD. *BTEC ExtDip:* MMM. Interview required. Portfolio required.

L68 LONDON METROPOLITAN UNIVERSITY
166-220 HOLLOWAY ROAD
LONDON N7 8DB
t: 020 7133 4200
e: admissions@londonmet.ac.uk
// www.londonmet.ac.uk

W2J4 BA Textile Design
Duration: 3FT Hon
Entry Requirements: *Foundation:* Merit. *GCE:* 240. *IB:* 28. Foundation Course required. Interview required. Portfolio required.

M40 THE MANCHESTER METROPOLITAN UNIVERSITY
ADMISSIONS OFFICE
ALL SAINTS (GMS)
ALL SAINTS
MANCHESTER M15 6BH
t: 0161 247 2000
// www.mmu.ac.uk

W232 BA Textiles in Practice
Duration: 3FT Hon
Entry Requirements: *GCE:* 280. *IB:* 27. Interview required. Portfolio required.

N23 NEWCASTLE COLLEGE
STUDENT SERVICES
RYE HILL CAMPUS
SCOTSWOOD ROAD
NEWCASTLE UPON TYNE NE4 7SA
t: 0191 200 4110 f: 0191 200 4349
e: enquiries@ncl-coll.ac.uk
// www.newcastlecollege.co.uk

W231 FdA Textile and Surface Design
Duration: 2FT Fdg
Entry Requirements: *Foundation:* Pass. *GCE:* 120-165. *OCR ND:* P2 *OCR NED:* P3 Foundation Course required. Interview required. Portfolio required.

N39 NORWICH UNIVERSITY COLLEGE OF THE ARTS

FRANCIS HOUSE
3-7 REDWELL STREET
NORWICH NR2 4SN
t: 01603 610561 f: 01603 615728
e: admissions@nuca.ac.uk
// www.nuca.ac.uk

W230 BA Textiles

Duration: 3FT Hon

Entry Requirements: *Foundation:* Merit. *GCE:* BBC. *BTEC Dip:* DM. *BTEC ExtDip:* MMM. *OCR ND:* M1 *OCR NED:* P1 Interview required. Portfolio required.

N41 NORTHBROOK COLLEGE SUSSEX

LITTLEHAMPTON ROAD
WORTHING
WEST SUSSEX BN12 6NU
t: 0845 155 6060 f: 01903 606073
e: enquiries@nbcol.ac.uk
// www.northbrook.ac.uk

W231 BA Textile Design

Duration: 3FT Hon

Entry Requirements: *GCE:* 160. Interview required. Portfolio required.

P65 PLYMOUTH COLLEGE OF ART (FORMERLY PLYMOUTH COLLEGE OF ART AND DESIGN)

TAVISTOCK PLACE
PLYMOUTH PL4 8AT
t: 01752 203434 f: 01752 203444
e: infoservices@plymouthart.ac.uk
// www.plymouthart.ac.uk

W231 BA (Hons) Textiles

Duration: 3FT Hon

Entry Requirements: Contact the institution for details.

W233 BA (Hons) Textiles (Top-Up)

Duration: 1FT Hon

Entry Requirements: Contact the institution for details.

S28 SOMERSET COLLEGE OF ARTS AND TECHNOLOGY

WELLINGTON ROAD
TAUNTON
SOMERSET TA1 5AX
t: 01823 366331 f: 01823 366418
e: enquiries@somerset.ac.uk
// www.somerset.ac.uk/student-area/considering-a-degree.html

W236 BA Design (Surface Design)

Duration: 3FT Hon

Entry Requirements: *Foundation:* Pass. *GCE:* 180. *IB:* 24. Interview required. Portfolio required.

S46 SOUTH NOTTINGHAM COLLEGE

WEST BRIDGFORD CENTRE
GREYTHORN DRIVE
WEST BRIDGFORD
NOTTINGHAM NG2 7GA
t: 0115 914 6400 f: 0115 914 6444
e: enquiries@snc.ac.uk
// www.snc.ac.uk

W231 FdA Textile Design

Duration: 2FT Fdg

Entry Requirements: Contact the institution for details.

S72 STAFFORDSHIRE UNIVERSITY

COLLEGE ROAD
STOKE ON TRENT ST4 2DE
t: 01782 292753 f: 01782 292740
e: admissions@staffs.ac.uk
// www.staffs.ac.uk

W233 BA Textile Surfaces

Duration: 3FT/4FT Hon

Entry Requirements: *Foundation:* Merit. *GCE:* 200-240. *IB:* 24. *BTEC Dip:* DD. *BTEC ExtDip:* MMM. Interview required. Portfolio required.

U65 UNIVERSITY OF THE ARTS LONDON

272 HIGH HOLBORN
LONDON WC1V 7EY
t: 020 7514 6000x6197 f: 020 7514 6198
e: c.anderson@arts.ac.uk
// www.arts.ac.uk

W231 BA Textile Design

Duration: 3FT Hon

Entry Requirements: *Foundation:* Pass. *GCE:* 80. *IB:* 28. Foundation Course required. Portfolio required.

W235 BA Textile Design

Duration: 3FT Hon

Entry Requirements: Interview required.

THEATRE & SCENIC ARTS AND SET DESIGN

B20 BATH SPA UNIVERSITY
NEWTON PARK
NEWTON ST LOE
BATH BA2 9BN
t: 01225 875875 f: 01225 875444
e: enquiries@bathspa.ac.uk
// www.bathspa.ac.uk/clearing

WW5F BA Dance/Visual Design
Duration: 3FT Hon
Entry Requirements: *Foundation:* Pass. *GCE:* 220-280. *IB:* 24.
Interview required.

D39 UNIVERSITY OF DERBY
KEDLESTON ROAD
DERBY DE22 1GB
t: 01332 591167 f: 01332 597724
e: askadmissions@derby.ac.uk
// www.derby.ac.uk

WW49 BA Creative Writing and Theatre Studies
Duration: 3FT Hon
Entry Requirements: *Foundation:* Distinction. *GCE:* 260-300. *IB:* 28. *BTEC Dip:* D*D*. *BTEC ExtDip:* DMM. *OCR NED:* M2

K24 THE UNIVERSITY OF KENT
RECRUITMENT & ADMISSIONS OFFICE
REGISTRY
UNIVERSITY OF KENT
CANTERBURY, KENT CT2 7NZ
t: 01227 827272 f: 01227 827077
e: information@kent.ac.uk
// www.kent.ac.uk

W000 BA The Visual and Performed Arts
Duration: 3FT Hon
Entry Requirements: *GCE:* AAB-ABB. *SQAH:* AAAAB-AAABB. *SQAAH:* AAB-ABB. *IB:* 33. *OCR ND:* D *OCR NED:* D1

N33 NEW COLLEGE STAMFORD
DRIFT ROAD
STAMFORD
LINCOLNSHIRE PE9 1XA
t: 01780 484300 f: 01780 484301
e: enquiries@stamford.ac.uk
// www.stamford.ac.uk

099W HND Performing Arts
Duration: 2FT HND
Entry Requirements: Interview required.

VISUAL AND VISION ARTS

A50 AMERICAN INTERCONTINENTAL UNIVERSITY - LONDON
110 MARYLEBONE HIGH STREET
LONDON W1U 4RY
t: 020 7467 5640 f: 020 7467 5641
e: admissions@aiulondon.ac.uk
// www.aiulondon.ac.uk

W213 BA Visual Communication
Duration: 4FT Hon
Entry Requirements: Contact the institution for details.

A66 THE ARTS UNIVERSITY COLLEGE AT BOURNEMOUTH (FORMERLY ARTS INSTITUTE AT BOURNEMOUTH)
WALLISDOWN
POOLE
DORSET BH12 5HH
t: 01202 363228 f: 01202 537729
e: admissions@aucb.ac.uk
// www.aucb.ac.uk

W215 BA Visual Communication
Duration: 3FT Hon
Entry Requirements: *Foundation:* Pass. *GCE:* BBC. *IB:* 24. *OCR ND:* M1 *OCR NED:* M1 Interview required. Portfolio required.

B20 BATH SPA UNIVERSITY
NEWTON PARK
NEWTON ST LOE
BATH BA2 9BN
t: 01225 875875 f: 01225 875444
e: enquiries@bathspa.ac.uk
// www.bathspa.ac.uk/clearing

WW82 BA Creative Writing/Visual Design
Duration: 3FT Hon
Entry Requirements: *Foundation:* Pass. *GCE:* 220-280. *IB:* 24.
Interview required.

WW42 BA Drama Studies/Visual Design
Duration: 3FT Hon
Entry Requirements: *GCE:* 220-280. *IB:* 24. Interview required.

WW32 BA Music/Visual Design
Duration: 3FT Hon
Entry Requirements: *Foundation:* Pass. *GCE:* 220-280. *IB:* 24.
Interview required.

C10 CANTERBURY CHRIST CHURCH UNIVERSITY
NORTH HOLMES ROAD
CANTERBURY
KENT CT1 1QU
t: 01227 782900 f: 01227 782888
e: admissions@canterbury.ac.uk
// www.canterbury.ac.uk

W900 BA Visual Arts: Visual Art
Duration: 3FT Hon
Entry Requirements: *GCE:* 240. *IB:* 24. Interview required.

C64 CITY COLLEGE COVENTRY
SWANSWELL
50 SWANSWELL STREET
COVENTRY CV1 5DG
t: 0800 616 202 f: 024 7622 3390
e: courses@covcollege.ac.uk
// www.covcollege.ac.uk

321W HND Visual Communications
Duration: 2FT HND
Entry Requirements: Contact the institution for details.

E84 UNIVERSITY OF EXETER
LAVER BUILDING
NORTH PARK ROAD
EXETER
DEVON EX4 4QE
t: 01392 723044 f: 01392 722479
e: admissions@exeter.ac.uk
// www.exeter.ac.uk

WW42 BA Drama and Visual Culture
Duration: 3FT Hon
Entry Requirements: *GCE:* AAA-AAB. *SQAH:* AAAAB-AAABB. *SQAAH:* AAB-ABB. *BTEC ExtDip:* DDD. Interview required.

WW24 BA Drama and Visual Culture with Study Abroad (4 years)
Duration: 4FT Hon
Entry Requirements: *GCE:* AAA-AAB. *SQAH:* AAAAB-AAABB. *SQAAH:* AAB-ABB. *BTEC ExtDip:* DDD. Interview required.

WQ23 BA English and Visual Culture
Duration: 3FT Hon
Entry Requirements: *GCE:* AAA-AAB. *SQAH:* AAAAB-AAABB. *SQAAH:* AAB-ABB. *BTEC ExtDip:* DDM.

WQF3 BA English and Visual Culture with Study Abroad (4 years)
Duration: 4FT Hon
Entry Requirements: *GCE:* AAA-AAB. *SQAH:* AAAAB-AAABB. *SQAAH:* AAB-ABB. *BTEC ExtDip:* DDM.

WV21 BA History and Visual Culture
Duration: 3FT Hon
Entry Requirements: *GCE:* AAB-ABB. *SQAH:* AAABB-AABBB. *SQAAH:* ABB-BBB. *BTEC ExtDip:* DDM.

WV12 BA History and Visual Culture with Study Abroad (4 years)
Duration: 4FT Hon
Entry Requirements: *GCE:* AAA-AAB. *SQAH:* AAAAB-AAABB. *SQAAH:* AAB-ABB. *BTEC ExtDip:* DDD.

WR29 BA Modern Languages and Visual Culture (4 years)
Duration: 4FT Hon
Entry Requirements: *GCE:* AAB-ABB. *SQAH:* AAABB-AABBB. *SQAAH:* ABB-BBB.

G43 THE GLASGOW SCHOOL OF ART
167 RENFREW STREET
GLASGOW G3 6RQ
t: 0141 353 4434/4514 f: 0141 353 4408
e: admissions@gsa.ac.uk
// www.gsa.ac.uk

W213 BA Communication Design
Duration: 4FT Hon
Entry Requirements: *GCE:* ABB. *SQAH:* AABB-ABBB. *IB:* 30. Interview required. Portfolio required.

G50 THE UNIVERSITY OF GLOUCESTERSHIRE
PARK CAMPUS
THE PARK
CHELTENHAM GL50 2RH
t: 01242 714501 f: 01242 714869
e: admissions@glos.ac.uk
// www.glos.ac.uk

W213 BA Visual Communication
Duration: 1FT Hon
Entry Requirements: Interview required. Portfolio required.

H36 UNIVERSITY OF HERTFORDSHIRE
UNIVERSITY ADMISSIONS SERVICE
COLLEGE LANE
HATFIELD
HERTS AL10 9AB
t: 01707 284800
// www.herts.ac.uk

WN22 FdA Visual Merchandising
Duration: 2FT Fdg
Entry Requirements: *GCE:* 60. Interview required. Portfolio required.

H49 UNIVERSITY OF THE HIGHLANDS AND ISLANDS
UHI EXECUTIVE OFFICE
NESS WALK
INVERNESS
SCOTLAND IV3 5SQ
t: 01463 279000 f: 01463 279001
e: info@uhi.ac.uk
// www.uhi.ac.uk

712W HNC Visual Communications
Duration: 1FT HNC
Entry Requirements: *GCE:* D. *SQAH:* C.

312W HND Visual Communications
Duration: 2FT HND
Entry Requirements: *GCE:* C. *SQAH:* CC.

K24 THE UNIVERSITY OF KENT
RECRUITMENT & ADMISSIONS OFFICE
REGISTRY
UNIVERSITY OF KENT
CANTERBURY, KENT CT2 7NZ
t: 01227 827272 f: 01227 827077
e: information@kent.ac.uk
// www.kent.ac.uk

W213 BA Visual Design and Communication (Top-Up)
Duration: 1FT Hon
Entry Requirements: Interview required. Portfolio required.

K84 KINGSTON UNIVERSITY
STUDENT INFORMATION & ADVICE CENTRE
COOPER HOUSE
40-46 SURBITON ROAD
KINGSTON UPON THAMES KT1 2HX
t: 0844 8552177 f: 020 8547 7080
e: aps@kingston.ac.uk
// www.kingston.ac.uk

WP21 BA Visual & Material Culture and Museum & Gallery Studies
Duration: 3FT Hon
Entry Requirements: *GCE:* 240.

L28 LEEDS COLLEGE OF ART
BLENHEIM WALK
LEEDS LS2 9AQ
t: 0113 202 8000 f: 0113 202 8001
e: info@leeds-art.ac.uk
// www.leeds-art.ac.uk

W211 BA Visual Communication
Duration: 3FT Hon
Entry Requirements: *Foundation:* Merit. *GCE:* 240. *IB:* 24. *BTEC Dip:* DD. *BTEC ExtDip:* MMM. Interview required. Portfolio required.

S21 SHEFFIELD HALLAM UNIVERSITY
CITY CAMPUS
HOWARD STREET
SHEFFIELD S1 1WB
t: 0114 225 5555 f: 0114 225 2167
e: admissions@shu.ac.uk
// www.shu.ac.uk

WP23 BA Media (Extended degree programme)
Duration: 4FT Hon
Entry Requirements: *GCE:* 220.

U20 UNIVERSITY OF ULSTER
COLERAINE
CO. LONDONDERRY
NORTHERN IRELAND BT52 1SA
t: 028 7012 4221 f: 028 7012 4908
e: online@ulster.ac.uk
// www.ulster.ac.uk

W210 BDes Design for Visual Communication
Duration: 3FT Hon
Entry Requirements: *GCE:* 240. *IB:* 24. Interview required. Portfolio required.

W25 WARWICKSHIRE COLLEGE
WARWICK NEW ROAD
LEAMINGTON SPA
WARWICKSHIRE CV32 5JE
t: 01926 884223 f: 01926 318 111
e: kgooch@warkscol.ac.uk
// www.warwickshire.ac.uk

212W HND Visual Communication
Duration: 2FT HND
Entry Requirements: *Foundation:* Pass. *GCE:* 160. Portfolio required.

OTHERS IN ART

B60 BRADFORD COLLEGE: AN ASSOCIATE COLLEGE OF LEEDS METROPOLITAN UNIVERSITY
GREAT HORTON ROAD
BRADFORD
WEST YORKSHIRE BD7 1AY
t: 01274 433008 f: 01274 431652
e: heregistry@bradfordcollege.ac.uk
// www.bradfordcollege.ac.uk/university-centre

W900 FdA Arts for the Creative Industries
Duration: 2FT Fdg
Entry Requirements: Contact the institution for details.

B77 BRISTOL, CITY OF BRISTOL COLLEGE
SOUTH BRISTOL SKILLS ACADEMY
CITY OF BRISTOL COLLEGE
PO BOX 2887 BS2 2BB
t: 0117 312 5000
e: HEAdmissions@cityofbristol.ac.uk
// www.cityofbristol.ac.uk

W900 FdA Creative Arts Therapies Studies
Duration: 2FT Fdg   CRB Check: Required
Entry Requirements: *GCE:* 140. Interview required.

B80 UNIVERSITY OF THE WEST OF ENGLAND, BRISTOL
FRENCHAY CAMPUS
COLDHARBOUR LANE
BRISTOL BS16 1QY
t: +44 (0)117 32 83333 f: +44 (0)117 32 82810
e: admissions@uwe.ac.uk
// www.uwe.ac.uk

W900 BA (Hons) Creative Practices
Duration: 1FT Hon
Entry Requirements: Contact the institution for details.

C10 CANTERBURY CHRIST CHURCH UNIVERSITY
NORTH HOLMES ROAD
CANTERBURY
KENT CT1 1QU
t: 01227 782900 f: 01227 782888
e: admissions@canterbury.ac.uk
// www.canterbury.ac.uk

W990 BA Arts Management
Duration: 3FT Hon
Entry Requirements: Contact the institution for details.

C93 UNIVERSITY FOR THE CREATIVE ARTS
FALKNER ROAD
FARNHAM
SURREY GU9 7DS
t: 01252 892960
e: admissions@ucreative.ac.uk
// www.ucreative.ac.uk

W900 BA Journalism
Duration: 3FT Hon
Entry Requirements: *GCE:* 220. *IB:* 24. *BTEC ExtDip:* PPP. Interview required. Portfolio required.

D39 UNIVERSITY OF DERBY
KEDLESTON ROAD
DERBY DE22 1GB
t: 01332 591167 f: 01332 597724
e: askadmissions@derby.ac.uk
// www.derby.ac.uk

VW19 BA Creative Writing and History
Duration: 3FT Hon
Entry Requirements: *Foundation:* Distinction. *GCE:* 260-300. *IB:* 28. *BTEC Dip:* D*D*. *BTEC ExtDip:* DMM. *OCR NED:* M2

NW19 BA Creative Writing and Marketing
Duration: 3FT Hon
Entry Requirements: *Foundation:* Distinction. *GCE:* 260-300. *IB:* 28. *BTEC Dip:* D*D*. *BTEC ExtDip:* DMM. *OCR NED:* M2

CW89 BA Creative Writing and Psychology
Duration: 3FT Hon
Entry Requirements: *Foundation:* Distinction. *GCE:* 260-300. *IB:* 28. *BTEC Dip:* D*D*. *BTEC ExtDip:* DMM. *OCR NED:* M2

D65 UNIVERSITY OF DUNDEE
NETHERGATE
DUNDEE DD1 4HN
t: 01382 383838 f: 01382 388150
e: contactus@dundee.ac.uk
// www.dundee.ac.uk/admissions/undergraduate/

VWL0 MA Arts and Social Sciences
Duration: 3FT Ord
Entry Requirements: *GCE:* BCC. *SQAH:* ABBB. *IB:* 30.

E42 EDGE HILL UNIVERSITY
ORMSKIRK
LANCASHIRE L39 4QP
t: 01695 657000 f: 01695 584355
e: study@edgehill.ac.uk
// www.edgehill.ac.uk

WW94 BA Creative Writing and Drama
Duration: 3FT Hon
Entry Requirements: GCE: 300. IB: 26. OCR ND: D OCR NED: M1
Interview required.

WQ93 BA Creative Writing and English
Duration: 3FT Hon
Entry Requirements: GCE: 280. IB: 26. OCR ND: D OCR NED: M2

WV91 BA Creative Writing and History
Duration: 3FT Hon
Entry Requirements: GCE: 280. IB: 26. OCR ND: D OCR NED: M2

G14 UNIVERSITY OF GLAMORGAN, CARDIFF AND PONTYPRIDD
ENQUIRIES AND ADMISSIONS UNIT
PONTYPRIDD CF37 1DL
t: 08456 434030 f: 01443 654050
e: enquiries@glam.ac.uk
// www.glam.ac.uk

W990 BA Art Practice
Duration: 3FT Hon
Entry Requirements: Foundation: Merit. GCE: BCC. IB: 24. BTEC
SubDip: M. BTEC Dip: D*D. BTEC ExtDip: DMM. OCR ND: D
OCR NED: M2 Interview required. Portfolio required.

H49 UNIVERSITY OF THE HIGHLANDS AND ISLANDS
UHI EXECUTIVE OFFICE
NESS WALK
INVERNESS
SCOTLAND IV3 5SQ
t: 01463 279000 f: 01463 279001
e: info@uhi.ac.uk
// www.uhi.ac.uk

209W HNC Contemporary Art Practice
Duration: 1FT HNC
Entry Requirements: SQAH: C. Interview required. Portfolio
required.

H60 THE UNIVERSITY OF HUDDERSFIELD
QUEENSGATE
HUDDERSFIELD HD1 3DH
t: 01484 473969 f: 01484 472765
e: admissionsandrecords@hud.ac.uk
// www.hud.ac.uk

W900 BA Contemporary Art
Duration: 3FT/4SW Hon
Entry Requirements: GCE: 300. SQAH: BBBB. IB: 28. Interview
required. Portfolio required.

L14 LANCASTER UNIVERSITY
THE UNIVERSITY
LANCASTER
LANCASHIRE LA1 4YW
t: 01524 592029 f: 01524 846243
e: ugadmissions@lancaster.ac.uk
// www.lancs.ac.uk

W900 BA Creative Arts
Duration: 3FT Hon
Entry Requirements: GCE: ABB. SQAH: BBBBB. SQAAH: BBB. IB:
32. Interview required.

L75 LONDON SOUTH BANK UNIVERSITY
ADMISSIONS AND RECRUITMENT CENTRE
90 LONDON ROAD
LONDON SE1 6I N
t: 0800 923 8888 f: 020 7815 8273
e: course.enquiry@lsbu.ac.uk
// www.lsbu.ac.uk

W9N2 BA Arts Management
Duration: 3FT Hon
Entry Requirements: GCE: 240. IB: 24.

N23 NEWCASTLE COLLEGE
STUDENT SERVICES
RYE HILL CAMPUS
SCOTSWOOD ROAD
NEWCASTLE UPON TYNE NE4 7SA
t: 0191 200 4110 f: 0191 200 4349
e: enquiries@ncl-coll.ac.uk
// www.newcastlecollege.co.uk

W000 BA Creative Practice (Top-up)
Duration: 1FT Hon
Entry Requirements: Interview required. Portfolio required. HND
required.

N36 NEWMAN UNIVERSITY COLLEGE, BIRMINGHAM
GENNERS LANE
BARTLEY GREEN
BIRMINGHAM B32 3NT
t: 0121 476 1181 f: 0121 476 1196
e: Admissions@newman.ac.uk
// www.newman.ac.uk

W900 BA Creative Arts
Duration: 3FT Hon
Entry Requirements: *Foundation:* Distinction. *GCE:* 260. *IB:* 24.
BTEC ExtDip: DMM. *OCR ND:* M2 *OCR NED:* M2

N37 UNIVERSITY OF WALES, NEWPORT
ADMISSIONS
LODGE ROAD
CAERLEON
NEWPORT NP18 3QT
t: 01633 432030 f: 01633 432850
e: admissions@newport.ac.uk
// www.newport.ac.uk

WX93 BA Creative and Therapeutic Arts
Duration: 3FT Hon   CRB Check: Required
Entry Requirements: *GCE:* 220. *IB:* 24. Interview required.

N82 NORWICH CITY COLLEGE OF FURTHER AND HIGHER EDUCATION (AN ASSOCIATE COLLEGE OF UEA)
IPSWICH ROAD
NORWICH
NORFOLK NR2 2LJ
t: 01603 773012 f: 01603 773301
e: he_office@ccn.ac.uk
// www.ccn.ac.uk

W990 FdA Arts and Well-Being
Duration: 2FT Fdg
Entry Requirements: *GCE:* CC.

R18 REGENT'S COLLEGE, LONDON (INCORPORATING REGENT'S BUSINESS SCHOOL, LONDON)
INNER CIRCLE, REGENT'S COLLEGE
REGENT'S PARK
LONDON NW1 4NS
t: +44(0)20 7487 7505 f: +44(0)20 7487 7425
e: exrel@regents.ac.uk
// www.regents.ac.uk/

W900 BA Creative Industries
Duration: 3FT Hon
Entry Requirements: *SQAH:* BBCC. *SQAAH:* CC.

S21 SHEFFIELD HALLAM UNIVERSITY
CITY CAMPUS
HOWARD STREET
SHEFFIELD S1 1WB
t: 0114 225 5555 f: 0114 225 2167
e: admissions@shu.ac.uk
// www.shu.ac.uk

N2W9 BSc Hospitality Business Management with Culinary Arts
Duration: 3FT/4SW Hon
Entry Requirements: *GCE:* 280.

W901 MArt Creative Art Practice
Duration: 4FT Hon
Entry Requirements: *GCE:* 280.

S30 SOUTHAMPTON SOLENT UNIVERSITY
EAST PARK TERRACE
SOUTHAMPTON
HAMPSHIRE SO14 0RT
t: +44 (0) 23 8031 9039 f: + 44 (0)23 8022 2259
e: admissions@solent.ac.uk
// www.solent.ac.uk/

W901 BA Art Enterprise
Duration: 3FT Hon
Entry Requirements: Contact the institution for details.

S72 STAFFORDSHIRE UNIVERSITY
COLLEGE ROAD
STOKE ON TRENT ST4 2DE
t: 01782 292753 f: 01782 292740
e: admissions@staffs.ac.uk
// www.staffs.ac.uk

WN91 BA Entrepreneurship for the Creative and Cultural Industries
Duration: 1FT Hon
Entry Requirements: Interview required. Portfolio required.

S82 UNIVERSITY CAMPUS SUFFOLK (UCS)
WATERFRONT BUILDING
NEPTUNE QUAY
IPSWICH
SUFFOLK IP4 1QJ
t: 01473 338833 f: 01473 339900
e: info@ucs.ac.uk
// www.ucs.ac.uk

W901 BA Arts Practice (Level 3 Entry Only)
Duration: 1FT Hon
Entry Requirements: Interview required. Portfolio required.

S84 UNIVERSITY OF SUNDERLAND
STUDENT HELPLINE
THE STUDENT GATEWAY
CHESTER ROAD
SUNDERLAND SR1 3SD
t: 0191 515 3000 f: 0191 515 3805
e: student.helpline@sunderland.ac.uk
// www.sunderland.ac.uk

W908 BA Arts & Design (4 years)
Duration: 4FT Hon
Entry Requirements: *GCE:* 80-220. *SQAH:* CCCC. *IB:* 22.
Interview required.

U40 UNIVERSITY OF THE WEST OF SCOTLAND
PAISLEY
RENFREWSHIRE
SCOTLAND PA1 2BE
t: 0141 848 3727 f: 0141 848 3623
e: admissions@uws.ac.uk
// www.uws.ac.uk

W900 BA Creative Industries Practice
Duration: 3FT/4FT Ord/Hon
Entry Requirements: *GCE:* CD.

W50 UNIVERSITY OF WESTMINSTER
2ND FLOOR, CAVENDISH HOUSE
101 NEW CAVENDISH STREET,
LONDON W1W 6XH
t: 020 7915 5511
e: course-enquiries@westminster.ac.uk
// www.westminster.ac.uk

W900 BA Contemporary Media Practice
Duration: 3FT Hon
Entry Requirements: *GCE:* BC. *SQAH:* CCCC. *IB:* 26. Interview required. Portfolio required.

PS